MW01383015

ADVANCES IN
FUTURES AND OPTIONS
RESEARCH

Volume 3 • 1988

ADVANCES IN FUTURES AND OPTIONS RESEARCH

A Research Annual

Editor: FRANK J. FABOZZI
Visiting Professor of Finance
Sloan School of Management
Massachusetts Institute of Technology

VOLUME 3 • 1988

 JAI PRESS INC.

Greenwich Connecticut　　　　　　　　　　　*London, England*

Copyright © 1988 JAI PRESS INC.
55 Old Post Road, No. 2
Greenwich, Connecticut 06836

JAI PRESS LTD.
3 Henrietta Street
London WC2E 8LU
England

ISBN: 0-89232-926-2

Manufactured in the United States of America

CONTENTS

ABSTRACTS

ON THE VALUATION OF AMERICAN PUT
OPTIONS ON DIVIDEND-PAYING STOCKS
Giovanni Barone-Adesi and
Robert E. Whaley

Pricing American put options on stocks with known dividends has largely been ignored in the option pricing theory literature because the problem is mathematically complex, and approximate option values are usually computed using expensive finite difference approximation methods. This paper provides a simple and fast nonlinear interpolation procedure that yields surprisingly accurate results.

FORWARD OPTIONS AND FUTURE
OPTIONS
Robert A. Jarrow and George S. Oldfield

American forward and futures call options are deceptively similar, yet different contracts. The purpose of this paper is to elucidate the differences between forward and futures options given stochastic interest rates. Special attention is given to considerations of early exercise. It is shown that American forward call options will never be exercised early, but American futures call options may. A characterization of the conditions under which American futures call options will never be exercised early is provided.

AN ANALYSIS OF THE BIAS IN OPTION
PRICING CAUSED BY A STOCHASTIC
VOLATILITY
John Hull and Alan White

This paper considers the errors caused by using the Black–Scholes model to price options on assets that have stochastic volatilities. It also considers the effect of a stochastic volatility on option replication strategies. The volatility is assumed to follow a stochastic process that may be instantaneously correlated with the stock price process, and may be mean reverting. The pricing error is evaluated in series form. It is shown that it exhibits a rich pattern of behavior. In some circumstances, Black–Scholes overprices whereas in other circumstances it underprices.

ANALYSIS OF BONDS WITH IMBEDDED
OPTIONS
   Farshid Jamshidian and Yu Zhu

A one-factor, price-based bond option model is developed to analyze bonds with imbedded options. It is shown that for a consistent bond option model, the instantaneous interest rate and the price volatility should satisfy the following two conditions: (1) when time approaches maturity, the difference between the instantaneous rate and bond yield should approach zero, and the price volatility should also approach zero; (2) if bond yield approaches zero, both the instantaneous rate and price volatility should approach zero. The bond option model is then applied to analyze the characteristics of bonds with imbedded options. Upper and lower bounds and asymptotic limits are derived for simple callable and putable bonds. For bonds with more complicated options, it is found that the first option largely determines the shape and location of these limits. For a callable bond, numerical calculation suggests that the first four to five call options are most important in capturing the impact of the whole call schedule. It is also found that bonds which are both callable and putable exhibit significantly less sensitivity to interest rate changes and tend to remain within narrow ranges of price and duration limits.

EMBEDDED CALL OPTIONS AND
REFUNDING EFFICIENCY
   C. Douglas Howard and
   Andrew J. Kalotay

Corporate bonds usually come equipped with early redemption provisions such as call and sinking fund acceleration options. These refunding features allow the issuer to reduce interest expense in suitable low rate environments. Only through active "liability management" can the value of these embedded options be efficiently extracted. This paper presents an option valuation-based approach to the management of embedded refunding provisions.

CAPITAL BUDGETING USING CONTINGENT CLAIMS ANALYSIS: A TUTORIAL
Peter Ritchken and Gad Rabinowitz

The purpose of this article is to explain the role of contingent claims analysis in capital budgeting, and to contrast this approach with net present valuation methods including decision tree approaches. The primary advantages of the contingent claims methodology are discussed and references are made to key studies that have applied this method. Simple examples are provided to illustrate the key ideas. One such example involving valuing flexibility in a system is discussed. This example clearly illustrates several advantages of contingent claims approach.

A CONCEPTUAL OPTION FRAMEWORK FOR CAPITAL BUDGETING
Lenos Trigeorgis

Traditional capital budgeting techniques undervalue investment opportunities by not properly capturing the value of managerial operating flexibility and other strategic concerns of practicing managers. This paper describes a general conceptual framework for viewing real investment opportunities as collections of options on real assets (an "expanded NPV" analysis) that integrates the important flexibility options (e.g., the options to defer or abandon a project early) with strategic/competitive interactions.

EVALUATION OF GOVERNMENT SUBSIDIES TO LARGE-SCALE ENERGY PROJECTS: A CONTINGENT CLAIMS APPROACH
Scott P. Mason and Carliss Y. Baldwin

Governments use financial incentives to induce private firms to take actions that are deemed socially desirable but are not privately profitable. This paper demonstrates that the options-based technique of contingent claims analysis (CCA) can be used to value complex government financial subsidies. However, in carrying out the valuation of loan guarantees for actual large-scale energy projects, the authors were struck by the fact that traditional project valuation techniques ignore the presence of "operating options." Operating options provide a quantitative representation of management's flexibility to revise its original operating strategy if future events turn out differently from those management expected at the outset. It is shown that CCA can also be used to value operating options and thus holds the promise of being able to recognize flexibility explicitly and quantify its impact on the value of particular undertakings.

EMPIRICAL REGULARITIES IN THE DEUTSCHE MARK FUTURES OPTIONS
David A. Hsieh and Luis Manas-Anton

This paper analyzes the Deutsche Mark futures options traded on the Chicago Mercantile Exchange, from January 24, 1984 to October 10, 1984. Transaction data were used to match the prices of the futures options and the underlying futures contracts.

In the data, there are very low rates of violations of early exercise boundary conditions and put–call parity conditions. This is indicative of well-synchronized markets and low transaction costs.

The analysis of implied volatilities revealed some interesting empirical regularities. (1) Implied volatilities are not constant over time. In fact, they appear to be serially correlated. (2) The moneyness bias is very strong, regardless of time to maturity. Deep-out-of-the-money options have the largest implied volatilities, and out-of-the-money options the second largest. In other words, the Black–Scholes model underprices deep-out-of-the-money options relative to at-the-money options. (The evidence is not conclusive for deep-in-the-money options, since they are not frequently traded.) (3) The maturity bias is also quite strong. Implied volatilities tend to rise as the options approach maturity. In other words, the Black–Scholes model underprices options that are closer to maturity relative to those that are further from maturity.

These systematic biases of the Black–Scholes model are unlikely to be caused by transaction costs and discontinuous trading. More likely, the distributional assumption of the Black–Scholes model is at fault. The conjecture is that a process with stochastic variance may be able to explain these biases.

PREFERENCE-FREE OPTION PRICES WHEN STOCK RETURNS CAN GO UP, DOWN, OR STAY THE SAME
Stylianos Perrakis

This paper examines preference-free option pricing in a multiperiod discrete-time model, in which the single-period stock return distribution is the three-state process where the stock price can go up, go down, or stay the same. Under the assumption of a positive beta stock four different orderings of the state-contingent discount factors in a one-period equilibrium model in incomplete financial markets are identified. For each such ordering the tightest possible call option price bounds are derived in a multiperiod context. The limits of these bounds are then found when the trading interval goes to zero, while the number of trades becomes infinite within a given time interval. The resulting bounds differ, depending on whether we have a diffusion or a jump process of stock returns. It is also shown that only one ordering exists that is capable of generating the Black–Scholes option price under diffusion as the limit of both its corresponding upper and lower bounds on option values. Thus, this ordering becomes a necessary and sufficient condition for a unique option price to emerge at the limit of continuous trading under diffusion. For a jump process, by contrast, no unique option prices emerge, even under such an ordering.

ON THE PROPERTIES OF THE VALUATION FORMULA FOR AN UNPROTECTED AMERICAN CALL OPTION WITH KNOWN DIVIDENDS AND THE COMPUTATION OF ITS IMPLIED STANDARD DEVIATION
Robert L. Welch and David M. Chen

Properties of the American Call Model with known dividends are derived by viewing it as a maximization of a deterministic function with the critical stock prices being the optimized decision variables. This simplifies the computation of the comparative statics of the call and its critical stock prices. Some of these results are then used to devise a simple and efficient search for the implied standard deviation (ISD) of a single call. Two examples are used to demonstrate the search process and the need to adjust for the exact early exercise premium in computing ISDs.

COMBINING VARIOUS FUTURES
CONTRACTS TO GET BETTER HEDGES
Laurie Goodman and N. R. Vijayaraghavan

Simple duration hedges work well if changes in the yield curve are flat and parallel. Both large changes in interest rates or changes in the steepness of the yield curve can greatly reduce the hedging effectiveness of a simple duration match. A hedge in which one matches duration and convexity will guard against both large changes in the level of rates and small changes in slope.

DEFAULT SPREADS IN THE FIXED AND IN
THE FLOATING INTEREST RATE MARKETS:
A CONTINGENT CLAIMS APPROACH
Ian Cooper and Antonio S. Mello

Yield spreads measuring the relative riskiness of two firms are usually different in the fixed rate market and in the floating rate market. For many this corresponds to an anomaly giving rise to arbitrage opportunity that can be successfully exploited by means of a swap transaction. This paper employs contingent claims analysis to evaluate the spreads due to credit differences of firms. It is shown that arbitrage pricing models are consistent with differences in quality spreads, since the relevant variables affecting risk vary in importance for different markets. The reason for the continuing growth of swaps must therefore be other than simply financial arbitrage.

T-BOND FUTURES PRICES:
CHEAPEST TO DELIVER VERSUS THE INDEX
Mark Castelino and Sris Chatterjee

An index comprising all deliverable bonds outperforms the cheapest to deliver in tracking Treasury bond futures prices. The superior performance of the index can be traced to the option-type properties of the contract. The existence of finite probabilities of delivery of all bonds in the index contributes to futures price changes that the cheapest to deliver by itself cannot. This result substantially diminishes the role of the cheapest to deliver bond for hedging purposes and, hence, argues for its replacement by the index.

INTRADAY RETURN AND VOLATILITY PATTERNS IN THE STOCK MARKET: FUTURES VERSUS SPOT
Joseph E. Finnerty and Hun Y. Park

We investigate the existence of intraday return and volatility patterns in the spot as well as in the futures markets of common stocks. Confirming the results of previous studies on weekend effects (i.e., the significant negative Monday return in the spot market but not in the futures market), we also provide new findings. The negative weekend effect in the spot market is found to start from around 1:30 P.M. on Friday (not from closing) and end at around 9:00 A.M. on Monday, 30 minutes after trading is open. We find a systematic and significant intraday volatility behavior of prices in the spot market, but no such occurrences in the futures market. A lunch hour effect is detected, where price movements are minimal during the lunch period in both the spot and futures markets. An unexplained anomaly is the persistent negative trend in prices for both spot and futures on Wednesday.

THE MONDAY EFFECT AND SPECULATIVE OPPORTUNITIES IN THE STOCK-INDEX FUTURES MARKETS
Dan R. Pieptea and Eliezer Prisman

This paper examines the weekend effect in the stock-index futures market. The S&P 500 spot index, nearby, and next to nearby contracts are included in the study and accounted for separately over the period April 1983–June 1986. Both expected return and risk components of the risk/expected-return tradeoff are investigated. We found a Monday effect consistent with previous literature for the spot index but the equal mean return hypothesis cannot be rejected for the futures contracts. A new intraweek seasonality effect related to systematic differences in the standard deviation of returns is identified. The standard deviation seasonality is found to persist in the futures market more than the mean-return effect. An explanation of the Monday effect is given based on investor's psychology.

CASH VERSUS FUTURES PRICES AND THE WEEKEND EFFECT: THE CANADIAN EVIDENCE
Trevor W. Chamberlain, C. Sherman Cheung and Clarence C. Y. Kwan

This study examines close to close price change data for TSE 300 Index futures for evidence of the so-called weekend effect, according to which measured returns for the trading day following a weekend are significantly negative. Unlike previous studies involving stock index futures, the results of which have been ambiguous, we find that a relatively strong weekend effect persists in the data. As such, our results parallel those obtained for cash markets in the United States and elsewhere.

THE EFFECT OF INDIVIDUAL STOCK OPTION EXPIRATIONS ON STOCK RETURNS BEFORE AND AFTER THE INTRODUCTION OF SP 100 INDEX OPTIONS
Joseph Vu and E. Mine Cinar

The results of this study show that the raw and excess returns of the underlying common stocks are negatively affected by the expiration dates of individual stock options. The impact is stronger after the introduction of the SP 100 index options.

A FURTHER INVESTIGATION OF THE RISK-RETURN RELATION FOR COMMODITY FUTURES
Hun Y. Park, K. C. John Wei and Thomas J. Frecka

Previous studies have examined the risk premium of futures contracts by estimating the beta using the CAPM and reached different conclusions depending upon the proxy chosen for the market portfolio. The main objective of this paper is to examine the risk–return relation for commodity futures, using an alternative pricing model, the APT, which does not accord a crucial role to the market porfolio. In addition, we reexamine the risk–return relation in the CAPM framework for comparison purposes. Empirical results in this paper provide evidence that neither the CAPM nor the APT is satisfactory for commodity futures contracts. In both models the residual variance appears to be the only important variable in pricing these assets. The results also suggest that the conflicting results in previous studies in a CAPM context may not be necessarily due to different proxies for the market portfolio, but instead due to the inconsistency of the risk–return relation with the CAPM and instability. The results from the APT models confirm this conclusion.

THE DAY-OF-THE-WEEK EFFECT FOR
DERIVATIVE ASSETS:
THE CASE OF GOLD FUTURES OPTIONS
Frank J. Fabozzi and Christopher K. Ma

While strong evidence of daily seasonality has been found in equity markets, recent studies show that this phenomenon is not significant in the derivative asset market. This paper identifies a strong day-of-the-week effect in returns of gold futures options. The daily effect is attributed, in part, to the underlying gold futures seasonality. It is further shown that both markets exhibit a positive weekend effect in a rising market, and a negative weekend effect in a declining market.

ON THE VALUATION OF AMERICAN PUT OPTIONS ON DIVIDEND-PAYING STOCKS

Giovanni Barone-Adesi[*] and Robert E. Whaley[**]

I. INTRODUCTION

The option pricing literature has developed enormously since Black–Scholes [2] (Merton [8]) derived valuation equations for the European call and put options written on zero (constant proportional) dividend yield stocks. Models now exist for pricing European and American options on a variety of underlying commodities ranging from financial assets such as common stocks and bonds to traditional agricultural futures contracts.[1]

[*]Faculty of Business, University of Alberta.
[**]Fuqua School of Business, Duke University.

This research was supported by the Futures and Options Research Center, Duke University, and the SSHRC.

Advances in Futures and Options Research, Vol. 3, pages 1–13.

Conspicuously absent from this literature is the valuation of American options written on commodities that have discrete cash payments during the life of the option. In particular, while an analytic valuation equation exists for the American call option written on a stock with known discrete dividends paid during the option's life (see Roll [10] and Whaley [12]), the valuation of the American put option on a stock with discrete dividends remains largely unaddressed. Usually the valuation of such put options involves implementing finite difference methods, and these methods are computationally expensive and impractical for real time pricing applications. Blomeyer [3] devised a fast algorithm that interpolates between known option values that surround the true unknown price. Unfortunately, however, his technique can lead to serious mispricing errors for typical parameter ranges. The purpose of this paper is to provide a fast and accurate approximation for the value of an American put option on a stock with known discrete dividend payments.

The outline of the paper is as follows. In Section II, the economics of the American put option valuation problem are discussed. First, the assumptions and definitions used in the analysis are presented. The problem is then formulated and the approximation method is presented and discussed. In Section III, the approximation method is applied and the results are compared with "true" put option values. For the stock option parameter ranges considered, the maximum pricing error is less than 1% and falls within the bid–ask spread. The paper concludes with a brief summary (Section IV).

II. THEORETICAL APPROXIMATION

A. Assumptions and Definitions

The approximation method relies on all of the standard Black–Scholes [2] assumptions, except that, in place of the no dividend assumption, it is assumed that the underlying stock pays a *single known* cash dividend during the option's life. Extensions to multiple known dividends are straightforward. The approximation itself, however, employs the valuation equations for European and American put options on stocks with no dividends. From Black–Scholes [2], the European put option formula is

$$p(S,T) = Xe^{-rT}N_1(-d_2) - SN_1(-d_1), \tag{1}$$

where

$$d_1 = \frac{\ln(S/X) + (r + \frac{1}{2}\sigma^2)T}{\sigma\sqrt{T}} \tag{1a}$$

and

$$d_2 = d_1 - \sigma\sqrt{T}. \tag{1b}$$

In Equation (1), S is the current stock price, X is the exercise price of the option, r is the riskless rate of interest, σ is the standard deviation of the instantaneous rates of return on the underlying stock, and T is the time to expiration of the option. $N_1(d)$ is the cumulative univariate normal density function with upper integral limit d. From MacMillan [7], the American put option valuation equation[2] is

$$P(S, T) = \begin{cases} p(S,T) + A_1 (S/S^*)^{q_1} & \text{where } S > S^*, \\ X - S & \text{where } S \leqslant S^*, \end{cases} \tag{2}$$

where

$$A_1 = -\frac{S^*\{1 - N[-d_1(S^*)]\}}{q_1}, \tag{2a}$$

$$q_1 = \frac{1 - n - \sqrt{(n-1)^2 + 4k}}{2}, \tag{2b}$$

$$n = \frac{2r}{\sigma^2}, \tag{2c}$$

$$k = \frac{2r}{\sigma^2(1 - e^{-rT})}, \tag{2d}$$

and S^* is the critical asset below above which the American put should be exercised immediately and is the solution to

$$X - S^* = p(S^*, T; X) - \{1 - N_1[-d_1(S^*)]\}S^*/q_1. \tag{2e}$$

In the approximation method for the American put option on a dividend-paying stock, the European and American put option valuation Equations (1) and (2) are used repeatedly for various stock prices and times to expiration. In addition, it is necessary to compute critical stock prices below which the American put will be exercised immediately. Henceforth, the notation $S^*(T)$ denotes the critical stock price below which the American put option written on a non-dividend-paying stock will be exercised immediately.

B. Put Option Pricing Problem

Before explaining the approximation method, the nature of the pricing problem for the American put option on a dividend-paying stock is discussed. To begin, dividends are ignored. In the absence of dividend payments on the underlying stock, the American put option may be exercised early because interest income can be earned on the exercisable proceeds of the option as soon as the option is exercised. Deferring exercise implicitly means interest income is being foregone. When the stock pays a dividend, however, the American put option holder is in a dilemma. If he continues to hold the put, he foregoes the interest; but, if he exercises immediately, he will not profit from the discrete upward jump in the exercisable proceeds of the put when the stock goes ex-dividend.

The tradeoff between the interest income and the dividend can be expressed more formally. Assume that the stock pays a dividend D at time t_D during the option's life. If the stock is zero today and the put option is exercised, the interest income that would be earned between now and the ex-dividend instant is $X(e^{rt_D} - 1)$. Now, if the dividend amount D at t_D is larger than the interest income, that is, if

$$D > X(e^{rt_D} - 1), \tag{3}$$

early exercise during the interval 0 to t_D is not rational and, if the American put is exercised at all, it will be during the time interval t_D to T.

Condition (3) can be used to gather further insight about the put option pricing problem. To do so, define t_N as a point in time before which it may be optimal to exercise the put early prior to ex-dividend, but after which it will not be optimal to exercise until after the dividend has been paid. This point in time is defined by the solution to

$$D = X[e^{r(t_D - t_N)} - 1], \tag{4}$$

and is

$$t_N = t_D - \frac{\ln(1 + D/X)}{r}. \tag{5}$$

Now, if t_N is negative, condition (3) holds and the American put will not be exercised during the interval 0 to t_D and may be exercised during the interval t_D to T. On the other hand, if t_N is positive, there exist three distinct time intervals during the option's life with different early exercise implications: during the interval 0 to t_N, there is a nonzero probability of early exercise; during the interval t_N to t_D, the probability of early exercise is zero; and during the interval t_D to T, there is a nonzero probability of early exercise.

C. Approximate Solution

The approximate solution to the put option pricing problem described in Section II,B has two parts—first where early exercise before the dividend is not possible and second where early exercise before the dividend is possible. In both cases, the approach to finding the solution is the same. Known option prices to which the true put option value $P(S, T; D, t_D)$ converges are identified and then weighted by the "probabilities" of their occurrence. The weighted average approximates the true option value.

The first case to be examined is where early exercise is precluded during the interval 0 to t_D, but is possible during the interval t_D to T (i.e., the case where $t_N \leqslant 0$). This occurs typically when the dividend paid during the option's life is large relative to the exercise price of the option. An upper bound for the put option $P(S, T; D, t_D)$ is the value of an American put written on a non-dividend-paying stock [i.e., Equation (2)], where the stock price net of the present value of the escrowed dividend, $S' = S - De^{-r t_D}$, replaces the stock price parameter, $P(S', T)$. This option necessarily overstates the true option value since it prices an early exercise premium over the entire option's life, when the early exercise premium between 0 and t_D is known to be equal to zero. But, as the stock price becomes large, the early exercise premium becomes small and the true value of the put converges to $P(S', T)$.

A lower price bound for $P(S, T; D, t_D)$ is found by subtracting the early exercise premium from 0 to t_D from the upper bound, that is,

$$P(S', T) - \varepsilon_P(S', t_D),\tag{6}$$

where the early exercise premium is defined by

$$\varepsilon_P(S', t_D) = P(S', t_D) - p(S', t_D).\tag{6a}$$

If the early exercise premium of an option decreased linearly as the option's life erodes (holding other factors constant), the lower price bound, $P(S', T) - \varepsilon_P(S', t_D)$, would, in fact, be the true price of the put. But, because the early exercise premium of an option decreases at an increasing rate,[3] the early exercise premium (6a) is larger than the early exercise premium imbedded in the American put and therefore the option value (6) provides an understatement of the true value of the put. The true option value converges to (6) as the stock price falls and the probability of early exercise at t_D grows large.

The upper and lower bounds of the true price are now weighted to provide an approximation for the true value. The approximation formula is

$$P(S, T; D, t_D) = w_1 P(S', T) + w_2 [P(S', T) - \varepsilon_P(S', t_D)],\tag{7}$$

where w_1 and w_2 sum to one.[4] The weight w_2 is the probability that the put will be exercised immediately after the dividend is paid.[5] To compute this probability, Equation (2) is first used to evaluate the price of an American put with time to expiration $T - t_D$. A by-product of the valuation is the computation of the critical stock price $S^*(T - t_D)$ below which the American put option holder will exercise at t_D. Note that the critical stock price is not a function of the stock price itself. With the critical stock price in hand, the probability of early exercise at t_D is then computed as

$$w_2 = N_1(-b) \tag{7a}$$

where

$$b = \frac{\ln[S'/S^*(T - t_D)] + (r - .5\sigma^2)t_D}{\sigma\sqrt{t_D}}. \tag{7b}$$

The weight,

$$w_1 = N_1(b), \tag{7c}$$

is the complement of (7a) or the probability that the put will not be exercised at time t_D.

It is instructive to note that the approximation (7) converges to its proper limits as the option goes deep in-the-money and out-of-the-money. As the put goes deep in-the-money (i.e., as the stock price falls), w_1 goes to zero, w_2 goes to one, and the value of (6) converges to the European put option values, $p(S', t_D)$.[6] This stands to reason. If $t_N \leqslant 0$, early exercise will not occur prior to ex-dividend. As the stock price moves lower and lower, the likelihood of exercising the put just after the dividend is paid approaches one. If exercise at t_D is certain, the American put option will have the same value as a European put expiring at t_D just after the dividend is paid, that is, $p(S', t_D)$. On the other hand, as the put goes deep out-of-the-money (i.e., the stock price rises), w_1 goes to one, w_2 goes to zero, and the American put price $P(S', T)$ approaches the European put price $p(S', T)$. That is, the deeper out-of-the-money the put option is, the lower the early exercise premium is, until eventually the American put is priced as if it were European.

The case where t_N is positive is slightly more complex because the premium arising from the prospect of early exercise between 0 and t_N must be recognized. If early exercise is certain to occur during the interval 0 to t_N, pricing the American put would be the straightforward problem of pricing an American put option on a non-dividend-paying stock. The price of such an option can be approximated using Equation (2), that is, $P(S, t_N)$. But, in general, early exercise between 0 and t_N is not certain so this additional put must be combined probabilistically with the other two in Equation (7). When $t_N > 0$, the approximation for the American put is

$$P(S, T; D, t_D) = w_1 P(S', T) + w_2[P(S', T) - \varepsilon_p(S', t_D)] + w_3 P(S, t_N), \tag{8}$$

where $w_1 + w_2 + w_3 = 1$.[7] The weight w_3 is the probability that the put will be exercised in the interval 0 to t_N, that is,

$$w_3 = N_1(-a) \tag{8a}$$

where

$$a = \frac{\ln[S/S^*(T - t_N)] + (r - .5\sigma^2)t_N}{\sigma\sqrt{t_N}}. \tag{8b}$$

Note that this probability is only an approximation in the sense that it is the probability that a put option written on a non-dividend-paying stock will be exercised at time t_N [8] [as reflected by the use of the critical stock price $S^*(T - t_N)$]. The weights w_1 and w_2 remain as above except that they are now joint probabilities. In order for the put life's to be extended beyond t_N, the weights must reflect the probability that the put is not exercised at t_N, that is, $N(a)$. The weights are now

$$w_1 = N_2(a, b; \sqrt{t_N/t_D}) \tag{8c}$$

and

$$w_2 = N_2(a, -b; -\sqrt{t_N/t_D}), \tag{8d}$$

where $N_2(a, b; \rho)$ is the cumulative bivariate normal density function with upper integral limits a and b and correlation coefficient ρ.[9] Note that the weights $w_1 + w_2$ sum to the probability of no early exercise at t_N, $N_1(a)$.

III. SIMULATION RESULTS

Before proceeding with a discussion of the accuracy of the approximation based on some simulation results, a simple example is constructed to illustrate the technique. Suppose that an American put option has an exercise price of 40 and a time to expiration of 0.3288 years. Assume that the current stock price is 40, that the stock pays a dividend of 0.50 exactly one-half way through the option's life, and that the standard deviation of the instantaneous rates of return of the stock net of the present values of the escrowed dividend is 20% annually. Assume also that the stock riskless rate of interest is 10% annually.

The first step is to compute the value of t_N using Equation (5). In this example, $t_N = 0.0402$. Since t_N is positive, Approximation Equation (8) is used. In (8), the critical stock price below which the put will be exercised at t_N, $S^*(T - t_N)$, is 35.96. The probability that the stock price will move from its current level of 40 to a value below 35.96 at t_N, w_3 is 0.0031, and the value of the American put expiring at t_N, $P(S, t_N)$, is 0.5724. If the put is not exercised at t_N, it may be exercised at t_D. The probability that the put will not be exercised at t_N and will be exercised at t_D, w_2, is 0.1271, and the value, $P(S', T) - \varepsilon_P(S', t_D)$ is $1.5735 - (1.2724 - 1.1966) = 1.4977$. Finally, the probability that the put is not exercised at t_N and is not exercised at

t_D, w_1, is 0.8698, and the value of the option, $P(S', T)$, is 1.5735. Substituting the numerical values into Equation (8),

$$P(40,.3288;.50,.1644) = .8698(1.5735)2.1271(1.4977)2.0031(.5724)$$
$$= 1.5607.$$

This put option value is reported in row 10 of Table 1.

Tables 1 and 2 contain the results of some simulations using the proposed nonlinear interpolation method. For comparison purposes, the values of the

Table 1. Comparison of American Put Option Approximation Values[a]
$(S = 40, r = .10, D = 0.50, t = T/2)$

No.	X	T	σ	APPX1[b]	APPX2[c]	True Value[d]	APPX3[e]
1	35	0.1644	0.20	0.06	0.06	0.06	0.06
2	40	0.1644	0.20	1.27	1.23	1.27	1.27
3	45	0.1644	0.20	5.35	5.34	5.18	5.21
4	50	0.1644	0.20	10.34	10.33	10.08	10.09
5	35	0.2466	0.20	0.12	0.12	0.12	0.13
6	40	0.2466	0.20	1.43	1.45	1.43	1.44
7	45	0.2466	0.20	5.30	5.29	5.09	5.05
8	50	0.2466	0.20	10.26	10.25	9.99	10.00
9	35	0.3288	0.20	0.18	0.19	0.18	0.19
10	40	0.3288	0.20	1.56	1.57	1.55	1.56
11	45	0.3288	0.20	5.31	5.25	5.04	5.10
12	50	0.3288	0.20	10.26	10.18	9.99	10.00
13	35	0.1644	0.30	0.30	0.30	0.30	0.30
14	40	0.1644	0.30	1.89	1.91	1.90	1.90
15	45	0.1644	0.30	5.48	5.52	5.45	5.42
16	50	0.1644	0.30	10.34	10.34	10.11	10.13
17	35	0.2466	0.30	0.49	0.49	0.49	0.50
18	40	0.2466	0.30	2.18	2.21	2.19	2.20
19	45	0.2466	0.30	5.58	5.62	5.55	5.52
20	50	0.2466	0.30	10.29	10.27	10.00	10.02
21	35	0.3288	0.30	0.66	0.67	0.66	0.67
22	40	0.3288	0.30	2.43	2.44	2.42	2.43
23	45	0.3288	0.30	5.71	5.73	5.64	5.56
24	50	0.3288	0.30	10.32	10.23	10.00	10.05

Notes: [a]The notation used in this table is as follows: S is the stock price, r is the riskless rate of interest, D is the amount of the cash dividend, t is the time to ex-dividend, X is the exercise price of the option, T is the time to expiration of the option, and σ is the standard deviation of the instantaneous rate of return on the stock.
[b]Blomeyer [3] dividend interpolation using Johnson [6] put approximation.
[c]Blomeyer [3] dividend interpolation using Geske–Johnson [5] put approximation.
[d]True option value computed using implicit finite difference method from Barone-Adesi and Whaley [1].
[e]Proposed nonlinear interpolation using MacMillan [7] put approximation.

true American put option, as computed using the implicit finite difference method, and the two approximations recommended by Blomeyer [3] are also presented. The parameters used to generate the option values are the same as those used by Blomeyer [3, p. 232] to facilitate comparisons. The results are quite interesting.

Table 1 contains the results for the most plausible set of parameters used in the Blomeyer analysis. A quarterly cash dividend of $.50 implies an annual dividend of $2.00, and, with a $40 share price, the annualized

Table 2. Comparison of American Put Option Approximation Values[a]
$$(S = 40, r = .10, D = 1.70, t = T/2)$$

No.	X	T	σ	APPX1[b]	APPX2[c]	True Value[d]	APPX3[e]
25	35	0.1644	0.20	0.13	0.14	0.13	0.14
26	40	0.1644	0.20	1.95	1.96	1.95	1.96
27	45	0.1644	0.20	6.34	6.33	6.33	6.35
28	50	0.1644	0.20	11.28	11.28	11.27	11.28
29	35	0.2466	0.20	0.22	0.23	0.23	0.24
30	40	0.2466	0.20	2.04	2.07	2.06	2.08
31	45	0.2466	0.20	6.21	6.19	6.18	6.24
32	50	0.2466	0.20	11.08	11.07	11.06	11.07
33	35	0.3288	0.20	0.30	0.32	0.32	0.33
34	40	0.3288	0.20	2.12	2.15	2.15	2.17
35	45	0.3288	0.20	6.10	6.07	6.07	6.16
36	50	0.3288	0.20	10.88	10.86	10.86	10.88
37	35	0.1644	0.30	0.47	0.47	0.47	0.48
38	40	0.1644	0.30	2.49	2.54	2.53	2.53
39	45	0.1644	0.30	6.46	6.49	6.49	6.48
40	50	0.1644	0.30	11.30	11.29	11.28	11.30
41	35	0.2466	0.30	0.69	0.70	0.70	0.71
42	40	0.2466	0.30	2.74	2.79	2.79	2.79
43	45	0.2466	0.30	6.44	6.51	6.51	6.49
44	50	0.2466	0.30	11.14	11.13	11.12	11.16
45	35	0.3288	0.30	0.88	0.89	0.89	0.90
46	40	0.3288	0.30	2.93	3.00	3.00	3.01
47	45	0.3288	0.30	6.46	6.55	6.54	6.54
48	50	0.3288	0.30	11.09	11.00	10.99	11.06

Notes: [a]The notation used in this table is as follows: S is the stock price, r is the riskless rate of interest, D is the amount of the cash dividend, t is the time to ex-dividend, X is the exercise price of the option, T is the time to expiration of the option, and σ is the standard deviation of the instantaneous rate of return on the stock.
[b]Blomeyer [3] dividend interpolation using Johnson [6] put approximation.
[c]Blomeyer [3] dividend interpolation using Geske–Johnson [5] put approximation.
[d]True option value computed using implicit finite difference method from Barone-Adesi and Whaley [1].
[e]Proposed nonlinear interpolation using MacMillan [7] put approximation.

dividend yield is 5%. With a $.50 dividend paid half way through the option's life, the proposed nonlinear interpolation values (7) or (8) reported in the column headed "APPX3" are remarkably close to the true values reported in the column headed "True Value." The largest errors tend to occur where the put is slightly in-the-money, but even in these cases the pricing errors are only about 1% and are less, in magnitude, than the bid–ask spread for such options. [10]

Another way in which the performance of the nonlinear interpolation can be gauged is by comparing its accuracy with the approximation techniques recommended by Blomeyer. Blomeyer's values are reported as columns "APPX1" and "APPX2" in Table 1. Without going into the details of the Blomeyer computations, it is obvious that his values are very misleading, with errors on order of 2–3%. [11]

Blomeyer [3, p. 232] also reports the results of his option price approxi-

Table 3. Comparison of American Put Option Approximation Value[a]
(S = 40, r = .10, D = 0.40, T = .25)

			σ = 0.20		σ = 0.30		σ = 0.40	
No.	X	t	True Value[b]	APPX3[c]	True Value[b]	APPX3[c]	True Value[b]	APPX3[c]
1	35	0.05	0.12	0.12	0.48	0.49	1.00	1.01
2	40	0.05	1.41	1.40	2.17	2.17	2.94	2.94
3	45	0.05	5.22	5.24	5.58	5.53	6.17	6.14
4	50	0.05	10.15	10.15	10.18	10.19	10.40	10.33
5	35	0.10	0.12	0.12	0.48	0.49	1.00	1.01
6	40	0.10	1.41	1.40	2.16	2.17	2.94	2.94
7	45	0.10	5.07	5.04	5.52	5.47	6.14	6.12
8	50	0.10	10.00	10.00	10.00	10.02	10.29	10.18
9	35	0.15	0.12	0.12	0.48	0.49	1.00	1.00
10	40	0.15	1.37	1.38	2.15	2.15	2.92	2.93
11	45	0.15	5.00	5.06	5.43	5.36	6.08	5.99
12	50	0.15	9.99	10.00	9.99	10.02	10.19	10.13
13	35	0.20	0.11	0.12	0.48	0.49	0.99	1.00
14	40	0.20	1.34	1.35	2.12	2.11	2.90	2.88
15	45	0.20	4.99	5.04	5.37	5.30	6.02	5.90
16	50	0.20	9.99	10.00	9.99	10.00	10.14	10.10

Notes: [a]The notation used in this table is as follows: S is the stock price, r is the riskless rate of interest, D is the amount of the cash dividend, t is the time to ex-dividend, X is the exercise price of the option, T is the time to expiration of the option, and σ is the standard deviation of the instantaneous rate of return on the stock.
[b]True option value computed using implicit finite difference method from Barone-Adesi and Whaley [1].
[c]Proposed nonlinear interpolation using MacMillan [7] put approximation.

mations for the case where the quarterly dividend is 1.70, and, for convenience, they are reported in Table 2. Here the Blomeyer approximations work about equally as well as the nonlinear interpolation, however, these results are of little practical value. A quarterly dividend of $1.70 on a $40 share price implies an annual dividend yield of a whopping 17%! This is not a typical common stock by any means.

Table 3 contains the simulation results for a different set of parameters. The parameters were chosen to correspond with more typical stock options. The dividend amount is $.40 on a $40 share price, implying an annual dividend yield of 4%. The standard deviation of the rate of return on the stock varies from 20 to 40%, and the times to ex-dividend vary from 0.05 to 0.20 years. The time to expiration is 0.25 years because the most actively traded stock options are typically the nearby contracts and the maximum time to expiration of a nearby contract is 3 months.

The results of Table 3 indicate that the nonlinear interpolation does reasonably well for the parameter ranges considered. Again, the put options slightly in-the-money have the greatest mispricing errors, but the magnitudes of the errors again fall within transaction costs bands. Overall, the nonlinear approximation works remarkably well considering that it takes less than 1/1000th of the time to compute the nonlinear interpolation than it does the finite difference value of these options.[12]

IV. SUMMARY

Pricing American put options on dividend-paying stocks has largely been ignored in the literature because the problem is mathematically complex and valuation usually resorts to expensive approximation procedures. This paper provides a simple and fast nonlinear interpolation procedure that yields surprisingly accurate results.

NOTES

1. Stoll and Whaley [11] develop a general framework for valuing options whose underlying commodities have constant continuous cost of carry rates. Barone-Adesi and Whaley [1] provide algorithms for pricing American options on such commodities.

2. Equation (2) is only an approximation of the true value of the American put option P(S, T). It was chosen over competing approximation methods (see, for example, Johnson [6] and Geske–Johnson [5]) because of its speed and accuracy. Johnson's method is fast but generally unreliable (see Barone-Adesi and Whaley [1] for evidence on this point). The Geske–Johnson compound option approach is accurate when a four-point extrapolation is used, but it requires the evaluation of a trivariate normal density function integral and routines for this integral evaluation are generally slow.

3.   To be more precise, the early exercise premium increases first at an increasing, then at a decreasing, rate as the time to expiration of the option grows large. The range of times to expiration over which the slope is increasing, however, is very close to zero and not relevant to the options being considered here. In general, the rate at which the premium increases diminishes as the time to expiration grows large because the American put option value approaches its asympotic limit. See Merton [8, pp. 173–174].

4.   For computational purposes, Equation (7) may be simplified to

$$P(S, T; D, t_D) = P(S', T) - w_2\varepsilon_P(S', t_D).$$

5.   The probabilities computed here are risk-neutral probabilities in the spirit of Cox and Ross [4].

6.   If the put is deep in-the-money, the American put option values, $P(S',T)$ in (6) and $P(S', t_D)$ in (6a), equal $X - S$. Thus, the value of (6) is $X - S - [X - S - p(S', t_D)]$ or simply $p(S', t_D)$.

7.   For computational purposes, Equation (8) may be simplified to

$$P(S, T; D, t_D) = (w_1 + w_2)P(S', T) - w_2\varepsilon_P(S', t_D) + w_3P(S, t_N).$$

8.   This critical stock price is computed implicitly for the American put option value $P(S, T - t_N)$ using the valuation equation (2).

9.   An algorithm for evaluating the bivariate normal integral is contained in Owen [9]. Alternatively, since the ratio t_N/t_D is usually small, reasonable approximations of the bivariate probabilities $N_2(a, b; \sqrt{t_N/t_D})$ and $N_2(a, -b; -\sqrt{t_N/t_D})$ are the products of the univariate probabilities $N_1(a)N_1(b)$ and $N_1(a) N_1(-b)$, respectively.

10.   The minimum bid–ask spread for options whose prices exceed \$3 is one-eighth or \$0.125. The minimum spread for options whose prices are below \$3 is one-sixteenth or \$0.0625.

11.   Generally speaking, as the dividend becomes small or as the time to ex-dividend grows large, the Blomeyer approximations become worse.

12.   The finite difference method used time steps of 0.20 days and stock prices steps of \$0.04.

REFERENCES

1.   Barone-Adesi, G., and R. E. Whaley, "Efficient Analytic Approximation of American Option Values," *Journal of Finance* 42 (June 1987), 301–320.

2.   Black, F., and M. Scholes, "The Pricing of Options and Corporate Liabilities," *Journal of Political Economy* 81 (May–June 1973), 637–659.

3.   Blomeyer, E. C., "An Analytical Approximation for the American Put Price for Options on Stocks with Dividends," *Journal of Financial and Quantitative Analysis* 21 (June 1986), 229–233.

4.   Cox, J. C., and S. A. Ross, "The Valuation of Options for Alternative Stochastic Processes," *Journal of Financial Economics* 3 (1986), 145–166.

5.   Geske, R., and H. E. Johnson, "The American Put Valued Analytically," *Journal of Finance* 39 (December 1984), 1511–1524.

6.   Johnson, J., "An Analytical Approximation for the American Put Price," *Journal of Financial and Quantitative Analysis* 18 (March 1983), 141–148.

7.   MacMillan, L. W., "Analytical Approximation for the American Put Option," *Advances in Futures and Options Research* 1 (1986), 119–139.

8. Merton, R. C., "The Theory of Rational Option Pricing," *Bell Journal of Economics and Management Science* 4 (1973), 141–183.
9. Owen, D. B., *Handbook of Statistical Tables*. Reading, Massachusetts: Addison-Wesley Publishing Company, 1962.
10. Roll, R., "An Analytic Valuation Formula for Unprotected American Call Options on Stocks with Known Dividends," *Journal of Financial Economics* 5 (1977), 251–258.
11. Stoll, H. R., and R. E. Whaley, "The New Option instruments: Arbitrageable Linkages and Valuation," *Advances in Futures and Option Research* 1 (1986), 25–62.
12. Whaley, R. E., "On the Valuation of American Call Options on Stocks with Known Dividends," *Journal of Financial Economics* 9 (1981), 207–211.

FORWARD OPTIONS AND FUTURES OPTIONS

Robert A. Jarrow* and George S. Oldfield*

I. INTRODUCTION

American forward and futures options are different types of contracts. If exercised early, a forward option's value equals the discounted difference between the striking price and the current forward price. A futures option's value, if exercised early, equals the simple difference between the striking price and the current futures price. This slight discrepancy is enough to prevent early forward option exercise and to allow early futures option exercise. Thus, American forward options can be treated like European options whereas American futures options cannot.

*S. C. Johnson Graduate School of Management, Cornell University.

We are grateful to Richard Furlaud of Paine Webber Inc. and the finance workshop at Cornell University for helpful comments.

Advances in Futures and Options Research, Vol. 3, pages 15–28.

Our purpose is to study the distinctions between American forward and futures options given stochastic interest rates. Futures options are considered in several recent papers: Ball and Torous [1], Ramaswamy and Sundaresan [14], and Brenner, Courtadon, and Subrahmanyan [4]. Our paper extends many of the results contained therein. For example, forward and futures prices and contracts are frequently treated as practically identical. From an empirical standpoint, this appears reasonable since forward and futures prices appear similar (see French [10] and Elton, Gruber, and Rentzler [9]). Yet, under stochastic interest rates, this practical equivalence cannot be extended to forward and futures options. The early exercise potential adds value to futures options. Moreover, this exercise potential depends critically on the statistical properties of forward and futures prices. For example, we show that a futures option's value depends upon the covariance between the spot price and a transform of the instantaneous reinvestment rate.

The next section describes forward options, shows that an American forward option can be treated like a European option, and describes a pricing technique. Section III presents some interesting special features of Treasury bill options. In Section IV, we define and analyze futures options. Section V presents an example, and a summary is given in the final section.

II. FORWARD OPTIONS

An agreement to trade immediately is settled at the cash or spot price. An agreement to trade in the future for a fixed price set now is a forward contract. Several types of financial forward contracts trade frequently. Banks commonly quote forward currency prices for commercial customers. Forward contracts on Treasury securities, called WI or "when issued" contracts, trade in the week prior to a Treasury auction. In addition, synthetic forward Treasury positions can be created with cash bills. Finally, packagers of mortgage-backed securities periodically short mortgage pools forward. These TBA or "to be allocated" GNMA, FNMA, and FHLMC mortgage-backed securities can be sold several months forward. Options on WIs and TBAs trade over the counter daily among wholesale dealers in the underlying cash securities.

We have many prices and contracts to differentiate so we begin with some definitions and symbols. Define the cash or spot price of a security at time s as $p(s, s)$ where $s \in [t, t^*]$. We assume that $p(s, s) > 0$ for all s. The forward price at time s for delivery and payment of a security at time t^* is $p(s, t^*)$. In this framework, a cash contract is a zero-term forward contract.

The forward price adjusts continually to make a new forward contract's value equal to zero. We denote the forward contract's value at the initiation date t as $f[p(t, t^*); k(t), t^*] = 0$ in which $k(t) = p(t, t^*)$ is the delivery price of the contract. For a long contract, the maturity value at time t^* is $f[p(t^*, t^*); k(t), t^*] = p(t^*, t^*) - k(t)$. It is easy to show (see Jarrow and Oldfield [12] and Cox, Ingersoll, and Ross [6]) that the current forward and spot prices are linked through a discount factor:

$$p(s, s) = p(s, t^*)b(s, t^*) \qquad \text{for all } s \in [t, t^*]. \tag{1}$$

In Equation (1), $b(s, t^*)$ denotes the time s price of a default free bill that matures and pays one dollar at time t^*. For convenience, to obtain expression (1) we assume that there are no storage costs for the spot asset. This assumption can be easily relaxed in the subsequent analysis. The relationship among the spot price, the forward price, and the discount factor is crucial for the subsequent pricing of forward options.

A forward call option is exercised at a stated exercise price in favor of the underlying forward contract. If a call is exercised, its owner receives a long forward contract written at the stated exercise price. This means that a forward call option's exercise value at time s is

$$c[p(s, t^*); K, \tau] = f[p(s, t^*); K, t^*] = [p(s, t^*) - K]b(s, t^*). \tag{2}$$

We label the call price $c[p(s, t^*); K, \tau]$ in which $p(s, t^*)$ is the current forward price, time s is between times t and τ, K is the stated exercise forward price, and τ is the expiration date ($t \leqslant \tau < t^*$). In words, Equation (2) means that an exercised call is worth the delivered forward contract. Note that K is *not* the price that a call's owner must pay to exercise. There is no cost to exercise the option.

Consider two alternative investment strategies at time $s \in [t, t^*]$. One can buy a European forward option that matures at τ and K bills that mature at t^* or one can buy the spot security. Suppose the spot security makes no interest or dividend payments prior to the forward option's expiration at time τ. At time τ, the value of the spot asset investment is $p(\tau, \tau)$. For the first investment strategy, if $p(\tau, t^*) < K$ (with positive probability), the call option's value is $c = 0$ and the investment's worth is $Kb(\tau, t^*)$. Since $p(\tau, t^*)b(\tau, t^*) = p(\tau, \tau)$, we get $Kb(\tau, t^*) > p(\tau, \tau)$. Conversely, if $p(\tau, t^*) \geqslant K$, the value of the first strategy involving the option and K bills is $[p(\tau, t^*) - K]b(\tau, t^*) + Kb(\tau, t^*) = p(\tau, \tau)$ and the second strategy's value is $p(\tau, \tau)$ too. This means that given $p(\tau, t^*) < K$ with positive probability then the initial value of the forward options and K bills strategy must exceed the value of the spot commodity. Thus,

$$c[p(s, t^*); K, \tau] > p(s, s) - Kb(s, t^*). \tag{3}$$

The value of an American call option is at least as great as a European call option's price (see Merton [13]). Thus, Equation (3) holds for an American call option too.

It is easy to show that an American option and a European option have the same price. Indeed, we simply establish that there is no incentive for early option exercise. If a forward call option is exercised before τ, say at time s, its rational value is $[p(s, t^*) - K]b(s, t^*)$ or equivalently, $p(s, s) - Kb(s, t^*)$. But from Equation (3), $c > p(s, s) - Kb(s, t^*)$. The option's value alive is greater than its exercised value. Thus, an American forward call option can be treated like a European call option.

To price a forward contract option, we rely upon the equivalent martingale framework described by Harrison and Pliska [11]. This is a generalization of the arbitrary preference, direct option pricing technique introduced by Cox and Ross [5]. In brief, given certain completeness, regularity, and no arbitrage conditions, an arbitrary stochastic price process can be transformed into a risk-neutral process. For example, the "pseudo-probabilities" in binomial option pricing are a discrete time representative of the general transformation (see Bartter and Rendleman [2] and Cox, Ross, and Rubinstein [7]). We assume that the spot, forward, and discount rate processes are imbedded in an economy that has an equivalent martingale transformation. [1] An explicit example of such an economy is given in Section V.

Let us define the interest rate process by $r(s) = \lim_{\Delta \to 0}\{[1 - b(s - \Delta, s)]/b(s - \Delta, s)\Delta\}$. The existence of an equivalent martingale measure, whose expectation is denoted by $\tilde{E}(\cdot)$, means that the term structure of interest rates accords with the expectations hypothesis. In other words, the price of a discount bond, $b(s, t^*)$, must relate to the interest rate process $r(s)$ in a simple way.

$$b(s, t^*) = \tilde{E}_s\{\exp[-\int_s^{t^*} r(y)\, dy]\}. \tag{4}$$

The subscript s in the $\tilde{E}_s(\cdot)$ operator reflects the fact that the expectation is conditional upon the information available at time s. Equation (4) means that in an equivalent risk-neutral world, arbitrage assures that all yields adjust on the basis of expected values alone.

It is convenient to specify an accumulation equation for instantaneous reinvestment. Define $B(\tau, t)$ by

$$B(\tau, t) = \exp[\int_t^\tau r(s)\, ds] \qquad \text{where } B(t, t) = 1. \tag{5}$$

This gives the value at time τ of one dollar continuously reinvested at $r(s)$ from time t to time τ. The discount factor for continuous reinvestment is the expected value of $1/B(\tau, t)$ as in expression (4).

A forward call option can be priced by using the equivalent martingale measure. Since the American call option's value equals the European call option's value, its price is its discounted expected value at expiration.

$$c[p(s, t^*); K, \tau] = \tilde{E}_s[\max\{[p(\tau, t^*) - K]b(\tau, t^*), 0\}/B(\tau, s)]$$
$$= \tilde{E}_s[\max\{p(\tau, t^*) - K, 0\}/B(t^*, s)] \tag{6}$$

This expression illustrates the present value operator in this economy. It corresponds to the generalization of expression (4) where the known cash flow of 1 dollar at time t^* was valued.

III. TREASURY BILL OPTIONS

Options on 13, 26, and 52 week U.S. Treasury bills trade over the counter among spot bill dealers. These options are tailored to a customer's specifications. Some standardization is effected, to provide liquidity in secondary trading. A common bill call option has some interesting features. It is written against $25,000,000 face value of 26 week bills and has a 6-month term until expiration. A bill call option can be exercised any time during its life for new 26 week bills delivered on Thursday of the next auction's delivery week (new 26 week bills are auctioned every Monday with payment and delivery on the following Thursday). Once exercised, the option's owner must pay the fixed delivery price when the bills are delivered. The delivery specifications introduce two unusual features. First, exercise is in terms of forward delivery. Second, the underlying forward contract changes every Friday. If a call option is exercised on or before Friday of the auction week, delivery and payment (at the exercise price) are effected on Thursday of the next week. In other words, delivery and payment always occur on Thursday after the next auction. The option expires on Friday of the last week. This scheme means that a call writer always has an auction for new bills in which to bid if delivery must be made.

The contract terms for a bill call option mean that the correct hedging instrument is a forward 26 bill. This forward bill can be a WI contract that settles on the next Thursday or a synthetic 26 week forward bill assembled from existing cash bills. A call is in the money when the 26 week forward price for the next delivery day exceeds the striking price. Over a weekend, the forward position switches to one that matures a week later. In effect the common type of Treasury bill call option comprises a compound option on a sequence of short duration forward or WI bills.

A recursive technique can be used to price a Treasury bill call option. Consider a call's owner on Friday afternoon 1 week before expiration. If the call is exercised immediately, the underlying forward price is $p(t, t^*)$. If the option is not exercised, the relevant forward price is $p(t, t^* + 1)$, in which time is measured in weeks. Thus, the owner must compute both the exercise value, $[p(t, t^*) - K]b(t, t^*)$ and the unexercised value, $c[p(t, t^* + 1); K, t^*]$. During the week prior to Friday, the option is a standard forward call and the contract should stay alive. The change in underlying forward price on Friday is like a dividend payment. In this case, the exercise alternative must be considered.

Pricing the option on Friday 1 week before it expires is straightforward. Solve Equation (6) given $p(t, t^* + 1)$ and compare the solution to $[p(t, t^*) - K]b(t, t^*)$. The larger value tells whether to hold or exercise. On Thursday or before, pricing involves a more complicated analysis. Again, one relies on the equivalent martingale framework to get an answer. In effect, the value on Thursday is the call's expected equivalent value on Friday, discounted 1 day. This reasoning applies for the whole week before Friday because before Friday the option is a normal forward call that will not be prematurely exercised. Thus, for any day t during the week, when Friday is denoted day s after day t, the call's value is:

$$c\,[p(t, t^*); \; k, \tau] = \tilde{E}_t\,[\max\{c\,[p(s, t^* + 1); \; K, \tau], \; [p(s, t^*) - K]b(t, t^*)\}/B(s, t)].$$
(7)

This recursive relationship gives forward call prices at any time before expiration at τ. The forward price resetting means that early exercise potential is a factor in pricing. The call is free to exercise at any time and K is paid on delivery of the spot bills.

IV.   FUTURES OPTIONS

Futures contracts are a lot like forward contracts. The main difference is that forward contracts have zero cash flows but change value, whereas futures contracts have continuous cash flows (equal to the change in the current futures price) but the contract's value is constant at zero. Prices adjust continually so that this is the case. We call the futures price $P(t, t^*)$ for a contract opened at time t for delivery at time t^*. The futures price for immediate delivery is the spot price so $P(s, s) = p(s, s)$.

As with forward contract options, the futures price–spot price relationship is essential for pricing futures options. It can be shown that the current futures price equals the equivalent expected spot price.

$$P(t, t^*) = \tilde{E}_t\,[p(t^*, t^*)]$$
(8)

The proof of this futures-spot relationship comes from Cox, Ingersoll, and Ross [6]. They show that the futures price is the present value of a security that pays $p(t^*, t^*)B(t^*, t)$ at time t^*. This security trades since we assume that markets are complete. In effect, a title to one unit of the spot commodity collateralizes a loan continuously reinvested at $r(s)$. The present value of this loan is $\tilde{E}_t\,[p(t^*, t^*)\,B(t^*, t)/B(t^*, t)]$, which gives the result in Equation (8). In words, the futures price represents the price of a synthetic traded asset. This observation will be significant in the subsequent analysis.

We can use the futures-spot relationship to show how forward and futures prices relate to one another. From Equation (1) and the valuation operator we write $p(t, t^*)b(t, t^*) = p(t, t)$ and $p(t, t) = \widetilde{E}_t[p(t^*, t^*)/B(t^*, t)]$. We also know that the accumulation factor, $B(t^*, t)$, is greater than unity since $r(s) > 0$ with positive probability. Thus, the present value of the future spot price is less than the current futures price, i.e., $E_t[p(t^*, t^*)/B(t^*, t)] < \widetilde{E}_t[p(t^*, t^*)]$. Given $\widetilde{E}_t[p(t^*, t^*)] = P(t, t^*)$ from Equation (8), we can rearrange the arguments above to write $p(t, t^*) b(t, t^*) < P(t, t^*)$, i.e., the discounted value of the current forward price is strictly less than the current futures price for the same commodity and delivery day. This is a testable implication of the above model.

A parallel argument relates the current futures price to the futures price at a later date. The futures price at a later date, from the discussion after expression (8), represents the value of a traded asset. Hence, it has a present value. Utilizing the valuation operator, the present value is $\widetilde{E}_t[P(\tau, t^*)/B(\tau, t)]$, where τ is before t^*. We claim that

$$P(t, t^*) > \widetilde{E}_t[P(\tau, t^*)/B(\tau, t)]. \tag{9}$$

The current futures price exceeds the present value of the subsequent futures price. The proof is straightforward. First, $\widetilde{E}_t[P(\tau, t^*)/B(\tau, t)] = \widetilde{E}_t\{\widetilde{E}_\tau[P(t^*, t^*)]/B(\tau, t)\}$. Since $B(\tau, t) > 1$ with positive probability, this last expression is less then $\widetilde{E}_t[P(t^*, t^*)]$. Finally, from expression (8), $\widetilde{E}_t[p(t^*, t^*)] = P(t, t^*)$ and this gives Equation (9). This result shows that the futures price today, $P(t, t^*)$, exceeds the present value of the futures price received at a later date, $\widetilde{E}_t[P(\tau, t^*)/B(\tau, t)]$. Hence, the futures price represents the price of a deteriorating asset, whose value declines over time by discounting at the accumulated spot rate.

With the spot, forward, and futures price relationship formalized, we can move to futures option pricing. We label the price of an American futures call option at time s by $C[P(s, t^*); K, \tau]$ in which $C(\cdot)$ denotes the call price, $P(s, t^*)$ the current futures price, K the exercise price, and τ the expiration date where $t \leqslant s \leqslant \tau < t^*$. The first concept to explore is the potential for early futures call exercise. We know that forward calls are not exercised early. This is not true for a futures call. From expression (9) we know that a futures price effectively has a "continuous dividend outflow" due to its deteriorating present value. Thus, early exercise of futures options is quite possibly optimal in some circumstances. We want to characterize these circumstances.

To find the conditions in which early exercise is optimal, we compare the exercised value of an American call option at time s to the unexercised value of a European call option at time s. If $P(s, t^*) - K$ exceeds the European call's price for some $P(s, t^*)$, then early exercise is optimal. Formally, early exercise is optimal with positive probability if and only if for some time s and some set of possible prices,[2]

$$P(s, t^*) - K \geqslant \pi + \widetilde{E}_s[P(\tau, t^*)/B(\tau, s)] - Kb(s, \tau) \tag{10}$$

where π is the price of a European futures put option. The left side of Equation (10) is the futures call's exercised value at time s. The right side, by the standard put–call parity relationship, is the European call's value at time s since $\widetilde{E}_s[P(\tau, t^*)/B(\tau, s)]$ represents the present value of the futures price, the underlying asset, at time s.

We restate Equation (10) by adding K to both sides and rearranging terms. Then early exercise is optimal with positive probability if and only if with positive probability

$$P(s, t^*) - \widetilde{E}_s[P(\tau, t^*)/B(\tau, s)] \geqslant \pi + K[1 - b(s, \tau)]. \tag{11}$$

The forward, future price expression in Equation (8) relates to the left side of Equation (11). Restated, the left-hand side is $\widetilde{E}_s[p(t^*, t^*) - p(t^*, t^*)/B(\tau, s)]$. Factoring inside the brackets gives the present value of the product, i.e., $\widetilde{E}_s\{p(t^*, t^*)[1 - 1/B(\tau, s)]\}$. This can be rewritten as the product of expected values plus a covariance term. Substituting this transformation and rearranging Equation (11) shows early exercise is optimal with positive probability if and only if with positive probability

$$P(s, t^*) \geqslant [\pi + K[1 - b(s, \tau)] - \widetilde{cov}_s\{p(t^*, t^*), [1 - 1/B(\tau, s)]\}]$$
$$/\widetilde{E}_s[1 - 1/B(\tau, s)]. \tag{12}$$

Roughly speaking, early exercise is optimal under some circumstances if the covariance term is positive and large enough so that the right side is below the futures price $P(s, t^*)$. Otherwise, early exercise need not be optimal. In particular, if the $\widetilde{cov}_s\{p(t^*, t^*), [1 - 1/B(\tau, s)]\}$ is sufficiently negative, it is quite possible that early exercise is never optimal. Thus, for each commodity, knowledge of this covariance term's magnitude is essential for identifying instances in which the American option pricing formula and the European option pricing formula coincide.

In some cases, a European formula can be used. In other cases, ones in which the relationship in expression (12) is satisfied, early exercise is a consideration. For example, if the spot rate process is statistically independent of the commodity's spot price process, then the covariance term is identically zero and expression (12) is satisfied with positive probability for large futures prices where $\pi \cong 0$. This example generalizes a result contained in Ball and Torous [1]. They consider deterministic interest rates where the statistical independence condition is trivially satisfied.

Next, to price futures call options, we consider two cases. The European case is first. This case occurs when expression (12) is never satisfied. Here, using the present value operator, the futures call value is

$$C[P(s, t^*); K, \tau] = \widetilde{E}_s[\max\{P(\tau, t^*) - K, 0\}/B(\tau, s)]. \tag{13}$$

It is revealing to contrast expression (13) with the value for the forward call option contained in expression (6). To make the comparison, we need to specify the relationship between forward prices and futures prices. It is easy to show that[3]

$$P(\tau, t^*) = p(\tau, t^*) + \tilde{cov}_\tau[p(t^*, t^*), 1 - 1/B(t^*, \tau)]/b(\tau, t^*). \qquad (14)$$

Substitution into expression (13) gives

$$C[P(s, t^*); K, \tau] = \tilde{E}_s[\max\{[p(\tau, t^*) + \tilde{cov}_\tau[p(t^*, t^*), 1 - 1/B(t^*, \tau)]$$
$$/b(\tau, t^*)] - K, 0\}/B(\tau, s)] \qquad (15)$$

The two call option values in expression (6) and (15) differ due to the covariance term within the maximum operator of expression (15) and the discounting factor. If the covariance term is zero or positive, then the European futures call option price exceeds the forward call's price. Conversely, if the covariance term is sufficiently negative, the forward call's price exceeds the European futures call's price. This situation corresponds to the case in which the forward price exceeds the futures price.

Finally, when expression (12) is satisfied with positive probability, early exercise is a consideration. To value the American futures call option in this case, one must first prespecify an early exercise policy (which depends on the information available at each date), and then value the European call under the value maximizing policy. This procedure is detailed in Bensoussan [3].

Futures price limit moves are an institutional reality in futures contract markets. It is easy to show that they do not influence futures option prices in our framework. The reason is simple. We can construct a synthetic security with the futures price value using the spot commodity and the discount factor [see Equation (8)]. Neither the spot commodity nor the discount factor is subject to exchange-defined limit moves. Thus, standard option pricing can proceed with the synthetic futures prices despite an arbitrary closing of the futures contract market.[4]

V. EXAMPLE

This section presents a simple example to illustrate the conclusions obtained in the previous sections. We study an economy lasting only two periods $(t = 0, 1, 2 = t^*)$. The stochastic structure of the economy is given in Figure 1. There are four states $\{1, 2, 3, 4\}$, each occurring with positive probability. At time 1, either event $\{12\}$ or $\{34\}$ occurs.

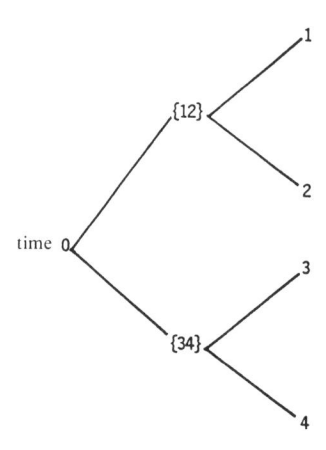

Figure 1. Resolution of uncertainty in the economy.

The spot commodities price follows a simple binomial process:

$$p(0, 0) = 1 \tag{16a}$$

$$p_{12}(1, 1) = e^{\alpha_u}, \ p_{34}(1, 1) = e^{\alpha_d} \tag{16b}$$

$$p_1(2, 2) = e^{2\alpha_u}$$

$$p_2(2, 2) = p_3(2, 2) = e^{\alpha_u + \alpha_d} \tag{16c}$$

$$p_4(2, 2) = e^{2\alpha_d}$$

where $\alpha_u > \alpha_d$. The subscripts on $p(t, t)$ represent the state of the economy. For example, $p_{12}(1, 1)$ is the spot price at time 1 in state {12}. The spot commodities price is normalized to be 1 at time 0. If state {12} occurs, then the price jumps "*up*" ($e^{\alpha_u} - 1$) percent, while if state {34} occurs, the price jumps "*down*" ($e^{\alpha_d} - 1$) percent. A similar pattern occurs from time 1 to time 2.

The accumulation factor (or spot rate) satisfies the following equations:

$$B(0, 0) = 1 \tag{17a}$$

$$B_{12}(1, 0) = B_{34}(1, 0) = e^{r(0)} \tag{17b}$$

$$B_1(2, 0) = B_2(2, 0) = e^{r(0) + r_d(1)}$$

$$B_3(2, 0) = B_4(2, 0) = e^{r(0) + r_u(1)} \tag{17c}$$

where $\alpha_u > r_u(1) > r_d(1) > \alpha_d$ and $\alpha_u > r(0) > \alpha_d$. Subscripts on $B(t, 0)$ represent the state of the economy at the appropriate time t. The spot rate over the first period is known to be r(0). At time 1, if state {12} occurs, then the spot rate is $r_d(1)$. If state {34} occurs, however, the spot rate is $r_u(1)$ where $r_u(1) > r_d(1)$. So, by construction spot rates are negatively correlated to the spot commodity's price.

The long-term bond process is given by

$$b(0, 2) = e^{-i_d - r_u(1)} = e^{-i_u - r_d(1)} \tag{18a}$$

$$b_{12}(1, 2) = e^{-r_d(1)}$$
$$b_{34}(1, 2) = e^{-r_u(1)} \tag{18b}$$

$$b_1(2, 0) = b_2(2, 0) = b_3(2, 0) = b_4(2, 0) = 1 \tag{18c}$$

where $i_u > i_d$. Again, the subscripts on b(t, s) represent the state of the economy at time t. By construction the bond's price is 1 at time 2. Since its value, b(0, 2), is known at time 0, expression (18a) expresses the constraint imposed on its returns over the next two periods. It earns the spot rate over the last period, and either a return of i_u over the first period if state {12} occurs, or a return of i_d if state {34} occurs where $i_u > i_d$.

Given there are only two possibilities at each time period, trading in the spot commodity and the accumulation factor guarantees that the market is complete. This completeness property means that any contingent claim related to these two traded assets can be duplicated by some dynamic portfolio strategy involving both assets. It also implies that an equivalent martingale measure exists. This measure is denoted by $\tilde{q}(w)$ for $w \in \{1, 2, 3, 4\}$ and can be shown to equal

$$\tilde{q}(\{12\}) = [e^{r(0)} - e^{\alpha_d}] / [e^{\alpha_u} - e^{\alpha_d}]$$
$$\tilde{q}(\{34\}) = 1 - \tilde{q}(\{12\}) \tag{19a}$$

$$\tilde{q}(\{1\} \mid \{12\}) = [e^{r_d(1)} - e^{\alpha_d}] / [e^{\alpha_u} - e^{\alpha_d}]$$
$$\tilde{q}(\{2\} \mid \{12\}) = 1 - \tilde{q}(\{1\} \mid \{12\}) \tag{19b}$$

$$\tilde{q}(\{3\} \mid \{12\}) = \tilde{q}(\{4\} \mid \{12\}) = 0$$

$$\tilde{q}(\{3\} \mid \{34\}) = [e^{r_u(1)} - e^{\alpha_d}] / [e^{\alpha_u} - e^{\alpha_d}]$$
$$\tilde{q}(\{4\} \mid \{34\}) = 1 - \tilde{q}(\{3\} \mid \{34\}) \tag{19c}$$

$$\tilde{q}(\{1\} \mid \{34\}) = \tilde{q}(\{2\} \mid \{34\}) = 0.$$

These are the "psuedo-probabilities" discussed in Section II. In addition, it is a straightforward exercise to show that [p(t, t)/B(t, 0)] is a martingale under the probability $\tilde{q}$.

Since the long-term bond is redundant in this economy, to avoid arbitrage, its value must equal

$$b(0, 2) = \widetilde{E}[1/B(2, 0)].$$

This condition is equivalent to

$$\tilde{q}(\{12\})e^{i_u} + \tilde{q}(\{34\})e^{i_d} = e^{r(0)}. \tag{20}$$

Together with condition (18a), condition (20) completely determines the parameters of the long-term bond process i_d and i_u as functions of $\{\alpha_d, \alpha_u, r_u(1), r_d(1), r(0)\}$. In particular, expression (20) implies that $i_u > r(0) > i_d$. Using conditions (1) and (8) from the previous sections (which can be directly proven in this simple economy), it can be shown that

$$p(0, 2) = e^{i_u + r_d(1)} \tag{21a}$$

and

$$\begin{aligned} P(0, 2) = p(0, 2) &+ [e^{r_d(1) + r(0)} - e^{r_d(1) + i_u}] \\ &+ [1 - \tilde{q}(12)]e^{r_d(1) + \alpha_d}[(e^{i_u}/e^{i_d}) - 1]. \end{aligned} \tag{21b}$$

The last two terms in expression (21b) are of different signs. The first is negative since $i_u > r(0)$, while the second is positive since $i_u > i_d$. For different values of the parameters, therefore, the forward price $p(0, 2)$ can exceed the futures price $P(0, 2)$, or be less than it. The sum of these two terms corresponds to the covariance component in expression (14).

For call options, using expression (15) and (6), the valuation formulas are (if the exercise price K is chosen so that there is a positive probability of exercise at time 1, $\tilde{q}[p(1, 2) > K] > 0$),

$$\begin{aligned} c\,[p(0, 2);\, K, 1] = \widetilde{E}\,[\max\{p(1, 2) - K, 0\}/B(2, 0)] \\ < \widetilde{E}\,[\max\{p(1, 2) - K, 0\}/B(1, 0)] = C\,[P(0, 2), K, 1] \end{aligned} \tag{22}$$

where $\tilde{cov}_1\,[p(2, 2),\, 1 - 1/B(2, 1)] = 0$ because $B(2, 1) = e^{r(1)}$ is known at time 1. This inequality verifies the results of the last section.

VI. SUMMARY

In this paper, we analyze the properties of forward options and futures options. Stochastic interest rates are assumed throughout. We derive several important results. First, in cases in which the spot asset makes no interim payments, a forward option will not be exercised before its expiration date. Thus, an American forward option can be treated like a European forward option. Second, an over the counter Treasury bill option can be treated like a compound forward option. This allows a recursive price technique based upon a series of European option pricing equations to be used. Finally, futures options may be exercised early. The futures option value depends critically on the covariance between the spot price and the expression $[1 - 1/B(t^*, \tau)]$. Since the term $B(t^*, \tau)$ represents an accumulation factor at time t^* for continuous reinvestment at the instantaneous risk free rate over $[\tau, t^*]$, the stochastic interest rate process is seen to influence the price of any futures option.

Options on spot, forward, and futures fixed income securities are widely traded. This paper gives a comprehensive analytic method based upon an equivalent martingale framework. Although the mathematic foundation is abstract, the direct pricing applications are based largely on algebraic relationships. The approach allows us to derive pricing equations for call options on forward and futures contracts with stochastic interest rates. An example is also provided to illustrate the main conclusions.

NOTES

1. The economy we consider is contained in Harrison and Pliska [11]. The market is complete and the trading strategies are admissible, allowing no arbitrage opportunities. Under these circumstances, Harrison and Pliska prove the existence of an equivalent martingale measure.

2. The proof of this statement follows. Suppose it is never optimal to exercise early. Then the American call's value unexercised is always strictly larger than its exercised value. But, the European call's value equals the American call's value in this case. Conversely, if early exercise is optimal with positive probability then there is some time s and some set of prices where $P(s, t^*) - K$ exceeds or equals the American call's value unexercised, which in turn exceeds or equals the European call's value. This completes the proof of this statement.

3. The proof is

$$p(\tau, t^*) = p(\tau, \tau)/b(\tau, t^*) = \tilde{E}_\tau[p(t^*, t^*)/B(t^*, \tau)]/b(\tau, t^*)$$
$$= \tilde{E}_\tau[p(t^*, t^*)]\tilde{E}[1/B(t^*, \tau)]/b(\tau, t^*)$$
$$- cov_\tau[p(t^*, t^*), 1 - 1/B(t^*, \tau)]/b(\tau, t^*)$$

which by expression (4) and (8) gives (14).

4. One can now value the futures option, based on the synthetic futures price. Here, the exchange set limit move restrictions on the futures price, influences the value of the option when exercised. These restrictions can be viewed as "new" boundary conditions on the option. The same technique as discussed in Section III can be applied.

REFERENCES

1. Ball, C. A., and W. N. Torous, "Futures Options and the Volatility of Futures Prices," *Journal of Finance* 4 (September 1986), 857–870.

2. Bartter, B., and R. Rendleman, "Two-State Option Pricing," *The Journal of Finance* 34 (December 1979), 1093–1110.

3. Bensoussan, A., "On the Theory of Option Pricing," *ACTA Mathematica*, 2 (1984), 159–184.

4. Brenner, M., G. Courtadon, and M. Subrahmanyan, "Options on the Spot and Options on Futures," *The Journal of Finance* 40 (December 1985), 1303–1317.

5. Cox, J., and S. Ross, "The Valuation of Options for Alternative Stochastic Processes," *Journal of Financial Economics* 3 (January/March 1976), 145–166.

6. Cox, J., J. Ingersoll, and S. Ross, "The Relation between Forward Prices and Futures Prices," *Journal of Financial Economics* 9 (December 1981), 373–382.

7. Cox, J., S. Ross, and M. Rubenstein, "Option Pricing: A Simplified Result," *Journal of Financial Economics* 7 (September 1979), 229–263.

8. Durrett, R., *Brownian Motions and Martingales in Analysis*, Wadsworth Advanced Books and Software, 1984.

9. Elton, E., M. Gruber, and R. Rentzler, "Intraday Tests of the Treasury Bill Futures Market," *Review of Economics and Statistics* LXVI (February 1984), 129–141.

10. French, K., "A Comparison of Futures and Forward Prices," *Journal of Financial Economics* 12 (November 1983), 311–342.

11. Harrison, J. M., and S. R. Pliska, "Martingales and Stochastic Integrals in the Theory of Continuous Trading," *Stochastic Processes and Their Applications* 11 (1981), 215–260.

12. Jarrow, R., and G. Oldfield, "Forward Contracts and Futures Contracts," *Journal of Financial Economics* 9 (December 1981), 373–382.

13. Merton, R., "The Theory of Rational Option Pricing," *The Bell Journal of Economics* 4 (Spring 1973), 141–183.

14. Ramaswamy, K., and S. Sundaresan, "The Valuation of Options on Futures Contracts," *Journal of Finance* 40 (December 1985), 1319–1340.

AN ANALYSIS OF THE BIAS IN OPTION PRICING CAUSED BY A STOCHASTIC VOLATILITY

John Hull[*] and Alan White[*]

I. INTRODUCTION

In a major breakthrough, Black and Scholes [1] produced a closed form solution for the price of a European call option on a stock. In order to derive the option pricing formula they assumed that markets are perfect, costless trading takes place continuously, the short-term interest rate is constant, the stock pays no dividends, and the stock price follows a geometric Brownian motion with a constant variance rate. These assumptions were subsequently relaxed by other authors.

Merton [25] dropped the assumption of a fixed interest rate and showed how, in this case, an option can be priced in terms of a bond price. This

[*]Faculty of Management, University of Toronto.

Advances in Futures and Options Research, Vol. 3, pages 29–61.
Copyright © 1988 by JAI Press Inc.
ISBN: 0-89232-926-2

solution methodology was later extended by Fischer [11], Margrabe [24], Stulz [32], and Johnson [19] who analyzed options to exchange one asset for another. The assumption of no dividends was addressed by Merton [25], Roll [28], and Geske [14]. Merton [25] also showed how the Black–Scholes formula can be extended to cover the situation in which the variance rate is a deterministic function of time.

Solutions to European option pricing problems for a variety of different stock price processes have also been derived. Merton [26], Cox and Ross [9], and Jones [22] determine the price of a call option if the stock price follows a discontinuous jump process or if it follows a mixed jump diffusion process. Cox and Ross [9] and Rubinstein [29] solve option pricing problems for situations in which the variance of the instantaneous rate of return is a function of the stock price. Geske [15] assumes that the variance rate of the firm value is fixed. Since the degree of financial leverage decreases as the firm value increases, this leads to a model in which stock price volatility declines as the stock price increases.

There has been some empirical work on the distribution of stock returns. Christie [6] finds that Geske's [15] model is supported by the data. However, the unexplained portion of changes in the variance is very large. This may be due to errors in estimating the variance or due to other random changes in the variance. Kon [23] finds that the observed distribution of stock returns is consistent with a randomly varying variance. Scott [31] using 258 monthly estimates of the variance of daily stock returns shows that the hypothesis that stock returns are distributed independently over time can be rejected. His results are consistent with a model in which the instantaneous variance of returns follows a mean reverting stochastic process. Bodurtha and Courtadon [2] and Hull and White [17] provide some evidence drawn from the prices of currencies and currency options that suggests that the variances of currency prices vary randomly. These empirical observations, coupled with the fact that there is no particular reason to assume that the variance rate of a stock price or a firm value is either constant or deterministic, suggest that the volatility should be modeled as a separate state variable. The Black–Scholes option pricing formula is then no longer correct.

A number of authors have examined option pricing problems when the volatility is stochastic. Johnson [20] was the first to consider this problem. He was able to derive the partial differential equation that such an option must satisfy. Although he was unable to solve this, he did infer some properties of the solution. More recent work has involved both analytic and numerical approaches. Johnson and Shanno [21] and Wiggins [33] produce numerical solutions to the problem. Scott [31] tests the hypothesis that observed option prices are consistent with a stochastic volatility. Hull and White [18] produce analytic results for the special case in which the volatility is uncorrelated with the stock price.

This paper derives an expression in series form for the pricing bias caused by a stochastic volatility. Unlike Hull and White [18], it allows the volatility to be instantaneously correlated with the stock price. Also, results are provided for the situation in which the volatility follows a mean reverting process as well as for the situation in which the volatility follows a stochastic process with no drift, a constant drift, or a constant proportional drift. The market price of the risk associated with the volatility is assumed constant. It might be guessed that the Black–Scholes price always under-prices when the volatility is stochastic. This paper shows that this is not the case. The bias shows a rich pattern of behavior. Whether underpricing or overpricing takes place is found to depend primarily on (1) the drift rate of the volatility, (2) the sign of the correlation between the stock price and volatility, and (3) the extent to which the option is in- or out-of-the-money.

This paper is similar in spirit to Dothan [10]. However the results here are more general than the results produced by Dothan in one respect. Dothan assumes, in the mean reverting case, that the rate at which the volatility is pulled toward its long run average level is small. This paper does not make that assumption. This paper also investigates a problem not considered by Dothan: the implications of a stochastic volatility for option replication strategies.

The solution technique in this paper is a particular case of a more general procedure for pricing two state variable contingent claims. The procedure is applicable when the price of the contingent claim is known when one of the variables is deterministic. Other work involving two state variable contingent claims has been done by Brennan and Schwartz [4, 5], Boyle and Kirzner [3], Stulz [32], and Richard [27].

The organization of this paper is as follows. Section II discusses the stochastic process that is assumed for the stock price. Section III provides a value for a European call option in series form. The results from using the series solution are compared with results from using Monte Carlo simulation in Section IV. Section V discusses the properties of the solution. Section VI discusses the implications of a stochastic volatility for option replication strategies. Conclusions are in Section VII.

II. PRICE DYNAMICS

Define

$S(t)$:   stock price at time t
$V(t)$:   variance of dS/S at time t
$\phi(t)$:   drift rate of dS/S at time t
$\eta(V)$:   drift rate of dV
ξ: instantaneous standard deviation of $dV/\sqrt{V}$
ρ: instantaneous correlation between dS/S and $dV/\sqrt{V}$

The stock price, S, and volatility, V, are assumed to obey the following stochastic processes:

$$\frac{dS}{S} = \phi \, dt + \sqrt{V} \, dz \tag{1}$$

$$dV = \eta \, dt + \xi\sqrt{V} \, dw \tag{2}$$

where dz and dw are Wiener processes.

Roughly speaking, the implication of the model proposed in (1) and (2) is that over the next short instant of time the rate of return earned by the stock will be drawn from a normal distribution with mean ϕ dt and variance V dt. At the same time the variance rate is itself changing to V + dV. Accordingly, in the following short instant of time, the rate of return earned by the stock will be drawn from a new normal distribution with mean ϕ dt and variance (V + dV) dt. The process for the unanticipated part of the stock price follows a martingale (as it must if markets are efficient) but it no longer follows a stationary process as has been traditionally assumed. Because the variance rate changes randomly, the probability density function of the stock price at some future time conditional on the current stock price is not lognormal.

The relation between V and S is captured by ρ, the instantaneous correlation between the Wiener processes dz and dw. Hull and White [18] analyze the case in which $\rho = 0$ while Cox and Ross [9] and Geske [15] examine the case in which $\rho = -1$. Dothan [10] produces a series solution for the general case $-1 \leqslant \rho \leqslant 1$. The empirical data of Kon [23] suggest that $-1 < \rho < 0$. This is in accord with casual observation. As stock prices rise, volatilities tend to decline but the correlation appears to be less than perfect.

We shall assume that ξ is constant and that the drift rate of V, η, is given by

$$\eta = a + bV, \tag{3}$$

where a and b are constants. In order to ensure that V remains nonnegative we require $a \geqslant 0$. Equation (3) can give a constant drift (b = 0), a constant proportional drift (a = 0), or a mean reverting process (a > 0, b < 0). In this latter case V tends to revert to a level $-a/b$ with a reversion rate $-b$.

Define EV(s,t) as the expected volatility at time s(s $\geqslant$ t) conditional on the volatility, V(t), at time t. The mean reverting model (a > 0, b < 0) is analogous to the model considered by Cox, Ingersoll, and Ross [8] for the short-term rate of interest. The expected volatility at time s is given by

$$EV(s, t) = [V(t) - \hat{V}]e^{b(s-t)} + \hat{V}, \tag{4}$$

where $\hat{V}$ is the reversion level, $-a/b$. The variance of V(s) conditional on

$V(t)$ is

$$V(t)\left(\frac{\xi^2}{-b}\right)[e^{b(s-t)} - e^{2b(s-t)}] + \hat{V}\left(\frac{\xi^2}{-2b}\right)[1 - e^{b(s-t)}]^2. \qquad (5)$$

Equations (4) and (5) allow us to infer some plausible parameters for the process for V. Equation (4) reveals that any deviations from the reversion value, $V - \hat{V}$, are expected to die away at an exponential rate. The time required for the expected deviation to be halved, the half-life, is given by $-0.693/b$. Values of b in the range from -10 to -1 per year give half-lives of from a few days to about half a year. Reasonable values for the reversion level, $\hat{V} = -a/b$, are in the range 0.05 to 0.10 per year.[1] Once a and b have been chosen, Equation (5) allows us to determine whether the long run variance of V for a given value of ξ is plausible. For example, if $a = 0.18$, $b = -2$, and $\xi = 0.10$ the long run standard deviation of V is 0.015 and the two standard deviation range for V is from 0.06 to 0.12 per year.[2]

III. CALL OPTION PRICING WHEN THE VARIANCE RATE IS STOCHASTIC

In this section we consider a European call option on a stock with an exercise price X and a maturity time T. The stock price is assumed to follow the process given by (1). If the variance rate, V, is constant then the option price, C, is the Black–Scholes price that satisfies the differential equation

$$\frac{\partial C}{\partial t} + \frac{1}{2} VS^2 \frac{\partial^2 C}{\partial S^2} - rC = -rS \frac{\partial C}{\partial S}. \qquad (6)$$

If the variance rate, V, obeys the stochastic process given by (2), the call price, c, depends on two state variables S and V. Garman [13] and Cox, Ingersoll, and Ross [7] show that a security f whose price depends on state variables θ_i must satisfy the differential equation

$$\frac{\partial f}{\partial t} + \frac{1}{2} \sum_{i,j} \rho_{ij}\sigma_i\sigma_j \frac{\partial^2 f}{\partial\theta_i\partial\theta_j} - rf = \sum_i \theta_i \frac{\partial f}{\partial\theta_i} [-\mu_i + \lambda_i\sigma_i] \qquad (7)$$

where σ_i is the instantaneous standard deviation of the proportional change in θ_i, ρ_{ij} is the instantaneous correlation between θ_i and θ_j, μ_i is the proportional drift rate of θ_i, and λ_i is the market price of risk for variable θ_i. When variable i is traded the ith element of the right-hand side of (7) is $-r\theta_i\partial f/\partial\theta_i$.

It follows that, for the two state variable case in question,

$$\frac{\partial c}{\partial t} + \frac{1}{2}\left[VS^2 \frac{\partial^2 c}{\partial S^2} + 2\rho V\xi S \frac{\partial^2 c}{\partial S\partial V} + \xi^2 V \frac{\partial^2 c}{\partial V^2} \right] - rc$$

$$= -rS\frac{\partial c}{\partial S} - [\eta - \lambda_V \xi\sqrt{V}]\frac{\partial c}{\partial V}$$

where λ_V is the market price of risk for variable V. Note that since λ_V depends on investor risk preferences, the option price will, in general, depend on investor risk preferences. We assume initially that λ_V is zero so that

$$\frac{\partial c}{\partial t} + \frac{1}{2}\left[VS^2 \frac{\partial^2 c}{\partial S^2} + 2\rho V\xi S \frac{\partial^2 c}{\partial S\partial V} + \xi^2 V \frac{\partial^2 c}{\partial V^2} \right] - rc = -rS\frac{\partial c}{\partial S} - \eta \frac{\partial c}{\partial V}. \qquad (8)$$

Later it will be shown the solution that is produced can be extended to accommodate the situation where λ_V is not zero, that is, where investors require compensation for bearing volatility risk.

Equation (8) is the differential equation that any security whose value is contingent on S and V must satisfy. If ξ and η are zero (8) devolves into (6), the Black–Scholes equation. If ξ is zero but η is nonzero then (8) becomes the differential equation that an option with a nonconstant deterministic variance rate must satisfy. This was solved by Merton [25].

In order to solve the option pricing problem when the volatility is stochastic, let us define the pricing bias

$$B = c - C.$$

This bias is the amount by which the actual option price when the variance rate is stochastic exceeds the Black–Scholes price when the variance is constant and equal to its initial value. Substituting $c = C + B$ in Equation (8) and using Equation (6) we obtain

$$\frac{\partial B}{\partial t} + \frac{1}{2}\left[VS^2 \frac{\partial^2 B}{\partial S^2} + 2\rho V\xi S \frac{\partial^2 B}{\partial S\partial V} + \xi^2 V \frac{\partial^2 B}{\partial V^2} \right] - rB$$

$$+ \rho V\xi S \frac{\partial^2 C}{\partial S\partial V} + \frac{1}{2}\xi^2 V \frac{\partial^2 C}{\partial V^2} = -rS\frac{\partial B}{\partial S} - \eta \frac{\partial B}{\partial V} - \eta \frac{\partial C}{\partial V} \qquad (9)$$

as the equation that the pricing bias must satisfy. The objective of this paper is to calculate B as a series in ξ

$$B = f_0 + f_1\xi + f_2\xi^2 + \cdots \qquad (10)$$

where the f_i are functions of S, V, and t.

Define a differential operator **D** as follows

$$\mathbf{D}f = \frac{\partial f}{\partial t} + \frac{1}{2} VS^2 \frac{\partial^2 f}{\partial S^2} - rf + rS \frac{\partial f}{\partial S}.$$

In terms of this operator, the Black–Scholes differential equation is $\mathbf{D}C = 0$. If Equation (10) is substituted into Equation (9) and terms are collected by powers of ξ and if (9) is to be satisfied for arbitrary ξ we obtain

$$\mathbf{D}f_0 + \eta \frac{\partial f_0}{\partial V} + \eta \frac{\partial C}{\partial V} = 0 \tag{11}$$

$$\mathbf{D}f_1 + \eta \frac{\partial f_1}{\partial V} + \rho VS \frac{\partial^2 f_0}{\partial S \partial V} + \rho VS \frac{\partial^2 C}{\partial S \partial V} = 0 \tag{12}$$

$$\mathbf{D}f_2 + \eta \frac{\partial f_2}{\partial V} + \rho VS \frac{\partial^2 f_1}{\partial S \partial V} + \frac{1}{2} V \frac{\partial^2 C}{\partial V^2} + \frac{1}{2} V \frac{\partial^2 f_0}{\partial V^2} = 0 \tag{13}$$

and

$$\mathbf{D}f_i + \eta \frac{\partial f_i}{\partial V} + \rho VS \frac{\partial^2 f_{i-1}}{\partial S \partial V} + \frac{1}{2} V \frac{\partial^2 f_{i-2}}{\partial V^2} = 0 \tag{14}$$

for $i > 2$.

Equations (11)–(14) define a family of differential equations that the coefficients of Equation (10) must satisfy. Every function f_i must satisfy the boundary conditions:

$$\begin{array}{llll} f_i = 0 & \text{when} & t = T & \\ f_i = 0 & \text{when} & S = 0 & \tag{15} \\ \partial f_i / \partial S \to 0 & \text{as} & S \to \infty. & \end{array}$$

The first of these follows from the fact that at $t = T$, $c = C = \max[0, S - X]$ regardless of the value of ξ. The second arises from $c = C = 0$ when $S = 0$. The third arises from the fact that both $\partial c / \partial S \to 1$ and $\partial C / \partial S \to 1$ as $S \to \infty$.[3]

The solutions to Equations (11)–(13) for the process for V given by (2) and (3) are

$$f_0 = C(\bar{V}) - C(V) \tag{16}$$

$$f_1 = \frac{\rho}{b^2 \delta} \{(a + bV)(1 - e^\delta + \delta e^\delta) + a(1 + \delta - e^\delta)\}S \frac{\partial^2 C(\bar{V})}{\partial S \partial \bar{V}} \tag{17}$$

$$f_2 = \frac{\phi_1}{T - t} S \frac{\partial^2 C(\bar{V})}{\partial S \partial \bar{V}} + \frac{\phi_2}{(T - t)^2} \frac{\partial^2 C(\bar{V})}{\partial \bar{V}^2} + \frac{\phi_3}{(T - t)^2} S \frac{\partial^3 C(\bar{V})}{\partial S \partial \bar{V}^2}$$

$$+ \frac{\phi_4}{(T - t)^3} \frac{\partial^3 C(\bar{V})}{\partial \bar{V}^3} \tag{18}$$

where

$$\phi_1 = \frac{\rho^2}{b^4}\left\{(a + bV)\left[e^\delta\left(\frac{1}{2}\delta^2 - \delta + 1\right) - 1\right] + a\,[e^\delta(2 - \delta) - (2 + \delta)]\right\}$$

$$\phi_2 = 2\phi_1 + \frac{1}{2b^4}\left\{(a + bV)(e^{2\delta} - 2\delta e^\delta - 1) - \frac{a}{2}(e^{2\delta} - 4e^\delta + 2\delta + 3)\right\},$$

$$\phi_3 = \frac{\rho^2}{2b^6}\{(a + bV)(e^\delta - \delta e^\delta - 1) - a(1 + \delta - e^\delta)\}^2,$$

$$\phi_4 = 2\phi_3,$$

$$\delta = b(T - t),$$

and $\overline{V}$ is the average expected variance rate in the interval (t, T), that is,

$$\overline{V} = \frac{1}{T - t}\int_t^T EV(s, t)\,ds.$$

The proof that f_0, f_1, and f_2 satisfy the differential Equations (11), (12), and (13) is given in the Appendix together with a procedure for calculating f_i for all values of i. It is not immediately obvious that f_0, f_1, and f_2 satisfy the boundary conditions in (15). A proof of this is given in Note 2 at the end of this paper. The higher order terms in the series are increasingly lengthy and complex, but are not difficult to derive.

When $\xi = 0$, the series gives

$$B = C(\overline{V}) - C(V)$$

or

$$c = C(\overline{V}).$$

This corresponds to the result in Merton [25] for the situation where the volatility is a deterministic function of time. When the volatility is constant $\overline{V} = V$ and the Black–Scholes result is obtained.

The special case $b = 0$ is found by taking the limits of (16)–(18). The value of f_0 is still given by (16),

$$f_1 = \rho\left[\frac{a(T - t)}{3} + V\right]\frac{(T - t)}{2}\,S\,\frac{\partial^2 C(\overline{V})}{\partial S \partial \overline{V}},$$

and f_2 is given by (18) where

$$\phi_1 = \rho^2\left[\frac{a(T - t)}{4} + V\right]\frac{(T - t)^3}{6}$$

$$\phi_2 = \left(2 + \frac{1}{\rho^2}\right)\phi_1$$

$$\phi_3 = \rho^2 \left[\frac{a(T - t)}{3} + V \right]^2 \frac{(T - t)^4}{8}$$

$$\phi_4 = 2\phi_3.$$

Up to now we have assumed that λ_V is zero. We consider two cases in which λ_V is not zero. First, if $\lambda_V \xi \sqrt{V}$ is a constant we can define a risk-adjusted drift rate, η^*, for V by

$$\eta^* = \eta - \lambda_V \xi \sqrt{V}.$$

If $a^* = a - \lambda_V \xi \sqrt{V}$, it follows that

$$\eta^* = a^* + bV.$$

Similarly, if $\lambda_V \xi \sqrt{V}$ is proportional to V we define $b^* = b - \lambda_V \xi / \sqrt{V}$ and

$$\eta^* = a + b^* V.$$

The solution to the problem where λ_V is not zero and the drift rate of V is η is identical to the solution of the problem where $\lambda_V = 0$ and the drift rate in V is η^*. The results in Equations (10), (16), (17), and (18) are therefore true with a replaced by a^* or b replaced by b^*.

IV. THE ACCURACY OF THE SERIES SOLUTION

In this section the bias obtained by taking the first three terms of the series solution is compared with an estimate of the bias using a Monte Carlo simulation. The advantage of using a Monte Carlo estimate as a benchmark is that the standard error of the estimate is known. The range of parameter values tested were

$$
\begin{aligned}
S/X: &\quad 0.90, 0.95, 1.00, 1.05, 1.10 \\
\rho: &\quad -1.0, -0.5, 0.0, 0.5, 1.0 \\
\xi: &\quad 0.075, 0.150 \text{ per year} \\
(a, b): &\quad (0,0), (0.18, -2), (0.90, -10). \\
V(0): &\quad 0.09 \text{ per year} \\
T: &\quad 180 \text{ days or } 0.493 \text{ years} \\
r: &\quad 0.
\end{aligned}
$$

The argument at the end of Section II shows that the selected values for ξ are reasonable.

The results are shown in Tables 1, 2, and 3. Each table shows the series solution, the Monte Carlo estimate, and the standard error of this estimate. The results report the bias as a percentage of the corresponding Black–Scholes price. The patterns revealed in Tables 1–3 are the same as those found by Hull and White [18] and Johnson and Shanno [21]. When the volatility is negatively correlated with the stock price, the Black–Scholes price is too high for out-of-the-money options and too low for in-the-money options. When the correlation is positive the reverse is true.

Note that for a sufficiently large sample size, the Monte Carlo result will differ from any imperfect estimate of the true value by more than two

Table 1. The Bias Induced in the Price of a Call Option When the Variance Rate Is Stochastic and Reverts Slowly to its Long-run Average Level[a]

				S/X		
ξ/year	ρ	0.90	0.95	1.00	1.05	1.10
0.15	− 1.0	− 7.57	− 3.41	− 0.95	0.39	1.03
		− 7.39	− 3.64	− 0.92	0.51	0.94
		(0.29)	(0.22)	(0.16)	(0.13)	(0.11)
	− 0.5	− 3.90	− 1.86	− 0.60	0.11	0.48
		− 3.87	− 2.00	− 0.53	0.22	0.56
		(0.16)	(0.11)	(0.09)	(0.07)	(0.06)
	0.0	− 0.35	− 0.33	− 0.26	− 0.18	− 0.11
		− 0.36	− 0.31	− 0.24	− 0.19	− 0.13
		(0.02)	(0.02)	(0.01)	(0.01)	(0.01)
	0.5	3.07	1.17	0.08	− 0.49	− 0.73
		3.21	1.17	− 0.07	− 0.51	− 0.68
		(0.15)	(0.10)	(0.08)	(0.06)	(0.06)
	1.0	6.37	2.64	0.41	− 0.82	− 1.39
		6.50	2.78	0.61	− 0.79	− 1.19
		(0.30)	(0.22)	(0.16)	(0.14)	(0.12)
0.075	− 1.0	− 3.63	− 1.61	− 0.41	0.25	0.56
		− 3.83	− 1.56	− 0.38	0.26	0.65
		(0.15)	(0.10)	(0.07)	(0.06)	(0.05)
	− 0.5	− 1.85	− 0.84	− 0.24	0.10	0.27
		− 1.85	− 0.84	− 0.20	0.09	0.25
		(0.07)	(0.05)	(0.04)	(0.04)	(0.03)
	0.0	− 0.09	− 0.08	− 0.07	− 0.05	− 0.03
		− 0.08	− 0.09	− 0.07	− 0.04	− 0.03
		(0.01)	(0.005)	(0.003)	(0.003)	(0.002)
	0.5	1.64	0.67	0.10	− 0.20	− 0.34
		1.57	0.65	0.12	− 0.25	− 0.37
		(0.06)	(0.06)	(0.04)	(0.03)	(0.03)
	1.0	3.33	1.41	0.27	− 0.35	− 0.65
		3.45	1.37	0.22	− 0.36	− 0.64
		(0.16)	(0.10)	(0.08)	(0.06)	(0.05)

[a]Bias is expressed as a percentage of the equivalent Black–Scholes price. The variance rate obeys the process $dV = (a + bV) dt + \xi V dz$. The option parameters are $\sqrt{V(t)} = 0.30$ per year, $r = 0$, $a = 0.18$, $b = -2$, and time to maturity $T - t = 180$ days or 0.493 years. Every cell in the table contains three numbers: the bias calculated using Equations (16)–(18), the Monte Carlo estimate of the bias based on a sample size of 40,000, and the standard error of the Monte Carlo estimate (in parentheses).

standard errors. If the Monte Carlo result differs from the series solution value by less than two standard errors we can conclude only that the series solution is not significantly different from the Monte Carlo result. On this basis, inspection of Tables 1, 2, and 3 reveals that the series solution is not significantly different from Monte Carlo estimates based on samples of size 40,000. These samples are chosen as 10,000 quadruplets using a two-dimensional antithetic variable approach. The Monte Carlo bias was calculated using a control variate approach (the Black–Scholes price and

Table 2. The Bias Induced in the Price of a Call Option When the Variance Rate Is Stochastic and has no drift[a]

		S/X				
$\xi/year$	ρ	0.90	0.95	1.00	1.05	1.10
0.15	− 1.0	− 10.42	− 4.66	− 1.30	0.51	1.36
		− 10.68	− 4.27	− 1.39	0.44	1.51
		(0.41)	(0.27)	(0.20)	(0.17)	(0.13)
	− 0.5	− 5.48	− 2.68	− 0.94	0.06	0.58
		− 5.45	− 2.62	− 0.87	− 0.07	0.67
		(0.19)	(0.17)	(0.11)	(0.11)	(0.08)
	0.0	− 0.69	− 0.65	− 0.52	− 0.36	− 0.22
		− 0.64	− 0.68	− 0.50	− 0.35	− 0.22
		(0.04)	(0.02)	(0.02)	(0.01)	(0.01)
	0.5	3.95	1.41	− 0.02	− 0.76	− 1.06
		4.17	1.46	− 0.11	− 0.63	− 0.97
		(0.20)	(0.14).	(0.10)	(0.09)	(0.07)
	1.0	8.46	3.52	0.54	− 1.12	− 1.92
		8.71	3.36	0.35	− 1.18	− 1.92
		(0.46)	(0.27)	(0.21)	(0.16)	(0.13)
0.075	− 1.0	− 4.96	− 2.19	− 0.56	0.33	0.75
		− 4.73	− 2.15	− 0.55	0.47	0.70
		(0.18)	(0.11)	(0.12)	(0.08)	(0.07)
	− 0.5	− 2.55	− 1.18	− 0.35	0.12	0.35
		− 2.54	− 1.21	− 0.39	0.17	0.29
		(0.10)	(0.07)	(0.06)	(0.04)	(0.04)
	0.0	− 0.17	− 0.16	− 0.13	− 0.09	− 0.06
		− 0.19	− 0.16	− 0.13	− 0.09	− 0.06
		(0.01)	(0.01)	(0.00)	(0.00)	(0.00)
	0.5	2.17	0.86	0.11	− 0.29	− 0.47
		2.15	0.83	0.17	− 0.25	− 0.47
		(0.09)	(0.07)	(0.06)	(0.05)	(0.03)
	1.0	4.47	1.90	0.37	− 0.48	− 0.89
		4.40	1.71	0.26	− 0.53	− 0.81
		(0.19)	(0.14)	(0.10)	(0.10)	(0.07)

[a]Bias is expressed as a percentage of the equivalent Black–Scholes price. The variance rate obeys the process $dV = (a + bV) \, dt + \xi V \, dz$. The option parameters are $V(t) = 0.30$ per year, $r = 0$, $a = b = 0$, and time to maturity $T - t = 180$ days or 0.493 years. Every cell in the table contains three numbers: the bias calculated using Equations (16)–(18), the Monte Carlo estimate of the bias based on a sample size of 40,000, and the standard error of the Monte Carlo estimate (in parentheses).

the stochastic volatility prices are estimated using the same random number streams). These procedures greatly increase the efficiency of the Monte Carlo estimate. (For a more detailed discussion of these approaches see Hammersely and Handscomb [16] and Hull and White [18].)

Table 3. The Bias Induced in the Price of a Call Option When the Variance Rate Is Stochastic and Reverts Quickly to its Long-run Average Level[a]

ξ/year	ρ	S/X				
		0.90	0.95	1.00	1.05	1.10
0.15	−1.0	−3.20	−1.43	−0.37	0.21	0.49
		−3.23	−1.50	−0.24	0.19	0.24
		(0.15)	(0.12)	(0.08)	(0.07)	(0.06)
	−0.5	−1.61	−0.73	−0.20	0.09	0.24
		−1.56	−0.66	−0.24	0.03	0.21
		(0.07)	(0.05)	(0.05)	(0.04)	(0.03)
	0.0	−0.06	−0.06	−0.04	−0.03	−0.02
		−0.05	−0.05	−0.03	−0.02	−0.02
		(0.01)	(0.01)	(0.01)	(0.01)	(0.00)
	0.5	1.45	0.59	0.10	−0.17	−0.29
		1.51	0.64	0.02	−0.12	−0.28
		(0.08)	(0.06)	(0.04)	(0.03)	(0.03)
	1.0	2.92	1.22	0.22	−0.32	−0.58
		2.79	1.10	0.32	−0.27	−0.57
		(0.13)	(0.10)	(0.09)	(0.08)	(0.06)
	−1.0	−1.56	−0.69	−0.17	0.12	0.25
		−1.57	−0.67	−0.12	0.15	0.24
		(0.08)	(0.05)	(0.04)	(0.04)	(0.03)
	−0.5	−0.78	−0.35	−0.09	0.06	0.13
		−0.79	−0.36	−0.12	0.09	0.13
		(0.05)	(0.03)	(0.02)	(0.02)	(0.02)
0.075	0.0	−0.02	−0.01	−0.01	−0.01	−0.00
		−0.01	−0.01	−0.01	−0.01	−0.00
		(0.00)	(0.00)	(0.00)	(0.00)	(0.00)
	0.5	0.74	0.31	0.06	−0.08	−0.14
		0.75	0.34	0.04	−0.06	−0.14
		(0.04)	(0.03)	(0.02)	(0.02)	(0.02)
	1.0	1.49	0.64	0.13	−0.15	−0.28
		1.48	0.60	0.14	−0.18	−0.29
		(0.08)	(0.06)	(0.04)	(0.04)	(0.03)

[a]Bias is expressed as a percentage of the equivalent Black–Scholes Price. The variance rate obeys the process $dV = (a + bV) dt + \xi V dz$. The option parameters are $\sqrt{V(t)} = 0.30$ per year, $r = 0$, $a = 0.90$, $b = -10$, and time to maturity $T - t = 180$ days or 0.493 years. Every cell in the table contains three numbers: the bias calculated using Equations (16)–(18), the Monte Carlo estimate of the bias based on a sample size of 40,000, and the standard error of the Monte Carlo estimate (in parentheses).

A more formal test of the accuracy of the series solution is based on the following t statistic

$$t = \frac{B(\xi) - B(MC)}{SE(MC)}$$

where $B(\xi)$ is the bias determined by the series, and $B(MC)$ and $SE(MC)$ are

Table 4. Comparison of Bias with that Produced by Dothan's model[a]

		S/X				
(a,b)	ρ	0.90	0.95	1.00	1.05	1.10
(0,0)	−1.0	−10.42	−4.66	−1.30	0.51	1.36
		−10.87	−5.01	−1.56	0.32	1.22
		−10.68	−4.27	−1.39	0.44	1.51
	−0.5	−5.48	−2.68	−0.94	0.06	0.58
		−5.60	−2.76	−1.01	0.01	0.55
		−5.45	−2.62	−0.87	−0.07	0.67
	0.0	−0.69	−0.65	−0.52	−0.36	−0.22
		−0.69	−0.65	−0.52	−0.36	−0.22
		−0.64	−0.68	−0.50	−0.35	−0.22
	0.5	3.95	1.41	−0.02	−0.76	−1.06
		3.84	1.33	−0.09	−0.80	−1.09
		4.17	1.46	−0.11	−0.63	−0.97
	1.0	8.46	3.52	0.54	−1.12	−1.92
		8.00	3.17	0.29	−1.31	−2.06
		8.71	3.36	0.35	−1.18	−1.92
(0.9, −10)	−1.0	−3.20	−1.43	−0.37	0.21	0.49
		4.64	1.72	−0.04	−1.02	−1.47
		−3.23	−1.50	−0.24	0.19	0.42
	−0.5	−1.61	−0.73	−0.20	0.09	0.24
		2.16	0.60	−0.25	−0.66	−0.80
		−1.56	−0.66	−0.24	0.03	0.21
	0.0	−0.06	−0.06	−0.04	−0.03	−0.02
		−0.69	−0.65	−0.52	−0.36	−0.22
		−0.05	−0.05	−0.03	−0.02	−0.02
	0.5	1.45	0.59	0.10	−0.17	−0.29
		−3.92	−2.04	−0.84	−0.13	0.26
		1.51	0.64	0.02	−0.12	−0.28
	1.0	2.92	1.22	0.22	−0.32	−0.58
		−7.51	−3.55	−1.23	0.03	0.64
		2.79	1.10	0.32	−0.27	−0.57

[a]Bias is expressed as a percentage of the equivalent Black–Scholes Price. Every cell in the table contains three numbers: the bias calculated using Equations (16)–(18), the bias calculated using Dothan's [10] solution, and the Monte Carlo estimate of the bias based on a sample size of 40,000. The variance rate obeys the process $dV = (a + bV) dt + \xi\sqrt{V} dz$. The option parameters are $\sqrt{V(t)} = 0.30$ per year, $r = 0$, $\xi = 0.15$ per year, and time to maturity $T - t = 180$ days or 0.493 years.

the estimated bias and the standard error of the estimate from the Monte Carlo calculation. Under the null hypothesis that the series solution is correct this statistic should be distributed as a standard unit normal. The t statistic for all the observations in Tables 1, 2, and 3 was tested to determine whether they are drawn from a standard unit normal (this gives a sample size of 150). The mean and variance of t were -0.08 and 0.93, respectively. The Kolmogorov D statistic was 0.06. Based on these results we are unable to reject at the 5% level the hypothesis that the mean is zero, the variance is 1, or that the distribution is normal. Thus, these Monte Carlo results do not permit us to distinguish between the series solution and the true value.

The solution given by Equations (10) and (16)–(18) is equivalent to a Taylor series expansion of the bias caused a stochastic volatility. Dothan [10] also produces a Taylor series expansion for the solution to Equation (8). The distinction between the two series solutions is that Dothan expands the series about the point $\eta = 0$ and $\xi = 0$. In this paper the expansion is about the point $\eta = \eta$ and $\xi = 0$. This suggests that both solutions should be approximately the same for small η and differ most widely when η is large.

Table 4 shows the biases computed using Equations (16)–(18) and those found using Dothan's solution for the cases $a = b = 0$ and $a = 0.9$, $b = -10$. As expected, when $\eta = 0$ the two solutions are very close but when η is large they differ substantially. The values $a = 0.9$, $b = -10$ are not extreme. They correspond to a variance rate that reverts to 0.09; perturbations from this reversion level die away with a half-life of about 25 days. Although not shown, we found that Dothan's approximation worked well when $b > -3$.

V. PROPERTIES OF THE SOLUTION

The impact of a stochastic volatility when ξ is small can be approximated by the first nonzero term in ξ in the series solution. If $\rho \neq 0$, and $V = -a/b$ (i.e., the variance rate is at the reversion value) then (17) approximates the bias as

$$B(\xi) \approx \frac{-\rho V}{b\delta}(1 + \delta - e^{\delta})S\,\frac{\partial^2 C(\bar{V})}{\partial S \partial \bar{V}}\,\xi$$

where

$$\frac{\partial^2 C(\bar{V})}{\partial S \partial \bar{V}} = \frac{-N'(d_1)d_2}{2\bar{V}}$$

$$d_1 = \frac{\ln(S/X) + r(T - t) + \bar{V}(T - t)/2}{\sqrt{\bar{V}(T - t)}}$$

$$d_2 = d_1 - \sqrt{\bar{V}(T - t)}$$

and $N(\cdot)$ is the cumulative normal distribution function. The sign of $B(\xi)$ is then the same as the sign of $-\rho d_2$. This means the bias is approximately zero when $d_2 = 0$ or when

$$\frac{S}{Xe^{-r(T-t)}} = e^{\bar{V}(T-t)/2}, \tag{19}$$

that is, when the option is slightly in the money. For the parameters in Tables 1–3 ($V = 0.09$ per year, $T - t = 180$ days) the bias changes sign when $S/Xe^{(T-t)} \approx 1.022$. Inspection of Tables 1–3 reveals that (19) is a reasonable approximation of the crossing point of the bias in all of the cases considered.

When the volatility and the stock price are uncorrelated ($\rho = 0$) and $V = -a/b$, the first nonzero term in the series expansion [see Equation (18)] gives

$$B(\xi) \approx \frac{V}{4b\delta^2} (e^{2\delta} - 4e^{\delta} + 2\delta + 3) \frac{\partial^2 C(\bar{V})}{\partial \bar{V}^2} \xi^2.$$

Since

$$\frac{\partial^2 C(\bar{V})}{\partial \bar{V}^2} = \frac{S\sqrt{T-t}}{4\bar{V}^{3/2}} N'(d_1)(d_1 d_2 - 1),$$

the sign of the bias is the same as the sign of $d_1 d_2 - 1$. Defining

$$k = \left[\left(\frac{\bar{V}(T-t)}{2} \right)^2 + \bar{V}(T-t) \right]^{1/2},$$

the bias is negative when

$$e^{-k} < \frac{S}{Xe^{-r(T-t)}} < e^{k} \tag{20}$$

and positive elsewhere. For the options in Tables 1–3, $e^{k} = 1.24$ and $e^{-k} = 0.81$. Thus, we see that in this case the Black–Scholes price is too high over a very wide range of stock prices around the exercise price. The properties in (19) and (20) have been derived under the assumption that $\bar{V} = V(t)$. When the current volatility differs from the average expected volatility [$\bar{V} \neq V(t)$], Equations (19) and (20) give the crossing points for the bias with respect to $C(\bar{V})$, the Black–Scholes price based on the mean expected volatility.

The $\rho = 0$ result can be understood from Hull and White [18] and Scott [31]. These papers show that when $\rho = 0$ the option price is the B–S price, C, integrated over the distribution of the mean volatility during the life of the option. In general C is a convex (concave) function of V for small (large) values of V. It follows that both underpricing and overpricing by B–S are possible. In the particular case where the option is at-the-money[4] C is always a concave function of V and overpricing always takes place.

The $\rho \neq 0$ results are consistent with the simulation results of Johnson and Shanno [21] and Hull and White [18]. They can be expressed in terms of the implied volatility, which is calculated using the B-S model. If $\rho > 0$ the implied volatility will tend to decrease as S/X increases. If $\rho < 0$ the implied volatility will tend to increase as S/X increases. It is interesting to compare these results with the empirical results of Rubinstein [30] who compared the implied volatility of options that differed only in exercise price. In the period 1976–1977 he found that as S/X increased there was a tendency for the implied volatility to decrease. For 1977–1978 the reverse was observed. Under our model this is consistent with a situation where the volatility was positively correlated with stock price in 1976–1977 and negatively correlated with stock price in 1977–1978.

Rubinstein also compared matched pairs of options differing only in time to maturity. He found that in the 1976–1977 period shorter term options had higher implied volatilities for out-of-the-money options. For at-the-money and in-the-money options the reverse was true. In the period 1977–1978 almost all options exhibited the property that shorter term options had higher implied volatilities. This is difficult to reconcile with Equations (16)–(18), and the above hypothesis about the sign of the correlation in the two time periods. The effect of a longer time to maturity is to generally exaggerate the biases and the distortions in the implied volatility.

As was discussed in Section III, when λ_V, which is a measure of the systematic risk of the variance rate V, is not zero we can define a risk adjusted drift rate, η^*,

$$\eta^* = a^* + bV \qquad \text{or} \qquad \eta^* = a + b^*V$$

where

$$a^* = a - \lambda_V \xi \sqrt{V} \qquad \text{and} \qquad b^* = b - \lambda_V \xi / \sqrt{V}.$$

The option price can then be determined in terms of the risk adjusted parameters a^* and b^*. One of the results of this is that $\overline{V}$ is no longer the mean expected variance rate. It is now a risk adjusted mean expected variance rate whose value is negatively related to λ_V. Thus $\partial f_0 / \partial \lambda_V < 0$ and, at least for relatively small values of ξ, $\partial B / \partial \lambda_V < 0$. An intuitive explanation of this result is as follows. As λ_V increases, the systematic risk of the option increases and the return required on the option increases. This means that, given the distribution of the terminal stock price, the option price, which is the discounted value of the expected payoff, will have a lower value than if the variance rate had no systematic risk. Therefore, if the variance rate's systematic risk can be varied without affecting the correlation between V and S, increasing the systematic risk of V lowers the option price and vice versa. Note that this effect is proportional to the time to maturity of the option. Thus, to the extent that it exists it will cause a marked trend in the implied volatilities of options of different maturities if these are computed using the Black–Scholes pricing equation.

VI.   IMPLICATIONS FOR OPTION REPLICATION STRATEGIES

Option replication strategies are of interest to investors who wish to buy portfolio insurance, market makers in options on an exchange, and financial institutions that write over-the-counter options. A stochastic volatility has serious implications for the effectiveness of option replication strategies that are based on the Black–Scholes model.

Suppose the stock price, variance rate, and time are S, V, and t, respectively, and the option price is $c(S, V, t)$. Applying Ito's lemma and using (1) and (2) gives

$$dc = \left[\eta \frac{\partial c}{\partial V} + \phi S \frac{\partial c}{\partial S} + \frac{\partial c}{\partial t} + \frac{1}{2}\left(\xi^2 V \frac{\partial^2 c}{\partial V^2} + VS^2 \frac{\partial^2 c}{\partial S^2}\right.\right.$$
$$\left.\left. + 2\xi VS\rho \frac{\partial^2 c}{\partial S\partial V}\right)\right] dt + S\sqrt{V}\frac{\partial c}{\partial S} dz + \xi\sqrt{V}\frac{\partial c}{\partial V} dw.$$

Consider the traditional Black–Scholes hedging portfolio that is short one call option and long $\partial C/\partial S$ shares. If the value of the portfolio is W,

$$dW = \frac{\partial C}{\partial S} dS - dc$$
$$= -\left[\eta \frac{\partial c}{\partial V} + \phi S\left(\frac{\partial c}{\partial S} - \frac{\partial C}{\partial S}\right) + \frac{\partial c}{\partial t} + \frac{1}{2}\left(\xi^2 V \frac{\partial^2 c}{\partial V^2} + VS^2 \frac{\partial^2 c}{\partial S^2}\right.\right.$$
$$\left.\left. + 2\xi VS\rho \frac{\partial^2 c}{\partial S\partial V}\right)\right] dt + S\sqrt{V}\left(\frac{\partial C}{\partial S} - \frac{\partial c}{\partial S}\right) dz - \xi\sqrt{V}\frac{\partial c}{\partial V} dw. \qquad (21)$$

This has two stochastic elements. The first of these is

$$-S\sqrt{V}\frac{\partial B}{\partial S} dz$$

and arises from the error, $\partial B/\partial S$, in the hedge ratio which is calculated from the Black–Scholes price. The second is

$$\xi\sqrt{V}\frac{\partial c}{\partial V} dw$$

and arises from the fact that the volatility risk is not hedged at all.

Consider first the sign of $\partial B/\partial S$. From Equation (10)

$$\frac{\partial B}{\partial S} = \frac{\partial f_0}{\partial S} + \frac{\partial f_1}{\partial S}\,\xi + \frac{\partial f_2}{\partial S}\,\xi^2 + \cdots.$$

When ξ is small the first nonzero term in this expansion is a good approximation. If $\rho \neq 0$, and $V = -a/b$ then

$$\frac{\partial B}{\partial S} \approx \frac{\partial f_1}{\partial S}\,\xi.$$

It can be shown that the sign of this is the same as the sign of

$$\rho\left(-d_2 + \frac{d_1 d_2 - 1}{\sqrt{\bar{V}(T-t)}}\right).$$

Define

$$k_1 = \frac{\bar{V}(T-t)}{2} - \sqrt{\bar{V}(T-t)}$$

$$k_2 = \frac{\bar{V}(T-t)}{2} + \sqrt{\bar{V}(T-t)}.$$

If

$$e^{k_1} < \frac{S}{Xe^{-r(T-t)}} < e^{k_2}$$

then $\partial f_1/\partial S$ has the same sign as $-\rho$. Near-the-money options are less (more) sensitive to changes in the stock price than the Black–Scholes equation suggests if there is positive (negative) correlation between S and V. For the parameters used in Tables 1–3 the range over which this phenomenon is observed is

$$0.83Xe^{-r(T-t)} < S < 1.26Xe^{-r(T-t)}.$$

This result may seem paradoxical. If the stock price is positively correlated with the volatility an increase in the stock price is likely to accompany an increase in the volatility. Both of these events raise the option value so one might expect an abnormally large increase in the option price as a result of an increase in the stock price. However, the hedge ratio calculation is the change in the option price for some change in the stock price with all else (in particular, the volatility) held constant.

It can be shown that in practice the absolute magnitude of $S\sqrt{V}\,\partial B/\partial S$ is very small. The degree of misshedging arising from the first stochastic term in Equation (21) is therefore minimal.

The size of the second stochastic term in Equation (21) can be assessed by approximating c and its derivatives with the corresponding Black–Scholes values. For an at-the-money option with $V = 0.09$ per year and $T - t = 0.493$ years (the parameters used in Tables 1–3), $\xi\sqrt{V}\partial c/\partial V$ is approximately $1.67\xi C$. For $\xi = 0.15$ this is about $0.25C$. In the situation where an option is being hedged using futures contracts, the actual wealth involved (ignoring margin requirements) is C so that the instantaneous standard deviation of the rate of return would then be 0.25 or 25% per year. Thus, failing to hedge the stochastic volatility imposes a risk on the investor comparable to the risk of holding the stock alone.

The impact of a stochastic volatility on a hedged option position was first noted by Galai [12]. Hull and White [17] test a variety of hedging schemes designed to control this risk. Their results show that a significant improvement in hedge performance can be achieved in practice by using other options on the same stock to eliminate the second stochastic term in (21).

VII. CONCLUSIONS

This paper uses a procedure to value two state variable contingent claims to derive a series solution for the price of a call option on a security with a stochastic volatility. The volatility may follow a mean reverting process and is allowed to be instantaneously correlated with stock price. When this correlation is positive it is shown that B-S tends to overprice out-of-the-money options and to underprice in-the-money options. When there is negative correlation the reverse is true. For reasonable values of the parameters the under- or overpricing is usually less than 1% of the B-S price for an at-the-money or in-the-money option. For an out-of-the-money option it can be considerably higher than this. It is possible that these pricing biases contribute to the results obtained by Rubinstein [30].

The results in this paper apply to a European call option on a non-dividend paying stock. They can be extended to European put options on the stock through the use of put–call parity, and, by using the results in Merton [25], to American call options on the stock. The solution technique employed in this paper can be used to determine the bias in the value of most one state variable contingent claims caused by a stochastic volatility.

APPENDIX

In this appendix we prove that Equations (16)–(18) are solutions to differential Equations (11)–(13) and provide a general technique to find all higher order terms. We start with a series of lemmas.

Lemma 1.

$$\mathbf{D}\left[\frac{\partial^n C(V)}{\partial V^n}\right] = -\frac{n}{T-t}\frac{\partial^n C(V)}{\partial V^n}.$$

Proof. Since $\mathbf{D}C = 0$ the result is true for $n = 0$. Assume that it is true for $n = k$:

$$\mathbf{D}\left[\frac{\partial^k C(V)}{\partial V^k}\right] = -\frac{k}{T-t}\frac{\partial^k C(V)}{\partial V^k} \qquad (A1)$$

From the structure of the $\mathbf{D}$ operator

$$\frac{\partial}{\partial V}\mathbf{D}x = \mathbf{D}\frac{\partial x}{\partial V} + \frac{1}{2}S^2\frac{\partial^2 x}{\partial S^2}$$

for any function x of S, V, and t. Putting $x = \partial^k C(V)/\partial V^k$ and using Equation (A1) we obtain

$$\mathbf{D}\left[\frac{\partial^{k+1} C(V)}{\partial V^{k+1}}\right] = -\frac{k}{T-t}\frac{\partial^{k+1} C(V)}{\partial V^{k+1}} - \frac{1}{2}S^2\frac{\partial^{k+2} C(V)}{\partial S^2 \partial V^k}. \qquad (A2)$$

From the known functional forms for the derivative of C:

$$\frac{1}{2}S^2\frac{\partial^2 C(V)}{\partial S^2} = \frac{1}{T-t}\frac{\partial C(V)}{\partial V}.$$

Hence

$$\frac{1}{2}S^2\frac{\partial^{k+2} C(V)}{\partial S^2 \partial V^k} = \frac{1}{T-t}\frac{\partial^{k+1} C(V)}{\partial V^{k+1}} \qquad (A3)$$

and Equation (A2) becomes

$$\mathbf{D}\left[\frac{\partial^{k+1} C(V)}{\partial V^{k+1}}\right] = -\frac{k+1}{T-t}\frac{\partial^{k+1} C(V)}{\partial V^{k+1}}$$

showing that the lemma is true for $n = k + 1$. It follows by mathematical induction that it is true for all n. ∎

Lemma 2.

$$\frac{\partial \overline{V}}{\partial t} + \eta \frac{\partial \overline{V}}{\partial V} = \frac{\overline{V} - V}{T-t}.$$

Proof. This result is generally true when η is a function of V and t. Here we demonstrate that it is true for the model considered by this paper. Since

$$EV(s, t) = (V - \hat{V})e^{b(s-t)} + \hat{V}$$

if follows that

$$\bar{V} = \frac{1}{T-t} \int_t^T [(V-\hat{V})e^{b(s-t)} + \hat{V}] \, ds$$

$$= \hat{V} + \frac{1}{b(T-t)} (V-\hat{V})(e^{b(T-t)} - 1), \tag{A4}$$

$$\frac{\partial \bar{V}}{\partial t} = \frac{1}{b(T-t)^2} (V-\hat{V})(e^{b(T-t)} - 1) - \frac{1}{T-t} (V-\hat{V})e^{b(T-t)},$$

and

$$\frac{\partial \bar{V}}{\partial V} = \frac{e^{b(T-t)} - 1}{b(T-t)}. \tag{A5}$$

Since

$$\eta = b(V-\hat{V}),$$

$$\frac{\partial \bar{V}}{\partial t} + \eta \frac{\partial \bar{V}}{\partial V} = \frac{V-\hat{V}}{T-t} \left[\frac{\partial \bar{V}}{\partial V} - 1 \right].$$

From Equation (A4)

$$V - \hat{V} = \frac{V - \bar{V}}{1 - \partial \bar{V}/\partial V}.$$

The lemma follows. ∎

Lemma 3.

$$\mathbf{D}\left[\frac{\partial^n C(\bar{V})}{\partial \bar{V}^n}\right] + \eta \frac{\partial}{\partial V}\left[\frac{\partial^n C(\bar{V})}{\partial \bar{V}^n}\right] = -\frac{n}{T-t} \frac{\partial^n C(\bar{V})}{\partial \bar{V}^n}.$$

Proof. Define $\theta(V) = \partial^n C(V)/\partial V^n$. Since $\bar{V}$ is a function of V and t, it follows from the structure of the $\mathbf{D}$ operator that

$$\mathbf{D}[\theta(\bar{V})] = \frac{\partial \theta(\bar{V})}{\partial t} + \frac{\partial \theta(\bar{V})}{\partial \bar{V}} \frac{\partial \bar{V}}{\partial t} + \frac{1}{2} VS^2 \frac{\partial^2 \theta(\bar{V})}{\partial S^2} - r\theta(\bar{V}) + rS \frac{\partial \theta(\bar{V})}{\partial S}$$

and

$$\mathbf{D}[\theta(V)]\bigg|_{V=\bar{V}} = \frac{\partial \theta(\bar{V})}{\partial t} + \frac{1}{2} \bar{V}S^2 \frac{\partial^2 \theta(\bar{V})}{\partial S^2} - r\theta(\bar{V}) + rS \frac{\partial \theta(\bar{V})}{\partial S}.$$

Hence

$$\mathbf{D}[\theta(\bar{V})] = \mathbf{D}[\theta(V)]\bigg|_{V=\bar{V}} + \frac{\partial \theta(\bar{V})}{\partial \bar{V}} \frac{\partial \bar{V}}{\partial t} + \frac{1}{2}(V-\bar{V})S^2 \frac{\partial^2 \theta(\bar{V})}{\partial S^2}.$$

Since

$$\frac{\partial \theta(\bar{V})}{\partial V} = \frac{\partial \theta(\bar{V})}{\partial \bar{V}} \frac{\partial \bar{V}}{\partial V}$$

it follows that

$$\mathbf{D}[\theta(\bar{V})] + \eta \frac{\partial \theta(\bar{V})}{\partial V} = \mathbf{D}[\theta(V)]\bigg|_{V=\bar{V}} + \frac{\partial \theta(\bar{V})}{\partial \bar{V}} \left[\frac{\partial \bar{V}}{\partial t} + \eta \frac{\partial \bar{V}}{\partial V} \right]$$

$$+ \frac{1}{2}(V - \bar{V})S^2 \frac{\partial^2 \theta(\bar{V})}{\partial S^2}.$$

From Lemma 1

$$\mathbf{D}[\theta(V)]\bigg|_{V=\bar{V}} = -\frac{n}{T-t} \frac{\partial^n C(V)}{\partial V^n}\bigg|_{V=\bar{V}}$$

$$= -\frac{n}{T-t} \frac{\partial^n C(\bar{V})}{\partial \bar{V}^n}.$$

From this and the result in Lemma 2

$$\mathbf{D}[\theta(\bar{V})] + \eta \frac{\partial \theta(\bar{V})}{\partial V} = -\frac{n}{T-t} \theta(\bar{V})$$

$$+ (V - \bar{V})\left[\frac{1}{2}S^2 \frac{\partial^2 \theta(\bar{V})}{\partial S^2} - \frac{1}{T-t} \frac{\partial \theta(\bar{V})}{\partial \bar{V}} \right].$$

Equation (A3) shows that the last term in this equation vanishes. The lemma follows from the definition of θ. ∎

Lemma 4.

$$\mathbf{D}C(\bar{V}) + \eta \frac{\partial C(\bar{V})}{\partial V} = 0.$$

Proof. This can be regarded as the particular case of Lemma 3 when $n = 0$. It is easily seen that the result is true by substituting $\theta(V) = C(V)$ and repeating the analysis in Lemma 3. ∎

Lemma 5.

$$\mathbf{D}\left[S \frac{\partial^n C(\bar{V})}{\partial \bar{V}^{n-1} \partial S} \right] + \eta \frac{\partial}{\partial V} \left[S \frac{\partial^n C(\bar{V})}{\partial \bar{V}^{n-1} \partial S} \right] = -\frac{n-1}{T-t} S \frac{\partial^n C(\bar{V})}{\partial \bar{V}^{n-1} \partial S}.$$

Proof. From the definition of the **D** operator

$$\mathbf{D}\left[S \frac{\partial x}{\partial S} \right] = S \frac{\partial}{\partial S} [\mathbf{D}x]$$

for any function x of S, V, and t. By substituting

$$x = \frac{\partial^{n-1} C(\bar{V})}{\partial \bar{V}^{n-1}}$$

into this and using Lemma 3 the result follows. ∎

The results in Lemmas 3, 4, and 5 enable Equations (11)–(13) to be solved. Lemma 4 shows that

$$f_0 = C(\bar{V}) - C(V) \tag{A6}$$

is a solution to Equation (11). Using this result, Equation (12) becomes

$$\mathbf{D}f_1 + \eta \frac{\partial f_1}{\partial V} + \rho VS \frac{\partial^2 C(\bar{V})}{\partial S \partial V} = 0$$

or

$$\mathbf{D}f_1 + \eta \frac{\partial f_1}{\partial V} + \rho VS \frac{\partial^2 C(\bar{V})}{\partial S \partial \bar{V}} \frac{\partial \bar{V}}{\partial V} = 0. \tag{A7}$$

Lemma 5 suggests that a solution to this is of the form

$$f_1 = \frac{\psi(V, t)}{T - t} S \frac{\partial^2 C(\bar{V})}{\partial S \partial \bar{V}}. \tag{A8}$$

To see why this is so, note first that from the structure of the **D** operator

$$\mathbf{D}(xy) = \frac{\partial x}{\partial t} y + x \mathbf{D} y$$

when x is a function of V and t, and y is a function of S, V, and t. Hence (A8) implies

$$\mathbf{D}f_1 = \left[\frac{1}{T - t} \frac{\partial \psi}{\partial t} + \frac{1}{(T - t)^2} \psi \right] S \frac{\partial^2 C(\bar{V})}{\partial S \partial \bar{V}} + \frac{\psi}{T - t} \mathbf{D}\left[S \frac{\partial^2 C(\bar{V})}{\partial S \partial \bar{V}} \right]. \tag{A9}$$

Also

$$\eta \frac{\partial f_1}{\partial V} = \left[\frac{\eta}{T - t} \frac{\partial \psi}{\partial V} + \frac{\eta \psi}{T - t} \frac{\partial}{\partial V} \right] \left[S \frac{\partial^2 C(\bar{V})}{\partial S \partial \bar{V}} \right]. \tag{A10}$$

Using Lemma 5 with n = 2

$$\mathbf{D}\left[S \frac{\partial^2 C(\bar{V})}{\partial S \partial \bar{V}} \right] = -\eta \frac{\partial}{\partial V}\left[S \frac{\partial^2 C(\bar{V})}{\partial S \partial \bar{V}} \right] - \frac{1}{T - t} S \frac{\partial^2 C(\bar{V})}{\partial S \partial \bar{V}}. \tag{A11}$$

From (A9), (A10), and (A11) it follows that (A7) is satisfied by (A8) when

$$\frac{\partial \psi}{\partial t} + \eta \frac{\partial \psi}{\partial V} + \rho V(T - t) \frac{\partial \bar{V}}{\partial V} = 0. \tag{A12}$$

This has the condition that $\psi(V, T) = 0$. Using standard techniques the solution is

$$\psi[\tau, V(\tau))] = -\int_{\tau}^{T} \rho\chi(s, k)(T - s) \left.\frac{\partial \overline{V}(t)}{\partial V(t)}\right|_{t=s} ds$$

where $V = \chi(t, k)$ is a solution to

$$\frac{dV}{\eta(V)} = dt$$

and k is the constant of integration. For the particular functional form of $\eta(V)$ given in Equation (3), the solution is

$$\psi(t, V) = \frac{-\rho}{b^3} \{(a + bV)(e^\delta - \delta e^\delta - 1) + a(e^\delta - \delta - 1)\} \qquad (A13)$$

where $\delta = b(T - t)$. This means that the second term in the series is

$$f_1 = \frac{\rho}{b^2\delta} \{(a + bV)(1 - e^\delta + \delta e^\delta) + a(1 + \delta - e^\delta)\} \, S \, \frac{\partial^2 C(\overline{V})}{\partial S \partial \overline{V}}. \qquad (A14)$$

Higher order terms are calculated similarly. Substituting (A6) and (A8) into Equation (13)

$$\mathbf{D}f_2 + \eta\frac{\partial f_2}{\partial V} + \rho VS\frac{\partial^2}{\partial S \partial V}\left[\frac{\psi}{T - t} S \frac{\partial^2 C(\overline{V})}{\partial S \partial \overline{V}}\right] + \frac{1}{2}V\frac{\partial^2 C(\overline{V})}{\partial V^2} = 0$$

which becomes

$$\mathbf{D}f_2 + \eta\frac{\partial f_2}{\partial V} + \rho VS\frac{\partial}{\partial S}\left[\frac{\psi_V S}{T - t} \frac{\partial^2 C(\overline{V})}{\partial S \partial \overline{V}} + \frac{\psi}{T - t} S \frac{\partial^3 C(\overline{V})}{\partial S \partial \overline{V}^2}\frac{\partial \overline{V}}{\partial V^2}\right] + \frac{1}{2}V\frac{\partial^2 C(\overline{V})}{\partial V^2} = 0$$

or

$$\mathbf{D}f_2 + \eta\frac{\partial f_2}{\partial V} + \rho VS \frac{\psi_V}{T - t} \frac{\partial^2 C(\overline{V})}{\partial S \partial \overline{V}} + \rho VS \frac{\psi}{T - t} \frac{\partial^3 C(\overline{V})}{\partial S \partial \overline{V}^2}\frac{\partial \overline{V}}{\partial V}$$

$$+ \rho VS^2 \frac{\psi_V}{T - t} \frac{\partial^3 C(\overline{V})}{\partial S^2 \partial \overline{V}} + \rho VS^2 \frac{\psi}{T - t} \frac{\partial^4 C(\overline{V})}{\partial S^2 \partial \overline{V}^2}\frac{\partial \overline{V}}{\partial V} + \frac{1}{2}V\frac{\partial^2 C(\overline{V})}{\partial V^2} = 0$$

where $\psi_V = \partial\psi/\partial V$. Since

$$S^2 \frac{\partial^2 C(\overline{V})}{\partial S^2} = \frac{2}{T - t} \frac{\partial C(\overline{V})}{\partial \overline{V}},$$

and from (A5)

$$\frac{\partial^2 \overline{V}}{\partial V^2} = 0,$$

this becomes

$$\mathbf{D}f_2 + \eta \frac{\partial f_2}{\partial V} + \frac{\rho V \psi_V}{T-t} S \frac{\partial^2 C(\overline{V})}{\partial S \partial \overline{V}} + \left[\frac{2\rho \psi_V}{(T-t)^2} + \frac{1}{2} \left(\frac{\partial \overline{V}}{\partial V} \right)^2 \right] V \frac{\partial^2 C(\overline{V})}{\partial \overline{V}^2}$$

$$+ \frac{\rho V \psi}{T-t} \frac{\partial \overline{V}}{\partial V} S \frac{\partial^3 C(\overline{V})}{\partial S \partial \overline{V}^2} + \frac{2\rho V \psi}{(T-t)^2} \frac{\partial \overline{V}}{\partial V} \frac{\partial^3 C(\overline{V})}{\partial \overline{V}^3} = 0. \tag{A15}$$

Lemmas 3 and 5 suggest

$$f_2 = \frac{\phi_1(V,t)}{T-t} S \frac{\partial^2 C(\overline{V})}{\partial S \partial \overline{V}} + \frac{\phi_2(V,t)}{(T-t)^2} \frac{\partial^2 C(\overline{V})}{\partial \overline{V}^2} + \frac{\phi_3(V,t)}{(T-t)^2} S \frac{\partial^3 C(\overline{V})}{\partial S \partial \overline{V}^2}$$

$$+ \frac{\phi_4(V,t)}{(T-t)^3} \frac{\partial^3 C(\overline{V})}{\partial \overline{V}^3}. \tag{A16}$$

When this is substituted into (A15) and the lemmas are used, a similar analysis to that for ψ gives the following first-order partial differential equations for the ϕ_i's:

$$\frac{\partial \phi_1}{\partial t} + \eta \frac{\partial \phi_1}{\partial V} + \rho V \psi_V = 0$$

$$\frac{\partial \phi_2}{\partial t} + \eta \frac{\partial \phi_2}{\partial V} + V \left[2\rho \psi_V + \frac{(T-t)^2}{2} \left(\frac{\partial \overline{V}}{\partial V} \right)^2 \right] = 0$$

$$\frac{\partial \phi_3}{\partial t} + \eta \frac{\partial \phi_3}{\partial V} + \rho V \psi \frac{\partial \overline{V}}{\partial V} (T-t) = 0 \tag{A17}$$

$$\frac{\partial \phi_4}{\partial t} + \eta \frac{\partial \phi_4}{\partial V} + 2\rho V \psi \frac{\partial \overline{V}}{\partial V} (T-t) = 0.$$

For the particular form of η given in Equation (3), these have solutions analogous to (A13),

$$\phi_1 = \frac{\rho^2}{b^4} \left\{ (a+bV) \left[e^\delta \left(\frac{1}{2} \delta^2 - \delta + 1 \right) - 1 \right] + a[e^\delta (2-\delta) - (2+\delta)] \right\}$$

$$\phi_2 = 2\phi_1 + \frac{1}{2b^4} \left\{ (a+bV)(e^{2\delta} - 2\delta e^\delta - 1) - \frac{a}{2} (e^{2\delta} - 4e^\delta + 2\delta + 3) \right\} \tag{A18}$$

$$\phi_3 = \frac{1}{2} \psi^2$$

$$\phi_4 = 2\phi_3.$$

Substituting these into (A16) gives f_2. Higher order terms are derived in exactly the same way; however, the algebra becomes increasingly complex.

The full proofs that (A13) satisfies (A12) and (A18) satisfy (A17) are given in Note 1 at the end of this paper.

NOTE 1: A PROOF THAT (A13) AND (A18) SATISFY (A12) AND (A17)

Equation (A13) is

$$\psi(t, V) = -\frac{\rho}{b^3}\{(a + bV)(e^\delta - \delta e^\delta - 1) + a(e^\delta - \delta - 1)\}$$

where $\delta = b(T - t)$.

$$\frac{\partial \psi}{\partial t} = -b\,\frac{\partial \psi}{\partial \delta}$$

$$= \frac{\rho}{b^2}\{(a + bV)(-\delta e^\delta) + a(e^\delta - 1)\}$$

$$\frac{\partial \psi}{\partial V} = -\frac{\rho}{b^2}(e^\delta - \delta e^\delta - 1). \qquad (1\text{-}1)$$

Since $\eta = a + bV$,

$$\frac{\partial \psi}{\partial t} + \eta\,\frac{\partial \psi}{\partial V} = \frac{\rho V}{b}(1 - e^\delta).$$

From Equation (A5)

$$\rho V(T - t)\,\frac{\partial \overline{V}}{\partial V} = -\frac{\rho V}{b}(1 - e^\delta),$$

so it follows that Equation (A12)

$$\frac{\partial \psi}{\partial t} + \eta\,\frac{\partial \psi}{\partial V} + \rho V(T - t)\,\frac{\partial \overline{V}}{\partial V} = 0$$

is satisfied.

For Equation (A18) first consider ϕ_1:

$$\phi_1 = \frac{\rho^2}{b^4}\left\{(a + bV)\left[e^\delta\left(\frac{1}{2}\delta^2 - \delta + 1\right) - 1\right] + a[e^\delta(2 - \delta) - (2 + \delta)]\right\}$$

$$\frac{\partial \phi_1}{\partial t} = -b\,\frac{\partial \phi_1}{\partial \delta}$$

$$= -\frac{\rho^2}{b^3}\left\{(a + bV)\frac{1}{2}\delta^2 e^\delta + a(e^\delta - \delta e^\delta - 1)\right\}$$

$$\frac{\partial \phi_1}{\partial V} = \frac{\rho^2}{b^3}\left[e^\delta\left(\frac{1}{2}\delta^2 - \delta + 1\right) - 1\right].$$

Since $\eta = a + bV$,

$$\frac{\partial \phi_1}{\partial t} + \eta \frac{\partial \phi_1}{\partial V} = \frac{\rho^2}{b^3} \{bV(e^\delta - \delta e^\delta - 1)\}$$

$$= \frac{\rho^2 V}{b^2} (e^\delta - \delta e^\delta - 1)$$

From Equation (1-1) the right-hand side of this is $-\rho V \psi_V$ so that

$$\frac{\partial \psi_1}{\partial t} + \eta \frac{\partial \phi_1}{\partial V} - \rho V \psi_V = 0 \qquad (1\text{-}2)$$

showing that ϕ_1 satisfies the first equation in (A17).

Next consider ϕ_2:

$$\phi_2 = 2\phi_1 + \psi_2$$

where

$$\psi_2 = \frac{1}{2b^4} \left\{ (a + bV)(e^{2\delta} - 2\delta e^\delta - 1) - \frac{a}{2} (e^{2\delta} - 4e^\delta + 2\delta + 3) \right\}.$$

Substituting this into the second equation in (A17) gives

$$2 \left[\frac{\partial \phi_1}{\partial t} + \eta \frac{\partial \phi_1}{\partial V} + \rho V \psi_V \right] + \frac{\partial \psi_2}{\partial t} + \eta \frac{\partial \psi_2}{\partial V} + V \frac{(T - t)^2}{2} \left(\frac{\partial \overline{V}}{\partial V} \right)^2 = 0.$$

We see from the first equation in (A17) that the first term is zero. Thus, ψ_2 must satisfy

$$\frac{\partial \psi_2}{\partial t} + \eta \frac{\partial \psi_2}{\partial V} + V \frac{(T - t)^2}{2} \left(\frac{\partial \overline{V}}{\partial V} \right)^2 = 0. \qquad (1\text{-}3)$$

Differentiating,

$$\frac{\partial \psi_2}{\partial t} = -b \frac{\partial \psi_2}{\partial \delta}$$

$$= -\frac{1}{2b^3} \{(a + bV)(2e^{2\delta} - 2e^\delta - 2\delta e^\delta) - a(e^{2\delta} - 2e^\delta + 1)\}$$

$$\frac{\partial \psi_2}{\partial V} = \frac{1}{2b^3} \{e^{2\delta} - 2\delta e^\delta - 1\}.$$

Since $\eta = a + bV$

$$\frac{\partial \psi_2}{\partial t} + \eta \frac{\partial \psi_2}{\partial V} = \frac{-1}{2b^3} \{bV(e^{2\delta} - 2e^\delta + 1)\}$$

$$= -\frac{V}{2b^2} (e^{2\delta} - 2e^\delta + 1).$$

From (A5)

$$\frac{\partial \bar{V}}{\partial V} = \frac{e^{\delta} - 1}{b(T - t)}$$

so

$$V \frac{(T - t)^2}{2} \left(\frac{\partial \bar{V}}{\partial V}\right)^2 = \frac{V}{2b^2} (e^{2\delta} - 2e^{\delta} + 1).$$

Thus,

$$\frac{\partial \psi_2}{\partial t} + \eta \frac{\partial \psi_2}{\partial V} + V \frac{(T - t)^2}{2} \left(\frac{\partial \bar{V}}{\partial V}\right)^2 = 0$$

which shows ψ_2 satisfies (1-3) and ϕ_2 satisfied the second equation in (A17).
Now consider ϕ_3,

$$\phi_3 = \frac{1}{2} \psi^2$$

$$\frac{\partial \phi_3}{\partial t} = \psi \frac{\partial \psi}{\partial t}$$

$$\frac{\partial \phi_3}{\partial V} = \psi \frac{\partial \psi}{\partial V}.$$

Thus

$$\frac{\partial \phi_3}{\partial t} + \eta \frac{\partial \phi_3}{\partial V} + \rho V \psi \frac{\partial \bar{V}}{\partial V} (T - t) = \psi \left[\frac{\partial \psi}{\partial t} + \eta \frac{\partial \psi}{\partial V} + \rho V \frac{\partial \bar{V}}{\partial V} (T - t)\right]$$

which (A12) shows to be zero. Thus, ϕ_3 satisfies the third equation in (A17). Given this, ϕ_4 trivially satisfies the fourth equation in (A17).

NOTE 2: A PROOF THAT (16)–(18) SATISFY THE BOUNDARY CONDITIONS (15)

The boundary conditions are

$$f_i = 0 \qquad \text{when} \qquad t = T \qquad\qquad (2\text{-}1)$$

$$f_i = 0 \qquad \text{when} \qquad S = 0 \qquad\qquad (2\text{-}2)$$

$$\lim_{S \to \infty} \frac{\partial f_i}{\partial S} = 0. \qquad\qquad (2\text{-}3)$$

First consider f_0:

$$f_0 = C(\bar{V}) - C(V)$$

when $t = T$, $\overline{V} = V$ so (2-1) is satisfied; when $S = 0$, $C(\overline{V}) = C(V) = 0$ so (2-2) is satisfied and

$$\lim_{S \to \infty} \frac{\partial f_0}{\partial S} = \lim_{S \to \infty} \frac{\partial C(\overline{V})}{\partial S} - \lim_{S \to \infty} \frac{\partial C(V)}{\partial S} = 0$$

so (2-3) is satisfied.

Now consider f_1. From (A8)

$$f_1 = \frac{\psi(V, t)}{(T - t)} S \frac{\partial^2 C(\overline{V})}{\partial S \partial \overline{V}}$$

where

$$\psi(V, t) = -\frac{\rho}{b^3} \{(a + bV)(e^\delta - \delta e^\delta - 1) + a(e^\delta - \delta - 1)\}$$

and

$$\delta = b(T - t).$$

To show that f_1 satisfies (2-1) we must show

$$\lim_{t \to T} \frac{\psi(V, t)}{(T - t)} = 0.$$

Expanding ψ in a series in δ and dropping all but the lowest order term gives

$$\lim_{t \to T} \psi(V, t) = -\frac{\rho}{b^3} \left\{ (a + bV) \left(-\frac{\delta^2}{2} \right) + a \left(\frac{\delta^2}{2} \right) \right\}$$

$$= \frac{1}{2} \rho V(T - t)^2.$$

Thus, $\lim_{t \to T}[\psi/(T - t)] = 0$. Since from the properties of $C(\overline{V})$, $(\partial^2 C/\partial S \partial \overline{V})|_{t=T} = 0$, it follows that f_1 satisfies (2-1).

To show that f_1 satisfies (2-3)

$$\frac{\partial f_1}{\partial S} = \frac{\psi}{T - t} \left[\frac{\partial^2 C(\overline{V})}{\partial S \partial \overline{V}} + S \frac{\partial^3 C(\overline{V})}{\partial S^2 \partial \overline{V}} \right]$$

which, making use of (A3), becomes

$$\frac{\partial f_1}{\partial S} = \frac{\psi}{T - t} \left[\frac{\partial^2 C(\overline{V})}{\partial S \partial \overline{V}} + \frac{2}{S(T - t)} \frac{\partial^2 C(\overline{V})}{\partial \overline{V}^2} \right].$$

From the properties of $C(\overline{V})$

$$\lim_{S \to \infty} \frac{\partial C(\overline{V})}{\partial S} = 1; \qquad \lim_{S \to \infty} \frac{\partial C(\overline{V})}{\partial \overline{V}} = 0$$

so

$$\lim_{S\to\infty} \frac{\partial^2 C(\bar{V})}{\partial\bar{V}\partial S} = 0 \quad \text{and} \quad \lim_{S\to\infty} \frac{\partial^2 C(\bar{V})}{\partial\bar{V}^2} = 0.$$

It follows that f_1 satisfies (2-3). Finally, f_1 trivially satisfies (2-2).

Now consider f_2. From (18)

$$f_2 = \frac{\phi_1(V,t)}{(T-t)} S \frac{\partial^2 C(\bar{V})}{\partial S\partial\bar{V}} + \frac{\phi_2(V,t)}{(T-t)^2} \frac{\partial^2 C(\bar{V})}{\partial\bar{V}^2} + \frac{\phi_3(V,t)}{(T-t)^2} S \frac{\partial^3 C(\bar{V})}{\partial S\partial\bar{V}^2}$$

$$+ \frac{\phi_4(V,t)}{(T-t)^3} \frac{\partial^3 C(\bar{V})}{\partial\bar{V}^3},$$

where

$$\phi_1 = \frac{\rho^2}{b^4}\left\{(a+bV)\left[e^\delta\left(\frac{1}{2}\delta^2 - \delta + 1\right) - 1\right] + a[e^\delta(2-\delta) - (2+\delta)]\right\}$$

$$\phi_2 = 2\phi_1 + \frac{1}{2b^4}\left\{(a+bV)(e^{2\delta} - 2\delta e^\delta - 1) - \frac{a}{2}(e^{2\delta} - 4e^\delta + 2\delta + 3)\right\}$$

$$\phi_3 = \frac{1}{2}\psi^2$$

$$\phi_4 = \psi^2.$$

To show that f_2 satisfies (2-1), expand the ϕ_i's in a series in δ keeping only the lowest order terms in δ and replacing δ with $b(T-t)$

$$\lim_{t\to T}\phi_1 = \frac{\rho^2}{b^4}\left\{(a+bV)\frac{\delta^3}{6} + a\left(\frac{-\delta^3}{6}\right)\right\}$$

$$= \frac{\rho^2 V}{6}(T-t)^3$$

$$\lim_{t\to T}\phi_2 = 2\lim_{t\to T}\phi_1 + \frac{1}{2b^4}\left\{(a+bV)\frac{\delta^3}{3} - \frac{a}{2}\left(\frac{2\delta^3}{3}\right)\right\}$$

$$= 2\frac{\rho^2 V}{6}(T-t)^3 + \frac{V}{6}(T-t)^3$$

$$\lim_{t\to T}\phi_3 = \frac{1}{2}\left[\lim_{t\to T}\psi\right]^2$$

$$= \frac{\rho^2 V^2}{8}(T-t)^4$$

$$\lim_{t\to T}\phi_4 = 2\lim_{t\to T}\phi_3$$

$$= \frac{\rho^2 V^2}{4}(T-t)^4.$$

With these results it is obvious that

$$\lim_{t \to T} f_2 = 0,$$

and f_2 satisfies (2-1).

From the properties of $C(\overline{V})$, $\partial/\partial S$ of the second and fourth terms in f_2 vanish as $S \to \infty$. By analogy to the arguments used for f_1, $\partial/\partial S$ of the first and third terms also vanish as $S \to \infty$. Thus,

$$\lim_{S \to \infty} \frac{\partial f_2}{\partial S} = 0$$

and f_2 satisfies (2-3).

Finally, when $S = 0$ the first and third terms in f_2 vanish. Applying (A3) to the second and fourth terms shows that they also vanish when $S = 0$. Thus, when $S = 0$, $f_2 = 0$ so f_2 satisfies (2-2).

NOTES

1. This corresponds to an instantaneous standard deviation of 22–32% per annum.
2. Hull and White [18] assumed that the volatility obeyed the process given by $dV = \hat{\xi}V\, dw$. The value of $\hat{\xi}$ which is comparable with the value of ξ used here is given by $\xi/\sqrt{V}$. If $\xi = 0.1$ and $V = 0.1$ the comparable $\hat{\xi}$ is about 0.3. Hull and White [17] provide some evidence indicating that for currencies $\hat{\xi}$ may be 1 or higher. However, it may be lower for stocks.
3. It should be noted that Equations (11)–(15) are true for any contingent claim C that satisfies Equation (6) and whose boundary conditions are independent of V. Thus, this solution technique can be used to determine the bias in the value of most one state variable contingent claims caused by a stochastic volatility.
4. At-the-money is defined as $S = Xe^{-r(T-t)}$.

REFERENCES

1. Black, F., and M. Scholes, "The Pricing of Options and Corporate Liabilities," *Journal of Political Economy* 81 (May–June 1973), 637–659.
2. Bodurtha, J. N., and G. Courtadon, "Empirical Tests of the Philadelphia Stock Exchange Foreign Currency Options Market," Ohio State University working paper WPS 84-69, 1984.
3. Boyle, P. P., and E. Kirzner, "Pricing Complex Options: Echo-Bay Ltd. Gold Purchase Warrants," *Canadian Journal of Administrative Studies* 2 (1985), 294–306.
4. Brennan, M. J., and E. S. Schwartz, "A Continuous Time Approach to the Pricing of Bonds," *Journal of Banking and Finance* 3 (1979), 133–155.
5. Brennan, M. J., and E. S. Schwartz, "An Equilibrium Model of Bond Pricing and a Test of Market Efficiency," *Journal of Financial and Quantitative Analysis* 17 (1982), 301–329.
6. Christie, A. A., "The Stochastic Behavior of Common Stock Variances," *Journal of Financial Economics* 10 (December 1982), 407–432.

7. Cox, J. C., J. E. Ingersoll, and S. A. Ross, "An Intertemporal General Equilibrium Model of Asset Prices," *Econometrica* 53 (March 1985), 363–384.

8. Cox, J. C., J. E. Ingersoll, and S. A. Ross, "A Theory of the Term Structure of Interest Rates," *Econometrica* 53 (March 1985), 385–407.

9. Cox, J. C., and S. A. Ross, "The Valuation of Options for Alternative Stochastic processes," *Journal of Financial Economics* 3 (March 1976), 145–166.

10. Dothan, M. U., A Random Volatility Correction for the Black–Scholes Option Pricing Formula," *Advances in Futures and Options Research* 2 (1987), 97–115.

11. Fischer, S., "Call Option Pricing When the Exercise Price Is Uncertain, and the Valuation of Index Bonds," *Journal of Finance* 33 (March 1978), 169–176.

12. Galai, D., "The Components of the Return from Hedging Options against Stocks," *Journal of Business* 56 (January 1983), 45–54.

13. Garman, M., "A General Theory of Asset Valuation under Diffusion State Processes," Working paper No. 50, University of California, Berkeley, 1976.

14. Geske, R., "The Pricing of Options with Stochastic Dividend Yield," *Journal of Finance* 33 (May 1978), 617–625.

15. Geske, R., "The Valuation of Compound Options," *Journal of Financial Economics* 7 (March 1979), 63–81.

16. Hammersley, J. M., and D. C. Handscomb, *Monte Carlo Methods.* London: Methuen, 1964.

17. Hull, J. C., and A. White, "Hedging the Risks from Writing Foreign Currency Options," *Journal of International Money and Finance* 6 (June 1987), 131–152.

18. Hull, J. C., and A. White, "The Pricing of Options on Assets with Stochastic Volatilities," *Journal of Finance* 42 (June 1987), 281–300.

19. Johnson, H. E., "The Pricing of Complex Options," Louisiana State University, Department of Finance, 1983.

20. Johnson, H. E., "Option Pricing When the Variance is Changing", Graduate School of Management working paper 11-79, University of California, Los Angeles, 1979.

21. Johnson, H. E., and D. Shanno, "Option Pricing When the Variance Is Changing," *Journal of Financial and Quantitative Analysis* 22 (June 1987), 143–151.

22. Jones, E. P., "Option Arbitrage and Strategy with Large Price Changes," *Journal of Financial Economics* 13 (1984), 91–114.

23. Kon, S. J., "Models of Stock Returns—a Comparison," *Journal of Finance* 39 (March 1984), 147–166.

24. Margrabe, W., "The Value of an Option to Exchange One Asset for Another," *Journal of Finance* 33 (March 1978), 177–186.

25. Merton, R. C., "The Theory of Rational Option Pricing," *Bell Journal of Economics and Management Science* 4 (Spring 1973), 141–183.

26. Merton, R. C., "Option Pricing When Underlying Stock Returns Are Discontinuous," *Journal of Financial Economics* 3 (March 1976), 125–144.

27. Richard, S. F., "An Arbitrage Model of the Term Structure of Interest Rates," *Journal of Financial Economics* 6 (1979), 33–57.

28. Roll, R., "An Analytic Valuation Formula for Unprotected American Call Options on Stocks with Known Dividends," *Journal of Financial Economics* 5 (November 1977), 251–258.

29. Rubinstein, M., "Displaced Diffusion Option Pricing," *Journal of Finance* 38 (March 1983), 213–217.

30. Rubinstein, M., "Nonparametric Tests of the Alternative Option Pricing Models Using All Reported Trades and Quotes on the 30 Most Active CBOE Option Classes from August 23, 1976 through August 31, 1978," *Journal of Finance* 40 (June 1986), 445–480.

31. Scott, L. O., "Option Pricing When the Variance Changes Randomly: Theory, Esti-

mation, and an Application," *Journal of Financial and Quantitative Analysis* 22 (December 1987), 419–438.

32. Stulz, R., "Options on the Minimum or the Maximum of Two Risky Assets," *Journal of Financial Economics*, 10 (1982), 161–185.

33. Wiggins, J. B., "Option Values under Stochastic Volatility: Theory and Empirical Evidence," *Journal of Financial Economics* 19 (1987), 351–372.

ANALYSIS OF BONDS WITH IMBEDDED OPTIONS

Farshid Jamshidian* and Yu Zhu*

I. INTRODUCTION

Many fixed income securities are imbedded with option-like features. Representatives of such securities are callable bonds, put bonds, convertible bonds, and mortgage-backed securities. Although most of these securities have either call or put options, but not both, some are both callable and putable. In today's market, the proliferated new products, designed to meet borrowers' and investors' needs, incorporate various option features in their structure. Thus, the importance of properly evaluating these securities and analyzing their risk characteristics cannot be overstated.

In general, the value decomposition principle can be used to analyze a bond with imbedded options. For example, a callable bond can be decomposed into an underlying bond and a short position of a call option

*Financial Strategies Group, Merrill Lynch Capital Markets.

Advances in Futures and Options Research, Vol. 3, pages 63–95.
Copyright © 1988 by JAI Press Inc.
All rights of reproduction in any form reserved.
ISBN: 0-89232-926-2

on that underlying bond. Similarly, a put bond is equivalent to an underlying bond plus a put option on the underlying bond. Applying this principle and using an option model, one can calculate the value of the underlying bond, and the value of the option on that underlying bond. The value of the option imbedded bond is their algebraic sum. This approach is easy to understand and also has resulted in many interesting findings.[1] The previous analyses are mainly for bonds with rather simple options, such as one European call option or put option. But most corporate bonds have multiple call options, and there are bonds with both multiple call and multiple put options. For those bonds with more complicated options, the value decomposition principle can still help us to understand the characteristics of the security. However, decomposing such a bond into its components and calculating the value of each component separately would be a very cumbersome procedure. Sometimes a naive decomposition may even lead to erroneous results.

In this paper, the value of a bond with imbedded options is considered as a solution to a bond option model. It is well known that a zero coupon bond and an option on that bond satisfy the same linear partial differential equation. They are distinguished only by their boundary conditions. By imposing approprite boundary conditions, the same differential equation gives the value of the bond with imbedded options.[2] Because of the linearity of the equation, the value decomposition principle is valid, hence this approach is consistent with the previous method.

For our applications we need a parsimonious and practical bond option model. Vasicek [14], Brennan and Schwartz [5], and Cox, Ingersoll, and Ross (CIR) [8], among others, developed one- or two-factor term structure models in which the short rate and/or long rate determine the whole term structure. Although primarily intended for deriving equilibrium bond prices, these models were also proposed for pricing interest rate contingent claims, as in the numerical procedures of Courtadon [7] and Brennan and Schwartz [6], and the closed form solution of Cox, Ingersoll, and Ross [8] for options on discount bonds. But there is a practical difficulty with such an approach. The contractual provisions of most contingent claims are in terms of bond prices not the level of the short-term rate. Since, in percentage terms, option prices are very sensitive to changes in price of the underlying bond, it is desirable, as a practical matter, to incorporate the price of the underlying security into the model in a direct way.

There are alternative price-based bond option models, which employ the price of the underlying security as the state variable and also incorporate short-term interest rate. The primary example is the classic Black–Scholes [3] model, which assumes constant interest rate and constant price volatility. In pricing debt options, however, these assumptions are often unacceptable. Several models were proposed to avoid these questionable assumptions. For example, Ball and Torous [1] proposed the Brownian bridge model, which is a specialization of Merton's [11] model to the case of constant volatility. In a framework similar to the Black–Scholes model, Schaefer and Schwartz [12] assumed a constant instantaneous riskless rate but a varying price volatility proportional to bond duration. However, as shown in this paper, these models do not satisfy certain consistency requirements for bond option pricing. For example, a call on a discount bond with a strike price greater than one should have a value of zero, since the price of that bond will never exceed unity. But these models give positive values for all strike prices. It should be noted that the term structure models such as CIR [8] and Courtadon [7] satisfy these consistency requirements because interest rates never become negative in their models.

Our model is a one-factor, continuous time arbitrage model. Similar to the Black–Scholes and the Schaefer and Schwartz model, it uses the price of the underlying bond as the state variable. In contrast to the above price-based models, we assume that both volatility and short-term rate are variable in a certain "well-posed" manner so as to guarantee the consistency requirements. These properties and its parsimony make the model a practical choice in our opinion. There remains the problem of incorporating more information from the market yield curve. CIR [8] and Ho and Lee [10] addressed this issue. But there are still difficulties. We shall return to this point in our conclusion.

The paper is organized as follows. Since the bond option model is important in its own right, we devote two sections to discussing the model's general setting and its specifications. First, in Section II we describe the general framework of the model. It is shown that put–call parity follows from the linearity of the model. Then, in Section III we discuss several conditions for a consistent model and compare our model with other related bond option pricing models. Section IV applies the model to study the characteristics of bonds with imbedded options. Following the common practice, we employ duration as the measure of the interest rate risk exposure. Based on the value decomposition principle and put–call parity, we derive theoretical bounds of the value and duration for simple cases and discuss their asymptotic properties. We also illustrate the characteristics of bonds with more complicated options by numerically solving the model. Section V summarizes the paper and briefly discusses the direction of our future research.

II. THE MODEL FRAMEWORK

We make the usual assumptions of markets for a continuous time setting: there is continuous trading, no taxes, and no transactions cost or other frictions. We assume that there is no default risk and the value of a contingent claim, F, is completely determined by the price of the underlying bond B, i.e.,

$$F = F(B, t).$$

The contingent claim can be a bond, an option on a bond, or a bond with imbedded options. The underlying bond pays continuously at a constant coupon rate D and has a (par) value of 100 at the maturity time T_M.[3] The price of the underlying bond follows a diffusion process B(t) with drift μ and diffusion coefficient σ:

$$\mu (B, t) \, dt = E \, [dB(t)/B(t) \mid B(t) = B]$$
$$\sigma^2 (B, t) \, dt = Var \, [dB(t)/B(t) \mid B(t) = B].$$

We also assume that the instantaneous riskless interest rate r is time varying and is determined by the bond price B, namely,

$$r = r(B, t).$$

The arbitrage argument used in deriving the Black–Scholes differential equation does not require the parameters r, μ, and σ to be constant. Moreover, that argument is still valid in the presence of coupon payment. Thus, by the same argument one obtains the differential equation for evaluating F(B, t):[4]

$$F_t + (1/2)\sigma^2(B, t)B^2 F_{BB} + [r(B, t) - D/B]BF_B - r(B, t)F + D_1 = 0 \quad (1)$$

where D_1 is the cash payment rate for the security F. We note that for a bond with imbedded options, we usually have $D_1 = D$, but if Equation (1) is used to evaluate a call or put on the underlying bond, then D_1 would be zero.

Clearly, the setting of Equation (1) is quite general. A specific choice of the function forms of volatility and riskless rate gives us a specific model. If both the volatility and riskless rate are constant and both D and D_1 are zero, we obtain the Black–Scholes model. Setting riskless rate constant and assuming volatility proportional to bond duration, we would have the Schaefer and Schwartz model [12]. In fact, different specifications corres- pond to different underlying stochastic processes and implied term struc- tures. In the next section we show that certain conditions should be satisfied in choosing these function forms.

The contractual provision of a bond with imbedded options is specified by its terminal value (payoff function) g(B):

$$F(B, T) = g(B), \quad (2)$$

where T is the time to option expiry. For a callable bond with a European call option the payoff function g(B) is equal to Min{B, K}, where K is the exercise (call) price. For a European put bond, $g(B) = \text{Max}\{B, K\}$. The value of $F(B, t)$ is then the solution of the terminal value problem (1) and (2).

A. Integral Representation of Solution

We note that the drift term $\mu(B, t)$ does not appear in Equation (1). It is replaced by a "risk-neutral" drift, $r(B, t) - D/B$. This implies that the value of a bond with imbedded options can be considered as based on a process $\bar{B}(t)$, the risk-neutral bond price process:

$$\frac{d\bar{B}(t)}{\bar{B}(t)} = [r(\bar{B}, t) - D/\bar{B}] \, dt + \sigma(\bar{B}, t) \, dz. \tag{3}$$

Based on an argument similar to the risk-neutrality argument, the solution Equation (1) with terminal condition (2) has the following integral representation:[5]

$$F(B, t) = E\left[g[\bar{B}(T)]\exp\left\{-\int_t^T r[\bar{B}(s), s] \, ds\right\} \Big| \bar{B}(t) = B\right]$$

$$+ D_1 \int_t^T B^*(1, s, 0) \, ds, \tag{4}$$

where T is the expiry date, and B^* is the value of a zero coupon bond. The arguments of B^*, $(1, s, 0)$, represent face value of 1, maturity time of s, and coupon of zero. The explicit expression of B^* is

$$B^*(1, s, 0) = E\left[\exp\left\{-\int_t^s r[\bar{B}(u), u] \, du \Big| \bar{B}(t) = B\right\}\right]. \tag{5}$$

Evidently, the first item on the right-hand side of (4) is the expected value (with respect to the risk-neutral process) of the discounted payoff of the claim, given the current underlying bond price of B. The second item is the sum of the discounted coupon payment stream. Thus, in the world described by (3), the value of a bond with imbedded options is an expected present value of its cash flow.

We shall see in the subsequent discussion that the integral representation (4) provides valuable insight into the model.

B. Put–Call Parity

Put–call parity is a fundamental relationship in option pricing theory. It states that for European call option C and put option P on an underlying bond B with time to expiry T and exercise price K, the following relationship holds:

$$C - P - B + B^*(K, T, D) = 0. \tag{6}$$

In the above equation $B^*(K, T, D)$ is the value of a bond that pays at the same coupon rate as the underlying bond, but matures at time T with par value of K. Subsequently we shall call B^* a "host bond" to expiry date. It should be noted that the underlying security in (6) is not necessarily a simple bond but can be a synthetic security, e.g., a callable bond.

Put–call parity does not depend on a particular option pricing model. Rather, a well-defined model should satisfy this relationship. To show that model (1) satisfies the put–call parity, we note that both B and $B^*(K, T, D)$ are solutions to Equation (1) with $D_1 = D$, while C and P satisfy the corresponding homogeneous equation. Hence, $C - P - B + B^*$ is a solution to Equation (1) with $D_1 = 0$. At expiry, the total payoff would be

$$Max\{B(T) - K, 0\} - Max\{K - B(T), 0\} - B(T) + K,$$

which is zero for all B(T). From the uniqueness of the terminal value problem (1) and (2), (6) holds for any time t before or at expiry.[6]

III. WELL-POSED CONDITIONS AND IMPLIED YIELD CURVE

There are two basic requirements in bond pricing. The first one says that a bond is always priced at par at maturity, and the second requirement is that the bond price at any time should not exceed the sum of all cash flows from holding the bond. We can write these two requirements as follows:

$$B(T_M) = 100 \tag{7a}$$

$$B(t) \leqslant B_{max} = 100 + D(T_M - t) \tag{7b}$$

If the second requirement is violated, one can sell the bond short, simply keep the proceeds in cash, pay all the obligations, and be left with an arbitrage profit. Obviously, any bond pricing model should at least meet these two requirements.

In model (1), we assume that the instantaneous riskless interest rate and the price volatility are functions of bond price and time. In this section we show that, in order to satisfy the constraints on bond price, we should impose certain restrictions on our choices of $r(B, t)$ and $\sigma(B, t)$. Since mathematically these restrictions are necessary for a well-posed model, we shall henceforth call them "well-posed" conditions.

As we mentioned in the previous section, the bond option value is directly related to the risk neutral process $\bar{B}$ rather than the underlying process B. We now show that for a consistent model, $\bar{B}$ should also satisfy the above two basic requirements. To see this, first we note that (7a) and (7b) are equivalent to the following requirements on the call value C:

$$C(B) \rightarrow B^*(1, T, 0)\text{Max}\{100 - K, 0\} \qquad \text{as } T \rightarrow T_M \qquad (8a)$$

and

$$C(B) = 0 \qquad \text{if } K \geqslant B_{max}. \qquad (8b)$$

Recall that $B^*(1, T, 0)$ is the discount factor. When the option expiry is very close to the bond maturity, the call value should be close to the discount value of the call's terminal payoff, $\text{Max}\{100 - K, 0\}$, and this justifies (8a). Equation (8b) is a direct consequence of (7b). To show that B should satisfy (7a) and (7b), we apply the integral representation (4). From (4) the call value can be written as

$$C(B) = E\left[\text{Max}\{\bar{B}(T) - K, 0\}\exp\left\{-\int_t^T r[\bar{B}(s), s] \, ds\right\}\right]. \qquad (9)$$

If $\bar{B}(T_M) = 100$, then (8a) is satisfied since, by definition,

$$B^*(1, T, 0) = E\left[\exp\left\{-\int_t^T r[\bar{B}(s), s] \, ds\right\}\right].$$

On the other hand, if (8a) is true for every K, $B(T_M)$ can only have a value of 100. Hence B satisfies (7a). Since the discount factor $\exp\{-\int_t^T r[B(s), s] \, ds\}$ is always positive, from (9) we have that (8b) is satisfied if and only if $B \leqslant \bar{B}_{max}$. Thus, $\bar{B}$ satisfies (7b).

We have shown that for a consistent bond option model, the risk-neutral bond price process has to meet the above two basic requirements. From these requirements we can now derive the following well-posed conditions in choosing r and σ.

A. Well-Posed Conditions

(a) When time t approaches maturity, the bond yield should approach the instantaneous riskless rate and the price volatility should approach zero.

To see that this condition guarantees that $\bar{B}(T_M) = 100$, let us examine the bond price formula:

$$B(y, t) = (100 - D/y)\exp\{-y(T_M - t)\} + D/y. \qquad (10)$$

Since B follows the risk-neutral process (3), the yield process defined by the above equation is the risk neutral yield process. To ensure that $B(T_M) = 100$, it requires that y is well behaved in the neighborhood of $t = T_M$, or the limit of y exists when t goes to T_M. From (10) we have

$$B_t = yB - D.$$

using this relationship and applying Ito's lemma, we can write the risk-neutral yield process as follows:

$$\frac{dy}{y} = \eta(y, t) \, dt + \delta(y, t) \, dz \qquad (11)$$

where

$$\eta(y, t) = [(r - y)B - (1/2) \, \delta^2 y^2 B_{yy}] / y B_y \qquad (12)$$

and

$$\delta(y, t) = B\sigma / y B_y \qquad (13)$$

Since B_y goes to zero when time is near maturity, for a well-behaved yield process, we need

$$r - y \to 0 \qquad \text{and} \qquad \sigma \to 0 \qquad \text{as } t \to T_M.$$

The intuition behind condition (a) is quite clear. Over time, a long-term bond becomes a shorter term bond. When time approaches maturity, the bond yield should be closer and closer to the instantaneous interest rate. On the other hand, a bond is always priced at par at maturity, hence the price volatility at maturity should not be anything but zero.

The second well-posed condition is

(b) Both the instantaneous riskless rate and price volatility should approach zero if bond yield goes to zero.

This is to meet requirement (7b). In fact, (7b) is equivalent to the statement that yield should be nonnegative. It is easy to see from (12) and (13) that for η and δ to be bounded, we need r and σ go the zero as y approaches zero. Although zero yield is acceptable, mathematically we would prefer that yield is always positive.[7] In other words, we would make the boundary (y = 0) inaccessible. In this case, condition (b) would be written as

$$r = 0(y) \qquad \text{and} \qquad \sigma = 0(y) \qquad \text{as } y \to 0.$$

It should be noted that in our model setting, if one assumes r and/or σ constant, these two conditions are violated. Therefore, the two basic requirements of bond pricing cannot be guaranteed. In fact, Equation (9) can be generalized as

$$C(B) = E[B^* \, \text{Max}\{\bar{B}(T) - K, 0\} \, | \, \bar{B}(t) = B] \qquad (14)$$

where B^* is a discount factor. Equation (14) is true for all continuous time option models based on the Kolmogorov backward differential equation. Since B^* is always positive, if the model does not have the aforementioned upper bound on the risk-neutral process $\bar{B}(t)$, then (8b) will be violated. For example, in the Brownian bridge process model the risk-neutral price B is lognormally distributed. For an exercise price K greater than B_{max}, C(B) will still be positive.[8] Similarly, when r is constant, the constant drift will cause $\bar{B}(T)$ to have positive probability density on the whole positive axis. This will lead to a positive $C(B)$ for all K, which again violates (8b). Similarly, (8a) is also violated in this case.

B. Example of $r(y, t)$ and $\sigma(y, t)$

In this subsection, we present a simple but practical example of r and σ that satisfies the well-posed conditions. Because of the nature of the two conditions, instead of defining these two functions in the price space, we choose yield as the state variable.[9] Assuming yield volatility δ constant, from (13) we have

$$\sigma = \delta y B_y / B. \tag{15}$$

It is easy to see that $\sigma(y, t)$ satisfies the well-posed conditions (a) and (b). Essentially, (15) assumes that the bond price volatility is proportional to its duration ($|B_y/B|$). An example of $r(y, t)$ is as follows:

$$r = \text{Max}\{0, y + (r_0 - y_0)(T_M - t)/(T_M - t_0)\}, \tag{16}$$

where the subscript 0 denotes initial values. For $r_0 < y_0$, conditions (a) and (b) are satisfied. Equation (16) implies parallel shifts in the yield curve, namely $\delta r/\delta y = 1$. The parallel shift is not a precise description of the yield curve movement, but it is nevertheless a good first approximation.[10]

Many other choices are of course possible. It should be noted that if the bond option has a short term to expiry, the solution to the problem (1) and (2) is not very sensitive to the function form $r(y, t)$.

Once $r(y, t)$ and $\sigma(y, t)$ are chosen, we can calculate not only the value of a bond with imbedded options, but also the values of a set of bonds with the same coupon rate and different (shorter) terms to maturity. Thus, given y_0 and r_0, the whole yield curve can be depicted, as shown in Figure 1. The three curves (cases 1, 2, and 3) correspond to three interest rate scenarios: r_0 is less than, equal to, and greater than y_0. All these curves look reasonable.

There is a relationship between model (1) and the one-factor term structure model. Let $\bar{r}(t) = r[\bar{B}(t), t]$ represent the risk-neutral interest rate process with

$$d\bar{r}(t) = \eta \, dt + a \, dz,$$

where η and a are obtained by using Equation (3) and applying Ito's lemma. Since the Kolmogorov backward equation is invariant under changes of coordinates, from (1) we get[11]

$$F_t + (1/2)a^2 F_{rr} + \eta F_r - rF + D_1 = 0 \tag{17}$$

which is the same as the differential equation of the one-factor term

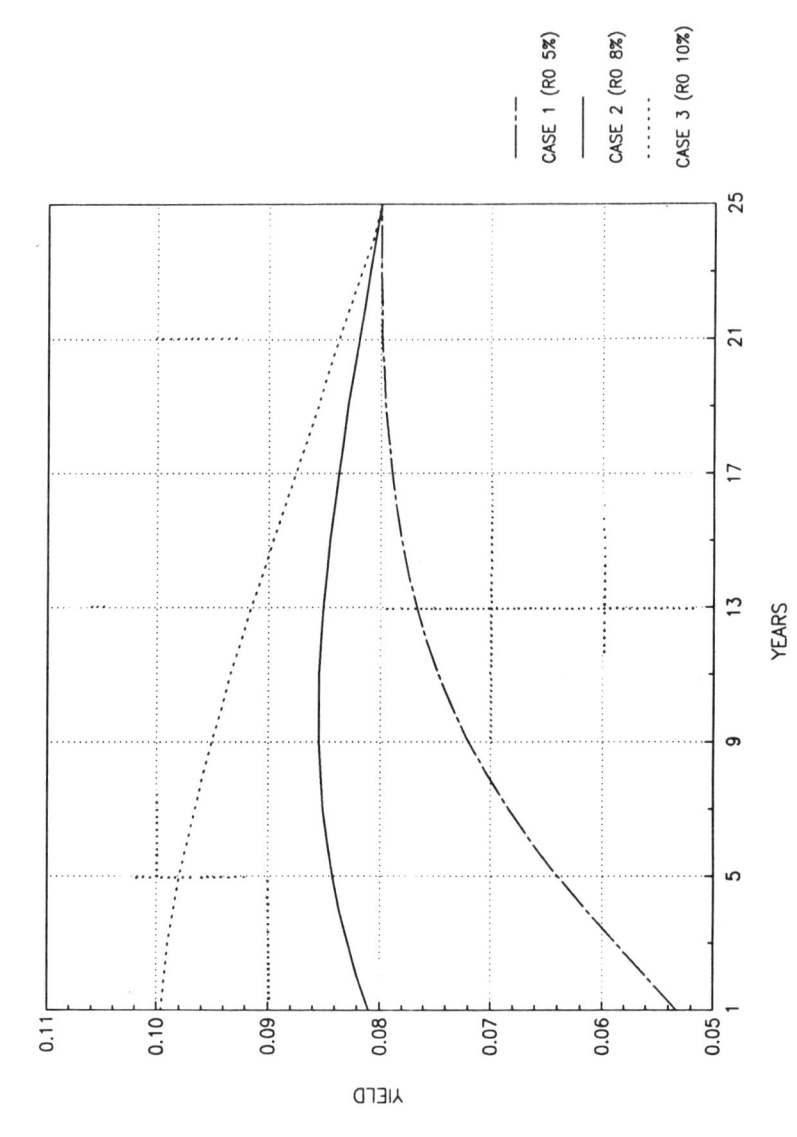

Figure 1. Implied yield curves for 8% coupon bond; yield volatility 20%.

structure model. (See, e.g., Equation (7a) in Courtadan [7].) Thus, particular function forms of r and σ determine the drift and the diffusion coefficients of the risk-neutral interest rate process, and vice versa.

The difference between model (1) and the one-factor term structure model is that the former accepts initial values of r_0 and B_0 (or y_0) as input, whereas the latter has only r_0 as its input. From model (1) one can obtain a reasonable yield curve. However, except at the two ends of the curve, the implied yield curve may not coincide with the observed market yield curve. The one-factor term structure model, on the other hand, is based on the market information to deduce an equilibrium term structure. But the calculated market price of the underlying security may differ significantly from the market price. As we mentioned earlier, this may cause serious errors in option pricing.

IV. CHARACTERISTICS OF BONDS WITH IMBEDDED OPTIONS

The model proposed in the previous sections provides a simple but useful tool to analyze bonds with imbedded options. In this section we study characteristics of callable bonds, put bonds, and callable–putable bonds. Based on the value decomposition principle and the put–call parity, we discuss the bounds and asymptotic properties of bond value and its duration. By specifying $r(y, t)$ and $\sigma(y, t)$ as in (15) and (16) and using a finite difference method to solve model (1) with terminal condition (2), we illustrate how bond value and duration change with interest rate. We note that these results are quite general, not depending on a particular model, but the calculation results show that our model conforms with these properties very well.

To find the value of a bond with one European call or put option, we can simply solve Equation (1) with the terminal condition

$$F(B, T) = Min\{B, K\}$$

if the option is a call, or

$$F(B, T) = Max\{B, K\}$$

if the option is a put. For complex imbedded options, we start from the last option expiry date, solve the model, then proceed to the next to last option expiry date, and so on. For example, suppose we are dealing with a bond with multiple call and put options. Say the last option is a European call with time to call T_N and call price $K_c(T_N)$ and the next-to-last option is a European put with put time T_{N-1} and put price $K_p(T_{N-1})$, etc. Since at time T_N, the call is on the underlying bond, the callable bond composed of this call and the underlying bond satisfies Equation (1) with $D_1 = D$ and the terminal condition

$$F_c(T_N) = \text{Min}\{B(T_N), K_c(T_N)\}.$$

At time T_{N-1} the put is on the callable bond, and the put and the callable bond constitute a callable–putable bond, denoted by F_{pc}. F_{pc} satisfies the same differential equation, but the terminal condition becomes

$$F_{pc}(T_{N-1}) = \text{Max}\{F_c(T_{N-1}), K_p(T_{N-1})\}.$$

By solving backward in this way, we can calculate the value of a bond with complex imbedded options.

We need some additional assumptions. First, we assume that the bond option model is "reasonable" in the sense that at time t the call delta (dC/dB) is positive, put delta (dP/dB) is negative, and call gamma (d^2C/dB^2) is positive.[12] This requires that the parameters and input data in model (1) be reasonable. Second, we assume that the imbedded option schedules are "reasonable." In particular, the exercise price K should not be so large that the duration of $B^*(K, T, D)$ would be longer than the duration of the underlying bond.

A. Callable Bond

We start from the simplest case. A simple callable bond is a bond imbedded with a short position of a European call option. If we use F_c to represent the value of the simple callable bond, we get

$$F_c = B - C. \tag{18}$$

The value of a simple callable bond has the following properties:

(a) $F_c \leqslant \text{Min}\{B, B_c^*\}$;
(b) F_c approaches B if y is very high,
     F_c approaches B_c^* if y is very low,

where B_c^* is the host bond to the call date: $B_c^* = B^*(K, T, D)$. Indeed, since C is nonnegative, $F_c \leqslant B$. From the put–call parity, we have

$$F_c = B_c^* - P, \tag{19}$$

where P is the put on the underlying bond with the same exercise price and expiry. So, $F_c \leqslant B_c^*$, which proves (a). When yield is high, B is small. So the call value would approach zero and F_c would approach B. When yield is low, the put is well out of the money, so that F_c would be close to B_c^*. Thus, we establish (b). This result says that the value of a simple callable bond is bounded above and approaches these bounds in the limit.

Figure 2 illustrates how the value of a callable bond changes with interest rates. This is a 10-year bond with a 7% coupon rate, and it can be called in 1 year at par. The figure shows clearly the upper bound and the asymptotic behavior of the value of that bond. It is interesting to note that the imbedded call option reduces the convexity of the bond. For our example, near the current yield level, the callable bond exhibits a negative convexity while the two host bonds (B and B^*) have positive convexities.

The duration of a callable bond is defined as

$$D_c = \frac{1}{F_c} \frac{dF_c}{dy} \tag{20}$$

where y denotes the yield of the underlying bond. The duration of a simple callable bond is also bounded and has similar asymptotic property as stated in the following:

(c) $D_B \geqslant D_c \geqslant D_c^*$;
(d) D_c approaches D_B (D_c^*) as y gets very high (low),

where D_B is the duration of the underlying bond and D_c^* is the duration of the host bond to the call date. From (18) it is easy to show that

$$D_B - D_c = \frac{D_B}{F_c} \left(B \frac{dC}{dB} - C \right). \tag{21}$$

Since $B\ dC/dB - C = 0$ if $B = 0$ and $(d/dB)\ (B\ dC/dB - C) = d^2C/dB^2 \geqslant 0$, we have $D_B - D_c \geqslant 0$. By differentiating (19) we obtain

$$D_c - D_c^* = \frac{1}{F_c} \left[PD_c^* + BD_B \left(-\frac{dP}{dB} \right) \right]. \tag{22}$$

Since we assume dP/dB is negative, $D_c \geqslant D^*$. Hence, (c) is true. And (d) follows similarly from (21) and (22).

Figure 3 illustrates the relationship between the duration and the interest rate for the same callable bond as in Figure 2. We note that within a wide range of yield changes, the duration of a callable bond increases with yield, while the durations of host bonds are decreasing with yield.

For a bond with more complicated call provisions we have

$$F_c \leqslant \text{Min}\{B, B_1^*\}$$

and

$$D_c \leqslant D_B.$$

B_1^* stands for the host bond to the first call date. In general, we do not have the lower bound for D_c, unless we assume that the put on a callable bond has a negative delta. But it can be shown in the Black–Scholes framework

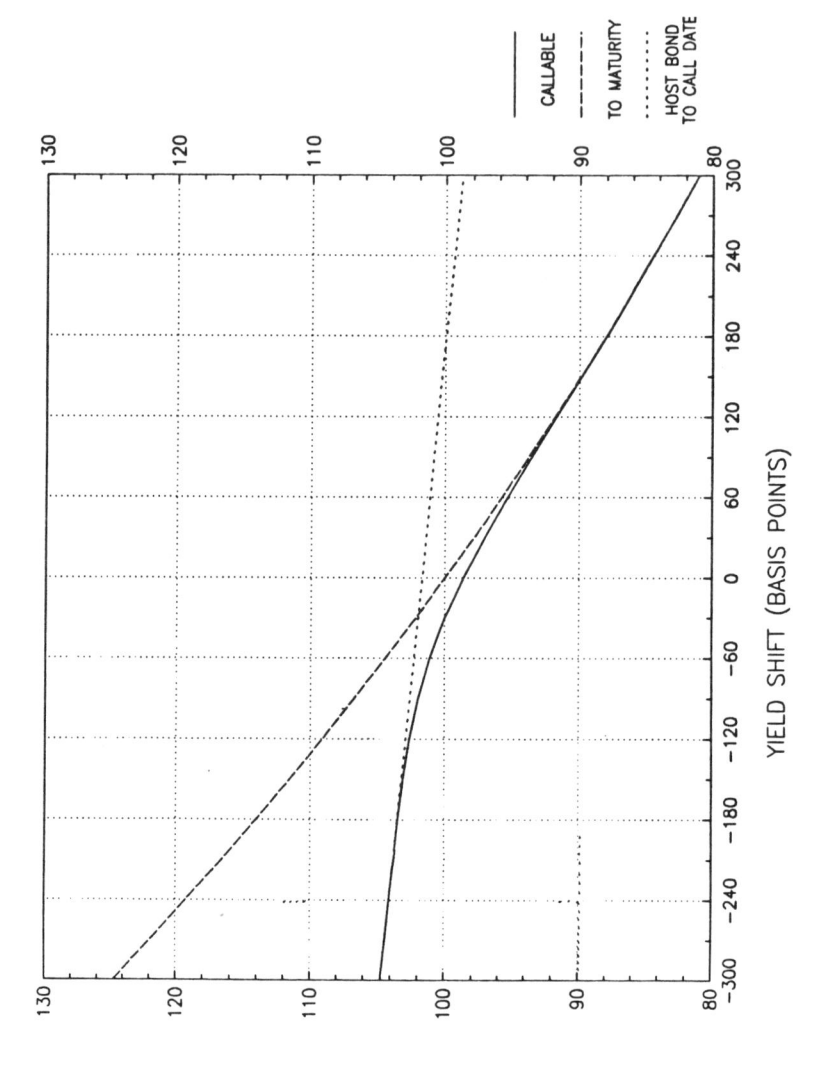

Figure 2. Callable bond. Change of bond value *vs.* yield shift: 10-year bond, CPN 7, 1 year to call at 100.

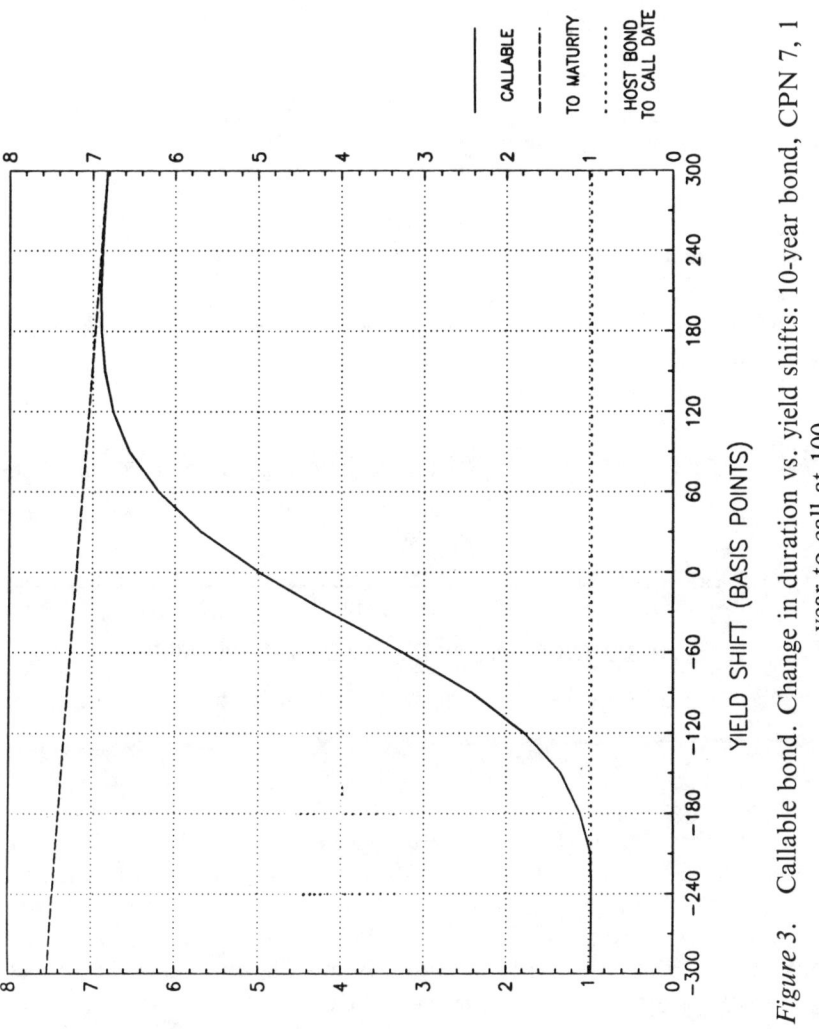

Figure 3. Callable bond. Change in duration vs. yield shifts: 10-year bond, CPN 7, 1 year to call at 100.

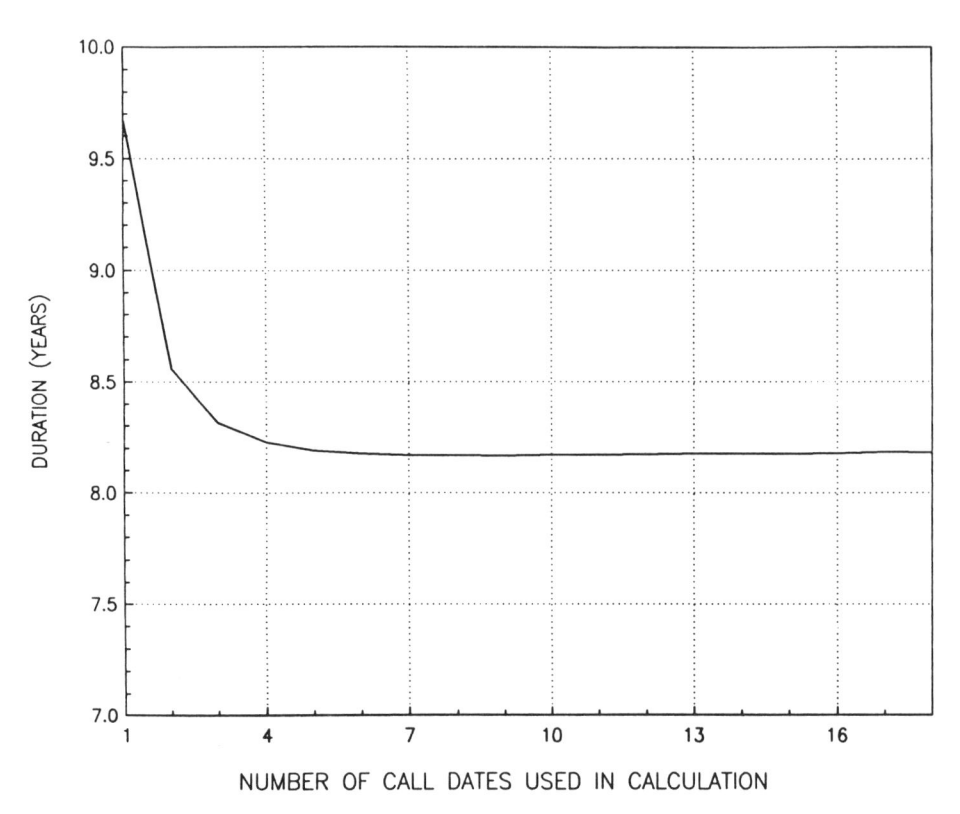

Figure 4.   Call adjusted duration with multiple call options: 22.5-year
bond, CPN 8.5, price 98.035.

that D_c is greater than D_1^*, the duration to the first call date.[13] The above
discussion suggests that the first call option plays an important role in
evaluating a callable bond. But other call options also have their impact.
Figure 4 shows how the duration of a callable bond changes when more
than one call option is used. The example is an 8.5% coupon bond with 22.5
years to maturity and priced at $98.039. The bond has multiple call options.
It can be called in 2 months at 105.76, then each year afterward at 105.49,
105.22, etc. The duration of the underlying bond is 10.13 years. If the first
call date is used, the duration becomes 9.68 years. If multiple call dates are
used in calculation, the duration will be adjusted successively to 8.56, 8.32,
8.23, etc. The shape of the curve suggests that, to calculate the call adjusted
duration of this bond, at least the first four to five call options should be
used to capture the impact of the whole call schedule.

B. Putable Bond

A simple putable bond is a bond imbedded with a long position of a European put. If F_p represents the value of a simple putable bond, we have

$$F_p = B + P. \tag{23}$$

By put–call parity, the value of a simple putable bond can also be written as

$$F_p = B_p^* + C, \tag{24}$$

where B_p^* is the host bond to the put date. A simple putable bond has the following properties:

(a) $F_p \geqslant \text{Max}\{B, B_p^*\}$;
(b) F_p approaches B (B_p^*) as y gets very low (high);
(c) $D_B \geqslant D_p \geqslant D_p^*$;
(d) D_p approaches D_B (D_p^*) as y gets very low (high),

where D_p is the duration of the putable bond and D_p^* is the duration of the host bond to the put date. Since these results are parallel to the case of a simple callable bond, we simply state them without proof. In contrast to a callable bond, the value of a putable bond is bounded below because the put option enhances the bond value. Figures 5 and 6 describe the change of value and duration of a bond with 26.5 years to maturity, putable in 3 years at par. We find that the put option increases the convexity of the underlying bond. Figure 6 shows that the duration of a putable bond decreases with yield.

For a more complicated putable bond we have

$$F_p \geqslant \text{Max}\{B, B_I^*\}$$

and

$$D_p \leqslant D_B.$$

C. Callable–Putable Bond

This is a more complicated and more interesting security: a bond imbedded with both call and put options. This security provides protections for both investors and issuers. If interest rates go up, investors can exercise the put option to prevent capital loss and reinvest the proceeds to obtain a higher yield. When interest rates fall, the issuer may call the bond and refinance the debt at a lower cost. The callable–putable bond is also more difficult to analyze. As we mentioned earlier, in the case of multiple call and put options, an earlier call (put) option is on a callable–putable bond.

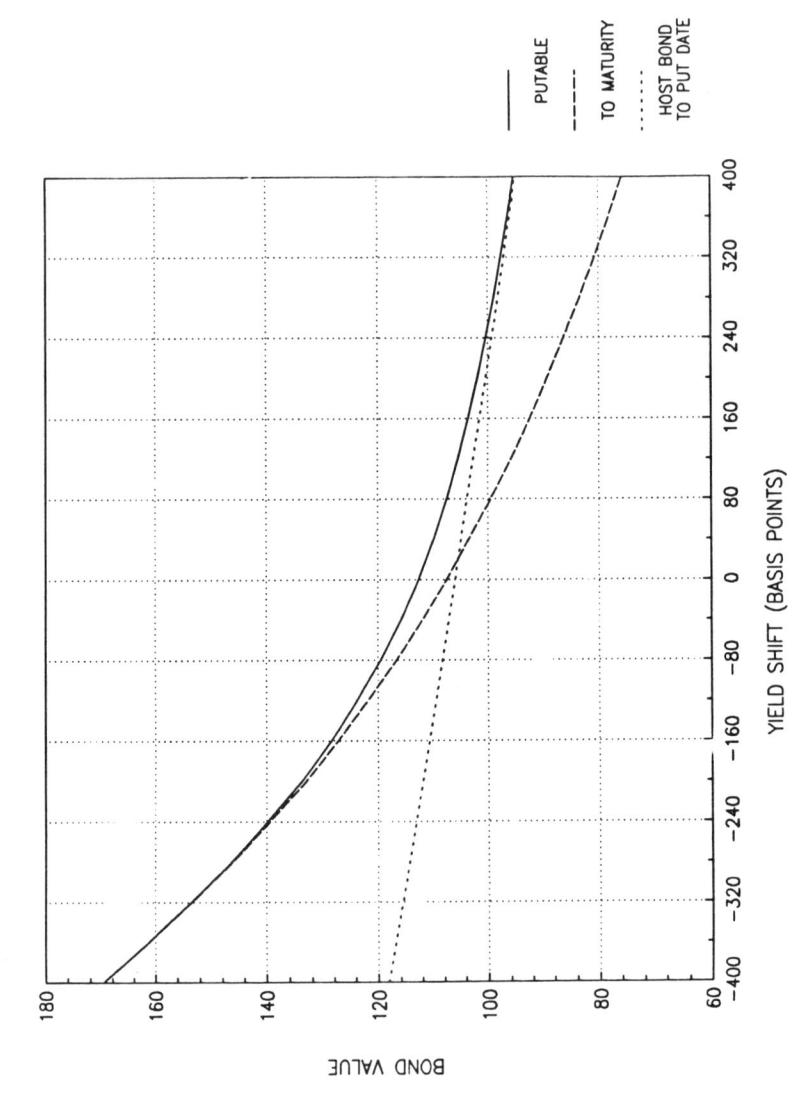

Figure 5. Putable bond. Change of bond value *vs.* yield shift: 26.5-year bond, CPN 9.75, putable in 3 years at 100.

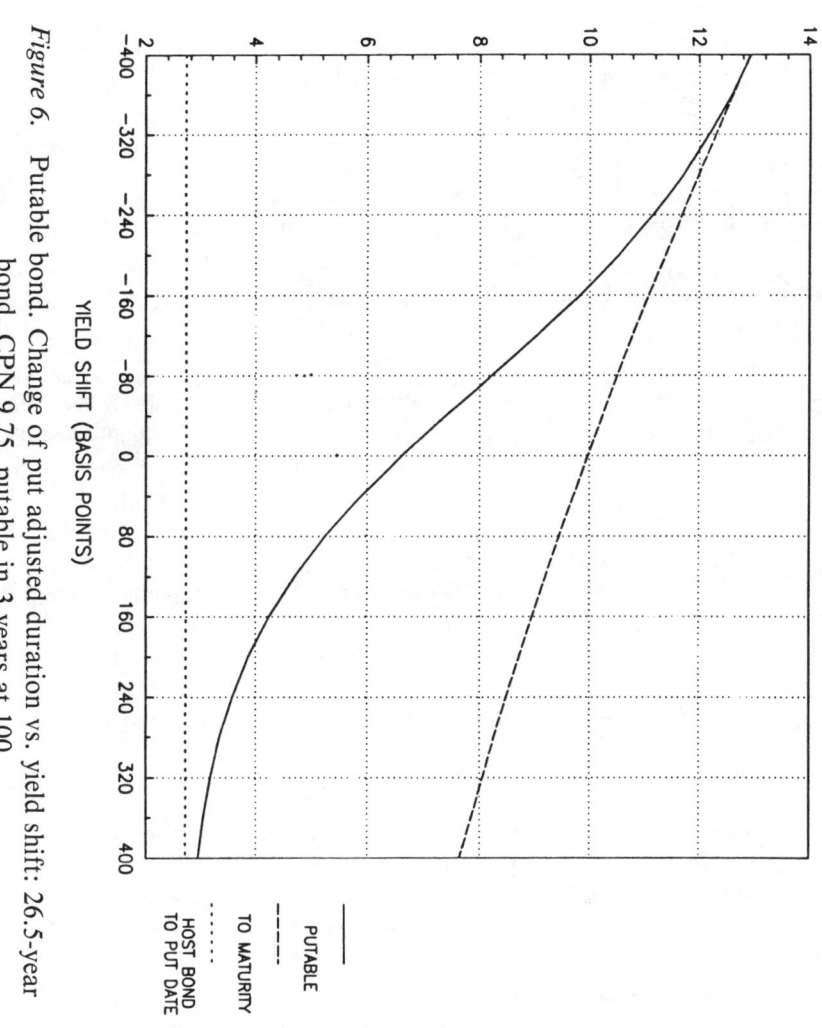

Figure 6. Putable bond. Change of put adjusted duration vs. yield shift: 26.5-year bond, CPN 9.75, putable in 3 years at 100.

Hence, except for very special cases, we need to use numerical methods to solve the terminal value problem (1) and (2) in order to calculate its value and measure its interest rate risk exposure.

A simple callable–putable bond is a bond with a short position in a European call option (with call price K_c and time to call T_c) and a long position in a European put option (with put price K_p and time to put T_p). If T_c is greater than T_p, then the call will be on the underlying bond, while the put is on the callable bond, and vice versa. If $T_c = T_p$, i.e., the call and the put expire at the same time, then both call and put are on the underlying bond. Only in this case the value of the callable–putable bond can be written as

$$F = B - C(B) + P(B). \qquad (25)$$

We note that in (25) the call price K_c should not be lower than the put price K_p. Otherwise, if the underlying bond price B at expiry is higher than K_c but lower than K_p, the investor would exercise the put option and the issuer would call the bond, causing conflict. For a simple callable–putable bond with $T_c = T_p$ and $K_p \leqslant K_c$, we have the following results:

(a) $B_c^* \geqslant F \geqslant B_p^*$;
(b) $D_B \geqslant D \geqslant \text{Max}\{D_p^*, D_c^*\}$.

Equality holds if $K_p = K_c$. As in the previous cases, we use put–call parity to prove these results. The value of the callable–putable bond can be expressed in the following two equivalent ways:

$$\begin{aligned} F &= B_c^* + P(B) - P_{kc}(B) \\ &= B_p^* - C(B) + C_{kp}(B), \end{aligned} \qquad (26)$$

where P_{kc} is a put on the underlying bond with exercise price K_c and C_{kp} is a call with exercise price K_p. Since $K_p \leqslant K_c$, we have $P(B) \leqslant P_{kc}$ and $C(B) \leqslant C_{kp}$, thus establishing (a). In order to show the duration D has an upper bound, we note that

$$D_B - D = \frac{D_B}{F} \left[B \frac{dC}{dB} - C + P - B \frac{dP}{dB} \right]. \qquad (27)$$

The right-hand side of (27) is positive because $\dfrac{d^2C}{dB^2} \geqslant 0$ and $dP/dB \leqslant 0$. Hence, $D_B \geqslant D$. We also have

$$D - D_c^* = \frac{P_{kc} - P}{F} D_c^* + \frac{BD_B}{F} \left[\frac{dP}{dB} - \frac{dP_{kc}}{dB} \right]. \qquad (28)$$

Since K_c is greater than K_p, we have $P_{kc} \geqslant P$. And it is also reasonable to assume that the put delta decreases with the exercise price.[14] Thus, $D_c \leqslant D$. Since $K_c \geqslant K_p$, we also have $D_c^* \geqslant D_p^*$ and (b) follows.

The above results show that the value of a callable–putable bond can change only within a very narrow range (B_p^*, B_c^*). In other words, the imbedded options reduce interest rate sensitivity substantially. As an example, let us study a 26.5-year bond with 9.75% coupon rate, callable at 115 and putable at par in 3 years. Figure 7 shows that with yield shift of ± 400 basis points the price of the underlying bond changes from 76 to 169 while the value of the callable–putable bond varies from 95 to 132. The smaller sensitivity to the interest rate is also reflected in a much smaller duration of a callable–putable bond (see Figure 8).

The callable–putable bond with $T_c = T_p$ is the simplest case. Since the call and the put are both on the underlying bond, we directly apply the value decomposition principle and obtain good results even by using a simple option model, such as the Black–Scholes model. For a more general case, however, one should be careful in applying the value decomposition principle. Suppose $T_c > T_p$. Since the put is now on a callable bond, the correct formula to evaluate the callable–putable bond is

$$F_{pc} = F_c + P(F_c)$$
$$= B - C(B) + P(F_c), \tag{29}$$

where $P(F_c)$ is the put value on the callable bond F_c. One might think that the value of the callable–putable bond can be approximated as if both put and call were on the underlying bond, as expressed by

$$F_1 = B - C(B) + P(B). \tag{30}$$

Or, one might calculate the current value of the callable bond $F_c = B - C(B)$, and then substitute this value into an option pricing formula to obtain the put value. By this method, we would have

$$F_2 = B - C(B) + P[B - C(B)]. \tag{31}$$

Figure 9 compares the results using method (29) with the two naive methods (30) and (31). This is a 26.5-year bond with coupon rate of 7.5% that can be called at par in 5 years and be put at par in 2 years. Figure 9 shows that the difference between F_{pc} and F_1 is small when interest rates are low, and the difference between F_{pc} and F_2 is small when rates are high. But in general, the error caused by using naive methods is not negligible. Figure 10 illustrates the errors in duration calculation caused by naive methods. It is interesting to note that the seemingly "better" method 2 produces more serious errors in duration calculation.

If one more call option (1 year at 105) and one more put option (7 years at par) are added, the above bond will have four imbedded options. Comparing Figure 11 with Figure 9, we find that the convexity near the current yield level is changed from positive to negative. The main reason for the change is that now the call becomes the first option, which seems to play a pivotal role

(*Text continues on page 92*)

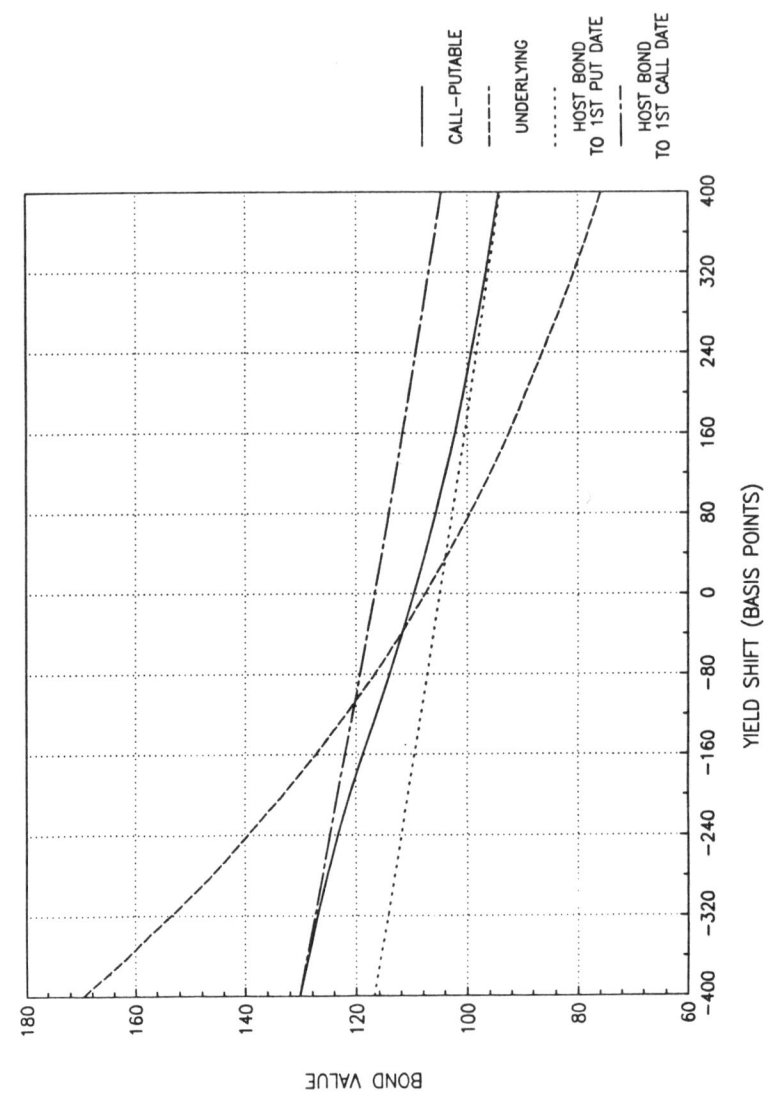

Figure 7. Simple callable–putable bond with TC = TP. Change of bond value vs, yield shift: 26.5-year bond, CPN 9.75, callable and putable in 3 years.

84

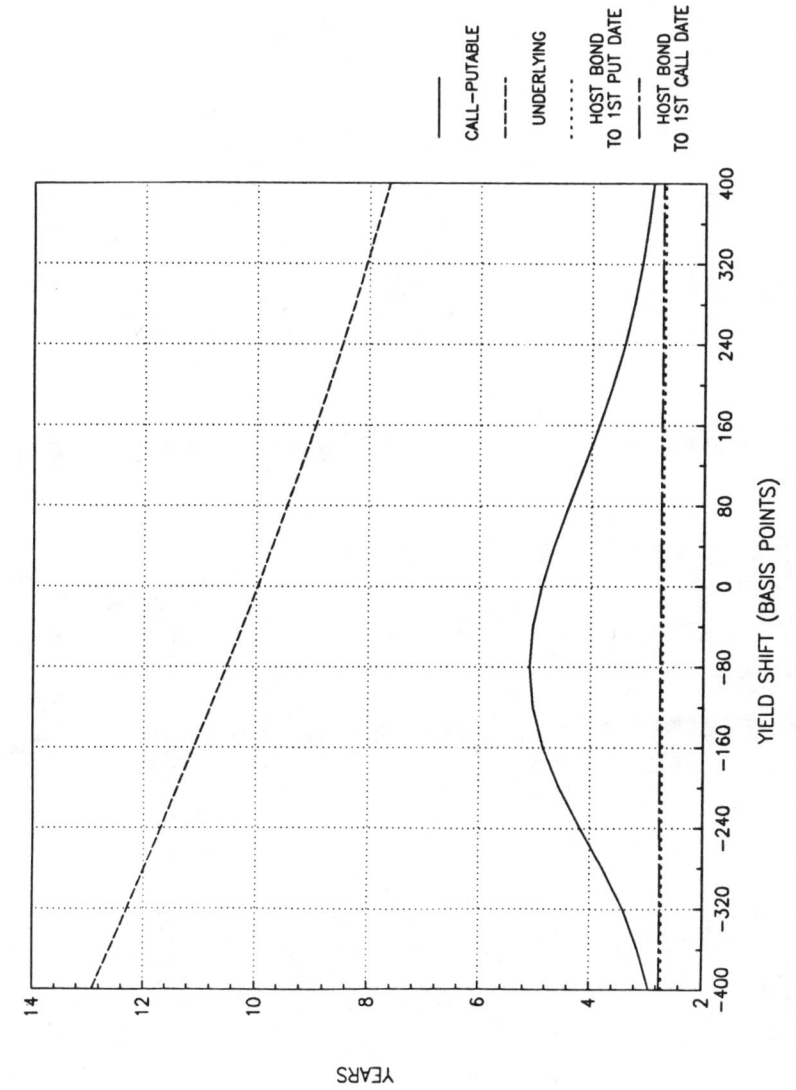

Figure 8. Simple callable–putable bond with TC = TP. Change of option adjusted duration vs yield shift: 26.5-year bond, CPN 9.75, callable and putable in 3 years.

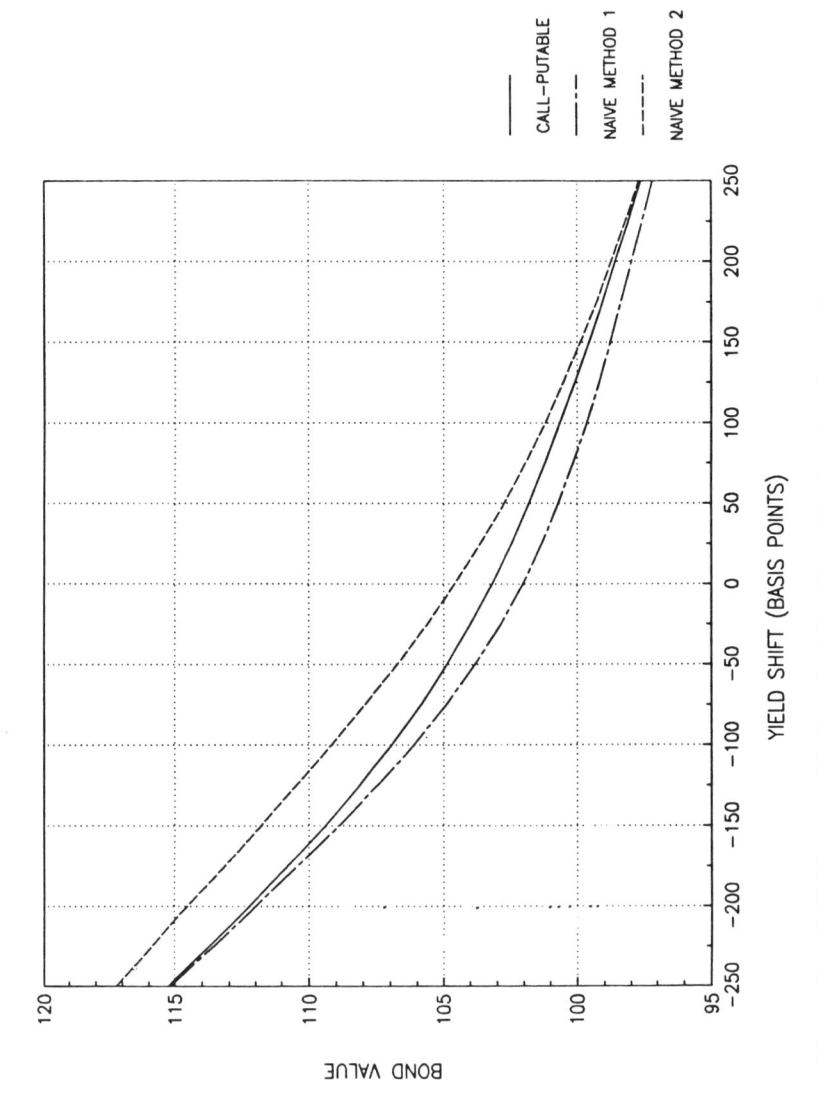

Figure 9. Callable–putable bond with TC > TP. Bond value: naive methods cause error: 26.5-year bond, CPN 7.5

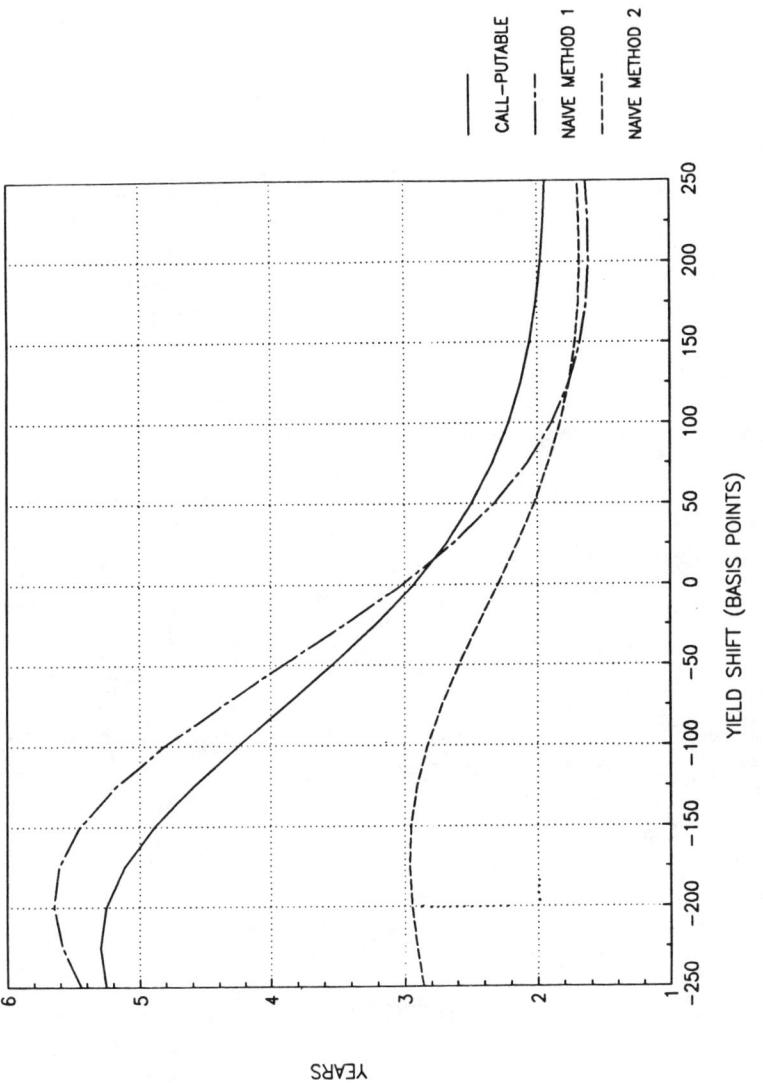

Figure 10. Callable–putable bond with TC > TP. Option adjusted duration: naive methods cause error: 26.5-year bond, CPN 7.5.

87

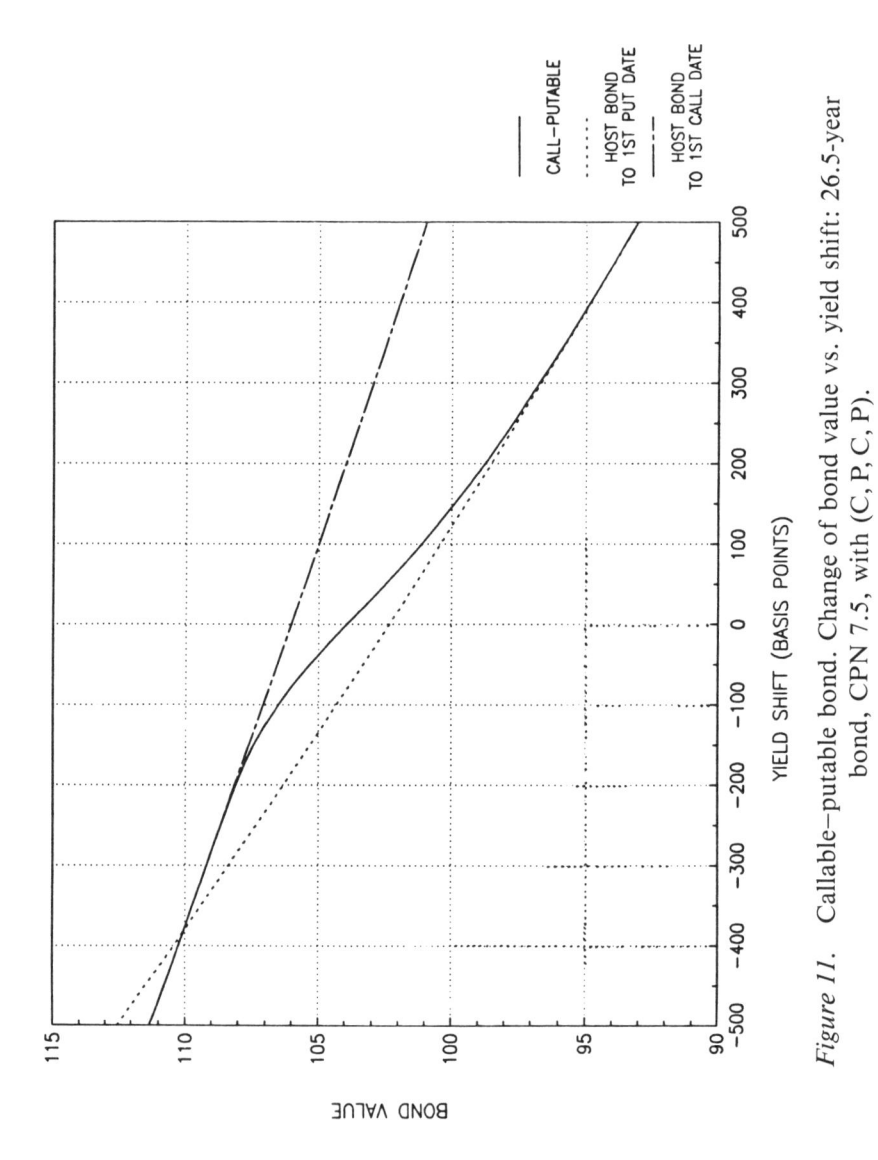

Figure 11. Callable–putable bond. Change of bond value vs. yield shift: 26.5-year bond, CPN 7.5, with (C, P, C, P).

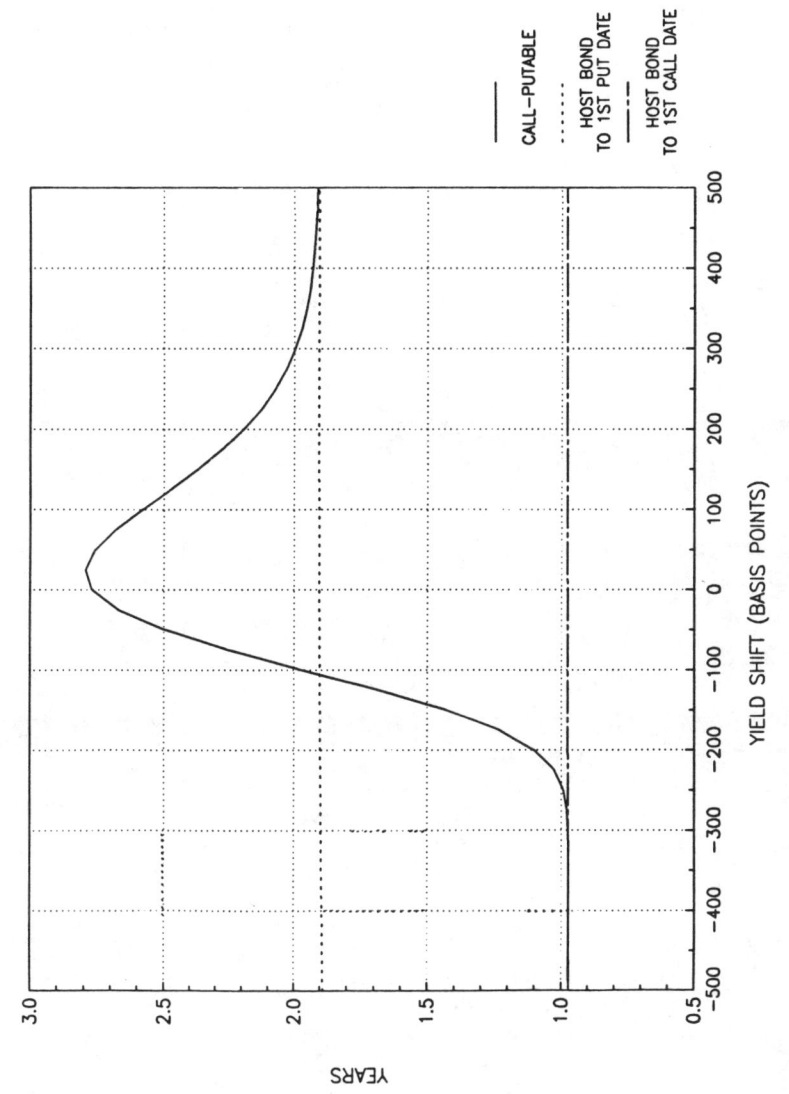

CALL–PUTABLE

....
HOST BOND
TO 1ST PUT DATE

— — —
HOST BOND
TO 1ST CALL DATE

YIELD SHIFT (BASIS POINTS)

YEARS

Figure 12. Callable–putable bond. Change of option and adjusted duration *vs.* yield shift: 26.5-year bond, CPN 7.5, with (C, P, C, P).

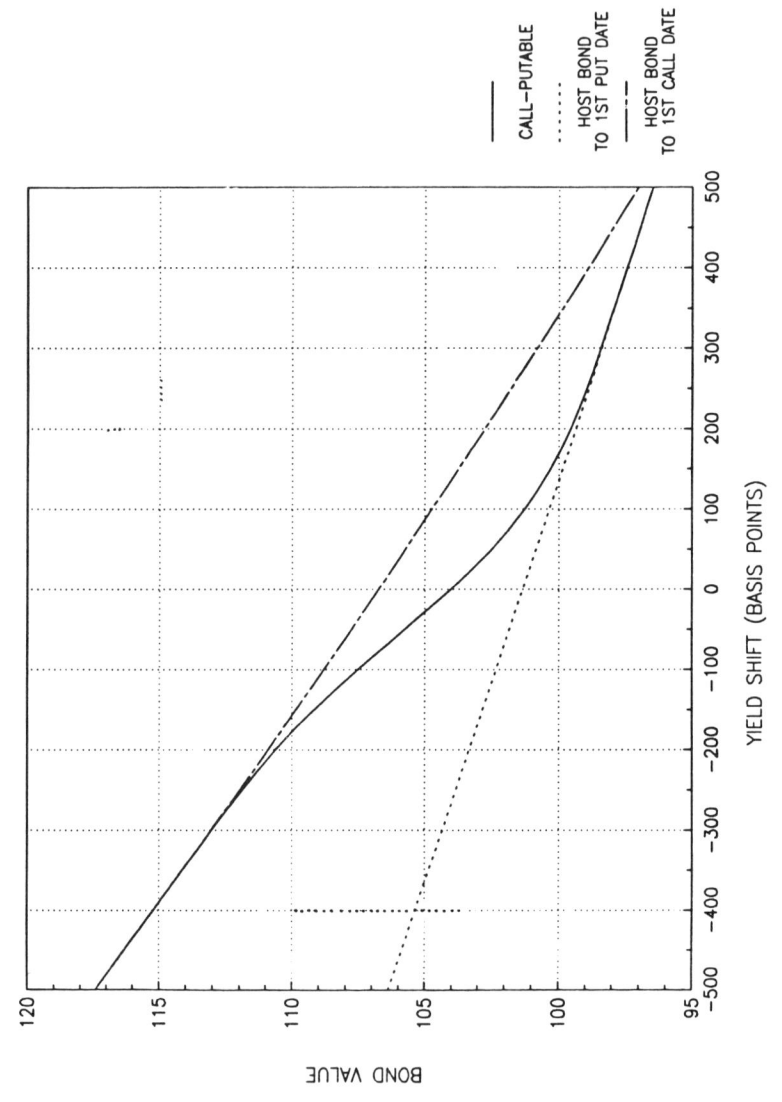

Figure 13. Callable–putable bond. Change of bond value *vs* yield shift: 26.5-year bond, CPN 7.5, with (P, C, P, C).

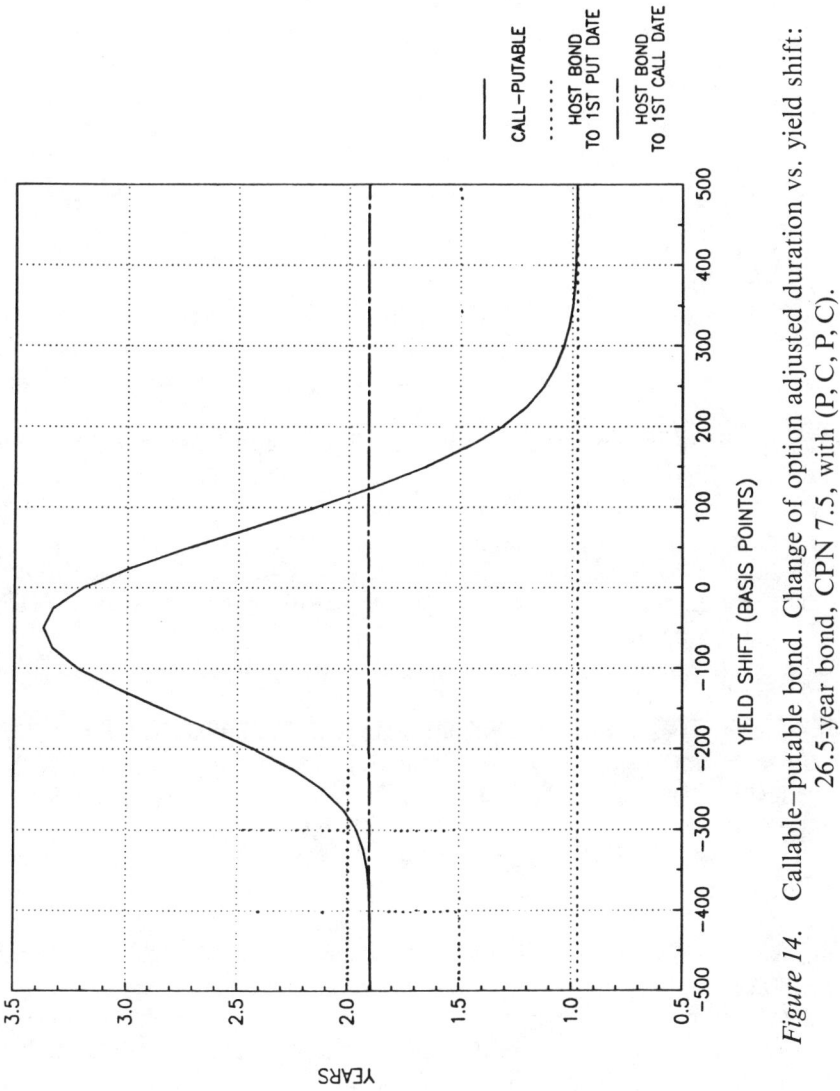

Figure 14. Callable–putable bond. Change of option adjusted duration *vs.* yield shift: 26.5-year bond, CPN 7.5, with (P, C, P, C).

in evaluating a bond with embedded options. Figures 11 and 12 show that the bond will behave like the host bond to the first call (put) date when yield is very low (high). If we change the imbedded option sequence from {call, put, call, put} to {put, call, put, call}, the curves in Figures 11 and 12 will "flip," as shown in Figures 13 and 14.[15] The convexity of the bond is now different, but the asymptotic properties are still the same.

V. CONCLUSION

This paper consists of two parts. First, based on an arbitrage argument in a continuous time setting, we develop a single-factor, price based bond option model. It satisfies the well-posed conditions for a consistent bond option model. Second, we apply the model to analyze bonds with imbedded options. Upper and lower bounds and asymptotic limits are found for simple callable and/or putable bonds. For bonds with more complex options, it is found that the first option largely determines the shape and location of these limits. Our numerical calculation suggests that, in many cases, the first four to five call options are most significant in determining the impact of the call schedule on a callable bond. It is also found that bonds that are both callable and putable exhibit significantly less sensitivity to interest rate changes and tend to remain within narrow ranges of price and duration limits.

The consistency and simplicity, the parsimony of input data, and the importance of the current bond price in option pricing make our bond option model a useful tool in evaluating bonds with imbedded options. Yet an obvious shortcoming of the model is that it takes into account only the current short-term rate and the bond yield, not the information of the whole yield curve.

Several authors have suggested ways to remedy this shortcoming. In an interesting discrete time framework, Ho and Lee [10] considered the movement of the whole term structure. In their model, prices of interest rate contingent claims are governed by the movement of the one period discount rate in a manner similar to the continuous time one-factor term structure model. Moreover, the movement of the one period rate is adjusted in such a way that prices of discount bonds fit the initial market term structure. But an inspection of their expression for the one period rate shows that it is not necessarily positive in all states. Hence, the second basic requirement of a bond option model (7b) or (8b) is not guaranteed. Cox, Ingersoll, and Ross [8] suggested introducing time-dependent drift into the square root model in such a way as to match the given initial term structure. Interest rates are positive here, but there is no simple closed form solution for the drift coefficient in terms of the initial discount function as there is in Ho and Lee [10] model.

Thus, our future research will have two aspects. One is to develop a bond option pricing model that is theoretically consistent and is able to incorporate more information from the current term structure, including the market price of the underlying bond. The other aspect would be to extend the application of the model in order to have a better understanding of bonds with imbedded options.

NOTES

1. See, for example, Bookstaber [4], Toevs [13], and Zhu and Jamshidian [15].

2. This statement is also true for coupon bonds. For a coupon bond, the bond satisfies a nonhomogeneous differential equation, while options satisfy the corresponding homogeneous equation.

3. This model does not require D to be constant. We make this assumption only for convenience. For European options we may eliminate the appearance of D in the differential equation by taking as state variable the bond price less the portion corresponding to coupon payments before option expiry.

4. To review the argument, let μ_1 and σ_1 denote the drift and the diffusion coefficients of the price process $F[B(t), t]$. Investing σ_1 in B and $-\sigma$ in F, we can remove the instantaneous uncertainty. Hence, the return of the portfolio should be proportional to rdt. One thus obtains

$$\sigma_1(\mu + D/B) - \sigma(\mu_1 + D_1/F) = \sigma_1 - \sigma)r,$$

or equivalently,

$$\frac{\mu + D/B - r}{\sigma} = \frac{\mu_1 + D_1/F - r}{\sigma_1}.$$

Substituting from Ito's lemma for μ_1 and σ_1 results in (1).

5. The differential equation (1) is an inhomogeneous Kolmogorov backward equation with potential $-r$, associated with the stochastic process (3). Assuming that boundary points are inaccessible, the terminal value problem (1) and (2) is well posed and the solution (4) is obtained by directly applying Theorem 6.5.3 in Friedman [9].

6. There is, however, no guarantee that the actual market price of $B^*(K, T, D)$ is the same as the computed price. For an option pricing model to prevent actual arbitrage, the market value of $B^*(K, T, D)$ (if observable) should be directly incorporated into the model.

7. By making the boundary $(y = 0)$ inaccessible, the terminal problem (1) and (2) is well posed without the necessity of spatial boundary conditions. It is also possible to assume a strictly positive inaccessible boundary. In this case r and σ are required to approach zero at this boundary.

8. As an example, we use the Brownian Bridge model to calculate a call option on a zero coupon bond. Given $B = 45.84$ (or yield of 6%), $T_M = 13$ years, $r = 6\%$, $K = 100$, volatility of the forward price of 0.08, and time to expiry of 9 years, the call value is 1.03, while it should be zero as the price of the bond can never exceed 100.

9. We found that it is numerically more efficient to solve our model in the yield space.

10. An alternative to (16) is a similar linear form but with $\partial r/\partial y$ at (r_0, t_0) being a given positive number. If $r_0 > Y_0$, one can choose a slightly different function to satisfy the well-posed conditions.

11.   Directly applying the chain rule produces the same result.

12.   Although these assumptions are intuitively reasonable, we note that in a bond option model, these properties are not always guaranteed. For example, if the short-term rate moves with the bond yield, a decrease in put value when bond price increases may be offset by the effect of the fall in the short rate, resulting in a positive delta.

13.   Let us consider a simple case of a callable zero coupon bond. Suppose the time to the first call date is T_1. Within the Black–Scholes framework, from (4) we have

$$F_c = \exp\{-rT_1\}f(B \exp\{-rT_1\})$$

for a certain function $f(\cdot)$. Assuming parallel shift in the yield curve, it is easy to show that the duration of the callable bond is

$$D = T_1 + (B/F_c)(dF_c/dB)(D_B - T_1).$$

Since for the zero coupon bond $D_B = T_M > T_1$ and dF_c/dB is nonnegative, we obtain $D \geqslant T_1$.

14.   Suppose $K_1 > K_2$. If $P_{Ki}(B)$ is a put on bond B with exercise price K_i and time to expiry T, then a portfolio $F = P_{K1}(B) - P_{K2}(B)$ satisifies Equation (1) with a terminal condition

$$g(B) = \text{Max}\{0, K_1 - B\} - \text{Max}\{0, K_2 - B\}.$$

Since g(B) is a nonincreasing function of B, it is reasonable to assume that F is also a nonincreasing function of B, or put delta is decreasing with the exercise price.

15.   In Figures 13 and 14 the bond can be called in 2 years at 105 and in 7 years at 100, and it can be put in 1 year and 5 years at par. All these imbedded options are assumed European.

REFERENCES

1.   Ball, C. B., and W. N. Torous, "Bond Price Dynamics and Options," *Journal of Financial and Quantitative Analysis* 18 (1983), 517–531.

2.   Black, F., and J. Cox, "Valuing Corporate Securities: Some Effects of Bond Indenture Provisions," *Journal of Finance* 31 (1976), 351–367.

3.   Black, F., and M. Scholes, "The Pricing of Options and Corporate Liabilities," *Journal of Political Economy* 8 (1973), 637–654.

4.   Bookstaber, R., "The Valuation and Exposure Management of Bonds with Imbedded Options," in *The Handbook of Fixed Income Securities* (F. J. Fabozzi and I. M. Pollack, eds.), 2nd ed. Dow Jones-Irwin, 1987.

5.   Brennan, M. J., and E. S. Schwartz, "A Continuous Time Approach to the Pricing of Bonds," *Journal of Banking and Finance* 3 (1979), 135–155.

6.   Brennan, M. J., and E. S. Schwartz, "Alternative Methods for Valuing Debt Options," *Finance* 4 (1983), 119–137.

7.   Courtadon, G., "The Pricing of Options on Default Free Bonds," *Journal of Financial and Quantitative Analysis* 17 (1982), 75–100.

8.   Cox, J. C., J. E. Ingersoll, and S. A. Ross, "A Theory of the Term Structure of Interest Rates," *Econometrica* 53 (1985), 385–407.

9.   Friedman, A., *Stochastic Differential Equations and Applications*, Vol. 1. New York: Academic Press, 1975.

10.   Ho, T. S., and S. Lee, "Term Structure Movements and Pricing Interest Rate Contingent Claims," *Journal of Finance* 41 (1986), 1011–1028.

11.   Merton, R. C., "Theory of Rational Option Pricing," *Bell Journal of Economics and Management Science* 4 (1973), 141–183.

12.   Schaefer, S., and E. Schwartz, "Time-Dependent Variance and the Pricing of Bond Options," Working Paper, University of British Columbia, 1986.

13. Toevs, A. L., "Interest Rate Risk and Uncertain Lives," *Journal of Portfolio Management* (Spring 1985), 45–56.

14. Vasicek, O. A., "An Equilibrium Characterization of the Term Structure," *Journal of Financial Economics* 5 (1977), 177–188.

15. Zhu, Y., and F. Jamshidian, "Call Adjusted Duration Model and Its Application in Bond Portfolio Management," in *The Handbook of Fixed-Income Options* (Frank J. Fabozzi, ed.), Probus Publishing, 1989.

EMBEDDED CALL OPTIONS AND REFUNDING EFFICIENCY

C. Douglas Howard* and Andrew J. Kalotay*

I. INTRODUCTION

A prudent liability manager will continuously monitor interest rates and will call a bond when the company's refunding rate is sufficiently low. Efficient use of embedded call options requires explicitly identifying this sufficiently low "target rate" [6]. This target rate depends on many factors, including the bond's coupon, the remaining time to maturity, the entire schedule of call prices, the perceived behavior of interest rates, tax considerations, the structure of the refunding issue, and the issuer's risk preference [1]. Refunding "efficiency" is the yardstick that measures the combined impact of these considerations. This paper focuses on the methodology underlying the computation of refunding efficiency and the target refunding rate.

*Salomon Brothers Inc.

Advances in Futures and Options Research, Vol. 3, pages 97–117.
Copyright © 1988 by JAI Press Inc.
All rights of reproduction in any form reserved.
ISBN: 0-89232-926-2

II.   THE BREAK-EVEN RATE: GOOD FOR A ONE-TIME CALL

The break-even rate is a fundamental element in refunding analysis. The traditional method for evaluating the savings from a refunding is to compute the present value of the resulting cash flow savings. [1] The break-even rate is the refunding rate that will generate a present value savings of 0%.

Consider for example, a 12% 40-year bullet bond callable after 5 years at a price 110.29% of par (the "long 12s"). Assume that the issuer loses the right to refund the bond if he passes up that opportunity in year 5. The issuer, therefore, has a "one-time" call option exercisable in year 5 of the bond's life (see Figure 1, Column 2).

Figure 2 shows the present value savings as a percentage of par for a refunding in year 5 at various refunding rate levels. The break-even rate occurs at 10.5%–11%. Specifically, a present value savings of 0% is generated by a refunding at 10.85%.

Because the call option is a one-time European-type option, the issuer should exercise it if the refunding rate is below the break-even rate. In this example, the issuer has nothing to lose by exercising the option, however small the savings may be.

Year	"One-Time" Call	"Two-Time" Call	Continuous Call
0–4	NR	NR	NR
5	110.29%	110.29%	110.29%
6	NR	109.94	109.94
7	NR	NR	109.59
35	NR	NR	100.35
36–40	NR	NR	100.00

NR Not refundable

Figure 1.   Schedule of optional call prices.

Refunding Rate	PV Savings from Refunding
9.00%	21.51%
9.50	15.00
10.00	9.05
10.50	3.60
11.00	− 1.41

Figure 2. One-time call option.

III. A HYPOTHETICAL "TWO-TIME" CALL OPTION

In reality, most call options are exercisable continuously at any time after the refunding protection expires. This complicates the decision, because in this case, the issuer has something to lose by exercising the option — namely, the opportunity to exercise the option at a later date, possibly achieving greater savings than are currently available. This could result from a decrease in interest rates or from a declining call price schedule.

To illustrate this complication, slightly modify the option so that the bond may *also* be called in year 6 at a price of 109.94% of par (see Figure 1, Column 3). The issuer now has two alternatives:

1. It can call the bond in year 5; or
2. It can wait until year 6 and call the bond then if savings are available. If the issuer chooses to wait a year, it will, in effect, in year 6 have a "one-time" option that should be exercised only if savings are positive.

If the issuer has a strong conviction about interest rate movements over the next year, the refunding decision is clear. The issuer will wait and call in year 6 if it believes that interest rates are declining, but call the bond in year 5 if it believes that interest rates are rising. The decision is much more difficult in the absence of such a conviction. However, given a reasonable model of interest rate behavior, one can still make a rational decision.

Suppose that in year 5, the issuer could refund the long 12s with a new 10% bond. As we have seen in Figure 2, the present value savings of such a refunding would be 9.05% of the par amount refunded. Instead of calling the bond and refunding in year 5, the issuer may wait and address the question 1 year later in a different refunding rate environment.

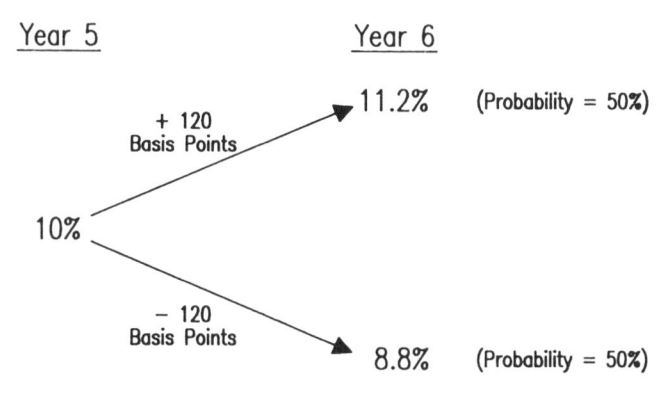

Figure 3.   A simple model of interest rate behavior.

For simplicity, assume that only two equally likely outcomes are possible. From year 5 to year 6, rates will rise or fall by 120 basis points from their current level of 10% (see Figure 3). This equates to an annual "volatility" of 1.2%/10%, or 12%.[2] If the refunding rate increases by 120 basis points to 11.2%, the savings decline to 0%. This is because 11.2% is above the break-even rate, and the option would not be exercised. If the refunding rate declines to 8.8%, the savings rise to 22.20% of par.[3] Because these two events are equally likely, the "expected value of waiting" to year 6 is $0.5 \times 0\% + 0.5 \times 22.20\%$, or 11.1%. The theoretical value of the call option in year 5 is equal to the *greater* of the savings that are available from a current exercise (9.05%) and the expected value of waiting (11.1%), or 11.1%.

Figure 4 shows current savings (in year 5), the expected value of waiting

Refunding Rate In Year 5	PV Savings of a Call In Year 5	Expected PVS of Waiting To Year 6	Theoretical Value of Call Option
9.00%	21.51%	21.22%	21.51%
9.50	15.00	15.21	15.21
10.00	9.05	11.10	11.10
10.50	3.60	8.37	8.37
11.00	−1.41	5.87	5.87

Figure 4.   Two-time call option.

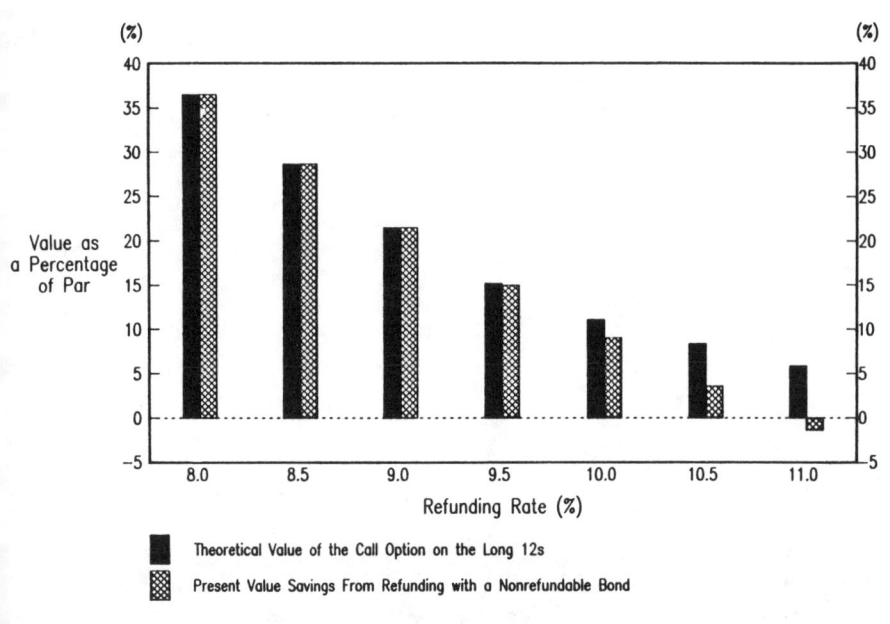

Figure 5. Option valuation applied to the long 12s ("two-time" call option).

and the theoretical option value over a range of refunding rate environments. In each refunding rate environment, the theoretical option value is the greater of current savings or the expected value of waiting. Figure 5 illustrates the option value and the savings of a current call. In refunding rate environments below roughly 9.5%, the savings generated by a refunding match the value of the call option. In contrast, if the refunding rate is roughly 10% or higher, the option value greatly exceeds the savings of a current refunding. The prudent liability manager will compare the savings generated by a refunding with the value of the option forfeited by the exercise of the call and will refund the bond only if the savings represent a substantial fraction of the option's value.

IV. EFFICIENCY

As a function of the refunding rate environment, the percentage of the option value that is captured by a refunding is shown in Figure 6. This is known as the "efficiency" of the refunding. For example, a refunding rate of 10% will generate 9.05% savings while the option value is 11.1%. The efficiency of this refunding would, therefore, be 81.5%.

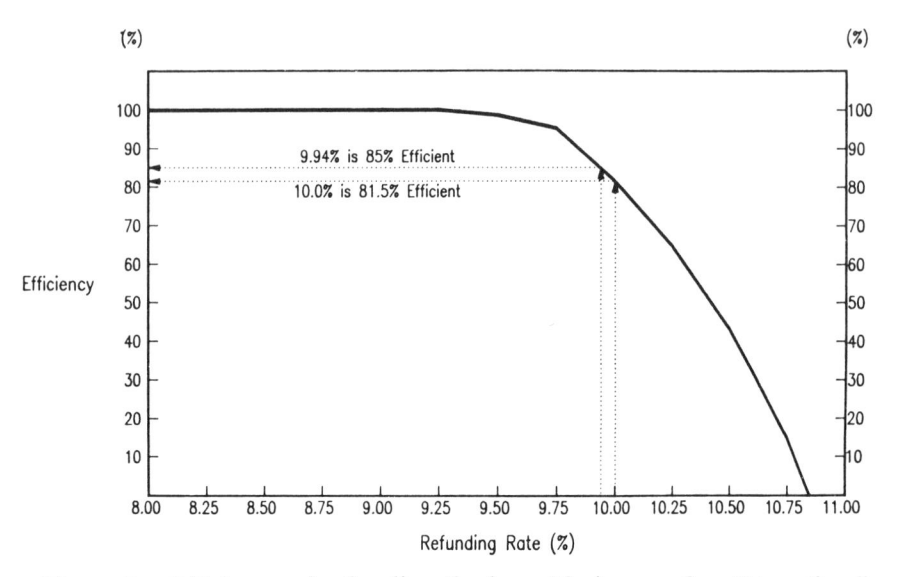

Figure 6.   Efficiency of refunding the long 12s in year five ("two-time" call option).

Each individual issuer must decide what degree of efficiency is sufficient to trigger a refunding. This decision should be made in the context of risk versus potential reward. A game of chance analogy illustrates the point. Suppose a coin is flipped, and if heads comes up, the player is paid $200. If tails comes up, the player is paid nothing. The "theoretical" value of the game to the player is $200 × 0.5 + $0 × 0.5, or $100. Now suppose the player is offered money to *not* play the game. How much would the player settle for? A risk-neutral player would settle for nothing less than the full $100 — the theoretical value of the game. However, a player with some degree of risk aversion would settle for less than the value of $100 just to avoid the possibility of ending up with nothing. The greater the degree of risk aversion, the less the player would settle for.

The debt issuer must make the same decision about the call option. Consider again the long 12s in a 10% refunding rate environment. The issuer can refund in year 5, settling for a certain 9.05% savings, or it can "flip a coin" and wait until year 6. In year 6, the issuer will either get 22.2% savings or nothing at all. Waiting is riskier, but the "expected" payoff of 11.1% savings (0.5 × 0% + 0.5 × 22.2%) is greater.

For a risk-averse issuer, there is some level of efficiency below 100% where the "expected" benefit of deferring a refunding will not justify the additional risk. In the absence of institutional, political, and regulatory considerations that dictate otherwise, we would recommend 85% efficiency as a reasonable balance between reward and risk. In the preceding coin-tossing analogy, this is equivalent to settling for $85 rather than playing the game.

For the long 12s with the hypothetical "two-time" call option, a refunding rate of 9.94% will lock in present value savings equal to 85% of the value of the call option (see Figure 6). This 85% efficiency "target refunding rate" means that the issuer would call the bond in year 5 only if the refunding rate is at or below 9.94%.

V. A CONTINUOUS OPTION

We simplified the preceding anaysis of the valuation of the call option in several respects. First, we assumed that the issuer could exercise the option at only two moments of the bond's life — the end of years 5 and 6. In reality, an embedded call option is usually exercisable at any time after the refunding protection expires. Figure 1 (Column 4) shows a realistic set of call prices declining to par 5 years prior to the maturity of the bond. Second, our model of refunding interest rate behavior (up or down from year to year) is simplistic. The "binomial" model can be improved by dividing a year into several steps. With each step, the refunding rate moves up or down. Figure 7 illustrates this process with four quarterly steps of 60 basis points up or down per year. Clearly this more closely approximates the actual continuous movement of interest rates. The magnitude of the quarterly movement is smaller than the annual movement in Figure 3 (60

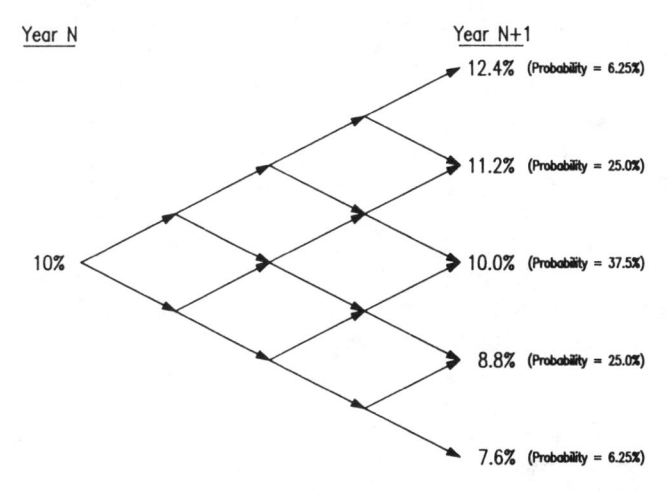

Figure 7. A more reasonable model of interest rate behavior.

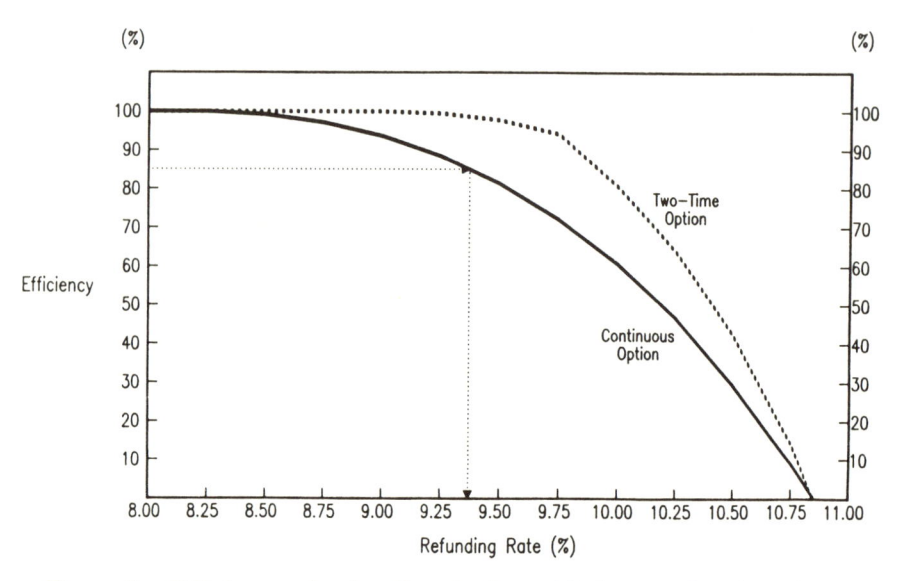

Figure 8.   Efficiency of refunding the long 12s in year five (continuous option).

basis points versus 120 basis points) to preserve the *annual* volatility of 12%. [4]

Figure 8 shows the efficiency of calling the long 12s if the option is exercisable at *any time* after year 5. For computational purposes, each year is divided into a sufficient number of discrete periods to very closely approximate the continuous nature of the option and of interest rate behavior.

At any given refunding rate level, the efficiency of calling the long 12s in year 5 is lower if the option is continuously exercisable than if it is exercisable only in years 5 and 6. This is because the issuer, when exercising and calling the bond, is parting with a much more valuable option. The theoretical option value now reflects the issuer's right to refund the bond at any opportune moment starting in year 5 — certainly a greater value than the "two-time" right to refund only in years 5 and 6. Since the option value is the denominator of the efficiency calculation, the higher option value translates into a lower efficiency. Therefore, a lower refunding rate environment is necessary to generate a specified level of efficiency. In fact, if the option is continuously exercisable, the 85% efficiency target refunding rate in year 5 is 9.37%, almost 60 basis points lower than the corresponding target rate on the "two-time" option.

VI. THE IMPORTANCE OF VOLATILITY

Remarkably, the only numerical assumption underlying the option valuation model is the volatility of the refunding rate, chosen in the preceding examples to be 12% annually. Because the option value is driven by prospective volatility, rather than historical volatility, the assumption is, at best, an estimate. Therefore, it is important to quantify the sensitivity of the decision to refund (or not refund) to the volatility assumption.

Figure 9 shows the efficiency of refunding the long 12s given three different interest rate volatilities. The larger the volatility assumption, the larger the theoretical option value and the lower the refunding efficiency for any given refunding rate environment.

This reflects the enhanced prospects of the refunding rate eventually drifting low enough to generate more savings from a later refunding. This effect translates into a lower target rate given a higher volatility. The 85% efficiency target rate declines to 9.07% given 15% volatility, and rises to 9.70% given a 9% volatility.

Figure 10 plots the 85% efficiency and 100% efficiency target rates as functions of the volatility assumption. Lower efficiency generates a target rate that is less sensitive to the volatility assumption. Fortunately, the ten-basis-point increment of the 85% efficiency target rate for a 1% change in volatility is not substantial. In addition, despite occasional peaks and

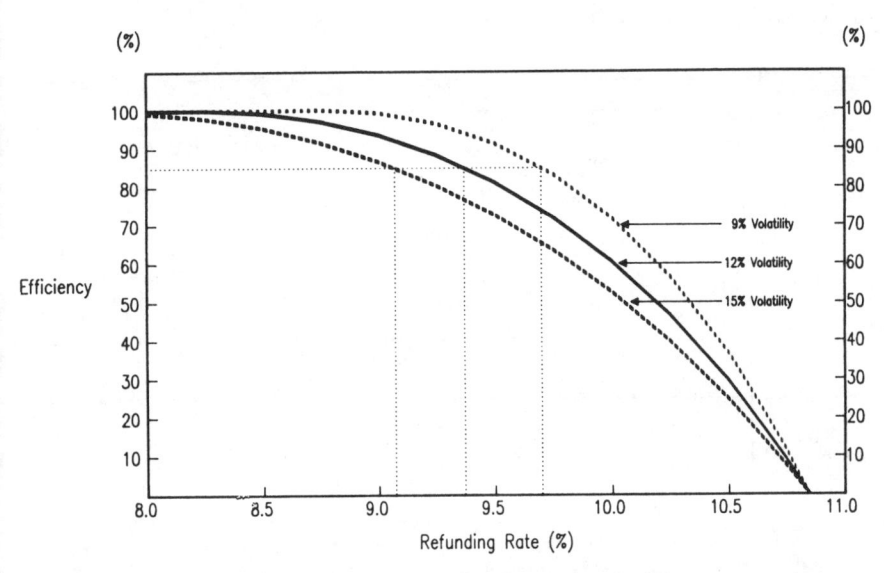

Figure 9. Refunding efficiency under several volatility assumptions.

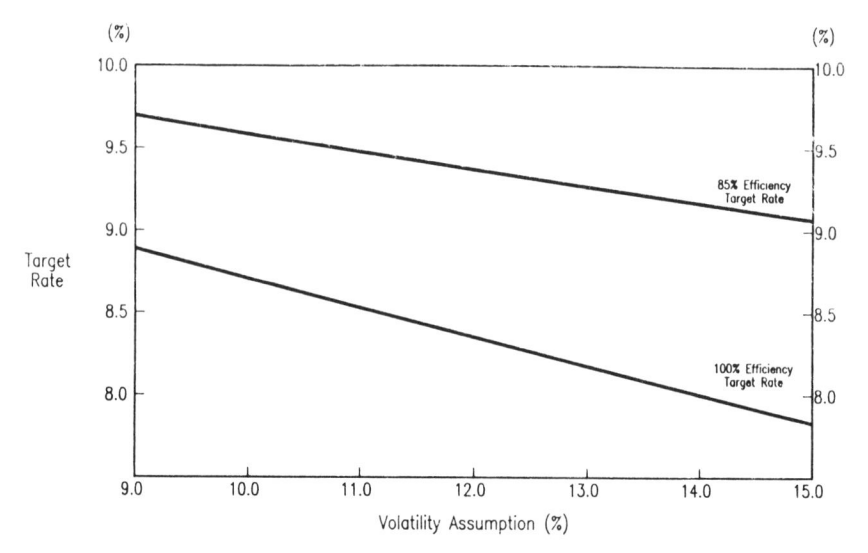

Figure 10. The sensitivity of target rates to the volatility assumption.

valleys, the volatility of long-term interest rates in recent years has generally remained in a range of 9–15% (see Figure 11). The sensitivity of the target rate in this example is increased by the 40-year term of the long 12s. Shorter term bonds, or bonds with less time to maturity, display less sensitivity to the volatility assumption.

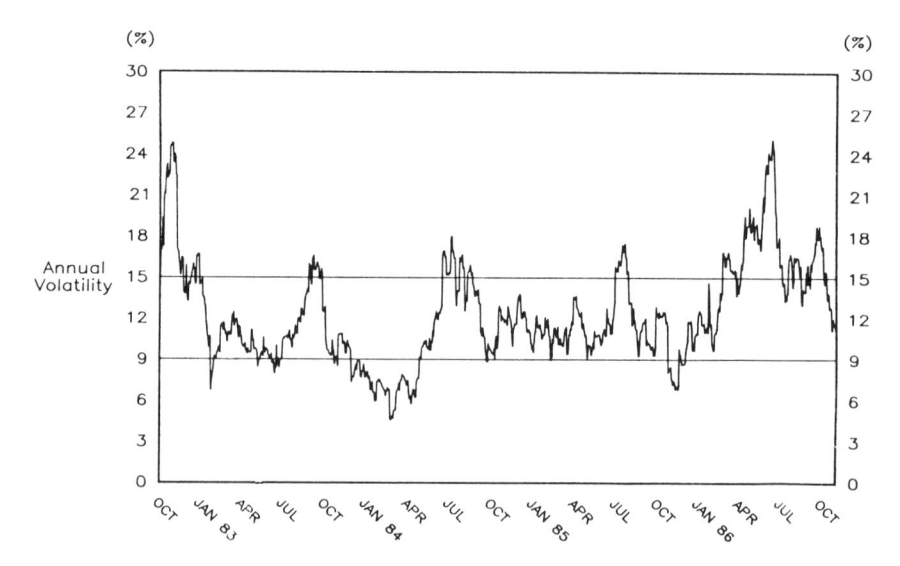

Figure 11. Recent historical volatility of long-term treasury bonds.

VII. THE STRUCTURE OF THE REFUNDING ISSUE

We have assumed that the long 12s will be refunded with a *nonrefundable* bond. This assumption is manifested in the nature of the present value savings calculation. This calculation is based on a matched-maturity refunding. The differential between the 12% coupon on the outstanding bond and the refunding issue coupon is present valued through the maturity of the outstanding issue. The call premium is subtracted from this number to obtain a net present value savings. The cash flows are deterministic, and no consideration is given to possible subsequent refundings of today's refunding issues.

If the refunding is effected with a *refundable* bond, this calculation understates the value of refunding by ignoring the potential for additional refundings. A simple two-step calculation is the remedy. First, compute the deterministic present value savings as previously described, pretending that the refunding issue is nonrefundable. Second, compute the value of a new call option on the refunding issue using theoretical option valuation. This option value by definition exactly captures the value of the potential for additional refundings. Therefore, when this new option value is added to the deterministic present value savings, the result is the total benefit of

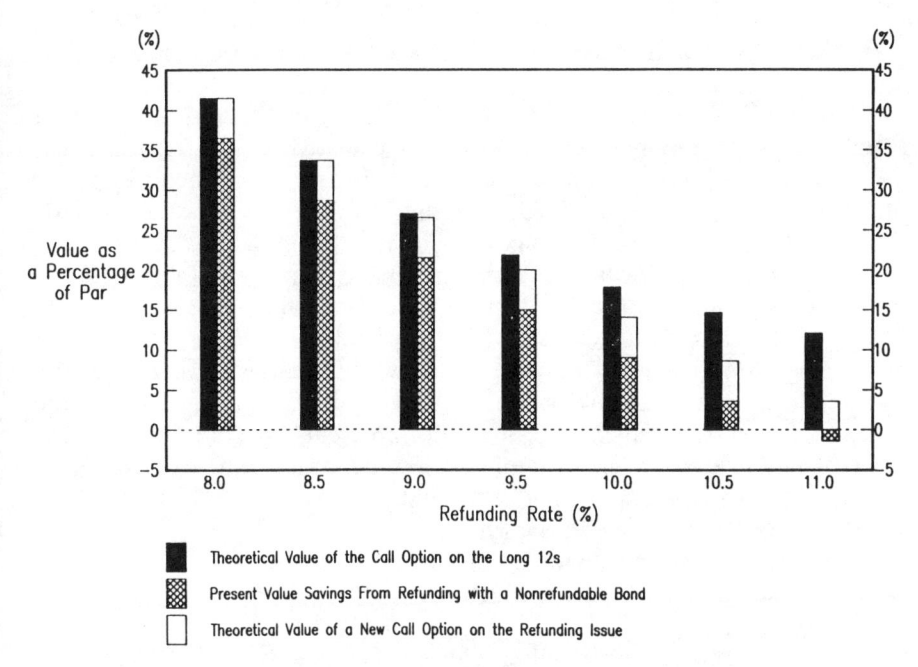

Figure 12. Option valuation with a refundable refunding issue.

refunding with a refundable bond. Figure 12 illustrates this as applied to the long 12s.

Figure 12 warrants several observations. Surprisingly, the value of the option on the *refunding* issue is virtually independent of the refunding rate. Moving right to left from an 11% rate environment to an 8% rate environment, one might expect this option value to increase as refunding rates decline. However, the coupon on the bond in which this option is embedded simultaneously declines from 11 to 8%. In other words, the relative degree to which this new option is "in the money" does not change. In contrast, the value of the option on the *refunded* issues (the long 12s) exhibits the expected behavior and substantially increases as the refunding rate declines from 11 to 8%. This reflects the fact that this option is embedded in a fixed-coupon (12%) bond, while the refunding rate environment is changed.

In addition, the value of the option on the refunding bond is much lower than the value of the option on the long 12s. Two factors contribute to this. First, in rate environments below the break-even rate of 10.85%, the option on the long 12s is "in the money." Second, the option on the long 12s is currently exercisable. The option on the refunding issue is not in the money and cannot be exercised until refunding protection expires in 5 years.

VIII.   TAX CONSIDERATIONS

Although we have disregarded taxes for illustrative purposes, in actual applications, refunding efficiency must be calculated on an after-tax basis. Taxes affect cash flows, the discount rate, and the value of the call option. Because of the reasons described, refunding efficiency on an after-tax basis is usually higher than on a pretax basis.

The most obvious tax benefit is that the entire premium above the issue's tax basis — which is usually at or close to face value — is immediately recognized as a current expense. This is particularly important in the case of repurchasing currently nonrefundable debt, because in that case, the premium can be considerably above the initial call price. Because the premium over the call price essentially represents the present value of incremental interest payments until the call date, its immediate deductibility is desirable. This effect is particularly important if the issuer's marginal tax rate is expected to decline in the future.

Figure 13 shows the refunding efficiency for the sample 12s assuming 0 and 34% marginal tax rates. It illustrates that the efficiency increases with higher tax rates.

The effect of taxes on refunding efficiency far exceeds the deductibility of

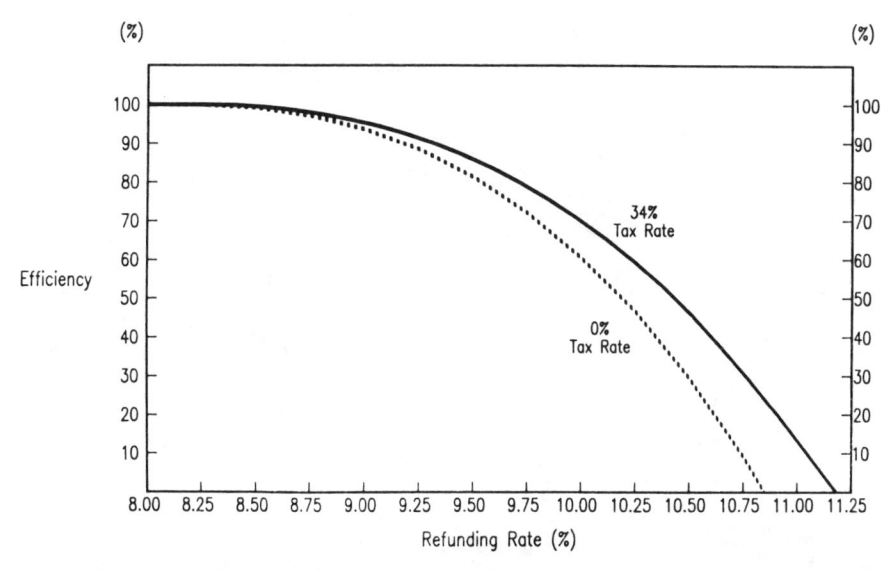

Figure 13. Efficiency in different tax environments.

the premium. The manner in which taxes affect the value of the call option on the refunding issue is much more subtle, but equally important. Boyce and Kalotay [2] showed that the expected value of this option is higher on an after-tax basis than on a pretax basis. For example, suppose that the market, which consists of essentially nontaxable institutions, demands 50 basis points in exchange for a call feature. Even if this is a fair price on a pretax basis, a taxable issuer should be willing to pay a higher coupon spread, perhaps as much as 80 basis points for the call feature. Because of this tax advantage, refunding with a refundable bond will generate a greater efficiency than refunding with a nonrefundabe bond.

IX. TARGET RATES CAN BE CALCULATED AT ANY TIME

For a specific bond, the target rate depends only on two inputs: the assumed interest rate volatility and the required level of efficiency. Once these inputs are specified, the target rate can be computed over the entire life of the issue. In fact, this calculation can be done at the time of issuance. Figure 14 displays the target rates for the long 12s beginning in year 5, when refunding protection expires.

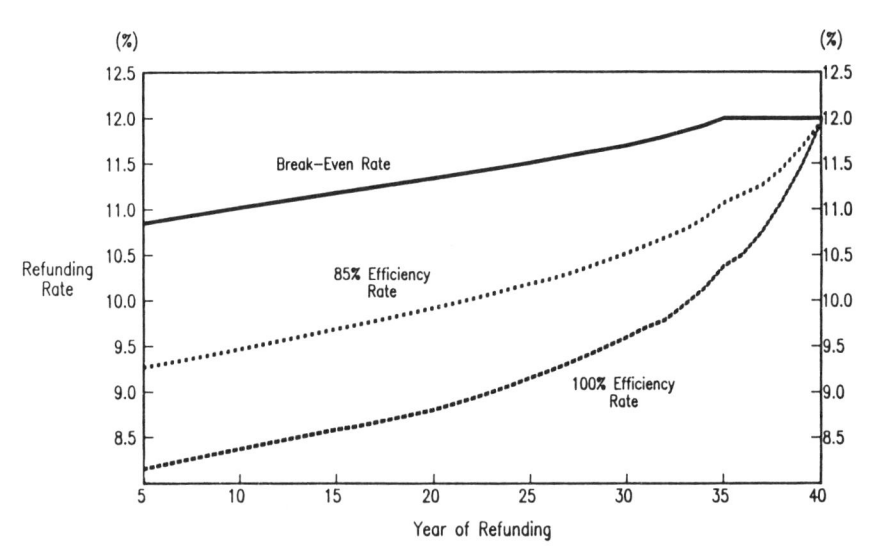

Figure 14.   Advance calculation of target rates for the long 12s.

X.   SINKING-FUND ISSUES ARE DELICATE[5]

Each sinking-fund payment should be considered as an individual bullet bond, with its own maturity and call price schedule. The original issue can be considered as a *portfolio* of bonds — one for each sinking-fund payment. At any time, the call price of each outstanding sinking-fund payment is the same. We can then determine the efficiency curve for each bond in this portfolio (that is, each sinking-fund payment). This is illustrated in Figure 15 for the long 12s, assuming a sinking-fund commencing in year 10. From these efficiency curves, we can determine the target refunding rate for each payment (see Figure 16).

Depending on its due date, each sinking fund has its own refunding rate, as determined by the issuer's yield curve. If this yield curve is flat (see Figure 17), the issuer should first call the balloon and then work backward, if appropriate. Conversely, if the yield curve is steeply upward sloping (see Figure 18), calling only some of the nearby payments may be optimal. As a general rule, each payment must be considered individually, and the optimum policy may entail calling only part of the issue.

Finally, two further considerations may be relevant in the analysis of sinking-fund issues: the acceleration provison such as a "double-up" and the delivery option. The former entitles the issuer to call at par some multiple of the mandatory sinking fund; the latter enables the issuer to deliver actual securities instead of cash. The delivery option is most valuable

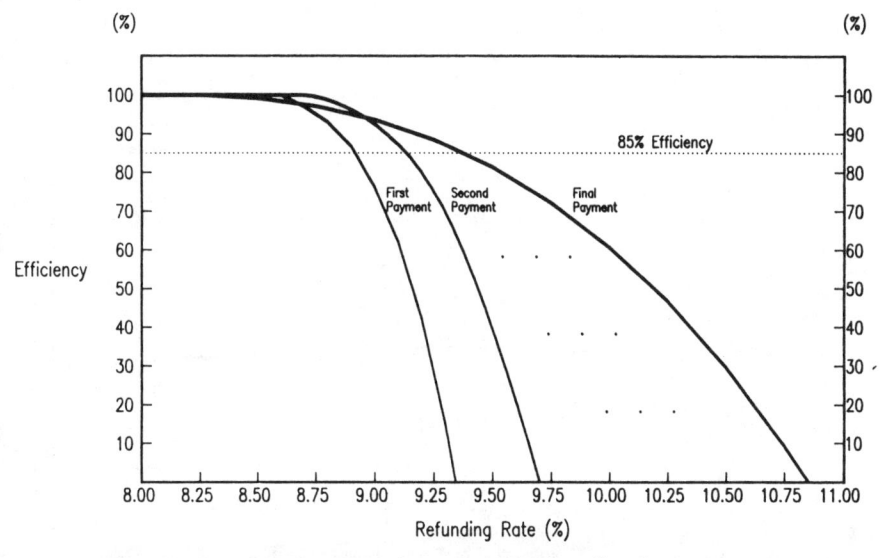

Figure 15. Efficiencies of several sinking-fund payments.

when the issue is selling at a discount.[6] If a bond is called, it cannot be doubled up against a subsequent sinking-fund payment or purchased at a price below par in the open market if interest rates rise. Because these options favor deferring redemption, their incorporation into the analysis will reduce current refunding efficiency.

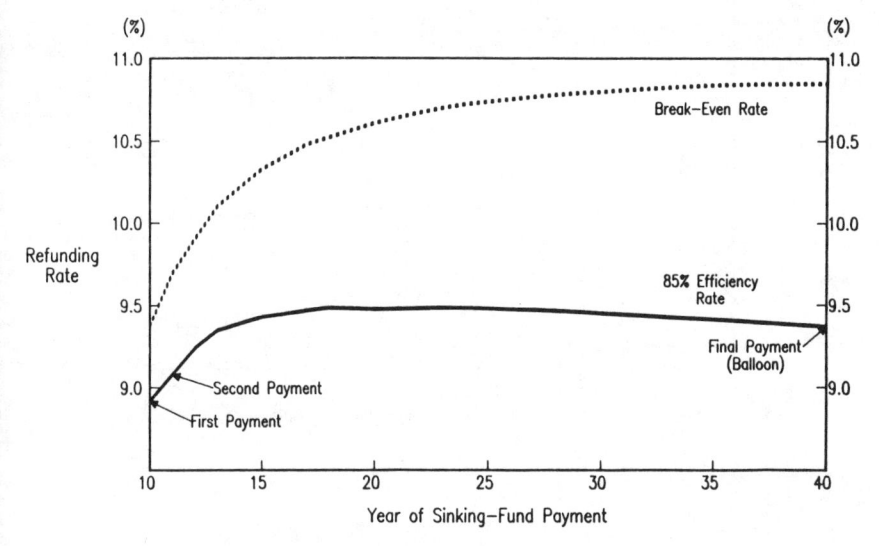

Figure 16. Year-five target rates for each sinking-fund payment.

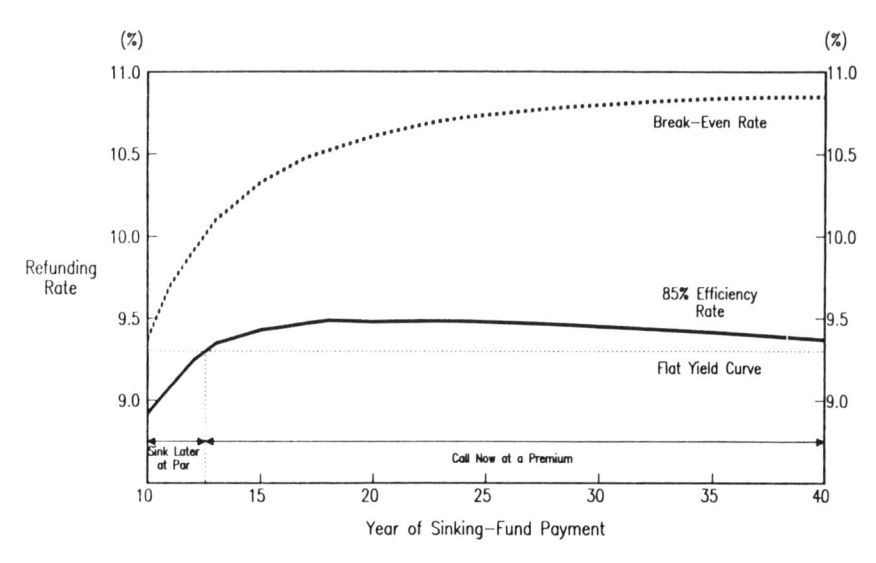

Figure 17. Sinking-fund strategy given a flat yield curve.

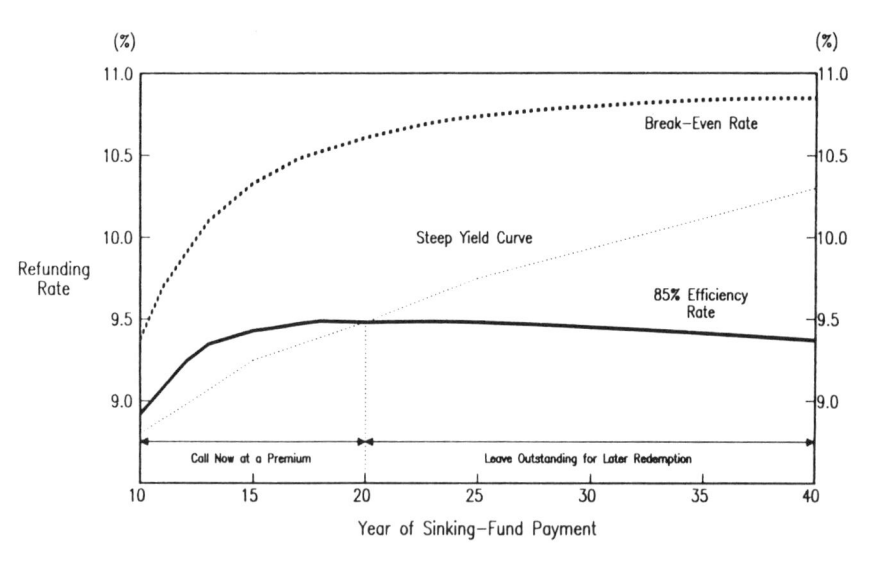

Figure 18. Sinking-fund strategy given a steep yield curve.

XI. EFFICIENCY HAS MORE GENERAL APPLICATIONS

Refunding efficiency is motivated by the idea that the interest savings gained from calling a bond should be compared with the theoretical value of the call option, which reflects current and *potential* opportunities. This concept readily applies to many situations other than a standard call that the issuer may wish to undertake to eliminate high-coupon debt and, thus, improve its debt service. Two obvious examples are repurchase programs for currently nonrefundable debt, either through tender offers or open market operations, and advance refunding of municipal issues. Another possible way of capturing the value of the call option is by utilizing the emerging market of options on interest rate swaps. There are various strategies for receiving, in the form of a cash payment, a high percentage of the theoretical value of the call option on the outstanding bond.

Although the call option is not involved directly, it plays a crucial role in these transactions. In the case of a repurchase, the bonds tend to be relatively cheap as they trade on a yield-to-call basis. This phenomenon is even more apparent in the case of "high to low" municipal refundings, in which the "effective purchase price" (that is, the size of the escrow account) is explicitly determined by the issuer's refunding rate and the initial call price of the outstanding issue.[7] The saving is essentially the difference between pricing the bond on a yield-to-maturity basis versus on a yield-to-call basis. This simple functional relationship between refunding rate and effective purchase price enables us to compute straightforwardly the efficiency of an advance refunding: The only determinant of future effective purchase price is the issuer's future refunding rate [3]. In contrast, the future price and refunding efficiency of a tender/repurchase candidate depend on the issuer's funding rate of matching maturity, the interest rate to call, and, even more importantly, supply/demand conditions.

XII. CONCLUSION

Prior to the advent of embedded option valuation and refunding efficiency, the refunding decision was usually based on a simple present value savings calculation. The issuer decided by "gut feel" if savings were sufficient in the prevailing interest rate environment to refund the bond. Unfortunately, the appropriate level of savings depends heavily on the specifics of the bond. For example, savings of 5% would probably not warrant refunding a long telephone bond but probably would be more than enough to refund an intermediate-term bond maturing in 2 or 3 years. Furthermore, the savings calculation considers only one side of an equation. Although this calculation values the benefit of a refunding, it entirely ignores the hidden cost of the refunding — namely the value of the call option that the issuer relinquishes to effect the refunding.

The efficiency benchmark overcomes both of these problems. The appropriate degree of efficiency (whether 85%, 90%, or even 100%) is related to the risk preference of the issuer and not to the specifics of the refunding candidate. If 85% efficiency is a good benchmark for a long bond, then it is also a good benchmark for an intermediate bond. More importantly, the efficiency calculation directly compares the value obtained from a refunding with the value of the forfeited option.

Today's volatile interest rate environment poses quite a challenge and opportunity for the liability manager to effectively and efficiently realize the full value of embedded call options.

APPENDIX

This appendix illustrates an intuitively appealing definition of interest rate volatility. However volatility is defined mathematically, conceptually it is intended to measure the degree of magnitude of future interest rate uncertainty. If interest rates are "highly volatile," one can estimate with only minimal confidence what interest rates will be after 1 year, for example. Conversely, low volatility implies that next year's rates can be predicted with a high degree of confidence.

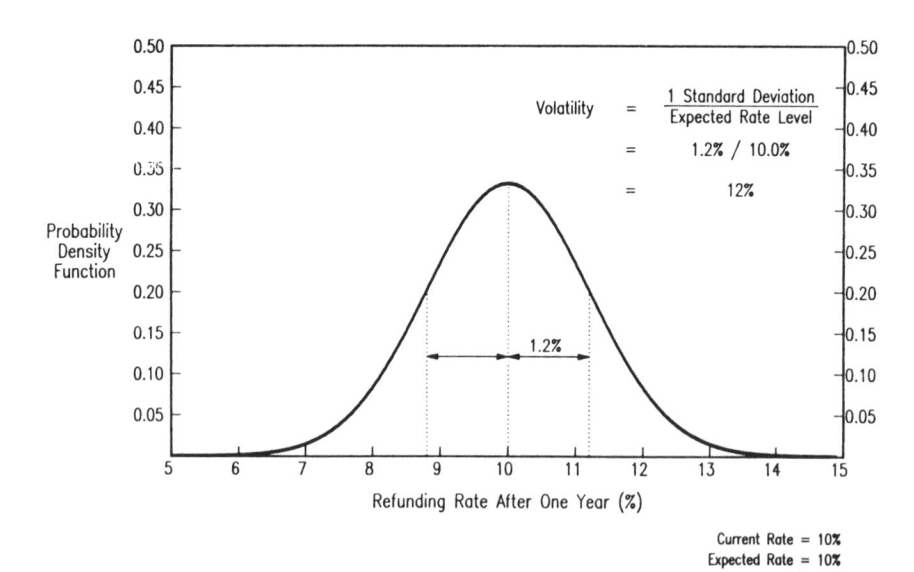

Figure A1. Volatility given a normal distribution.

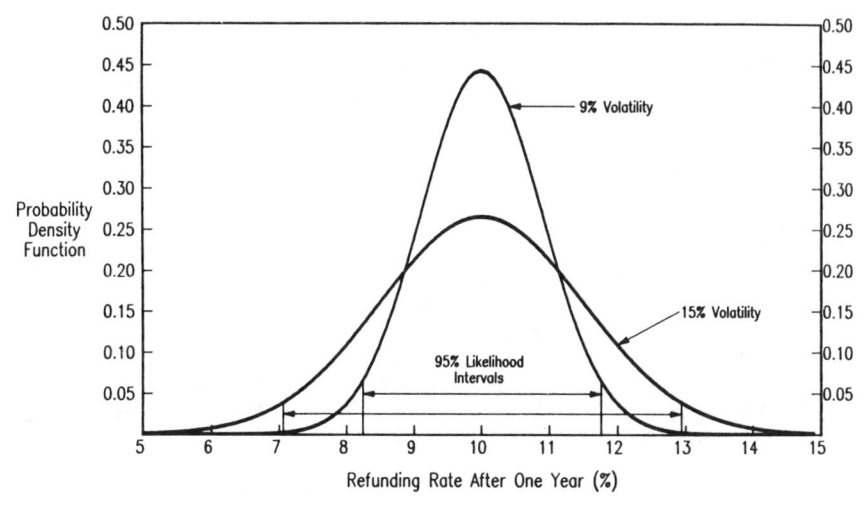

Figure A2.   Normal distributions with 9 and 15% volatility.

Suppose, for example, that the refunding rate for the issuer of the long 12s is currently 10%. The issuer cannot know what the refunding rate will be after 1 year, but assume that it is known that the rate is normally distributed with a mean of 10% and a standard deviation of 1.2% (see Figure A1). Volatility is defined to be the standard deviation of 1.2%

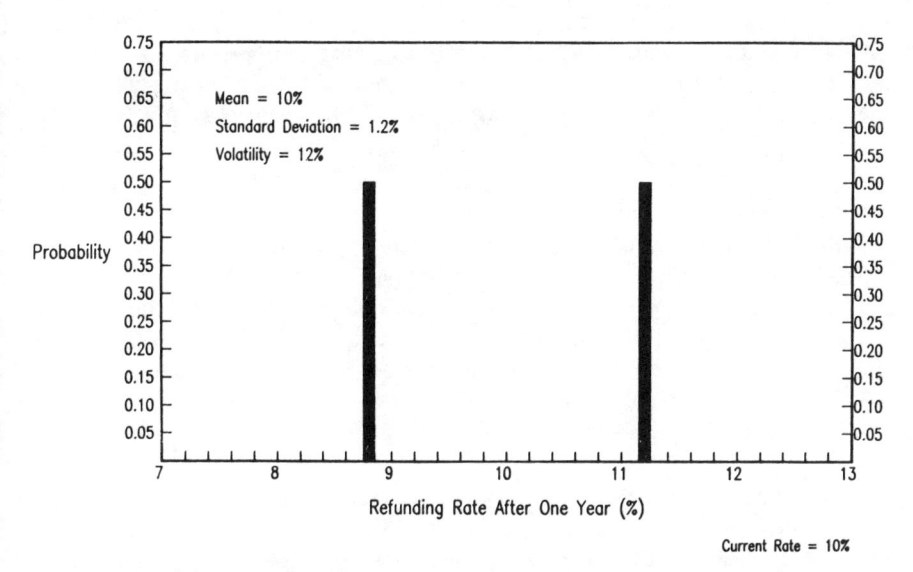

Figure A3.   Discrete distribution with one step per year.

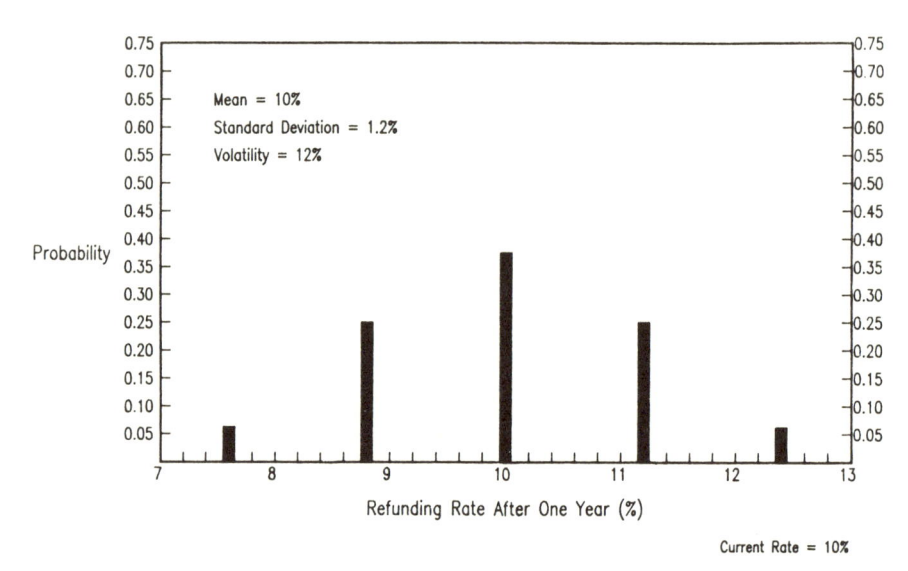

Figure A4.   Discrete distribution with four steps per year.

divided by next year's "expected" rate level (which is also the current rate level) — expressed as a percentage. In this example, interest rate volatility is 1.2%/10% × 100%, or 12%.

The standard deviation (and, therefore, volatility) is a direct measure of the issuer's degree of uncertainty about next year's refunding rate. Figure A2 illustrates the link between volatility and future interest rate uncertainty. In this exhibit, the probability distributions of next year's refunding rate are shown assuming 9 and 15% volatility and a normal distribution. The 95% confidence interval for each distribution shows the interval centred at 10% in which one can be 95% certain that next year's interest rate will fall. A higher volatility gives rise to a larger interval and, therefore, greater interest rate uncertainty.

This definition of volatility works for any type of future interest rate probability distribution — not just the normal distribution. Figures A3 and A4 show the discrete probability distributions resulting from the interest rate behavior illustrated in Figures 3 and 7, respectively. In both cases, the standard deviation around the mean of 10% is 1.2%. This equates to a volatility of 1.2%/10%, or 12%.

NOTES

1. For a discussion about alternative approaches to this problem, with regard to the specification of the cash flows and the choice of discount rate, see Kalotay [7].

2. See Appendix.

3. To be comparable with the 9.05% savings in year 5, the savings available in year 6 is discounted back to year 5.

4. See Appendix.

5. For further information, see Kalotay and McIntyre [8].

6. See Kalotay [5].

7. Advance refunding is mathematically equivalent to the index call. See Leibowitz [4].

REFERENCES

1. Boyce, W. M., and A. J. Kalotay, "Optimum Bond Calling and Refunding," *Interfaces* (November 1979).

2. Boyce, W. M., and A. J. Kalotay, "Tax Differentials and Callable Bonds," *Journal of Finance* (September 1979).

3. Gurwitz, A. S., A. J. Kalotay, and D. Howard, *Call Provisions and Efficient Refunding in Municipal Finance*. Salomon Brothers Inc, March 1987.

4. Leibowitz, M. L., *The Index Call*, Salomon Brothers Inc, April 1981.

5. Kalotay, A. J., *The Effect of Sinking Funds on the Cost of Debt*. Salomon Brothers Inc, September 1981.

6. Kalotay, A. J., *The Interest Rate Risk of Callable Bonds*. Salomon Brothers Inc, September 1982.

7. Kalotay, A. J., "On the Structure and Valuation of Debt Refundings," *Financial Management* (Spring 1982).

8. Kalotay, A. J., and P. McIntyre, *Sinking Fund Issues: A Challenge for the Active Manager*. Salomon Brothers Inc, November 1984.

CAPITAL BUDGETING USING CONTINGENT CLAIMS ANALYSIS:

A TUTORIAL

Peter Ritchken[*] and Gad Rabinowitz[*]

I. INTRODUCTION

Classical net present value analysis (NPV) has replaced cruder payback and accounting rate of return methods and is used by a majority of corporations to evaluate projects. The method involves a comparison between the cost of an investment and the present value of the cash flows generated by the project, which are computed according to the equation

$$PV = \frac{C_1}{(1 + k)} + \frac{C_2}{(1 + k)^2} + \cdots + \frac{C_n}{(1 + k)^n} \qquad (1)$$

[*]Weatherhead School of Management, Case Western Reserve University.

We thank Alo Ghosh, Shanjaw Kuo, Juan Ocampo, Jonathan Weiner, and other participants of the Options Group in McKinsey and Company for helpful discussions.

Advances in Futures and Options Research, Vol. 3, pages 119–143.

where C_i is the cash flow in period i and k is the appropriate discount rate. Equation (1) is used to price a bond where C_i is the coupon payment, C_n is the final repayment of principal, and k is the interest rate. The application of the bond equation to valuation of *risky* projects is made possible by two major assumptions. First, uncertain future cash flows are replaced by their expected values and treated as given at the outset. Second, the discount rate k is assumed known and constant and depends solely upon the risk of the project. These two assumptions are known to be quite severe for many projects. First, by assuming the expected future cash flows to be known at the outset presupposes a *static* approach to investment decision making that ignores the possibility that future managerial decisions, made in reponse to market conditions, could create additional value [17]. Second, by using the same discount rate in each period, the NPV equation presupposes that managerial actions over the lifetime of the project do not alter risks. Clearly projects in which management has the ability to take actions to control downside losses (for example, by abandoning projects in response to adverse market conditions) are less risky than if no such actions are available (for example, if projects are committed). The only way an NPV approach can deal with this risk effect is through some ad hoc adjustment of the discount rate. Even without managerial intervention, the risk of projects need not remain constant over time. For example, projects entering their second phases after successful first phases may be less risky than similar projects whose first phases failed. Hence, not only will discount rates vary according to active managerial actions, and with time, but they also may be uncertain. Finally, even if it were true that the discount rates were deterministic and constant, the problem of estimating the appropriate value is still formidable. In principle the appropriate discount rate is determined by the rate of return offered in capital markets by equivalent risk securities. Since identifying a portfolio of similar firms is often extremely difficult, in practice a company may choose to adopt a single corporate discount rate (based on the weighted average cost of capital) by which all projects are evaluated regardless of their risk.

To some extent the drawback of these static assumptions may be overcome by employing techniques such as Monte Carlo simulation and decision tree analysis. Decision tree analysis (DTA) helps management structure decision problems by mapping all feasible alternative actions contingent on all future possible states of nature. By properly taking into account actions, conditional on the appropriate states of nature, DTA can, in principle, be used to compute unconditional expected cash flows. As such it is particularly useful, especially in analyzing complex *sequential* investment decisions. The main drawback of DTA, however, regards the problem of determining appropriate discount rates to be used in working back through the decision tree. In addition, these methods not only require mutually exclusive scenarios to be established in advance, but they also require probability estimates of the likelihoods of their occurrence. In many instances there is a wide range of scenarios, and prespecifying probabilities of their occurrence may be extremely difficult. In this tutorial some of the problems associated with using decision tree methods are examined.

A new approach to capital budgeting, referred to as contingent claims analysis (CCA), enables management to quantify aspects of extra value of economic desirability ignored by a standard NPV analysis [9]. Specifically, CCA is able to value the *operating flexibility* and *strategic options* within a single project. The operating flexibility refers to the additional project value that is derived by the fact that management can revise operating decisions in response to market conditions. Examples of operating options include the option to defer expansion, to alter outlays for maintenance and replacement, to shut down, abandon, expand, or contract facilities, and to alter mixes of factor inputs. The strategic options associated with a project result from its interdependence with future and follow-up investments [13]. By not investing in the project future possible opportunities are closed off (or delayed). The value of retaining options to these future projects is embedded into the value of the strategic options.

The existence of "flexibility options" in any project provides management with the tools necessary to adapt its future actions (contingent on future events) in such a way that the upside potential of projects can be improved while downside losses can be limited. By ignoring the value of these flexibility options, traditional NPV analysis may misvalue projects of strategic importance.

In the next section an example is provided that illustrates the key concepts behind the net present value model. In Section III a decision tree model is used to evaluate the net present value of a project where future decisions are made in response to market conditions. The example serves to highlight the failings behind some of the traditional decision tree models. The contingent claims methodology is then presented in Seciton IV. The advantages of this methodology are carefully outlined. In Section V the relationships between contingent claims analysis and decision tree methods are made clear. It is shown that in many instances decision tree methods can be readily modified to value operating and strategic options. Sections VI and VII provide extensions of the simple contingent claims pricing model. In Section VIII, a second example is presented that serves to illustrate the general power of contingent claims analysis. Section IX considers compound options and their valuation. Section X provides a brief literature review and some comments on the limitations of the approach.

II. CAPITAL BUDGETING USING NET PRESENT VALUE

Consider a firm that is deciding whether to purchase a plant. For simplicity we assume the investment horizon is two periods and that all cash flows from the plant in the first period are reinvested into the plant. The final value of the plant is indicated in the tree diagram below.

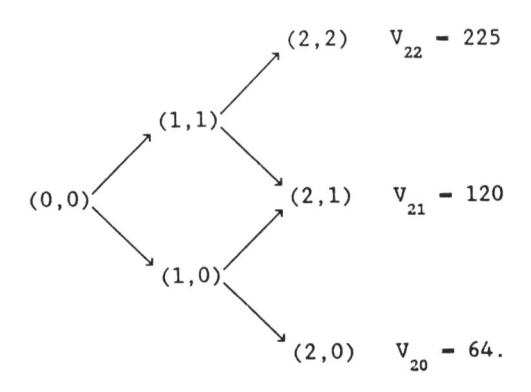

In the diagram, node (i, j) represents time period i, and state j, where j counts the number of up movements from time 0. Let V_{ij} be the plant value in period i of the state is j. Notice that from each period only one of two states can be reached. The initial investment required for this project is $I_0 = \$90$ and the risk-free interest rate per period is 5%.

Let $p(q)$ be the probability that in each period an up-state (down-state) will occur. Then a traditional NPV analysis requires that the expected cash flows be obtained, and then appropriately discounted. For the above problem the expected cash flow in period 2, $E\{\tilde{V}_2\}$ is

$$E\{\tilde{V}_2\} = p^2 V_{22} + 2pq V_{21} + q^2 V_{20}.$$

For $p = 0.5$ we obtain

$$E\{\tilde{V}_2\} = (0.25)225 + (0.5)120 + (0.25)64 = 132.25.$$

The present value of the project is obtained by discounting this expected value by an appropriate discount rate. The appropriate rate is determined by the rate of return offered by equivalent risk securities in capital markets. Assume that there exists a firm whose operations consist of a project similar to the one being considered. The stock price of this firm is S_0 and its future prices conditional on the states of nature are shown below:

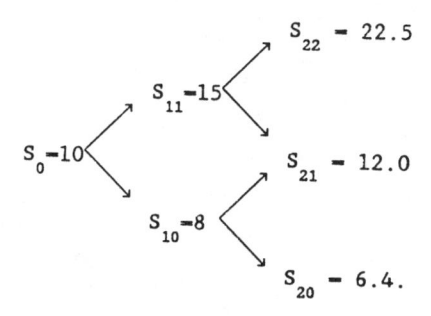

We assume the stock pays no dividends. Notice that in each period the stock price either increases by 50% or declines to 80% of its value. The expected return in any period from holding this stock is $(1.5p + 0.8q) - 1$. With $p = 0.5$, the expected return in each period is 15% and hence the appropriate discount rate for the stock is 15%.

Notice that by purchasing 10 shares of this firms stock, the payouts in period 2 are identical to the payouts of the project. Hence, to avoid arbitrage opportunities, we conclude that the current value of the project is $100. Equivalently, since the project is perfectly correlated to the payments of the stock, the appropriate discount rate for the project must equal that of the stock, and hence from Equation (1) we obtain

$$V_0 = E(\tilde{V}_2)/(1 + k)^2 = 132.25/(1.15)^2 = 100.$$

Using 15% as the discount rate, the value of the project in each period and state is given as follows:

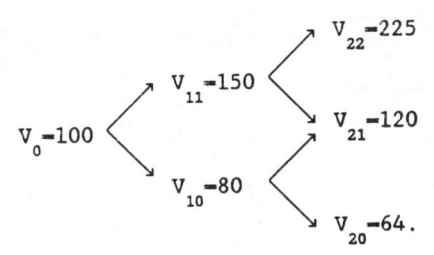

II. DECISION TREE ANALYSIS APPROACH FOR VALUING GROWTH OPTIONS

We now extend the static investment problem to one in which decisions made over the lifetime of the project influence cash flows. In so doing we illustrate how DTA can be used for capital budgeting. Assume that in the initial period, management is able to purchase a licence that provides it with the option to double the scale and value of the plant in period 1, for costs that are established today. Specifically, according to the licencing agreement, if an up-state occurs (in period 1) then management may expand at a cost of $X_{11} = 120$, while if a down-state occurs, the expansion cost is $X_{10} = 90$. The sequence of decisions and nature states is given by

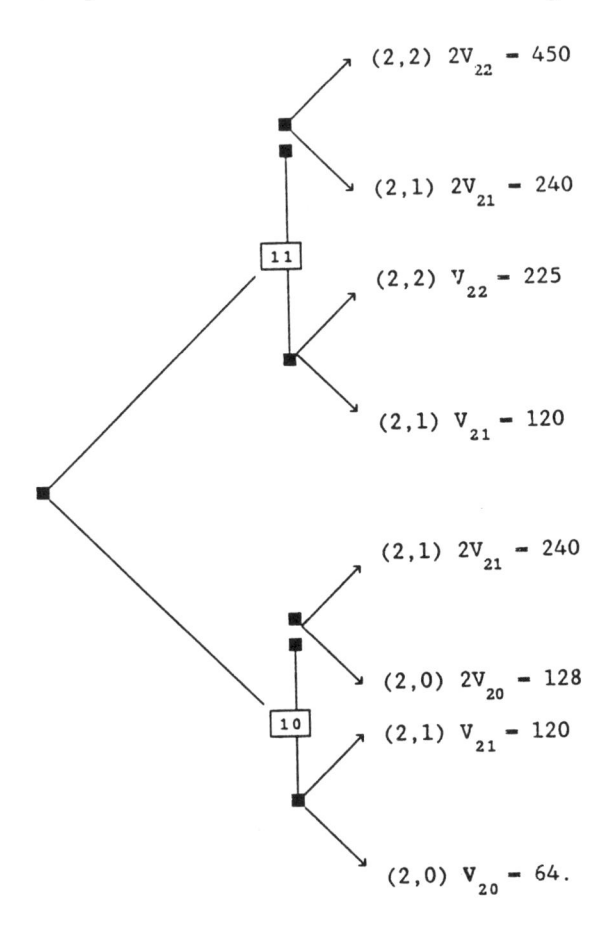

At the end of period 1, management will either double the scale and value of the plant or not, depending on whether it is in their interests. The value of the plant in node (1, 1) is $V_{11} = 150$. By paying $X_{11} = \$120$ the total value of the expanded plant can be increased to \$300. Clearly under this state of nature it is optimal for the firm to make its expansion. Indeed the value of the project in node (1, 1), W_{11} say, can be written as

$$W_{11} = V_{11} + C_{11}$$

where V_{11} is the present value of the single plant without the expansion and C_{11} is the value of a call option on the net present value of the expansion given by

$$C_{11} = \max(V_{11} - X_{11}, 0) = \max(150 - 120, 0) = \$30.$$

Similarly the optimal decision if state $(1, 0)$ is reached is not to expand since the present value of the expansion (\$80) is below its cost (\$90). Let C_{10} be the value of the option to expand in state $(1, 0)$. Then

$$C_{10} = \max(V_{10} - X_{10}, 0) = \max(80 - 90, 0) = \$0.$$

Collapsing the decision tree back to stage zero, we have

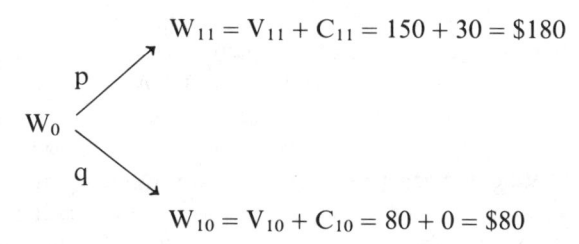

$$W_{11} = V_{11} + C_{11} = 150 + 30 = \$180$$
$$W_{10} = V_{10} + C_{10} = 80 + 0 = \$80$$

where W_0 represents the present value of the project and is computed by first evaluating the expected project value in period 1 and discounting:

$$W_0 = \frac{W_{11}p + W_{10}q}{1 + k^*}.$$

Using the discount rate for the project (with no options), i.e., 15%, we obtain

$$W_0 = \frac{108(0.5) + 80(0.5)}{1.15} = \$113.0.$$

One may argue that a 15% discount rate is not appropriate. Indeed it could be argued that only the values V_{11} and V_{10} should be discounted at 15% and that the values derived from the expansion option should be discounted at a different rate.

Then

$$W_0 = \frac{pV_{11} + qV_{10}}{(1 + k)} + C_0$$

where C_0 represents the present value of a claim worth C_{11} in state $(1, 1)$ and C_{10} in state $(1, 0)$. Clearly, since the present value of the project with no options is $V_0 = 100$, we obtain

$$W_0 = V_0 + C_0$$

or

$$W_0 = 100 + C_0$$

where

$$C_0 = \frac{p(30) + q(0)}{1 + k^*}.$$

The problem now is to establish an appropriate discount rate, k^*, for the growth option.

In the next section we illustrate how contingent claims analysis (CCA) can be used to derive the appropriate value for the growth option, C_0. Surprisingly, this value can be established without requiring knowledge of the up and down probabilities. It turns out that the correct present value for this project is $110.4, which is less than the present value obtained using the decision tree analysis. This difference can be explained by the failure of DTA to provide appropriate discount rates. DTA requires the discount rates to be specified *exogenously*, whereas CCA implicitly provides the appropriate discount rates. The appropriate discount rates are obtained by using readily available stock prices and riskless interest rate information provided in the capital markets, and by recognizing the fact that participants in these markets are free to trade and borrow funds and will do so if it is in their best interests. The next section illustrates the key ideas behind the CCA methodology.

IV. A CONTINGENT CLAIMS APPROACH FOR VALUING GROWTH OPTIONS

To establish the true value of the project with growth options, we need a method for valuing a contingent claim C_0. We have a stock currently priced at £10 and whose period 1 values are either 15 or 8 (i.e., $u = 1.5$, $d = 0.8$).

$$S_0 = 10 \begin{array}{c} \nearrow S_{11} = uS_0 = 15 \\ \\ \searrow S_{10} = dS_0 = 8. \end{array}$$

Since the riskless rate is 5%, we have bonds that provide payouts of $1.05 for every dollar invested, regardless of the state.

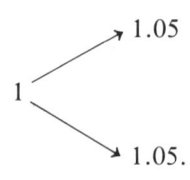

$$1 \begin{array}{c} \nearrow 1.05 \\ \\ \searrow 1.05. \end{array}$$

Now consider a portfolio of H shares of stock partially financed by borrowing \$B. The payoffs of the portfolio in period 1 are

$$HS_0 - B_0 \nearrow \quad HS_{11} - (1 + r)B$$
$$\searrow \quad HS_{10} - (1 + r)B.$$

We shall choose H and B such that the payouts of this portfolio are equal to the value of the growth option in period 1. That is,

$$HS_{11} - (1 + r)B = C_{11}$$
$$HS_{10} - (1 + r)B = C_{10}$$

where C_{11} and C_{10} are the value of the contingent claims in states $(1, 1)$ and $(1, 0)$, respectively ($C_{11} = 30, C_{10} = 0$).

Solving for H and B we obtain

$$H^* = \frac{C_{11} - C_{10}}{S_{11} - S_{10}}$$
$$B^* = (H^* S_{10} - C_{10})/(1 + r).$$

Since this portfolio provides the same payouts as the expansion option, their current values should be the same. That is, the current fair value of the expansion option should be

$$C_0 = H^* S_0 - B^*.$$

Substituting for H^* and B^*, and uS and dS for S_{11} and S_{10}, and rearranging terms we obtain

$$C_0 = [\theta C_{11} + (1 - \theta)C_{10}]/(1 + r)$$

where

$$\theta = (1 + r - d)/(u - d).$$

In our problem

$$\theta = (1.05 - 0.8)/(1.5 - 0.8) = 0.35714$$

and hence

$$C_0 = \frac{(0.35714)(30) + 0}{1.05} = 10.2.$$

We have shown that a claim that pays out \$30 in state $(1, 1)$ and \$0 in state $(1, 0)$ is currently worth \$10.2. Since the expansion option pays out \$30 in state 1 and \$0, otherwise, it too must be worth \$10.2. That is the fair value of the licencing arrangement (growth option) is worth \$10.2 and the value of the project is

$$W_0 = \$100 + \$10.2 = \$110.2.$$

If the project were priced at the DTA value of \$113, then the value of the growth option would incorrectly be computed as \$13. To see that this is incorrect notice that if the price of this contract was \$13 then its payoffs could be represented by

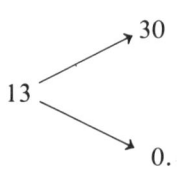

However, using the information provided by the capital markets the same terminal payouts could be obtained for \$10.20. Specifically by buying $H^* = 4.285$ shares of stock partially financed by borrowing $B^* = 32.65$ dollars at the riskless rate yields the same payouts as the expansion option as shown below:

Payout of Option   *Payouts of the Replicating Portfolio*

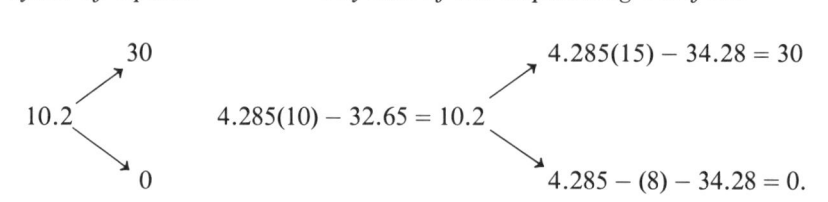

Since the same payouts can be achieved at lower cost, there is no reason for management to pay a higher feee than \$10.2 for the option to expand at the predetermined costs.

Notice that in establishing the price of the option no information on the probabilities of the up- and down-state was required. That is, the value of the expansion option does not explicitly depend on p. Finally, note that if the present value of the claim is 10.2 then for $p = 0.5$ the appropriate discount rate is $1 + k^* = E(\tilde{C}_1)/C_0 = 15/10.2 = 1.47$. Hence for $p = 0.5$ the appropriate discount rate to use for the option in the DTA is $k^* = 47\%$.

VI.   CONTINGENT CLAIM ANALYSIS AND DECISION TREE METHODS

In this section we show that CCA can be viewed as a corrected form of DTA where the appropriate discount rate is established endogenously. Notice that in our example $\theta = 0.35714$. We shall now treat this value as the probability of an up-movement in the decision tree, and assume that all investors in the economy are risk neutral (RN). This being the case all investors will discount the expected cash flows at the riskless discount rate of 5%.

The expected value of the project (without the expansion option) in period 2, $E\{V_2^{RN}\}$, is given by

$$E\{V_2^{RN}\} = \theta^2 V_{22} + 2\theta(1 - \theta)V_{21} + (1 - \theta)^2 V_{20}$$
$$= \theta^2(225) + 2\theta(1 - \theta)(120) + (1 - \theta)^2 64$$
$$= 110.25$$

and the value of the project, V_0^{RN}, would be

$$V_0^{RN} = E\{V_2^{RN}\}/(1 + r)^2$$
$$= (110.25)/(1.05)^2 = 100.$$

Notice that this answer coincides with the true value of the project obtained in our real economy.

Similarly, the present value of the project with expansion options in our risk-neutral economy, W_0^{RN}, is given by the present value of the project without the expansion option, V_0^{RN}, together with the present value of the expansion option, C_0^{RN}. Let $E\{C_1^{RN}\}$ be the expected value of the expansion option in period one. Then we have

$$W_0^{RN} = E\{V_2^{RN}\}/(1 + r)^2 + E\{C_1^{RN}\}/(1 + r)$$
$$= 100 + [\theta C_{11} + (1 - \theta)C_{10}]/(1 + r)$$
$$= 100 + 10.2$$
$$= 110.2.$$

In both cases the project value obtained by adjusting the probability of an up-movement from p to θ and then discounting the cash flows at the riskless rate yields the same answer as those obtained earlier.

The example illustrates the fact that CCA can be viewed as an economically adjusted version of DTA. These adjustments involve a redistribution of probability mass such that risk is reallocated in a way that allows the appropriate discount factor to be the riskless rate. This redistribution of probability mass, together with the use of the riskless discount rate, results in the value of the project being set at its appropriate fair value, the fair value representing the price at which participants in the capital markets would be prepared to pay for bearing equivalent risks. The adjustments to the DTA calculations result in valuations superior to the usual decision tree methods because the latter method fails to recognize that the appropriate discount rates can be extracted from market information. Rather than exogenously provide ad hoc discount factors, CCA uses market information to endogenously compute them in such a way that the resulting value precludes the possibility of riskless arbitrage opportunities arising. Moreover, by using the risk-adjusted probability measures in the decision tree, the decision maker is relieved of having to specify probabilities of each possible scenario.

VI. MULTIPERIOD PRICING OF CONTINGENT CLAIMS

In Section IV, the valuation of a contingent claim expiring in one period was accomplished by establishing a portfolio of stocks and bonds in the capital markets that produced identical payouts to the contingent claim. Since a replication exists, the current value of the claim can be computed either as the present value of the replicating portfolio, or as the discounted expected terminal value of the claim, where the expectation is computed using the risk-adjusted probabilities and the discount factor is the riskless rate.

We now consider the problem of valuing a claim with a strike price of $10 that expires in two periods where the number of terminal states is three. The values of the stock and the terminal values of the option are as follows:

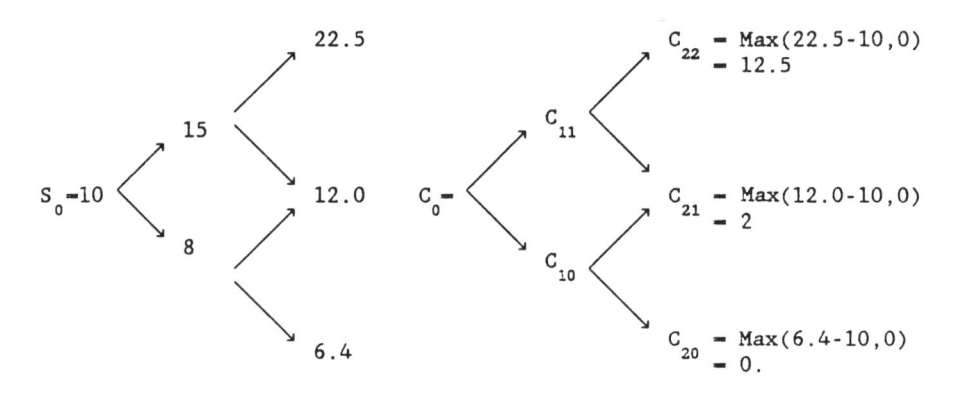

To value the call we again consider a portfolio of H shares partially financed by borrowing B_0 dollars. The final payouts of this portfolio are shown below:[1]

$$10H - B_0 \begin{cases} 22.5H - (1.05)^2 \\ 12H - (1.05)^2 B \\ 6.4H - (1.05)^2 B. \end{cases}$$

Equating the portfolio value to the terminal call value we obtain

$$22.5H - (1.05)^2 B = 12.5$$
$$12.0H - (1.05)^2 B = 2$$
$$6.4H - (1.05)^2 B = 0.$$

Unfortunately, since there are three equations and only two variables, no unique solution exists and the call option cannot be replicated. More specifically, the payouts of the claim cannot be replicated by a *static* strategy of buying a portfolio of stocks and bonds. However, the payouts of the claim can be replicated by a *dynamic* strategy in which the portfolio composition is revised in the first period in a way that depends on which state occurred. The revisions must be done in such a way that no additional funds are injected into or withdrawn from the replicating portfolio at each revision point (node). That is, while the composition of the portfolio is adjusted at each node, the way the adjustments are made leaves the replicating portfolio value unchanged.[2]

Given the ability to replicate the payoffs of the contingent claim, the value of the claim can be obtained by discounting its expected terminal value (using risk-adjusted probabilities) at the risk free rate. That is,

$$C_0 = \frac{12.5P_{22} + 2P_{21} + 0P_{20}}{(1.05)^2}$$

where P_{2j} = the risk adjusted probability of being in state j (j = 0, 1, 2) in period two and is computed by

$$P_{2j} = \binom{2}{j} \theta^j (1 - \theta)^{2-j} \qquad j = 0, 1, 2.$$

In general if the terminal call option can take on n values, then provided there are (n − 1) opportunities to revise portfolios, a replication is possible and the value of the claim can be computed by

$$C_0 = \sum_{j=0}^{n} C_{nj} P_{nj}/(1 + r)^n$$

where C_{nj} is the value of the claim in period n given j upward movements have occurred and P_{nj} is the probability that in n periods (trials) j upward movements would occur. Specifically,

$$P_{nj} = \binom{n}{j} \theta^j (1 - \theta)^{n-j} \qquad j = 0, 1, 2, 3, ..., n$$

where θ is the risk-adjusted probability value that is used in the decision tree for each period and r is the riskless rate per period. The price obtained by using the above equation is referred to as the binomial option price [4].

Table 1. Sensitivity of Option Prices.

Factor Increases	Direction of Change in Price of Option
Stock price	Increases
Strike	Decreases
Interest rate	Increases
Volatility	Increases
Time	Increases

As the number of states increases the number of revision opportunities increases. In the limiting case, we obtain a situation where there is a market with continuous trading opportunities. If the period by period up and down parameters of the stock process are specified in a particular way then, as the frequency of trading opportunities in the period increases, the binomial price process can be made to converge onto a lognormal price process. In this special limiting case the binomial model reduces to the Black–Scholes equation [1].

$$C_0 = S_0 N(d_1) - Xe^{-rT}N(d_2)$$

where

$$d_1 = [\ln(S_0/X) + (r + \sigma^2/2)T]/\sigma\sqrt{T}$$
$$d_2 = d_1 - \sigma\sqrt{T}$$

where S_0 is the current price of the underlying instrument (stock), X is the strike price, T is the time to maturity, r is the riskless rate, σ is the instantaneous volatility of the stock, and $N(\cdot)$ is the cumulative normal distribution.

Table 1 indicates how the option price responds to changes in each of the terms. From the equation for the pricing of contingent claims it can be noted that their value is greater in more uncertain environments and when interest rates are high. Moreover, the longer the life of the claim the greater its value. *Thus, contrary to a traditional NPV analysis, higher uncertainty, higher interest rates, and longer investment horizons are not necessarily damaging to an investment opportunity.* Specifically while these factors reduce the value of a project using the traditional NPV model given by Equation (1), they increase the value of managerial flexibility. Indeed the increase in this latter value may more than offset the decrease given by discounting static cash flows.

VIII.   REPLICATION AND EQUILIBRIUM OPTION PRICING MODELS

Option prices derived from formulas that are based on the replication approach are seemingly independent of considerations relating to capital market equilibrium. Alternative derivatives for establishing fair option prices, called "equilibrium derivations," evolve from the requirement that the option earn an expected rate of return commensurate with the risk involved in holding the option as an asset. If the underlying security is a financial asset that pays no dividends, then the two approaches produce equivalent values. However, if the underlying security is a commodity that possesses a convenience yield and/or pays dividends, then the full return on the security is not totally determined by price changes. In this case the equilibrium expected rate of return necessary to compensate investors for bearing risk of holding the asset, α say, exceeds the expected rate of return measured by price changes alone, α_p say. Since the option is a claim on prices, in this case the option is a claim on an asset that earns a below-equilibrium rate of return. For such assets, adjustments must be made to the Black–Scholes model [12]. Specifically we have:

$$C_0 = S_0 e^{-\delta T} N(d_1^*) - X^{-rT} N(d_2^*)$$

where

$$\delta = \alpha - \alpha_p$$
$$d_1^* = [\ln(S_0/X) + (r - \delta + \sigma^2/2)T]/\sigma\sqrt{T}$$

and

$$d_2^* = d_1^* - \sigma\sqrt{T}.$$

Hence the call price now depends on a "convenience yield like" term, δ.

Such adjustments are typically necessary in capital budgeting problems, where the underlying securities replicating the payoffs may not be financial assets where total return is reflected in price changes.

VIII.   VALUING FLEXIBILITY USING SIMPLE OPTIONS

In this section we consider the valuation of flexibility in projects where managerial decisions can be made in each period. To facilitate exposition of the problem we initially consider a problem involving the valuation and comparison of alternative flexible manufacturing systems.

Consider a project whose profits from using a machine, A, which uses technology a in each period, are given below.

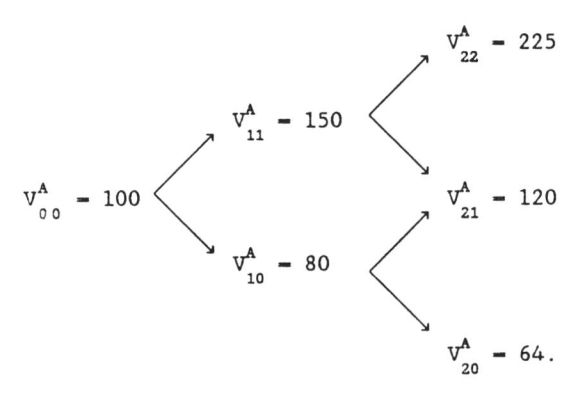

The profits generated by an alternative "machine," B say, which uses technology b, is shown below:

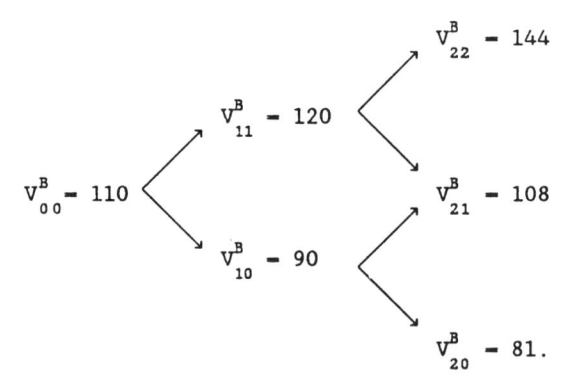

Assume information from the capital markets indicates that the risk adjusted probability θ in each period is $\theta = 0.5$. Then the present value of profits using machine A is given by

$$PV(A) = 100 + \frac{150(0.5) + 80(0.5)}{1.05} + \frac{225(0.25) + 120(0.5) + 64(0.25)}{(1.05)^2}$$

$$= 329.5.$$

Similar calculations for machine B yield

$$PV(B) = 310.0.$$

We now consider a machine D, that can switch between technology a and b at no cost. Clearly D is more valuable than either machine A or B, whose uses are limited to a single technology. Hence

$$PV(D) \geq \max\{PV(A), PV(B)\}$$

A firm using machine D can be viewed as a firm that uses technology b in each period unless the profit from using technology a is higher. Let $F^D(b, a)$ represent the current value of flexibility that machine D derives beyond that of machine B (attributable to the fact that it can switch from technology b to a).

$$F^D(b, a) = PV(D) - PV(B).$$

A firm using machine D can be viewed as a firm that uses B but in addition in each of the three periods has the option to switch to technology a if it is in their best interests. Let $C_0^D(b, a)$, $C_1^D(b, a)$, and $C_2^D(b, a)$ be the current value of these three options. Then

$$F^D(b, a) = \sum_{j=0}^{2} C_j(b, a).$$

Let $d_{ij}(b, a)$ be the value of switching from b to a in state (i, j). Then

$$d_{ij}(b, a) = \max(V_{ij}^a - V_{ij}^b, 0)$$

and the values of this flexibility switching in each state are shown below:

$C_0(b) = d_{00}(b, a) = 0$

$C_1(b, a)$
- $d_{11}(b, a) = \max(150 - 120, 0) = 30$
- $d_{10}(b, a) = \max(80 - 90, 0) = 0$

$C_2(b, a)$,
- $d_{22}(b, a) = \max(225 - 144, 0) = 81$
- $d_{21}(b, a) = \max(120 - 108, 0) = 12$
- $d_{20}(b, a) = \max(64 - 81, 0) = 0.$

Clearly the value of being able to switch from b to a in the current period, $C_0(b, a)$ is \$0. The current value of being able to switch in the second period is

$$C_1(b, a) = (30\theta + 0)/(1 + r) = 15/1.05 = 14.3$$

and the current value of being able to switch in the second period is

$$C_2(b, a) = [81\theta^2 + 24(1 - \theta)\theta]/(1 + r)^2$$
$$= [81(0.25) + 24(0.25)]/(1.05)^2 = 23.8.$$

Hence the value of being able to switch from a rigid technology b to a,

$F^D(b, a)$, is

$$F^D(b, a) = \sum_{j=0}^{2} C_j(b, a) = 0 + 14.3 + 23.8 = 38.1$$

and the total value of machine D is

$$PV(D) = PV(B) + F^D(b, a)$$
$$= 310.0 + 38.1 = 348.1.$$

In a similar way a firm that uses machine D can be viewed as a firm that uses a machine A unless the profit from using technology b is higher. In this case

$$PV(D) = PV(A) + F^D(a, b)$$

where

$$F^D(a, b) = \sum_{j=0}^{2} C_j(a, b)$$

where each option provides the owner of machine D to switch to technology b if it is in their interests. The terminal values associated with each of the three options of being able to switch are shown below:

$$C_0(a, b) = b_{00}(a, b) = 10$$

$$C_1(b, a) \nearrow d_{11}(a, b) = \max(120 - 150, 0) = 0$$
$$\searrow d_{10}(b, a) = \max(90 - 80, 0) = 10$$

$$C_2(a, b) \begin{cases} \nearrow d_{22}(a, b) = \max(144 - 225, 0) = 0 \\ \rightarrow d_{21}(b, a) = \max(108 - 120, 0) = 0 \\ \searrow d_{20}(b, a) = \max(81 - 64, 0) = 17. \end{cases}$$

Using CCA we obtain

$$C_0(a, b) = 10, \qquad C_1(a, b) = 4.76, \qquad C_2(a, b) = 3.85$$

and hence

$$F^D(a, b) = 10 + 4.76 + 3.85 = 18.6.$$

Hence

$$PV(D) = PV(A) + F^D(a, b) = 329.5 + 18.6 = 348.1$$

which is the same result we obtained earlier. Note that $F^D(a, b)$ exceeds

$F^D(b, a)$. That is, the value of flexibility is greater for an owner of machine A then B.

Of course machine D can be valued directly, by recognizing that the payoffs in each period are established according to the maximum of two possible payouts, i.e. $V_{ij} = Max(V_{ij}^a, V_{ij}^b)$. Hence the cash flows are

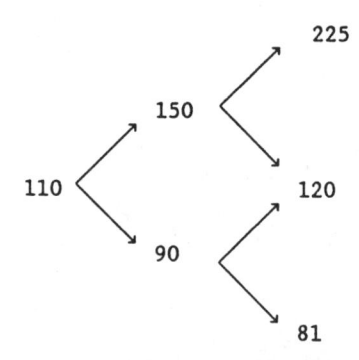

and

$$PV(D) = 110 + \frac{150\theta + 90(1 - \theta)}{(1 + r)} + \frac{225\theta^2 + 240\theta(1 - \theta) + 81(1 - \theta)^2}{(1 + r)^2}$$

$$= 348.1.$$

IX. VALUING FLEXIBILITY USING COMPOUND OPTIONS

For machine D, there was no cost involved in switching between modes a and b. Thus, the optimal technology to use in any period did not depend on the current technology being used. We now consider a machine E, which is not as flexible as machine D. Specifically, we assume that technology switching involves a cost. Let $X^E(a, b)$ be the cost of switching machine E from a to b.[3] In our example

$$X^E(a, b) = 5$$
$$X^E(b, a) = 90.$$

In this case a firm using machine E cannot be viewed as a firm that uses machine A and in addition has simple options to switch from a to b in each period. Indeed, we now illustrate why the value of flexibility associated with machine E, beyond that of A is not equal to the sum of three simple options, i.e.,

$$F^E(a, b) \neq \sum_{j=0}^{2} C_j(a, b).$$

Before we value machine E, note that it is more valuable than either A or B but less valuable than D, i.e.,

$$\max[PV(A), PV(B)] \leqslant PV(E) \leqslant PV(D).$$

Let $F^E(a, b)$ be the value of flexibility provided by E beyond that of machine A, i.e.,

$$F^E(a, b) = PV(E) - PV(A).$$

Then $0 \leqslant F^E(a, b) \leqslant F^D(a, b)$.

The valuation of the flexibility of machine E is difficult because, unlike machine D, the values of the three switching options are not independent. In the case of machine D whether the first option to switch was exercised or not had no impact on the second option. However, faced with switching costs, this independence breaks down. Specifically in the case of machine E, the nature of the switching option held in the second period depends on whether the first option was exercised. If machine E enters period 1 in mode a then the option held is an option to switch to be for a price of 5. However if period 1 is entered in mode b then the option held is to switch to a for a price of 90.

For machine D, the benefits of switching equal the benefits that arise in the immediate period. However, for machine E, the act of switching not only impacts benefits in the current period but also impacts cash flows and switching decisions in future periods. In essence by switching technologies (exercising an option), not only are payouts in the current period being altered, but also a new sequence of options to switch nodes in future periods is obtained. Options that when exercised result in the creation of new options are referred to as *compound* options [1, 6]. In order to value the flexibility of machine E, we have to value a compound option. We now consider valuation of such options using a backward dynamic process.

Let $K^E_{ij}(a)$ be the present value of profits at time i from node (i, j) given that the state is entered in mode a and optimal decisions are made thereafter. Let $I_{ij}(a)$ represent the optimal technology to use in state (i, j) given state (i, j) was entered using technology a. Thus,

$$K^E_{22}(a) = \max[V^A_{22}, V^B_{22} - X(a, b)]$$
$$= \max[225, 144 - 5] = 225$$

and $I_{22}(a) = a$. Similarly,

$$K^E_{22}(b) = \max[V^B_{22}, V^A_{22} - X(b, a)]$$
$$= \max[144, 225 - 90] = 144$$

and $I_{22}(b) = b$.

Hence given node $(2, 2)$ is reached the optimal decision is not to switch modes. Similar calculations for node $(2, 1)$ and $(2, 0)$ yield

$$K_{21}^E(a) = 120, \qquad I_{21}(a) = a,$$
$$K_{21}^E(b) = 108, \qquad I_{21}(b) = b,$$
$$K_{20}^E(a) = 76, \qquad I_{20}(a) = b,$$
$$K_{20}^E(b) = 81, \qquad I_{20}(b) = b.$$

Hence, the only time a switch should occur is if state $(2, 1)$ is reached in mode a.

We now backtract to period 1. Assume node $(1, 1)$ was entered into in mode a. Then if mode a is maintained in this state the present value is

$$V_{11}^A + \frac{\theta K_{22}^K(a) + (1 - \theta)K_{21}^E(a)}{1 + r} = 150 + 164.3 = 314.3$$

while if a switch is made the present value is

$$V_{11}^B - X(a, b) + \frac{\theta K_{22}^E(b) + (1 - \theta)K_{21}^E(b)}{1 + r} = 120 - 5 + 120 = 235.$$

Hence $K_{11}(a) = \max[314.3, 235] = 314.3$ and the optimal decision is $I_{11}(a) = a$. Similarly,

$$K_{11}^E(b) = \max\left[V_{11}^B + \frac{\theta K_{22}^E(b) + (1 - \theta)K_{21}^E(b)}{(1 + r)}, \; V_{11}^A - X(b, a) \right.$$
$$\left. + \frac{\theta K_{22}^E(a) + (1 - \theta)K_{21}^E(a)}{(1 + r)} \right]$$
$$= \max[120 + 120, 150 - 90 + 150] = 240$$

and $I_{11}(b) = b$.

Similar calculations for node $(1, 0)$ yield

$$K_{10}^E(a) = \max[80 + 93.3, 90 - 5 + 90] = 175.0 \text{ and } I_{10}(a) = b.$$
$$K_{10}^E(b) = \max[90 + 90, 80 - 90 + 93.3] = 180 \text{ and } I_{10}(b) = b.$$

Finally in the current node we have

$$K_0^E(a) = \max\left[V_0^A + \frac{\theta K_{11}^E(a) + (1 - \theta)K_{10}^E(a)}{(1 + r)}, \; V_0^B - X(a, b) \right.$$
$$\left. + \frac{\theta K_{11}^E(b) + (1 - \theta)K_{10}^E(b)}{(1 + r)} \right]$$
$$= \max[100 + 232.2, 110 - 5 + 200] = 332.2$$

and $I_0(a) = a$. Similarly

$$K_0^E(b) = \max[110 + 200, 100 - 90 + 232.2] = 310.0$$

and $I_0(b) = b$. Notice that in this example $K_0^E(b) = PV(B)$ because given machine E starts in mode b, the optimal schedule never involves switching to mode a.

Assuming no initial set up costs, the present value of E is given by

$$PV(E) = \max[K_0^E(a), K_0^E(b)] = 332.2,$$

and the optimal operating schedule is shown below:

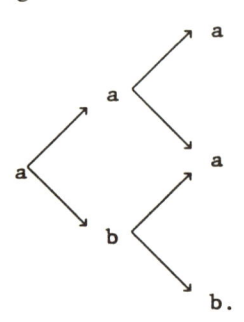

Notice that the value of flexibility $F^E(a, b)$ beyond that of A is given by

$$F^E(a, b) = PV(E) - PV(A) = 332.2 - 329.5 = 2.7.$$

Similarly

$$F^E(b, a) = PV(E) - PV(B) = 332.2 - 310.0 = 22.2.$$

Furthermore, the additional value of flexibility of machine D over E is given

Table 2.   Examples of Flexibility Options.

	Mode	Stochastic Variables	Option	Strike
A	Produce	Output price	Option to shut	Variable cost
B	Shut down		down	
A	Delay	Value of plant	Option to invest	Cost of
B	Invest	(project)	(build)	investment
A_i	Production rates	Output price	Option to alter production rate	Switching costs
A_i	Different products	Prices of competing products	Option to select product	Variable and switching costs
A_i	Selecting inputs (technologies for processing inputs)	Input price of competing raw materials	Option to switch raw materials	Variable and switching costs

by PV(D) − PV(E) = 348.1 − 332.2 = 15.9. That is, for this particular problem, a firm should be prepared to pay $15.9 more for machine D above the price of E.

The example clearly illustrates how the pricing of flexibility can become complex when the underlying valuation involves compound options. The example contains several interesting cases. Specifically by redefining "technologies" as "decision alternatives" and by redefining "machines," the switching options problem just described can be used in several other capital budgeting areas. Specifically, if mode a represents the strategy of not expanding and mode b represents expanding, then by defining $X_{ij}^c(a, b)$ to be the cost of expansion, and $X_{ij}^c(b, a) = \infty$, the problem reduces to the expansion growth option problem discussed in Section III. Note by forcing $X_{ij}^c(b, a)$ to be infinity, one is assuming that expansion projects are irreversible. Table 2 summarizes other possible interpretations of "modes" in the flexibility options problem.

X. COMMENTS

In the last decade numerous papers have appeared that apply CCA to capital budgeting. The option to defer investment in an irreversible project is examined by McDonald and Siegel [11]. Paddock, Siegel, and Smith value offshore petroleum leases [15]. In their analysis an undeveloped reserve is viewed as an option that if exercised results in a developed reserve. Majd and Pindyck examine the flexibility of delaying construction activities in projects that produce no cash flows until completed [8]. Myers and Majd value options associated with abandonment possibilities [14]. McDonald and Siegel value options to shut down production whenever output prices fall to values not sufficient to cover variable costs [10]. Brennan and Schwartz consider the problem of valuing a mine with limited resources with options to open, shut down, reopen, and abandon [3]. Finally, Mason and Merton provide an excellent overview of CCA theory in capital budgeting [9]. All these studies have highlighted the importance of incorporating the value of these options into valuation calculations. Indeed, the value of these options can be so important that ignoring them may lead to serious undervaluation [10]. However, the value of these options taken simultaneously does not equal the sum of their values taken separately. Indeed, the incremental value of an additional option is lower the greater the number of options present. Thus, neglecting a few particular options while including many others may not cause significant valuation errors [17]. At this time it remains somewhat of an art to establish which options are of primary importance to be included in the analysis. Kester has provided a taxonomy of claims that may be of some assistance [7].

In most realistic capital budgeting problems, the options to be valued are complex compound options, whose value may depend on several sources of uncertainty. Unlike simple stock options, the underlying state variables may not be easily identifiable or, for that matter, observable. In this case a substitute portfolio of securities has to be established that mimics the payouts of the project. The ability to achieve this depends critically on the assumption of market completeness.[4]

Since most capital budgeting problems require valuing complex compound options, the formulation of the problems, together with their mathematical solutions, can be difficult. As an example, the actual numerical methods required to solve the resource valuation model of Brennan and Schwartz is nontrivial [3]. It remains for future research to establish methods for solving large, complex problems in an efficient fashion. Toward this goal, simulation procedures may offer an attractive alternative to the numerical methods that are currently being used to solve these problems. [2]

XI. CONCLUSION

This tutorial has attempted to introduce the reader to contingent claims methods and techniques used in capital budgeting. This approach can be viewed as an adjusted decision tree method in which the appropriate discount rates to be used are provided endogenously. Valuation of projects using contingent claims analysis is rapidly being adopted in many organizations. The advantage of these procedures is that they clearly establish the value added by managerial decision making in response to market forces.

NOTES

1. The riskless rate is 5% per period.
2. For a discussion of how this dynamic strategy works see [4], [5], and [16].
3. In general the switching costs could depend on the state (i, j) and on the number of switches.
4. If no portfolio of securities can be established to replicate the payoff of the project, then the uniqueness of the project would expand the investment opportunity set and using option pricing or any other net present value method would produce equally inaccurate results.

REFERENCES

1. Black, F., and M. Scholes, "The Pricing of Options and Corporate Liabilities," *Journal of Political Economy* 3 (1973), 637–659.

2. Boyle, P., "Options: A Monte Carlo Approach," *Journal of Financial Economics* (May 1977), 323–338.

3. Brennan, M., and E. Schwartz, "Evaluating Natural Resource Investments," *Journal of Business* (January 1985), 135–157.

4. Cox, J., S. Ross, and M. Rubinstein, "Option Pricing: A Simplified Approach," *Journal of Financial Economics* 7 (September 1979), 229–263.

5. Cox, J., and M. Rubinstein, *Options Markets*. Englewood Cliffs, N.J.: Prentice-Hall, 1985.

6. Geske, R., "The Valuation of Options," *Journal of Financial Economics* 7 (1979) 63–82.

7. Kester, W. C., "Todays Options for Tomorrows Growth," *Harvard Business Review* (March–April 1984), 153–161.

8. Majd, S., and R. Pindyck, "Time to Build, Option Value and Investment Decisions," *Journal of Financial Economics* 18 (1987), 7–27.

9. Mason, S., and R. C. Merton, "The Role of Contingent Claims Analysis in Corporate Finance," in *Recent Advances in Corporate Finance* (E. Altman and M. Subrahmanyam, eds.). Irwin, 1985.

10. McDonald, R., and D. Siegel, "Investment and the Valuation of Firms When There Is an Option to Shut Down," *International Economic Review* XXVI (June 1985), 331–349.

11. McDonald, R., and D. Seigel, "The Value of Waiting to Invest," *Quarterly Journal of Economics* (November 1986), 707–727.

12. McDonald, R., and D. Seigel, "Option Pricing When the Underlying Asset Earns a Below-Equilibrium Rate of Return: A Note," *Journal of Finance* 39 (March 1984), 261–265.

13. Myers, S., "Determinants of Corporate Borrowing," *Journal of Financial Economics* 5, 2 (1977), 147–175.

14. Myers, S., and Majd, S., "Calculating Abandonment Value Using Option Pricing Theory," Working Paper No. 1462-83, Sloan School of Management, MIT, Cambridge, MA.

15. Paddock, J., D. Seigel, and J. Smith, "Option Valuation of Claims on Physical Assets: The Case of Offshore Petroleum Leases," MIT Energy Lab, Working Paper No. MIT-EL 83-005WP, February 1983.

16. Ritchken, P., *Options: Theory, Strategy and Applications*: Glenview, IL: Scott Foresman & Co., 1987.

17. Trigeorgis, L., and S. P. Mason, "Valuing Managerial Operating Flexibility," Harvard Business School, June 1985.

18. Trigeorgis, L., "Valuing Real Investment Opportunities: An Options Approach to Strategic Capital Budgeting," Ph.D. Dissertation, Harvard University, 1986.

A CONCEPTUAL OPTIONS FRAMEWORK FOR CAPITAL BUDGETING

Lenos Trigeorgis*

I. INTRODUCTION

Recent studies of the practice of corporate management verify that there continues to be a discrepancy between traditional finance theory and corporate practice. Many managers, dissatisfied with the current state of capital budgeting, are often willing to overrule conventional net present value (NPV) analysis or other discounted cash flow (DCF) techniques

*College of Management, University of Massachusetts, Boston.

I am grateful to W. Carl Kester, Scott P. Mason, and Stewart C. Myers who, through their writings and discussions, left their marks on the following pages. Any errors are my own.

Advances in Futures and Options Research, Vol. 3, pages 145–167.

because they see additional value in projects beyond that resulting from directly measurable cash flows.

Specifically, many practitioners recognize two aspects of extra value that are not adequately addressed in a conventional NPV analysis: (1) the "operating flexibility" of a project that is simply a collection of options enabling management to make or revise decisions at some future time (e.g., to defer, expand, or abandon a project early), and (2) the "strategic value" of a project resulting from its interdependencies with future, follow-up investments and from competitive interaction.

Several academics have also recognized that traditional capital budgeting techniques may often misvalue projects due to the presence of such strategic interactions and managerial operating options. For example, Myers [20] notes the inability of conventional DCF techniques to capture the time-series interactions among contingent investments. Kester [12] uses Myers' initial concept of looking at growth investment opportunities as options on real assets to explore qualitatively the "strategic" and competitive interaction aspects of real projects. Trigeorgis and Mason [33] use options-based contingent claims analysis to practically quantify the value of managerial operating flexibility embedded in a variety of operating options. All agree that corporate finance theory needs to be extended by using option valuation techniques to deal with real investment opportunities and bridge the existing gap between traditional financial theory and strategic planning.

Other approaches that have been proposed to overcome the shortcomings of static NPV analysis such as simulation (Hertz [8]) and decision tree analysis (DTA), as applied to capital budgeting by Magee [13], basically stumble on the problem of determining the appropriate discount rate.[1] The fundamental problem, as we will see next, lies in the valuation of investment opportunities whose claims are not symmetric. In general, asymmetric claims on the value of a project do not have the same discount rate as the project value itself. More specifically, using a constant risk-adjusted discount rate is incorrect if uncertainty is not resolved continuously at a constant rate over time as is the case with growth or compound investment opportunities where early stages of a project are contingent (or can be seen as options) on follow-up stages. It is time to recognize that managerial flexibility creates several interacting real options in most investment projects that may add value due to their inherent asymmetry.[2]

II. NPV AND MANAGERIAL FLEXIBILITY/ASYMMETRY

The basic inadequacy of the NPV or other DCF approaches to capital budgeting is that they ignore, or cannot properly capture, management's

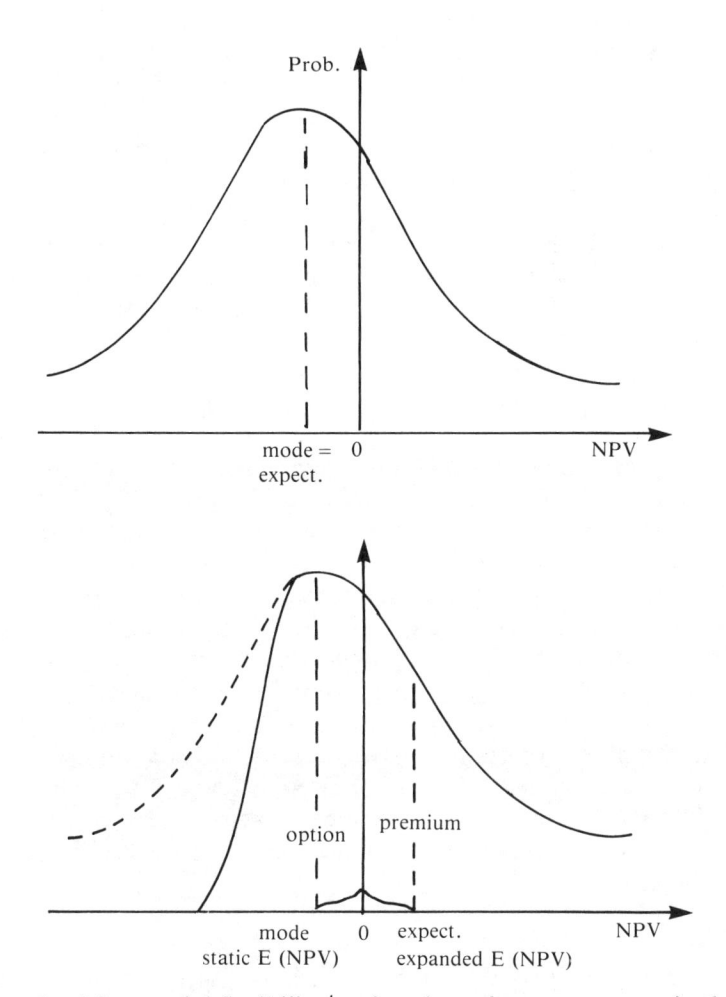

Figure 1. Managerial flexibility/options introduce asymmetry in the probability distribution of NPV. (Top) Symmetric distribution of NPV in the absence of managerial flexibility. The (static) expected NPV coincides with the mode (or most likely estimate). (Bottom) Asymmetric (skewed to the right) distribution of NPV caused by managerial flexibility (e.g., options to defer, abandon). The (expanded) expected value exceeds the mode (= static expected NPV):   expanded NPV = static NPV + "option premium."

flexibility to adapt and revise later decisions. Traditional NPV in particular makes implicit assumptions concerning an "expected scenario" of cash flows and presumes management's commitment to a certain "operating strategy." Typically, an *expected* pattern of cash flows over a *prespecified* life is discounted at a risk-adjusted rate to arrive at the project's NPV. Treating projects as *independent* investment opportunities, an *immediate* accept or reject decision is then made by accepting all projects for which NPV is positive. In effect, it is as if management makes at the outset an irrevocable commitment to an "operating strategy" — e.g., to take the project immediately and operate it continuously until the end of its prespecified expected useful life — from which it cannot depart regardless of whether nature remains faithful to or deviates from its expected scenario of cash flows.

In the real world of uncertainty and competitive interactions, however, the realization of cash flows will probably differ from what management originally expected. As new information arrives and uncertainty about future cash flows is gradually resolved, management may find that various projects allow it varying degrees of flexibility to depart from and revise the operating strategy it originally anticipated to follow. For example, management may be able to defer, expand, abandon, or in various other ways alter a project at different stages during its useful life.

Management's flexibility to adapt its future actions depending on the future environment introduces an asymmetry or skewness in the probability distribution of NPV that expands the investment opportunity's true value by improving its upside potential while limiting downside losses relative to management's initial expectations (see Figure 1).[3] This asymmetry necessitates using an expanded NPV rule reflecting both components of an opportunity's value, the traditional (static or passive) NPV of direct cash flows and a premium for the flexibility inherent in its operating options, i.e.,

$$\text{Expanded NPV} = \text{Static (Passive) NPV} + \text{Option Premium.}$$

Note that such an "expanded NPV" framework does not seek to do away with traditional (static) NPV but rather uses it as a necessary (although not necessarily the only) value component.

III.   TOWARD A CONCEPTUAL REAL OPTIONS FRAMEWORK

As we just pointed out, the operating flexibility and strategic value aspects of various projects cannot be properly captured by traditional DCF techniques due to their discretionary asymmetric nature and dependence on future events that are uncertain at the time of the initial decision. These important aspects can, nevertheless, be properly analyzed by thinking of investment opportunities as being bundles of options on real assets (or "real options") through the options-based technique of contingent claims analysis (CCA) (see, for instance, Trigeorgis and Mason [33]). Just as the owner of an American call option on a financial asset has the right — but not the obligation — to acquire the asset by paying a prespecified price (the "exercise price") on or before a predetermined date (the "exercise or maturity date"), and he will exercise the option if and when it is to his best interest to do so, so will the holder of options on real assets. The owner of a discretionary investment opportunity has the right — but not the obligation — to acquire the (gross) present value of expected cash flows by making an investment outlay on or before the anticipated date when the investment opportunity will cease to exist.[4] Thus, there exists a close analogy between such real investment opportunities (or real options) and call options on stocks (as shown in Figure 2).[5,6]

Even if no other associated real options exist, the *flexibility to defer* or decide when to initiate the project, as may be provided by a lease to drill for oil, the property rights to extract mineral reserves, or a patent to develop a new product, has a positive value even if immediate undertaking of the project has a negative (static) NPV of cash flows. Such flexibility gives management the right to wait and make the investment (i.e., exercise the option) only if (for instance, the price of the oil or the mineral rises, or the demand for the new product develops enough so that) project value turns out to exceed the necessary outlay, without imposing any symmetric obligation to invest and lose if the opposite scenario occurs.[7]

More generally, when other real options in addition to the option to defer the investment are present, a discretionary investment opportunity can be seen as a call option on a collection or portfolio consisting of the project value, V, and other real call or put options. For example, the *option to expand* the scale of a project by e% by making an additional investment I′ can be formally seen as analogous to a call option to acquire e% of the

Stock Call Option	*Real Option*
Current Value of Stock	— (Gross) PV of Expected Cash Flows
Exercise Price	— Investment Cost
Time to Expiration	— Time until Opportunity disappears
Stock Value Uncertainty	— Project Value Uncertainty
Riskless Interest Rate	— Riskless Interest Rate

Figure 2. Comparison between call options on stocks and real options.

(gross) project value (the underlying "asset") with exercise price of I'. If market conditions are uncertain, management may, for example, find it preferable to build excess production capacity enabling it to produce at a faster rate, on a larger scale, or for a longer period if, as uncertainty resolves itself, it turns out that its product is more enthusiastically received in the market than originally anticipated.

Similarly, the *option to contract* the scale of a project's operation by c% to save on certain preplanned advertising or maintenance expenditures of magnitude I'' can be seen as a put option on c% of the project value with exercise price I''. For instance, management may find it justifiable to build a plant with lower initial construction costs and higher maintenance expenditures in order to acquire the flexibility to contract operations by cutting down on maintenance costs if the product turns out to do worse than initially expected. Management may also have the *flexibility to temporarily shut down* production (or not to operate) in any given year if cash revenues are not adequate to cover the variable costs of operating in that year; one may thus look at operation in each year as a call option on that year's cash revenue with exercise price the variable cost of operating.[8]

Management may also have the flexibility to terminate a project in its current use earlier than initially expected by switching to its future best alternative use (switching between alternative inputs/outputs) or selling its assets in a second-hand market for their "salvage value." Consider, for example, the decision to build a chemical plant involving the choice between a plant with lower initial construction costs that can use only a single input (e.g., electricity) to produce a single output (e.g., vitamins), and an otherwise identical plant with somewhat higher costs (and higher resale value) but allowing the flexibility to receive diverse inputs (either electricity or coal) to produce a variety of outputs (say vitamins or aspirins). Even though the first plant may have a higher (static) NPV, management may find the second plant more desirable as market conditions change and the relative prices of inputs, outputs, or the plant resale value fluctuate as it may switch to a cheaper input, a more profitable output, or sell the plant's assets in a second-hand market. This *option to switch use* can be seen as a put option on the opportunity's value (in its current use) with exercise price its value in the best alternative use. Furthermore, management may also have the *option to abandon* a project during construction by "defaulting" on subsequent preplanned investment cost "installments" if a coming "installment" exceeds the value from continuing the project. This option to abandon can be looked at either as a compound call option on the opportunity with exercise prices the set of individual investment "installments" or alternatively as a put option on the opportunity with exercise price the cumulative value of subsequent cost savings.[9]

Most of the important payoffs of managerial flexibility can be captured by combining these simple options as building blocks. If many such real options are present simultaneously then the total investment opportunity can be seen as a collection of such real call and put options and can be, in most cases, analyzed numerically via a more involved contingent claims analysis.[10] But even in complex cases when numerical routines are not available, an options-based conceptual framework can offer significant payoffs to qualitative understanding.

IV. DEVELOPING A NEW PROJECT CLASSIFICATION

In practice, firms often classify projects according to risk or functional characteristics (e.g., replacement or new product introduction) to simplify the capital budgeting process. These schemes are incomplete, however, in that they overlook the option aspects of projects described earlier. To motivate a new options-based classification and be better able to appreciate the various elements that it encompasses, let us first start from simple NPV and gradually build up the framework highlighting one aspect at a time. After introducing the flexibility to defer or abandon a project, we will then focus on the concept of compoundness first within and later among projects, and finally highlight interactions introduced by competition.

To see things in a broader perspective, let us first distinguish between two basic types of decision problems that a manager may face: (1) "games against nature," in which the manager's problem is to optimize in the face of random fluctuations in the (gross) value of cash flows from the investment, V (mostly applicable to fully competitive markets), and (2) "strategic games against competition," in which the manager's investment decisions are made with the explicit recognition that they would invite competitive reaction that would in turn impact the value of the investment opportunity (generally found in oligopolistic markets).

A. Static (Passive) NPV

Traditional NPV addresses decision problems of the first type since it typically ignores strategic competitive interactions. But even in dealing with "games against nature" passive NPV is limited in that it implicitly presumes that all decisions are unequivocally taken up front as if management did not have the flexibility to review its original plans in response to nature's deviation from its expected scenario of cash flows. As explained earlier, in the absence of such managerial flexibility or real options, static NPV would be correct: management would make an *immediate* investment outlay, I (considering for now the simplest case of a *single* one-time expenditure), only in return for a higher present value of expected cash inflows, V. The difference, i.e., NPV ($= V - I$) is of course the current value of the *investment*, provided the manager had no other choice but to "take it (immediately) or leave it."

B. Opportunity to Defer

What should really be of interest, however, is not the value of immediate investment per se, but rather the value of the investment *opportunity*. As explained earlier, in a world of uncertainty where nature can play games (V may fluctuate randomly) the opportunity to invest can be more valuable than immediate investment since it allows management the flexibility to defer undertaking the investment until circumstances turn most favorable or back out altogether if they turn unsatisfactory. The investment *opportunity* is thus formally *equivalent* to a call *option* on V with exercise price the one-time investment outlay I. The value of this opportunity to invest therefore exceeds the NPV of cash flows from immediate investment by the value of the flexibility to defer the investment. Such an investment opportunity may thus be economically desirable even if the investment itself may have a negative NPV (i.e., $V < I$). It would therefore be very useful to distinguish between opportunities that allow management the flexibility to defer their undertaking (such as projects with patents or leases) and projects that do not (such as an expiring offer to immediately expand capacity to meet extra demand by an impatient client).

Even if management lacks the flexibility to defer the undertaking of a project when faced with an immediate accept/reject decision, it may still have the flexibility to abandon a once undertaken project for its "salvage value" before the end of its expected life if it turns out to perform worse than expected.[11] The flexibility to abandon a project early should therefore be explicitly accounted for in the investment decision whenever appropriate.

C. Intraproject Compoundness

Let us, for the moment, suppress the flexibility to defer undertaking the project or abandon it for its salvage value. Consider, however, the investment outlay, I, no longer as a single one-time expenditure at the outset but rather as a sequence of investment "installments" starting immediately and extending throughout (much of) the life of the investment (e.g., annual maintenance expenditures during the life of a machine or plant). In such a case the investment is actually a compound option where an earlier investment cost installment represents the exercise price required to acquire a subsequent option to continue operating the project until the next installment comes due, and so on. This is the idea of compoundness within the same project — an intraproject interaction. If managerial flexibility is reintroduced, then intraproject compoundness highlights a series of distinct points in time — just before a subsequent investment installment comes due — when the project might be better discontinued if it turns out not to perform satisfactorily. DCF techniques and particularly NPV that deal with the sequence of investment installments simply by subtracting their present value from that of the expected cash inflows or even by including all but the first investment installment costs in the so called "net cash flows" clearly undervalue such compound investments.

D. Interproject Compoundness

Let us now return to the simple case of a single one-time investment outlay at the start of each project. Consider, however, the case of contingent projects where undertaking the first is a prerequisite for the next or provides the opportunity to acquire at maturity the benefits of the new investment by making a new outlay (e.g., a research project provides at completion the opportunity to acquire the revenues of the developed product upon incurring a production outlay). This idea of interproject compoundness is remarkably similar in structure when looking at a sequence of projects to the intraproject compoundness described above (see Figure 3), with the difference that each "investment installment" now provides the opportunity to begin a new project rather than continue the

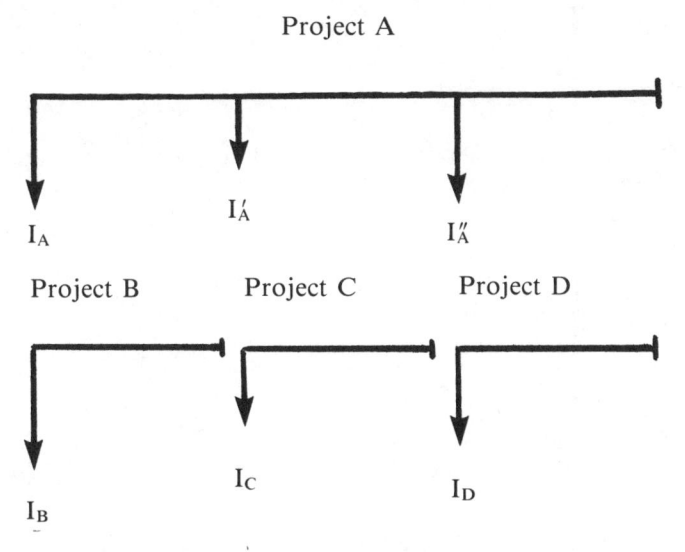

Figure 3. (Top) Intraproject compoundness. (A single project A with many investment installments, I_A, I_A', I_A''). (Bottom) Interproject compoundness. (A sequence of many single-outlay interdependent projects B, C, D).

same one. Compoundness between projects is an interaction of strategic importance since it may justify the undertaking of projects with negative NPV of direct cash flows on the basis of opening up subsequent future investment opportunities.

E. Competitive Interaction

Another dimension to the valuation of investment opportunities is introduced by competitive interaction. Here we may distinguish between two forms of analysis depending on the type of interaction between competitors. If the impact of competitive entry can be considered exogenous and pertains basically to the threat of capturing part of the value of the investment away from the incumbent firm, then its management still faces an "optimization problem" — although a more complex one — in that it

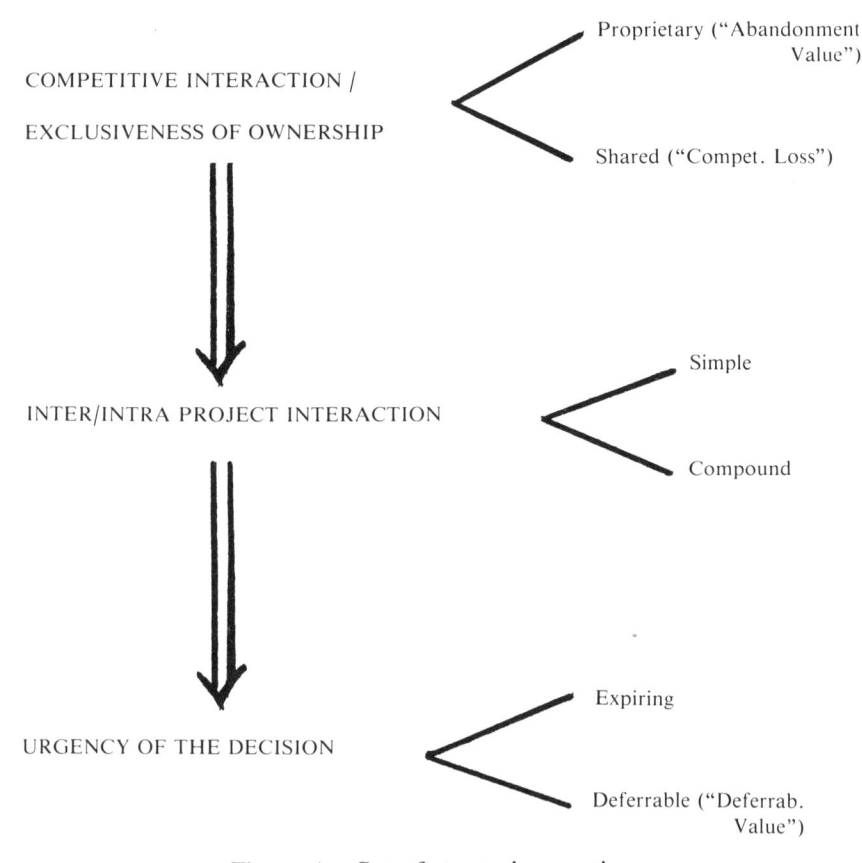

Figure 4. Set of strategic questions.

has to incorporate the impact of competition in its own investment decision but can ignore any reciprocal effects of that decision on competitors' actions. If, however, each competitor's investment decisions are contingent upon and sensitive to the other's moves then a more complex "game-theoretic" treatment becomes necessary. Investing earlier than one otherwise would to preempt competitive entry is a simple case of such "strategic games against competition". The absence or presence (and type) of competitive interaction can therefore serve as another "cut" for classifying and valuing real investment opportunities. We are thus led to propose the set of "strategic questions" for corporate management presented in Figure 4.

V. "STRATEGIC QUESTIONS" FOR CAPITAL BUDGETING ANALYSIS

The first question that management must address in the evaluation process refers to the *exclusiveness of option ownership* and the *effect of competition* on the firm's ability to fully appropriate for itself the option value. If the firm retains an exclusive right as to whether and when to invest, unaffected by competitive initiatives, then its investment opportunity is classified as a *proprietary option*. Investment opportunities with high barriers of entry for competitors such as a patent for developing a product having no close substitutes, or a unique knowhow of a technological process, or market conditions that competitors are unable to duplicate for at least some time, are just a few examples of such real proprietary options. In such cases, management may have the flexibility to abandon a project early (i.e., the project has additional "abandonment value"), or even temporarily interrupt the project's operation in certain "unprofitable" periods. [12] If, however, competitors share the right to exercise and may be able to take part (or all) of the project's value away from the firm, then the option is *shared*. [13] Shared real options can be seen as jointly held opportunities of a number of competing firms or of a whole industry, and can be exercised by any one of their collective owners. Such shared real options are, for example, the opportunity to introduce a new product unprotected by possible introduction of close substitutes, or to penetrate a new geographic market without barriers to competitive entry. The loss in value suffered by an incumbent firm as a result of competitive interaction when a competitive firm exercises its shared rights will be subsequently called "competitive loss."

The second question concerns *inter- (or intra-) project interactions*, specifically compoundness. [14] Is an investment opportunity valuable in and of itself or is it a prerequisite for subsequent investment opportunities? If the opportunity is a real option leading upon exercise to further discretionary investment opportunities or an option whose payout is another option then it is classified as *compound*. Such real options on options may have a more "strategic" impact on a firm and are more complicated to analyze; they can no longer be looked at as independent investments, but rather as links in a chain of interrelated projects the earlier of which are prerequisites for the ones to follow. A research and development (R&D) investment, a lease for an undeveloped tract with potential oil reserves, and an acquisition of an unrelated company are just a few examples of such compound options that may be undertaken not just for their direct cash flows but also (or perhaps primarily) for the new opportunities that they may open up (a new technological breakthrough, large reserves of oil, or access to a new market). On the other hand, if the project can be evaluated as a stand-alone investment opportunity, it is called a *simple option*. Such independent opportunities whose value upon exercise is limited only to the underlying project in and of itself are, for instance, standard replacement or maintenance projects.

The last "strategic question" refers to the *urgency of the decision*. Management must distinguish between those projects that need an immediate accept/reject decision, i.e., *expiring* investment opportunities, and those that management can defer for future action, i.e., *deferrable* options. We will subsequently refer to the value of the flexibility to defer undertaking a project as the "deferrability value" of the project. Deferrable projects require a more extensive analysis of the optimal timing of investment since management must compare the net value of taking the project today with the net value of taking it at all possible future years. Thus, management must analyze the relative benefits and costs of waiting in association with other strategic considerations (e.g., the threat of competitive entry in a shared-deferrable option may justify early capital commitment for preemptive purposes). This mode of analysis leads us to the real options classification scheme shown in Figure 5. [15]

This eight-fork classification scheme is intended to focus management's attention on the important characteristics of investment opportunities as options on real assets as described above. And although the distinctions between the various categories may at times be more relative rather than absolute, most real investment opportunities including strategic can find a place in one of the eight branches of the options-based classification tree. For example, routine maintenance could be classified and analyzed as a proprietary–simple–expiring (P–S–E) option, plant modernization as proprietary–simple–deferrable, bidding for purchase of assets as shared–simple–expiring, a new product introduction with close substitutes as shared–simple–deferrable, an immediate franchise offer as proprietary–compound–expiring, research and development of a unique product as

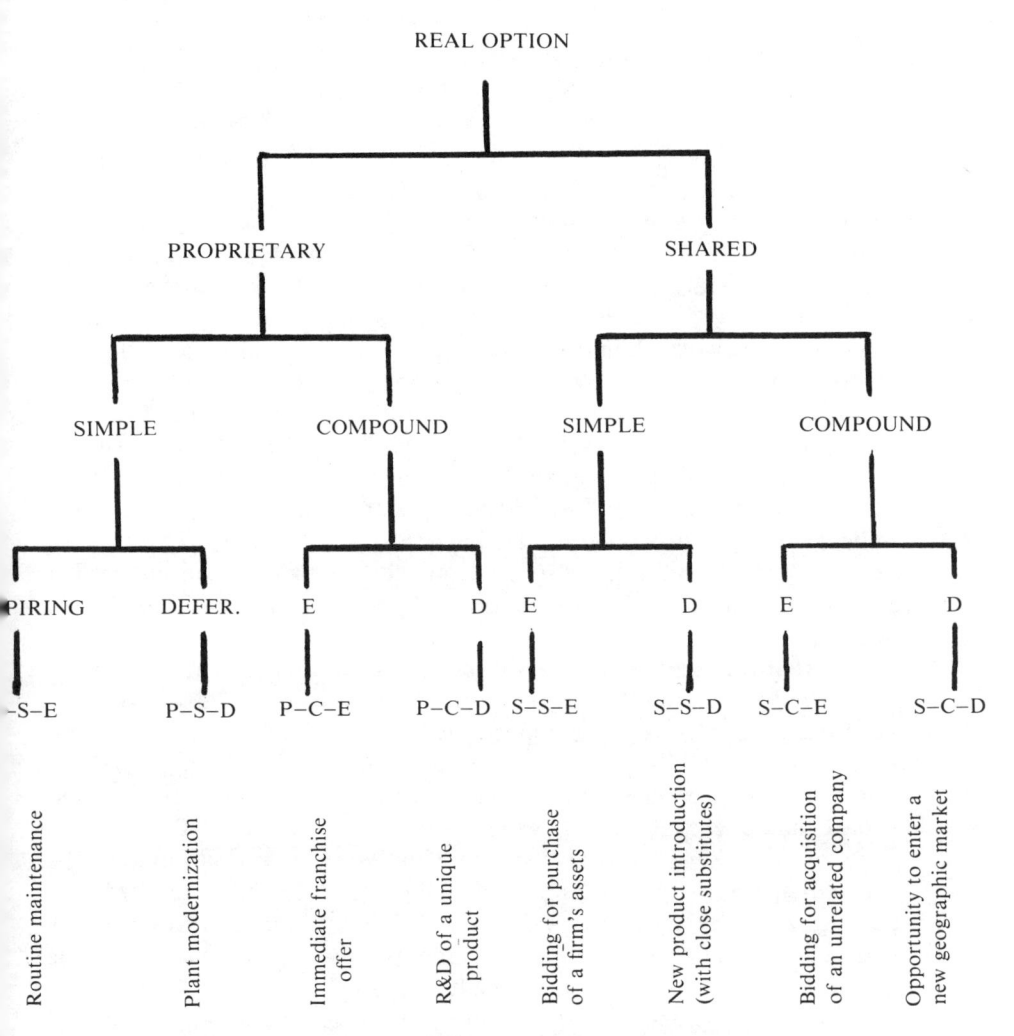

Figure 5. Proposed real options classification.

proprietary–compound–deferrable, bidding for the acquistion of an unrelated company as shared–compound–expiring, and the opportunity to enter a new geographic market as shared–compound–deferrable.

It is worth noting that under this real options classification scheme conventional (static) NPV investments are properly seen as a special case under the leftmost branch of proprietary–simple–expiring options since such investments are typically evaluated as if they were exclusively owned (hence "proprietary"), independent (hence "simple"), and immediate (hence "expiring") opportunities.

VI.   OPTIONS CLASSIFICATION, OPERATING STRATEGY, AND VALUE COMPONENTS

The options-based classification scheme also helps uncover management's implicit "operating strategy" as well as the different value components comprising the "option premium" part of an investment opportunity's "expanded NPV." Figure 6 shows different "operating strategies" and the corresponding real option value ("expanded NPV") for various simple investment categories under the options classification scheme. Again, the proposed framework should be seen as a practical aid in recognizing and understanding some frequently recurring options combinations.

In Figure 6, Part A shows the basic operating strategy assumed (appropriately so in the absence of managerial flexibility) by conventional (static) DCF techniques: management starts the project (indicated by "↓") at time 0 and operates it continuously (indicated by a solid line "—") until the end (indicated by "↑") of its preestimated expected useful life (T). The value of the real opportunity in this case is adequately captured by the static NPV component (since there is no "option premium" in the absence of real options).

In Part B different operating strategies may be found preferable when circumstances turn out differently from what was originally expected. In a proprietary–simple–expiring opportunity the possibility of abandonment at an earlier time ($T' < T$) may become valuable. The value of the real opportunity would then be its value if no departure from the expected scenario and operating strategy were to occur (i.e., the static NPV) plus the value of abandonment. In a shared–simple–expiring real option, the project is again taken immediately but competitive entry (denoted by " ↯ ") may cause erosion in project value, so the option premium may actually have negative value (competitive loss). In a proprietary–simple–deferrable opportunity the option premium results from management's flexibility to defer the project (unit T_1) and possibly from its additional incremental ability to abandon it early, i.e., "option premium" = "deferrability value" + "abandonment value."

Finally, in a shared–simple–deferrable investment opportunity the value of the real option ("expanded NPV") is

static NPV + ("deferrability value" – "competitive loss").

If this "expanded NPV" turns positive before the investment opportunity expires, the project should be undertaken. Exactly when, however, would depend on the trade-off between "deferrability value" and "competitive loss": the longer management defers the investment, the higher its deferrability value, but also the greater the risk of competitive loss.

OPTION CLASSIFIC.	OPERATING STRATEGY	REAL OPTION VALUE

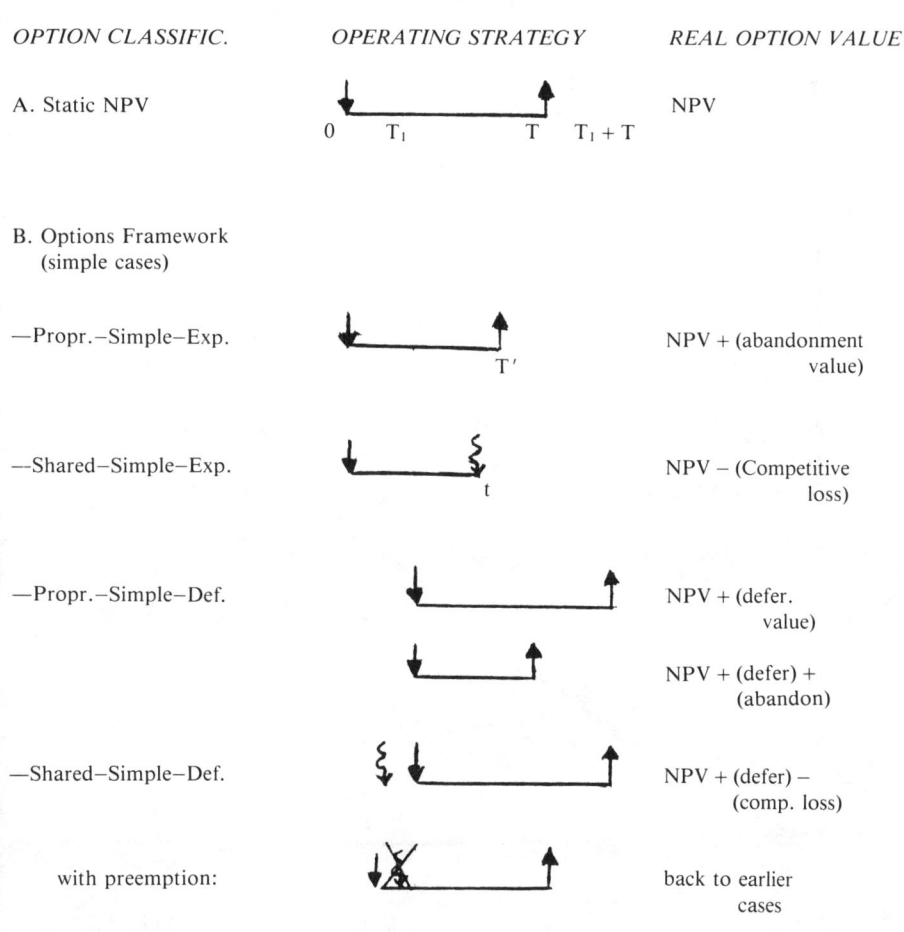

A. Static NPV — NPV

B. Options Framework (simple cases)

—Propr.–Simple–Exp. — NPV + (abandonment value)

—Shared–Simple–Exp. — NPV − (Competitive loss)

—Propr.–Simple–Def. — NPV + (defer. value)

NPV + (defer) + (abandon)

—Shared–Simple–Def. — NPV + (defer) − (comp. loss)

with preemption: — back to earlier cases

Figure 6. Option classification, "operating strategies," and components of real option value. T, expected project life; T_1, period to defer (e.g., duration of patent or lease); ↓, management's decision to start the project; ↑, management's decision to end the project; ≨, competitive entry (out of management's control).

Figure 7, based on an analogy with call options, is intended to give a simplified visual impression of the various components of value for the last case of the shared–simple–deferrable option. It shows total real option value (expanded NPV), R, as a function of (gross) project value, V, and is based on the assumption that a competitor's entry causes a drop in project value from V to V′, with the exact magnitude of the drop (which may, for instance, be due to loss of market share to the competitor) depending on market structure characteristics. This project value drop translates into a

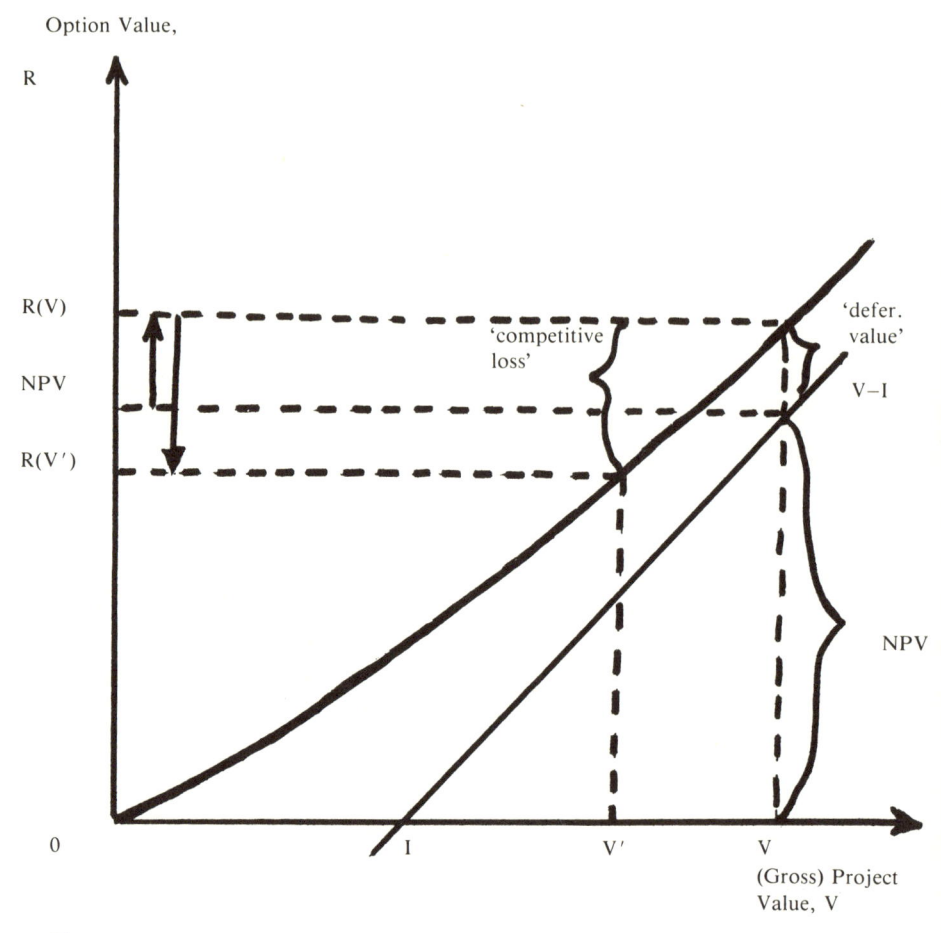

Figure 7.   Value components for a shared–simple–deferrable investment
opportunity.

smaller damage in real option value attributed to competition from R(V) to
R(V′) (the "competitive loss").

Notice that the real option value exceeds the static NPV component of
project value (given by the vertical distance to the 45 degree line which
equals V − I), and is nonnegative even if the project's NPV is negative. The
"deferrability value" component of the option premium is here represented
by the vertical distance equivalent to R(V) − NPV. Observe that either the
"deferrability value" or the "competitive loss" parts of the option premium
may dominate, depending on the severity of the impact of competitive entry
on (gross) project value.

VII. IMPLICATIONS FOR CAPITAL BUDGETING

Viewing opportunities to invest as collections of options on real assets provides new insight into investment decision making and enables managers to draw several important implications for capital budgeting, some of which may provide direct challenge to established popular beliefs.

1. An "expanded NPV" analysis. Management should broaden its valuation horizon by moving toward an "expanded NPV" criterion in order to capture the flexibility of operating strategies it may implement as well as other strategic interactions. Under the expanded framework, the total economic desirability of an investment opportunity is explicitly seen as the sum of its static NPV of directly measurable expected cash flows and of the option premium reflecting the value of managerial operating flexibility and strategic interactions. The incremental contribution of (and any interactions among) these additional sources of value (e.g., "deferrability value," "abandonment value," "competitive loss") comprising the "option premium" should be added to the static NPV, so that an investment opportunity is now desirable if

$$\text{expanded NPV} = \text{static NPV} + \text{option premium} > 0.$$

By looking at real investment opportunities through this expanded conceptual options valuation lens managers can now better appreciate that:

(a)   traditional (static) NPV may indeed undervalue projects (by suppressing the "option premium" or flexibility component of total value), as previously suggested by Kester [12] and other critics, mainly from corporate strategy;

(b)   it may be justified to accept projects with negative (static) NPV if the value of managerial flexibility (i.e., the option premium) exceeds the negative NPV of the project's direct expected cash flows; [16]

(c)   the value of managerial flexibility — and the extent to which managers should make investment outlays in excess of what is dictated by traditional standards — can now be quantified through options pricing, unlike other suggestions by previous critics.

2.   The options framework also indicates that, other things remaining the same, the value of managerial flexibility ("option premium"):

(a)   is higher in more uncertain environments, again a direct consequence of the asymmetry it introduces. (This beneficial impact of risk on real option value implies that in more uncertain environments real compound options, having a higher option premium component, are relatively more valuable than, say, simple deferrable investment opportunities, which in turn are more valuable than simple expiring projects);

(b)   may be higher during periods of high real interest rates;

(c)   may be higher for investment opportunities of longer duration. (This implies that in the special case of a proprietary real option without any form of "dividends" — such as competitive arrivals or intermediate cash flows — management may find it optimal to wait until close to maturity before deciding whether to exercise its real option or not. [17] The value implicit in having control over the timing of exercising such a proprietary real option may help explain the striving by many firms to achieve a dominant competitive position in their industry.)

Note that, contrary to conventional popular belief, higher uncertainty, greater interest rates, or more time before undertaking a project (though implying more distant cash flows) are not necessarily hurting the value of an investment opportunity. Although all these factors do certainly damage its (static) NPV component as traditionally recognized — their negative impact shown by down-pointing arrows in Figure 8 — they may nevertheless substantially enhance managerial flexibility and bear the opposite effect on the "option premium" component of value — the possibility of a positive impact indicated by upward-pointing arrows. Thus, the overall impact of these factors is not clear-cut a priori, although it *may* prove beneficial for the total value of an investment opportunity or "expanded NPV" (if it increases the "option premium" more than it reduces the "static NPV" component of value).

3.   The presence of competitive interactions in shared options may justify earlier exercise. [18]

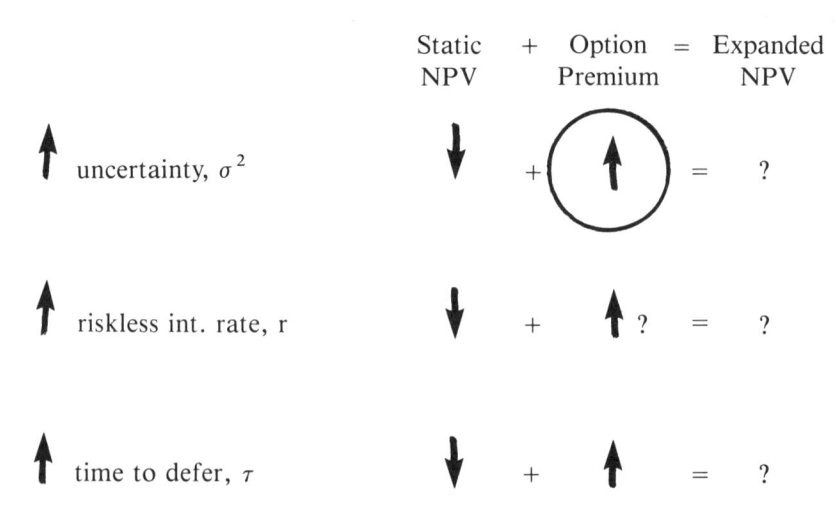

Figure 8.   Impact of various factors on investment opportunity value
components.

As Kester [10] first recognized, competitive actions may cause erosion in a real option's value that may not be avoidable simply by selling the option to others (as most real options may not be tradeable) so that an early preemptive investment may at times be the only available response to prevent such undesirable competitive value losses. The effect of such competitive erosions in real option value in a preemptive equilibrium setting may be thought of as analogous to the effect of dividends on the value of a call option in justifying early exercise. [19]

In general, management may find it justifiable to exercise relatively early (a) when its real option is shared with competitors and the anticipated loss in project value due to competitive entry is large and can be preempted, (b) when competitive pressure is intense, (c) when project uncertainty and, generally, interest rates are low, and (d) when the "competitive loss" preempted exceeds the "deferrability value" sacrificed by early exercise, or more generally when the value of managerial flexibility (or option premium) is low relative to the (static) NPV of the project.

VIII. CONCLUSION

This paper sought to describe a general conceptual framework for analyzing investment opportunities seen as collections of options on real assets, with special emphasis on the operating flexibility and strategic/competitive dimensions that are left out of conventional discounted cash flow analyses. A new project classification scheme and strategic questions for capital budgeting analysis have been proposed, and their use in helping uncover management's implicit operating strategy and the various option value components has been described. Our framework is intended as a practical aid in recognizing and understanding the frequently encountered combinations of real options.

The options-based framework presented here promises to offer an expanded and unifying evaluation approach for all real investment decisions by integrating capital budgeting and strategic planning under the single roof of value maximization. Moreover, since the options methodology has been used already in the valuation of most financial securities, options-based analysis has the potential not only to integrate all real investment decisions ("strategic" with "normal"), but also to marry the real with the financing decisions of the firm under a common paradigm.

NOTES

1.   In decision analysis the tree is built forward using the actual probabilities and expected rate of return; thus, when moving backward to calculate project value, it is inconsistent to

discount at the riskless rate of return and the appropriate discount rate remains indeterminable.

In option pricing, however, the no-arbitrage hedge attainable under continuous trading allows a solution that is independent of risk attitudes and that therefore may be conveniently obtained in a world of risk neutrality. In essence, we may obtain the solution by building forward an equivalent tree using "risk-neutral" probabilities so that when moving backward we may consistently discount the expected terminal cash flows at the risk-free rate. Thus, in its discrete form options pricing can be seen as a special though economically corrected version of DTA that recognizes open market opportunities to trade and borrow (see Trigeorgis and Mason [33]).

2.   Option pricing techniques can simultaneously compute the correct discount rate and determine the optimal exercise of operating options inherent in a project.

3.   In the absence of such managerial flexibility, the probability distribution of NPV would be reasonably symmetric, in which case the (static) expected NPV (or mean of the symmetric distribution) would coincide with its mode or most likely estimate (see top part of Figure 1). When managerial flexibility (such as the options to defer or abandon a project early) is significant, however, by basically providing a protection against (or adaptation to) future events turning out differently from what management expected at the outset, it introduces a truncation (typically at or below the mode) so that the resulting actual distribution is skewed to the right (bottom part of Figure 1). The true expected value of such an asymmetric distribution — which we will refer to as the "expanded" expected NPV, "expanded" in that it incorporates managerial flexibility — exceeds its mode — which is the same as the mode of the corresponding symmetric distribution and hence the static expected NPV — by an "option premium" reflecting the value of managerial flexibility.

4.   The "investment outlay" does not necessarily have to be a single one-time investment, but may actually be a series of investment "installments."

5.   The value of a call option on a stock is of course higher, other things constant, the greater the stock price and the lower the required exercise price, the greater the volatility of stock returns (since it increases the upside profit potential while the downside risk is limited due to the option asymmetry), the higher the risk-free interest rate (since it lowers the present value of the future exercise price), and the longer the time to maturity (both through a higher total uncertainty of stock returns and a lower present value of the exercise cost). For a more detailed exposition of option pricing see Cox and Rubinstein [4] or Brealey and Myers [2, Chapter 20].

6.   Although the analogy between stock call options and real options is a close one, it is not exact. Some of the main differences that we incorporate in our framework later are (1) stock call options are proprietary (exclusively owned) while real options may often be shared with competitors; (2) unlike stock call options, real options are generally not tradeable (which may motivate early exercise to preempt competitors); (3) real options may often be interdependent (compound options).

7.   The option to initiate has been examined by Tourinho [30] in valuing reserves of natural resources, by McDonald and Siegel [19], and by Siegel, Smith, and Paddock [27] in valuing offshore petroleum leases. The latter found, for example, that longer leases allowing more flexibility as to when, if at all, to develop the petroleum tracts are more valuable, especially when oil prices are highly uncertain. Majd and Pindyck [14] recently value the option to delay sequential construction (or time to build).

8.   The option to shut down has been analyzed by McDonald and Siegel [18] using quantitative option pricing techniques.

9.   The option to abandon has first been treated by Robichek and Van Horen [25] using simulation techniques. Recently Myers and Majd [21] employ quantitative option pricing methodology to analyze the same option seen as formally equivalent to an American put on a dividend-paying stock.

The problem of switching between inputs or outputs has not yet been solved explicitly, although some related work has appeared in the literature. Margrabe [15], for example, values an option to exchange one asset for another. Stultz [29] analyzes options on the maximum (or minimum) of two risky assets, which incidentally provides an approach for valuing opportunities allowing the flexibility to choose upon exercise among two mutually exclusive uses (or related risky streams of cash flows). A good example would be the opportunity to buy a piece of land that can be used either for a house or office space. Recently, Kensinger [9] examines the option to exchange [convert] one set of commodities for [into] another.

10.   The simultaneous presence of several such real options may give rise to (typically negative) interaction effects (such as between the options to expand and abandon), necessitating the use of options-based numerical analysis techniques for solving the more complex problems. See Trigeorgis [32] for a numerical analysis of projects with multiple interacting real options.

11.   "Salvage value" or value in the best alternative use may come from the value of expected cash flows from switching use (or inputs/outputs), a market price for which the project may sell in a second-hand market or, in situations where subsequent expenditures are due, the value of subsequent cost savings from discontinuing the project.

12.   To simplify exposition we will ignore for the rest of the paper the option (not) to operate, as well as the options to expand/contract the scale of operations.

13.   As pointed out earlier, shared options can be differentiated further depending on whether the impact of competition is taken as exogenous or causes endogenous strategic counteractions.

14.   There are, of course, other forms of interproject dependence such as "mutually exclusive" projects where undertaking of one project precludes undertaking the other, or "synergistic" projects that enhance each other's cash flows when taken together; we will choose to ignore these interactions in this paper and concentrate instead on compoundness.

15.   The basic form of this classification is similar to that first proposed by Kester [12].

16.   It may also be justified to defer projects with positive NPV if the benefits of deferral would exceed associated costs (as can be more clearly seen in the shared–simple–deferrable situation described earlier).

17.   This, of course, holds under the assumed Weiner diffusion dynamics for an asset earning an equilibrium expected rate of return. Other authors using different dynamic structures have similarly found, for example, that a monopolist firm would delay exercising its option to innovate or explore relative to a competitive situation (see, for example, Dasgupta and Stiglitz [5] and Pindyck [22]). If competition is present or if the project earns an expected return below the market equilibrium, then the "dividend effect" may turn premature exercise into an optimal action.

18.   The idea that competition will induce premature exercise is also supported in the economic literature. For example, Dasgupta and Stiglitz [5] show that competitive threat may induce a firm to innovate earlier, and Reinganum [24] finds that competitors may stimulate innovation through their provocation of incumbent firms.

19.   See Trigeorgis [31] for a quantitative treatment of the impact of competitive entry seen as analogous to dividends.

REFERENCES

1.   Black, F., and M. Scholes, "The Pricing of Options and Corporate Liabilities," *Journal of Political Economy* 3 (1973), 637–659.

2.   Brealey, R., and S. Myers, *Principles of Corporate Finance*. New York: McGraw-Hill, 1984.

3. Brennan, M., and E. Schwartz, "A New Approach to Evaluating Natural Resource Investments," *Midland Corporate Finance Journal* (Spring 1985).
4. Cox, J., and M. Rubinstein, *Options Markets*. Englewood Cliffs, N.J.: Prentice-Hall, 1985.
5. Dasgupta, P., and J. Stiglitz, "Uncertainty, Industrial Structure and the Speed of R/D," *Bell Journal of Economics* 11 (Autumn 1980), 1–28.
6. Gehr, A., Jr, "Risk Adjusted Capital Budgeting Using Arbitrage," *Financial Management* (Winter 1981), 14–19.
7. Geske, R., "The Valuation of Compound Options," *Journal of Financial Economics* 7 (1979), 63–82.
8. Hertz, D., "Risk Analysis in Capital Investment," *Harvard Business Review* 42 (January–February 1964), 95–106.
9. Kensinger, J. W., "Adding the Value of Active Management into the Capital Budgeting Equation," *Midland Corporate Finance Journal* (Spring 1987), 31–42.
10. Kester, W. C., "Evaluating Growth Options: A New Approach to Strategic Capital Budgeting," Working Paper 83-38, Harvard Business School (November 1982).
11. Kester, W. C., "Turning Growth Options into Real Assets," Harvard Business School (January 1984).
12. Kester, W. C., "Today's Options for Tomorrow's Growth," *Harvard Business Review* (March/April 1986).
13. Magee, J., "How to Use Decision Trees in Capital Investment," *Harvard Business Review* (September–October 1964).
14. Majd, S., and R. Pindyck, "Time to Build, Option Value, and Investment Decisions," *Journal of Financial Economics* (March 1987), 7–27.
15. Margrabe, W., "The Value of an Option to Exchange One Asset for Another," *Journal of Finance* 33, 1 (March 1978), 177–186.
16. Mason, S. P., and C. Y. Baldwin, "Evaluation of Government Subsidies to Large-Scale Energy Projects: A Contingent Claims Approach," *Advances in Futures and Options Research*, this volume.
17. Mason, S. P., and R. C. Merton, "The Role of Contingent Claims Analysis in Corporate Finance," in *Recent Advances in Corporate Finance* (E. Altman and M. Subrahmanyam, eds.). Irwin, 1985.
18. McDonald, R., and D. Siegel, "Investment and the Valuation of Firms When There Is an Option to Shut Down," *International Economic Review* (1985).
19. McDonald, R., and D. Siegel, "The Value of Waiting to Invest," *Quarterly Journal of Economics* (November 1986), 707–727.
20. Myers, S., "Finance Theory and Financial Strategy," *Interfaces* 14, 1 (January–February 1984), 126–137; reprinted in *Midland Corporate Finance Journal* (Spring 1987), 6–13.
21. Myers, S., and S. Majd, "Calculating Abandonment Value Using Option Pricing Theory," Working Paper No. 1462-83, Sloan School of Management, MIT, Cambridge, MA (revised January 1984).
22. Pindyck, R., "Uncertainty and Exhaustible Resource Markets," *Journal of Political Economy* 86 (December 1980), 1203–1225.
23. Rao, R., and J. Martin, "Another Look at the Use of Option Pricing Theory to Evaluate Real Asset Investment Opportunities," *Journal of Business Finance and Accounting* 8, 3 (Autumn 1981), 421–430.
24. Reinganum, J., "Uncertain Innovation and the Persistence of Monopoly," *American Economic Review* 73, 4 (September 1983), 741–748.
25. Robichek, A., and J. Van Horn, "Abandonment Value and Capital Budgeting," *Journal of Finance* (December 1967), 577–590.

26. Schwab, B., and P. Lusztig, "A Note on Investment Evaluations in Light of Uncertain Future Opportunities," *Journal of Finance* 27, 5 (December 1972), 1093–1100.

27. Siegel, D., J. Smith, and J. Paddock, "Valuing Offshore Oil Properties with Option Pricing Models," *Midland Corporate Finance Journal* (Spring 1987), 22–30.

28. Smith, C., "Option Pricing: A Review," *Journal of Financial Economics* 3 (January/March 1976), 3–51.

29. Stultz, R., "Options on the Minimum or Maximum of Two Risky Assets: Analysis and Applications," *Journal of Financial Economics* 10, 2 (January 1982), 161–185.

30. Tourinho, O., "The Option Value of Reserves of Natural Resources," Working Paper, University of California, Berkeley (1979).

31. Trigeorgis, L., "The Impact of Competitive Interaction on the Value of Real Investment Opportunities," Harvard Business School (December 1984).

32. Trigeorgis, L., "Projects with Multiple Real Options: A Numerical Investigation," Harvard Business School (December 1985).

33. Trigeorgis, L., and S. P. Mason, "Valuing Managerial Flexibility," *Midland Corporate Finance Journal* (Spring 1987), 14–21.

EVALUATION OF GOVERNMENT SUBSIDIES TO LARGE-SCALE ENERGY PROJECTS:

A CONTINGENT CLAIMS APPROACH

Scott P. Mason[*] and Carliss Y. Baldwin[*]

I. INTRODUCTION

Because of lower oil prices and a lessening of fear about the disruption of foreign oil supplies, most synthetic fuel projects in both the United States and Canada have been postponed. Higher oil prices or increased fear of supply disruptions could bring about the reconsideration of government

[*]Harvard Business School.

We thank Donald Lessard (MIT), Richard Ruback (Harvard), Donald Tate (Canadian Ministry of Finance), and Robert Stobaugh (Harvard) for helpful comments and discussions.

Advances in Futures and Options Research, Vol. 3, pages 169–181.

subsidies to synthetic fuel, but more importantly, the issues raised in the valuation of subsidies to energy projects are relevant to the analysis of government financial incentives in general. In spite of their prevalence, the cost of financial incentives to governments and their value to private recipients are not well understood. In attempting to control costs and measure the benefits of incentives, many governments have established credit and tax expenditure budgets. But, unfortunately, the actual outflows associated with guarantees, tax abatements, price supports, subsidized loans, or equity participations are often determined by uncertain, future events. The need to deal with uncertainty makes estimating the initial cost of such financial incentives extremely difficult.[1]

The authors have had the opportunity to apply financial techniques in evaluating proposed government financial incentives to actual large-scale energy projects. Specifically, we were concerned with the analysis of complex government subsidies whose values were significantly affected by uncertainty surrounding the projects being considered. In the process of working out project and subsidy valuation methods, it became clear that neither the projects nor the proposed subsidies could be evaluated without taking into account so-called "operating options." Such options reflect managers' ability to respond to future events in ways that enhance the value of the basic opportunity. For example, if prices of an output fall, managers may be able to change the product mix, or in extreme circumstances, shut down some capacity. Operating options can have a material effect on a project's value; moreover financial incentives, such as government guarantees, can change the way managers exercise their options, further complicating the task of project and subsidy valuation.

This paper has two objectives. In Section II, we demonstrate how options valuation techniques may be applied in estimating the cost of complex financial subsidies and incentives. Specifically, we discuss the case of a loan guarantee to a generic large-scale energy project. In Section III, we go on to describe more fully how operating options affect the value of the project and the subsidy. We contend that classical valuation techniques, which do not properly account for such options, may gravely misrepresent the value of projects from both a public and a private perspective. In Section IV, we assess the significance of options valuation techniques for project evaluation and capital budgeting in general.

II.   ESTIMATING THE COST OF COMPLEX FINANCIAL SUBSIDIES AND INCENTIVES USING OPTIONS VALUATION TECHNIQUES

We begin with a stylized financial model of a large-scale synthetic fuels plant. The model is representative of projects such as American Natural

Resources' Great Plains Project (coal gasification in Beulah, North Dakota), Exxon's Colony Project (oil shale in Piceance Creek Basin, Colorado), or Gulf's Alsand's Project (tar sands in the Athabasca region of Alberta). Assume that as of the present, $t = 0$, it will take until $t = t_1$ to construct the plant. The plant will operate until $t = t_2$. The necessary initial investment is known with certainty and has a present value, as of $t = 0$, of I. To begin with, this project may be valued by estimating expected cash flows over the operations phase $(t = t_1 \ldots t_2)$, and then discounting these cash flows by properly risk-adjusted discount rates. In line with standard capital budgeting practice, all information about the expected time path of energy prices, operating expenses, and interest rates is assumed to be properly reflected in the expected cash flows and discount rates.[2]

Let V be the value of the project calculated in this way, but neglecting the initial investment. The project will require outside (in this case, government) support, if the cost I exceeds its value. The minimum subsidy, S, necessary to induce private investment is

$$S = I - V. \tag{1}$$

In a well-functioning capital market, a subsidy can be constructed in a variety of ways. It may take the form of an immediate cash grant, a concessionary loan, purchase commitments, price supports, tax reductions, a direct investment, or a loan guarantee. Whatever form the subsidy takes, the private market will assign a value to the contract, taking account of the time pattern and risk characteristics of the subsidy. Once the value is established, the subsidy can be "capitalized," that is, its cash flows can be sold, pledged as collateral, used as the basis for an equity issue, or otherwise be traded for current resources. With the capital market as intermediary, even risky or contingent claims on public resources can be exchanged for real resources today.

In the case of large-scale projects, a common form of subsidy is a government loan guarantee. When the government guarantees a project's debt, it becomes a "cosigner" of the loan, much like one person cosigning a bank loan for another person. Should the firm fail to repay the debt, the government is obliged to assume the liability, and make good the payments. Thus, when its debt is guaranteed, a firm has acquired an insurance policy that ensures the repayment of its debt. Just as insurance policies are assets to policyholders, loan guarantees are assets to recipient firms. And, just as policies are liabilities of insurance companies, loan guarantees are liabilities of governments.

The value of a guarantee is usually recognized by lenders through a reduced rate of interest and by their willingness to extend more credit than otherwise would be made available. Since the full faith and credit of both the firm and the government stand behind the loan, the interest rate should be close to the government's borrowing rate (assuming, as is generally the case, that the government borrows at a lower rate than the firm), and the project's debt capacity should be at least as large as the amount of the guarantee.

Government loan guarantees are readily capitalized in financial markets and thus are an effective means of conveying a subsidy to the project. But, to be efficient, the terms of the guarantee, G, must be set so that

$$G = S. \tag{2}$$

If the value of the guarantee exceeds the minimum necessary subsidy, then the government may be overcompensating the project's private sponsor.

The value of a loan guarantee can be estimated through the technique of contingent claims analysis (CCA), developed by Black and Scholes [3] and Merton [12]. CCA is a general methodology for the valuation of arbitrary contingent claims. In its essential form, CCA relies on the following assumptions:

(A.1)   "Frictionless markets": there are no transaction costs or differential taxes. Trading takes place continuously in time. Borrowing and lending are unrestricted and the borrowing rate equals the lending rate. Short sales are unrestricted, with full use of proceeds

(A.2)   The riskless short-term rate, r(t), is known over time.

(A.3)   The dynamics for the value of the project V, through time, can be described by a diffusion-type stochastic process:

$$dV = [\alpha V - P(V, t)] \, dt + \sigma V \, dz. \tag{3}$$

In Equation (3) α denotes the instantaneous expected rate of return on the project per unit time, $P(V,t)$ is the total contractual dollar payouts by the project per unit time, σ is the instantaneous standard deviation of the return on the project per unit time, and dz is a standard Gauss Wiener process.

Black and Scholes [3] and Merton [12] demonstrated that any claim whose value can be written as a function of the project value V and time is exactly correlated with the project value over short intervals. (That is, small changes in project value generate proportional changes in the value of the so-called "contingent" claim.) This initial insight was first applied to the pricing of options on common stocks. Extending the methodology, Merton [13] derived a dynamic portfolio strategy that involves mixing positions in the firm with the risk-free asset to produce patterns of return that can exactly replicate the return to *any* corporate liability of the firm. The replicating portfolio must be continually adjusted in response to changes in the value of the firm and the passage of time. The continuous application of this replication argument results in a fundamental partial differential equation that must be satisfied by the prices of all of the firm's liabilities.

For example, equity, $E(V,t)$, must satisfy

$$1/2\sigma^2 V^2 E_{VV} + [r(t)V - P(V, t)]E_V + E_t - r(t)E + p(V, t) = 0 \qquad (4)$$

where subscripts denote partial derivatives, and $p(V, t)$ represents the payments made or received by equity during the life of the project. The value of a loan guarantee, $G(V, t)$, is also contingent on the value of the project and therefore must obey

$$1/2\sigma^2 V^2 G_{VV} + [r(t)V - P(V, t)]G_V + G_t - r(t)G = 0. \qquad (5)$$

The derivation of Equations (4) and (5) depends crucially on the project and its claims being traded in a frictionless capital market, where a "no-arbitrage" condition holds.[3] Thus, one may question whether such equations provide a valid description of capital projects that are not traded. In response, we would note that all capital budgeting procedures have as an objective the estimation of the value of a project *as if* it were traded. The CCA technique thus has the same capacities and limitations as any financial valuation method. The prime caveat, which applies to all valuation techniques presently in use, is the following: if undertaking the project changes the opportunity set available to capital market investors, then using either standard DCF techniques or contingent claims techniques will lead to an error in the project's value. For example, if undertaking a particular large-scale energy project were to change the future price of oil, then the project's value is ambiguous: it would have one value given present prices, and another value given the prices that would prevail if the project were undertaken. Financial techniques can be used to calculate the project's value under each price scenario, but neither valuation correctly captures the project's impact on the economy. However, as a practical matter, projects with measurable impacts on prices and therefore the market's opportunity set are rare. Even a multibillion dollar energy project would not by itself change oil prices, although a collection of such projects might.

Returning to our analysis of a project with a government loan guarantee, to be specified completely, the valuation Equations (4) and (5) require terminal and boundary conditions. These conditions serve to give a unique representation to each contingent claim. To illustrate, assume that the project in question is financed by equity and government guaranteed debt. Of the total necessary investment, I, assume that B dollars are raised through the issuance of guaranteed debt and $I_E = I - B$ are contributed by equity. Assume that σ is estimated by studying the return series of other companies involved in oil production.[4] Interest rate projections are exogenously specified. Recall that V is the value of the fully constructed project, and that $P(V, t) = 0$ for $0 < t < t_1$ (this means that no resources are being drawn out of the project during construction). For $t_1 < t < t_2$, $P(V, t)$ reflects the time pattern of resource withdrawals, i.e., the pattern of depletion of the natural resource deposit or the physical plant. We assume that all construction money is put up at the start:

$$p(V, 0) = -I_E = -I + B$$

$$p(V, t) = 0 \qquad\qquad 0 < t \leqslant t_1.$$

After construction, for $t_1 < t \leqslant t_2$, $p(V, t)$ reflects the dividends paid to equity over the project's life. The initial quantity V is determined from the DCF project evaluation (described above).

The terminal condition for equity at the end of the project's life ($t = t_2$) is

$$E(V, t_2) = \max[0, V - DP(t_2)] \qquad (4a)$$

where $DP(t_2)$ is the contractually due payment on the government guaranteed debt at time t_2. The repayment schedule is assumed to be defined for $t_1 < t \leqslant t_2$. The boundary conditions are

$$E(V, t) = 0 \qquad \text{for } V \leqslant DP(t) \qquad (4b)$$

$$E(V, t)/V \to 1 \qquad \text{as } V \to \infty. \qquad (4c)$$

Condition (4b) says that if the value of the project should ever drop to or below the currently due payment on the guaranteed debt then the equity is worthless. Condition (4c) says that as the value of the project becomes large, the value of equity approaches but does not exceed the value of the project.

The terminal condition for the guarantee is

$$G(V, t_2) = \min[0, DP(t_2) - V] \qquad (5a)$$

which says the government must pay the minimum of the difference between the due payment and the value of the project, and zero. The boundary conditions are

$$G(V, t) = B(t) \qquad \text{for } V \leqslant DP(t) \qquad (5b)$$

$$G(V, t)/V \to 0 \qquad \text{as } V \to \infty. \qquad (5c)$$

Condition (5b) says that if the project defaults, the guarantor must pay the remaining principal, $B(t)$, which is defined over $0 < t < t_2$. Condition (5c) says that as the value of the project gets larger the value of the guarantee approaches zero.

For a particular set of data on the project and loan guarantee terms, Equations (5), (5a), (5b), and (5c) can be solved numerically and the value of the guarantee, $G(V, 0)$, estimated.[5] This quantity can then be compared to S, the necessary subsidy. If $G < S$ then a more generous guarantee must be offered (more principal, slower repayment); conversely, if $G > S$ then a less generous guarantee may be considered (less principal, faster repayment). [An equivalent, sometimes easier task is to estimate the value of equity, using (4), (4a), (4b), and (4c). If the value of equity is positive then the guarantee is too valuable and if the value is negative the guarantee is not sufficiently valuable.]

The authors have used CCA in conjunction with classical discounted cash flow valuation methods to estimate the value of loan guarantees to actual proposed energy projects. However, in carrying out this work, we became aware of an interesting problem. DCF approaches to capital budgeting cannot properly account for management's ability to revise its original operating strategy if future events turn out differently from those management expected at the outset. Unlike other approaches, the options-based technique of CCA can explicitly recognize and place a value on managerial flexibility. Such flexibility introduces an "asymmetry" or "skewedness" in the distribution of the value of the project because future decisions can improve project gains while at the same time limiting project losses. The asymmetry introduced by managerial flexibility calls for an expanded NPV criterion that reflects both sources of a project's value, the traditional "static" NPV of directly measurable cash flows and premium for flexibility. The value of flexibility can be estimated by valuing a variety of "operating options" that may be associated with the project. The next section will refine our concept of operating options and discuss their potential impact on the subsidies necessary to induce private investment.

III.   OPERATING OPTIONS AND PROJECT AND SUBSIDY VALUE

In operating a project, management usually has numerous options, which can be exercised to improve the project's performance as events unfold. For example, in responding to a change in market prices, management can often change the mix of inputs or outputs, or increase or decrease production within certain bounds. Traditional discounted cash flow valuation techniques generally ignore or improperly account for these managerial options. The existence of options increases a project's value, thus, by ignoring them, traditional valuation techniques tend to undervalue projects. While ignoring any single operating option may not change a project's value by a large amount, ignoring all operating options can introduce significant biases in the analysis.

Let us start with a well known operating option: the *option to abandon*, first analyzed by Robichek and Van Horne [16] and more recently studied by Myers and Majd [14]. In the construction phase of the project, if the value V declines significantly, it may be economic to halt or delay further construction. Traditional discounted cash flow valuation techniques tend to ignore this option, but the CCA technique outlined in Section II can value it and thus estimte the error implicit in the DCF valuation. In the case of the generic energy project defined above, suppose that the initial investment, instead of being funded entirely at the outset (at $t = 0$), can be funded over the construction period according to a preset schedule. Let $I_E(t)$ (for $0 < t \leqslant t_1$) be the time pattern of money that equity would contribute at each point during the construction phase. The correct CCA formulation of the equity valuation problem in this case is Equation (4) with

$$p(V, t) = -I_E(t) \qquad \text{for } 0 < t \leqslant t_1.$$

A new boundary condition

$$E[\bar{V}(t), t] = 0 \qquad \text{for } 0 < t \leqslant t_1 \tag{4b'}$$

would then reflect the equity investor's option to abandon the project by halting the inflow of construction money if the project's value falls too low [below $\bar{V}(t)$]. This formulation, (4), (4a), (4b'), and (4c), is a free boundary problem where a schedule of abandonment values, $\bar{V}(t)$, is identified as part of the solution to the problem. The difference between the value of equity computed here and that computed in Section II is the value of the option to abandon. The existence of the option increases the value of the project and hence reduces the necessary subsidy. The value of the guarantee in the presence of the option to abandon can be determined by rewriting condition (5b)

$$G[\bar{V}(t), t] = B(t) \qquad \text{for } 0 < t \leqslant t_1 \tag{5b'}$$

when $\bar{V}(t)$ is idenitified in the solution of the equity valuation problem.[6]

Implicit in most traditional project valuations are assumptions about the scale and life of the plant. Specifically, cash flow projections usually allow for maintenance expenses or new investment to maintain the scale and life of the proposed facility. However, such expenditures represent *options to expand or contract capacity*. As uncertainty is resolved during the operating phase of a plant, management can use these options to respond to changing market conditions. For example, in the case of a synthetic fuels plant, if after 5 years of operation the price of energy falls substantially then management may decrease maintenance expenditures, and take more cash out in the short run. Similarly, if the price of energy has risen dramatically, then management may decide to increase capital spending, in order to expand the scale or extend the life of the plant.

Unfortunately, the CCA treatment of this option is very difficult because of the sheer number of potential combinations of decisions to expand or contract plant size and extend or shorten plant life. However, if it is reasonable to constrain the set of choices management might face, a partial analysis is possible. For example, one could assume that at particular times, management has the option to invest a given amount to continue at the present scale, may invest more to expand to a known larger scale, or may invest less and contract to a smaller scale. Such a simplification of manager's actual choices, although approximate, may be more realistic than ignoring management's options entirely. In the case of a subsidized investment, the option to expand or contract capacity at the margin clearly has value and thus its presence should cause the size of the necessary subsidy to decrease.

The *option to operate* is another option that is of value in the private sector. Traditional project valuation typically assumes cash flows will occur in each year of the proposed project's life. However, in any given year, if revenues are expected to fall short of ongoing direct costs, it may be optimal to shut down. Although the option to operate clearly has value, estimation of its impact on the project is extremely difficult, especially if a shutdown extends the plant's life (as would be true for resource-deposit-based facilities). McDonald and Siegel [11] look at this problem. Holding the plant's life constant, they view each year's operation as a call option, and value the project as the sum of these options.

Another operating option is the *option to change inputs or outputs*. A project can be viewed as a means of transforming inputs purchased at one price into outputs sold at another price. Certain pieces of capital have the property that they can take diverse inputs or make diverse outputs or both. Oil refineries and chemical plants are good examples of potentially flexible capital: they can be designed to process different combinations of inputs and/or outputs, but such flexibility usually comes at some incremental cost. The work of Margrabe [10] on valuing options to exchange one risky asset for another, of Stultz [17] on valuing options on the minimum or maximum, and of Baldwin and Ruback [2] on the option value implicit in short-lived assets when prices are uncertain are each attempts to value the flexibility implicit in particular technologies. As with the option to abandon and the option to expand or contract capacity, the option to operate and the option to change inputs or outputs tend to increase the value of a project and therefore should reduce the magnitude of necessary subsidies.

An example of an operating option that *increases* necessary subsidies is the *option to initiate*. A company that possesses a proprietary technology or a lease on lands containing coal, oil shale, or tar sands has an option to begin the construction of an extraction plant when it is optimal to do so. It may be the case that this option is currently "out of the money," that is,

$$V < I,$$

but the option has a positive value none the less. Thus, a subsidy of value

$$S = I - V$$

will systematically undercompensate the equityholders. The equityholders are justified in requesting a subsidy that compensates them for exercising their valuable option. Even if the project valuation suggests that

$$V > I$$

in other words, the project is presently profitable, the equityholders may still be justified in requesting a subsidy to build now if they can demonstrate that it is not optimal to exercise their option prematurely. For example, if construction costs are fixed or slowly rising, and lease payments on producing properties are low, it may be optimal to defer the start of construction. In contrast, if construction costs are expected to rise sharply or if lease payments are high, then it may be optimal to start without delay. In the first case, a private sponsor may need to be paid to accelerate construction. Options to initiate have been identified by Tourinho [18] in studying the value of natural resources and Paddock, Siegel, and Smith [15] in studying corporate bids for hydrocarbon leases. Majd and Pindyck [9] model a multistage construction project as a series of compound options in which each unit of investment buys an option on the next unit.

One final point about the interaction of subsidies and operating options deserves mention: frequently the contractual terms of a subsidy will change the way in which private sponsors exercise an operating option. These changes in managerial decisions will in turn change both the project's value and the value of the subsidy. The interdependence of project, subsidy, and option values can work to the benefit or detriment of the government. On the one hand, if the subsidies are designed poorly, the project may be managed in ways that run counter to the public interest. On the other hand, if subsidies are designed to take account of the private sponsor's options, the government may be able to increase the efficiency of its financial interventions.

To illustrate the interaction of operating options and subsidies, consider our generic energy project, in the case where the investment takes place over time and hence the option to abandon has value. The investment is funded partly by private equity and the remainder by government guaranteed debt. If the debt funds are paid in first, and the equity later, then the private sponsor may be inclined to abandon the project more quickly [that is, at higher values, $V(t)$] than is optimal from the government's perspective. The reason is that equity will garner positive returns only after the project's debt is repaid. Faced with the need to invest, and very little promise of return, the private sponsor may optimally elect to withhold its funds. In contrast, if the equity funds are invested first, and debt later, then the private equityholder would never voluntarily abandon the project. From equity's perspective, its investment cost is sunk; subsequent expenditures that utilize government-guaranteed loans are always worth pursuing, even if the chance of return is slim. The private sponsor's incentives to pursue the project at any price means that the government cannot rely on the sponsor's "economic" decisions, but must independently assess the merits of continuing to fund the project.

There are no hard and fast rules on how to design a perfect interface between operating options and financial subsidies. The optimal subsidy contract depends critically on the government's ongoing ability to evaluate and respond to project-related events as they unfold. However, the interaction of options and subsidies can have an important effect on both project and subsidy values. Contingent claims analysis can be used to assess optimal strategies and probable outcomes under different subsidy structures. Thus, the CCA technique may be applied not only to value complex financial subsidies and particular operating options, but through iterated application, may be used to improve the design of government incentives in order to bring public and private goals closer together.

IV. CONCLUSION

This paper demonstrates that techniques currently exist to value even quite complex government financial subsidies. However, in carrying out the valuation of loan guarantees for actual large-scale energy projects, the authors were struck by the fact that traditional project valuation techniques ignore an important set of variables that we have labeled "operating options." While we first became intrigued by operating options through the rather specialized exercise of valuing subsidies, we feel that the recognition of these options and their explicit incorporation in capital budgeting procedures may have far-reaching consequences for firms' capital investment decisions.

It has been argued that classical capital budgeting techniques systematically undervalue projects.[7] Suggestions on how to counter this bias range from setting the discount rate at zero (so as not to value future cash flows less than present dollars) to deciding on major investments on the basis of judgment and strategy alone, without subjecting them to "distortive" quantitative analysis. This paper supports the contention that traditional capital budgeting may undervalue projects, because it ignores valuable operating options. However, techniques such as contingent claims analysis may be used to value some of these options.

Operating options provide a quantitative representation of the elusive property of managerial "flexibility." Managers have always implicitly recognized the value of flexible projects and technology. Contingent claims analysis can recognize flexibility and quantify its impact on the value of particular undertakings. Using CCA, the value of managerial flexibility can be measured objectively and weighed in relation to other factors as part of an overall project evaluation and resource allocation process.

NOTES

1. See Baldwin, Lessard, and Mason [1] for a discussion of the issues arising in the treatment of loan guarantees and other financial incentives in the Canadian federal budget. Also see Congressional Budget Office Study [5] on the budgetary treatment of U.S. government credit assistance.

2. In negotiations between a government and the private sponsor of a project, government analysts usually must rely on the sponsor to supply data on capital investment, operating costs, and production rates. Usually these data cannot be independently verified. (Other important data, such as estimates of future energy prices, interest rates, risk-adjusted discount rates, and tax treatments can be verified by government analysts.) Lack of objective information is a serious problem that can be addressed although not eliminated by appropriate incentives. However, for purposes of this discussion, we assume that the data have been checked as far as possible, and that all parties have agreed on the inputs to the analysis.

3. "No-arbitrage" refers to the requirement that perfectly correlated securities with identical returns must have the same price. Otherwise, market agent could profit by arbitrage transactions.

4. Ideally σ would be estimated from historical data on the total return to similar projects. As a practical matter, σ is usually estimated by calculating the standard deviation of returns on the equity of related enterprises and then adjusting the resulting figure for the companies' debts. If the companies in question have inhomogeneous capital structures, more complicated procedures may be warranted.

5. See Brennan and Schwartz [4], Geske and Johnson [6], and Geske and Shastri [7] on numerical techniques for valuing contingent claims.

6. As a computational matter, the analyst no longer has the choice of which claim to value first. The equity claim must be valued and the value-maximizing strategy with respect to abandonment identified before the guarantee's value can be assessed.

7. See, for example, Hayes and Garvin [8].

REFERENCES

1. Baldwin, C. Y., D. R. Lessard, and S. P. Mason, "Budgetary Time Bombs: Controlling Government Loan Guarantees," *Canadian Public Policy* 9, No. 3 (1983).
2. Baldwin, C. Y., and R. S. Ruback, "Inflation, Uncertainty and Investment," *Journal of Finance* 41, No. 3 (1986), 657–668.
3. Black, F., and M. Scholes, "The Pricing of Options and Corporate Liabilities," *Journal of Political Economy* 81 (1973), 637–659.
4. Brennan, M. J. and E. S. Schwartz, "The Valuation of American Put Options," *Journal of Finance* 32, No. 2 (1977), 449–462.
5. Congressional Budget Office, "New Approaches to the Budgetary Treatment of Federal Credit Assistance," March (1984).
6. Geske, R., and H. E. Johnson, "The American Put Valued Analytically," *Journal of Finance* 39, No. 5 (1984), 1511–1524.

7. Geske, R., and K. Shastri, "Valuation by Approximation: A Comparison of Alternative Valuation Techniques," *Journal of Financial and Quantitative Analysis* 20, No. 1 (1985), 45–71.

8. Hayes, R. H., and D. A. Garvin, "Managing as if Tomorrow Mattered," *Harvard Business Review* 50, No. 3 (1982), 70–79.

9. Majd, S., and R. Pindyck, "Time to Build, Option Value and Investment Decisions," *Journal of Finanical Economics* 8, No. 1 (1987), 7–27.

10. Margrabe, W., "The Value of an Option to Exchange One Asset for Another," *Journal of Finance* 33, No. 1 (1978), pp. 177–186.

11. McDonald, R. L., and D. R. Siegel, "Investment and the Valuation of Firms When There Is an Option to Shut Down," *International Economic Review* 26, No. 2 (1985), 331–349.

12. Merton, R. C., "The Theory of Rational Option Pricing," *Bell Journal of Economics and Management Science* 4, No. 1 (1973), 141–183.

13. Merton, R. C., "On the Pricing of Contingent Claims and the Modigliani-Miller Theorem," *Journal of Financial Economics* 15, No. 2 (1977), 241–250.

14. Myers, S. C., and S. Majd, "Calculating Abandonment Value Using Option Pricing Theory," Working Paper No. 1462-83, Alfred P. Sloan School of Management, MIT, Cambridge, Ma., 1983.

15. Paddock, J. L., D. Siegel, and J. L. Smith, "Option Valuation of Claims on Real Assets: The Case of Offshore Petroleum Leases," *Quarterly Journal of Economics* 103, No. 3 (1988), 479–508.

16. Robichek, A. A., and J. C. Van Horne, "Abandonment Value in Capital Budgeting," *Journal of Finance* 22, No. 5 (1967), 577–590.

17. Stultz, R., "Options on the Minimum or Maximum of Two Risky Assets: Analysis and Applications," *Journal of Finance* 10, No. 2 (1982), 161–185.

18. Tourinho, O. A. F., "The Option Value of Reserves of Natural Resources," Unpublished Working Paper, University of California, Berkeley, Ca., 1979.

EMPIRICAL REGULARITIES IN THE DEUTSCHE MARK FUTURES OPTIONS

David A. Hsieh[*] and Luis Manas-Anton[**]

I. INTRODUCTION

Most studies of options pricing use the Black–Scholes [7] model, which assumes that the price of the underlying asset is a Wiener process whose variance remains constant over the life of the option. In the foreign exchange market, this assumption is often violated. Burt, Kaen, and Booth

[*]Graduate School of Business, University of Chicago.

[**]Department of Economics, University of Chicago, and the World Bank.

We would like to thank Robert Whaley for providing valuable assistance in obtaining the approximate solution of the American options, and the Chicago Mercantile Exchange for providing the data used in this study.

Advances in Futures and Options Research, Vol. 3, pages 183–208.

[11], Westerfield [34], and Rogalski and Vinso [27] have all found that the rate of change of spot currency prices are nonnormal. In addition, Hsieh [20] and Manas-Anton [23] have found that these price changes are not independent and identically distributed, and that they are better described by Engle's [14] autoregressive conditional heteroscedasticity model (ARCH) or Bollerslev's [9] generalized autoregressive conditional heteroscedasticity model (GARCH). The main goal of this paper is to ascertain whether options in foreign currencies behave in a manner consistent with an ARCH model.

We examine the options on the Deutsche Mark (DM) futures contract traded on the Chicago Mercantile Exchange (CME). These options have been studied by Ball and Torous [2], who use closing option prices and corresponding settlement futures prices from January 24, 1984 to March 1, 1985. Cox and Rubinstein [13, p. 134] expresssed some reservations on the use of closing prices. Hence, in our work, we use transaction data obtained from the CME.

There are two reasons for choosing options on currency futures. In the first place, the options on DM futures are traded in a pit on the CME only a few feet away from the pit where the underlying DM futures are traded. Floor traders can observe prices and conduct trades in both markets very easily. These two markets are "well synchronized" in the sense of Galai [16]. In addition, the cost of trading in DM futures and futures options appears to be small. Ball and Torous [2, p. 864] write: "Transaction costs to trading in futures contracts and futures option contracts are minimal. For floor traders in a particular contract, round trip transaction costs to a position in that instrument are on the order of 24c per contract. These costs include a service charge of 2c per contract per side payable to the exchange, and a clearing charge of 10c per contract per side payable to the clearing firm. However, for floor traders in a particular contract taking a position in a different instrument, say, a futures option trader taking a position in the underlying futures contract, an additional round trip service charge of approximately $3 per contract is levied." The round trip transaction costs for a floor trader arbitraging between the futures option and the underlying futures contract are less than $3.50.

The paper is organized as follows. Section II reviews the theoretical models for pricing futures options. Section III describes the data. Section IV tests for violations of boundary conditions in the data. Section V analyzes the implied volatilities of the data. Section VI provides a summary of the results.

II. THE PRICING OF OPTIONS ON DEUTSCHE MARK FUTURES CONTRACT

In this section, we review the Black–Scholes model for pricing options on futures contracts. For this purpose, we shall use the following notation. Let S denote the cash price of Deutsche Mark (DM) currency in terms of U.S. Dollars. Let i be the instantaneous U.S. riskless interest rate, and i^* the instantaneous German riskless interest rate. Both are assumed to be known and constant. There is no spread between borrowing and lending rates in both currencies. Furthermore, there are no transaction costs, and trading is conducted continuously over time.

Under these conditions, costless arbitrage ensures that the futures price of Deutsche Mark, F, must satisfy the following relation:

$$F = S \exp[(i - i^*)T'], \tag{1}$$

where T' is the time to maturity of the futures contract, measured in the same time units as the interest rates.

A standard assumption for pricing option and futures contracts is to suppose that S can be described by the following continuous time stochastic process:

$$dS/S = \mu \, dt + \sigma \, dZ, \tag{2}$$

where Z is a standard Wiener diffusion process. We use the term "Black–Scholes model" to denote any options pricing model that assumes Equation (2). This assumption also means that F must be characterized by

$$dF/F = (\mu - i + i^*) \, dt + \sigma \, dZ. \tag{3}$$

Now, consider a European call option on the futures contract, with time to maturity $T(< T')$, and strike price K. Then using a riskless hedge between the option and the futures contract, and noting that the carrying cost of the latter is zero, one obtains the Black [5] formula for pricing a call option on futures contract:

$$C(F, T, K) = \exp(-iT)[FN(d_1) - KN(d_2)], \tag{4}$$

where

$$d_1 = [\log(F/K) + \sigma^2 T/2]/[\sigma\sqrt{T}], \tag{5}$$

$$d_2 = d_1 - \sigma\sqrt{T}, \tag{6}$$

and

$$N(x) = \left[\int_{-\infty}^{x} \exp(-u^2/2) \, du\right]/\sqrt{2\pi}. \tag{7}$$

Similarly, one obtains the price of a put option:

$$P(F, T, K) = \exp(-iT)[KN(-d_2) - FN(-d_1)]. \tag{8}$$

Several comments on the Black–Scholes model are relevant. First, the forward price and the futures price of DM are the same under the above assumptions, if the two contracts mature at the same time. Hence, these pricing formulas for European futures options are identical to those for European cash options found in Biger and Hull [4], Garman and Kohlhagen [17], Giddy [18], and Grabbe [19].

Second, the DM futures options traded on the CME are American options, which differ from European options in that their owners can exercise the option at any time prior to maturity. Ramaswamy and Sundaresan [26] have shown that there are some circumstances in which the value of an American option would be greater than that of an identical European option. Consider the case in which the futures price F is much higher than the strike price K. For a call option, the European formula will give a price approximately equal to $\exp(-iT)$ [F − K]. If the American call option is exercised immediately, the owner receives [F − K]. Hence, the American option must command a higher price than its European counterpart. In fact, the American option must sell for a price no less than [F − K], the value of early exercise.

Shastri and Tandon [32] have shown that the potential early exericse bias tends to be small for call options in currencies, especially when the domestic interest rate is higher than the foreign interest rate. However, prices of American and European put options frequently differ by important amounts. We must take this into account.

Unfortunately, there is no simple closed form solution to evaluate American options. Numerical methods or approximations must be performed. In this paper, we use the technique described in Barone-Adesi and Whaley [3]. They point out that the difference between the value of an American option and that of an identical European option is the early exercise premium of the former. Since the same partial differential equation (which results from the riskless hedge between the option and the underlying asset) applies to both the American and the European option, it also applies to the early exercise premium of the American option. Barone-Adesi and Whaley employ a quadratic approximation for this partial differential equation, and obtain a closed form (approximate) solution for the early exercise premium. When this is added to the value of the European option, it gives an approximation of the value of the American option. They show that this method not only gives accurate approximations of the value of the American option, but also is one of the fastest computational methods available for pricing American options.

Third, the distributional assumption of the Black–Scholes model may not be appropriate. If dS/S is not a Wiener process, then the model may give biased option values. Rubinstein [28] shows that if dS/S is a mixture of a Wiener process and a Poisson jump process, then there are systematic biases in the Black–Scholes model if one ignores the jump component. In particular, the Black–Scholes model overprices out-of-the-money calls relative to at-the-money calls, and very-near-maturity calls relative to middle-maturity calls.

Our strategy is to determine whether the Black–Scholes model prices deviate systematically from the observed prices. In particular, we are interested in finding out whether the observed prices are consistent with ARCH or GARCH models, which are consistent with the behavior of spot currencies. Mustafa [25] calculates theoretical prices for call options written on assets that follow IGARCH processes, and compares them to the Black–Scholes model. His results indicate that the Black–Scholes model underprices out-of-the-money calls relative to at-the-money calls, and very-near-maturity calls relative to middle-maturity calls.

III. THE DATA

The data consist of quotes on the Deutsche Mark (DM) futures contract and quotes on the options on the DM futures contract, traded on the Chicago Mercantile Exchange (CME). Each DM futures contract is for the delivery of 125,000 DM. Each DM option contract is written on one DM futures contract. The futures contract was first traded on May 16, 1972, while the option did not start until January 24, 1984. The price of the futures contract as well as the options is quoted in U.S. cents per DM. Each tick of the options and the futures equals $12.50, which is the minimum price change for both contracts.

The data were provided by the CME, and are generally known as "quote capture" information. The data set contains the time and price of every transaction in which the price has changed from the previous transaction. In addition, bid and ask prices are also recorded if the bid price is above or the ask price is below the price of the previous transaction. There is no information regarding the number and volume of transaction at a particular price. The data used in this study covered DM futures and futures options quotes from January 23, 1984 to October 10, 1984. (Figure 1 plots the daily closing prices of the spot DM contract. Over this period, the DM has consistently depreciated against the U.S. Dollar.)

We eliminated all bid and ask quotes from the data, since they do not represent transaction prices. From the remaining quotes, we extracted a very small subsample of data. On each trading day, we found the last traded price for each option nearest to noon Chicago time, and then matched it

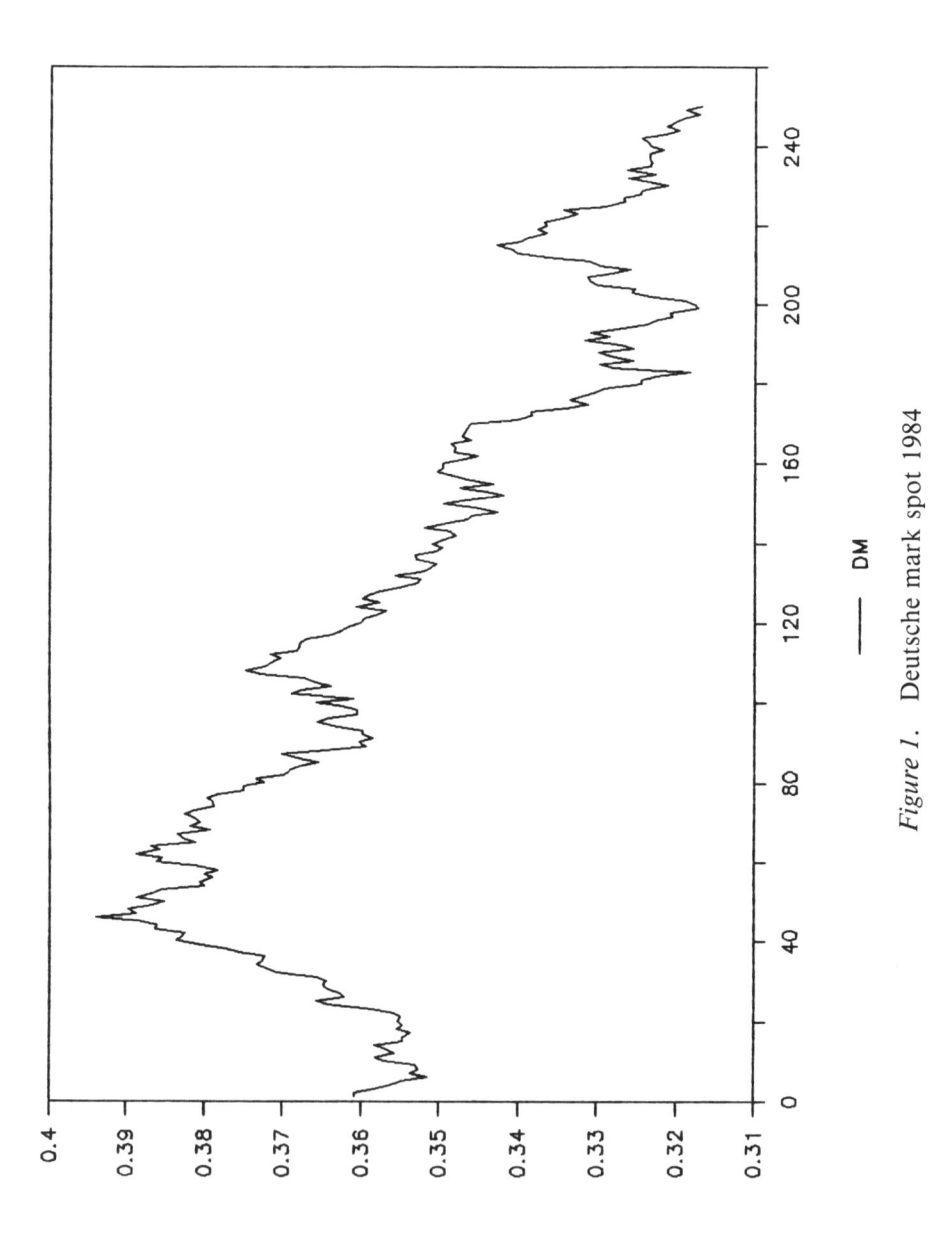

Figure 1. Deutsche mark spot 1984

to the price of the underlying futures contract that traded most closely preceding the option. On average, the time between an option transaction and the preceding futures transaction was only 152 seconds. We have a total of 1560 observations on call options and 824 on put options in our sample. The smaller number of observations on puts is due to the fact that puts are less frequently traded than calls. Table 1 gives a complete breakdown of these options by strike price and by maturity date.

We do not have any transaction data for interest rate. Instead, we use the

Table 1. Number of Days with Traded Options: January 23, 1984–October 10 1984.

Strike Price	Maturity Date				
	8403	*8406*	*8409*	*8412*	*8503*
	Call Options				
30	—	—	—	—	—
31	—	—	—	—	—
32	—	—	—	23	5
33	—	—	—	28	21
34	3	—	14	40	25
35	9	7	45	60	25
36	25	52	68	74	22
37	31	90	76	74	15
38	22	91	81	87	—
39	13	72	70	39	—
40	—	58	75	19	—
41	—	37	39	—	—
42	—	19	6	—	—
Total	103	426	474	444	113
	Put Options				
30	—	—	—	11	—
31	—	—	—	23	6
32	—	—	—	29	5
33	—	—	7	36	2
34	—	—	40	37	—
35	9	18	76	33	—
36	19	59	67	24	—
37	18	79	58	—	—
38	7	68	26	—	—
39	6	45	4	—	—
40	—	12	—	—	—
41	—	—	—	—	—
42	—	—	—	—	—
Total	59	281	278	193	13

3-month treasury bill rate in the Federal Reserve G.13 Release as the riskless U.S. interest rate (i). This should not cause too much of a problem in pricing options, since interest rates are not nearly as volatile as exchange rates, and option prices are not very sensitive to small changes in interest rates.

IV. TESTING FOR VIOLATIONS OF BOUNDARY CONDITIONS

In this section, we test for violations of the early exercise boundary conditions and the put–call parity conditions in the data. These boundary conditions are of interest, since they are derived merely from arbitrage arguments and not from any particular model of option pricing.

A. Early Exercise Boundary Conditions

As pointed out in Section II, American options on futures contracts must sell for at least the value of early exercise, if there is to be no profitable arbitrage. These boundary conditions are

$$C(F, K, T) \geqslant \max\{0, F - K\} \tag{9}$$

and

$$P(F, K, T) \geqslant \max\{0, K - F\}. \tag{10}$$

Table 2 summarizes our findings of violations of the above boundary conditions. For call options, we found 16 violations out of 1560 observations, at a rate of 1.03%. These violations occurred only in the options maturing in March and June of 1984. In fact, all but one of these violations occurred before March 9, 1984. The size of the violations is quite small. The maximum violation is 4 ticks or $50. For the calls maturing in March 1984, 4 violations involved the discrepancy of 1 tick, 2 violations involved 2 ticks, 2 violations involved 3 ticks, and 2 more involved 4 ticks. For the calls maturing in June 1984, 1 violation involved the discrepancy of 1 tick, another involved 2 ticks, 3 violations involved 3 ticks, and 1 involved 4 ticks.

For put options, we found 5 violations out of 824 observations, at a rate of 0.61%. All violations involved options maturing in June and September 1984. Here, too, the size of the violations is small. The maximum violation is 2 ticks or $25.00. For the put options maturing in June 1984, 3 violations involved only 1 tick, and 1 violation involved 2 ticks. For the put options maturing in September 1984, there was only 1 violation involving 2 ticks.

These results contrast interestingly with those in previous studies. Ball and Torous [2], using closing DM futures option prices and settlement DM

Table 2. Violations of Early Exercise Boundary Conditions

	Maturity Date				
	8403	*8406*	*8409*	*8412*	*8503*
Call Options: $C \geqslant \max\{0, F - K\}$					
Number of violations	10	6	0	0	0
Percentage of violations	9.7%	1.4%	0%	0%	0%
Maximum size of violation					
(Ticks)	4	4	0	0	0
(Dollars)	$50.00	$50.00	$0	$0	$0
Average size of violation					
(Ticks)	2.20	2.67	0	0	0
(Dollars)	$27.50	$33.33	$0	$0	$0
Put Options: $P \geqslant \max\{0, K - F\}$					
Number of violations	0	4	1	0	0
Percentage of violations	0%	1.4%	0.4%	0%	0%
Maximum size of violation					
(Ticks)	0	2	2	0	0
(Dollars)	$0	$25.00	$25.00	$0	$0
Average size of violation					
(Ticks)	0	1.25	2	0	0
(Dollars)	$0	$15.63	$25.00	$0	$0

futures prices from January 24, 1984 to March 1, 1985, found 2.70% violations for calls and 7.08% for puts. Shastri and Tandon [30], using closing prices for cash options and cash currencies from December 14, 1982 to November 22, 1983, found 1.66% violation for calls and 17.60% for puts. Bodurtha and Courtadon [8], using transaction prices for cash options and cash currencies from February 28, 1983 to September 14, 1984, found 0.77% violations in call observations, and 8.26% violations for puts. Thus, our results find a similar rate of violation in calls, but a substantially lower rate for puts.

We speculate that the high rate of violation for puts in Ball and Torous [2] resulted from the use of closing prices. As mentioned earlier, puts are much less frequently traded than calls. Closing prices for puts are probably not synchronous with the corresponding settlement futures prices. This may also explain the high rate of violation for puts in Shastri and Tandon [30].

But this cannot explain the high rate of violation for puts in Bodurtha and Courtadon [8], who used transaction data. Bodurtha and Courtadon themselves showed that if transaction costs were taken into account, then these violations disappeared.

B. Put–Call Parity Conditions

Besides the early exercise boundary conditions, there are other arbitrage restrictions between the prices of puts and calls. Ramaswamy and Sundaresan [26] provide a relation between call and put options with similar contractual terms:

$$C(F, K, T) \leqslant P(F, K, T) + F - Kb(T), \tag{11}$$

where $b(T)$ is the price of a unit discount bond paying \$1 with time to maturity T. This relation is called "the upper put–call parity" in Ball and Torous [2], and holds even if interest rates are stochastic. Stoll and Whaley [33] provide a second relation:

$$C(F, K, T) \geqslant P(F, K, T) - Fb(T) + K. \tag{12}$$

This condition is called the "lower put–call parity" in Ball and Torous [2], and holds only if interest rates are constant over time.

We checked for violations of the two parity conditions in the data. We assumed a constant interest rate, and used the 3-month treasury bill rate (i) to calculate the price of the discount bond as

$$b(T) = \exp(-iT). \tag{13}$$

Table 3 summarizes our findings. For the lower put–call parity, there were only three violations out of 592 observations, a rate of 0.51%. Two violations occurred in the option with a strike price of 39c maturing on March 1984, when the options were 1 and 2 days prior to expiration. The maximum violation was only 3.98 ticks (\$49.75). The third violation occurred in the options with a strike price of 34c, but it was only 1 tick (\$12.50). For the upper put–call parity, there were only four violations out of 592 observations, a rate of 0.68%. The largest violation was 9.97 ticks (\$124.50). This appears to be sizable. However, it turns out that the put and the call traded 1 hour and 21 minutes apart, during which time, the futures price moved 11 ticks (\$137.50). The second largest violation was 6.14 ticks (\$76.75). In this case, the put and the call traded more than 4 hours apart, during which time the futures price moved 18 ticks (\$225.00). These two instances should not be considered violations of the upper put–call parity condition, since the puts and calls could not be traded simultaneously. The remaining two violations consist of 1.99 ticks (\$25.00) and 0.97 ticks (\$12.50).

Table 3. Violations of Put–Call Parity Conditions

	Maturity Date				
	8403	*8406*	*8409*	*8412*	*8503*
Number of observations	55	219	183	131	4
Test of Upper Put–Call Parity: $C(F, K, T) \leqslant P(F, K, T) + F - Kb(T)$					
Number of violations	2	0	1	0	0
Percentage of violations	3.6%	0%	0.5%	0%	0%
Maximum size of violation					
(Ticks)	3.98	0	1	0	0
(Dollars)	$49.75	$0	$12.50	$0	$0
Average size of violation					
(Ticks)	2.5	0	1	0	0
(Dollars)	$31.25	$0	$12.50	$0	$0
Test of Lower Put–Call Parity: $C(F, K, T) \geqslant P(F, K, T) - Fb(T) + K$					
Number of violations	1	3	0	0	0
Percentage of violations	1.8%	1.4%	0%	0%	0%
Maximum size of violation					
(Ticks)	6.14	9.96	0	0	0
(Dollars)	$76.75	$124.50	$0	$0	$0
Average size of violation					
(Ticks)	6.14	4.31	0	0	0
(Dollars)	$76.25	$53.83	$0	$0	$0

Our results are similar to the findings of other authors. For the lower and upper put–call parity conditions, Ball and Torous [2] found violation rates of 0.58 and 0.73%, respectively, while Bodurtha and Courtadon [8] found violation rates of 0.05 and 0.32%, respectively. Shastri and Tandon [30] found violation rates of 28.25 and 46.10%, respectively, but Bodurtha and Courtadon argued that these results were caused by using closing prices.

On the whole, we found that we have very low rates of violation of the early exercise boundary conditions and the put–call parity conditions. These results compare very favorably with those in previous work. For the few violations we found, we cannot attribute them to transaction costs and nonsynchronized trading. We do not believe that these violations are evidence of market inefficiency. Rather, there may be other explanations. It is possible that, when the DM futures options were first traded, there was little liquidity. Bid and ask prices may have been more than several ticks apart, causing some transactions to appear to violate the boundary conditions. As the liquidity in these options increased, the bid–ask spread narrowed, and so these apparent violations disappeared over time. It is also possible that, when the options were first traded, the quote capture reporting procedures may not have been very accurate. The recorded time for an option price may be different from the actual trading time. We therefore observed some discrepancies that never existed in real time. The reporting procedures may have been improved at a later date, so we do not observe these violations any more.

V.   ANALYSIS OF IMPLIED VOLATILITIES

In this section, we document the deviations of the Black–Scholes model prices from the observed prices. For this purpose, let us denote the theoretical or model price of a call option on the DM futures contract as $C(F, K, T; \sigma, i)$, and that of a put option as $P(F, K, T; \sigma, i)$. We observe the variables F (the price of the underlying futures contract), K (the strike price), T (time to maturity), i (the riskless interest rate, assumed to be the 3-month Treasury bill rate), and the market value of the option. The only unknown is σ (the instantaneous standard deviation of the underlying contract).

We proceed along the methodology in Rubinstein [28] by finding the value of σ that equates the model price to the observed market price. We denote this value by V, which is known as the "implied volatility" of that option. For example, suppose we observe the price of a call option with strike price K, time to maturity T, interest rate i, futures price F, and observed price C. Then we find V that satisfies

$$C(F, K, T, V, i) = C. \qquad (14)$$

This is a nonlinear equation, and is solved by an iterative Newton–Raphson procedure. One implied volatility is calculated for each observation. The implied volatilities are then used to examine the validity of the Black–Scholes model.

First, σ is constant in the Black–Scholes model, and so the implied volatility, V, should be the same over time. Any change in V can be attributable only to measurement error. Assuming that these errors are not correlated over time, the V's should not be correlated over time.

Second, σ should be the same for all options, regardless of the strike price. Therefore, the implied volatility of an option with a lower strike price should equal that of an option with a higher strike price.

Third, σ should be the same for all options, regardless of the time to maturity. Therefore, the implied volatility of an option with a short time to maturity should equal that of an option with a longer time to maturity.

A. Serial Correlation of Implied Volatilities

Table 4 presents some time series statistics of the implied volatilities. For both puts and calls, it is quite clear that the first- and second-order serial correlation coefficients, ρ_1 and ρ_2, are very different from zero. It therefore appears to be the case that the implied volatilities contain a systematic error term, contrary to the assumptions of the Black–Scholes model. This finding is consistent with a time-varying σ. The Black–Scholes model can be generalized, as in Merton [24], to handle the case when σ is time-varying but nonstochastic. But there are no simple results when σ is stochastic, as in the case of an ARCH model.

Table 4. Time Series Statistics of Implied Volatilities.

Strike Price	Number of Observation	Mean $\times 10^2$	Max $\times 10^2$	Min $\times 10^2$	SD $\times 10^2$	ρ_1	ρ_2
		Calls Maturing 8403					
35	8	0.45	0.50	0.40	0.05	0.63	0.26
36	21	0.55	1.30	0.40	0.24	0.46	0.01
37	24	0.49	0.57	0.43	0.03	0.56	0.20
38	20	0.60	1.41	0.47	0.20	0.15	0.09
39	13	0.72	1.10	0.60	0.12	0.05	−0.01
		Calls Maturing 8406					
36	44	0.54	0.76	0.42	0.071	0.46	0.32
37	90	0.54	0.74	0.44	0.056	0.61	0.67
38	91	0.59	1.50	0.43	0.137	0.64	0.48
39	72	0.63	2.36	0.48	0.245	0.51	0.34
40	58	0.72	3.61	0.52	0.441	0.46	0.27
41	37	0.63	0.70	0.56	0.037	0.68	0.49
42	19	0.66	0.73	0.58	0.049	0.75	0.58
		Calls Maturing 8409					
34	14	0.70	1.07	0.52	0.135	0.09	0.13
35	45	0.64	0.74	0.51	0.044	0.56	0.48
36	68	0.65	0.97	0.52	0.068	0.90	0.82
37	76	0.64	0.85	0.51	0.077	0.90	0.86
38	81	0.64	0.96	0.53	0.094	0.87	0.78
39	70	0.64	0.99	0.52	0.091	0.85	0.69
40	75	0.67	1.32	0.53	0.139	0.82	0.62
41	35	0.66	1.34	0.55	0.130	0.26	0.16
42	6	0.69	0.82	0.58	0.089	0.40	0.03

Continued

Table 4. *(Continued)*.

Strike Price	Number of Observation	Mean $\times 10^2$	Max $\times 10^2$	Min $\times 10^2$	SD $\times 10^2$	ρ_1	ρ_2
			Calls Maturing 8412				
32	23	0.87	0.93	0.79	0.039	0.70	0.51
33	28	0.86	0.92	0.70	0.060	0.73	0.49
34	40	0.81	0.96	0.63	0.115	0.93	0.87
35	60	0.77	1.00	0.60	0.138	0.95	0.91
36	74	0.76	1.06	0.57	0.152	0.95	0.91
37	74	0.77	1.09	0.59	0.156	0.96	0.91
38	57	0.73	1.05	0.60	0.116	0.90	0.79
39	39	0.74	1.13	0.57	0.133	0.82	0.61
40	19	0.74	0.82	0.61	0.061	0.72	0.64
			Puts Maturing 8403				
35	9	0.49	0.51	0.46	0.02	−0.01	−0.06
36	19	0.49	0.57	0.42	0.04	0.70	0.53
37	18	0.51	0.63	0.40	0.07	0.73	0.53
38	7	0.63	0.70	0.53	0.06	0.43	−0.15
39	6	0.76	0.94	0.65	0.11	−0.31	−0.09
			Puts Maturing 8406				
35	18	0.55	0.68	0.44	0.083	0.76	0.60
36	59	0.58	1.21	0.44	0.105	0.39	0.34
37	79	0.57	0.90	0.44	0.070	0.66	0.47
38	63	0.57	0.87	0.47	0.066	0.46	0.40
39	43	0.58	0.80	0.49	0.051	0.28	0.24
			Puts Maturing 8409				
34	40	0.67	0.85	0.57	0.060	0.55	0.45
35	74	0.63	0.82	0.51	0.048	0.48	0.33
36	66	0.62	0.83	0.55	0.052	0.72	0.59
37	58	0.61	0.87	0.48	0.067	0.72	0.49
38	26	0.58	0.66	0.53	0.035	0.49	0.20
39	4	0.60	0.64	0.56	0.060	0.64	0.34
			Puts Maturing 8412				
30	11	0.95	1.00	0.88	0.047	0.41	0.28
31	23	0.91	0.96	0.81	0.041	0.66	0.43
32	29	0.87	0.96	0.71	0.062	0.72	0.57
33	36	0.82	0.92	0.64	0.089	0.89	0.83
34	37	0.78	0.94	0.64	0.100	0.90	0.83
35	33	0.70	0.92	0.58	0.085	0.84	0.69
36	24	0.65	0.82	0.57	0.050	0.36	0.07

B. Moneyness Bias

The Black–Scholes model has been found to work well for at-the-money options, but often misprices deep-in-the-money and deep-out-of-the-money options. For our study, we created five categories of moneyness. A call option is deep-out-of-the-money (DOM) if the ratio of the futures price to the strike price (F/K) is less than 0.95, it is out-of-the-money (OM) if F/K is between 0.95 and 0.98, it is at-the-money (AM) if F/K is between 0.98 and 1.02, it is in-the-money (IM) if F/K is between 1.02 and 1.05, and deep-in-the-money (DIM) if F/K is greater than 1.05. The moneyness of put options is defined similarly, except for reversing the order of the definition of moneyness.

Table 5 summarizes our findings. In the first row, we compare the implied volatilities of deep-out-of-the-money calls with those of the other four categories of call options. The comparison against the at-the-money calls is in the second column. In our data, there are 570 days with observations for

Table 5. Comparison of Implied Volatilities across Moneyness[a].

	OM	AM	IM	DIM
		Call Options		
DOM	-10.0	-14.1	-11.9	-15.2
	$(23,451)^c$	$(16,570)^c$	$(13,192)^c$	$(1,24)^c$
OM		-5.9	-5.5	-8.5
		$(68,441)^c$	$(35,169)^c$	$(9,45)^c$
AM			-1.5	-0.8
			$(68,182)^c$	$(13,44)^c$
IM				-0.7
				$(13,28)$
		Put Options		
DOM	-4.0	-5.6	-4.8	-2.0
	$(25,111)^c$	$(19,134)^c$	$(11,49)^c$	$(5,11)$
OM		-3.4	-0.4	3.0
		$(58,235)^c$	$(43,93)$	$(11,20)$
AM			2.4	6.8
			$(90,144)$	$(17,24)$
IM				2.4
				$(7,17)$

[a] The numbers in the table are the averages of the logarithm of the implied volatility of the less out-of-the-money option minus that of the more out-of-the-money option. The first number in parentheses is the number of times the implied volatility of the less out-of-the-money option exceeds that of the more out-of-the-money option. The second number is the total number of such comparisons.

[b] Definition of moneyness:

Puts	Calls	
DIM:	DOM:	Futures/Strike $\leqslant 0.95$
IM:	OM:	$0.95 <$ Futures/Strike $\leqslant 0.98$
AM:	AM:	$0.98 <$ Futures/Strike $\leqslant 1.02$
OM:	IM:	$1.02 <$ Futures/Strike $\leqslant 1.05$
DOM:	DIM:	$1.05 <$ Futures/Strike.

[c] Denotes statistical significance at the 5% level of the one-tailed test, that the implied volatilities of the less out-of-the-money option is smaller than that of the more out-of-the-money option, using the nonparametric test in Rubinstein [28].

both categories. Of these, only 16 pairs (2.81%) contain at-the-money calls with implied volatilities greater than deep-out-of-the-money calls. The implied volatilities of the at-the-money calls are less than those of the deep-out-of-the-money calls at the 5% significance level, using the nonparametric test in Rubinstein [28]. On average, the implied volatilities of the at-the-money calls are 10.0% smaller than those of the deep-out-of-the-money calls. Figure 2 contains a plot of the two implied volatilities for the calls maturing in September 1984, and shows that the deep-out-of-the-money calls consistently have higher implied volatilities than the at-the-money calls. A glance at Table 5 reveals that, as a rule, the deep-out-of-the-money calls have the largest implied volatilities, and the out-of-the-money calls the second largest. The rankings are not conclusive for the remaining calls, probably because these options are not traded as frequently.

The comparison for puts gives similar results. Table 5 shows that the deep-out-of-the-money puts have the largest implied volatilities, and the out-of-the-money puts the second largest. Again, the rankings are not conclusive for the remaining puts. Figure 3 contains a plot of the implied volatilities of the out-of-the-money puts and the at-the-money puts, and shows that the out-of-the-money puts consistently have higher implied volatilities than the at-the-money puts.

Our results show that the Black–Scholes model underprices out-of-the-money calls and puts relative to at-the-money options. Borenstein and Dooley [10] find the same phenomenon in options on cash currencies. However, Whaley [35] finds that the model overpriced out-of-the-money calls but underpriced out-of-the-money puts for options on the Standard and Poors 500 futures contract.

To check the robustness of our results, we performed regression tests using options that are identical except for strike prices. The results are consistent with those above. They show that options with lower strike prices have lower implied volatilities. (These results are not reported in the paper, but are available upon request.)

To check if the moneyness bias changes with time to mturity, we recomputed Table 5 for options with maturities of 0–2 weeks, 3–4 weeks, 5–6 weeks, 7–10 weeks, and 10 or more weeks. The results are in Appendices 1 to 5. They show very clearly that the moneyness bias continues to hold, regardless of the time to maturity. In fact, the moneyness bias becomes more pronounced as time to maturity shortens. For example, the average difference in implied volatilities between out-of-the-money calls and deep-out-of-the-money calls is 7.1% when both options have 10 or more weeks until maturity. This difference rises to 11.0, 21.7, 23.1, and 45.9% as the time to maturity falls to 7–10 weeks, 5–6 weeks, 3–4 weeks, and 0–2 weeks, respectively.

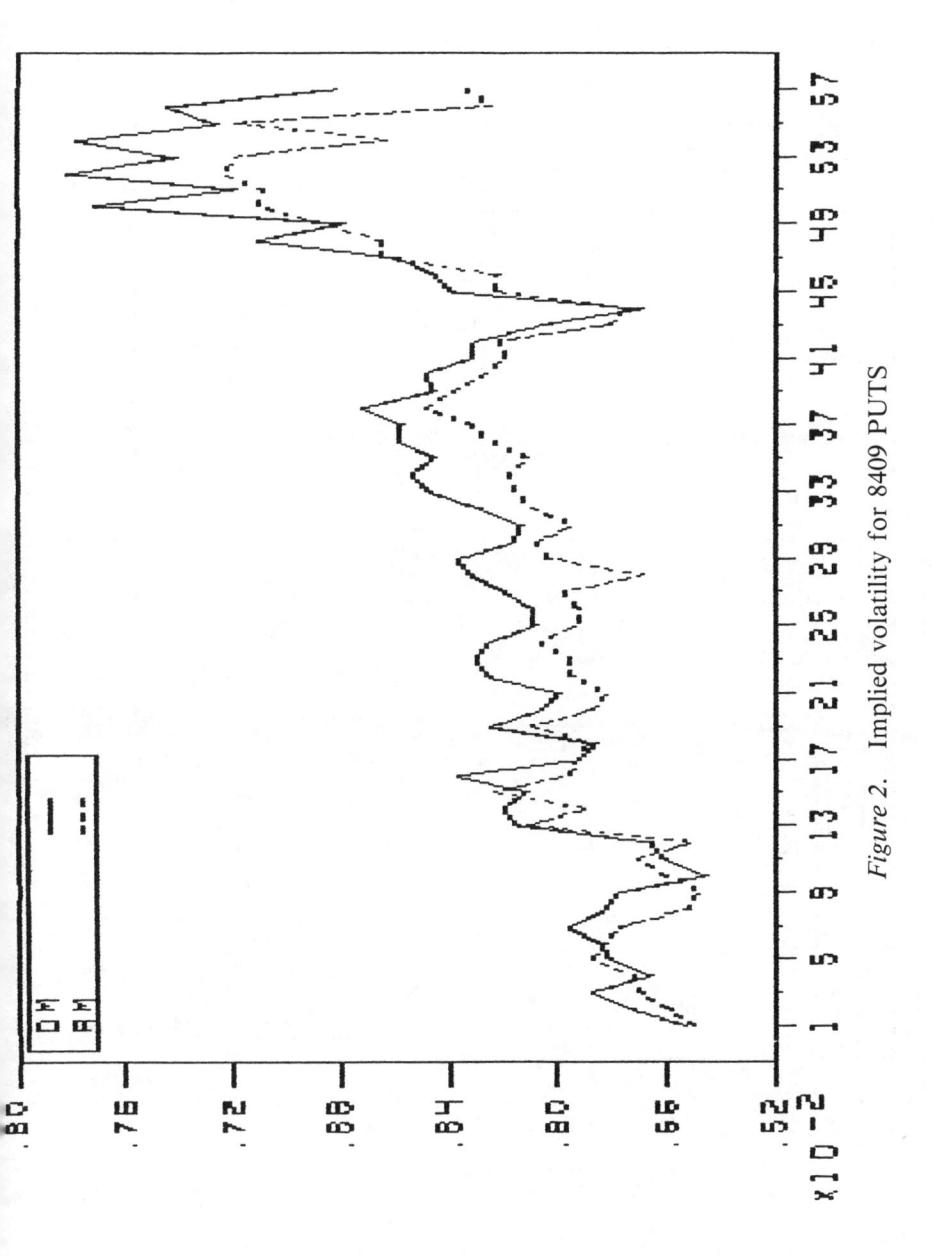

Figure 2. Implied volatility for 8409 PUTS

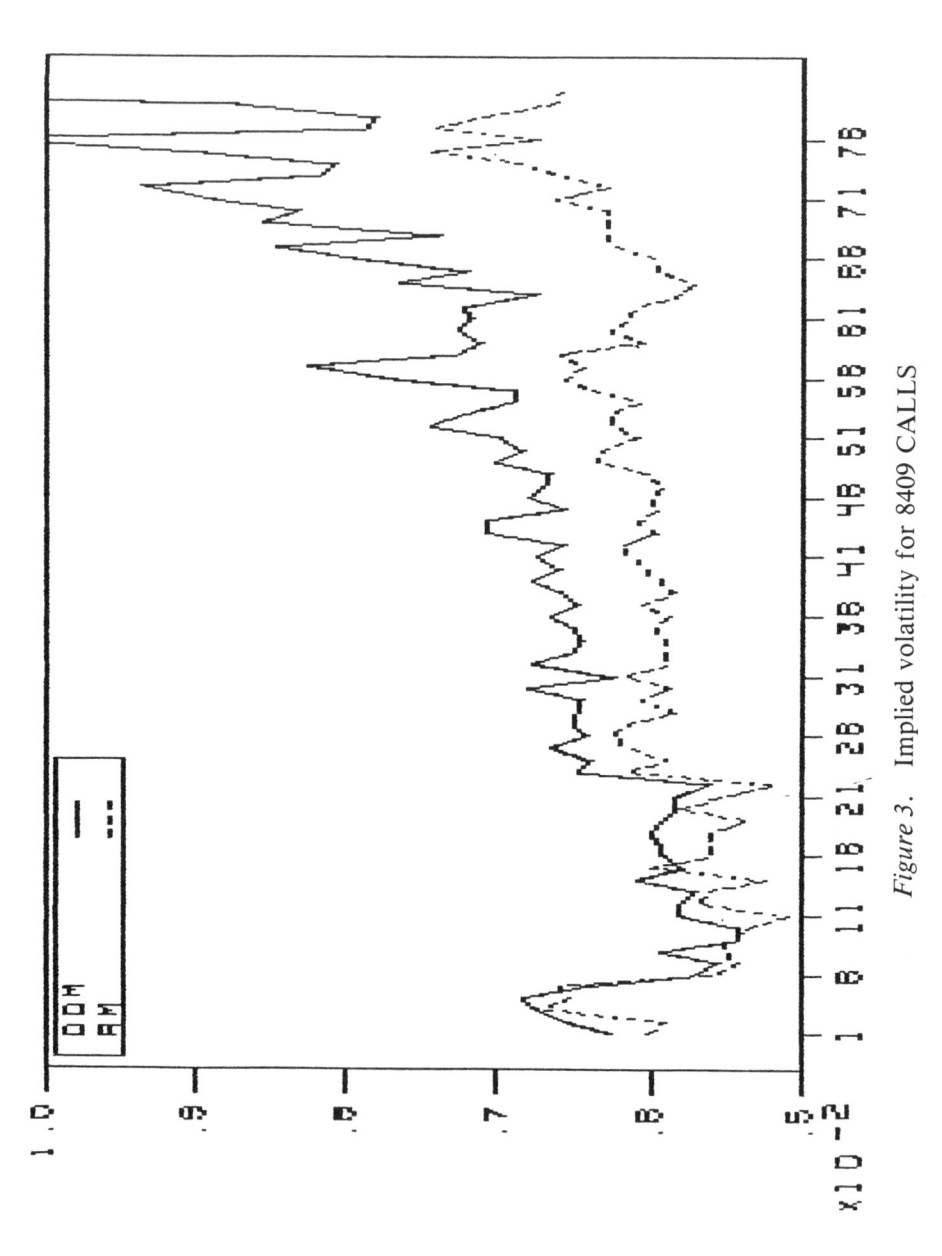

Figure 3. Implied volatility for 8409 CALLS

C. Maturity Bias

Ball and Torous [2] observed that implied volatilities of DM futures options increased as the time to maturity decreased. They regressed the implied volatilities of at-the-money options on their maturity times, and find a positive and statistically significant coefficient for most of the sample.

We also find the same phenomenon in our data. But we obtain our results using the nonparametric test of Rubinstein [28]. We compared the implied volatilities of pairs of options that are identical except that they mature 3 months apart. For example, we compared the implied volatility of the 38c call maturing in June with that of the 38c call maturing in September, as they move through time. In this way, we hold constant all other aspects except time to maturity. We performed the same analysis holding fixed moneyness as well. Under the assumptions of the Black–Scholes model, the implied volatilities should not differ between options with different times to maturity.

The findings are in Table 6. Let us first examine the effect of maturity alone. For call options, this is in the sixth row of the table, and for put options, in the last row. In our sample, there are 50 pairs of options that are identical except they mature 3 months apart, and the shorter term option has 0–2 weeks remaining until expiration. There are 38 pairs (76%) in which the shorter term option has the larger implied volatility. The difference is 27.7% on average. The results are equally striking for those matched pairs in which the shorter term option has 3–4 weeks and 5–6 weeks remaining until expiration. The evidence is not conclusive for the remaining pairs.

For puts, when the shorter term option has 4 or fewer weeks remaining to expiration, it also tends to have a higher implied volatility than the longer term option. The evidence is not conclusive for the remaining pairs.

To check if the maturity bias is affected by the moneyness of the options, we performed the same comparisons holding fixed moneyness. The first row in Table 6 shows that for deep-out-of-the-money calls, the shorter term option always has a higher implied volatility, regardless of time to maturity. This, however, does not hold for the other call options. The second row in Table 6 shows that for out-of-the-money calls, the shorter term option has a higher implied volatility only if it has less than 6 weeks to maturity. Similarly, the third row in Table 6 shows that for at-the-money calls, the shorter term option has a higher implied volatility only if it has less than 4 weeks to maturity. The evidence is inconclusive for in-the-money and deep-in-the-money calls. For put options, there are also too few observations to give any definitive conclusions about any effects moneyness has on the maturity bias.

Our results indicate that the Black–Scholes model underprices very-near-maturity options relative to middle-maturity options. Borestein and Dooley

Table 6.   Comparison of Implied Volatilities between across Maturity[a]

Moneyness	Weeks 0–2	to 3–4	Maturity 5–6	of 7–10	Shorter 10+	Option Total
			Call Options			
DOM	116.5	26.0	22.6	11.7	11.5	24.6
	(3,3)	(10,10)	(21,21)	(17,19)	(8,8)	(59,61)
OM	57.6	14.8	5.6	0.7	−2.4	7.4
	(8,8)	(21,21)	(26,34)	(19,36)	(11,26)	(85,125)
AM	14.6	2.6	0.4	−4.4	−4.9	2.3
	(26,36)	(29,43)	(19,37)	(7,39)	(3,16)	(84,171)
IM	b	−2.1	b	b	b	−2.5
	(1,3)	(2,10)	(1,3)	(1,2)	(1,2)	(6,20)
DIM	—	b	—	—	b	15.0
	(0,0)	(2,2)	(0,0)	(0,0)	(1,1)	(3,3)
Total	27.7	9.3	7.1	0.7	−1.3	7.4
	(38,50)	(64,86)	(67,95)	(44,96)	(24,43)	(237,380)
			Put Options			
DOM	—	—	b	—	—	b
	(0,0)	(0,0)	(1,1)	(0,0)	(0,0)	(1,1)
OM	—	b	2.1	—	—	5.9
	(0,0)	(1,1)	(5,8)	(0,0)	(0,0)	(6,9)
AM	18.1	2.1	0.1	−3.2	b	4.9
	(24,27)	(18,26)	(14,33)	(4,14)	(0,2)	(60,102)
IM	21.3	5.8	1.3	b	b	6.1
	(4,5)	(12,13)	(7,10)	(2,3)	(0,1)	(25,32)
DIM	—	b	b	—	—	8.6
	(0,0)	(1,1)	(1,1)	(0,0)	(0,0)	(2,2)
Total	20.5	13.7	4.4	−1.3	b	6.0
	(28,32)	(32,41)	(28,53)	(6,17)	(0,3)	(94,146)

[a] The numbers are the averages of the logarithm of the implied volatility of the closer-to-maturity option minus that of the further-to-maturity option. The first number in parentheses is the number of times the implied volatility of the closer-to-maturity option is greater than that of the further-to-maturity option.
[b] Less than five comparisons.

[10] find similar results in options on cash currencies. However, Whaley [35] finds that the model overprices very-near-maturity options relative to middle-maturity options.

VI.   CONCLUSION

In our analysis of the DM futures options, we found that futures options have very low rates of violations of early exercise boundary conditions and put–call parity conditions. This is indicative of well-synchronized markets and low transaction costs.

In our analysis of implied volatilities, we found the following empirical regularities:

1. Implied volatilities are not constant over time. In fact, they appear to be serially correlated.
2. The moneyness bias is very strong, regardless of time to maturity. The Black–Scholes model underprices out-of-the-money options relative to at-the-money options.
3. The maturity bias is also important. The Black–Scholes model underprices very-near-maturity options relative to middle-maturity options.

These empirical regularities imply that there are systematic biases in the Black–Scholes model. These biases are unlikely to be caused by transaction costs and discontinuous trading. Trading costs are very low, and currencies can almost be traded around the clock. Rather, the biases of the Black–Scholes model is likely to result from an incorrect distributional assumption — that the underlying asset price is a Wiener diffusion process. There are several alternative explanations that may account for the moneyness and maturity biases.

The first candidate is that the underlying process contains a jump component. Rubinstein [28] show that the mixed jump diffusion process can cause the Black–Scholes model to underprice deep-out-of-the-money options relative to at-the-money options, and very-near-maturity options relative to middle-maturity options. Borenstein and Dooley [10] cite the pure jump process as a possible explanation for the moneyness and maturity biases. There is, however, additional evidence that contradicts this explanation. The pure jump process and the mixed jump diffusion process imply that incremental changes in the exchange rate are independent and identically distributed. This is not consistent with the findings in Hsieh [20] and Manas-Anton [23] that the rates of change of spot exchange rates are not independent and identically distributed, and that variances are changing over time.

The second candidate is the Samuelson [29] hypothesis that the variance of the futures price increases as the contract nears maturity. This was used in Ball and Torous [2] to explain the maturity bias. If the Samuelson conjecture is true, one should observe widening daily trading ranges as a future contract nears maturity. Plots of the daily highs and lows for the four DM futures contracts maturing in 1984 (available upon request) show little evidence to support the Samuelson conjecture. In addition, even if the Samuelson hypothesis is true, it can explain only the maturity bias, not the moneyness bias.

The third candidate is that the cash and futures prices follow ARCH or GARCH processes. Simulations conducted by Mustafa [25] for call options indicate that the Black–Scholes model underprices out-of-the-money options relative to at-the-money options, and near-maturity options relative to middle-maturity options. Thus, the ARCH or GARCH models can explain the moneyness and maturity biases in our data. Furthermore, ARCH and GARCH models are consistent with the observation that rates of change of spot currency prices are not independent, and that their variances are changing over time. Thus, the ARCH family of models appears to be the best explanation of the empirical regularities in options prices, futures prices, and cash prices in the foreign exchange markets.

REFERENCES

1. Ball, C. A., and W. N. Torous, "Our Jumps in Common Stock Prices and Their Impact on Call Option Pricing," *Journal of Finance* 40 (1985), 155–173.
2. Ball, C. A., and W. N. Torous, "Futures Options and the Volatility of Futures Prices," *Journal of Finance* 41 (1986), 857–870.
3. Barone-Adesi, G., and R. Whaley, "Efficient Analytic Approximation of American Option Values," *Journal of Finance* 42 (1987), 301–320.
4. Biger, N., and J. Hull, "The Valuation of Currency Options," *Financial Management* 12 (1983), 24–28.
5. Black, F., "The Pricing of Commodity Contracts," *Journal of Financial Economics* 3 (1976), 167–179.
6. Black, F., and M. Scholes, "The Valuation of Option Contracts and a Test of Market Efficiency," *Journal of Finance* 27 (1972), 399–417.
7. Black, F., and M. Scholes, "The Pricing of Options and Corporate Liabilities," *Journal of Political Economy* 81 (1973), 637–654.
8. Bodurtha, J. N., and G. R. Courtadon, "Efficiency Tests of the Foreign Currency Options Market," *Journal of Finance* 41 (1986), 151–162.
9. Bollerslev, T,. "Generalized Autoregressive Conditional Heteroskedasticity," *Journal of Econometrics* 31 (1986), 307–327.
10. Borenstein, E. R., and M. P. Dooley, "Options on Foreign Exchange and Exchange Rate Expectations," unpublished manuscript, International Monetary Fund, 1987.
11. Burt, J., F. R. Kaen, and G. G. Booth, "Foreign Market Efficiency under Flexible Exchange Rates," *Journal of Finance* 32 (1977), 1325–1330.
12. Cox, J. C., J. E. Ingersoll, Jr., and S. A. Ross, "The Relation between Forward Prices and Futures Prices," *Journal of Financial Economics* 9 (1981), 321–346.
13. Cox, J. C., and M. Rubinstein, *Options Markets*. Englewood Cliffs, N.J.: Prentice-Hall, 1985.
14. Engle, R. E., "Autoregressive Conditional Heteroscedasticity with Estimates of the Variance of United Kingdom Inflation," *Econometrica* 50 (1982), 987–1007.
15. French, D. W., "The Weekend Effect on the Distribution of Stock Prices: Implications for Option Pricing," *Journal of Financial Economics* 13 (1984), 547–559.
16. Galai, D., "Empirical Tests of Boundary Conditions for CBOE Options," *Journal of Financial Economics* 6 (1978), 187–211.
17. Garman, M. B., and S. W. Kohlhagen, "Foreign Currency Option Values," *Journal of International Money and Finance* 2 (1983), 231–238.

18. Giddy, I., "Foreign Exchange Options," *Journal of Futures Markets* 3 (1983), 143–166.
19. Grabbe, J. O., "The Pricing of Call and Put Options on Foreign Exchange," *Journal of International Money and Finance* (1983), 239–254.
20. Hsieh, D. A., "The Statistical Properties of Daily Foreign Exchange Rates: 1974–1983," *Journal of International Economics* (1988), 129–145.
21. Luft, C. F., and B. D. Fielitz, "Am Empirical Test of the Commodity Option Pricing Model Using Ginnie Mae Call Options," *Journal of Financial Research* 9 (1986), 137–151.
22. Luft, C. F., and A. Ghoshal, "Foreign Currency Option Values: A Comparison of Historical and Implied Volatilities," unpublished manuscript, DePaul University, 1986.
23. Manas-Anton, L. A., "Empirical Behavior of Flexible Exchange Rates: Statistical Analysis and Consistent Models," unpublished Ph.D. dissertation, University of Chicago, 1986.
24. Merton, R. C., "A Theory of Rational Option Pricing," *The Bell Journal of Economics and Management Science* 4 (1973), 141–183.
25. Mustafa, C., "Option Valuation with Integrated GARCH Processes," unpublished manuscript, University of California at San Diego, 1987.
26. Ramaswamy, K., and S. M. Sundaresan, "The Valuation of Options on Futures Contracts," *Journal of Finance* 40 (1985), 1319–1340.
27. Rogalski, R. J., and J. D. Vinson, "Empirical Properties of Foreign Exchange Rates," *Journal of International Business Studies* 9 (1978), 69–79.
28. Rubinstein, M., "Nonparametric Tests of Alternative Option Pricing Models Using All Reported Trades on the 30 Most Active CBOE Option Classes from August 23, 1976 Through August 31, 1978," *Journal of Finance* 40 (1985), 455–480.
29. Samuelson, P. A., "Proof That Properly Anticipated Prices Fluctuate Randomly," *Industrial Management Review* 6 (1965), 41–49.
30. Shastri, K., and K. Tandon, "Arbitrage Tests of the Efficiency of the Foreign Currency Options," *Journal of International Money and Finance* 4 (1985), 455–468.
31. Shastri, K., and K. Tandon, "Valuation of Foreign Currency Options: Some Empirical Tests," *Journal of Financial and Quantitative Analysis* 21 (1986), 145–160.
32. Shastri, K., and K. Tandon, "On the Use of European Models to Price American Options on Foreign Currency," *Journal of Futures Markets* 6 (1986), 93–108.
33. Stoll, H. R., and R. E. Whaley, "New Option Instruments: Arbitrage Linkages and Valuation," *Advances in Futures and Options Research* 1 (1986), 25–62.
34. Westerfield, J. M., "An Examination of Foreign Exchange Risk under Fixed and Floating Rate Regimes," *Journal of International Economics* 7 (1977), 181–200.
35. Whaley, R. E., "Valuation of American Futures Options: Theory and Empirical Tests," *Journal of Finance* 41 (1986), 127–150.

APPENDIX 1: PAIRWISE COMPARISON OF IMPLIED VOLATILITIES ACROSS MONEYNESS

	OM	AM	IM	DIM
	Call Options with More Than 10 Weeks To Maturity			
DOM	− 7.1	− 9.4	− 10.8	− 15.2
	(19,296)	(15,361)	(10,132)	(1,24)
OM		− 2.5	− 5.1	− 8.5
		(62,255)	(20,115)	(9,45)
AM			− 2.6	− 7.4
			(37,112)	(9,40)
IM				− 0.7
				(13,28)
	Put Options with More Than 10 Weeks to Maturity			
DOM	− 3.6	− 5.3	− 4.5	− 2.2
	(20,85)	(17,100)	(7,29)	(4,8)
		− 2.0	− 1.0	− 0.4
OM		(39,123)	(17,37)	(4,9)
			− 1.0	0.4
AM			(28,49)	(6,9)
IM				0.1
				(3,8)

See notes in Table 5.

APPENDIX 2: PAIRWISE COMPARISON OF IMPLIED VOLATILITIES ACROSS MONEYNESS

	OM	AM	IM	DIM
	Call Options with 7–10 Weeks To Maturity			
DOM	− 11.0	− 14.8	− 12.0	—
	(2,101)	(1,141)	(2,44)	
OM		− 5.2	− 3.4	—
		(5,94)	(8,29)	
AM			0.3	—
			(19,39)	
IM				—
	Put Options with 7–10 Weeks to Maturity			
DOM	− 4.6	− 6.9	− 4.9	*a*
	(5,23)	(2,29)	(4,14)	(0,1)
OM		− 2.6	− 0.3	*a*
		(12,61)	(16,33)	(0,3)
AM			2.2	*a*
			(34,53)	(0,3)
IM				*a*
				(0,3)

See notes in Table 5.
*a*Less than five comparisons.

APPENDIX 3: PAIRWISE COMPARISON OF IMPLIED VOLATILITIES ACROSS MONEYNESS

	OM	*AM*	*IM*	*DIM*
	Call Options with 5–6 Weeks To Maturity			
DOM	− 21.7	− 28.3	− 27.9	—
	(0,36)	(0,42)	(0,11)	
OM		− 7.0	− 9.1	—
		(1,41)	(1,10)	
AM			− 5.2	—
			(2,12)	
IM				—
	Put Options with 5–6 Weeks to Maturity			
DOM	a	− 4.9	a	a
	(0,3)	(0,5)	(0,3)	(1,2)
OM		− 6.3	− 1.6	12.4
		(6,26)	(6,16)	(6,7)
AM			2.8	16.3
			(17,27)	(10,11)
IM				13.9
				(4,6)

See notes in Table 5.
[a]Less than five observations.

APPENDIX 4: PAIRWISE COMPARISON OF IMPLIED VOLATILITIES ACROSS MONEYNESS

	OM	*AM*	*IM*	*DIM*
	Call Options with 3–4 Weeks To Maturity			
DOM	− 23.1	− 39.2	− 4.2	—
	(2,14)	(0,21)	(1,5)	
OM		− 14.5	− 7.0	—
		(0,37)	(6,14)	
AM			4.7	—
			(10,17)	
IM				—
	Put Options with 3–4 Weeks to Maturity			
DOM	—	—	—	—
OM		− 6.5	− 0.7	a
		(1,18)	(2,5)	(1,1)
AM			2.0	—
			(8,12)	
IM				—

See notes in Table 5.
[a]Less than five comparisons.

APPENDIX 5: PAIRWISE COMPARISON OF IMPLIED VOLATILITIES ACROSS MONEYNESS

	OM	AM	IM	DIM
	Call Options with 0–2 Weeks To Maturity			
DOM	*a*	− 105.5	—	—
	(0,4)	(0,5)		
OM		− 47.1	*a*	—
		(0,14)	(0,1)	
			a	*a*
AM			(0,2)	(4,4)
IM				—
	Put Options with 0–2 Weeks to Maturity			
DOM	—	—	—	—
OM		− 18.3	*a*	—
		(0,7)	(2,2)	
AM			*a*	—
			(3,3)	
IM				—

See notes in Table 5.
*a*Less than five comparisons.

PREFERENCE-FREE OPTION PRICES WHEN THE STOCK RETURNS CAN GO UP, GO DOWN, OR STAY THE SAME

Stylianos Perrakis*

I. INTRODUCTION

This paper derives preference-free European option prices for assets whose returns over a single time period are generated by a trinomial process. The only restriction on such a process is that the return under the middle one of the three states must be equal to 1. In other words, the stock return in an elementary time period must go up, go down, or stay the same with positive

*Faculty of Adminstration, University of Ottawa.

I wish to thank Peter Ryan for many helpful discussions leading to the development of this paper.

Advances in Futures and Options Research, Vol. 3, pages 209–235.

probabilities. As argued in [15], this three-state process is a more realistic model for options on individual stocks than the widely used two-state process, originally developed in [3] and [11].

Under the two-state process it is always possible to construct a riskless hedge involving the stock, the option, and the riskless asset. Consequently, it is also possible to derive European option prices that are both exact and preference-free. As shown in [4, pp. 366–367] the two-state assumption is both necessary and sufficient for the derivation of such option prices. Hence, any attempts to relax this assumption must either introduce specific preferences, or accept the possibility that option prices may not be uniquely determined solely by arbitrage considerations. In [15] Stapleton and Subrahmanyam followed the first approach: they introduced the assumption of constant proportional risk-aversion (CPRA) utilities for the representative investor,[1] and showed that with these preferences the trinomial process corresponded to the same option price as the two-state process. Here, by contrast, we adopt the second possibility: option prices may not be exactly determined by the arbitrage requirements implicit in stock market equilibrium. This approach, originally introduced in [10] and subsequently extended in [8], [9], and [12], derives upper and lower bounds on European option prices based on the entire distribution of stock returns. As shown in [8], these bounds are generalizations of the binomial option price, coinciding with it under the two-state assumption.

Although the bounds of [8], [9], [10], and [12] are valid for any return distribution and, hence, include the trinomial as a special case, they are not completely preference-free. They were developed under the assumption that the state-contingent discount factors implicit in stockmarket equilibrium were monotonically ordered with respect to the stock return. These state-contingent discount factors were identified in [13] as the normalized expected marginal utility of consumption of the representative investor, conditional on the occurrence of a particular state (stock return value). Hence, the monotonicity assumption embodied some restrictions on investor preferences that were, however, more general than CPRA utilities. No such restrictions are adopted in this paper, even though the methodology used is very similar to that of [8], [9], [10], and [12]. It follows, therefore, that the derived bounds are wider than those of the earlier studies, even though they are also based on the same data for their derivation.

A question that was left unanswered in the earlier studies was the asymptotic behavior of the option bounds as the length of the elementary time period shrinks to zero, while the number of such periods tends to infinity within a fixed time interval. As shown in [3] the two-state bound tends to the familiar Black–Scholes option pricing of [1] when subjected to such a limiting process, provided that the stock return distribution follows a diffusion process; otherwise the option price tends to the one corresponding to a jump process [3, p. 255]. The conditions for such limiting stock return distributions were investigated in detail in [7]. In this paper the derived preference-free bounds are also subjected to the same limiting process under diffusion. This asymptotic behavior produces a Black–Scholes type option price for the upper bound, but with a variance different from that of the basic process. For positive beta stocks this upper bound is directly related to the probability of the middle (stay-the-same) state. The lower bound, on the other hand, tends to the well-known bound already identified by Merton in [6].

The situation is different if the stock returns follow asymptotically a jump process. Then the preference-free lower bound tends to a two-state option price corresponding to a jump process. The upper bound, on the other hand, tends to the trivial bound represented by the price of the stock.

Last, the asymptotic behavior of the bounds under diffusion is examined for all possible preference patterns arising out of the three-state process. It is then shown that the *only pattern* capable of generating the Black–Scholes price as a unique equilibrium value is the one corresponding to the monotone ordering assumption used in [8], [9], [10], and [12]. This assumption, therefore, constitutes a necessary, as well as a sufficient condition for Black–Scholes pricing to emerge out of the trinomial process.

The importance of these results can perhaps be judged from the brief presentation and analysis in [4, pp. 367–368] of the stock return process used in this paper. The authors of that book noted that the three-state process had the same mean and variance, and the same asymptotic behaviour as the two-state process. They also conjectured that the option price would tend asymptotically to the same bound as the two-state process, namely the Black–Scholes price. The conjecture *is not verified*: the asymptotic behavior of options on stocks that follow the three-state process of one-period returns is not independent of the pattern of preferences. These options *may* tend to an exact price, but only if the monotone ordering of preferences of [8], [9], [10], and [12] is assumed. Otherwise, a range of possible option prices exists even under asymptotic conditions.

The organization of this paper is as follows. The next section sets up the notation and assumptions of the general model. Section III examines the option bounds under various preference structures, and determines the smallest and largest among these bounds. Finally, Sections IV and V examine the limiting stock return process under diffusion and jump process, respectively, and derive the behavior of the two extreme option bounds with such processes. A numerical simulation has also been included.

II. THE MODEL AND ITS ASSUMPTIONS

Let S denote the price of the stock and X the exercise price of the option. The stock return per dollar invested[2] Z may take exactly three values z_i in one period, with corresponding probabilities p_i, $i = 1, 2, 3$, and $z_1 < z_2 < z_3$. It will be assumed that $z_2 = 1$, so that one period later the stock price becomes Sz_1, S, or Sz_3. There are no taxes or dividends. Let R denote one plus the riskless rate of interest, which is assumed nonrandom and constant in every period.

As Rubinstein [13] and Brennan [2] showed, the value V[ ] of a contingent claim $g(Z)$ on such a stock is given by

$$V[g(Z)] = \frac{1}{R} E[\hat{Y}(Z)g(Z)], \tag{1}$$

where $\hat{Y}(Z)/R$ are the state-contingent discount factors. The function $\hat{Y}(Z)$ is not unique in an incomplete market, in which the number of possible states of the world exceeds the number of available securities. Similarly, it is not necessary that $\hat{Y}(Z)$ be the same for all investors. If, however, we adopt a number of additional assumptions, spelled out in detail in [13], then it was shown in that same paper that $\hat{Y}(Z)$ can be interpreted as the conditional marginal utility of consumption of a representative investor, normalized by its expectation. In other words, $\hat{Y}(z) \equiv E[Y \mid Z = z]/E[Y]$, where Y is the marginal utility. As already noted, such additional assumptions are not necessary for the models of this paper. Accordingly, the only assumptions adopted here are (1) the single-price law, (2) nonsatiation, and (3) homogeneous expectations on the part of all investors concerning the disribution of stock returns.[3]

A comparison of these assumptions with the corresponding assumptions of the discrete-time option models of [2], [13], [15], and [8], [9], [10], [12] shows very clearly the gains in generality achieved here. Thus, investor utilities of the constant proportional risk aversion (CPRA) class were assumed for all investors in [2], [13], and [15], together with specific forms of the joint (Y, Z) distribution. In the more general models of [8], [9], [10], and [12], on the other hand, $\hat{Y}(z)$ was assumed monotone nonincreasing or nondecreasing, a shape that is implied by the distributional assumptions of the other models. Here, by contrast, $\hat{Y}(z)$ is unrestricted in shape.

Let $\hat{z} \equiv E[Z] = \sum_{i=1}^{3} p_i z_i$ denote the expectation of Z. By the definition of $\hat{Y}(z)$ we have $E[Z\hat{Y}(Z)] = R$, and $E[\hat{Y}(Z)] = 1$. From (1) and the definition of Z these relations imply simply that the current value of the one-period return on $1 invested in the stock is $1, and that the value of $1 received with certainty one period later is $1/R$. Since $R = E[Z\hat{Y}(Z)] = E[Z]E[\hat{Y}(Z)] + Cov[Z, \hat{Y}(Z)] = \hat{z} + Cov[Z, \hat{Y}(Z)]$, we have $R \gtrless \hat{z}$ depending on whether $Cov[Z, \hat{Y}(Z)] \gtrless 0$. Hereafter we shall assume without loss of generality that $\hat{z} \geq R$, or that our stock is a "positive beta" security. As noted in [9], such securities form the overwhelming majority of stocks. The pricing of options on negative beta securities can be done very easily and with minimal reformulation by following the methodology of this paper.

The assumption that $\hat{z} \geqslant R$ imposes certain restrictions on the shape of $\hat{Y}(z)$. Specifically, the relative order of the three values $\hat{Y}(z_i)$, $i = 1, 2, 3$, must be one of the following four alternatives: (1) $\hat{Y}(z_1) \geqslant \hat{Y}(z_2) \geqslant \hat{Y}(z_3)$, (2) $\hat{Y}(z_1) \geqslant \hat{Y}(z_3) \geqslant \hat{Y}(z_2)$, (3) $\hat{Y}(z_2) \geqslant \hat{Y}(z_1) \geqslant \hat{Y}(z_3)$, or (4) $\hat{Y}(z_2) \geqslant \hat{Y}(z_3) \geqslant \hat{Y}(z_1)$. Of these, (1) and (3) are consistent only with $\hat{z} \geqslant R$, while (2) and (4) are consistent with both $\hat{z} \geqslant R$ and $\hat{z} \leqslant R$. The orders $\hat{Y}(z_3) \geqslant \hat{Y}(z_1) \geqslant \hat{Y}(z_2)$ and $\hat{Y}(z_3) \geqslant \hat{Y}(z_2) \geqslant \hat{Y}(z_1)$, on the other hand, are possible only if $\hat{z} \leqslant R$, and are excluded otherwise.

Let $C_n(S, X)$ denote the price of an n-period European call option on a stock of value S with exercise price X. This price will, in general, depend upon the structure of preferences, represented in this case by the function $\hat{Y}(Z)$. Let the superscript (i) denote the corresponding case of relative order of the three factors $\hat{Y}(z_j)$, $i = 1, \ldots, 4$, $j = 1, 2, 3$. For instance, $C_n^{(1)}(S, X)$ represents the option price under the preference structure $\hat{Y}(z_1) \geqslant \hat{Y}(z_2) \geqslant \hat{Y}(z_3)$. In [8], [9], [10], and [12] it was shown that $C_n^{(1)}(S, X)$ was contained between an upper and a lower limit.[4] In the next section it will be shown that the same is true for option prices under each one of the four preference structures $C_n^{(i)}(S, X)$, $i = 1, \ldots, 4$, $n = 1, 2, \ldots$. Hence, the largest and smallest of these limits for all four structures represent the preference-free bounds, between which the true option value lies for all rational investors.

III. OPTION BOUNDS UNDER VARIOUS PREFERENCE STRUCTURES

Let $\bar{C}_n^{(i)}(S, X)$ and $\underline{C}_n^{(i)}(S, X)$ represent, respectively, the upper and lower bounds on the call value $C_n(S, X)$ under preference structure (i), $i = 1, \ldots, 4$. In [8], [9], [10], and [12] these bounds were derived for $i = 1$ by two alternative approaches, arbitrage and linear programming (LP). It is this latter method that will be adopted for this paper. The derivations will be carried out in detail for structure (2), the remaining cases being treated as extensions. As in the previous studies [8], [9], and [10], the derivation is recursive, starting from $n = 1$.

Since $\hat{Y}(z_1) \geqslant \hat{Y}(z_3) \geqslant \hat{Y}(z_2)$, we set

$$\hat{Y}(z_2) = x_2, \qquad \hat{Y}(z_3) = x_2 + x_3, \qquad \hat{Y}(z_1) = x_1 + x_2 + x_3 \qquad (2)$$

where $x_i \geqslant 0$, $i = 1, 2, 3$. We also define $c_j(S, X) \equiv \max\{0, Sz_j - X\}$, $j = 1, 2, 3$. Since a call option price $C_1(S, X)$ is, by definition of the discount factors $\hat{Y}(z_i)$, equal to $1/R \sum_{j=1}^{3} p_j \hat{Y}(z_j) c_j(S, X)$, where $E[\hat{Y}(Z)] = 1$, $E[Z\hat{Y}(Z)] = R$, any set of discount factors satisfying the last two relations and respecting the relative order of magnitude $\hat{Y}(z_1) \geqslant \hat{Y}(z_3) \geqslant \hat{Y}(z_2)$ yields a possible option price consistent with preference structure (2). Such prices lie between the bounds $\bar{C}_1^{(2)}(S, X)$ and $\underline{C}_1^{(2)}(S, X)$, which are found by, respectively, solving the following LPs:

$$\max(\min)\{\sum_{j=1}^{3} p_j \hat{Y}(z_j) c_j(S, X)\} \tag{3a}$$

subject to

$$\sum_{j=1}^{3} p_j \hat{Y}(z_j) z_j = R \tag{3b}$$

$$\sum_{j=1}^{3} p_j \hat{Y}(z_j) = 1. \tag{3c}$$

Substituting (2) into (3a, b, c) and rearranging, we get for (3b, c)

$$p_1 z_1 x_1 + x_3(p_1 z_1 + p_3 z_3) + x_2 \hat{z} = R, \qquad p_1 x_1 + x_3(p_1 + p_3) + x_2 = 1.$$

The last transformation consists of setting $Y_1 \equiv x_1 p_1$, $Y_2 \equiv x_2$, and $Y_3 \equiv x_3(p_1 + p_3)$. Set also $\hat{z}_{13} = (p_1 z_1 + p_3 z_3)/(p_1 + p_3)$, $\hat{C} = \sum_{j=1}^{3} p_j c_j$, and $\hat{C}_{13} = (p_1 c_1 + p_3 c_3)/(p_1 + p_3)$, where the arguments of the c_j's were omitted for notational simplicity. The systems (3a, b, c) then become

$$\max(\min)\{Y_1 c_1 + Y_2 \hat{C} + Y_3 \hat{C}_{13}\} \tag{4a}$$

subject to

$$Y_1 z_1 + Y_2 \hat{z} + \hat{Y}_3 \hat{z}_{13} = R \tag{4b}$$

$$Y_1 + Y_2 + Y_3 = 1 \tag{4c}$$

$$Y_j = 0, \qquad j = 1, 2, 3.$$

We note that[5] $\hat{z} < \hat{z}_{13}$, and similarly $\hat{C} < \hat{C}_{13}$.

The system (4a, b, c) can now be solved very easily by inspection, along the lines introduced in [12]. Since the graph formed by the three points $\{z_j, c_j, j = 1, 2, 3\}$ on a (z, C) plane is convex, the graph of the points $\{(z_1, c_1), (\hat{z}, \hat{C}), (\hat{z}_{13}, \hat{C}_{13})\}$ is also convex, since its coordinates were obtained by linear transformations of the coordinate of the initial graph.[6] Figure 1 shows the general shape of the transformed graph.[7]

From Figure 1 it is now clear that the set of possible option prices consistent with our preference structure is represented by points within the triangle. Because of constraint (4b) only the points along the line segment AB, with abscissas equal to R, are admissible. It is clear that the solution of the maximization (minimization) problem is represented by point A (B). This point is a convex combination of c_1 and $\hat{C}_{13}$ ($\hat{C}$). From the geometry of the figure it follows that

$$\bar{C}_1^{(2)}(S, X) = \frac{\hat{z}_{13} - R}{(\hat{z}_{13} - z_1)R} c_1(S, X) + \frac{R - z_1}{(\hat{z}_{13} - z_1)R} \hat{C}_{13}(S, X) \tag{5a}$$

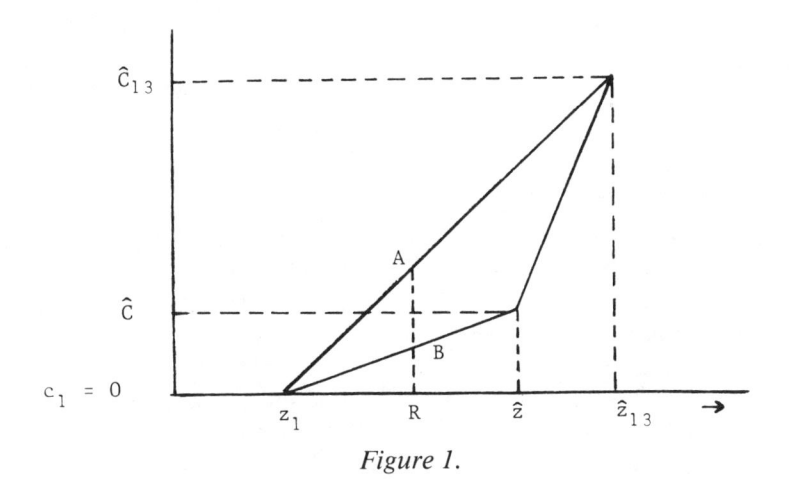

Figure 1.

$$\underline{C}_1^{(2)}(S, X) = \frac{\hat{z} - R}{(\hat{z} - z_1)R} c_1(S, X) + \frac{R - z_1}{(\hat{z} - z_1)R} \hat{C}(S, X). \tag{5b}$$

A comparison of these results with the corresponding bounds of [9] and [12], derived under preference structure (1), shows that preference structure (2) yields uniformly *higher* call option prices than (1). Indeed, the lower bound $\underline{C}_1^{(2)}(S, X)$ coincides with the upper bound $\overline{C}_1^{(1)}(S, X)$. Further, the middle state with return $z_2 = 1$ plays no role in the derivation of the upper bound.

The derivation of the one-period bounds under preference structure (3) can now be summarized briefly, since it follows a pattern similar to that of (2). Under preference structure (3), where $\hat{Y}(z_2) \geqslant \hat{Y}(z_1) \geqslant \hat{Y}(z_3)$, we define again nonnegative variables x_i, $i = 1, 2, 3$, with $\hat{Y}(z_3) = x_3$, $\hat{Y}(z_1) = x_1 + x_3$, $\hat{Y}(z_2) = x_1 + x_2 + x_3$, and substitute them into the two LPs of (3a, b, c). Then we set $Y_3 = x_3$, $Y_1 = x_1(p_1 + p_2)$ and $Y_2 = x_2 p_2$, and define $\hat{z}_{12} = (p_1 z_1 + p_2 z_2)/(p_1 + p_2) = (p_1 z_1 + p_2)/(p_1 + p_2)$, $\hat{C}_{12} = (p_1 c_1 + p_2 c_2)/(p_1 + p_2)$. The two bounds are now found from the LPs:

$$\max(\min)\{Y_1 \hat{C}_{12} + Y_2 c_2 + Y_3 \hat{C}\} \tag{6a}$$
$${}_{\{Y_i\}}$$

subject to

$$Y_1 \hat{z}_{12} + Y_2 + Y_3 \hat{z} = R \tag{6b}$$

$$Y_1 + Y_2 + Y_3 = 1 \tag{6c}$$

where $\hat{z}_{12} < z_2 (=1) < \hat{z}$. It can be easily shown that for any $\delta > 0$ $\delta \hat{C}_{12} + (1 - \delta)\hat{C} \geqslant c_2$. Hence, a convex graph similar[8] to Figure 1 is also formed by the three pairs of coordinates $\{(\hat{z}_{12}, \hat{C}_{12}), (1, c_2), (\hat{z}, \hat{C})\}$.

Applying the same reasoning as in the previous case, we may easily derive

$$\overline{C}_1^{(3)}(S, X) = \frac{\hat{z} - R}{(\hat{z} - \hat{z}_{12})R} \hat{C}_{12}(S, X) + \frac{R - \hat{z}_{12}}{(\hat{z} - \hat{z}_{12})R} \hat{C}(S, X) \tag{7a}$$

$$\underline{C}_1^{(3)}(S, X) = \frac{\hat{z} - R}{(\hat{z} - 1)R} c_2(S, X) + \frac{R - 1}{(\hat{z} - 1)R} \hat{C}(S, X). \tag{7b}$$

Preference structure (4), though, with $\hat{Y}(z_2) \geqslant \hat{Y}(z_3) \geqslant \hat{Y}(z_1)$ is different. It can be transformed in the same way as the other three structures, but it now defines a *concave* graph, as in Figure 2. This graph is formed by the pairs of coordinates $\{(1, c_2), (\hat{z}, \hat{C}), (\hat{z}_{23}, \hat{C}_{23})\}$, where $z_{23} \equiv (p_2 + p_3 z_3)/(p_2 + p_3)$, $\hat{C}_{23} \equiv (p_2 c_2 + p_3 c_3)/(p_2 + p_3)$.

It can be easily shown that for any $\delta > 0$ we have $\hat{C} > \delta c_2 + (1 - \delta)\hat{C}_{23}$, implying a graph similar to Figure 2, rather than Figure 1. Since $R < \hat{z}$, the upper and lower bounds are at points B and A, respectively. The two option bounds now become

$$\overline{C}_1^{(4)}(S, X) = \frac{\hat{z} - R}{(\hat{z} - 1)R} c_2(S, X) + \frac{R - 1}{(\hat{z} - 1)R} \hat{C}(S, X) \tag{8a}$$

$$\underline{C}_1^{(4)}(S, X) \equiv \frac{\hat{z}_{23} - R}{(\hat{z}_{23} - 1)R} c_2(S, X) + \frac{R - 1}{(\hat{z}_{23} - 1)R} \hat{C}_{23}(S, X). \tag{8b}$$

For the sake of completeness we also provide the bounds for preference structure (1), already derived in the earlier studies:

$$\overline{C}_1^{(1)}(S, X) = \frac{\hat{z} - R}{(\hat{z} - z_1)R} c_1(S, X) + \frac{R - z_1}{(\hat{z} - z_1)R} \hat{C}(S, X) \tag{9a}$$

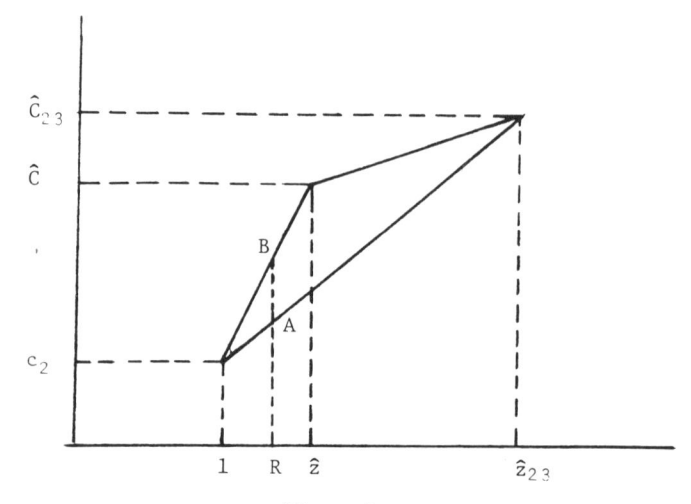

Figure 2.

$$\underline{C}\{^{(1)}(S, X) = \frac{\hat{z} - R}{(\hat{z} - \hat{z}_{12})R} \hat{C}_{12}(S, X) + \frac{R - \hat{z}_{12}}{(\hat{z} - \hat{z}_{12})R} \hat{C}(S, X). \tag{9b}$$

A comparison of (7a) and (9b) shows that $\underline{C}\{^{(1)}(S, X) = \overline{C}\{^{(3)}(S, X)$, implying that preference structure (3) generates lower call option prices than structure (1). Similarly, (7b) and (8a) show that $\underline{C}\{^{(3)}(S, X) = \overline{C}\{^{(4)}(S, X)$, implying lower option prices for (4) than for (3). Since we already saw that structure (2) has higher option prices than (1), we may easily conclude:

PROPOSITION 1. The preference-free call option prices in a single period for a three-state stock return distribution are contained within the lower and upper bounds $\underline{C}\{^{(4)}(S, X)$ and $\overline{C}\{^{(2)}(S, X)$, respectively given by (8b) and (5a).

The next step is the extension of the bounds to more than one period until expiration of the option. It is clear from the various expressions (5), (7), (8), and (9) that the bounds have all the properties of option prices, first derived in [6]. For their multiperiod extensions it will be assumed that successive stock returns Z are independent and identically distributed random variables.[9] Also, it is assumed that preferences are *consistent* between periods, or that the same structure of preferences exists in every period.[10] Given such an assumption, it is possible to formulate a recursive derivation of the bounds, based on an extension of the LP approach. The derivation will be done for preference structure (2) the remaining cases being very similar.

Suppose that we are at $n = 2$, two periods before expiration of the option, and that the option pricing function $C_1(S, X)$ is known. Then at the end of the period the call will become $C_1(Sz, X)$, The price $C_2(S, X)$, therefore, would be equal to $1/R \sum_{j=1}^{3} p_j \hat{Y}(z_j) C_1(Sz_j, X)$, where for structure (2) $\hat{Y}(z_1) \geq \hat{Y}(z_3) \geq \hat{Y}(z_2)$, and the factors $\hat{Y}(z_j)$ satisfy (3b) and (3c). In such a case it would be sufficient to solve the LP problems (3a, b, c), with $C_1(Sz_j, X)$ replacing the factors c_j, in order to find bounds on $C_2(S, X)$ under preference structure (2). Such bounds would be valid for the given call price function $C_1(S, X)$. The bounds for *all possible* first-period call option prices would obviously correspond to LP problems, in which the first-period bounds $\overline{C}\{^{(2)}(S, X)$ and $\underline{C}\{^{(2)}(S, X)$ have replaced the unknown function $C_1(S, X)$, respectively, in the maximization and minimization problems.

Applying the same transformation on the state-contingent discount factors $\hat{Y}(z_j)$, $j = 1, 2, 3$, as in the single-period case, we derive the following LPs for the upper and lower bounds:

$$\max_{\{Y_j\}} \{Y_1 \overline{C}\{^{(2)}(Sz_1) + Y_2 \hat{\overline{C}}\{^{(2)}(S) + Y_3 \hat{\overline{C}}\{^{(2)}_{,13}(S)\} \tag{10a}$$

$$\min_{\{Y_j\}}\{Y_1\underline{C}_1^{(2)}(Sz_1) + Y_2\hat{\underline{C}}_1^{(2)}(S) + Y_3\hat{\underline{C}}_{1,13}^{(2)}(S)\} \tag{10b}$$

subject to the constraints (4b) and (4c), namely

$$Y_1z_1 + Y_2\hat{z} + Y_3\hat{z}_{13} = R, \quad Y_1 + Y_2 + Y_3 = 1, \qquad Y_j \geqslant 0, \qquad j = 1, 2, 3. \tag{10c}$$

In (10a) we have defined

$$\hat{\overline{C}}_1^{(2)}(S) \equiv E[\overline{C}_1^{(2)}(SZ, X)], \quad \hat{\overline{C}}_{1,13}(S) \equiv \frac{p_1\overline{C}_1^{(2)}(Sz_1, X) + p_3\overline{C}_1^{(2)}(Sz_3, X)}{p_1 + p_3},$$

and omitted the argument X for notational simplicity. Similar definitions hold for $\underline{C}_1^{(2)}(S)$ and $\hat{\underline{C}}_{1,13}^{(2)}(S)$. In other words, the functions $\overline{C}_1^{(2)}(Sz, X)$ and $\underline{C}_1^{(2)}(Sz, X)$ replaced the function $\max\{Sz - X, 0\}$ in defining the two-period bounds.

Given the convexity of $\overline{C}_1(S)$ and $\underline{C}_1(S)$, it is easy to see that the three coordinate pairs $\{[z_1, \overline{C}_1^{(2)}(Sz_1)], [\hat{z}, \hat{\overline{C}}_1^{(2)}(S)], [\hat{z}_{13}, \hat{\overline{C}}_{1,13}^{(2)}(S)]\}$, and $\{[z_1, \underline{C}_1^{(2)}(Sz_1)], [\hat{z}, \underline{C}_1^{(2)}(S)], [\hat{z}_{13}, \underline{C}_{1,13}^{(2)}(S)]\}$ form triangular covex graphs similar[11] to Figure 1. The geometric solution of the two LPs (10a, b, c) is, therefore, identical to that of the single-period case: the upper bound is a convex combination of the first and last points of the triangle, and the lower bound a combination of the first and second points. In both cases, the weights are the same as in the single period bounds.

Since the convexity in S of the bounds is preserved in the recursive derivation, it is easy to see that the bounds can be extended without reformulation to any number of periods. Hence, we have

$$\overline{C}_n^{(2)}(S, X) \equiv \frac{\hat{z}_{13} - R}{(\hat{z}_{13} - z_1)R}\overline{C}_{n-1}^{(2)}(Sz_1, X) + \frac{R - z_1}{(\hat{z}_{13} - z_1)R}\hat{\overline{C}}_{n-1,13}(S, X) \tag{11a}$$

$$\underline{C}_n^{(2)}(S, X) = \frac{\hat{z} - R}{(\hat{z} - z_1)R}\underline{C}_{n-1}^{(2)}(Sz_1, X) + \frac{R - z_1}{(\hat{z} - z_1)R}\hat{\underline{C}}_{n-1}^{(2)}(S, X) \tag{11b}$$

where

$$\hat{\overline{C}}_{n-1,13}^{(2)}(S, X) \equiv E[\overline{C}_{n-1}^{(2)}(SZ, X)|Z \neq 1], \quad \text{and} \quad \hat{\underline{C}}_{n-1}^{(2)}(S, X) \equiv E[\underline{C}_{n-1}^{(2)}(SZ, X)].$$

The derivation of the n-period bounds for the three other preference structures is done in the same spirit as for structure (2). Thus, we have

$$\overline{C}_n^{(3)}(S, X) = \frac{\hat{z} - R}{(\hat{z} - \hat{z}_{12})R}\hat{\overline{C}}_{n-1,12}^{(3)}(S, X) + \frac{R - \hat{z}_{12}}{(\hat{z} - \hat{z}_{12})R}\hat{\overline{C}}_{n-1}^{(3)}(S, X) \tag{12a}$$

$$\underline{C}_n^{(3)}(S, X) = \frac{\hat{z} - R}{(\hat{z} - 1)R}\underline{C}_{n-1}^{(3)}(S, X) + \frac{R - 1}{(\hat{z} - 1)R}\hat{\underline{C}}_{n-1}^{(3)}(S, X) \tag{12b}$$

where

$$\hat{\overline{C}}_{n-1,12}^{(3)}(S, X) \equiv E[\overline{C}_{n-1}^{(3)}(SZ, X)|Z \leqslant 1], \quad \hat{\overline{C}}_{n-1}^{(3)}(S, X)$$
$$\equiv E[\overline{C}_{n-1}^{(3)}(SZ, X)], \quad \hat{\underline{C}}_{n-1}^{(3)}(S, X) \equiv E[\underline{C}_{n-1}(SZ, X)].$$

Similarly,

$$\overline{C}_n^{(4)}(S, X) = \frac{\hat{z} - R}{(\hat{z} - 1)R} \overline{C}_{n-1}^{(4)}(S, X) + \frac{R - 1}{(\hat{z} - 1)R} \hat{C}_{n-1}^{(4)}(S, X) \tag{13a}$$

$$\underline{C}_n^{(4)}(S, X) = \frac{\hat{z}_{23} - R}{(\hat{z}_{23} - 1)R} \underline{C}_{n-1}^{(4)}(S, X) + \frac{R - 1}{(\hat{z}_{23} - 1)R} \hat{C}_{n-1, 23}^{(4)}(S, X). \tag{13b}$$

Finally, preference structure (1) yields

$$\overline{C}_n^{(1)}(S, X) = \frac{\hat{z} - R}{(\hat{z} - z_1)R} \overline{C}_{n-1}^{(1)}(Sz_1, X) + \frac{R - z_1}{(\hat{z} - z_1)R} \hat{C}_{n-1}^{(1)}(S, X) \tag{14a}$$

$$\underline{C}_n^{(1)}(S, X) = \frac{\hat{z} - R}{(\hat{z} - \hat{z}_{12})R} \hat{C}_{n-1, 12}^{(1)}(S, X) + \frac{R - \hat{z}_{12}}{(\hat{z} - \hat{z}_{12})R} \underline{C}_{n-1}(S, X). \tag{14b}$$

All these bounds will be used in the next section. Since each bound was derived recursively, it follows that the relative order of magnitude of the single-period bounds is preserved in n-periods. Hence, we have the following result:

Proposition 2: If $\overline{C}_n(S, X)$ and $\underline{C}_n(S, X)$ denote the n-period preference-free upper and lower bounds for a three-state stock return distribution then we have

$$\overline{C}_n(S, X) = \overline{C}_n^{(2)}(S, X), \qquad \text{given by (11a)}$$
$$\underline{C}(S, X) = \underline{C}_n^{(4)}(S, X), \qquad \text{given by (13b)}.$$

The next section will examine the asymptotic behavior of these two bounds as the number of periods tends to infinity, while the length of each period tends to zero. The derivation follows the approach introduced in [3] for the two-state process, and generalized in [7]. The diffusion model will be initially assumed for the stock returns.

IV. THE LIMITS UNDER DIFFUSION

Let T denote the length of the total trading horizon (time to expiration of the option), and Δt the length of time between successive trades. The one-period distribution of the stock return Z will depend on Δt. The limiting form of its successive convolutions over n-periods is derived by letting $\Delta t \to 0$ as $n \to \infty$, while $n \Delta t$ remains fixed and equal to T. This limiting distribution is lognormal under a diffusion process. The conditions for such a process to emerge were investigated in detail in [7], and will be only briefly summarized here. [12]

In the notation of [7], let $o(\Delta t)$ denote all functions $f(\Delta t)$ such that $\lim_{\Delta t \to 0}[f(\Delta t)/\Delta t] = 0$. Similarly, $0(\Delta t)$ denotes functions $f(\Delta t)$ such that $\lim_{\Delta t \to 0}[f(\Delta t)/\Delta t]$ is a constant. Thus, $o(\Delta t)$ and $0(\Delta t)$ are functions that tend to zero, respectively, faster and as fast as Δt. Last, the symbol $\sim$ is used to denote asymptotic proportionality at the limit as $\Delta t \to 0$.

The various limiting forms of the stock return distribution were investigated in [7] under six fundamental assumptions governing the mathematical and economic properties of stock returns. These assumptions are standard features of contingent claims models, and will be adopted here as well. Some of them, like (A.6), which assumes a Markovian structure of stock returns, have already been adopted in this paper. Similarly, (A.1), (A.2), and (A.3) of [7] assume that the stock return variance is bounded, nonvanishing, and more or less uniformly spread out over all trading periods as $\Delta t \to 0$, with the result that at the limit the variance is proportional to Δt. Assumption (A.5) stipulates that the expected rate of return per unit time over the trading horizon is finite. Finally, assumption (A.4) is a key condition for a diffusion process to emerge. It stipulates that in the expression for the variance $\sum_{i=1}^{3} p_i(z_i - \hat{z})^2$ both p_i and $(z_i - \hat{z})$ are sufficiently "well-behaved" functions of Δt that may be approximated by polynomials of $\Delta t^{\frac{1}{2}}$ in the vicinity of $\sqrt{\Delta t} = 0$. The limiting properties of $p_i(z_i - \hat{z})^2$ as $\Delta t \to 0$ would depend on its lowest power component, which must be proportional to Δt for at least two of the events $i = 1, 2, 3$. Further, as shown in [7], if $p_i \sim (\Delta t)^{a_i}$, $(z_i - \hat{z}) \sim (\Delta t)^{b_i}$, $i = 1, 2, 3$, where a_i and b_i are the lowest power components of p_i and $(z_i - \hat{z})$, a diffusion emerges if $a_i = 0$, $b_i = 1/2$ for at least two i's. This is the structure of security returns that will be adopted in this paper.

Let $Z_t^{(n)}$ denote the product of n successive realizations of the trinomial random variable Z. By assumption, $Z_t^{(n)}$ tends to a lognormal random variable as $n \to \infty$, $\Delta t \to 0$, $n\Delta t = T$. Let also $\lim_{\Delta t \to 0}^{n \to \infty} E[\ln Z_t^{(n)}] \equiv \mu T$, $\lim_{\Delta t \to 0}^{n \to \infty} \text{var}[\ln Z_t^{(n)}] \equiv \sigma^2 T$, so that $\lim_{\Delta t \to 0}^{n \to \infty} E[Z_t^{(n)}] = e^{(\mu + \sigma^2/2)T}$. Similarly, let $R \equiv e^{r\Delta t}$, where r is the instantaneous riskless rate of interest, with $r \leqslant \mu + \sigma^2/2$ by assumption. The general structure of the security returns Z as $\Delta t \to 0$ is given below, after incorporating the assumptions necessary for the convergence to a diffusion process:

$$z_1 = e^{-\alpha_1 \sigma \sqrt{\Delta t}}, \ p_1 = \gamma_1 - \delta\mu/\sigma\sqrt{\Delta t}; \quad z_2 = 1, \ p_2 = \gamma_2; \quad z_3 = e^{\alpha_3 \sigma \sqrt{\Delta t}},$$

$$p_3 = \gamma_3 + \delta\mu/\sigma\sqrt{\Delta t}; \quad \alpha_i > 0, \ \delta > 0, \ \gamma_i > 0, \ i = 1, 2, 3 \qquad (15)$$

where the coefficients must satisfy

$$\sum_{i=1}^{3} \gamma_i = 1, \quad \gamma_1\alpha_1 = \gamma_3\alpha_3, \quad \gamma_1\alpha_1^2 + \gamma_3\alpha_3^2 = 1, \quad \delta(\alpha_1 + \alpha_3) = 1. \qquad (16)$$

Frequently it is also assumed [13] ([3], [4]) that $z_3 = z_1^{-1}$, or that $\alpha_1 = \alpha_3 \equiv \alpha$, in which case $\gamma_1 = \gamma_3 \equiv \gamma$ and $\gamma\alpha^2 = 1/2$, $\alpha\delta = 1/2$, $\delta = \gamma\alpha$. With this assumption the process becomes

$$z_1 = e^{-\alpha\sigma\sqrt{\Delta t}}, \quad p_1 = \gamma\left[1 - \frac{\alpha\mu}{\sigma}\sqrt{\Delta t}\right]; \quad z_2 = 1, \quad p_2 = 1 - 2\gamma; \quad z_3 = e^{\alpha\sigma\sqrt{\Delta t}},$$

$$p_3 = \gamma\left[1 + \alpha\frac{\mu}{\sigma}\sqrt{\Delta t}\right]. \tag{17}$$

This is the structure that will be adopted here. The trinomial process in [4, pp. 367–368] is a special case of (17) for $\gamma = 1/4$, $\alpha = \sqrt{2}$. Note also that (15) and (16) imply

$$\hat{z} = 1 + (\mu + \sigma^2/2)\Delta t + o(\Delta t). \tag{18}$$

Given now this limiting process for the stock returns, we must derive the limiting behavior of the expressions given by (5a)–(11a) and (7b)–(13b), respectively, for the upper and lower bounds. Let $P \equiv (\hat{z}_{13} - R)/(\hat{z}_{13} - z_1)$, $Q \equiv (\hat{z}_{23} - R)/(\hat{z}_{23} - 1)$, and let also $Z_{13}^{(n)}$ and $Z_{23}^{(n)}$ denote the products of n successive independent binomial stock returns Z, respectively, with states z_1 and z_3 and probabilities $p_1/(p_1 + p_3)$, $p_3/(p_1 + p_3)$, and states z_2 and z_3 and probabilities $p_2/(p_2 + p_3)$ and $p_3/(p_2 + p_3)$. By successive applications of (11a) and (13b) we find that the two bounds are given by the following sums:

$$\overline{C}_n(S, X) = \frac{1}{R^n} \sum_{j=0}^{n} \binom{n}{j} P^j (1 - P)^{n-j} E\left[\max\{Sz_1^j Z_{13}^{(n-j)} - X, 0\}\right] \tag{19}$$

$$\underline{C}_n(S, X) = \frac{1}{R^n} \sum_{j=0}^{n} \binom{n}{j} Q^j (1 - Q)^{n-j} E\left[\max\{SZ_{23}^{(n-j)} - X, 0\}\right]. \tag{20}$$

Hence, the preference-free option bounds are seen from (19)–(20) to be n-period expected call payoffs over the successive one-period *two-stage* stock return processes, shown in Figures 3a and 3b for the upper and lower bounds, respectively. These two processes are, however, a *two-state* (z_1, z_3) process with hedging probabilities $P + (1 - P)[p_1/(p_1 + p_3)] \equiv A$ and $(1 - P)[p_3/(p_1 + p_3)] = 1 - A$, and a *two-state* $(1, z_3)$ process with probabilities, $Q + (1 - Q)[p_2/(p_2 + p_3)]$, $(1 - Q)[p_3/(p_2 + p_3)]$ denoted by B and $1 - B$.

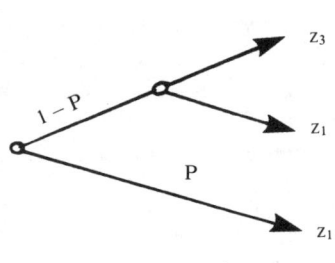

Figure 3a.

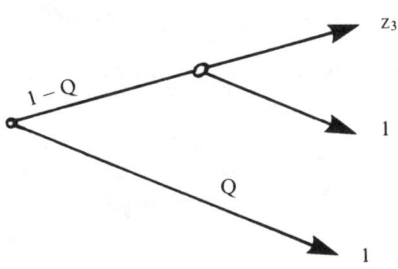

Figure 3b.

From (19) and (20), therefore, the call option upper and lower bounds are given by

$$\overline{C}_n(S, X) = \frac{1}{R^n} \sum_{j=0}^{J} \binom{n}{j} A^j (1 - A)^{n-j} [Sz_1^j z_3^{n-j} - X] \tag{21}$$

$$\underline{C}_n(S, X) = \frac{1}{R^n} \sum_{i=0}^{I} \binom{n}{i} B^i (1 - B)^{n-i} [Sz_3^{n-i} - X] \tag{22}$$

where J and I are the largest integers j and i, respectively, such that $Sz_1^j z_3^{n-j} \geqslant X$ and $Sz_3^{n-i} \geqslant X$. In other words, both bounds are binomial option prices concentrated on the states (z_1, z_3), and (z_2, z_3). Their asymptotic behavior can be found easily when the stock returns are given by the diffusion process (17). Let $B(S, X; r, T, \sigma)$ denote the Black–Scholes option price.

$$B(S, X; r, T, \sigma) = SN\left[\frac{\ln S/X + (r + \sigma^2/2)T}{\sigma\sqrt{T}}\right]$$

$$- Xe^{-rT} N\left[\frac{\ln S/X + (r - \sigma^2/2)T}{\sigma\sqrt{T}}\right]. \tag{23}$$

Then we have:

PROPOSITION 3: The preference-free price of a European call option when the stock return follows a trinomial diffusion given by (17) within a time horizon T has an upper bound given by $B(S, X; r, T, \alpha\sigma)$, where $\alpha = \sqrt{1/(1 - p_2)}$, p_2 is the probability of no stock price change in the trinomial process, and $B(\ )$ is the Black–Scholes price (23). The lower bound, on the other hand, tends asymptotically to $\max\{0, S - Xe^{-rT}\}$.

Proof.   For the upper limit: since

$$A = P + (1 - P) \frac{p_1}{p_1 + p_3} = \frac{\hat{z}_{13} - R}{\hat{z}_{13} - z_1} + \frac{R - z_1}{\hat{z}_{13} - z_1} \frac{p_1}{p_1 + p_3},$$

we can easily find, from the definition of $\hat{z}_{13}$, that $A = (z_3 - R)/(z_3 - z_1)$, $1 - A = (R - z_1)/(z_3 - z_1)$. Hence, (21) denotes the expected call payoff of a two-state process concentrated on z_1 and z_3. From (17) the standard deviation of such a process is $\alpha\sigma$, and the limit of its call price for $n \to \infty$, $\Delta t \to 0$, $n\,\Delta t = T$ is given by (23), with $\alpha\sigma$ replacing σ, Q.E.D.

The lower bound corresponds similarly to a two-state process, concentrated on 1 and z_3, with B and $1 - B$, respectively, equal to $(z_3 - R)/(z_3 - 1)$ and $(R - 1)/(z_3 - 1)$. The one-period mean of this process is still R, but the variance of its logarithm is [14]

$$\frac{R - 1}{z_3 - 1} \alpha^2 \sigma^2 \, \Delta t - \left[\alpha\sigma\sqrt{\Delta t} \, \frac{R - 1}{z_3 - 1}\right]^2 = \alpha^2 \sigma^2 \, \Delta t \, \frac{(R - 1)(z_3 - R)}{(z_3 - 1)^2} = o(\Delta t),$$

implying that

$$\lim_{\substack{n \to \infty \\ \Delta t \to 0}} [n \ \text{var}(\ln Z)] = 0.$$

It is well-known [4, p. 216], however, that for $\sigma \to 0$ the Black–Scholes price (2) tends to the Merton lower bound $\max[0, S - Xe^{-rT}\}$, Q.E.D.

A careful examination of the lower bound given in (22) shows that for all in or at-the-money options $(S \geqslant X)$ the value $\underline{C}_n(S, X)$ is automatically equal to the Merton lower bound $S - (X/R^n)$ of [6], even without the limiting process. Indeed, an option on a stock following the binomial return process concentrated on 1 and z_3 will never become worthless at expiration as long as $S \geqslant X$. This means that its value will be equal to $S - (X/R^n)$. What Proposition 3 shows is that even when $S < X$, in which case $\underline{C}_n(S, X)$ in (22) exceeds the Merton bound $S - (X/R^n)$, there is asymptotic convergence to this bound at the limit as $n \to \infty$, $\Delta t \to 0$, $n \Delta t = T$.

Thus, a unique preference-free option price based solely on arbitrage does not exist even asymptotically for the trinomial process where the stock can go up, go down, or stay the same. The possible option prices lie between the limits established by Proposition 3. The upper limit depends not only on the observables such as the time to expiration, the stock and exercise prices, and the riskless rate of interest as well as the variance of the stock return, but also on the probability that the stock price does not change. The conjecture, therefore, in [4, pp. 367–368] that the value of call options for such a process also converges to the original Black–Scholes prices is not verified.

The next question that arises is the emergence of Black–Scholes prices for the trinomial process under restricted preferences. What are, in other words, the *minimal* assumptions on investor preferences that yield a single option price at the limit under diffusion? As noted in [15, p. 1526], the trinomial process is probably a more "reasonable" assumption to use for options on individual stocks than the two-state process of [3] and [11]. It was shown in that paper that a set of *sufficient* conditions for Black–Scholes option pricing to emerge as an equilibrium price in the trinomial process was that (1) future stock price (or return) and aggregate wealth have a joint multiplicative binomial distribution; (2) the representative investor's utility of wealth is of the CPRA class. The next proposition formulates *necessary*, as well as sufficient conditions on preferences for Black–Scholes option pricing under the three-state process, given consistent preferences for the representative investor in every period. [15]

PROPOSITION 4: The Black–Scholes option price (23) is the equilibrium price of a positive beta stock whose return distribution follows the trinomial diffusion given by (17) *if and only if* the representative investor's state-contingent discount factors are inversely monotonically ordered with respect to the stock returns in every period.

Proof. For the sufficiency we must show that both option price bounds derived under preference structure (1) and given by (14a, b) converge to the Black–Scholes price (23) under diffusion. If sufficiency is proven then necessity can be proven easily by contradiction. For suppose that the n-period option price tends at the limit to the Black–Scholes price. The representative investor cannot have preference structure (2), since this preference has uniformly higher option prices than (1). Similarly preference structure (4) yields lower option prices than (1). We will also show that structure (3) has asymptotically lower prices than the Black–Scholes value: since the upper bound $\bar{C}_n^{(3)}(S, X)$ is the same as $\underline{C}_n^{(1)}(S, X)$, it suffices to show that

$$\lim_{\substack{n \to \infty \\ \Delta t \to 0}} \underline{C}_n^{(3)}(S, X) < B(S, X; r, T, \sigma).$$

Let $Z_{12}^{(n)}$ denote the product of n successive realizations of the two-state random return $\{[z_1, p_1/(p_1 + p_2)], [z_2, p_2/(p_1 + p_2)]\}$. As already noted, $Z_t^{(n)}$ is the product of n successive realizations of the original three-state process. Let also $Q_{(1)} \equiv (\hat{z} - R)/(\hat{z} - z_1)$, $P_{(1)} \equiv (\hat{z} - R)/(\hat{z} - \hat{z}_{12})$. With this notation (14a, b) can be written as

$$\bar{C}_n^{(1)}(S, X) = \frac{1}{R^n} \sum_{j=0}^{n} \binom{n}{j} Q_{(1)}^j (1 - Q_{(1)})^{n-j} E[\max\{[Sz_1^j Z_t^{(n-j)} - X, 0]\}] \quad (24a)$$

$$\underline{C}_n^{(1)}(S, X) = \frac{1}{R^n} \sum_{j=0}^{n} \binom{n}{j} P_{(1)}^j (1 - P_{(1)})^{n-j} E[\max\{[SZ_{12}^{(j)} Z_t^{(n-j)} - X, 0]\}]. \quad (24b)$$

These expressions are discounted expected call payoffs over n-periods to expiration for the successive independent realizations of the *two-stage* one-period stock return distributions shown in Figures 4a and 4b for the upper and lower bound, respectively. These distributions are trinomials (z_i, T_i) and (z_i, U_i), $i = 1, 2, 3$, where

$$T_1 = Q_{(1)} + p_1(1 - Q_{(1)}); \qquad T_j = [1 - Q_{(1)}]p_j, \qquad j = 2, 3 \quad (25a)$$

$$U_j = p_j\left[1 - P_{(1)} + \frac{P_{(1)}}{p_1 + p_2}\right], \qquad j = 1, 2; \qquad U_3 = [1 - P_{(1)}]p_3. \quad (25b)$$

In the derivation of the bounds they can be used *as if* risk-neutrality were prevailing. Hence, they are equivalent to the *hedging probabilities* of the two-state process.

From (25a) and (25b) it is easy to see that $\sum_{i=1}^{3} T_i z_i = \sum_{i=1}^{3} U_i z_i = R$. Similarly, $(z_i - R) \sim \Delta t$, $i = 1, 3$, and $(1 - R)^2 = o(\Delta t)$. Further, (25a, b) and

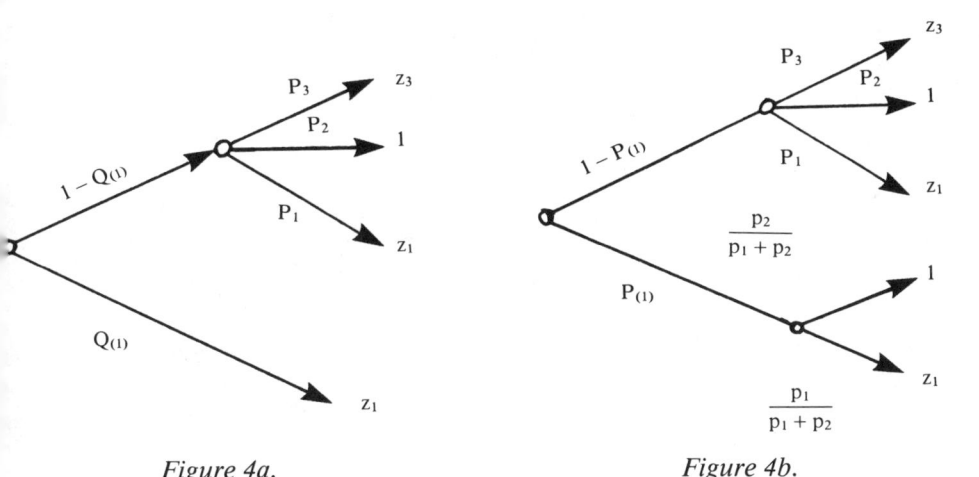

Figure 4a.　　　　　　　　　Figure 4b.

(17) show that the probabilities T_i and U_i, $i = 1, 2, 3$, tend to constant terms as $\Delta t \to 0$. Hence, the limiting distributions of the trinomial random variables corresponding to the two bounds are lognormal, given that they satisfy the Lindeberg condition, as shown in [7, pp. 27–29]. The mean of these distributions is equal to

$$\lim_{\substack{n \to \infty \\ \Delta t \to 0}} R^n = \lim_{\substack{n \to \infty \\ \Delta t \to 0}} e^{nr\Delta t} = e^{rT},$$

while the one-period variances of their logarithms are $\sum_{i=1}^{3} T_i (\ln z_i)^2 - [\sum_{i=1}^{3} T_i \ln z_i]^2$ and $\sum_{i=1}^{3} U_i (\ln z_i)^2 - [\sum_{i=1}^{3} U_i \ln z_i]^2$. From (17) and (25a, b) these variances both turn out to be $\sigma^2 \Delta t + o(\Delta t)$, which implies that at the limit as $\Delta t \to 0$ and $n \to \infty$ the variance of the logarithm is $\sigma^2 T$. Hence, at the limit both (24a) and (24b) tend to the discounted expected call payoff of a lognormal distribution with mean rT and logarithmic variance $\sigma^2 T$. This limit, however, is the Black–Scholes price[16] (23), Q.E.D. This proves the sufficiency part of Proposition 4.

For the necessity, all that remains to be shown is that

$$\lim_{\substack{n \to \infty \\ \Delta t \to 0}} \underline{C}_n^{(3)}(S, X) < B(S, X; r, T, \sigma).$$

From (12b), setting $P_{(3)} \equiv (\hat{z} - R)/(\hat{z} - 1)$ and applying (12b) recursively, we get

$$\underline{C}_n^{(3)}(S, X) = \frac{1}{R^n} \sum_{j=0}^{n} \binom{n}{j} P_{(3)}^j (1 - P_{(3)})^{n-j} E[\max\{SZ_t^{(n-j)} - X, 0\}]. \quad (26)$$

As with preference structure (1), this expression is the discounted expected

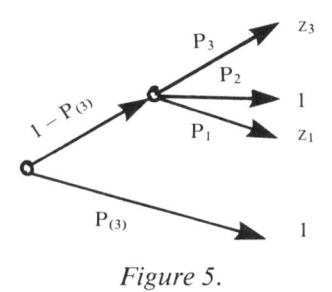

Figure 5.

call payoff of the successive independent two-stage processes over n-period shown in Figure 5. As before, this turns out to be a discounted expected call payoff with the following trinomial (z_i, W_i, $i = 1, 2, 3$) hedging probabilities

$$W_i = p_i[1 - P_{(3)}], \qquad i = 1, 3; \qquad W_2 = P_{(3)} + p_2[1 - P_{(3)}].$$

This distribution tends to a lognormal with the same mean e^{rT} as in the other structures. The variance of the logarithm though, is different. Since

$$1 - P_{(3)} = \frac{R - 1}{\hat{z} - 1} = \frac{r \, \Delta t + o(\Delta t)}{(\mu + \sigma^2/2) \, \Delta t + o(\Delta t)},$$

it is easy to see that

$$\sum_{i=1}^{3} W_i (\ln z_i)^2 - \left[\sum_{i=1}^{3} W_i \ln z_i \right]^2$$

$$= [1 - P_{(3)}][p_1(\ln z_1)^2 + p_3(\ln z_3)^2] - (\mu \, \Delta t)^2 = \frac{r\sigma^2}{\mu + \sigma^2/2} \, \Delta t + o(\Delta t),$$

implying that the limiting lognormal distribution has logarithmic variance equal to $r\sigma^2 T/(\mu + \sigma^2/2)$, which is less than $\sigma^2 T$ by assumption. Hence, the call option price tends to $B(S, X; r, T, \sqrt{[r/(\mu + \sigma^2/2)]}\sigma)$, which is less than the Black–Scholes price (23), Q.E.D.

Proposition 4 gives, therefore, the minimal set of assumptions capable of generating Black–Scholes prices for European options out of the basic three-state stock return process. These are, in addition to the single-price law, the nonsatiation and the absence of arbitrage assumptions inherent in the basic stock market equilibrium model, weak aggregation and monotone ordering of state-contingent discount factors in each period. The assumption of weak aggregation[17] guarantees the existence of a representative investor, while monotone ordering of preferences by such an investor yields Black–Scholes option prices for positive beta stocks; an almost identical proof also hold for the rarely encountered negative beta stocks. It should be noted that the Black–Scholes price emerges under such assumptions at the limit, when the number of trading periods becomes infinitely large and the length of each trading period tends to zero. Otherwise, these assumptions produce only upper and lower bounds for option prices, within which the "true" option price lies.

V. THE EXTENSION TO JUMP PROCESSES

If the three-state stock return does not follow a diffusion then it can only be a jump process. Such processes correspond to the "discontinuous sample paths with rare events" case of [7]. In such a case let d and u denote the sizes of z_3 and z_1, respectively, and λ_3 and λ_1 the corresponding arrival intensities. Instead of (17) the one-period stock return process would then have the following structure:

$$z_1 = d < 1, \quad p_1 = \lambda_1 \, \Delta t; \quad z_2 = 1, \, p_2 = 1 - (\lambda_1 + \lambda_3) \, \Delta t; \quad (27)$$
$$z_3 = u > 1, \quad p_3 = \lambda_3 \, \Delta t.$$

This is the case of a *thinly traded* stock, in which the price stays the same almost always, while price changes occur rarely, in up or down jumps. [18]

For this process the preference-free upper and lower bounds $\overline{C}_n(S, X)$ and $\underline{C}_n(S, X)$ are still given by (21)–(22), but Proposition 3 is no longer valid. Each bound is a binomial option price whose stock returns do not converge to 1 but remain constant as $\Delta t \to 0$. Then we have:

PROPOSITION 5: The preference-free price of a European call option when the stock return follows the trinomial jump process given by (27) within a time horizon T has the stock price S as the least upper bound, while the lower bound tends to

$$\underline{C}(S, X) = S\psi[x; y] - Xe^{-rT}\psi[x; y/u] \qquad (28)$$

where $y \equiv ruT/(u - 1)$, x denotes the smallest nonnegative integer greater than $(1/\ln u)(\ln X/S)$, and $\psi[x; y] \equiv \sum_{i=x}^{\infty} (e^{-y}y^i/i!)$.

Proof. The lower bound follows immediately from [3, pp. 254–255]: as already noted, $\underline{C}_n(S, X)$ is a binomial option price with stock returns concentrated on 1 and $z_3 = u$, and corresponding hedging probabilities $(u - R)/(u - 1)$ and $(R - 1)/(u - 1) = [r/(u - 1)]\Delta t + o(\Delta t)$. This option price was estimated in [3, p. 255] and is given by (28), Q.E.D. The upper bound, on the other hand, is a binomial option price with stock returns concentrated on d and u, with hedging probability $p \equiv (R - d)/(u - d)$. Hence, if $p' \equiv (u/R)p$ we know [3, pp. 238–239] that $\overline{C}_n(S, X) = S\phi[\alpha; n, p'] - (X/R^n) \, \phi[\alpha; n, p]$, where $\alpha \equiv$ the smallest nonnegative integer greater than $\ln(X/Sd^n)/\ln(u/d)$, and $\phi[\ ]$ denotes the complementary binomial distribution function. It is easy to show [19] that $\phi[\alpha; n, p] \to 0$

and $\phi[\alpha; n, p'] \to 1$ as $n \to \infty$, implying that

$$\lim_{\substack{n \to \infty \\ \Delta t \to 0}} \bar{C}_n(S, X) = S, \qquad \text{Q.E.D.}$$

We note that (28) corresponds to the Merton [6] lower bound $S - Xe^{-rT}$ for in-the-money stocks ($S \geqslant X$), but to a *higher* lower bound for out-of-the-money stocks. The upper bound, on the other hand, is the same as the one found by Merton [6] by arbitrage methods.

Last, we examine the convergence of the two bounds corresponding to preference structure (1), the monotonic ordering of the state-contingent discount factors. Here, in contrast to diffusion, it can be shown that the bounds converge to two *different* expressions. Hence, no unique option price emerges for stocks whose returns follow jump processes, even under the necessary and sufficient conditions, under which such a unique price emerges in diffusion. The convergence results are given by:

PROPOSITION 6.   If the representative investor's state-contingent discount factors are in every period inversely monotonically ordered with respect to the stock returns, then the European call option price for the trinomial stock return process given by (27) lies asymptotically between the upper and lower bounds $\bar{C}^{(1)}(S, X)$ and $\underline{C}^{(1)}(S, X)$, where

$$\bar{C}^{(1)}(S, X) = E_{j_1}[J(Sd^{j_1}e^{[[u-1]\lambda_3 - r]T}, X; x(j_1), u\lambda_3 T]$$

$$= \sum_{j_1=0}^{\infty} \frac{e^{-\theta T}(\theta T)^{j_1}}{j_1!} J(Sd^{j_1}e^{[[u-1]\lambda_3 - r]T}, X; x(j_1), u\lambda_3 T) \quad (29)$$

$$\underline{C}^{(1)}(S, X) = E_{j_1}[J(Sd^{j_1}e^{[[u-1]\phi - r]T}, X; x(j_1), u\phi T]$$

$$= \sum_{j_1=0}^{\infty} \frac{e^{-\lambda_1 T}(\lambda_1 T)^{j_1}}{j_1!} J(Sd^{j_1}e^{[[u-1]\phi - r]T}, X; x(j_1), u\phi T) \quad (30)$$

where $\theta \equiv [(u - 1)\lambda_3 - r]/(1 - d)$, $\phi \equiv [(1 - d)\lambda_1 + r]/(u - 1)$, $x(j_1)$ denotes the smallest nonnegative integer greater than $(1/\ln u)$ $[\ln(X/S) - j_1 \ln d]$, $J(S, X; x, v) \equiv S\psi[x; v] - Xe^{-rt}\psi[x; v/u]$, and $\psi(x; v) \equiv \sum_{i=x}^{\infty} (e^{-v}v^i/i!)$.

Proof.   As shown in the proof of Proposition 4, the n-period option bounds under preference structure (1) are expected call payoffs, computed as if the stock returns were following trinomial probabilities, respectively given by (25a) and (25b). Here p_i and z_i, $i = 1, 2, 3$, correspond to the process given by (27). It suffices to take the limit of these expectations for $n \to \infty$, $\Delta t \to 0$, $n\Delta t = T$.

For both upper and lower bounds it can be shown that the limiting distributions of the stock return $Su^{j_3} d^{j_1}$ under such conditions have j_1 and j_3

distributed as a double Poisson process. For this it suffices to apply the approach of [7]. For instance, the upper bound's one-period trinomial process (T_i, z_i), with T_i given by (25a), $i = 1, 2, 3$, has moments $T_i[z_i - \hat{z}]^k$, $i = 1, 2, 3, k = 1, 2, 3, \ldots$, that turn out to be proportional to Δt. Similarly, it turns out that $T_1 = \theta \Delta t + o(\Delta t)$, $T_3 = \lambda_3 \Delta t + o(\Delta t)$, implying at the limit a double Poisson process with parameters nT_i, $i = 1, 3$, or θT and $\lambda_3 T$. The expectation of the call payoff under such a process can be easily seen to be equal to (29), Q.E.D. The proof for the lower bound is identical, with the trinomial process (U_i, z_i), $i = 1, 2, 3$, defining an n-period stock return $Su^{j_3}d^{j_1}$, with j_1 and j_3 asymptotically distributed as a double Poisson process with parameters $\lambda_1 T$ and ϕT, Q.E.D.

In the next section the empirical significance of the above results is evaluated by computing the bounds given by (29) and (30). The parameters used were estimated from real data on a thinly traded stock in the Toronto stock market.

VI. SOME NUMERICAL RESULTS

In this section we first present some numerical simulation results on the speed of convergence of the various option bounds to their respective Black–Scholes values. In particular, we are interested in the influence of the parameter α, which is directly related to the probability p_2 of the middle (stay-the-same) state by the relation $\alpha = \sqrt{1/(1 - p_2)}$. In other words, α is a measure of the "thinness of trading" of the stock. By Proposition 3 we know that the preference-free upper bound increases with α, while the lower bound stays the same. Hence, the range of uncertainty of the preference-free option prices also increases with α. Intuitively, therefore, one expects that this increased uncertainty will also carry over to the convergence of the various option prices to their limiting values.

Tables 1, 2, and 3 present the simulation results for options on stocks following a diffusion process, with $S = X = 100$ and with the following values of their instantaneous parameters and time to expiration:

$$r = 0.1 \qquad \sigma = 0.2 \qquad \mu = 0.1 \qquad T = 1$$

The values of the parameter α are $\sqrt{1.5}$, $\sqrt{2}$, and $\sqrt{3}$, corresponding to p_2 equal to $1/3$, $1/2$, and $2/3$, for Tables 1, 2, and 3, respectively. All three tables share the following landmark option values:

$$\text{Black–Scholes value } B(S, X; r, T, \sigma) = 13.269$$

$$\text{Merton lower bound } S - Xe^{rT} = 9.516.$$

The asymptotic upper bounds, on the other hand, are, for each value of α

Table 1. $p_2 = 1/3$

				n				
	2	5	10	15	20	30	40	50
$\overline{C}_n^{(1)}$	12.870	13.155	13.223	13.245	13.255	13.264	13.268	13.271
$\underline{C}_n^{(1)}$	12.675	13.024	13.134	13.173	13.193	13.214	13.225	13.232
$\overline{C}_n$	13.669	15.153	14.555	14.918	14.677	14.718	14.739	14.750

Table 2. $p_2 = 1/2$

				n				
	2	5	10	15	20	30	40	50
$\overline{C}_n^{(1)}$	12.753	13.103	13.208	13.240	13.254	13.267	13.275	13.275
$\underline{C}_n^{(1)}$	12.325	12.875	13.053	13.115	13.147	13.180	13.197	13.208
$\overline{C}_n$	14.841	16.563	15.848	16.272	15.987	16.033	16.056	16.070

Table 3. $p_2 = 2/3$

				n				
	2	5	10	15	20	30	40	50
$\overline{C}_n^{(1)}$	12.267	12.972	13.163	13.218	13.242	13.265	13.274	13.279
$\underline{C}_n^{(1)}$	11.517	12.578	12.906	13.012	13.066	13.122	13.151	13.169
$\overline{C}_n$	16.846	18.960	18.056	18.580	18.222	18.278	18.307	18.327

and p_2:

$$p_2 = 1/3 \qquad 1/2 \qquad 2/3$$
$$\alpha = \sqrt{1.5} \qquad \sqrt{2} \qquad \sqrt{3}$$
$$B(S, X; r, T, \alpha\sigma) = 14.801 \qquad 16.127 \qquad 18.391.$$

The tables yield values of $\overline{C}_n^{(1)}, \underline{C}_n^{(1)}$, and the preference-free upper bound $\overline{C}_n$ for various values on n.

As the tables show very clearly, these three trinomial processes, which have the same limiting stock return distribution, have vastly different ranges of option values. Not only does the preference-free upper bound $\overline{C}_n$ increase dramatically with α, but the convergence of $\overline{C}_n^{(1)}$ and $\underline{C}_n^{(1)}$ to the common Black–Scholes value of 13.269 is a decreasing function of the stay-the-same probability. On the other hand, this convergence is fairly rapid, even for $p_2 = 2/3$.

Table 4. $\underline{C}_n(100,105)$

				n				
	2	5	10	15	20	30	40	50
$p_2 = 1/3$	7.396	6.726	6.185	5.886	5.693	5.551	5.509	5.451
$p_2 = 1/2$	7.664	7.002	6.444	6.123	5.908	5.634	5.562	5.531
$p_2 = 2/3$	7.999	7.372	6.817	6.479	6.243	5.929	5.726	5.584

The last set of simulation results examines the convergence of the preference-free lower bound to its asymptotic value. Table 4 is computed with the same instantaneous parameters, with $X = \$100$ and $T = 1$, but with an exercise price $X = \$105$. For that value the Merton lower bound is $\$4.992$.

The conclusion with respect to the preference-free lower bound is identical to those of the similar upper bound. In other words, the convergence to the asymptotic lower bound is an inverse function of p_2. In this case, though, the convergence is much slower in all cases.

Hence, in any real-life case the asymptotic bound may not be reached for short times to expiration of the option, since not enough trading periods may fit within the interval to ensure convergence. It may thus be possible to use the discrete-time bound for trading purposes, instead of its asymptotic value.

Last, we examine the practical significance of the results stated in Proposition 6, when there is reason to believe that the stock returns are generated by a jump, rather than by a diffusion process. As noted in the previous section, the terminal stock price during any fixed time interval T is in this case equal to $Sd^{j_1}u^{j_3}$, where j_i has a Poisson distribution with parameter $\lambda_i T$, $i = 1, 3$. The four parameters d, u, λ_1, and λ_3 of this process can be estimated from a sample of observations on stock returns over nonoverlapping time intervals of equal length T, together with the corresponding "down" and "up" moves j_1 and j_3.

For this estimation an optioned stock was chosen that had the lowest volume of trading over a randomly selected number of weeks during 1986. For that stock (Total Petroleum), we obtained a record of all trades that took place over an 8-week period during the fall of 1986. Then, choosing $T = 1$ day, an unbiased estimate of λ_1 and λ_3 was derived immediately, by taking the average numbers of the observed down and up trades over the total number of days in our sample, given that $E[j_i] = \lambda_i T$, $i = 1, 3$. d and u, on the other hand, can be estimated by fitting to the data the regression $D = j_1 \ln d + j_3 \ln u + \varepsilon$ where D is the daily stock return, j_1 and j_3 the observed numbers of down and up trades within that day, and ε is a random term. Each day constitutes a separate observation.

Table 5. $\overline{C}^{(1)}, \underline{C}^{(1)}$, and B

	Days to Expiration								
	5	10	15	20	30	40	50	60	75
$\overline{C}$	0.455871	0.655257	0.811306	0.945000	1.173710	1.370833	1.547750	1.71029	1.934376
$\underline{C}$	0.414273	0.596707	0.739758	0.862517	1.072955	1.254763	1.418268	1.568756	1.776637
B	0.439158	0.629601	0.779091	0.907377	1.127178	1.31691	1.487399	1.6442	1.860601

The data generated the following estimates: $\lambda_1 = 1.605$ $\lambda_3 = 1.9488$, implying that, on average, there were less than four trades in a day for that stock, for which a price change was recorded. Since this is clearly a thinly traded stock, the regression on the (approximately) 40 daily returns over the 8-week period was run, producing the estimates u = 1.0077874 and d = 0.9922523.

Table 5 shows the estimated call option bounds $\underline{C}^{(1)}$ and $\overline{C}^{(1)}$ generated by the above parameter values for the double Poisson process for various numbers of days to expiration. The remaining parameters used in the estimates were S = X = \$32.5, r = 0.00018127. The table also gives the Black–Scholes value B corresponding to these parameters, and to the logarithmic variance generated by the Poisson process, equal to $[\lambda_1(\ln d)^2 + \lambda_3(\ln u)^2]^{1/2} = 0.0146413$.

The results of Table 5 show a gap of the order of 10% between the two bounds for this stock, which followed a pattern of very thin trading during the period covered by the data. The Black–Scholes value lay between the bounds, but in all cases closer to the upper, rather than the lower bound. Work is at present continuing on extending these comparisons to other, less extreme cases of thin trading.

VII. CONCLUSIONS

This paper has examined the valuation of European call options under preference-free conditions when the elementary one-period stock return process is the trinomial up, down, and stay the same. As noted in [15], there are reasons to believe that such a return process is a correct description of the actual formation of stock price changes. If the continuous-time trading assumption of the original Black–Scholes derivation is relaxed then the trinomial process emerges as a prime candidate for its replacement by a discrete-time model. It is a more general, as well as more realistic model than the two-state process of [3] and [11], which generates the Black–Scholes price at the limit.

As shown in this paper, the tightest limits of perefence-free option prices under the three-state process in continuous time are a function of the thinness of trading of the stock, as well as the type of limiting stock return distribution (diffusion or jump process) that emerges in continuous time. In diffusion the upper limit is a Black–Scholes-type expression that is an increasing function of the probability of the stay-the-same state, i.e., the thinness of trading in the stock. When the stock return is a jump process, on the other hand, the option price is bound from above by the stock price. Conversely, the lower bound under diffusion is the European option lower bound identified in [6], but it is a higher valued expression in the jump process case.

These preference-free bounds are not very tight. The question that arises, therefore, is what are the *minimal* assumptions capable of generating either exact prices or tighter bounds. Answers to this question under diffusion were provided in Propositions 4 and 6 and their proofs. It was shown that only one preference assumption was capable of generating an exact option price at the limit under diffusion. This was the monotonic ordering of the state-contingent discount factors, which was introduced for the first time in [10]. This assumption generates the Black–Scholes option price as the limit of both upper and lower bound. In other words, even though the monotone ordering assumption does not define a unique option price but only upper and lower bounds on admissible prices, these bounds converge to the same Black–Scholes value at the limit under diffusion, as we go to continuous trading. All other preferences define intervals of admissible option prices even at the continuous time limit. [20]

On the other hand, meaningful preference-free option bounds were also derived here for a finite number of trading periods. Thus, for "short" times to expiration, and given data on the amplitude of individual stock price changes, it is possible to generate preference-free option bounds that may be used for trading purposes. The trinomial asumption is the only assumption used for the derivation of these bounds, but their tightness is a function of the amplitude of price changes and becomes, thus, an empirical matter. Some numerical simulation results were presented to illustrate this point.

For a jump process, by contrast, no single price emerges even under monotone ordering. The limiting upper and lower bounds under such an ordering were estimated with real data, and shown to differ by less than 10% in most cases. Hence, the monotone ordering is able to generate useful results for trading purposes even when no unique price emerges at the limit.

As a final comment, it should be noted that the results of this paper may also be seen as completing the link between discrete and continuous-time contingent claims pricing, which was established rigorously in [7]. The conclusions, however, are somewhat pessimistic. The nature of the limiting stock return distribution is not sufficient to define unique contingent claims prices without restrictions on investor preferences, not even at the limit of continuous trading, unless the one-period returns are a two-state process. In other words, two stocks with identical return distributions over finite time intervals may correspond to different prices for their contingent claims over the same intervals if their one-period return distributions differ.[21]

Restrictions on preferences along the lines of [2], [13], or [15] become, therefore, indispensable in order to generate meaningful claims prices from discrete-time trading. As already noted, the monotone ordering is the most general such restriction, compatible with a single Black–Scholes price in the trinomial process used in this paper.

NOTES

1. They also examined a model with additive random factors in its price change and constant absolute risk aversion for the representative investor.

2. Hereafter Z denotes the random variable and z its realized value.

3. This condition is implied if the existence of a representative investor is assumed, but is considerably more general than this latter assumption, since a common pattern of preferences is not assumed.

4. The limits used here were also shown in [12] to be the tightest possible limits under our assumptions. In [18] and [10], by contrast, the same upper bound but a looser lower bound were derived. However, it was shown in [9] that the two models are equivalent, and that the tighter lower bound of [12] should be used.

5. This is easy to see if we set $\hat{z} = p_2 z_2 + (1 - p_2)\hat{z}_{13}$.

6. See [12, p. 1227]; the convexity is also very easy to prove directly in this case: it suffices to show that $\hat{C}$ is less than any convex combination of c_1 and $\hat{C}_{13}$.

7. In Figure 1 c_1 was assumed equal to zero, since otherwise the triangle degenerates into a straight line, and both points A and B converge to the Merton [6] lower bound $S - X/R$.

8. The only difference is that the end-point $\hat{C}_{12}$ need not be zero in order for a triangle to emerge as long as $Sz_1 < X < S$.

9. The asumption is a standard feature of most option models (e.g., [3], [6], [11], and [15]).

10. This assumption is not necessary for Propositions 2, 3, and 5 (the preference-free bounds), but it is used in Proposition 4, deriving the Black–Scholes value. It is adopted at this point only because it simplifies the exposition.

11. Here, however, $\bar{C}_1^{(2)}(Sz_1)$ and $\underline{C}_1^{(2)}(Sz_1)$ are not necessarily zero.

12. The main requirement is the so-called *Lindeberg condition* [5, pp. 518–521] that guarantees the validity of the Central Limit Theorem.

13. Again this assumption is not necessary, but it does simplify the presentation.

14. Note that $[(R - 1)(z_3 - R)]/(z_3 - 1)^2 \sim (r/\alpha\sigma)\sqrt{\Delta t}$.

15. In other words we assume weak aggregation [13, p. 411] or that a representative investor exists, such that financial assets' prices are formed as if all investors were identical to that investor. This assumption can be weakened somewhat by requiring that only the rank ordering of preferences must be identical between all investors.

16. See the theorem in [14, p. 16]

17. See note 15.

18. For this process the stock price after n-periods is equal to $Sd^{j_1}u^{j_3}$, where (j_1, j_3) have a double Poisson distribution with parameters $\lambda_1 T$ and $\lambda_3 T$.

19. The proof is identical to the one given in [3], and is based on the fact that the one-period logarithmic means tend to $[(1 - d)/(u - d)] \ln u + [(u - 1)/(u - d)] \ln d < 0$ and $[u(1 - d)/(u - d)] \ln u + [d(u - 1)/(u - d)] \ln d > 0$.

20. In fact, it is clear from the proofs of Propositions 3 and 4 that each preference corresponds at the limit to option prices located in nonoverlapping intervals: (4) lies between $\max\{0, S - Xe^{-rT}\}$ and $B(S, X; r, T, \sqrt{r/(\mu + \sigma^2/2)}\sigma)$; (3) has this latter expression as a lower limit and $B(S, X; r, T, \sigma)$ as an upper; $B(S, X; r, T, \sigma)$ is the sole limit of (1) and the lower limit of (2), while (2)'s upper limit is $B(S, X; r, T, \alpha\sigma)$.

21. For instance, the binomial and trinomial models in [4, pp. 367–[68], which have respectively unique and nonunique contingent claims prices derived from identical assumptions.

REFERENCES

1. Black, F., and M. Scholes, "The Pricing of Options and Corporate Liabilities," *Journal of Political Economy* 81, 3 (May–June 1973), 637–659.

2. Brennan, M. J., "The Pricing of Contingent Claims in Discrete Time Models," *Journal of Finance* 34, 1 (March 1979), 53–68.

3. Cox, J. C., S. Ross, and M. Rubinstein, "Option Pricing: A Simplified Approach," *Journal of Financial Economics* 7, 1 (March 1979), 229–263

4. Cox, J. C., and M. Rubinstein, *Options Markets*. Englewood Cliffs, N.J.: Prentice-Hall, 1985.

5. Feller, W., *An Introduction to Probability Theory and its Applications,* Vol. II, 2nd Ed. New York: Wiley, 1971.

6. Merton, R. C., "The Theory of Rational Option Pricing," *The Bell Journal of Economics and Management Science* 7, 1 (Spring 1973), 141–183.

7. Merton, R. C., "On The Mathematics and Economics Assumptions Of Continuous-Time Models," in *Financial Economics: Essays in Honor of Paul Cootner* (W. F. Sharpe and C. M. Cootner, eds.), pp. 9–51. Englewood Cliffs, N.J.: Prentice-Hall, 1982.

8. Perrakis, S., "Options Bounds in Discrete Time: Extensions and the Pricing of the American Put," *Journal of Business* 59, 1 (January 1986), 119–142.

9. Perrakis, S., "Options Bounds in Discrete Time and the Pricing of Corporate Debt," *Advances in Futures and Options Research* 2 (1987), 179–207.

10. Perrakis, S., and P. Ryan, "Option Pricing Bounds in Discrete Time", *Journal of Finance* 39, 2 (June 1984), 519–525.

11. Rendleman, R. J., and B. J. Bartter, "Two-State Asset Pricing," *Journal of Finance* 34, 5 (December 1979), 1093–1110.

12. Ritchken, P., "On Option Pricing Bounds," *Journal of Finance* 40, 4 (September 1985), 1219–1233.

13. Rubinstein, M., "The Valuation of Uncertain Income Streams and the Pricing of Options", *The Bell Journal of Economics* 7, 2 (Autumn 1976), 407–425.

14. Smith, C. W., "Option Pricing: A Review," *Journal of Financial Economics* 3, (1976), 3–51.

15. Stapleton, R. C., and M. G. Subrahmanyam, "The Valuation of Options When Asset Returns Are Generated by a Binomial Process", *Journal of Finance* 39, 5 (December 1984), 1525–1539.

ON THE PROPERTIES OF THE VALUATION FORMULA FOR AN UNPROTECTED AMERICAN CALL OPTION WITH KNOWN DIVIDENDS AND THE COMPUTATION OF ITS IMPLIED STANDARD DEVIATION

Robert L. Welch* and David M. Chen**

I. INTRODUCTION

The deterministic relationship between the value of a European call option and its set of underlying variables is well known. This fact has been widely

*Brock University, St. Catharines, Ontario.
**State University of New York at Buffalo.
  This paper is partially based on an appendix of David Chen's dissertation [4] and he would like to thank his committee's chairman, Professor Thomas J. Frecka, for encouragement. We would also like to thank the associate editor, Robert Whaley, for helpful comments.

Advances in Futures and Options Research, Vol. 3, pages 237–256.

used to derive the market's implied standard deviation of stock returns (hereafter, ISD) from the current option price given the other observable parameters and a specified valuation model (e.g., see Chiras and Manaster [5] and Latané and Rendleman [13]).

Roll [18], Geske [7], and Whaley [23] have presented a valuation formula for the unprotected American call written on a stock with known dividends (hereafter, the RGW or American call model). Considering the relative stability of the timing and magnitude of dividends over the short time interval of a call option's effective life, the assumption of known dividends seems to offer a logical way to deal with the positive probabilities of early exercise associated with unprotected American calls at the ex-dividend instants.

In spite of the theoretical advantage of the American call model and some empirical results favoring its specification (see Whaley [24] and Sterk [21]), it is used less often. Part of the reason may be that it is more difficult to determine ISDs from the American call model as compared to the Black and Scholes' [3] model (hereafter, the European call model).

As a result some authors introduce a potential "modeling" bias by assuming the probability of early exercise is zero or one, while others introduce a "sampling" bias by only using calls with a zero probability of early exercise.

The former (modeling) bias arises when the pseudo-American call model is used either to value the call (as in Black [2]) or as a criterion of elimination (as in Rubinstein [19]). One possible manifestation of this assumption is the direct and/or inverse striking price bias as explained by Geske and Roll [9].

The latter (sampling) bias arises from tests restricted to calls that either have no dividend prior to maturity (as in Geske and Roll [10]) or whose dividends are smaller than the opportunity interest cost incurred by paying the exercise price prior to maturity (see Merton [15]). The former results in short maturity samples while the latter restricts the sample to low dividend paying stocks and/or particular ex-dividend dates (i.e., with respect to maturity).

In order to control for the biases created by improper modeling or sampling, future research should use ISDs from the American call model. Some of this research will require the computation of a large number of ISDs because of the inherent problems with closing prices and the availability of (near) continuous data such as the Berkeley Options Data Base. An immediate requirement will be an efficient ISD procedure. Furthermore, researchers in related areas will also be able to increase the accuracy of their results by explicitly modeling the probability for early exercise (e.g., Patell and Wolfson [16, 17]).

In order to devise this ISD search, certain properties of the American call will be needed. These can be obtained in a straightforward manner by viewing the American call holder as a maximizing agent. Since the holder must decide when to exercise the call, he will do so rationally and thereby maximize its value. Thus, he will only exercise early just prior to the ex-dividend dates if the stock price at these times reaches an optimal value. These optimal future stock prices have been called critical prices by Roll [18]. One benefit of this approach is the application of the envelope theorem in computing derivatives of the call such that the functional dependence of the critical prices on the parameters can be ignored.

Treating the American call as a maximization of a deterministic function and the subsequent application of comparative static techniques is of interest by itself. Furthermore it sets the stage for the computation of all the call's derivatives — not just those required for the ISD search. Because it is important to detail the behavior of the American call in the presence of dividends, we present all the derivatives of the call and its critical stock prices as well as provide some intuitive discussion. In spite of the advantages afforded by the envelope theorem, these computations are not simple and we provide some essential information in this regard.

Thus, our purpose is to analyze the properties of the American call model and, based on the analytical results, to devise some procedures for a simple but efficient numerical search for the ISD.

The remainder of this paper proceeds as follows. In Section II, the two-dividend American call is presented as a standard maximization of a deterministic function, with the future stock prices at the ex-dividend instants playing the role of decision variables.[1] The call's derivatives and the comparative statics of the critical stock prices are detailed in Appendixes A and B, respectively. Some of these results are used in Section III to devise an efficient numerical search procedure for the ISD. This is followed by two examples to illustrate the process in Section IV. Last, a summary of the results and conclusions is contained in Section V.

The following notation is in part adapted from Roll [18] and is used throughout the paper:

$\widetilde{P}_t$ = stock price at time t,
t_1 = time until the first ex-dividend instant,
t_2 = time until the second ex-dividend instant,
T = time until expiration,
D_1 = known dividend to be paid at t_1 with certainty,
D_2 = known dividend to be paid at t_2 with certainty,
r = instantaneous riskless interest rate,
$\widetilde{S}_t$ = stock price at time t net of the present value of escrowed dividends,
    i.e.,

$$\widetilde{S}_t = \widetilde{P}_t - e^{-r(t_1 - t)}D_1 - e^{-r(t_2 - t)}D_2 \text{ for } t_0 \leqslant t < t_1,$$
$$\widetilde{S}_t = \widetilde{P}_t - e^{-r(t_2 - t)}D_2 \text{ for } t_1 \leqslant t < t_2, \text{ and}$$
$$\widetilde{S}_t = \widetilde{P}_t \text{ for } t_2 \leqslant t \leqslant T,\ ^2$$

$S_{t_1}^*, S_{t_2}^* =$ critical stock prices at t_1, t_2, above which the American call will be exercised early,

$N_1(a) =$ standard univariate normal distribution with upper integral limit a,

$N_2(a, b; \rho) =$ standard bivariate normal distribution with upper integral limits a and b and correlation coefficient ρ,

$N_3(a, b, c; \rho_{12}, \rho_{13}, \rho_{23}) =$ standard trivariate normal distribution[3] with upper integral limits a, b, and c and correlation coefficients ρ_{12}, ρ_{13}, and ρ_{23},

$n_1(x)$, $n_2(x, y; \rho)$, and $n_3(x, y, z; \rho_{12}, \rho_{13}, \rho_{23}) =$ the standard uni-, bi-, and trivariate normal density, respectively,

$\sigma =$ instantaneous standard deviation of returns on $\widetilde{S}_t$,

$X =$ exercise price,

$\widetilde{C}_t =$ value of the American call option at time t,

$\tilde{c}_t =$ value of the European call option at time t,

$CP =$ current (time t_0) market price of the American call option.

II. APPLYING STANDARD COMPARATIVE STATIC TECHNIQUES TO C_{t_0}

For convenience we state the formula for the two-dividend American call in Equation (1).

$$
\begin{aligned}
C_{t_0} = {} & S_{t_0}[1 - N_3(-f_1, -g_1, -h_1; \rho_{12}, \rho_{13}, \rho_{23})] \\
& - X[e^{-rt_1}N_1(f_2) + e^{-rt_2}N_2(-f_2, g_2; -\rho_{12}) \\
& + e^{-rT}N_3(-f_2, -g_2, h_2; \rho_{12}, -\rho_{13}, -\rho_{23})] + D_1 e^{-rt_1}N_1(f_2) \\
& + D_2 e^{-rt_2}[N_1(f_2) + N_2(-f_2, g_2; -\rho_{12})]
\end{aligned}
\tag{1}
$$

where

$$\rho_{12} = \sqrt{t_1/t_2}, \qquad \rho_{13} = \sqrt{t_1/T}, \qquad \rho_{23} = \sqrt{t_2/T},$$

$$f_2 = \left[\ln(S_{t_0}/S_{t_1}^*) + \left(r - \frac{\sigma^2}{2}\right)t_1\right]\Big/\sigma\sqrt{t_1}, \qquad f_1 = f_2 + \sigma\sqrt{t_1},$$

$$g_2 = \left[\ln(S_{t_0}/S_{t_2}^*) + \left(r - \frac{\sigma^2}{2}\right)t_2\right]\Big/\sigma\sqrt{t_2}, \qquad g_1 = g_2 + \sigma\sqrt{t_2},$$

$$h_2 = \left[\ln(S_{t_0}/X) + \left(r - \frac{\sigma^2}{2}\right)T\right]\Big/\sigma\sqrt{T}, \qquad h_1 = h_2 + \sigma\sqrt{T}.$$

The two-dividend American call model price, C_{t_0}, is a deterministic function of 11 variables, 9 of which are given parameters ($S_{t_0}, X, r, \sigma, T, t_1, t_2, D_1, D_2$) and two future stock prices (S_{t_1}, S_{t_2}) that are determined by the call holder in choosing an early exercise strategy. C_{t_0} reaches its maximum value at the optimal values ($S_{t_1}^*$ and $S_{t_2}^*$) of these future stock prices that are commonly referred to as critical stock prices. If the two-dividend model is well defined, a maximum exists by the Weierstrass theorem (e.g., see Intriligator [11]) because C_{t_0} is a continuous function on a compact domain. For example, if a critical price becomes infinite, the probability of early exercise at that instant is zero and the two-dividend model reduces to a one-dividend model. Essentially the dimensionality of the problem is reduced. Letting the vector θ represent the parameters and the vector S represent decision variables (S_{t_1}, S_{t_2}), we have: [4]

$$\max_{S} C_{t_0}(S, \theta) \equiv C_{t_0}[S_{t_1}^*(\theta), S_{t_2}^*(\theta), \theta] \equiv C_{t_0}^*(\theta)$$

$C_{t_0}^*$ is commonly referred to as the Roll–Geske–Whaley model. The first-order (necessary) conditions for a maximum require the gradient of C_{t_0} with respect to S to equal 0 at the critical stock prices. That is,

$$\nabla_S C_{t_0}^* \equiv 0.$$

The second-order (sufficient) conditions require the Hessian matrix of second partial derivatives with respect to S to be negative definite (n.d.). Thus

$$\nabla_S^2 C_{t_0}^* < 0.$$

The first-order conditions yield:

$$C_1 \equiv \frac{\partial C_{t_0}}{\partial S_{t_1}^*} = -e^{-rt_1}n_1(f_2)[S_{t_1}^* - X + D_1 + D_2 e^{-r(t_2 - t_1)} - C_{t_1}^*]/S_{t_1}^*\sigma\sqrt{t_1} \equiv 0 \qquad (2)$$

$$C_2 \equiv \frac{\partial C_{t_0}}{\partial S_{t_2}^*} = -e^{-rt_2}n_1(g_2)N_1\left(\frac{-f_2 + \rho_{12}g_2}{\sqrt{1 - \rho_{12}^2}}\right)[S_{t_2}^* - X + D_2 - C_{t_2}^*]/S_{t_2}^*\sigma\sqrt{t_2} \equiv 0 \quad (3)$$

where $C_{t_1}^*$ ($C_{t_2}^*$) is the value of an American call at t_1 (t_2) with one (no) dividend remaining. That is,

$$C_{t_1}^* = S_{t_1}^*[1 - N_2(-a_1, -b_1; \rho)] - X[e^{-r(t_2 - t_1)}N_1(a_2) \\ + e^{-r(T - t_1)}N_2(-a_2, b_2; -\rho)] + D_2 e^{-r(t_2 - t_1)}N_1(a_2) \qquad (4)$$

$$C_{t_2}^* = S_{t_2}^*N_1(v_1) - Xe^{-r(T - t_2)}N_1(v_2) \qquad (5)$$

where $\rho = \sqrt{(t_2 - t_1)/(T - t_1)}$,

$$a_2 = \left[\ln(S_{t_1}^*/S_{t_2}^*) + \left(r - \frac{\sigma^2}{2}\right)(t_2 - t_1)\right]\Big/\sigma\sqrt{t_2 - t_1}, \qquad a_1 = a_2 + \sigma\sqrt{t_2 - t_1},$$

$$b_2 = \left[\ln(S_{t_1}^*/X) + \left(r - \frac{\sigma^2}{2}\right)(T - t_1)\right]\Big/\sigma\sqrt{T - t_1}, \qquad b_1 = b_2 + \sigma\sqrt{T - t_1},$$

$$v_2 = \left[\ln(S_{t_2}^*/X) + \left(r - \frac{\sigma^2}{2}\right)(T - t_2)\right]\Big/\sigma\sqrt{T - t_2}, \qquad v_1 = v_2 + \sigma\sqrt{T - t_2}.$$

We note that the first-order conditions (2) and (3) hold if and only if

$$H \equiv S_{t_1} - X + D_1 + D_2 e^{-r(t_2 - t_1)} - C_{t_1} = 0 \tag{6}$$

and

$$G \equiv S_{t_2} - X + D_2 - C_{t_2} = 0. \tag{7}$$

These are the familiar definitions of $S_{t_1}^*$ and $S_{t_2}^*$ as being the stock prices (net of dividends) at which the holder of a call is indifferent to exercising at t_1 and t_2.

The second-order conditions are satisfied as[5]

$$C_{11} \equiv \frac{\partial^2 C_{t_0}}{\partial S_{t_1}^{*2}} = -e^{-rt_1}n_1(f_2)N_2(-a_1, -b_1; \rho)/S_{t_1}^*\sigma\sqrt{t_2} < 0$$

$$C_{22} \equiv \frac{\partial^2 C_{t_0}}{\partial S_{t_2}^{*2}} = -e^{-rt_2}n_1(g_2)N_1\left(\frac{-f_1 + \rho_{12}g_1}{\sqrt{1 - \rho_{12}^2}}\right)N_1(-v_1)/S_{t_2}^*\sigma\sqrt{t_2} < 0$$

and

$$\frac{\partial^2 C_{t_0}}{\partial S_{t_1}^*\partial S_{t_2}^*} = \frac{\partial^2 C_{t_0}}{\partial S_{t_2}^*\partial S_{t_1}^*} = 0.$$

To see that C_{t_0} reaches a unique maximum at the critical prices, we first refer to (7). At $S_{t_2}^*$ the exercise value $(S_{t_2} - X + D_2)$ just equals the value of not exercising — namely, C_{t_2}. If a value less (greater) than $S_{t_2}^*$ is used then the exercise value decreases (increases) by more than the ex-dividend call value (i.e., $\Delta S_{t_2} \geqslant \Delta C_{t_2}$) and yet early exercise would occur more (less) often. A similar argument holds for $S_{t_1}^*$ in (6). Thus, the premium for early exercise would be smaller at any prices other than the critical stock prices and the call would be undervalued.

As a result, when computing derivatives of the RGW model with respect to the parameters (θ), the functional dependence of the critical prices on those parameters can be ignored.[6] This is just the envelope theorem and it simplifies the computations considerably.[7]

The derivatives of the two-dividend RGW model are detailed in Appendix A where it is shown that $C_{t_0}^*$ is positively (negatively) related to S_{t_0}, σ, r, T, t_1, and t_2 (X, D_1, and D_2). The derivatives with respect to T, t_1, and t_2 require special attention because the correlation coefficients are time dependent. By using the lemmas in Appendix A it is possible to show that all such terms sum to zero.

Furthermore, the implicit function theorem holds because C_{t_0} is twice continuously differentiable with respect to the domain and (by definition) reaches a maximum at S^*. Thus, the comparative statics of the critical prices can be determined. Specifically,

$$\nabla_\theta S = - [\nabla_s^2 C_{t_0}]^{-1} [\nabla_\theta (\nabla_s C_{t_0})]$$

where $[\nabla_\theta (\nabla_s C_{t_0})]$ is the matrix of cross partials with respect to S and θ. For example, we solve for $\nabla_\sigma S$:

$$\frac{\partial S_{t_1}^*}{\partial \sigma} = \frac{(\partial C_1/\partial \sigma) C_{22}}{C_{11} C_{22}} = \frac{\partial C_{t_1}/\partial \sigma}{N_2(-a_1, -b_1; \rho)} > 0$$

$$\frac{\partial S_{t_2}^*}{\partial \sigma} = \frac{(\partial C_2/\partial \sigma) C_{11}}{C_{22} C_{11}} = \frac{\partial C_{t_2}/\partial \sigma}{N_1(-v_1)} > 0.$$

Appendix B details the formulas for $\nabla_\theta S$, while Table 1 provides a summary of the signs of these derivatives.

In Table 1 the critical prices ($S_{t_i}^*$, for i = 1, 2) are positively (negatively) related to X, r, σ, and T (t_i, D_i). In addition, $S_{t_1}^*$ is a positive (negative) function of t_2 (D_2) while $S_{t_2}^*$ is not dependent on t_1 or D_1. The intuition for these derivatives can be seen from the necessary conditions (6) and (7) by comparing the change in exercise value against the change in the ex-dividend call value when there is a small movement in a parameter.

We discuss four derivatives as examples and note that an increase (decrease) in a critical price decreases (increases) the probability of early exercise. First, as σ increases, C_{t_i} increases, which makes early exercise less attractive and hence $S_{t_i}^*$ increases in order to decrease the probability of early exercise. Second, as X increases, the decrease in exercise value exceeds the decline in C_{t_i}, hence $S_{t_i}^*$ increases. Third, the probability of early exercise at t_1 increases as t_1 increases because C_{t_1} decreases due to a shorter time to maturity (i.e., $T - t_1$) and early exercise is made more attractive by the

Table 1. Comparative Statics of Critical Stock Prices ($S_{t_1}^*$, $S_{t_2}^*$)

S	S_{t_0}	X	r	σ	T	t_1	t_2	D_1	D_2
					θ				
$S_{t_1}^*$	0	+	+	+	+	−	+	−	−
$S_{t_2}^*$	0	+	+	+	+	0	−	0	−

increase in the present value of D_2. Last, $S_{t_1}^*$ is a positive function of t_2 because C_{t_1} is positively related to t_2 and the value of exercising at t_1 decreases by the decrease in the present value of D_2.

Because of the interrelationships between t_1, t_2, and T it is worthwhile to note that the following relationship holds:

$$\frac{\partial S_{t_1}^*}{\partial t_1} + \frac{\partial S_{t_1}^*}{\partial t_2} + \frac{\partial S_{t_1}^*}{\partial T} = 0.$$

Last, it is important to note that this methodology can be applied to any option model dependent on critical asset prices (e.g., the American put by Geske and Johnson [8], American options on futures by Whaley [25], the short sale constrained options by Welch [22], the RGW model with three (or even one) dividends, and the compound option model by Geske [6]).

The next section uses the direction of these derivatives to establish the logic behind an efficient numerical search for the ISD in the presence of two or fewer dividends.

III. THE SEARCH FOR ISDs

A. The European Call Model

For the European call model [i.e., see (5) where t_2 and $S_{t_2}^*$ are replaced by t_0 and S_{t_0}, respectively], it can be shown that

$$\frac{\partial c}{\partial S_{t_0}} = N_1(h_1) > 0, \tag{8}$$

$$\frac{\partial c}{\partial \sigma} = \sqrt{T} S_{t_0} n_1(h_1) > 0. \tag{9}$$

Furthermore,

$$\frac{\partial^2 c}{\partial \sigma^2} = \frac{1}{\sigma} \sqrt{T} S_{t_0} n_1(h_1) h_1 h_2 = \frac{1}{\sigma} h_1 h_2 \frac{\partial c}{\partial \sigma} \tag{10}$$

which is positive if either $h_1 < 0$ or $h_2 > 0$. By the definition of h_1 and h_2 in (1), we can infer $\partial^2 c/\partial \sigma^2 > 0$ if

$$\sigma < w = \left(\left| 2\left(\frac{1}{T} \ln(S_{t_0}/X) + r\right) \right| \right)^{1/2}. \tag{11}$$

Therefore, c is a strictly increasing, convex function of σ for the domain $0 < \sigma < w$. Similarly, $\partial^2 c/\partial \sigma^2 < 0$ if $h_1 > 0$ and $h_2 < 0$, which is equivalent to saying $\partial^2 c/\partial \sigma^2 < 0$ if $\sigma > w$. Hence, c is a strictly increasing, concave function of σ for the domain $\sigma > w$.

Define a funciton F such that $F(\sigma) = c(\sigma) - CP$ and let σ^* be the solution of $F(\sigma^*) = 0$, or equivalently, $c(\sigma^*) = CP$. If there is no other better candidate, we can start from the initial point w to search for σ^* along the linear-approximation search sequence $(\sigma^{(n)})$ of the function F such that

$$\sigma^{(n+1)} = -F(\sigma^{(n)})/F'(\sigma^{(n)}) + \sigma^{(n)}, \tag{12}$$

where $F'(\sigma^{(n)}) = \partial c(\sigma^{(n)})/\partial\sigma$. Then $(\sigma^{(n)})$ will converge to σ^* from the right for $\sigma^* < w$ and from the left for $\sigma^* > w$. Because of the convexity or concavity of the function F with respect to each partial domain of σ, the convergence will be achieved without oscillation.[8]

For any given $\sigma > 0$,

$$c(P_{t_0}, \sigma) \geqslant C(S_{t_0}, \sigma) \geqslant c(S_{t_0}, \sigma).$$

The former inequality is due to dividend payments and the latter to premiums of early exercise for American calls. Conversely, let σ_L be determined by solving $c(P_{t_0}, \sigma_L) = CP$, σ^* by $C(S_{t_0}, \sigma^*) = CP$, and σ_u by $c(S_{t_0}, \sigma_u) = CP$, then

$$\sigma_L \leqslant \sigma^* \leqslant \sigma_u.$$

We will use these lower and upper bounds in our search for ISDs of American calls.

B. The One-Dividend Adjusted American Call Model

If there is only one dividend before maturity, we will use model C_{t_1} [i.e., see (4)] for our analysis. One can simply regard t_1 as t_0 and $S_{t_1}^*$ as S_{t_0}. It can be shown that

$$\frac{\partial C_{t_1}}{\partial S_{t_1}} = 1 - N_2(-a_1, -b_1; \rho) > 0, \tag{13}$$

$$\frac{\partial C_{t_1}}{\partial \sigma} = \sqrt{T - t_1} S_{t_1} n_1(b_1) N_1 \left(\frac{-a_1 + \rho b_1}{\sqrt{1-\rho^2}} \right) + \sqrt{t_2 - t_1} S_{t_1} n_1(a_1) N_1(-v_1) > 0. \tag{14}$$

Hence, the American call model price is a strictly increasing function of S_{t_1} and σ, the same as its European counterpart. Clearly, if $S_{t_2}^* = +\infty$ (i.e., $a_1 = -\infty$) then (13) and (14) reduce to (8) and (9), respectively.

If it is desired to search for the ISD of a set of unprotected American calls simultaneously by minimizing the sum of squared differences between model prices and actual prices (see Whaley [24] pp. 39–40), Equation (14) can be used. Equation (14) can be used to search for the ISD of an individual option, but the curvature of C_{t_1} with respect to σ is not easy to determine. Furthermore, $S_{t_2}^*$, the critical stock price above which the option will be exercised just before the ex-dividend instant, is also a function of σ.

Therefore, the search process for $S_{t_2}^*$ must be addressed before continuing the search process for σ^*.

We note that $C_{t_1}(S_{t_2}^*)$ is the $\max_{S_{t_2}} C_{t_1}(S_{t_2})$. It can be shown that the first order condition $[(\partial C_{t_1}/\partial S_{t_2}^*) \equiv 0]$ holds if and only if G [see (7)] is zero. In other words the exercise value at t_2 just equals the ex-dividend call value, C_{t_2}. Using (8) we have

$$G' \equiv \frac{\partial G}{\partial S_{t_2}} = 1 - N_1(v_1) > 0.$$

$$G'' \equiv \frac{\partial^2 G}{\partial S_{t_2}^2} = -(S_{t_2}\sigma\sqrt{T-t_2})^{-1}n_1(v_1) < 0.$$

Hence, G is a strictly increasing, concave function of S_{t_2}. Let $S_{t_2}^*$ be the solution of $G(S_{t_2}^*) = 0$. If we start from an initial point $S_{t_2}^{(0)}$ smaller than $S_{t_2}^*$, then the linear-approximation search sequence $(S_{t_2}^{(n)})$ defined as

$$S_{t_2}^{(n+1)} = -G(S_{t_2}^{(n)})/G'(S_{t_2}^{(n)}) + S_{t_2}^{(n)} \tag{15}$$

will converge from the left to $S_{t_2}^*$ without oscillation because of the concavity of the function G. Since $C_{t_2} \geqslant 0$, setting $S_{t_2}^{(0)} = X - D_2$ will guarantee that $S_{t_2}^{(0)} \leqslant S_{t_2}^*$.

As σ changes, $S_{t_2}^*$ as a function of σ also changes. Using the comparative static techniques in Section II, $S_{t_2}^*$ is an increasing function of σ as

$$\frac{\partial S_{t_2}^*}{\partial \sigma} = \sqrt{T-t_2}S_{t_2}^*n(v_1)/N_1(-v_1) > 0.$$

Therefore, $S_{t_2}^*(\sigma_1) > S_{t_2}^*(\sigma_2)$ whenever $\sigma_1 > \sigma_2$.

The properties of $S_{t_2}^*$ discussed above coupled with the fact that σ^* has a lower bound σ_L such that $c(P_0, \sigma_L) = CP$ and an upper bound σ_u such that $c(S_0, \sigma_u) = CP$ suggest the following binary search process for σ^*.

Step 1. a. Let $\sigma^* = \sigma_L$ and $S_{t_2}^{(0)} = X - D_2$.
   b. Search for $S_{t_2}^*(\sigma^*)$ using (15). If $S_{t_2}^*$ goes to positive infinity,[9] then set $\sigma^* = \sigma_u$ and stop the search process. Otherwise, set $S_{t_2}^{(0)} = S_{t_2}^*(\sigma^*)$.

Step 2. a. Let $\Delta = (1/2)(\sigma_u - \sigma_L)$. If Δ is sufficiently small, terminate the search process. Otherwise, $\sigma^* = \sigma_L + \Delta$.
   b. Search for $S_{t_2}^*(\sigma^*)$ using (15). If $S_{t_2}^*(\sigma^*)$ goes to infinity, set $\sigma^* = \sigma_u$ and terminate the search process.[10] Otherwise compute C_{t_0} according to model C_{t_1} [i.e., (4)].
   c. If C_{t_0} is sufficiently close to CP, terminate the search process. If $C_{t_0} > CP$, set $\sigma_u = \sigma^*$ and repeat Step 2.[11] Otherwise, set $\sigma_L = \sigma^*$, $S_{t_2}^{(0)} = S_{t_2}^*(\sigma^*)$, and repeat Step 2.

C. The Two-Dividend Adjusted American Call Model

For the two-dividend adjusted model of Section II, it was shown that C_{t_0} increases with σ and S_{t_0}. These derivatives are given in Appendix A and notice that they reduce to (8) and (9), respectively, if both $S_{t_1}^*$ and $S_{t_2}^*$ go to infinity but reduce to (13) and (14) if only one of them becomes infinite.

The search process for σ^* is similar to that of the one-dividend adjusted model. The only issue remaining to be addressed is the search process for $S_{t_1}^*$. From the first-order conditions it can be shown that H [i.e., see (6)] is an increasing concave function of S_{t_1}. Specifically,

$$H' = \partial H/\partial S_{t_1} = N_2(-a_1, -b_1; \rho) > 0 \text{ [see (13)]}.$$

$$H'' = \partial H'/\partial S_{t_1} = -\frac{n_1(a_1)N_1(-v_1)}{S_{t_1}\sigma\sqrt{t_2 - t_1}} - \frac{n(b_1)}{S_{t_1}\sigma\sqrt{T - t_1}} N_1\left(\frac{-a_1 + \rho b_1}{\sqrt{1 - \rho^2}}\right) < 0.$$

Setting the initial value, $S_{t_1}^{(0)} = X - D_1 - e^{-r(t_2 - t_1)}D_2$, will guarantee a convergence to $S_{t_1}^*$ from the left without oscillation. The search sequence $(S_{t_1}^{(n)})$ is defined similar to (15). We also know from Section II that $S_{t_1}^*$ is an increasing function of σ. Thus $S_{t_1}^*(\sigma_1) > S_{t_1}^*(\sigma_2)$ whenever $\sigma_1 > \sigma_2$. We can now devise the following search process for σ^* of the two-dividend adjusted model:

Step 1. a. Set $\sigma^* = \sigma_L$, $S_{t_1}^{(0)} = X - D_1 - e^{-r(t_2 - t_1)}D_2$, and $S_{t_2}^{(0)} = X - D_2$.
   b. Search for $S_{t_2}^*(\sigma^*)$. If $S_{t_2}^*(\sigma^*)$ becomes infinite, go to the search process of the one-dividend adjusted model. Otherwise, $S_{t_2}^{(0)} = S_{t_2}^*(\sigma^*)$.
   c. Search for $S_{t_1}^*(\sigma^*)$. If $S_{t_1}^*(\sigma^*)$ becomes infinite,[12] go to the search process of the one-dividend adjusted model. Otherwise, $S_{t_1}^{(0)} = S_{t_1}^*(\sigma^*)$.

Step 2. a. Let $\Delta = (1/2)(\sigma_u - \sigma_L)$. If Δ is sufficiently small, terminate the search process. Otherwise, $\sigma^* = \sigma_L + \Delta$.
   b. Search for $S_{t_2}^*(\sigma^*)$ and then $S_{t_1}^*(\sigma^*)$. If both $S_{t_2}^*(\sigma^*)$ and $S_{t_1}^*(\sigma^*)$ become infinite, set $\sigma^* = \sigma_u$ and terminate the search process. If one of them is infinite, compute C_{t_0} using model C_{t_1} [see (4)]. Otherwise, compute C_{t_0} using the model in (1).
   c. If C_{t_0} is sufficiently close to CP, terminate the search process. If $C_{t_0} > CP$, set $\sigma_u = \sigma^*$ and repeat Step 2. For $C_{t_0} < CP$, if $S_{t_1}^*$ is infinite, set $S_{t_2}^{(0)} = S_{t_2}^*$. If $S_{t_2}^*$ is infinite, set $S_{t_1}^{(0)} = S_{t_1}^*$. For either case, then set $\sigma_L = \sigma^*$ and go to the search process of the one-dividend adjusted model. Otherwise, set $S_{t_1}^{(0)} = S_{t_1}^*$, $S_{t_2}^{(0)} = S_{t_2}^*$, $\sigma_L = \sigma^*$, and repeat Step 2.

To calculate the trivariate normal integral, notice that $\rho_{13} - \rho_{12}\rho_{23} = 0$, hence,

$$N_3(f, g, h; \rho_{12}, \rho_{13}, \rho_{23}) = \int_{-\infty}^{g} N_1\left(\frac{f - \rho_{12}y}{\sqrt{1 - \rho_{12}^2}}\right) N_1\left(\frac{h - \rho_{23}y}{\sqrt{1 - \rho_{23}^2}}\right) n_1(y)\, dy.$$

The integrand becomes a normal density function multiplied by two univariate normal integrals (see Geske [6]).[13]

IV. SPECIFIC EXAMPLES

The following two examples demonstrate the numerical search process discussed above and the need to adjust for the exact early exercise premium when computing ISDs.

Example 1. CP = 4.5, P_{t_0} = 68.25, X = 70, r = 0.1294, D_1 = 0.8, D_2 = 0.8, t_1 = 0.1726, t_2 = 0.45479, and T = 0.46575 (S_{t_0} = 66.71339).

σ_L	$c(P_{t_0}, \sigma_L)$	σ_u	$c(S_{t_0}, \sigma_u)$
0.38740	8.28782	0.17490	3.57583
0.17631	4.52469	0.22645	4.50056
0.17490	4.50001		

σ^*	$S_{t_1}^{(0)}$	$S_{t_1}^*$	$S_{t_2}^{(0)}$	$S_{t_2}^*$	$C(S_{t_0}\sigma^*)$
0.17490	68.4287	∞	69.2	69.5548	3.90071
0.20067			69.5548	69.6820	4.35341
0.21356			69.6820	69.7494	4.58039
0.20712			69.6820	69.7156	4.46686
0.21034			69.7156	69.7330	4.52361
0.20873			69.7156	69.7224	4.49523
0.20953			69.7224	69.7287	4.50942
0.20913			69.7224	69.7266	4.50233

The search process starts with finding the lower bound (σ_L) of σ^* by solving $c(P_{t_0}, \sigma_L) = CP$. The initial value 0.3874 is computed according to (11). This example shows that it takes three iterations to find σ_L at 0.1749. Also, the value of a European call is positively related to the standard deviation of returns on its underlying stock. σ_L is then used as the initial value to search for the upper bound (σ_u) of σ^* by solving $c(S_{t_0}, \sigma_u) = CP$.

It takes only one more iteration to find σ_u at 0.22645. Note that for $\sigma_L = \sigma_u = 0.1749$, $c(P_{t_0}) = 4.50001 > c(S_{t_0}) = 3.57583$. Since $P_{t_0} > S_{t_0}$, the value of a European call is positively related to the price of its underlying stock. σ_L is again used as the initial point to search for σ^*, the ISD of the American call. The initial value of the critical stock price at time t_1, $S_{t_1}^{(0)}$, is determined by $X - D_1 - e^{-r(t_2-t_1)}D_2 = 68.4287$. Similarly, $S_{t_2}^{(0)} = X - D_2 = 69.2$. This example shows that when σ^* is at its lower bound, 0.1749, $S_{t_1}^*$ is infinite and $S_{t_2}^*$ is finite. Hence, the value of the American call can be calculated according to the one-dividend adjusted model (4). This gives $C_{t_0} = 3.90071$, which is smaller than $CP = 4.5$. Analytically, the positive relationship between C and σ is shown in (14) and Appendix A. Hence, it takes a larger σ to have $C(\sigma) = CP$. Since $S_{t_1}^*$ is an increasing function of σ, it is impossible to have a finite $S_{t_1}^*$ later in the search process. Therefore, this two-dividend case can be treated as a one-dividend case. The binary search results show that $C(\sigma)$ and $S_{t_2}^*$ are positively related to σ. $S_{t_2}^*$, however, is not quite as sensitive to changes in σ. It usually takes only two iterations from $S_{t_2}^{(0)}$ to $S_{t_2}^*$. The final σ^* will be between 0.20873 and 0.20913. The number of iterations required to find σ^* will depend on the degree of accuracy desired. [14]

This example demonstrates the need to adjust for the exact early exercise premium. The dividend payments are only 2.34% of the stock price but σ_L is 16.38% lower than σ^* while σ_u is 8.28% higher than σ^*.

Example 2. Change t_1 from 0.1726 to 0.4; the other parameters are the same as specified in Example 1 ($S_{t_0} = 66.7361$).

σ_L	$c(P_{t_0}, \sigma_L)$	σ_u	$c(S_{t_0}, \sigma_u)$
0.38740	8.28782	0.17490	3.58864
0.17631	4.52469	0.22574	4.50061
0.17490	4.50001		

σ^*	$S_{t_1}^{(0)}$	$S_{t_1}^*$	$S_{t_2}^{(0)}$	$S_{t_2}^*$	$C(S_{t_0}\sigma^*)$
0.17490	68.4057	71.2804	69.2	69.5548	4.01897
0.20032	71.2804	71.9390	69.5548	69.6801	4.45881
0.21303	71.9390	72.2839	69.6801	69.7465	4.67980
0.20667	71.9390	72.1051	69.6801	69.7132	4.56923
0.20350	71.9390	72.0239	69.6801	69.6967	4.51400
0.20191	71.9390	71.9825	69.6801	69.6884	4.48640
0.20270	71.9825	72.0041	69.6884	69.6926	4.50020

By changing t_1 from 0.1726 to 0.4, $S_{t_1}^*$ becomes finite. Thus, Example 2 shows that the closer the ex-dividend date is to the expiration date, the higher the probability of early exercise is at the ex-dividend date (Roll [18]). Also $S_{t_1}^*$ is positively related to σ. The explanation of the other results is similar to that provided in Example 1.

V. SUMMARY

The two-dividend RGW model is viewed as a maximization of a deterministic function where the critical stock prices represent the optimized decision variables. This simplifies the computation of the call's derivatives, the comparative statics of the critical stock prices, and other properties (i.e., such as concavity). The application of the envelope theorem plays an important role in these calculations.

In spite of the advantages afforded by the envelope theorem the computation of the comparative statics is still complicated and three lemmas are provided in this regard. All the comparative statics are presented in detail and an intuitive discussion of the signs of some of these derivatives is given.

In applying the formula to inversely derive the market's implied standard deviation of the stock (ISD), the following facts are utilized:

1. When the probability of early exercise goes to zero, the American call model reduces to the European call model.
2. The European call model can be used to derive the lower and upper bounds on the ISD by using, respectively, the current stock price and the current stock price less the present value of escrowed dividends as the arguments.
3. The value of an American call and its critical stock prices are "smooth" increasing functions of the total risk of the stock.

A binary search process is suggested to determine the ISD. This eliminates the need to compute the more complicated partial derivatives required by gradient search routines. Logical choices of initial points for the search process are also recommended. The proximity of the upper and lower bounds to each other, the nested sequencing of the 0, 1, 2 dividend cases, and the binary search all combine to yield a simple and efficient search routine. Furthermore, two examples are provided to demonstrate the numerical search process discussed in the paper.

As a result a large number of ISDs can now be calculated from a simple algorithm using the RGW model. This should facilitate future empirical work with calls. It is also noted that these techniques can be applied to any option involving critical asset prices (i.e., puts and futures options).

APPENDIX A: DERIVATIVES OF THE TWO-DIVIDEND RGW MODEL

$$\frac{\partial C_{t_0}}{\partial S_{t_0}} = \frac{\partial C_{t_0}}{\partial P_{t_0}} = 1 - N_3(-f_1, -g_1, -h_1; \rho_{12}, \rho_{13}, \rho_{23}) > 0$$

$$\frac{\partial C_{t_0}}{\partial \sigma} = S_{t_0}\left\{ \sqrt{t_1}\, n_1(f_1)N_2(-a_1, -b_1; \rho) + \sqrt{t_2}\, n_1(g_1)N_1\left(\frac{-f_1 + \rho_{12}g_1}{\sqrt{1-\rho_{12}^2}}\right)N_1(-v_1) \right.$$

$$\left. + \sqrt{T}\, n_1(h_1)N_2\left(\frac{-f_1 + \rho_{13}h_1}{\sqrt{1-\rho_{13}^2}}, \frac{-g_1 + \rho_{23}h_1}{\sqrt{1-\rho_{23}^2}}; \rho_{12}\sqrt{1-\rho^2}\right) \right\} > 0$$

$$\frac{\partial C_{t_0}}{\partial r} = X[t_1 e^{-r t_1} N_1(f_2) + t_2 e^{-r t_2} N_2(-f_2, g_2; -\rho_{12})$$

$$+ T e^{-rT} N_3(-f_2, -g_2, h_2; \rho_{12}, -\rho_{13}, -\rho_{23})]$$

$$+ t_1 D_1 e^{-r t_1}[N_1(-f_2) - N_3(-f_1, -g_1, -h_1; \rho_{12}, \rho_{13}, \rho_{23})]$$

$$+ t_2 D_2 e^{-r t_2}[N_2(-f_2, -g_2; \rho_{12})$$

$$- N_3(-f_1, -g_1, -h_1; \rho_{12}, \rho_{13}, \rho_{23})] > 0$$

$$\frac{\partial C_{t_0}}{\partial X} = -[e^{-r t_1} N_1(f_2) + e^{-r t_2} N_2(-f_2, g_2; -\rho_{12})$$

$$+ e^{-rT} N_3(-f_2, -g_2, h_2; \rho_{12}, -\rho_{13}, -\rho_{23})] < 0$$

$$\frac{\partial C_{t_0}}{\partial T} = \frac{S_{t_0}\sigma}{2\sqrt{T}}\, n_1(h_1)N_2\left(\frac{-f_1 + \rho_{13}h_1}{\sqrt{1-\rho_{13}^2}}, \frac{-g_1 + \rho_{23}h_1}{\sqrt{1-\rho_{23}^2}}; \rho_{12}\sqrt{1-\rho^2}\right)$$

$$+ Xre^{-rt}N_3(-f_2, -g_2, h_2; \rho_{12}, -\rho_{13}, -\rho_{23}) > 0$$

$$\frac{\partial C_{t_0}}{\partial t_1} = \frac{S_{t_0}\sigma}{2\sqrt{t_1}}\, n_1(f_1)N_2(-a_1, -b_1; \rho) + rXe^{-r t_1} N_1(f_2)$$

$$+ re^{-r t_1} D_1[N_1(-f_2) - N_3(-f_1, -g_1, -h_1; \rho_{12}, \rho_{13}, \rho_{23})] > 0$$

$$\frac{\partial C_{t_0}}{\partial t_2} = \frac{S_{t_0}\sigma}{2\sqrt{t_2}}\, n_1(g_1)N_1\left(\frac{-f_1 + \rho_{12}g_1}{\sqrt{1-\rho_{12}^2}}\right)N_1(-v_1) + Xre^{-r t_2}N_2(-f_2, g_2; -\rho_{12})$$

$$+ re^{-r t_2} D_2[N_2(-f_2, -g_2; \rho_{12}) - N_3(-f_1, -g_1, -h_1; \rho_{12}, \rho_{13}, \rho_{23})]$$

$$> 0$$

$$\frac{\partial C_{t_0}}{\partial D_1} = -e^{-r t_1}[N_1(-f_2) - N_3(-f_1, -g_1 - h_1; \rho_{12}, \rho_{13}, \rho_{23})] < 0$$

$$\frac{\partial C_{t_0}}{\partial D_2} = -e^{-r t_2}[N_2(-f_2, -g_2; \rho_{12}) - N_3(-f_1, -g_1, -h_1; \rho_{12}, \rho_{13}, \rho_{23})]$$

$$< 0$$

The following lemmas are useful when computing the comparative statics of C_{t_0} — especially with respect to t_1, t_2, and T.

Lemma 1. Let the upper integral limits (a, b) and the correlation coefficient (ρ) of $N_2(a, b; \rho)$ be functions of some parameter t. Then

$$\frac{\partial}{\partial t} [N_2(a(t), b(t); \rho(t))] = \frac{\partial a}{\partial t} n_1(a)N_1\left(\frac{b - \rho a}{\sqrt{1 - \rho^2}}\right)$$

$$+ \frac{\partial b}{\partial t} n_1(b)N_1\left(\frac{a - \rho b}{\sqrt{1 - \rho^2}}\right) + \frac{\partial \rho}{\partial t} n_2(a, b; \rho).$$

Lemma 2. Let the upper integral limits (a, b, c) of $N_3(a, b, c; \rho_{12}, \rho_{13}, \rho_{23})$ be functions of some parameter t, but ρ_{12} ρ_{13}, and ρ_{23} be independent of t. Then $\left(\frac{\partial}{\partial t}\right) N_3[a(t), b(t), c(t); \rho_{12}, \rho_{13}, \rho_{23}]$

$$= \frac{\partial a}{\partial t} n_1(a)N_2\left[\frac{b - \rho_{12}a}{\sqrt{1 - \rho_{12}^2}}, \frac{c - \rho_{13}a}{\sqrt{1 - \rho_{13}^2}}; \frac{\rho_{23} - \rho_{12}\rho_{13}}{\sqrt{(1 - \rho_{12}^2)(1 - \rho_{13}^2)}}\right]$$

$$+ \frac{\partial b}{\partial t} n_1(b)N_2\left[\frac{a - \rho_{12}b}{\sqrt{1 - \rho_{12}^2}}, \frac{c - \rho_{23}b}{\sqrt{1 - \rho_{23}^2}}; \frac{\rho_{13} - \rho_{12}\rho_{23}}{\sqrt{(1 - \rho_{12}^2)(1 - \rho_{23}^2)}}\right]$$

$$+ \frac{\partial c}{\partial t} n_1(c)N_2\left[\frac{a - \rho_{13}c}{\sqrt{1 - \rho_{13}^2}}, \frac{b - \rho_{23}c}{\sqrt{1 - \rho_{23}^2}}; \frac{\rho_{12} - \rho_{13}\rho_{23}}{\sqrt{(1 - \rho_{13}^2)(1 - \rho_{23}^2)}}\right].$$

Lemma 3. Let $\rho_{12} = \sqrt{t_1/t_2}$, $\rho_{13} = \sqrt{t_1/T}$, and $\rho_{23} = \sqrt{t_2/T}$ in $N_3(a, b, c; \rho_{12}, \rho_{13}, \rho_{23})$ and assume the upper integral limits are independent of t_1, t_2, and T. Then,

(1) $\quad \dfrac{\partial N_3}{\partial t_1} = \dfrac{\rho_{12}}{2t_1} n_2(a, b; \rho_{12})N_1\left(\dfrac{c - \rho_{23}b}{\sqrt{1 - \rho_{23}^2}}\right) - \dfrac{\rho_{13}}{2t_1} n_2(a, c; \rho_{13})N_1(R)$

(2) $\quad \dfrac{\partial N_3}{\partial t_2} = -\dfrac{\rho_{12}}{2t_2} n_2(a, b; \rho_{12})N_1\left(\dfrac{c - \rho_{23}b}{\sqrt{1 - \rho_{23}^2}}\right)$

$$+ \dfrac{\rho_{23}}{2t_2} n_2(b, c; \rho_{23})N_1\left(\dfrac{a - \rho_{12}b}{\sqrt{1 - \rho_{12}^2}}\right)$$

(3) $\quad \dfrac{\partial N_3}{\partial T} = -\dfrac{\rho_{23}}{2T} n_2(b, c; \rho_{23})N_1\left(\dfrac{a - \rho_{12}b}{\sqrt{1 - \rho_{12}^2}}\right) + \dfrac{\rho_{13}}{2T} n_2(a, c; \rho_{13})N_1(R)$

where

$$R = \left[b - \frac{\rho_{12}(1 - \rho_{23}^2)a}{(1 - \rho_{13}^2)} - \frac{\rho_{23}(1 - \rho_{12}^2)c}{(1 - \rho_{13}^2)}\right]\bigg/\left[\frac{(1 - \rho_{12}^2)(1 - \rho_{23}^2)}{(1 - \rho_{13}^2)}\right]^{1/2}.$$

APPENDIX B: CRITICAL STOCK PRICE COMPARATIVE STATICS

$$\frac{\partial S_{t_1}^*}{\partial \sigma} = S_{t_1}^*\left[\sqrt{T - t_1}n_1(b_1)N_1\left(\frac{-a_1 + \rho b_1}{\sqrt{1 - \rho^2}}\right)\right.$$

$$\left. + \sqrt{t_2 - t_1}n_1(a_1)N_1(-v_1)\right]\Big/N_2(-a_1, -b_1; \rho) > 0$$

$$\frac{\partial S_{t_2}^*}{\partial \sigma} = \frac{\sqrt{T - t_2}S_{t_2}^*n_1(v_1)}{N_1(-v_1)} > 0$$

$$\frac{\partial S_{t_1}^*}{\partial D_1} = \frac{-1}{N_2(-a_1, -b_1; \rho)} < 0$$

$$\frac{\partial S_{t_1}^*}{\partial D_2} = \frac{-e^{-r(t_2 - t_1)}N_1(-a_2)}{N_2(-a_1, -b_1; \rho)} < 0$$

$$\frac{\partial S_{t_2}^*}{\partial D_2} = \frac{-1}{N_1(-v_1)} < 0$$

$$\frac{\partial S_{t_1}^*}{\partial r} = \{e^{-r(t_2 - t_1)}(t_2 - t_1)D_2N_1(-a_2)$$

$$+ X[(t_2 - t_1)e^{-r(t_2 - t_1)}N_1(a_2)$$

$$+ (T - t_1)e^{-r(T - t_1)}N_2(-a_2, b_2; -\rho)]\}/N_2(-a_1, -b_1; \rho) > 0$$

$$\frac{\partial S_{t_2}^*}{\partial r} = (T - t_2)e^{-r(T - t_2)}XN_1(v_2)/N_1(-v_1) > 0$$

$$\frac{\partial S_{t_1}^*}{\partial X} = [1 - e^{-r(t_2 - t_1)}N_1(a_2) - e^{-r(T - t_1)}N_2(-a_2, b_2; -\rho)]/N_2(-a_1, -b_1; \rho) > 0$$

$$\frac{\partial S_{t_2}^*}{\partial X} = [1 - e^{-r(T - t_2)}N_1(v_2)]/N_1(-v_1) > 0$$

$$\frac{\partial S_{t_1}^*}{\partial t_1} = \left\{-S_{t_1}^*\left[n_1(a_1)\frac{\sigma}{2\sqrt{t_2 - t_1}}N_1(-v_1)\right.\right.$$

$$\left. + n_1(b_1)\frac{\sigma}{2\sqrt{T - t_1}}N_1\left(\frac{-a_1 + \rho b_1}{\sqrt{1 - \rho^2}}\right)\right]$$

$$- Xre^{-r(t_2 - t_1)}[N_1(a_2) + e^{-r(T - t_2)}N_2(-a_2, b_2; -\rho)]$$

$$\left. - rD_2e^{-r(t_2 - t_1)}N_1(-a_2)\right\}/N_2(-a_1, -b_1; \rho) < 0$$

$$\frac{\partial S_{t_1}^*}{\partial t_2} = \left[re^{-r(t_2 - t_1)}[D_2 N_1(-a_2) + XN_1(a_2)] \right.$$

$$\left. + S_{t_1}^* \frac{\sigma n_1(a_1)}{2\sqrt{t_2 - t_1}} N_1(-v_1) \right] / N_1(-a_1, -b_1; \rho) > 0$$

$$\frac{\partial S_{t_2}^*}{\partial t_2} = -\frac{\partial S_{t_2}^*}{\partial T} = -Xe^{-r(T - t_2)} \left[rN_1(v_2) + n_1(v_2) \frac{\sigma}{\sqrt{T - t_2}} \right] / N_1(-v_1) < 0$$

$$\frac{\partial S_{t_1}^*}{\partial T} = Xe^{-r(T - t_1)} \left[rN_2(-a_2, b_2; -\rho) \right.$$

$$\left. + \frac{\sigma n_1(b_2)}{2\sqrt{T - t_1}} N_1 \left(\frac{-a_2 + \rho b_2}{\sqrt{1 - \rho^2}} \right) \right] / N_2(-a_1, -b_1; \rho) > 0$$

NOTES

1. Although, the derivation process can be somewhat tedious, the extension of the two-dividend case to the general n-dividend case is straightforward. It is our experience with empirical data that an American call with three-dividend payments before maturity seldom has a detectable positive probability of early exercise at the first ex-dividend instant. Also Black [2] and Geske [7] observe that most American calls would only be exercised at the last ex-dividend instant. Hence, the one- and two-dividend cases are the only empirically relevant ones.

2. We assume that the stock price decreases at the ex-dividend instant by the amount of the dividend payment and leave the difference between the actual price decrease and the dividend payment to be an inherent part of the stochastic process generating the stock price. See Barone-Adesi and Whaley [1] for a recent discussion and test of the issue. Hereafter, unless specifically mentioned, stock price refers to $\tilde{S}_t$ rather than $\tilde{P}_t$.

3. See Johnson and Kotz [12] for discussion of the multivariate normal distribution.

4. An alternative equivalent definition of the RGW model ($C_{t_0}^*$) is

$$\max_{S_{t_1}} C_{t_0}(S_{t_1}, \theta_2, \max_{S_{t_2}} C_{t_1}(S_{t_2}, \theta_1 | S_{t_1}))$$

where C_{t_1} is the one dividend American call model at t_1 and $\theta_1(\theta_2)$ are the parameters.

5. We note that C_{t_0} is strictly concave with respect to S_{t_1} and S_{t_2} as both C_{11} and C_{22} are negative. This should not be confused with the convexity of C_{t_0} with respect to S_{t_0} (e.g., see Merton [15] p. 179).

6. Geske and Johnson [8] in their footnote 3 note that this functional dependence results in terms that cancel each other and hence can be ignored when computing derivatives of the American put. Since their put model has the same structure as a multiple dividend RGW call we can apply the maximization view of this paper to their put model. Hence, the envelope theorem explains why all such terms cancel.

7. We can also obtain a more general view of the envelope theorem by forming:

$$L(S, \theta) = C_{t_0}(S, \theta) - C_{t_0}^*(\theta).$$

By definition L reaches a maximum of 0 at S^*, and therefore $\nabla_{s, \theta} L = 0$ and $\nabla_{s, \theta}^2 L \leqslant 0$ (e.g., see

Silberberg [20]). From these second-order conditions we have the concavity of C_{t_0} with respect to the critical prices and that $\partial^2 C_{t_0}/\partial\theta_i^2 \leqslant \partial^2 C_{t_0}^*/\partial\theta_i^2$ (where θ_i is one of the parameters).

8. This cannot be guaranteed if σ^* falls into the irrational (not in mathematical sense) domain of $\sigma < 0$. We can terminate the search process if σ becomes very small and still $c(\sigma) > CP$. For a similar development of the European ISD see Manaster and Koehler [14].

9. $S_{t_2}^*$ goes to infinity if for any $S_{t_2}^{(n)}$, $N_1(v_1)$ is close to one and still $S_{t_2}^{(n)} + D_2 - X - C_{t_2}(S_{t_2}^{(n)}) < 0$.

10. If $S_{t_2}^*(\sigma^*)$ is infinite, then only for $\sigma < \sigma^*$ can we have finite $S_{t_2}^*(\sigma)$. But $CP = c(S_{t_0}, \sigma_u) > c(S_{t_0}, \sigma^*) = C(S_{t_0}, \sigma^*) > C(S_{t_0}, \sigma)$, hence we set $\sigma^* = \sigma_u$.

11. Once in our search sequence we find a σ such that $C_{t_0}(\sigma) > CP$ and $S_{t_2}^*(\sigma)$ is finite, we will never find any σ such that $S_{t_2}^*(\sigma)$ is infinite.

12. $S_{t_1}^*$ becomes infinite if for any $S_{t_1}^{(n)}$, $N_2(-a_1, -b_1 : \rho)$ is close to zero and still $S_{t_1}^{(n)} + D_1 + e^{-r(t_2 - t_1)}D_2 - X < C_{t_1}(S_{t_1}^{(n)})$.

13. The IMSL library provided by International Mathematical and Statistical Library, Inc. has subroutines for univariate and bivariate normal distribution functions and numerical integration.

14. It appears from the examples that the binary search process takes many oscillations at points near convergence. Using extrapolation at the near convergent points seems to be a good alternative. However, it took only a small fraction of a computing second to provide results for the examples, since using the binary search process eliminates the need to calculate partial derivatives.

REFERENCES

1. Barone-Adesi, G., and R. Whaley, "The Valuation of American Call Options and the Expected Ex-Dividend Stock Price Decline," *Journal of Financial Economics* 17 (1986), 91–111.

2. Black, F., "Fact and Fantasy in the Use of Options," *Financial Analysts Journal* 31 (1975), 36–41, 61–72.

3. Black, F., and M. Scholes, "The Pricing of Options and Corporate Liabilities," *Journal of Political Economy* 81 (1973), 637–654.

4. Chen, D., "The Information Content of Quarterly Earnings Data and the Market's Revision of Risk Predictions Implied in Option Prices," Unpublished Ph.D. dissertation, University of Illinois at Urbana–Champaign, 1986.

5. Chiras, D., and S. Manaster, "The Information Content of Option Prices and a Test of Market Efficiency," *Journal of Financial Economics* 6 (1978), 213–234.

6. Geske, R., "The Valuation of Corporate Liabilities as Compound Options," *Journal of Financial and Quantitative Analysis* 13 (1977), 541–552.

7. Geske, R., "A Note on an Analytical Valuation Formula for Unprotected American Call Options on Stocks with Known Dividends," *Journal of Financial Economics* 7 (1979), 375–380.

8. Geske, R., and H. Johnson, "The American Put Option Valued Analytically," *Journal of Finance* 39 (1984), 1511–1524.

9. Geske, R., and R. Roll, "On Valuing American Call Options with the Black–Scholes European Formula," *Journal of Finance* 39 (1984), 443–455.

10. Geske, R., and R. Roll, "Isolating Observed Bias in American Call Option Pricing: An Alternative Variance Estimator," February Working Paper, U.C.L.A., #4-84, 1984.

11. Intriligator, M., *Mathematical Optimization and Economic Theory*. Englewood Cliffs, N.J.: Prentice-Hall, 1971.

12. Johnson, N., and S. Kotz, *Distribution in Statistics: Continuous Multivariate Distributions*, pp. 84–102. New York: Wiley, 1972.

13. Latané, H., and R. Rendleman, Jr., "Standard Deviations of Stock Price Ratios Implied in Option Prices," *Journal of Finance* 31 (1976), 369–381.

14. Manaster, S., and G. Koehler, "The Calculation of Implied Variances from the Black–Scholes Model: A Note," *Journal of Finance* 37 (1982), 227–230.

15. Merton, R., "Theory of Rational Option Pricing," *Bell Journal of Economics and Management Science* 4 (1973), 141–183.

16. Patell, J., and M. Wolfson, "Anticipated Information Releases Reflected in Call Option Prices," *Journal of Accounting and Economics* 1 (1979), 117–140.

17. Patell, J., and M. Wolfson, "The Ex Ante and Ex Post Price Effects of Quarterly Earnings Announcements Reflected in Option and Stock Prices," *Journal of Accounting Research* 19 (1981), 434–458.

18. Roll, R., "An Analytic Valuation Formula for Unprotected American Call Options on Stocks with Known Dividends," *Journal of Financial Economics* 5 (1977), 251–258.

19. Rubinstein, M., "Non-parametric Tests of Alternative Option Pricing Models Using Reported Trades and Quotes on the 30 Most Active CBOE Option Classes from August 23, 1976 through August 31, 1978," *Journal of Finance* 40 (1985), 455–480.

20. Silberberg, E., *The Structure of Economics: A Mathematical Analysis*, pp. 263–284. New York: McGraw-Hill, 1978.

21. Sterk, W., "Comparative Performance of the Black–Scholes and Roll–Geske–Whaley Option Pricing Models," *Journal of Financial and Quantitative Analysis* 18 (1983), 345–354.

22. Welch, R., "Short Sale Restrictions — The Implications for Equity and Option Markets," Unpublished Ph.D. dissertation, 1989, SUNY at Buffalo.

23. Whaley, R., "On the Valuation of American Call Options on Stocks with Known Dividends," *Journal of Financial Economics* 9 (1981), 207–211.

24. Whaley, R., "Valuation of American Call Options on Dividend-Paying Stocks: Empirical Tests," *Journal of Financial Economics* 10 (1982), 29–58.

25. Whaley, R., "Valuation of American Futures Options: Theory and Empirical Tests," Working Paper, 1984, University of Alberta, Edmonton.

COMBINING VARIOUS FUTURES CONTRACTS TO GET BETTER HEDGES

Laurie Goodman* and N. R. Vijayaraghavan**

I. INTRODUCTION

In many market situations the participants have to hold positions in fixed income securities for indeterminate periods of time. This leaves them exposed to interest rate fluctuations. For example, a market maker in bonds will necessarily have to hold a certain cash inventory of bonds. A mortgage originator will necessarily be exposed to rate commitments he makes to his clients. These and other similar situations might warrant hedging against

*Goldman, Sachs & Co.
**Drexel Burnham Lambert.
This paper was written when the authors were employed by Citicorp Investment Bank.

Advances in Futures and Options Research, Vol. 3, pages 257–268.
Copyright © 1988 by JAI Press Inc.
All rights of reproduction in any form reserved.
ISBN: 0-89232-926-2

interest rate fluctuations. Duration is a commonly used measure in designing such hedges. However, in the face of large yield changes and shifts in the slope of the yield curve, using duration alone as a hedging condition provides incomplete protection. In this paper, we present a better method for hedging fixed income portfolios that can be easily implemented. Essentially, the hedger combines different futures contracts to more accurately match the behavior of his bond portfolio.

II. DURATION AND SIMPLE HEDGES

Modified duration (D), is the percentage change in price of an instrument resulting from a one percentage point change in yield:

$$-D = \frac{\Delta P/P}{\Delta Y} \tag{1}$$

where

ΔP = change in price of the instrument
P = initial price of the instrument
ΔY = change in yield on the instrument.

In terms of actual cashflows, it can be easily shown that modified duration can be expressed as the present value weighted average of the times of the cashflows, divided by one plus the semiannual yield as follows:

$$D = \sum_{i=1}^{n} \frac{iw_i}{2(1 + Y/2)} \tag{2}$$

where

i = semiannual period
w_i = the fraction of present value of cashflow at semiannual period i with respect to price of the instrument
Y = initial yield to maturity
n = horizon of cashflows.

If we were to plot the price against the yield of the instrument as in Figure 1, duration is approximated simply by the negative of the slope of the curve at the initial yield Y.[1] For small changes in yields (ΔY), the price changes (ΔP) of the bond can be closely approximated by the indicated tangent line.

Duration is often used to hedge one instrument with another. For example, suppose you own $1 million of the 7 1/4 of '96 priced at 100 : 05. A five basis point change in its yield would cause a $3355 change in its value. If you were hedging with the 7 1/2 of '16, priced at 100 : 01 $1 million par would change in value by $5775 for a five basis point yield change. An

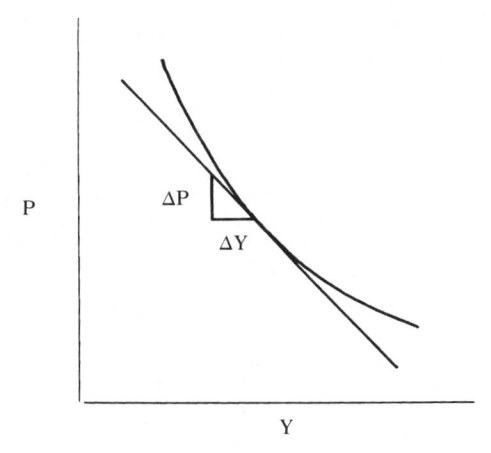

Figure 1. Price-yield curve.

appropriate hedge would, therefore, seem to be 0.58 long bonds for each 10-year note: (0.58) ($5775) = $3355. The hedge ratio 0.58 could also be calculated by using the durations of the two securities and their market prices:

$$\text{Hedge ratio} = \frac{P_1 D_1}{P_2 D_2} \qquad (3)$$

where

P_1 = price of instrument 1 (portfolio security)
D_1 = duration of instrument 1
P_2 = price of instrument 2 (hedge security)
D_2 = duration of instrument 2.

Since the 7 1/4 of '96 priced at 100:05 has a duration of 6.71 years and the 7 1/2 of '16 priced at 100:01 has a duration of 11.55 years, the hedge ratio selected would be 0.58. There are, however, two big implicit assumptions for the simple duration method in Equation (3) to work: small yield changes and parallel yield curve shifts. We next look at specific examples to see how these culprits can spoil our duration-based hedge.

III. THE FIRST CULPRIT: LARGE YIELD CHANGES

The conventional duration method fails when there are sudden, large yield changes in the market. In Table 1, we show how much the price of the 7 1/4 of '96 would change if yields changed by varying amounts (column 1). For example, its price would rise $3.54 (column 2) if its yield declined by 50

Table 1.   Hedge of 7 1/4 of '96 with 7 1/2 of '16

Yield Change Percent	Value Change: 7 1/4 of '96	Value Change: Hedge	Loss on Portfolio	Duration: 7 1/4 of '96	Duration: Hedge
− 3.0	23.63	28.34	− 4.71	7.11	14.52
− 2.0	15.04	16.87	− 1.83	6.98	13.48
− 0.5	3.54	3.58	− 0.04	6.78	12.01
− 0.1	0.69	0.69	0.00	6.72	11.64
0.0	0.00	0.00	0.00	6.71	11.55
+ 0.1	− 0.69	− 0.69	0.00	6.69	11.45
+ 0.5	− 3.37	− 3.27	− 0.10	6.64	11.10
+ 2.0	− 12.61	− 11.44	− 1.17	6.43	9.86
+ 3.0	− 18.15	− 15.79	− 2.36	6.29	9.11

basis points. If you had shorted 0.58 par of the 7 1/2 of '16, the change in the value of your short position would be as shown in column 3. The effectiveness of the hedge is the net difference between the value changes as shown in column 4.

For small yield changes (up to 10 basis points), the duration hedge works well (as shown by zero losses on the portfolio). For larger yield changes, the hedge loses more value than the portfolio security when yields fall and the hedge gains less than the portfolio security when yields rise. The result is that the hedged portfolio loses value for any large yield movement.

The last two columns shed light on why this happens; they show that the durations of the instruments vary when yields change. The duration of the hedge increases relatively more rapidly when yields fall (creating a larger price increase and hence a larger loss on the short position) and declines relatively rapidly when yields rise (creating more moderate price declines and hence a smaller gain on the short position).

In setting our original hedge ratio at 0.58, implicitly we assumed that the durations on the two insruments would stay constant, resulting in equal price changes on both instruments. However, suppose we were interested in looking at how the hedge would perform if interest rates rose by 300 basis points. As yields rise, the hedge ratio rises from 0.58 to 0.69. Thus, over the 300 basis point move, the hedge ratio averages 0.635. Therefore, setting the hedge ratio to be 0.58 certainly would produce errors for this move. This loss could be prevented by more frequent rebalancing if yield changes are small, thereby accommodating the changing duration. But if yield changes are large, the opportunity to rebalance within the course of that change is not available and hence we cannot prevent losses. We conclude that it is not enough to just measure duration alone, but also the *potential for the changes in duration in hedging portfolios.*

"Convexity" is the name given to the change in dollar duration (defined as price weighted duration) that occurs when the yield changes. In simple terms, it measures the drift in dollar duration when yields change. This can be expressed as

$$C = \frac{-1}{P} \cdot \frac{\Delta(PD)}{\Delta Y}$$

where

C = convexity
$\Delta(PD)$ = change in dollar duration
ΔY = change in yield.

Convexity can also be expressed as the present value weighted average of the squares of the times of the cashflows as follows:

$$C = \sum_{i=1}^{n} \frac{i^2 w_i}{4(1 + Y/2)} \tag{4}$$

where

i = semiannual period
w_i = present value fraction at semi annual period i
Y = initial yield to maturity.

Therefore, C is like duration, but it involves the square of each year instead of simply the year itself. That is, it is the second-order moment of duration. It is this measure that will be useful for us to compensate for the effects of large level changes and small slope changes in the yield curve.

You can see it in Figure 2; convexity is the curvature of the price–yield relationship. It measures the drift in duration per unit change in yield. In the figure, bond B_2 has a higher convexity than bond B_1, even though both bonds have the same duration. In our example, this propensity to change

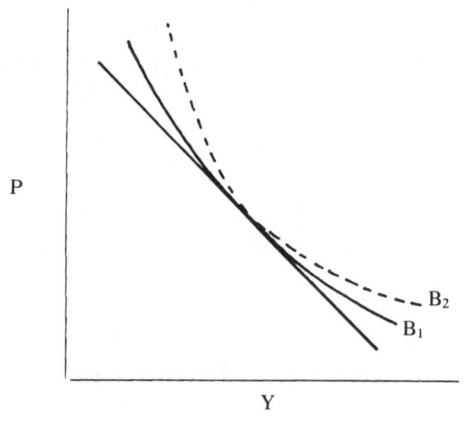

Figure 2. Convexity of bonds.

duration is higher for the hedge than for the cash, resulting in higher convexity for the hedge. As we have a short position in the hedge, the result is net negative convexity for the overall hedged portfolio.

The hedge in our example was selected only to match duration. However, we have seen that to better match price changes we need to hedge on two counts: duration and convexity. With a single hedge instrument, though, we have control over only one duration moment. Once, for example, D is chosen to be equal to that of the cash portfolio, that constraint automatically dictates the hedge ratio, and we cannot exercise any control over the convexity, C. We need two instruments to achieve hedging on both D and C.

IV. THE SECOND CULPRIT: CHANGES IN THE SHAPE OF THE YIELD CURVE

The simple duration measure also fails when the yield curve changes shape, rather than shifting in a parallel fashion. If we use the simple duration hedging method involving two bonds with different cash flows, and the slope of the yield curve changes, price changes on these instruments could be different.

Suppose you owned $100 of 7 1/4 of '96 and wanted to hedge by shorting the 7 1/2 of '16, as discussed in Table 1. The yields, on these two instruments are 7.225 and 7.50, respectively (plotted in Figure 3 along a linear duration-yield curve, C_0). The hedge ratio based on duration alone was 0.58. Assume now that the slope of the yield curve increases such that yield increases in proportion to duration; that is, if the duration of one instrument is twice as large as another, the yield change will be twice as large. In the particular case shown in Figure 3 (curve C_1), the yield on the '96 rises by 10 basis points to 7.325 and the yield on the '16 rises by 17 basis points to 7.67. The '96 loses $0.69 as in Table 1, and the $58 par '16 hedge loses $1.16. Therefore, there is a net difference of price changes of $0.47

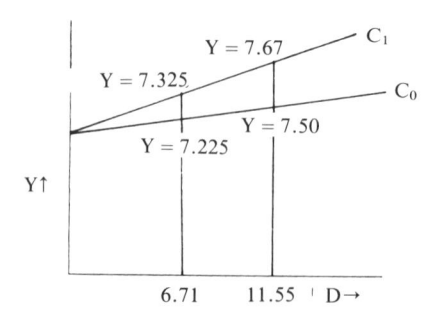

Figure 3.   Yield curve changes.

between the portolio security and the duration hedge. In this case, it so happens that this will be a net gain for the portfolio. However, if the yield curve slope had dropped by the same amount, there would have been a net loss.

The reason why this happened is because the yield changes were not the same for the '96 and the '16. The simple duration hedge ratio works only on the assumption that yield changes were the same for instruments of all maturities. Had rates on both risen by 10 basis points, the duration matching strategy would have sufficed. However, the assumed slope change implies higher yield changes for longer duration instruments, which means that the price of our hedge changes more. This implies different price changes on the two instruments, depending on whether the slope change is positive or negative. When the slope change is positive, the higher yield change on the hedge makes it gain more (because it is shorted) relative to a situation that has the same yield changes on both instruments. This could produce an overall gain for the portfolio, which is what happened above. On the other hand, when the slope change is negative, the higher yield change on the hedge makes it lose a lot more than the cash instrument gains. Let us now see how we can get the correct hedge ratio for the current case, still using only a single hedge instrument.

Specifically, we assumed a slope change in the yield curve with respect to duration. This implies that the yield changes were proportional to the individual instruments' duration. We can represent the yield change of the '16 as follows:

$$\Delta Y_2 = \Delta Y_1 \frac{D_2}{D_1} \tag{5}$$

where

ΔY_2 = yield change on the '16 = 17 basis points
ΔY_1 = yield change on the '96 = 10 basis points
D_2 = duration of '16 = 11.55 years
D_1 = duration of '96 = 6.71 years.

But we also know that the price changes on the two instruments will be as follows (from the basic definition of duration):

$$\Delta P_1 = P_1 D_1 \, \Delta Y_1$$
$$\Delta P_2 = P_2 D_2 \, \Delta Y_2.$$

In simple duration hedging we *assumed* that ΔY_1 and ΔY_2 were the same. The hedge ratio was determined as [shown in (3)]:

$$\text{Hedge ratio} = \frac{P_1 D_1 \, \Delta Y_1}{P_2 D_2 \, \Delta Y_2} = \frac{P_1 D_1}{P_2 D_2}.$$

However, in our current case, we have a slope change in the yield curve in proportion to the duration. Therefore, ΔY_1 and ΔY_2 are related as shown above in (5). We get

$$\text{Hedge ratio} = \frac{P_1 D_1 \; \Delta Y_1}{P_2 D_2 \; \Delta Y_1 D_2/D_1} = \frac{P_1 D_2^1}{P_2 D_2^2}.$$

The value of this hedge ratio is 0.3365. If we had chosen this hedge ratio initially, our price change on the position in the '16 would have been 0.69, matching that on the '96. This is the correct hedge ratio for this specific example. Note that we are still using a single instrument as a hedge. What we have demonstrated is that for a pure slope change a single instrument can still be used as a hedge, provided we adjust the hedge ratio as mentioned above. In fact, this new hedge ratio can be interpreted as a *pure convexity hedge.* [2] Just as in the case of small level changes where a pure duration hedge was sufficient, in the current situation with small slope changes, a pure convexity hedge works. However, it is important to note that when there are both level and slope changes we cannot hedge with one instrument alone. We need a minimum of two instruments.

The example clearly shows that simple duration hedge ratios do not work when there are shape changes in the yield curve. The shape changes produce different yield changes at different maturities, and this in combination with convexity produces price changes that are different from those predicted by the simple duration measure.

The correct hedge should adjust for different yield changes with respect to maturity. This is discussed in the following section.

V. THE SOLUTION

Let us now summarize our findings: we have identified two problems — large yield changes (even when yield curves are level) and yield curve shape changes — which make simple duration hedging imperfect. We have also shown the following:

1. When yield changes are *parallel and small,* simple duration hedging works.
2. When yield changes are *parallel and large,* we need to hedge for both duration and convexity. Two hedging instruments are needed here.
3. When yield changes comprise *only small slope changes,* single instrument hedging still works. However, the hedge ratio now is that of price weighted convexities (the pure convexity hedge).

4. When there are changes *in both yield level (whether small or large) and slope (only small changes),* simultaneous duration and convexity hedging should work. We need a minimum of two hedge instruments again.

It is also very important to note that we are not imposing any constraints on the initial form of the yield curve. All our references above have been only with respect to *changes* in the yield curve. Duration and convexity hedging are fairly sufficient for price protection as long as the changes in the yield curve consist only of level changes (small or large) and small slope changes. Therefore, we need to find a hedge that matches both the cash instruments' duration, D, and its convexity, C.

It should be noted that even if we match both D and C, the hedge may not be perfect for general yield changes that are of higher order than slope (for example, changes in curvature). This is because the cash portfolio's third and higher order moments will generally be different from those of the hedge. Therefore, to further increase the accuracy of the hedge, we need to match the higher order moments for the cash and the hedge. But for precise higher order hedging, we need as many instruments as the number of moments we wish to take into account. This increases the (transaction) cost and the complexity of the hedge. However, we have found that simpler hedges that account only for D and C are sufficient to produce relatively accurate hedges.

Another way to interpret our results is to take a look at two polar cases. The first is the perfect hedge, which would match all cashflows (i.e., a dedicated portfolio) of the underlying instrument with zero coupon bonds. This match requires as many bonds as the underlying cashflows, and hence could be cumbersome and expensive. Conventional duration hedging with a single zero coupon bond may be interpreted as the other extreme, where the hedging is performed by a single (duration equivalent zero) cashflow. Here, the hedge is simple and inexpensive, but could be inaccurate due to the problems discussed earlier. Multiple duration hedging, such as using D and C, occupies a middle position by allowing combinations of more than one hedging instrument, which results in control over as many terms of the duration vector as the number of instruments we have in our hedge. The number of instruments could be considerably fewer than the cashflow-matched hedge, and the accuracy of the hedge can be considerably higher than that of conventional single-instrument duration hedging. Therefore, multiple duration hedging should be viewed as a convenient alternative between the relatively inaccurate but simple conventional duration hedging and the relatively expensive but accurate cashflow-matched complete hedge.

VI.   HEDGING WITH MULTIPLE INSTRUMENTS

Consider a cash portfolio of $100 market value of the 7 1/4 of 11/15/96, priced at $100:05$. For this security, $D = 6.71$, $C = 57.46$. Now assume that we use two instruments to hedge, say the 6 5/8 of '92 and the 7 1/2 of '16. The yields are 7.225 for the cash instrument and 6.86 and 7.50 for the two hedges, respectively. Further, $D = 4.21$, $C = 20.51$ for the 6 5/8 of '92 and $D = 11.55$, $C = 226.8$ for the 7 1/2 of '16. We then set up the following two equations:

$$x_1(4.21) + x_2(11.55) = 6.71$$
$$x_1(20.51) + x_2(226.8) = 57.46$$

where x_1 and x_2 are market values of the 6 5/8 of '92 and 7 1/2 of '16, respectively.

Solving the two equations we get $x_1 = 1.192$ and $x_2 = 0.145$. Therefore, the $100 of the 7 1/4 of '96 should be hedged with $119.2 of the 6 5/8 of '92 and $14.5 of the 7 1/2 of '16. Note that these are market values and not face values. In general, we can weight any two hedge instruments so as to match both duration and convexity of the portfolio.

Now, let us calculate what happens when there is a 50 basis point yield changes in all instruments, i.e., a large parallel shift in the yield curve. The $100 of the cash instrument loses $3.37, the $119.2 of 6 5/8 of '92 gains $2.521, and the $14.5 of 7 1/2 of '16 gains $0.823. The net gain on the hedges is $3.34, closely matching the $3.37 loss on the cash security. The net portfolio loss is only $0.03 compared to the $0.10 we had earlier with the simple duration hedge. Therefore, it is clear that our multiple hedge improves protection for large yield level changes.

Now let us evaluate the situation with the pure slope change mentioned earlier: the cash security yield increases by 10 basis points, the 7 1/2 of '16 increases by 17 basis points and the 7 5/8 of '92 by 6.3 basis points (calculated on the basis of its duration). We now see that the cash security loses $0.69, the gain on the 6 5/8 of '92 is $0.339, and the gain on the 7 1/2 of '16 is $0.298. Thus, the total gain on the hedges is $0.64 compared to the loss of $0.69 on the cash. This gives a net loss of $0.05[3] on the portfolio, compared to a net gain of $0.47 with the simple hedge. Given that perfect hedging is our goal, this example shows that multiple hedging sharply reduces the errors obtained with simple hedging.

Note that in both the situations above, we have not imposed any constraints on the inital yield curve. It is also straightforward to extrapolate the situation to a case where a combination of the above happen, i.e., both a large level yield change and small slope change. It can be easily shown that our hedge will also work in such a situation.

Also note that as the level yield changes becomes very large, it may be necessary to include third and higher order moments of duration to improve the accuracy of the hedge. Likewise, large slope changes and higher order curvature changes in the shape of the yield curve might require consideration of higher order duration moments. These are the sources of errors that are likely to be induced by just considering duration and convexity alone for hedging.

VII. USING MULTIPLE FUTURES CONTRACTS FOR BETTER DURATION HEDGING

Fixed income cash portfolios are often hedged with futures portfolios as the futures market is extremely liquid, has lower transaction costs, and (usually) is highly correlated to cash market fluctuations. However, the number of futures portolios available is limited, and portfolio managers have to "design" appropriate combinations of futures to suit their particular hedge requirements. The volatility of the yield curve determines the number of terms in the multiple duration measure that have to be matched. Usually two terms (to cover level and slope changes) should account for a substantial portion of the variation in the yield curve.

Table 2 shows the duration data on futures instruments as of January 21, 1987. Note that the value of D increases at a slower rate than C as the underlying maturity of the instrument increases. Table 3 shows the hedges required for balancing a dollar of the underlying portfolio of various actively traded Treasury securities of different maturities with pairs of futures on eurodollar, T-notes, and T-bonds on the same day.[4]

The hedges required for various cash securities are generally in accord with intuition. For example, as the underlying cash maturity increases, we find that the relative proportion of the note content goes up in the eurodollar–note combination. Beyond about 7 years cash maturity, it makes more sense to use a note–bond combination rather than a eurodollar–note combination. The former combination is more representative of the part of the yield curve in which the cash security lies and is likely to produce a better duration moment match. Again, it can be seen that the bond proportion goes up as the cash maturity increases from 7 to 30 years in

Table 2. Duration Data on Futures

Futures Contract	D	C
Eurodollar	0.22	0.14
Note	4.66	29.24
Bond	8.47	123.06

Table 3. Hedges Per Unit Dollar of Cash[a]

Underlying Cash Maturity	Eurodollar, Note Futures	Note Bond Futures	Eurodollar, Bond Futures
2 years	$-6.21, -0.09$	$-0.59, \quad 0.11$	$-7.42, -0.02$
3 years	$-7.31, -0.25$	$-0.84, \quad 0.13$	$-10.50, -0.05$
4 years	$-6.78, -0.40$	$-0.95, \quad 0.12$	$-11.88, -0.09$
5 years	$-4.87, -0.65$	$-1.04, \quad 0.08$	$-13.40, -0.14$
7 years	$0.71, -1.20$	$-1.14, -0.01$	$-14.31, -0.26$
10 years	$13.33, -2.10$	$-1.04, -0.23$	$-13.00, -0.47$
20 years	$59.76, -4.82$	$-0.04, -1.07$	$-0.59, -1.08$
30 years	$128.30, -8.63$	$1.63, -2.29$	$20.46, -1.93$

[a]Negative signs indicate short positions, positive signs long positions.

both the note–bond (third column) and eurodollar–bond (fourth column) combinations.

However, when using multiple futures, the additional convexity hedging might sometimes result in nonintuitive hedges. For example, in the case of hedging 2–5 year cash maturities, the requirement is a *long* position in bond futures in the note–bond combination. This is because note futures held in a simple duration hedge against 5-year notes provide too much convexity. The long position in bond futures *subtracts* out some of the convexity. Since convexity rises faster than duration, subtracting bond from note futures reduces convexity proportionally more than duration.

NOTES

1. The slope of the curve is actually $\Delta P/\Delta Y$, which for par bonds, is $100[(\Delta P/P)/\Delta Y] = -100D$. For other bonds, though, the percentage change in price, $100 \ \Delta P/P$, is not equal to the change in price, ΔP, so that the approximation is inexact. An exact graphic representation of duration that would hold for all bonds would have the natural log of price ($\ln P$) on the vertical axis. However, for expositional ease, we will refer to the slope of Figure 1 as duration.

2. If yields are defined with respect to maturity, this hedge ratio would have been P_1C_1/P_2C_2, where C is given in (4).

3. Pure slope change, in the light of the definition of convexity as in (4), should be defined with respect to maturity. However, we have maintained our earlier definition of slope change defined with respect to duration, strictly for comparison with the earlier example. Note that the values of C calculated utilized the definition of (4). This will introduce errors in the magnitude of the hedge losses in the calculations.

4. The cheapest to deliver instrument on the bond futures has a call feature whose duration and convexity features were accounted for in our calculations in Table 3.

DEFAULT SPREADS IN THE FIXED AND IN THE FLOATING INTEREST RATE MARKETS:

A CONTINGENT CLAIMS APPROACH

Ian Cooper* and Antonio S. Mello**

I. INTRODUCTION

Bonds issued by corporations are subject to default risk. Sometimes borrowers fail to make a scheduled payment of either interest or principal on the debt. Returns promised to corporate bondholders are, therefore, not certain as they are in the case of returns on treasury securities. The difference must be reflected on the low price investors are prepared to pay for a corporate bond relative to a government bond with comparable

*London Business School
**Massachusetts Institute of Technology

Advances in Futures and Options Research, Vol. 3, pages 269–289.
ISBN: 0-89232-926-2

features. The magnitude of the discount is a function of the probability of default during the life of the bond, of the contractual provisions protecting the interests of the debt claimants, and of the market prices required for equivalent issues.

Corporations have the choice to borrow at a fixed rate or at a rate that varies over time with the level of short-term interest rates. As Cornell [3] argued, this choice should reflect the firm's operating exposure to unexpected changes in the rate of inflation. For companies whose operating cash flow is positively correlated with inflation, floating rate debt provides a long-term hedge against inflation risk. In periods of rising inflation, higher interest payments are matched with higher cash flows. The real costs of floating rate financing are relatively fixed and help to reduce the variability of the cash flow to equity for such a business. By contrast, companies whose operating profits do not keep pace with unanticipated inflation could eliminate interest rate risk by fixing the amount of interest payments on the debt.

Rational investors perceive the firm's exposure to inflation risk and the associated problem of finding an optimal debt structure. For this reason natural floating rate borrowers get relatively better terms in that market, while natural fixed rate borrowers get relatively better rates in the fixed interest rate market. Therefore, for any two firms, investors in each market may demand premiums that reflect the risks of default on the different types of debt. If these risks vary with each firm across markets, in equilibrium the relative spreads should differ in different debt markets. Though this conclusion seems to be confirmed by the facts, different yield spreads in the fixed and in the floating interest rate markets are usually described as market anomalies. Behind this view lies the notion that the differentials should be the same since they are the price of the same thing: the difference in the quality of the two borrowers. Since they are not the same, an opportunity for arbitrage is presented. Indeed, many believe that this difference in spreads is the principal reason for the growth of interest rate swaps (see Bicksler and Chen [2] and Lipsky and Elhalaski [6]). Yet, years after the opening of the swaps market and a value of hundreds of billions of dollars in transactions, yield differentials still persist.

In this study we use option pricing theory for valuing securities (see Black and Scholes [1]) and measure yield spreads in the fixed interest rate market and in the floating interest rate market. We follow the traditional approach to modeling default risk as developed by Merton [8] and extend it to the case of floating rate debt, relying on a method that values options to exchange one risky asset for another (see Margrabe [7]). We wish to see whether arbitrage pricing models of corporate debt are consistent with differentials in the yield spreads when borrowers have differing credit risk. In doing the analysis we assume capital markets are perfect. This is because the "equal yield spreads" view reasons that arbitrage opportunities are the result of institutional constraints and other distortions that render markets imperfect.[1] If spread "anomalies" of the size that drive swap transactions can be generated in perfect markets, this throws some doubt on the motive for swaps.

The plan of the paper is as follows: In Section II the Merton [8] model for computing the risk structure of interest rates is applied to measure the credit differentials on corporate debt with fixed payouts. In Section III, we develop a similar framework to measure the credit differentials on corporate debt with floating payouts. In Section IV we extend the analysis to risky coupon bonds and compare the spread due to credit differences in the fixed rate market and in the floating rate market. Section V contains some concluding comments.

II. DEFAULT SPREAD ON RISKY DISCOUNT BONDS: THE FIXED RATE CASE

In this section we follow the work on pricing risky debt presented by Merton [8]. The following assumptions are considered:

A1. Capital markets are perfect: There are no transaction costs or taxes. Information is costless and market participants are price takers. There are no limits on short sales.

A2. There exists a riskless asset paying a known and constant interest rate r.

A3. Trading in all assets takes place continuously.

A4. The dynamic behavior of the value of the firm is independent of its capital structure and of the probability of default. There are no bankruptcy costs or claim dilution.

A5. The value of the firm follows a diffusion process with instantaneous variance proportional to the square root of the value.

Under these assumptions the basic valuation equation for any security is

$$1/2\sigma^2 V f_{vv} + [Vr - C(V, t)]f_v - fr + C'(V, t) = -f_t \qquad (1)$$

where f is the generic label for any of the firm's securities. V is the value of the firm, σ^2 is the instantaneous variance of the return on the firm, t denotes time, $C(V, t)$ is the net total dollar payout made by the firm per unit time, and $C'(V, t)$ is the payout per unit time promised by security f. Suppose the firm has outstanding only equity and a bond that pays no coupons until maturity T. At this time, bondholders receive a promised final payment of F or they take over the assets leaving nothing to shareholders. So at time T, the bond will have the value min(V, F), and at any time $t < T$ its value will be greater than zero and less than V. The relevant form of the valuation Equation (1) for this discount bond, B, is

$$1/2\sigma^2 V^2 B_{vv} + VrB_v - Br = -B_t \qquad (2)$$

with boundary condition

$$B(V, T) = min(V, F).$$

To solve (2) subject to the maturity condition above we recall that with limited liability the equity of the firm is identical to a European call option with an exercise price at T equal to the amount promised to bondholders, F. Then

$$B(V, \tau) = V - [VN(h_1) - Fe^{-r\tau}N(h_2)] \qquad (3)$$

where $\tau = T - t$. Following Merton [8] we can rewrite (3) by defining $d = Fe^{-r\tau}/V$,

$$B(V, \tau) = Fe^{-r\tau}[N(h_2) + N(-h_1)/d] \qquad (4)$$

where the upper limits of integration take values, respectively, of

$$-h_1 = [\log(d) - 1/2\sigma^2\tau]/\sigma\sqrt{\tau}$$
$$h_2 = -[\log(d) + 1/2\sigma^2\tau]/\sigma\sqrt{\tau}.$$

The premium demanded by investors aware of the possibility that the firm might default on its obligations can be derived from the promised yield on the bond, $R(\tau) = -\log[B(V, \tau)/F]/\tau$. Then the default premium over and above the yield on a riskless discount bond with the same maturity is

$$R(\tau) - r = -\log[N(h_2) + N(-h_1)/d]/\tau \qquad (5)$$

provided that the firm does not default, R(t) is the return to bondholders. The risk premium required by investors is a function of two factors, in addition to the maturity of the bond: (1) the variance of the returns on the firm as a proxy for the earnings variability, and (2) the level of financial leverage represented by the ratio of the present value of the final payment promised to bondholders, discounted to the riskless rate of interest, to the current value of the firm.[2]

Consider now the case of two corporations each promising to pay the same amount at maturity. The two firms are in different risk "classes," with firm 2 riskier than firm 1, in the sense that it has either a higher variance of returns, a higher quasi-debt-to-firm value ratio, or a higher value for both of these variables. When both firms issue bonds promising a fixed amount F at maturity, the yield for the bond issued by firm i is

$$R_i(\tau) = -\log[B_i(V_i, \tau)/F]/\tau \qquad (6)$$

and the relative spread on these two bonds represents the compensation for different probability of default. We write this spread as

$$\beta f(\tau) = R_2(\tau) - R_1(\tau) \tag{7}$$

and taking (6) and (7) together we have

$$\beta f(\tau) = -\log[B_2(V_2, \tau)/B_1(V_1, \tau)]/\tau. \tag{8}$$

Using (4) in (8) we can write the spread due to credit differences of the two firms issuing fixed-rate debt as

$$\beta f(\tau) = -\frac{1}{\tau} \log\left[\frac{N(h_{22}) + N(-h_{12})/d_2}{N(h_{21}) + N(-h_{11})/d_1}\right] \tag{9}$$

where h_{kj} denotes the upper limit of integration k in the case of firm j. Note that the value of the spread when both firms promised to pay an equal fixed amount at maturity, F, depends only upon the relative values of σ and d.

Defining s to be equal to the expression inside the brackets in (9), we can obtain comparative statics results of the spread by taking the derivative of s with respect to the relevant parameters and knowing that β_f is a decreasing function of s.

$$s_{\sigma_1} = \phi_2\phi_1^{-2}N'(h_{21})\sqrt{\tau} > 0, \qquad \text{and } \beta f_{\sigma_1} < 0 \tag{10a}$$

$$s_{\sigma_2} = -\phi_1^{-1}N'(h_{22})\sqrt{\tau} < 0, \qquad \text{and } \beta f_{\sigma_2} > 0 \tag{10b}$$

$$s_{d_1} = \phi_2\phi_1^{-2}N(-h_{11})/d_1^2 > 0, \qquad \text{and } \beta f_{d_1} < 0 \tag{10c}$$

$$s_{d_2} = -\phi_1^{-1}N(-h_{12})/d_2^2 < 0, \qquad \text{and } \beta f_{d_2} > 0 \tag{10d}$$

where $\phi_i = N(h_{2i}) + N(-h_{1i})/d_i$ and $N'(h_{kj})$ denotes the standardized normal density function at h_{kj}. These results state that the default risk spread for fixed discount bonds increases if the volatility of the returns or the quasi-debt to value of the riskier firm (firm 2) increase, and falls if the volatility of the returns or the quasi-debt to value of the less risky firm (firm 1) increase. The intuition of these results is immediate.

This can be seen in Figures 1 and 2 plotting the spread for different values of the ratio of the firms' volatilities, σ_2/σ_1. The value of the spread increases as firm 2 becomes riskier relative to firm 1 and for the same value of the ratio of volatilities, the spread decreases as both firms become less risky (d_i and/or σ_i decrease). Figure 3 shows how the value of the spread changes with the maturity of the debt. Making $d_1 = d_2$ and both equal to 0.4, one can see that for shorter maturities the spread widens with an increase in the maturity of the debt, while it declines for longer maturity values. This effect is clearly more pronounced for cases when the ratio σ_2/σ_1 is higher. In summary, the sign of the partial derivatives of the value of the default yield spread for discount bonds paying a fixed amount at maturity is

$$\begin{array}{cccccc} - & + & - & + & 0 & +/- \end{array}$$
$$\beta f = \beta f(d_1, d_2, \sigma_1, \sigma_2, r, \tau). \tag{11}$$

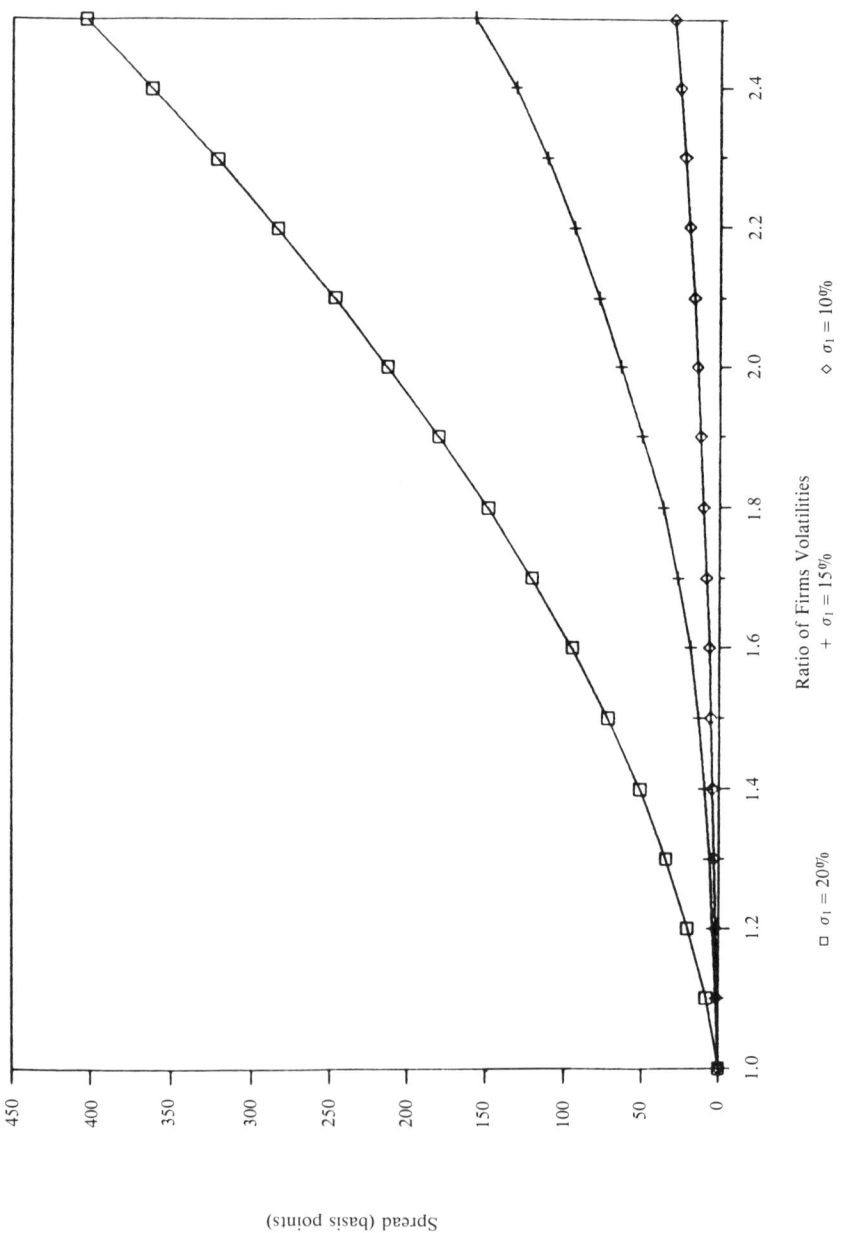

Figure 1. Fixed interest rate spread and firms' volatilities. Both firms have same quasi-debt-to-firm value ratio (d = 0.4); $\sigma_2 = K\sigma_1$, $K \in [1.0, 2.5]$, and $\sigma_1 = 0.20$. Debt maturity is 5 years. R = 0.10.

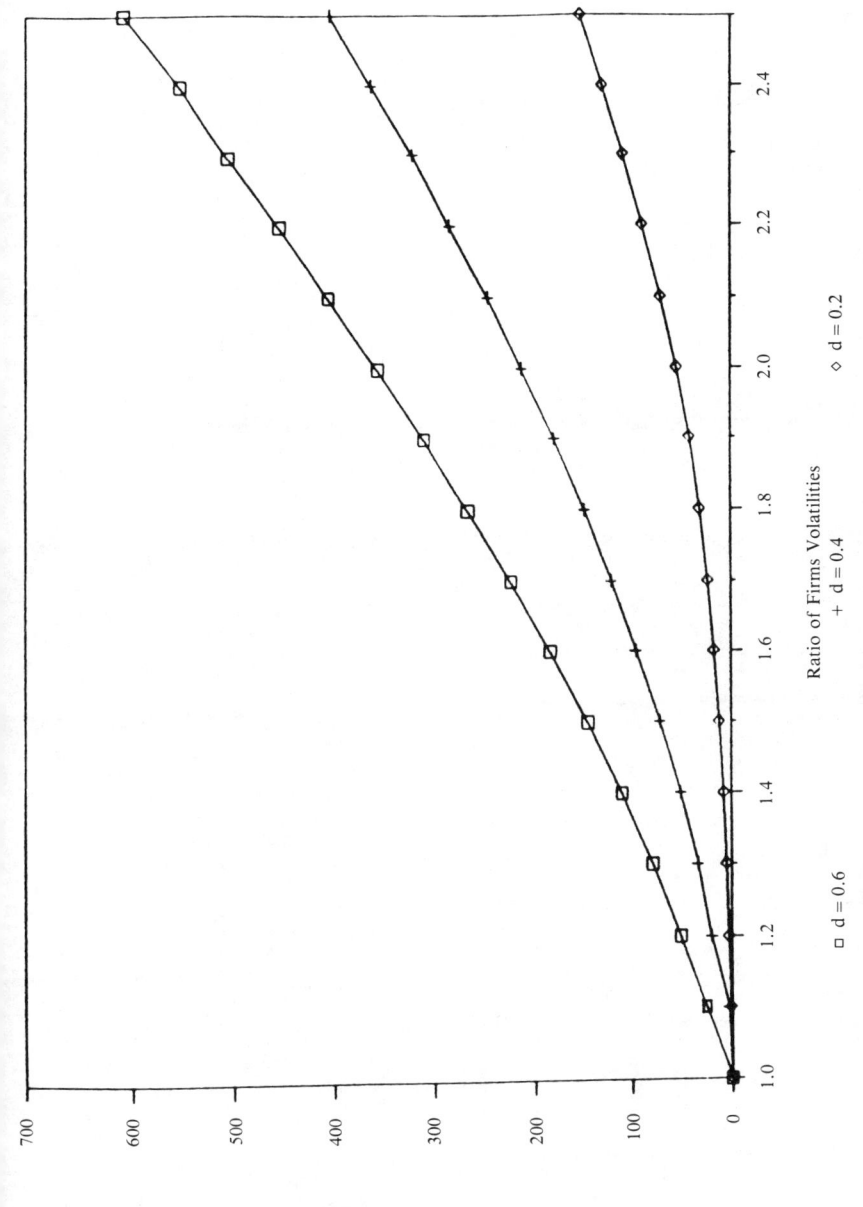

Figure 2. Fixed interest rate spread and quasi-debt-to-firm value ratio. Both firms have same quasi-debt-to-firm value ratio; $\sigma_2 = K\sigma_1$, $K \in [1.0, 2.5]$, and $\sigma_1 = 0.20$. Debt maturity is 5 years. R = 0.10.

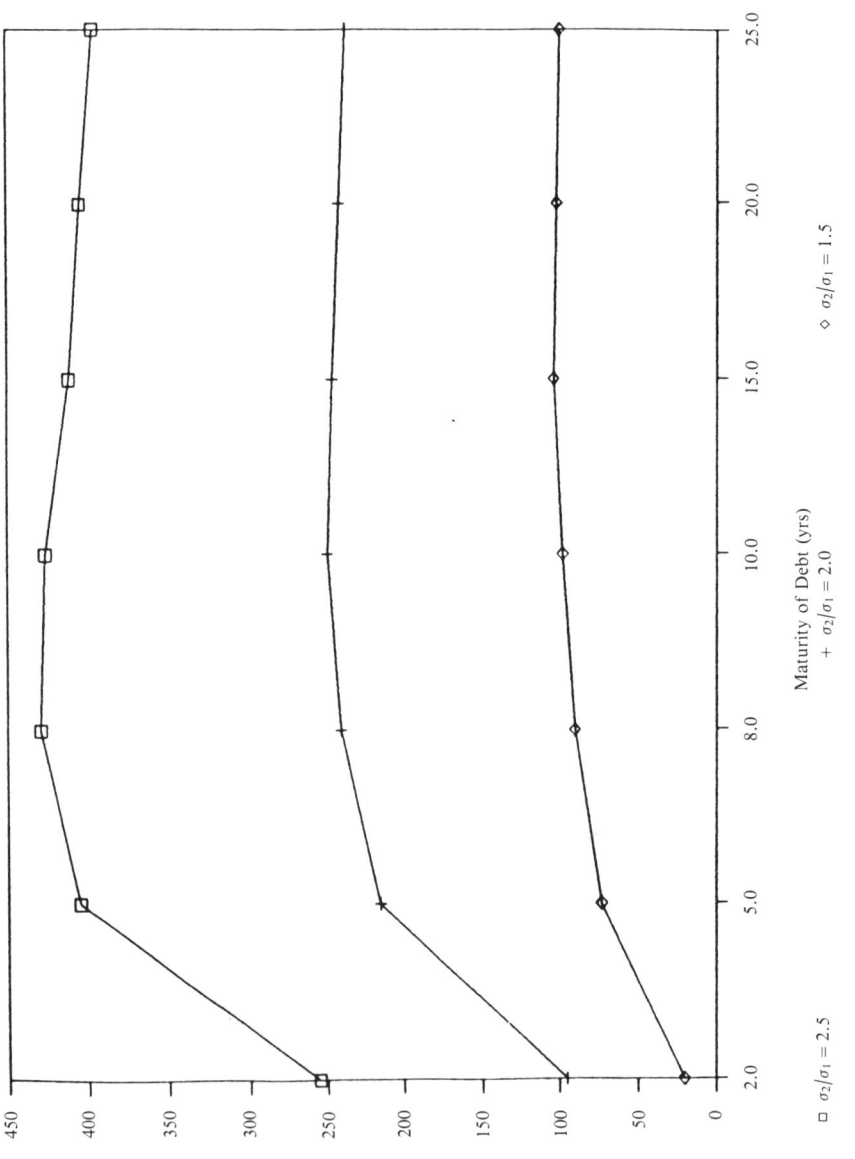

Figure 3. Fixed interest rate spread and debt maturity. Both firms have same quasi-debt-to-firm value ratio; $\sigma_2 = K\sigma_1$, $K \in [1.0, 2.5]$, and $\sigma_1 = 0.20$. R = 0.10.

□ $\sigma_2/\sigma_1 = 2.5$ + $\sigma_2/\sigma_1 = 2.0$ ◇ $\sigma_2/\sigma_1 = 1.5$

III. DEFAULT SPREAD ON RISKY DISCOUNT BONDS: THE FLOATING RATE CASE

One thing that limits the application of Merton's work to the case of floating rate notes is the assumption that no uncertainty results from shifts in the term structure of interest rates. If a deterministic term structure is assumed, the payout associated with a floating rate note will become known and this type of debt will be essentially indistinguishable from fixed rate debt. To overcome this difficulty in the pricing of floaters, several authors have suggested alternative ways of modeling interest rate uncertainty (see Cox, Ingersoll, and Ross [4] and Ramaswamy and Sundaresan [9]). In our case, a different problem occurs, since at this stage, we assume no intermediate payments of any kind. The distinction between fixed rate debt and floating rate debt, when no coupons are assumed, is made possible only through the amount promised at maturity. In the fixed rate case this amount is known with certainty, whereas in the floating rate case it is unknown and random. As a result, the value of the floater is a function of the value of the firm, as in the fixed rate case, but also of the value of the random final payment, in addition to time. Therefore, we need to make another assumption:

A6. The dynamics of the value of the riskless principal amount, X, to be paid at maturity to the holder of the floating rate bond are described by a diffusion type stochastic process with instantaneous variance proportional to the square root of the value.

Under assumptions A1 to A6 the value of the floating rate bond, L, at any point in time is the solution to the following equation:

$$1/2(\sigma_v^2 V^2 L_{vv} + \sigma_x^2 X^2 L_{xx} + 2\rho_{vx}\sigma_v\sigma_x VXL_{vx}) + VrL_v + XrL_x - Lr = -L_t \quad (12)$$

with boundary condition

$$L(V, X, T) = \min(V, X)$$

with either V and X having zero or positive, but stochastic, values. To solve (12) subject to the maturity condition above we can use again the relationship that values the equity of the firm as a European call option. In this case, however, the option gives the right to exchange one risky asset, V, for another, L, at time T. If shareholders exercise the option they will get $V - X$ or nothing if they do not exercise it. Their position is equivalent to a call option on the firm's assets with exercise price X, and a put option on an asset that pays X with exercise price V. The value of such portfolio is given in Margrabe [7] and equals

$$E(V, X, \tau) = VN(K_1) - XN(K_2) \quad (13)$$

where

$$K_1 = [\log(V/X) + 1/2\sigma^2\tau]\sigma\sqrt{\tau}$$

$$K_2 = K_1 - \sigma\sqrt{\tau}$$

$$\sigma^2 = \sigma_v^2 + \sigma_x^2 - 2\rho_{vx}\sigma_v\sigma_x$$

recalling that $L(V, X, \tau) = V - E(V, X, \tau)$ and defining $\bar{d} = X/V$ as the ratio of the current riskless value of the random amount promised at maturity to the current value of the firm, we can write the expression for the value of the risky discount bond as

$$L(V, X, \tau) = X[N(\bar{h}_2) + N(-\bar{h}_1)/\bar{d}] \tag{14}$$

where

$$-\bar{h}_1 = [\log(\bar{d}) - 1/2\sigma^2\tau]/\sigma\sqrt{\tau}$$

$$\bar{h}_2 = -[\log(\bar{d}) + 1/2\sigma^2\tau]/\sigma\sqrt{\tau}.$$

Expression (14) is the floating rate equivalent to expression (4) in the fixed rate case. The expected yield on this floating rate bond is $R(\tau) = -\log[L(V, X, \tau)/X(\tau)]/\tau$, being $X(\tau)$ the payment bondholders expect to receive when there is no risk of default. Then $X(t) = X(\tau)e^{-r\tau}$, and the default risk premium demand by investors is

$$\bar{R}(\tau) - r = -\log[N(\bar{h}_2) + N(-\bar{h}_1)/\bar{d}]/\tau. \tag{15}$$

Note that in the case of the floating rate bond the premium required by bondholders is a function of (1) the variance of the firm's returns, (2) the ratio of the present value of the expected final payment promised to bond holders, discounted at the riskless rate of interest, to the current value of the firm, (3) time until maturity, (4) the variance of the shocks the random final payment is likely to suffer, and (5) the correlation parameter between the firm's value and the value of that random principal amount. It is expected that these last two variables will have an impact on the value of the spread for risky floating rate bonds. We write this spread as

$$\beta 1(\tau) = \bar{R}_2(\tau) - \bar{R}_1(\tau) \tag{16}$$

and assuming equal current riskless values of the final payments under the bonds issued by both firms, the spread becomes

$$\beta 1(\tau) = -\frac{1}{\tau} \log\left[\frac{N(\bar{h}_{22}) + N(-\bar{h}_{12})/\bar{d}_2}{N(\bar{h}_{21}) + N(-\bar{h}_{11})/\bar{d}_1}\right]. \tag{17}$$

It is important to note that the spread does not depend upon the unknown value of the principal payment bondholders get at maturity. To obtain comparative statics results of $\beta 1(\tau)$ we define z as the expression inside the brackets of (17) and note that $\beta 1(\tau)$ is a decreasing function of z.

$$z_{\sigma_1} = \psi_2 \psi_1^{-2} N'(\bar{h}_{21}) \sqrt{\tau}(\sigma_1 - \rho_{1x}\sigma_x)/\sigma(1)^{1/2} \lessgtr 0, \qquad \text{and } \beta 1_{\sigma_1} \lessgtr 0 \quad (18a)$$

$$z_{\sigma_2} = -\psi_1^{-1} N'(\bar{h}_{22}) \sqrt{\tau}(\sigma_2 - \rho_{2x}\sigma_x)/\sigma(2)^{1/2} \gtrless 0, \qquad \text{and } \beta 1_{\sigma_2} \lessgtr 0 \quad (18b)$$

Note that $\beta 1_{\sigma_1} < 0$ as long as $\sigma_1 > \sigma_x$, and $\beta 1_{\sigma_2} > 0$ as long as $\sigma_2 > \sigma_x$. Also

$$z_{d_1} = \psi_2 \psi_1^{-2} N(-\bar{h}_{11})/\bar{d}_1^2 > 0, \qquad \text{and } \beta 1_{d_1} < 0 \quad (18c)$$

$$z_{d_2} = -\psi_1^{-1} N(-\bar{h}_{12})\bar{d}_2^2 < 0, \qquad \text{and } \beta 1_{d_2} > 0 \quad (18d)$$

$$z_{\sigma_x} = \psi_1^2 [\psi_2 N'(\bar{h}_{21})(\sigma_x - \rho_{1x}\sigma_1)/\sigma(1)^{1/2}$$
$$- \psi_1 N'(\bar{h}_{22})(\sigma_x - \rho_{2x}\sigma_2)/\sigma(2)^{1/2}]\sqrt{\tau} \gtrless 0, \qquad \text{and } \beta 1_{\sigma_x} \lessgtr 0 \quad (18e)$$

$$z_{\rho_{1x}} = -\psi_2 \psi_1^{-2} N'(\bar{h}_{21}) \sqrt{\tau}[\sigma_1\sigma_x/\sigma(1)^{1/2}] \gtrless 0, \qquad \text{and } \beta 1_{\sigma_{1x}} > 0 \quad (18f)$$

$$z_{\rho_{2x}} = \psi_1^{-1} N'(\bar{h}_{22}) \sqrt{\tau}[\sigma_2\sigma_x/\sigma(2)^{1/2}] > 0, \qquad \text{and } \beta 1_{\rho_{2x}} < 0 \quad (18g)$$

where $\sigma(i) = \sigma_i^2 + \sigma_x^2 - 2\rho_{ix}\sigma_i\sigma_x$ and $\psi_i = N(\bar{h}_{2i}) + N(-\bar{h}_{1i})/\bar{d}_i$; $N'(\bar{h}_{kj})$ denotes the standardized normal density function at $\bar{h}_{kj}$, as before. The results presented in (18) show that the default risk spread for floating discount bonds is an increasing function of the volatility and of the quasi-debt to value of firm 2, with higher σ, and a decreasing function of the risk parameters of firm 1, with lower σ. Figure 4 plots the spread for different values of the ratio of the volatilities of the two firms, σ_2/σ_1. Also the spread increases if the correlation between the value of firm 1 and the random final payment, X, increases, and falls if the correlation between the value of firm 2 and the random final payment, X, increases.

The effect of a change in the volatility of the final payment, σ_x, is ambiguous, and can be better seen in combination with the correlation parameters. For values of these parameters such that $\rho_{1x} > 0$ and $\rho_{2x} < 0$, the spread is an increasing function of the value of σ_x. Conversely, for $\rho_{1x} < 0$ and $\rho_{2x} > 0$, that is, when the value of firm 1 is negatively correlated with X and the value of firm 2 is positively correlated with X, the spread is a decreasing function of the value of σ_x. The importance of the correlation parameters in determining the size of the spread can be immediately seen by inspection of Figure 5. As for the time to maturity, computed values confirm the findings for the fixed rate case, in that the changes in the value of the spread can have either sign.

We present below the sign of the partial derivatives of the value of the default yield spread for discount bonds paying a random amount at maturity.

$$\overset{\quad - \quad + \quad - \quad + \quad +/- \quad + \quad - \quad\ 0\ +/-}{\beta 1 = \beta 1(d_1, d_2, \sigma_1, \sigma_2, \sigma_x, \quad \rho_{1x}, \rho_{2x}, r, \tau)} \qquad (19)$$

It is interesting to see how the correlations can affect the relative riskiness of the two bonds, reflected in the default risk spread for floating rate debt. Other things being equal, a high correlation between an individual

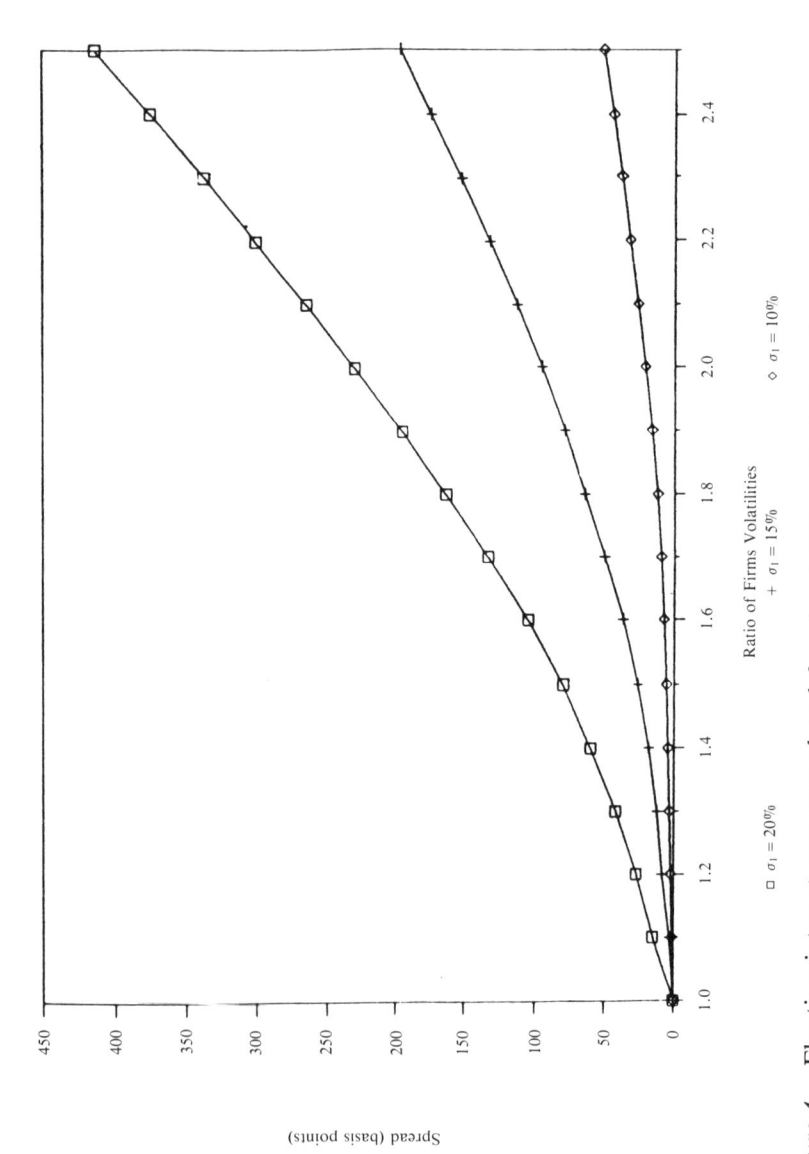

Figure 4. Floating interest rate spread and firms' volatilities. Both firms have quasi-debt-to-firm value ratio ($\bar{d} = 0.4$); $\sigma_2 = K\sigma_1$, $K \in [1.0, 2.5]$, and $\sigma_1 = 0.20$, $\sigma_x = .05$, $\rho_{1x} = \rho_{2x} = 0.0$. Debt maturity is 5 years. $R = 0.10$.

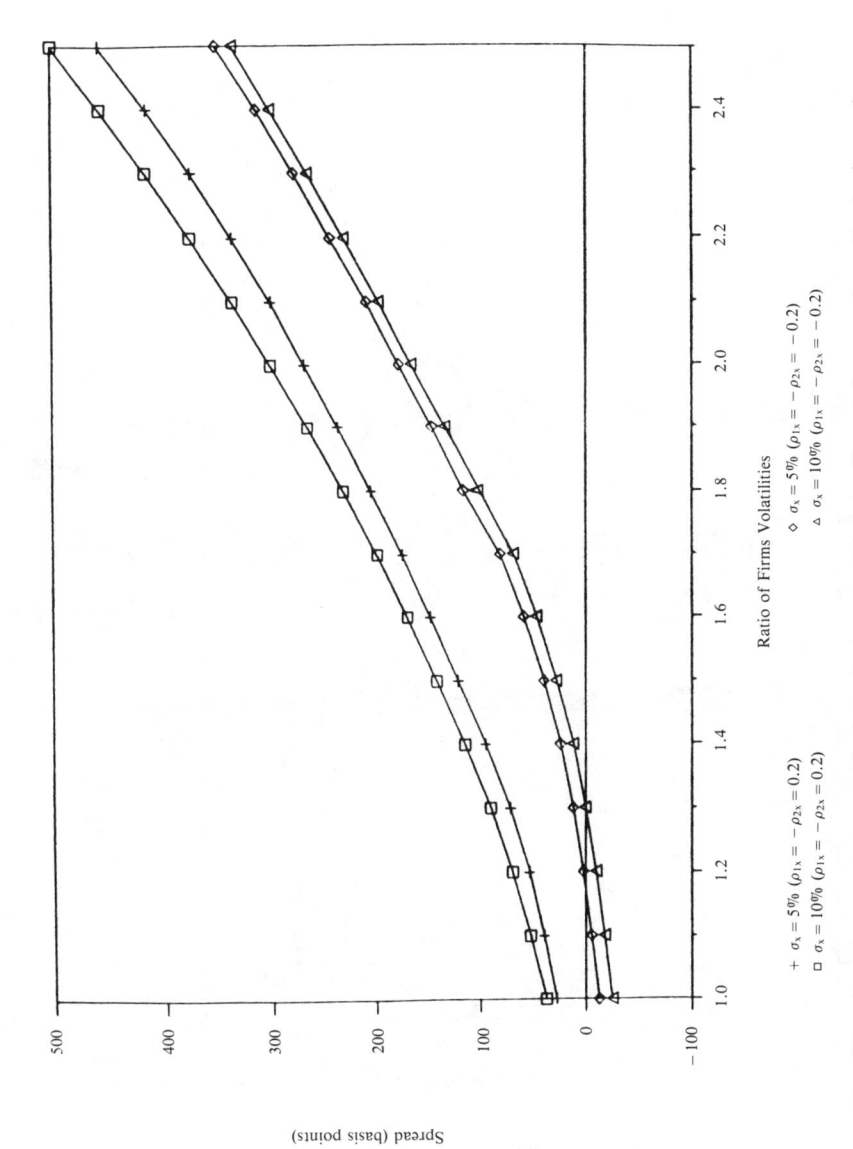

Figure 5. Floating interest rate spread and the combined effect of σ_x and ρ. Both firms have same quasi-debt-to-firm value ratio ($\bar{d} = 0.4$); $\sigma_2 = K\sigma_1$, $K \in [1.0, 2.5]$, and $\sigma_1 = 0.20$. Debt maturity is 5 years. $R = 0.10$.

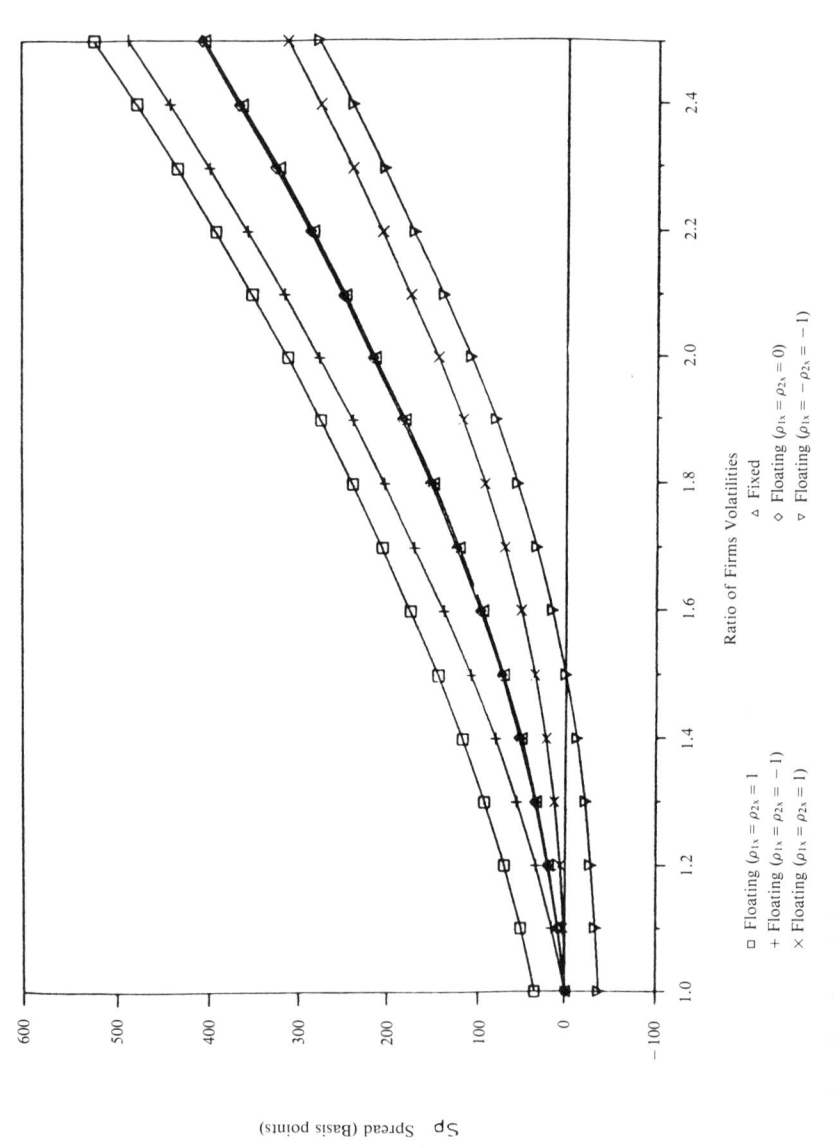

Figure 6. Fixed and floating interest rate spreads and the correlation factor. Both firms have same quasi-debt-to-firm value ratio (d = 0.4), with d = d̄; $\sigma_2 = K\sigma_1$, $K \in [1.0, 2.5]$, and $\sigma_1 = 0.20$, $\sigma_x = .05$. Debt maturity is 5 years. R = 0.10.

company's level of profitability and the economic variable affecting the size of the payment to bondholders means default occurring in fewer occasions. Companies with the same variability of returns and equal degree of financial leverage pay equal premiums on equal probability of default on fixed rate debt [see Equation (5)]. Within the same risk class, however, companies whose operating returns keep pace with variable debt payments have a comparative advantage in borrowing floating rate. This must be translated into smaller margins in this market. Yield spreads measuring the difference in the quality of two borrowers are no longer equal in equilibrium, simply because they depend on differing sets of relevant risk factors.

Figure 6 shows the exact situation. By assumption $d_1 = \bar{d}_1$, $d_2 = d_2$, and $d_1 = d_2$. Thus, if firm 2 issues fixed rate debt it must face a higher yield to maturity than firm 1, because $\sigma_2 > \sigma_1$. However, the situation in the floating rate debt market also depends on the relative values of ρ_{1x} and ρ_{2x}. In fact, for values of $\rho_{2x} > 0$, the yield differential is always smaller in the floating rate market than in the fixed rate market. In a few cases it may even be that the fixed rate spread is positive, $\beta f > 0$, and for the same two firms the floating rate spread is negative, $\beta 1 < 0$. In that case, firm 1 has an absolute advantage in the fixed rate debt market, while firm 2 has an absolute advantage in the floating rate debt market.[3]

Table 1 repeats the computations for values of $d_1 = \bar{d}_1$, $d_2 = \bar{d}_2$, and $d_1 \neq d_2$. The results presented are as one would have expected. The relative change in the spreads from the previous case ($d_1 = d_2$) is very much a function of the signs of the correlation coefficients. If d_2 decreases relative to d_1, the reduction in the value of the spread is greater (smaller) in the floating rate case than in the fixed rate case if $\rho_{2x} > 0$ ($\rho_{2x} < 0$). If, on the other hand, d_2 increases relative to d_1, the increase in the value of the spread is smaller (greater) in the floating rate case than in the fixed rate case if $\rho_{2x} > 0$ ($\rho_{2x} < 0$).

Table 1. Spreads (Basis Points) for Fixed and Floating Rate Discount Bonds.

	$d_1 = 0.4; d_2 = 0.4$			$d_1 = 0.4; d_2 = 0.5$			$d_1 = 0.5; d_2 = 0.4$		
σ_2/σ_1	βf	$\beta 1^{(a)}$	$\beta 1^{(b)}$	βf	$\beta 1^{(a)}$	$\beta 1^{(b)}$	βf	$\beta 1^{(a)}$	$\beta 1^{(b)}$
1	0	− 38	36	20	− 30	80	− 23	− 82	29
1.5	72	0	144	138	44	230	50	− 44	139
2.0	213	108	312	314	194	428	190	64	307
2.5	404	277	524	531	392	661	382	232	518

[a]Corresponds to $\rho_{1x} = -\rho_{2x} = -1$. [b]Corresponds to $\rho_{1x} = -\rho_{2x} = 1$. In all cases $d_i = \bar{d}_i$ and $\sigma_1 = 20\%$, $r = \log(1.10)$, $\tau = 5$ years.

To complete our analysis of the default risk spread on risky discount bonds we now show under what conditions the yield differentials are equal in both the floating interest rate and the fixed interest rate markets. Since the present value, at the riskless rate, of the promised payment to bondholders is equal for both cases, $Be^{-r\tau} = X(t)$, for a given pair of values (d_1, d_2), the yields for fixed and for floating rate debt depend solely on the volatility parameters. Moreover, the spread is a monotonically increasing function of the ratio of volatilities. To see why, take the case of the fixed-rate spread, where

$$\beta f = -\log(s)/\tau \tag{20}$$

call $g = \sigma_2/\sigma_1$ and assume that $g > 1$. Then

$$s_g = -\phi_1^{-1} N'(h_{22})\sigma_1\sqrt{\tau} < 0 \qquad \text{and} \quad \beta f_g > 0. \tag{21}$$

For each value of g, there is a unique value of βf.[4] Note that for floating rate bonds, the relevant parameters are given in expression (13). The inverse function rule allows us to say that, for a given value of (d_2, d_1) with $d_i = \bar{d}_i$, βf equals $\beta 1$ only when[5]

$$\sigma_2^2/\sigma_1^2 = (\sigma_2^2 + \sigma_x^2 - 2\rho_{2x}\sigma_2\sigma_x)/(\sigma_1^2 + \sigma_x^2 - 2\rho_{1x}\sigma_1\sigma_x) \tag{22}$$

or

$$\sigma_2^2/\sigma_1^2 = (\sigma_x - 2\rho_{2x}\sigma_2)/(\sigma_x - 2\rho_{1x}\sigma_1). \tag{23}$$

In particular the yield spreads will be equal across markets when the following equality holds:[6]

$$\sigma_2/\sigma_1 = \rho_{1x}/\rho_{2x} \tag{24}$$

that is, the spread differentials are equal in the two markets when the ratio of correlation coefficients for both firms also equals the inverse of the ratio of the firm's volatilities. Note that, since we have assumed that $\sigma_2 > \sigma_1$, the less risky firms must also have returns more correlated with the value of the payment promised in the floating rate issue, $\rho_{1x} > \rho_{2x}$.

IV.   DEFAULT SPREAD ON RISKY COUPON BONDS

Most corporate debt and certainly all floating rate securities available pay coupons. With coupon bonds the equity of the firm is equivalent to a compound call option. At every coupon date the stockholders have the choice between continuing to service the debt or forfeiting the firm to bondholders. Default risk is, therefore, not independent across payments of different maturity.

In this section we determine the value of the spread due to credit differences of two firms when the bonds issued pay coupons. As before, we assume that the default premium demanded in the market reflects the value of the firm, V. If at any point in time this value falls below the current coupon payment times the number of periods until maturity, bondholders take over the assets leaving nothing to shareholders. It is assumed that the firm is free to enter both the floating rate market and the fixed rate market and issue debt accordingly. Thus, we need to specify the correspondent coupon payment formulas. When the firm issues fixed rate bonds it pays continuous coupons at a known and constant rate. If, however, the firm decides to issue floating rate bonds the continuous coupon payout will adjust to reflect changes in interest rates. More precisely, the coupon rate will always equal the current short-term rate plus a constant mark-up.[7] For simplicity, consider that the term structure of interest rates is adequately specified by the short-term rate, with dynamics given by

$$dr = \alpha(m - r)\,dt + \sigma_r\sqrt{r}\,dz_r.$$ (25)

Expression (25) simply states that short-term rates always tend to revert to a long-term mean value, m.[8] In this framework we can value bonds employing continuous rebalancing arguments, knowing that the expected payoff on a replicating portfolio of existing assets equals that on a derivative security, in order to eliminate arbitrage opportunities. Bond values will depend on two state variables, in addition to time: (1) the market value of the issuing firm that follows the stochastic process specified in A5, and (2) the current rate of interest that evolves according to expression (25).

It is worth noting that by making bond values depend on the current interest rate we depart from the approach developed by Merton [8], assuming a deterministic term structure. Clearly, we could have valued fixed rate bonds employing this simpler approach and rely on V alone, and used instead our two state variable model for the purpose of valuing floating rate bonds. That, however, would make the default risk spreads in the two markets depend on different factors. To ensure consistency of the results, bonds paying either fixed rate coupons or floating rate coupons will be valued taking both V and r as the relevant variables. Then, it can be shown that the valuation equation for a coupon bond $F(V, r, \overline{C}, t)$ issued by firm V is:

$$1/2(\sigma_v^2 V^2 F_{vv} + \sigma_r^2 r F_{rr} + 2\rho_{vr}\sigma_v\sigma_v V\sqrt{r} F_{vr}) + \alpha(m - r)F_r$$
$$+ (rV - \overline{C})F_v + \overline{C} - Fr = -F_t \quad (26)$$

with boundary condition

$$F(V, r, \overline{C}, T) = \min(V, P)$$

where $\overline{C} = cP$, when the bond pays fixed coupons, and $\overline{C} = (r(t) + \theta)P$, when the bond pays floating coupons. Note that in either case the amounts actually paid depend on the value of the firm, since for values of V below the time-varying lower boundary the firm defaults on its obligations.

There are no known closed form solutions to the valuation Equation (26). Thus, we have employed the numerical method of finite differences to approximate the partial derivatives, solving the equation for a particular set of contractual features.[9] The results of the valuations were then used to determine the default risk spreads. For that the following procedure was employed: First we computed the coupon rates, $\bar{C}/P$, that would be paid if the bonds were default-free. Next, we determined what these rates should be if the default risk bonds were to sell to a current price equal to par value. By subtracting the first coupon rate from the second we obtained the values of the default risk spread. For fixed coupon bonds this was simply the difference between two constant rates, $c(V, r, T) - c(r, T)$. Cox, Ingersoll, and Ross [4] have shown that $F(r, t, T) = P$, at all times, for a floating rate bond paying continuous coupons of $r(t)P$. Thus, the default spread for floaters is measured by the fixed premium set at the time of issuance, $\theta(V, r, T)$.

This same approach can be employed to value the relative spread for bonds issued by corporations with different credit risk. In the rest of this section we present the results of the coupon spreads for two firms issuing either fixed rate bonds or floating rate notes. The current rate of interest $r(t)$ evolves according to equation (25), with parameters $k = 1.0$, $m = 0.10$ and $\sigma_r^2 = 0.0025$. Firm 1 is assumed to be in a lower "risk class", with $\sigma_1^2 = 0.04$. The riskier firm, Firm 2, has $\sigma_2^2 \in [0.04, 0.25]$. In other words the volatility of the returns on the riskier firm is between one and two and a half times the volatility of the return on the less risky firm. For both firms, the correlation between the firm's value and the short term interest rate is either 0.2 or -0.2. Figure 7 contains the results corresponding to $\underline{d} = 0.4$ for bonds maturing in 5 years. Note that in this case, $\underline{d}$ is the true debt to firm value ratio, where the current price of the risky bond $F(V, r, \bar{C}, T)$ is equal to P. In all cases the fixed coupon spreads differ from the floating coupon spreads. For fixed rate bonds, the spread appears to be decreasing in ρ_{ir} and the same occurs for floating rate bonds. Hence, the correlation factor seems to have a positive impact in reducing the risk of default for floating rate bonds that is shared too by fixed rate bonds. When the riskier firm, Firm 2, is positively correlated with the short term interest rate, $\rho_{2r} = 0.2$, the floating coupon spread is smaller than the fixed coupon spread. When the opposite occurs, that is $\rho_{2r} = -0.2$, the floating coupon spread is bigger than the fixed coupon spread. It is also worth noting that the spread is more sensitive to the value of the correlation parameter in the case of floating rate bonds. We examined these issues for coupon bonds maturing in 10 years. The results were quite similar, although the relative values for the spreads increased slightly.

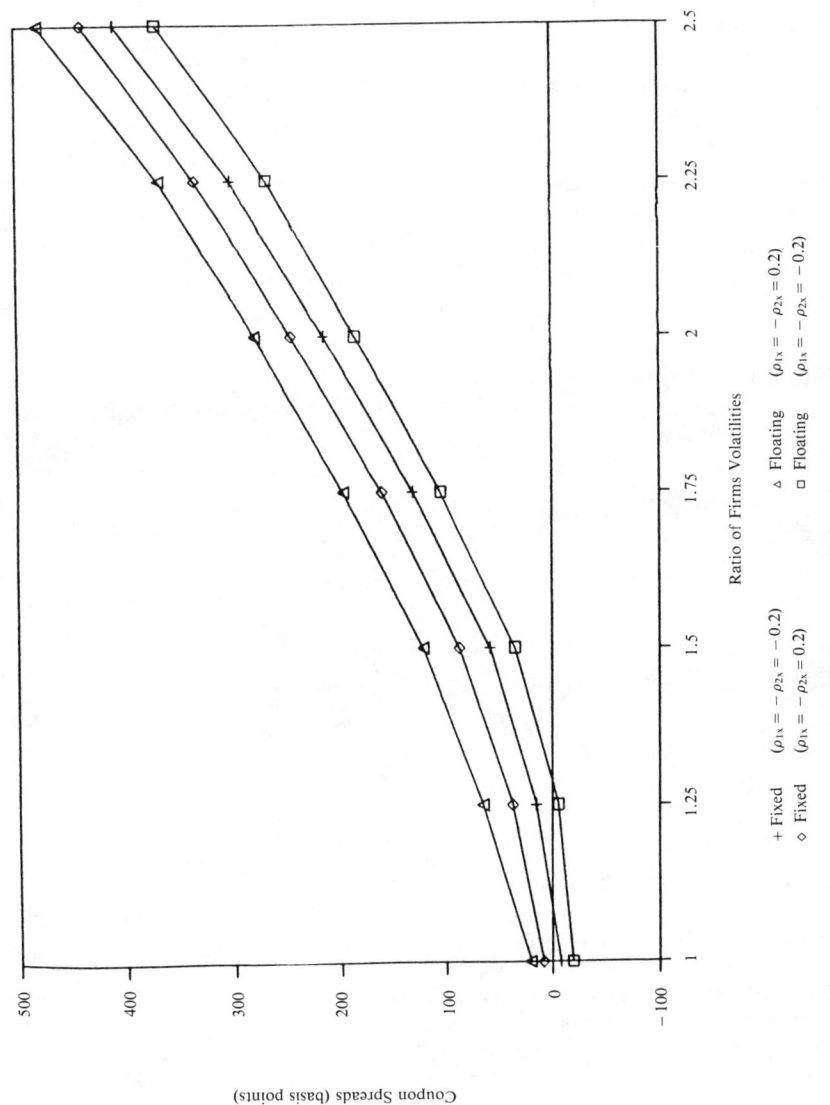

Figure 7. Fixed and floating coupon spreads and the correlation factor. The interest rate r evolves as a diffusion $dr = \alpha(m - r) \, dt + \sigma_r \sqrt{r}$, where $\alpha = 1.0$, $m = 0.10$, $\sigma^2 = 0.0025$. $\rho_{vr} = 0.2$ or -0.2. Both firms have same debt to firm value ratio ($\underline{d} = 0.4$), $\sigma_2 = K\sigma_1$, $K \in [1.0, 2.5]$ and $\sigma_1 = 0.20$. Debt maturity is 5 years.

V. CONCLUSIONS

In this work we have applied methods for the valuation of the spread due to credit differences of two firms in the fixed rate market and in the floating rate market. The results presented do not lend support to the view that reasons that the yield differentials should be the same in both markets. Arbitrage pricing models are consistent with differences in quality spreads because the set of relevant variables affecting the value of these spreads differ. In particular, a definition of relative riskiness just on the basis of the variance of the firm's returns is misleading in the case of floating rate debt, for the degree of correlation between the company's level of profitability and the payments on the debt has great importance in the likelihood of default. Though showing that the spreads are not necessarily equal, we do not explain why the spreads in the fixed rate market are greater than in the floating rate market. There are a few reasons which may account for the fact. Perhaps corporate managers do not always distinguish between interest rate risk and inflation risk in long-range financial planning. Alternatively, the model is not an accurate description of the market and we may be missing some sort of segmentation. Solving the question is a matter for empirical testing.

NOTES

1.   This argument is expressed in nearly every article on swaps.
2.   Merton calls this upward biased estimate of the market value debt-to-firm value ratio, the quasi debt-to-firm value ratio.
3.   This corresponds to the absolute swap case.
4.   Alternatively, one can take $s(\sigma_1, \sigma_2)$ and apply the transformation, such that $s(\sigma_1, \sigma_2) = s(g, u)$ with $g = \sigma_2/\sigma_1$ and u some known variable. Then s_g can be determined as part of the Jacobian of the transformation.
5.   Note that $d_i = \bar{d}_i$ does not imply equality between the present values of the promised payments under the different types of debts, if discounted at the risk adjusted rate of interest.
6.   This is the case when $\sigma_i^2 = \sigma_i^2 + \sigma_x - 2\rho_{ix}\sigma_i\sigma_x$, for both firms.
7.   Other more general coupon paying formulas would increase the number of state variables rendering the valuation problem virtually intractable.
8.   This process has been used in many other studies and appears to provide a sensible description of the behavior of interest rates over time.
9.   The method solves the partial differential equation alternating in the directions of V and r. For the lower boundary condition with respect to V (at $V = 0$), the bond has value zero. At $r = 0$, the valuation equation itself serves as the lower boundary. $F_{rr} = 0$ served as the upper boundary condition for r, and $F_v = 0$ serves as the upper boundary condition for V. The range of values for r is $(0, 30\%)$ and for V is $(0, 1200)$. The increment in the direction of r is 0.25% and in the direction of V is $10.00. In both cases 120 mesh points were employed. Bond prices were computed for 5 and 10 years, using 120 mesh points (time-steps of 0.5 and 1 month).

REFERENCES

1. Black, F., and M. Scholes, "The Pricing of Options and Corporate Liabilities," *Journal of Political Economy* (May–June 1973).
2. Bicksler, J., and A. Chen, "An Economic Analysis of Interest Rate Swaps," *Journal of Finance* (July 1986).
3. Cornell, B., "The Future of Floating Rate Bonds," *Chase Financial Quarterly* (Spring 1981).
4. Cox, J., T. Ingersoll, and S. Ross, 'An Analysis of Variable Rate Loan Contracts," *Journal of Finance* (May 1980).
5. Jain, M. K., *Numerical Solution of Differential Equations*. New York: John Wiley, 1984.
6. Lipsky, T., and S. Elhalaski, "Swap-Driven Primary Issuance in the International Bond Market," Salomon Brothers (January 1986).
7. Margrabe, W., "The Value of an Option to Exchange One Asset for Another," *Journal of Finance* (March 1978).
8. Merton, R., "On the Pricing of Corporate Debt: The Risk Structure of Interest Rates," *Journal of Finance* (June 1974).
9. Ramaswamy, K., and S. Sundaresan, "The Valuation of Floating-Rate Instruments," *Journal of Financial Economics* (June 1986).

T-BOND FUTURES PRICES:

CHEAPEST TO DELIVER VERSUS THE INDEX

Mark Castelino* and Sris Chatterjee**

I. INTRODUCTION

The CBT Treasury Bond futures contract has been the subject of much research for several years. Academics have focused most of their attention on the option-type properties of the contract, particularly as they relate to equilibrium pricing.[1] Practitioners on the other hand have devoted most of their attention to the usefulness and effectiveness of the contract for

*Department of Business Administration, Rutgers University, Newark.
**School of Business, Rutgers University, New Brunswick.

We gratefully acknowledge a grant from the Coordinating Council of Business Studies at Rutgers University.

Advances in Futures and Options Research, Vol. 3, pages 291–300.

hedging purposes.[2] Central to the discussion of either approach has been the role of the "cheapest to deliver" bond.

Equilibrium pricing approaches generally invoke an arbitrage condition to generate forward prices for all deliverable bonds. The lowest of these forward prices corresponds to the bond that is cheapest to deliver. Since it is always advantageous to the short seller to deliver the cheapest bond that can be purchased in the cash market, the forward price obtained for such a bond serves as the benchmark for pricing the futures contract. In fact, it serves as the upper bound for the price of the contract because of the existence of several "delivery options" that belong exclusively to the short seller.[3] The equilibrium futures price is obtained by adjusting the forward price of the cheapest to deliver bond by the cumulative value of the delivery options.[4] A further adjustment to this price is made to account for the daily "mark to market" requirement typical of futures markets.[5]

Where hedging is concerned, it has been argued[6] that since futures contracts price off the cheapest to deliver bond, the price sensitivity of the contract should parallel that of the cheapest to deliver. Thus, regardless of whether one uses a regression or a duration based approach, the price behavior of the cheapest to deliver bond is the critical variable in the design and construction of effective hedges. The option type features of the contract plays no explicit role in determining hedge ratios, although it is recognized that their existence increases the risk (basis) of the hedge.[7]

The primary focus of this paper is to question the emphasis placed on cheapest to deliver bond in determining changes in futures prices and consequently its singular role in hedge ratio determination. The cheapest to deliver bond might be adequate for tracking actual futures prices if the identity of this bond remained unchanged from the day a hedge is placed to the day the hedge is lifted. But such is not the case.[8] Therefore, the change in the daily futures price should equal the change in the forward price implied by the cheapest to deliver minus the change in the value of the implied delivery options. The impact of this last component can be quite large, particularly since the identity of the cheapest to deliver bond often changes quite frequently.[9] Since the cheapest to deliver bond cannot capture the changes in option value, the task is to find a proxy that can better track the changes in the value of the delivery option.[10] We believe that such a proxy exists in the form of an index composed of all economically deliverable bonds. Intuitively, since there is a finite probability that any bond in the deliverable set may be delivered, the proxy should be based on the entire set of such bonds. Using daily futures and cash price data for all contracts from March 1984 to December 1985 we show that an index of derived prices of all deliverable bonds consistently outperforms the cheapest to deliver bond in explaining changes in futures prices. We believe such a finding substantially diminishes the role of the cheapest to deliver bond for hedge construction and, just as importantly, suggests that futures prices are driven by fundamental factors that drive the prices of all bonds rather than those of a specific one. Section II discusses the existing theory and describes our hypothesis. Section III reports the results and Section IV concludes with suggestions for further research.

II. THEORETICAL DISCUSSION

The upper bound on the price of a futures contract is found by using the Cost of Carry model that imposes a no-arbitrage condition between shorting one T-Bond futures contract, buying a Treasury bond in the cash market, and holding it for delivery at expiration of the futures contract. The standard Treasury bond designated for delivery by the CBT carries an 8% coupon with at least 15 years to maturity/call from the first delivery day of the contract month. However, actual delivery by the short need not be made with this standard bond. The CBT allows delivery of any treasury bond as long as the maturity/call condition is met. Since bonds with coupons higher (lower) than 8% will sell at a premium (discount) compared to the standard bond, the CBT has established an adjustment for nonpar deliveries. This adjustment is known as the "conversion factor" adjustment. The conversion factor for the deliverable bond simply equals the fraction of par value for which the deliverable bond would sell if it were priced at an 8% yield to maturity.

If the yield curve were flat at 8%, then the conversion factor would be unbiased. But in reality these factors are biased[11] causing a preference for delivery of a specific bond in the deliverable set. Such a bond is called the "cheapest to deliver." Since it is to the greatest advantage for the short trader to carry this bond to meet delivery requirements, its implied forward price[12] is a major determinant of equilibrium futures prices. If we define $f_1(t)$, $f_2(t)$, ..., $f_n(t)$ as implied forward prices of all deliverable bonds and $F(t)$ as the equilibrium futures price at time "t," then

$$F(t) < \min[f_1(t), f_2(t), ..., f_n(t)]$$

or (1)

$$F(t) < f_{cd}(t)$$

where

$$f_{cd}(t) = \min[f_1(t), f_2(t), ..., f_n(t)]$$
$$= \text{implied forward price of the cheapest to}$$

deliver bond.

The strict inequality in (1) derives from two sources. The first is the "mark to market" requirement typical of futures markets (see Cox, Ingersoll, and Ross [5], Jarrow and Oldfield [11], and Richard and Sundaresan [22]). Second, and more importantly, is the existence of several options belonging exclusively to the short trader with regard to the type and timing of actual delivery. (See notes 3 and 13.) There have been extensive studies that have attempted to price these options both individually and cumulatively (see Gay and Manaster [10], Kane and Marcus [16], and Arak and Goodman [1]). The consensus has been that the options do have value, but the extent to which they depress futures prices relative to the forward price of the cheapest to deliver is much disputed. By explicitly accounting for the existence of the option, inequality (1) can be rewritten as Equation (2):

$$F(t) = f_{cd}(t) - OP(t) \qquad (2)$$

where

$$OP(t) = \text{cumulative value of delivery options.}$$

Hence, changes in future prices can be expressed as

$$\Delta F(t) = \Delta f_{cd}(t) - \Delta OP(t). \qquad (3)$$

It is clear from Equation (3) that the cheapest to deliver bond can at best explain only a part (albeit a large one) of the total movement in the futures prices. The remainder is explained by changes in the cumulative value of the options. This in turn implies that any hedge ratio construct based solely on the cheapest to deliver is necessarily incorrect and the estimated hedge ratio is inefficient. In fact, this is precisely the implication of the recent studies by Kamara and Siegel [13] and Johnson [12]. Kamara and Siegel directly address the derivation of the hedge ratio in the presence of quality options, but both of these papers explicitly model the probability that one deliverable asset may replace another at the expiration of the futures contract.

The intuition behind these two recent studies lies in the fact that the quality option is an option to deliver one out of several available bonds. The futures contract can therefore be thought of as a combination of a futures contract on an actually existing bond plus an option to exchange that bond for one of several other bonds. The pricing of this exchange option in the case of only two deliverable (available) assets is demonstrated in Margrabe [20], Garbade and Silber [8], and Gay and Manaster [9]. Cheng [4] and Johnson [12] have extended this analysis to the case of multiple deliverable assets. Empirical estimates of the value of the quality option corresponds to a discount of between 1.9 and 6.2% for a 3-month contract from the equilibrium futures prices that would emerge in the absence of the delivery option. This result is taken from Kane and Marcus [15] who carry out a Monte Carlo simulation of term structure dynamics. To the best of our knowledge, there is no empirical analysis on the quality option with actual market data. We hope that our analysis will fill this gap.

The explicit recognition of the delivery probabilities in the studies of Johnson [12] and Kamara and Siegel [13] suggests that an appropriately weighted index of all deliverable bonds should track futures prices better than the cheapest to deliver bond. This is precisely our hypothesis. The existence of such an index has direct implication for hedge ratio construction, as it would replace the cheapest to deliver bond as the fundamental force behind change in futures prices. In constructing the index, intuition suggests a weighting scheme that reflects the probability of delivery of each bond in the deliverable set. However, ex ante, there is no simple empirical way to measure these probabilities. The use of historical data will be both inaccurate and inadequate. The inaccuracy stems from the requirement that the term structure dynamics in the future replicate the past. On the other hand, it would be inadequate because new Treasury issues often become the cheapest to deliver soon after entering the market, and sometimes stay that way until the expiration of the futures contract. In the absence of any systematic way to measure the delivery probabilities, an index of all deliverable bonds is constructed giving each bond equal weight. The index is therefore an equally weighted index of the implied forward prices of all deliverable bonds.

In order to test the hypothesis that the T-Bond futures price tracks the index better than the cheapest to deliver, we ran the following regressions:

$$\Delta F(t) = a + b \Delta f_{cd}(t) + e(t) \tag{4}$$

$$\Delta F(t) = a_1 + b_1 \Delta \text{ Index}(t) + \varepsilon(t) \tag{5}$$

where $\Delta F(t)$, $\Delta f_{cd}(t)$, and Δ Index(t) are price differences over a period of 5 days. $F(t)$ is the actual futures price for a specific contract. $f_{cd}(t)$ is the implied forward price for the same contract based on the cheapest to deliver bonds. Index(t) is the index of implied forward prices based on the entire set of deliverable bonds. Each of these three price series starts 12 months prior to maturity and ends on the last trading day of the month preceding expiration. For example, the price series constructed by us for the December 1985 contract will start on January 1 and end on November 30, 1985.

Our sample is based on eight futures contracts extending from March 1984 to December 1985. For each contract the deliverable bonds are first identified. For some contracts the number of deliverable bonds is as high as 27. For any trading day we calculate the implied future price with respect to each deliverable bond as shown in footnote 12. The 3-month LIBOR rate is used to represent the opportunity cost of money. The minimum implied price on any day is taken as the estimated futures price for that day and the bond that has this minimum implied price is identified as the 'cheapest to deliver." The trading days for any contract extend from 1 month to 12 months before maturity. For some contracts as many as 11 bonds have been the cheapest to deliver at one time or another over this period. The number of times that the cheapest to deliver changes for a contract is much larger than the number of cheapest to deliver bonds because the same bond may become the cheapest to deliver at different time during a contract's life. These switches only indicate the significance of the quality option.

III. EMPIRICAL RESULTS

The results of the regressions on Equations (4) and (5) are reported in Table 1. The following conclusions can be drawn:

1. For every single contract from March 1984 to December 1985, the index outperforms the cheapest to deliver in its ability to explain changes in futures prices. The consistently higher R^2 confirms this.

2. The performance differentials (differences in R^2) is as high as 11.3% for the June 1984 contract and less than 1% for the September 1984 contract. The average improvement in performance of the index over the cheapest to deliver is approximately 14.2%.

3. The average beta coefficient for the index is 1.042 while that for the cheapest to deliver is 0.969, suggesting that futures prices are more volatile than the index of implied forward prices, but less volatile than the implied forward prices based on cheapest to deliver.

4. Even with the improved performance of the index, substantial basis risk remains. In the best performance case (September 1985) as much as 10% of the movement in futures prices cannot be explained by the index.

5. The number of different bonds that acquire the cheapest to deliver status during the life of the futures contract may be taken as an indicator of the degree of delivery risk implicit in the quality option. Our discussion in Section II would suggest that there should be some positive relation between the relative performance of the index and the measure of delivery risk. To a limited extent, this is true for our data: the performance differentials cluster around 3–4% for the contracts from December 1984 to December 1985 when the number of cheapest to deliver bonds was also fewer in comparison. However, our results are neither conclusive nor consistent in this regard: for example, both the June 1984 and September 1984 contracts had as many as 11 different cheapest to deliver bonds; however, the former had a performance differential of more than 11%, while the latter less than 1%, in favor of the index. This aspect of the problem requires further study and analysis.

Table 1. Regression Results of Futures Prices versus Index and Cheapest to Deliver

Contract	Independent Variable	Constant[a]	Slope	R^2	Number of Bonds[b]	NOBS
March '84	Index	0.1481 (0.536)	1.00658 (31.228)	0.79921	—	246
	Chp	0.00272 (0.081)	0.87692 (21.049)	0.70243	11	246
June '84	Index	0.00177 (0.066)	0.99069 (31.424)	0.80121	—	246
	Chp	−0.0156 (−0.463)	0.8429 (23.282)	0.68871	11	246
Sep '84	Index	0.00859 (0.372)	1.0492 (35.893)	0.84022	—	246
	Chp	0.02011 (0.868)	0.93411 (35.874)	0.84007	11	246
Dec '84	Index	0.01281 (0.595)	1.08005 (43.377)	0.88437	—	247
	Chp	0.03031 (1.272)	0.99468 (38.587)	0.85821	6	247
Mar '85	Index	0.01561 (0.701)	1.06538 (45.635)	0.89435	—	247
	Chp	0.02029 (0.791)	0.99204 (45.635)	0.85986	5	247
Jun '85	Index	0.02839 (1.244)	1.0445 (43.809)	0.89174	—	234
	Chp	0.04682 (1.847)	1.01487 (38.690)	0.86531	5	234
Sep '85	Index	0.02807 (1.248)	1.04948 (48.148)	0.90548	—	243
	Chp	0.04545 (1.723)	1.05551 (40.176)	0.86962	4	243
Dec '85	Index	0.00026 (0.011)	1.05569 (43.472)	0.88898	—	237
	Chp	0.01483 (0.530)	1.04867 (36.477)	0.84936	3	237

[a]All quantities in parenthese are t-statistics.
[b]Number of bonds that achieved "cheapest to deliver" status during test period.

IV. CONCLUSION

An index of all deliverable bonds outperforms the cheapest to deliver in explaining changes in futures prices. This result was confirmed for all contracts starting from March 1984 and ending on December 1985. Using the cheapest to deliver bond to obtain hedge ratios would give rise to substantial basis risk because none of the delivery options is factored into the hedging procedures. The evidence that the index tracks futures prices better than the cheapest to deliver suggests that the index implicitly captures the contribution made by these options. The implication of this result is that the index should supplant the cheapest to deliver in hedging procedures.

Further research in this area should focus on the construction of the index in a way that could more appropriately account for the delivery probabilities of the different bonds.

NOTES

1. See Margrabe [20], Kilcollin [17], Garbade and Silber [8], Gay and Manaster [9], and Kane and Marcus [15].

2. See Pitts [21], Toevs and Jacob [23], Arak and Goodman [1], and Arak, Goodman, and Ross [2].

3. The delivery rules provide the short seller with four types of delivery options: (1) a quality option and (2) three types of timing options: (a) a delivery day option because the short may choose any business day in the delivery month to make a delivery; (b) an end of month option that arises because trading in the futures contract is suspended during the last 7 business days in the delivery month and invoice prices are set on the last day of futures trading for all deliveries occurring during the end of the month; (c) a wild card option that arises because deliveries on any day may be announced as late as 8:00 P.M. for invoice prices that are fixed as of 2:00 P.M. Chicago time. The quality option arises because the underlying asset on the CBT T-Bond futures contract is a government bond with a hypothetical 8% coupon (and 15 years to maturity) and because actual deliveries are related to this bond by an imperfect adjustment known as "conversion factor." See Garbade [7] and Gay and Manaster [10] for details. For empirical estimates of the value of different kinds of delivery options, see Gay and Manaster [10], Kane and Marcus [16], and Arak and Goodman [1].

4. The theoretical value of this option in the presence of multiple assets is derived independently in Cheng [4] and Johnson [12].

5. See Cox, Ingersoll, and Ross [5] for the distinction between the forward and futures prices in the presence of marking to market. See Benninga and Smirlock [3] for an empirical analysis.

6. See Figlewski [6] and Toevs and Jacob [23].

7. See Figlewski [6].

8. The interaction of yield with the coupons and maturity structure of the cheapest to deliver bond is analyzed in Livingston [18, 19]. The analysis is tractible only for parallel shifts in the yield curve and there is no simple rule for predicting the cheapest to deliver in the case of general reshapings of the yield curve. More importantly, when the treasury issues a new bond that bond often becomes the new cheapest to deliver.

9. For an example of how frequently the cheapest to deliver bond may change, consider the June 1984 contract. Eleven bonds acquired the status of cheapest to deliver at one time or another during the 12 months preceding maturity of the contract. During this period, there were 81 switches among these 11 bonds. In other words, there were 81 changes in the cheapest to deliver bond. Actual deliveries also seem to suggest that the futures market is not tied to a single bond even when the contract has matured; for example, 16 bonds were delivered against the March 1986 contract. Traders in the futures market confirm that actual deliveries are made

with bonds that are less liquid or have some other unattractive features. Such bonds may not be identified as the cheapest to deliver by the cost of carry model.

10. Kamara and Siegel [13] have recently demonstrated the construction of the theoretically correct hedge ratio when there are only two deliverable qualities. But the extension of this methodology to the case of multiple deliverable qualities is almost impossible. This is what makes the search for an adequate proxy so much more important.

11. When the interest rate is above 8%, the bias in the conversion factor favors delivery of low (high) coupon bonds with long (short) maturities. See Arak, Goodman, and Ross [2] and Livingston [18, 19].

12. If cc denotes the cost of carry, then the ex-ante equilibrium forward price is given by

$$f = [P_j/Q_j] + cc$$

where P_j is the current cash price of the jth bond and Q_j is the bond's conversion factor and

$$cc = 1/Q_j\{[P_j + A_j][rT/360] - C_j\,T/365\}$$

where

A_j = Accrued interest up to cash settlement day since the last coupon date

r = Cost of funds (e.g., a suitable short-term rate)

T = Number of days from settlement date to futures expiration

C_j = Annual coupon of the cash bond.

13. In contrast to the attention paid to the quality option, much more attention seems to have been paid to the actual value of the timing options, in particular the "wild card option." Both Gay and Manaster [10] and Kane and Marcus [16] analyze the wild card options in detail. Of these two studies, the analysis in Kane and Marcus is more accurate. In testing their model, Kane and Marcus assume that the futures price converges to the spot price at the termination of the contract and find that the value of the wild card option "at the start of the delivery month is consistent with the futures price being bid down by approximately 1/5th of a point." This is somewhat less than the value imputed by Gay and Manaster who did not consider the impact of the wild card option on the futures price. Arak and Goodman [1] criticize Kane and Marcus [16] for ignoring (1) the quality option in the delivery month and (2) the end-of-the-month option. When these options are built in, the wild card option becomes even less valuable. Arak and Goodman conclude that even the daily option does not have much value when compared to the quality option and the end-of-the-month option.

REFERENCES

1. Arak, M., and L. Goodman, "Treasury Bond Futures: Valuing the Delivery Options," *Journal of Futures Market* 7 (June 1987), 269–286.
2. Arak, M., L. Goodman, and S. Ross, "The Cheapest to Deliver Bond on the Treasury Bond Futures Contract," *Advances in Futures and Options Research* 1 (1986), 29–49.
3. Benninga, S., and M. Smirlock, "An Empirical Analysis of the Delivery Option, Marking to Market and the Pricing of T-Bond Futures," *Journal of Futures Market* 5 (Fall 1985), 361–374.
4. Cheng, S. T., "Multi Asset Contingent Claims in Stochastic Interest Rate Environments," Working Paper, Columbia University, March 1987.
5. Cox, J. C., J. E. Ingersoll, and S. A. Ross, "The Relation between Forward and Futures prices," *Journal of Financial Economics* 9 (December 1981), 321–346.
6. Figlewski, S., *Hedging With Interest Rate Futures for Institutional Investors: From Theory To Practice,* Massachusetts: Ballinger Publishing, 1985.

7. Garbade, K. D., "Treasury Bond Futures: Contract Provisions and Relation to Cash Market Bonds, *Topics in Money and Security Markets,* No. 13, Bankers Trust Company, New York, May 1985.

8. Garbade, K. D., and W. Silber, "Futures Contracts on Commodities with Multiple Varieties: An Analysis of Premiums and Discounts," *Journal of Business* 56 (July 1987), 249–272.

9. Gay, G. D., and S. Manaster, "The Quality Option Implicit in Futures Contracts," *Journal of Financial Economics* 13 (September 1984), 353–370.

10. Gay, G. D., and S. Manaster, "Implicit Delivery Options and Optimal Delivery Strategies for Financial Futures Contracts," *Journal of Financial Economics* 16 (May 1986), 41–72.

11. Jarrow, R. A., and G. S. Oldfield, "Forward Contracts and Futures Contracts," *Journal of Financial Economics* 9 (December 1981), 373–382.

12. Johnson, H., "Options on the Maximum and Minimum of Several Assets", *Journal of Financial and Quantitative Analysis* 22 (September 1987), 277–283.

13. Kamara, A., and A. F. Siegel, "Optimal Hedging in Futures Markets with Multiple Specifications," *Journal of Finance* 42 (September 1987), 1007–1021.

14. Kane, A., and A. Marcus, "Conversion Factor Risk and Hedging in T-Bond Futures Market, *Journal of Futures Market* 4 (Spring 1984), 55–64.

15. Kane, A., and A. Marcus, "The Quality Option in the T-Bond Futures Market: An Empirical Assessment", *Journal of Futures Market* 6 (Summer 1986), 231–248.

16. Kane, A., and A. Marcus, "Valuation and Optimal Exercise of the Wild Card Option in the Treasury Bond Futures Market," *Journal of Finance* 41 (March 1986), 195–207.

17. Kilcollin, T. E., "Difference Systems in Financial Futures Markets," *Journal of Finance* 37 (December 1982), 1183–1197.

18. Livingston, M., "The Cheapest to Deliver Bond for the CBT Treasury Bond Futures Contract," *Journal of Futures Market* 4 (1984), 161–172.

19. Livingston, M., "The Effect of Coupon Level on Treasury Bond Futures Delivery," *Journal of Futures Market* 7 (June 1987), 303–309.

20. Margrabe, W. E., "The Value of an Option to Exchange One Asset for Another," *Journal of Finance* 33 (March 1978), 177–186.

21. Pitts, M., "Managing Risk with Interest Rate Futures," in *The Handbook of Fixed Income Securities* (F. J. Fabozzi and I. Pollack, eds.), pp. 891–917. Dow Jones-Irwin, 1987.

22. Richard, S., and M. Sundaresan, "A Continuous Time Equilibrium Model of Forward Prices and Futures Prices in a Multigood Economy," *Journal of Financial Economics 9* (December 1981), 347–371.

23. Toevs, A., and D. Jacob, "A Comparison of Alternative Hedge Ratio Methodologies with Interest Rate Futures," *The Handbook of Fixed Income Securities,* 918–938.

INTRADAY RETURN AND VOLATILITY PATTERNS IN THE STOCK MARKET:
FUTURES VERSUS SPOT

Joseph E. Finnerty* and Hun Y. Park*

I. INTRODUCTION

One of the mind-boggling issues in finance research recently is the systematic pattern of stock returns during the week, i.e., the weekend effect. A number of studies have examined the daily common stock returns (e.g., French [3], Gibbons and Hess [5], Lakonishok and Levi [8], Rogalski [10], and Keim and Stambaugh [7]). The common conclusion in the previous studies is that Monday returns tend to be negative and less than those on the other weekdays, and that the differences between Monday returns and

*University of Illinois

Advances in Futures and Options Research, Vol. 3, pages 301–317.
ISBN: 0-89232-926-2

average weekday returns are statistically significant and pervasive across securities. A recent study (Lakonishok and Levi [9]) documented the negative Monday effect using the Dow Jones Industrial Average for 90 years. However, the causes for the weekend effects are not fully understood and remain puzzling, at least at the present time, although some studies have debated whether the Monday negative returns might be due to a different institutional settlement procedure, transaction costs, or measurement error.[1]

In a recent study Cornell [1] tested the weekend effects in the S&P 500 spot and futures markets utilizing opening and closing prices. He found that the Monday effect exists due to the peculiar behavior of cash prices during nontrading hours. The return from Friday's close to Monday's open was found to be significantly negative in the S&P 500 spot index for the period of May 3, 1982–July 24, 1984. However, he did not find a similar pattern for S&P 500 futures for the sample period. He also found notably that on an open-to-close basis, Monday average returns were higher than any other day of the week not only in the spot but in the futures index.

The purpose of this study is multifold. First, we further investigate the weekend effects in the spot as well as in the futures markets, using actually transacted closing and opening prices of the Major Market Index (MMI) and its futures contracts. The MMI is a price-weighted index of 20 blue chips, 15 of which are included in the Dow Jones 30 Industrials; see Appendix for the companies included in the MMI. Second, we examine intraday returns for the spot and futures, in an attempt to examine exactly from what time on Friday to what time on Monday the weekend effect takes place, and to investigate whether a systematic pattern of prices during the day exists. To the authors' best knowledge, there is only one study concerning intraday price patterns. Harris [6] used intraday data to analyze returns on NYSE stocks for the 14 months between December 1981 and January 1983. The most notable finding was that the negative Monday returns accrued mostly in the first 45 minutes of trading, and on Tuesday thropugh Friday, prices rose significantly in the first 45 minutes of trading. He also found that the very large positive returns accrued over the last 15 minutes of trading on all weekdays. This paper further investigates the intraday systematic return patterns in the spot stock market and compares them with those in the futures market. This test will be particularly interesting to traders who wish to time their trades, since the presence of a systematic intraday return pattern may lead to a profitable timing strategy. Third, we also examine the intraday volatility behavior of prices in both futures and spot markets to better understand the intraday return patterns, if any.

The next section describes the data and presents empirical results. Confirming the results of the previous studies on the weekend effect, we provide new findings. First, we find that the weekend effect takes place starting from around 1:30 P.M. on Friday until around 9:00 A.M. on Monday, 30 minutes after trading is open. Second, the volatility of spot prices for the first 30 minutes of trading is shown to be abnormally high compared to other trading hours during the day, and the volatility for the last 30 minutes of trading prior to the close of the market is relatively low. However, we could not find the intraday volatility pattern in the futures market as significant as that in the spot market. Third, we show a lunch hour effect, where price movements are minimal during the 12 to 1 hour in both the spot and futures markets. Fourth, and more interestingly, a significantly negative trend in prices for both the spot and futures markets is detected on Wednesday, which we find puzzling. The last section contains a brief conclusion.

II. DATA AND EMPIRICAL RESULTS

The data consist of all intraday spot and futures prices of the Major Market Index over the period July 23, 1984 to July 15, 1986. The initial data base included every transaction as reported for the futures contracts and the values of the spot index occurring one to four times every minute of the trading day, so that a percentage change was available for each minute of trading at minimum. For the weekly return pattern part of the study, the opening and closing prices for the MMI and the most actively traded MMI futures contract were used. Following Cornell [1], all holidays and the days following holidays are excluded from the sample so that all daily returns in this paper are one-day and weekend returns. For the sample period, there are 16 holidays, 5 on Monday, 2 on Tuesday, 3 on Wednesday, 3 on Thursday, and 4 on Friday. For the intraday return portion of the study, prices were taken at 15-minute intervals starting from the opening and ending at the close. For the majority of the contracts this was 8:45 A.M. to 3:15 P.M., however, for the more recent contracts the opening had been moved to 8:15 A.M. The most actively traded futures contract in general was the nearby contract except for the delivery month when the next contract became the most actively traded.

The closing prices for the MMI are plotted in Figure 1 for the period July 1984 to July 1986. During this period the MMI stocks increased by over 60%, therefore on average we would expect to find positive daily returns.

The results for the day of the week effect portion of the study are reported in Table 1. For the spot and futures prices these returns are calculated (1) close to close, (2) close to open, and (3) open to close. Their means and standard deviations, and two F-statistics for each day are reported. The first F-statistic is for the hypothesis that the means of the

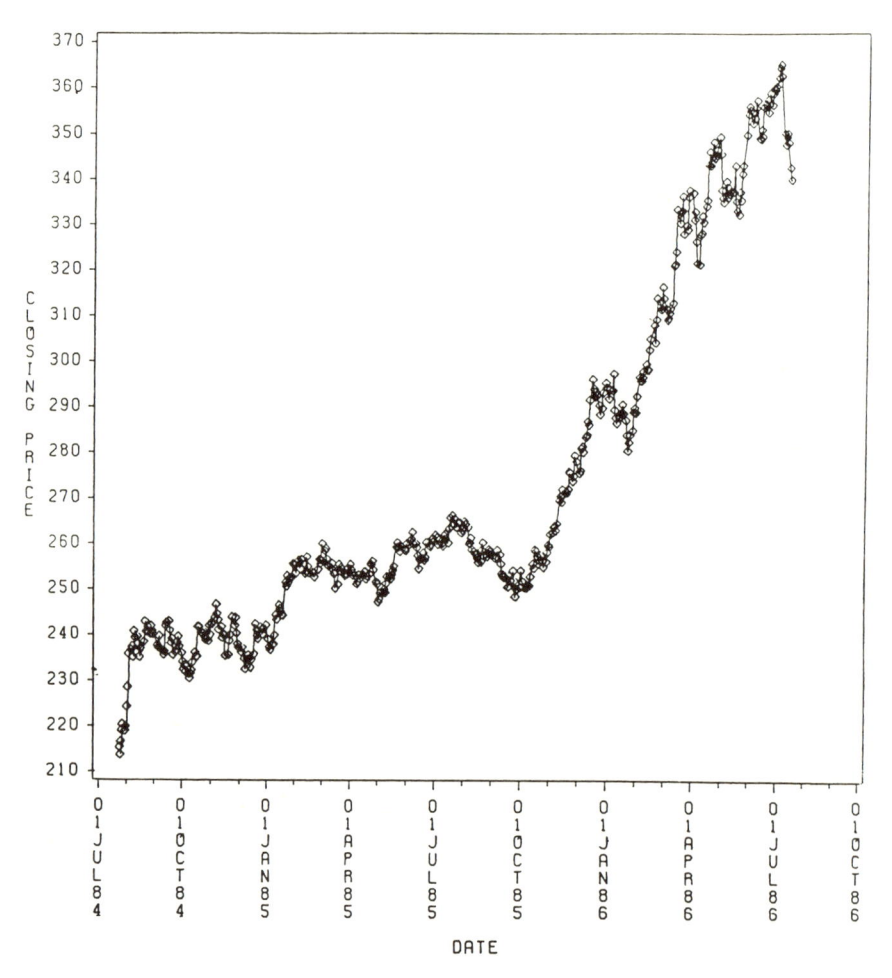

Figure 1.   Trend of spot closing price (July 23, 1984–July 15, 1986).

daily returns are equal during the week, and the second F-statistic is for the hypothesis that all of them are equal to zero.

For the spot index, the results confirm the findings of Cornell [1], Rogalski [10], and Gibbons and Hess [5]. The return from Friday's close to Monday's open is significantly negative indicating the existence of a weekend effect. However, the negative return is offset by the high return when trading is occurring, so that the return from close to close is positive. All of the other daily average returns are not significantly different from zero, indicating that there is no day of the week effect except for Monday. The results for the futures shows no significant day of the week effects on

Table 1. Day of the Week Returns for MMI Spot and Futures (%) (July 23, 1984 to July 15, 1986)

	Monday	Tuesday	Wednesday	Thursday	Friday	F-statistic[a]
Observations	94	96	97	96	96	
MMI spot close to close						
Mean	−0.005	0.154	−0.036	0.208	0.136	0.863
SD	0.788	0.840	0.087	0.862	0.887	1.209
MMI spot close to open						
Mean	−0.121[b]	0.006	0.006	0.004	0.077	2.323[b]
SD	0.061	0.043	0.033	0.045	0.051	2.428[b]
MMI spot open to close						
Mean	0.116	0.148	−0.043	0.203	0.059	0.830
SD	0.781	0.829	0.870	0.847	0.977	1.323
MMI futures close to close						
Mean	0.141	0.169	−0.047	0.215	0.017	1.630
SD	0.745	0.871	0.910	0.866	0.858	1.779
MMI futures close to open						
Mean	0.027	0.104	0.028	0.026	0.016	1.505
SD	0.329	0.232	0.259	0.260	0.334	1.754
MMI futures open to close						
Mean	0.114	0.066	−0.076	0.189	0.001	1.458
SD	0.692	0.883	0.869	0.843	0.866	1.628

[a]The first F-statistic is for the hypothesis that all the coefficients are equal in the regression $R_t = b_1 D_1 + b_2 D_2 + b_3 D_3 + b_4 D_4 + b_5 D_5 + \varepsilon_t$, where R_t is the return on the spot or futures and D_1 through D_5 represent day-of-the-week dummies. The second F-statistic is for the hypothesis that all the coefficients in the regression are equal to zero.
[b]Significant at the 5% level.

any day, thereby providing support for the efficient market hypothesis with respect to futures trading.

It is interesting, however, to observe that only on Wednesday, the returns from open to close for both spot and futures markets are negative, which indicates the downward trend of prices during the day. This becomes clearer when we examine the intraday return patterns.

The intraday return patterns allow us to look at specific periods during the trading day when price changes are more likely to occur. If the readers have ever had the opportunity to visit an exchange and view the trading activity, there seems to be great importance associated with the opening and closing of the market. As the bell rings, the traders burst into a cacophony of sound and motion, likewise at the close, the trading reaches a feverish pitch, then at the bell, silence.

In order to assess any systematic trading patterns that may be present during various part of the trading day, the spot and futures price data were analyzed over 15-minute intervals. An adjustment was made for the change in the opening of the MMI futures contract trading from 8:15 A.M. to 8:45 A.M. by treating those contracts that were opened at 8:15 A.M. as if they opened at 8:45 A.M. This adjustment affected only the first 15-minute trading period for the futures contracts results. The opening price at 8:15 A.M. was used to calculate the interval return as

$$\frac{f_{9:00 \text{ A.M.}} - F_{8:15}}{f_{8:15}} \times 100 = \% \text{ of return}$$

where $F_{8:15}$ is the opening price of the MMI contract. The earlier MMI futures and spot interval returns were calculated by

$$\frac{P_t - P_{OPEN}}{P_{OPEN}} \times 100 = \% \text{ return}$$

Table 2.   Cumulative 15-Minute Intraday Percentage Returns — MMI Futures.

	Monday	*Tuesday*	*Wednesday*	*Thursday*	*Friday*
Open–9:00 A.M.	− 0.018	0.020	0.008	0.009	0.018
9:00–9:15	− 0.017	− 0.005	− 0.002	0.039	0.049
9:15–9:30	− 0.014	0.038	0.002	0.017	0.059
9:30–9:45	0.012	0.029	− 0.0003	0.031	0.032
9:45–10:00	− 0.0001	− 0.002	− 0.034	0.037	0.054
10:00–10:15	0.004	− 0.014	− 0.064	0.059	0.052
10:15–10:30	− 0.0003	− 0.008	− 0.023	0.037	0.023
10:30–10:45	0.006	0.013	− 0.040	0.064	0.045
10:45–11:00	0.007	0.040	− 0.027	0.068	0.077
11:00–11:15	0.017	0.037	− 0.002	0.071	0.058
11:15–11:30	0.057	0.049	− 0.032	0.088	0.077
11:30–11:45	0.035	0.041	− 0.022	0.128	0.080
11:45–12:00	0.083	0.036	− 0.035	0.115 ⎫	0.089
12:00–12:15 P.M	0.071	0.064 ⎫	− 0.069	0.115 ⎬ [a]	0.129 ⎫
12:15–12:30	0.051 ⎫	0.061 ⎬ [a]	− 0.043 ⎫	0.115 ⎭	0.128 ⎬ [a]
12:30–12:45	0.052 ⎬ [a]	0.065 ⎭	− 0.042 ⎬ [a]	0.142	0.063
12:45–1:00	0.051 ⎭	0.003	− 0.048	0.139	0.057
1:00–1:15	0.067	0.024	− 0.050	0.102	0.029
1:15–1:30	0.056	0.046	− 0.077	0.135	0.069
1:30–1:45	0.034	0.048	− 0.059	0.170	0.080
1:45–2:00	0.080	0.063	− 0.108	0.149	0.034
2:00–2:15	0.088	0.050	− 0.143	0.152	0.056
2:15–2:30	0.113	0.070	− 0.114	0.108	− 0.002
2:30–2:45	0.124	0.073	− 0.102	0.137	− 0.026
2:45–3:00	0.135	0.082	− 0.111	0.174	− 0.033
3:00–Close	0.127	0.094	− 0.100	0.174	0.005

[a]Changes are not significantly different from zero at the 10% level of significance.

where P_t is the price at 15-minute intervals during the day and P_{open} is the opening price on the respective market.

These cumulative 15-minute interval returns are presented in Table 2 for the MMI futures contracts and in Table 3 for the spot MMI index.

The results from Table 2 are plotted in Figure 2 to make the comparison between days easier. The symbols are M = Monday, T = Tuesday, W = Wednesday, H = Thursday, F = Friday. In comparing the various days of MMI futures contracts, Wednesday stands out as a day where on average prices trend continually lower. Monday, Tuesday, and Thursday trend upward, while Friday with the most volatility winds up with little change. The MMI futures contract on average opens down on Monday for the first half hour and then trends upward for the remainder of the day. All of the other days on average have a positive return for the first 15 minutes of trading. Interestingly, there does appear to be a lunch hour effect from

Table 3. Cumulative 15-Minute Intraday Percentage Returns — MMI Futures.

	Monday	Tuesday	Wednesday	Thursday	Friday
Open–9:00 A.M.	− 0.015	− 0.011	0.026	0.005	0.003
9:00–9:15	− 0.055	0.045	0.027	0.032	0.060
9:15–9:30	− 0.046	0.068	0.028	0.016	0.11
9:30–9:45	− 0.026	0.050	0.028	0.011	0.088
9:45–10:00	− 0.024	0.056	0.008	0.032	0.018
10:00–10:15	− 0.023	0.050	− 0.014	0.048	0.082
10:15–10:30	− 0.021	0.039	− 0.014	0.049	0.063
10:30–10:45	− 0.016	0.057	− 0.006	0.054	0.087
10:45–11:00	− 0.021	0.053	− 0.017	0.056	0.086
11:00–11:15	− 0.011	0.076	− 0.005	0.062	0.084
11:15–11:30	− 0.001	0.077	0.008	0.077	0.090
11:30–11:45	0.013	0.083	0.004	0.094	0.087
11:45–12:00	0.025	0.089	− 0.021 [a]	0.115	0.104 [a]
12:00–12:15 P.M	0.028 [a]	0.100	− 0.022	0.131	0.103
12:15–12:30	0.028	0.099 [a]	− 0.028	0.127	0.114
12:30–12:45	0.027	0.103	− 0.031	0.127 [a]	0.113
12:45–1:00	0.007	0.096	− 0.049	0.129	0.090
1:00–1:15	0.008	0.074	− 0.026	0.125	0.089
1:15–1:30	0.007	0.083	− 0.038	0.131	0.098
1:30–1:45	− 0.007	0.092	− 0.036	0.141	0.099
1:45–2:00	0.021	0.110	− 0.052	0.139	0.070
2:00–2:15	0.040	0.103	− 0.054	0.161	0.065
2:15–2:30	0.071	0.146	− 0.070	0.131	0.045
2:30–2:45	0.064	0.128	− 0.069	0.117	0.033
2:45–Close	0.096	0.134	− 0.041	0.167	0.031

[a]Changes are not significantly different from zero at the 10% level of significance.

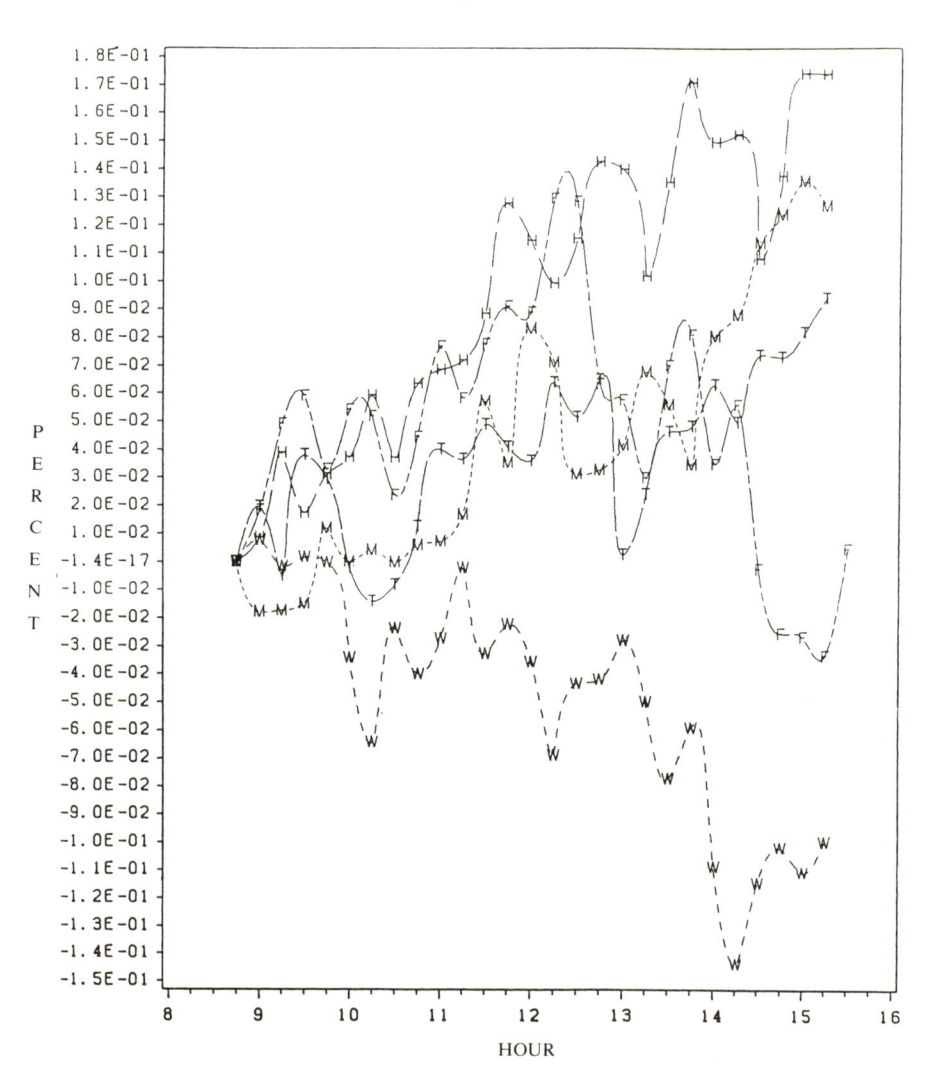

Figure 2.   Cumulated 15-minute intraday returns (futures).

noon to 1 P.M. where price changes tend to diminish except Monday and Wednesday.

From these results, while there appears to be difference between the mean returns during a given day, the difference may not be economically significant if you have to pay commissions. However, if you wish to incorporate these results in the timing of your purchase and sales of futures contracts, you may be better off buying near the close on Wednesday afternoon and selling near the close on Thursday.

In Figure 3, the cumulative intraday returns are plotted for the spot MMI. The weekend effect of negative returns on Mondays open is easily seen. Again of interest is the continual downward trend of prices on Wednesday. The lunch hour effect seems to be a little longer in the spot market lasting from noon to 1:30 P.M. where prices seem to decline. At the close prices are up on average for all days but Friday. On Friday prices begin trending downward at 1:30 P.M. and continue their downward trend until the close. Judging from Figure 3, the negative weekend effect in the spot

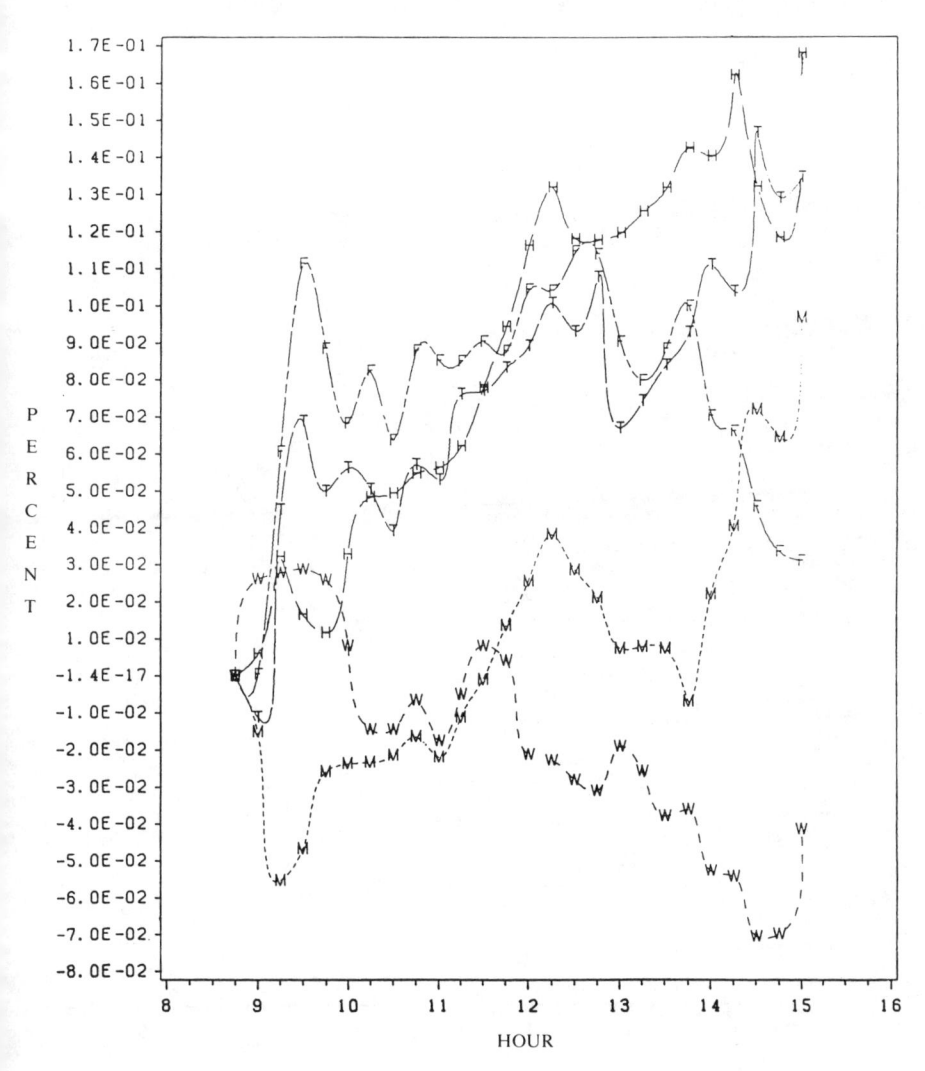

Figure 3.   Cumulated 15-minute intraday returns (spot).

market appears to start from around 1:30 P.M., not from the close on Friday, and end at around 9:00 A.M. on Monday. The return from 1:30 P.M. on Friday to 9:00 A.M. on Monday is calculated to be -0.1479% (with the standard deviation 0.0686), which is much lower than the return from close to open on Monday in Table 1.[2]

In an attempt to better understand the intraday return pattern and the day of the week effect, we examined the intraday volatility behavior in each day of the week. Figures 4 and 5 present the volatility of futures prices and spot prices, respectively, from the opening time to 9:00 A.M. and for every

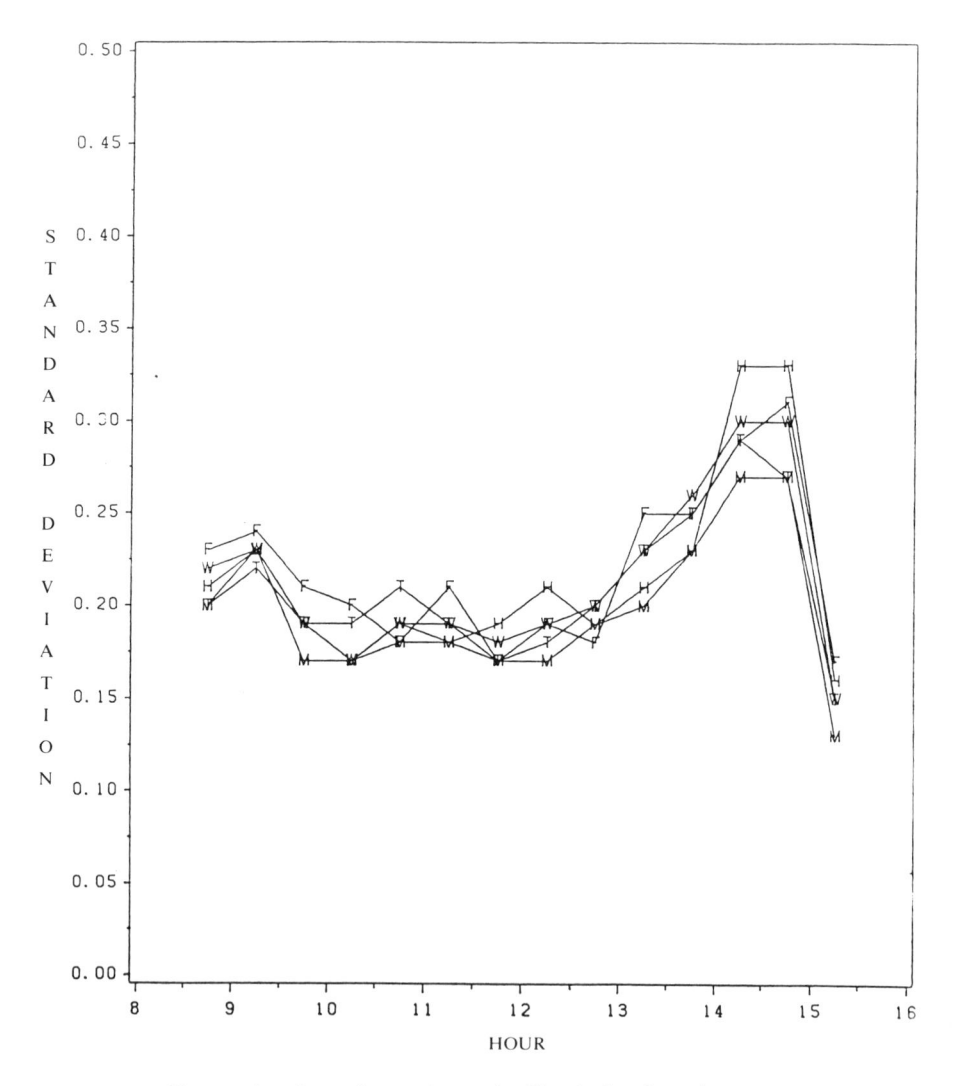

Figure 4.   Intraday price volatility behavior (futures).

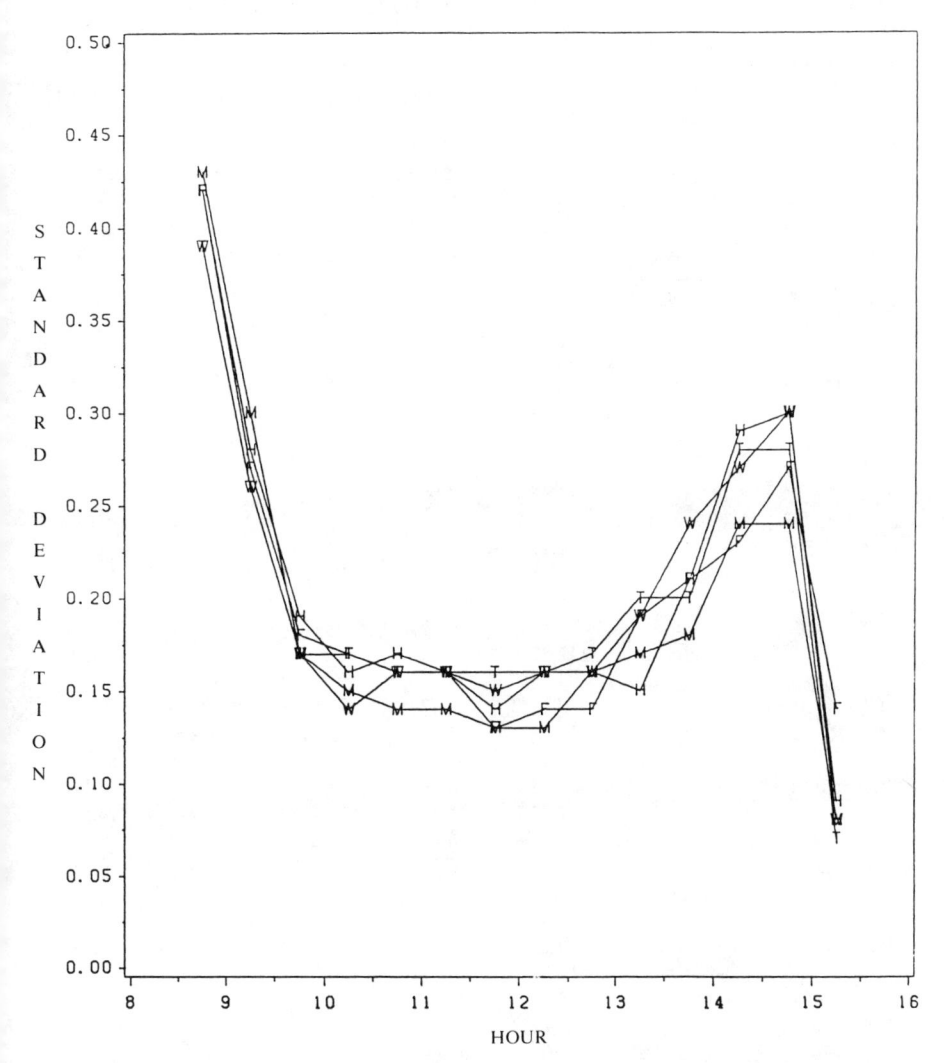

Figure 5. Intraday price volatility behavior (spot).

30 minutes thereafter. Since the index and its futures prices were reported at least once every minute and in some cases three or four times per minute, we had enough observations to calculate the volatility (the standard deviation) of prices. The number of observations for each calculation of the average standard deviation ranges from 82 to 102. Figure 5 presents the dramatic volatility behavior of spot prices. However, in Figure 4, it does not appear that such a significant pattern of volatility exists in the futures market, even though the volatility tends to decline around the closing time.

The volatility of spot prices is very high around the opening time (i.e.,

Time		Monday	Tuesday	Wednesday	Thursday	Friday
Open–9:00 A.M.	$\bar{\sigma}$	0.2045	0.2017	0.2178	0.2061	0.2317
	t-statistics	15.45	14.84	14.74	13.26	14.38
	Observations	88	93	92	94	95
9:00–9:30	$\bar{\sigma}$	0.2332	0.2250	0.2258	0.2308	0.2448
	t-statistics	18.05	16.91	15.70	15.00	15.19
	Observations	92	98	97	96	95
9:30–10:00	$\bar{\sigma}$	0.1742	0.1858	0.1862	0.1870	0.2076
	t-statistics	13.34	13.67	12.61	12.15	12.88
	Observations	90	94	92	96	95
10:00–10:30	$\bar{\sigma}$	0.1721	0.1912	0.1720	0.1703	0.2007
	t-statistics	13.18	14.22	11.57	10.89	12.26
	Observations	90	96	91	93	92
10:30–11:00	$\bar{\sigma}$	0.1799	0.2078	0.1893	0.1921	0.1845
	t-statistics	13.15	14.96	12.74	12.02	11.33
	Observations	82	90	91	89	93
11:00–11:30	$\bar{\sigma}$	0.1757	0.1882	0.1940	0.1755	0.2053
	t-statistics	13.15	13.62	12.92	11.17	12.27
	Observations	86	91	89	92	88
11:30–12:00	$\bar{\sigma}$	0.1685	0.1705	0.1784	0.1875	0.1699
	t-statistics	12.39	12.54	11.94	11.93	10.27
	Observations	83	94	90	92	90
12:00–12:30 P.M.	$\bar{\sigma}$	0.1654	0.1748	0.1913	0.2113	0.1880
	t-statistics	12.45	12.93	13.16	13.66	11.30
	Observations	87	95	95	95	89
12:30–1:00	$\bar{\sigma}$	0.1878	0.1983	0.1994	0.1949	0.1763
	t-statistics	14.05	14.75	13.42	12.46	10.59
	Observations	86	96	91	93	89
1:00–1:30	$\bar{\sigma}$	0.2033	0.2263	0.2335	0.2097	0.2540
	t-statistics	15.31	16.92	15.80	13.56	15.51
	Observations	87	97	92	95	92
1:30–2:00	$\bar{\sigma}$	0.2325	0.2473	0.2614	0.2304	0.2469
	t-statistics	17.80	18.39	18.26	14.98	15.16
	Observations	90	96	98	96	93
2:00–2:30	$\bar{\sigma}$	0.2672	0.2853	0.3021	0.3266	0.2934
	t-statistics	21.02	21.44	21.21	21.34	18.11
	Observations	95	98	99	97	94
2:30–3:00	$\bar{\sigma}$	0.2702	0.2697	0.2954	0.3281	0.3126
	t-statistics	21.14	20.58	20.64	21.43	19.40
	Observations	94	101	98	97	95
3:00–Close	$\bar{\sigma}$	0.1320	0.1476	0.1492	0.1603	0.1747
	t-statistics	10.38	11.09	10.37	10.53	11.01
	Observations	95	98	97	98	98
F-statistic[b]		9.72	8.39	9.95	11.35	7.60

[a]All of the statistics are significant at the 1% level.
[b]The F-statistic is for the hypothesis that all the coefficients are equal in the regression $\sigma_t = \alpha_1 D_1 + \alpha_2 D_2 + \cdots \alpha_{14} D_{14} + e_t$, where σ_t is the standard deviation of prices for the segmented time period t during the day and D_1 through D_{14} represent the segmented time dummies during the day.

Table 5.   Intraday Price Volatility (Spot)[a] (July 23, 1984 to July 15, 1986)

Time		Monday	Tuesday	Wednesday	Thursday	Friday
Open–9:00 A.M.	$\bar{\sigma}$	0.4260	0.3780	0.3882	0.4190	0.4231
	t-statistics	19.64	14.19	13.86	16.62	16.82
	Observations	40	39	39	40	41
9:00–9:30	$\bar{\sigma}$	0.2967	0.2597	0.2621	0.2843	0.2746
	t-statistics	21.40	15.30	14.91	17.83	17.79
	Observations	98	102	99	100	97
9:30–10:00	$\bar{\sigma}$	0.1700	0.1686	0.1717	0.1856	0.1791
	t-statistics	12.26	9.93	9.76	11.65	11.01
	Observations	98	102	99	100	98
10:00–10:30	$\bar{\sigma}$	0.1475	0.1683	0.1397	0.1633	0.1741
	t-statistics	10.64	9.91	7.95	10.25	10.70
	Observations	98	102	99	100	98
10:30–11:00	$\bar{\sigma}$	0.1448	0.1582	0.1614	0.1661	0.1561
	t-statistics	10.44	9.32	9.18	10.42	9.59
	Observations	98	102	99	100	98
11:00–11:30	$\bar{\sigma}$	0.1389	0.1536	0.1615	0.1592	0.1578
	t-statistics	10.02	9.05	9.19	9.98	9.70
	Observations	98	102	99	100	98
11:30–12:00	$\bar{\sigma}$	0.1293	0.1594	0.1529	0.1364	0.1335
	t-statistics	9.33	9.39	8.70	8.56	8.20
	Observations	98	102	99	100	98
12:00–12:30 P.M.	$\bar{\sigma}$	0.1284	0.1640	0.1643	0.1629	0.1364
	t-statistics	9.26	9.66	9.35	10.22	8.38
	Observations	98	102	99	100	98
12:30–1:00	$\bar{\sigma}$	0.1626	0.1736	0.1602	0.1596	0.1374
	t-statistics	11.73	10.23	9.113	10.01	8.44
	Observations	98	102	99	100	98
1:00–1:30	$\bar{\sigma}$	0.1682	0.1964	0.1872	0.1533	0.1924
	t-statistics	12.14	11.57	10.65	9.62	11.76
	Observations	98	102	99	100	97
1:30–2:00	$\bar{\sigma}$	0.1786	0.2013	0.2374	0.2099	0.2146
	t-statistics	12.89	11.86	13.51	13.17	13.12
	Observations	98	102	99	100	97
2:00–2:30	$\bar{\sigma}$	0.2416	0.2756	0.2736	0.2865	0.2336
	t-statistics	17.43	16.23	15.56	17.92	14.29
	Observations	98	102	99	100	97
2:30–3:00	$\bar{\sigma}$	0.2353	0.2786	0.2952	0.3033	0.2672
	t-statistics	16.97	16.41	16.79	19.03	16.34
	Observations	98	102	99	100	97
3:00–Close	$\bar{\sigma}$	0.0835	0.0709	0.0834	0.0937	0.1365
	t-statistics	5.87	4.10	4.70	5.82	8.22
	Observations	93	98	97	98	94
F-statistic[b]		25.52	14.19	14.75	20.89	15.20

[a]All of the statistics are significant at the 1% level.
[b]The F-statistic is for the hypothesis that all the coefficients are equal in the regression $\sigma_t = \alpha_1 D_1 + \alpha_2 D_2 + \cdots \alpha_{14} D_{14} + e_t$, where σ_t is the standard deviation of prices for the segmented time period t during the day and D_1 through D_{14} represent the segmented time dummies during the day.

from opening to 9:00 A.M.) and in general declines until noon and goes up after the lunch hour.[3] It is also noticeable that the volatility drops significantly prior to the close in each day. Tables 4 and 5 present the average intraday volatility of prices and its t-statistic and F-statistic in each day during the week for the futures and spot markets, respectively. The F-statistic is for the hypothesis that the average volatilities in all the segmented trading hours during the day are equal. All of the F-statistics in Tables 4 and 5 are significant at the 1% level, which implies that there exists a systematic volatility pattern in the futures and spot market. Note, however, that the F-statistics in the spot market are much higher than those in the futures market, which is attributable to the high volatility of prices around the opening time in the spot market.

The high volatility of spot prices around the opening time may not be surprising since the information created in nontrading hours is likely to affect stock prices when the market is open. French and Roll [4], using returns from closing to closing prices of common stocks listed in the New York and American Stock Exchanges, compared the return variance during trading hours with that during nontrading hours and found that the former is much higher than the latter. They suggested three hypotheses for the observed volatility pattern: (1) more public information arrival during trading hours, (2) private information only affecting prices through the trading of informed investors, particularly when the market is open, and (3) the trading noise such as investors overreaction to each other's trades that might increase the volatility of prices when the market is open. Our results are consistent with the second and third hypotheses. If investors expect the higher volatility after the market is open, the price may decline for a short period of time so that we may observe negative returns from closing to opening prices. Note, however, that the volatility of spot prices around the opening time remains the same across all days during the week. If the volatility is proportional to the number of nontrading hours, then Monday's volatility is presumably at least three times as much as other days. The same level of volatility around the opening time across all days and the negative return from closing to opening prices only on Monday still leave the Monday effect puzzling. Nevertheless, the absence of the existence of a significant volatility pattern in the futures market suggests that the well-documented day of the week effect may be attributable to some institutional factors that are present only in the spot market.[4]

III. CONCLUSIONS

The day of the week results reported here confirm the findings of other studies: there is a weekend effect that on average depresses prices on

Monday for the stocks of the MMI index. No such day of the week effect is present in MMI futures contracts.

However, using the intraday data, we provide new findings in this paper. First, the negative weekend effect in the spot market is found to take place starting from around 1:30 P.M. on Friday (i.e., not from closing) until around 9:00 A.M. on Monday, 30 minutes after trading is open. Second, the volatility of spot prices from the opening time to 9:00 A.M. is found to be abnormally high compared to other trading hours. However, we could not find a similar intraday volatility pattern in the futures market. The absence of such a volatility pattern in the futures market, and the similar level of volatility in the spot market around the opening time across all days leave the negative Monday effect still puzzling, but at least the results suggest that the day of the week effect in the spot market may be attributable to some institutional factors unique to the spot market. Third, there appears to be a lunch hour effect, where price movements are minimal during the 12 to 1 hour in both the futures and spot market. Most puzzling of all was the negative trend in prices for both the spot and futures markets on Wednesday. Further work needs to be done to explain this mid-week occurrence.

APPENDIX: THE MAJOR MARKET INDEX COMPANIES [5]

1. American Express
2. AT&T (new)
3. Chevron
4. Dupont
5. Eastman Kodak
6. Exxon
7. General Electric
8. General Motors
9. IBM
10. Inter Paper
11. Merck
12. Minn M&M
13. Procter & Gamble
14. Sears, Roebuck
15. U.S. Steel
16. Coca Cola
17. Dow Chemical
18. Johnson and Johnson
19. Mobil
20. Phillip Morris

NOTES

1.   For example, Lakonishok and Levi [8] argue that Friday trades carry slightly different settlement procedures, requiring 5 business days plus an additional day for check clearance. Due to the placement of Friday in the week, two additional weekend days are required before payment can be cleared. Thus, the normal settlement process initiated on Friday increased from 8 to 10 days. Dyl and Martin [2] tested this hypothesis. Noting that the settlement period was only 4 days prior to 1968, they calculated daily returns prior to and after this period and found that the Monday effect was not affected from one sample to another, rejecting Lakonishok and Levi's hypothesis. Lakonishok and Levi [9] argued in turn that 4 day settlement was not honored in practice prior to 1968 and they diluted their hypothesis, suggesting that settlement procedures could explain only a portion of negative returns on Monday.

2.   For the futures, the return from 1:30 P.M. on Friday to 9:00 A.M. on Monday is −0.1089% (with the standard deviation 0.6186), which is also much lower than the close-to-open return on Monday in Table 1, although it is not still statistically significant.

3.   It is likely that all of the stocks in the MMI index do not begin to be traded simultaneously. If some of the stocks were not traded for a short period of time after the market is open, the volatility of the index would be lower than the case where all of the stocks are traded at the same time. Thus, the volatility of the index reported in this paper would be a conservative measure and the comparison of volatilities between the spot and futures markets is intact since the spot price volatility is much higher than the futures price volatility.

4.   We also examined the intraday trading volume of futures to see whether the intraday return and volatility patterns are related to the trading activities during the day. In general, trading is most active on Tuesday, followed by Wednesday, Monday, Thursday, and Friday. Regardless of the day, the trading volume increases significantly in an hour after the market is open until around 11:00 A.M. and becomes less active for about 2 hours thereafter. It regains activity from 1:00 P.M. until the market is closed. However, the intraday return patterns of futures do not appear to be influenced by the trading activity during the day. The trading volume for the spot MMI is not available since it is not an actually traded portfolio. However, if the intraday trading volumes of the stocks in the MMI were available, it may confirm similar findings in the spot market.

5.   The first 15 companies are also included in the DJIA, the price-weighted average of 30 NYSE blue chip stocks.

REFERENCES

1.   Cornell, B., "The Weekly Pattern in Stock Returns: Cash versus Futures: A Note," *Journal of Finance* 40 (June 1985), 583–588.

2.   Dyl, E. A., and S. A. Martin, Jr., "Weekend Effects on Stock Return: A Comment," *Journal of Finance* 40 (March 1985), 347–350.

3.   French, K. R., "Stock Returns and Weekend Effect," *Journal of Financial Economics* 8 (1980), 55–69.

4.   French, K. R., and R. Roll, "Stock Return Variances: The Arrival of Information and The Reaction of Traders," working paper, University of Chicago, 1985.

5.   Gibbons, M. R., and P. Hess, "Day of the Week Effects and Asset Returns," *Journal of Business* 54 (1981), 579–596.

6.   Harris, L., "How to Profit from Intradaily Stock Returns," *Journal of Portfolio Management* (Winter 1986), 61–64.

7. Keim, D., and R. Stambaugh, "A Further Investigation of the Weekend Effect in Stock Returns," *Journal of Finance* 39 (1984), 819–835.

8. Lakonishok, J., and M. Levi, "Weekend Effects on Stock Returns: A Note," *Journal of Finance* 37 (1982), 883–889.

9. Lakonishok, J., and M. Levi, "Weekend Effects on Stock Returns: A Reply," *Journal of Finance* 40 (1985), 351–352.

10. Rogalski, R. J., "New Findings Regarding Day of the Week Returns over Trading and Nontrading Periods," unpublished working paper, Dartmouth College, 1984.

THE MONDAY EFFECT AND SPECULATIVE OPPORTUNITIES IN THE STOCK-INDEX FUTURES MARKET

Dan R. Pieptea* and Eliezer Prisman**

I. INTRODUCTION

Extensive evidence supporting the existence of the Monday effect has been presented in the literature. Discovered by Cross [3], the Monday effect is a seasonality of the stock market: equity issues earn systematically lower returns on Mondays than on any other day of the week. Early studies

*University of Texas at Dallas.
**Bar-Ilan University.

The paper has benefited considerably from comments and discussions with Robert Daigler, Edward Dyl, Joanne Hill, Joseph Finnerty, Michael Rozeff, Lemma Senbet, and Laura Starks. The usual disclaimer applies.

Advances in Futures and Options Research, Vol. 3, pages 319–328.

conducted by French [6], Gibbons and Hess [7],[1] Lakonishok and Levi [10, 11], and later by Jaffe and Westerfield [9], Smirlock and Starks [13], and Harris [8] document this seasonality. Covering different periods and employing distinct statistical techniques, all the studies agree on the existence of the Monday effect but no consensus exists over an explanation of this potential market inefficiency.

The reason this inefficiency has persisted (even after it was discovered and publicized) may be due to the difficulty in taking advantage of the speculative opportunities created by it. Uncertainty of returns and transaction costs make it impossible to speculate on this kind of market inefficiency in the spot market.[2] However, the introduction of stock index futures has made it possible to take on a large amount of market risk, and join or exit the market at an extremely low transaction cost in a timely fashion. And because margin requirements for stock-index futures can be satisfied with T-bill holdings, it is possible to speculate on the Monday effect at virtually no cost,[3] provided the weekend seasonality also persists in the futures market. The important question that this paper addresses is whether there are any speculative opportunities in the stock-index futures market generated by the Monday effect.

Although this subject has not been fully explored, controversy already exists. Using data covering the first 27 months after S&P 500 index futures started trading on April 21, 1982, Cornell [2] finds no evidence of a Monday effect in the S&P 500 futures market. Cornell's results contrast markedly with those reported by Dyl and Maberly [4] who used a similar procedure for a slightly different period and confirm the existence of a close-to-open weekend effect in the S&P 500 Index Futures. This controversy, due in part to the unavailability of data over a long period for a mature market at the time the studies were conducted, calls for reconsideration of intraweek seasonalities of the stock-index futures.

This paper extends the discussion of the Monday effect in the stock-index futures markets in several directions. (1) It studies the Friday close to Monday close effect for the S&P 500 cash index and index futures contracts over a more recent and mature period of the index futures market, after options on S&P 500 index futures started trading. (2) It investigates futures market efficiency as a function of time to expiration of the contract. The S&P 500 spot index, nearby, and next to nearby contracts are included in the study and accounted for separately. (3) Both expected return and risk components of the risk/expected-return tradeoff are investigated.

We found a Monday effect consistent with previous literature for the spot index but the equal mean return hypothesis cannot be rejected for the futures contracts. Surprisingly, the next to nearby contract is even more efficient than the nearby contract. A new intraweek seasonality effect related to systematic differences in the standard deviation of returns is identified. The lower standard deviation of Monday returns adds meaning to the weekend effect. Not only are expected returns lower but they are consistently so, with a lower standard deviation than on other weekdays. The standard deviation seasonality is found to persist somewhat more in the futures market than the mean-return effect.

The index futures market is found consistent with the efficient market hypothesis with no evidence of speculative opportunities based on intra-week seasonalities. The paper also finds that the seasonal pattern in the spot market has been affected by the presence of index futures and predicts that extended use of program trading will render the spot market even more efficient.

Section II describes the data and methodology used, while Section III presents the results and their meaning. Evidence of efficiency of stock-index futures is found and a new explanation based on investor's psychology is given for the Monday effect. Section IV summarizes the conclusions.

II. DATA AND METHODOLOGY

To ensure a mature and liquid index futures market in which contracts are priced efficiently relative to the underlying spot index is used, the sample period begins after options on the futures contract started trading on the Chicago Mercantile Exchange. Statistical tests were conducted using daily S&P 500 data for the period March 18, 1983 to June 27, 1986.

There are four futures contracts on the S&P 500, each expiring on the third Friday of their delivery month.[4] The data consist of daily closing prices collected from the *Wall Street Journal* for all the contracts that were traded on a particular day, namely the nearby contract, the next to nearby contract, and the most distant contract. In a few instances where the cash index was missing, closing prices were obtained from the Chicago Mercantile Exchange.

Earlier studies (e.g., French [6] and Rogalski [12]) found statistically significant differences between weekend, holiday, and holiday-weekend returns. To avoid data contamination, a total of 28 holiday and holiday-weekend data were eliminated from the data set.

The delivery months for the S&P 500 index futures contracts are March, June, September, and December. Only up to three contracts are traded at a given time. Statistics for the nearby and next to nearby contracts were calculated. Contracts further into the future were disregarded due to a low open interest and lack of market liquidity that ultimately results in irrelevant closing quotes. However, the most distant contract of previous Friday was used to calculate the return of a contract for the first Monday on which it became next to nearby.

DAN R. PIEPTEA and ELIEZER PRISMAN

Returns net of dividends for the cash index were based on closing prices. By analogy, returns for the futures contracts are defined as $R_t = (P_{t+1} - P_t)/P_t$. R_t should not be interpreted as fractional return on the investor's position but rather offers a base of comparison between the spot and futures market (e.g., Black [1]).

The test was conducted in two phases. In the first step the return distribution across the week is investigated. The ex-post expectation and standard deviation of daily annualized returns and correlation coefficients between the futures contracts and the spot index have been calculated by day of the week. Unbiased estimators were used for mean and variance of returns. The results are listed in Table 1. In comparing our results with those reported by other studies, the reader is reminded that we report returns on an annualized basis.

In the second phase the statistical hypotheses of equal average and equal standard deviations of returns were tested. The standard t test procedure for normal populations with unknown means and variance is employed. Tables 2 and 3 present the level of statistical significance for the equal mean return and equal standard deviation tests for all adjacent days of the week. The results are discussed in the next section.

Confidence intervals were calculated at the .9 probability level for the difference of expected returns for pairwise adjacent days. A symmetric confidence interval around zero indicates equal expected rates, while an asymmetric one indicates different expected returns. The results are listed in Table 4. For comparisons of standard deviations, confidence intervals were constructed for the ratios of standard deviations at the probability level of .9. Equal return standard deviations are indicated by symmetry around one. The results are tabulated in Table 5.

Table 1. Average and Standard Deviation Return by Day of Week[a]

	Mon	Tue	Wed	Thr	Fri
1. Avg(R_I)	-4.93	42.33	3.16	23.5	32.59
2. Avg(R_{NC})	19.35	9.10	4.83	23.57	6.75
3. Avg(R_{NNC})	17.61	16.18	6.61	17.08	13.65
4. $\sigma(R_I)$	2.11	2.45	2.41	1.97	2.23
5. $\sigma(R_{NC})$	2.04	2.41	2.45	2.13	2.09
6. $\sigma(R_{NNC})$	2.09	2.46	2.48	2.07	2.12
7. $\rho(R_I, R_{NC})$	.81	.78	.83	.87	.85
8. $\rho(R_I, R_{NNC})$	.81	.78	.83	.87	.85
9. Observations	153	156	166	163	162

[a]Avg(R_I), Avg(R_{NC}), Avg(R_{NNC}) = average annualized return for the spot index, nearby, and next to nearby contracts, respectively; $\sigma(R_I)$, $\sigma(R_{NC})$, $\sigma(R_{NNC})$ = standard deviation of the annualized returns for the index, nearby, and next to nearby contracts, respectively; $\rho(R_I, R_{NC})$, $\rho(R_I, R_{NNC})$ = correlation coefficients between spot index and the two futures contracts.

Table 2. Equal Mean Return Hypothesis: Statistical Significance α[a]

	Mon/Tue	Tue/Wed	Wed/Thr	Thr/Fri	Fri/Mon
Spot	.07	.15[b]	.40[b]	.71[b]	.09
	(302)	(318)	(316)	(313)	(312)
NC	.69[b]	.88[b]	.47[b]	.48[b]	.59[b]
	(300)	(319)	(322)	(322)	(312)
NNC	.96[b]	.73[b]	.68[b]	.88[b]	.87[b]
	(301)	(319)	(318)	(322)	(312)

[a]NC, NNC = nearby and next to nearby contract, respectively. Each cell represents the level of statistical significance for the equal mean returns. Numbers in parentheses represent the degrees of freedom of the t-distribution.
[b]Significant at the .10 level.

Table 3. Equal Return Variance Hypothesis: Statistical Significance[a]

	Mon/Tue	Tue/Wed	Wed/Thr	Thr/Fri	Fri/Mon
Spot	.07	.85[b]	.01	.03	20[b]
NC	.05	.84[b]	.08	.78[b]	.80[b]
NNC	.05	.92[b]	.03	.77[b]	.90[b]

[a]NC, NNC = nearby and next to nearby contract, respectively. Each cell represents the level of statistical significance for the equal standard deviation of returns.
[b]Significant at the .10 level.

Table 4. Difference of Expected Returns: Confidence Intervals[a]

	Mon/Tue	Tue/Wed	Wed/Thr	Thr/Fri	Fri/Mon
Spot	(−.90, −.41)	(−.15, .84)	(−.61, .20)	(−.49, .31)	(−.03, .90)
NC	(−.31, .52)	(−.40, .49)	(−.60, .23)	(−.21, .55)	(−.51, .26)
NNC	(−.42, .44)	(−.36, .55)	(−.51, .31)	(−.35, 41)	(−.43, .35)

[a]For example, column Mon/Tue indicates the confidence interval for $E_{Monday}(R) - E_{Tuesday}(R)$. NC, NNC = nearby and next to nearby contract, respectively. Confidence intervals correspond to a probability level of 90%.

Table 5. Ratio of Standard Deviations: Confidence Intervals[a]

	Mon/Tue	Tue/Wed	Wed/Thr	Thr/Fri	Fri/Mon
Cash	(.56, .96)	(.79, 1.34)	(1.15, 1.93)	(.55, .93)	(.94, 1.59)
NC	(.55, .94)	(.75, 1.25)	(1.01, 1.70)	(.80, 1.35)	(.80, 1.35)
NNC	(.56, .95)	(.75, 1.28)	(1.02, 1.86)	(.74, 1.24)	(.78, 1.33)

[a]Column Mon/Tue describes the ratio of standard deviations of returns $\sigma_{Monday}(R)/s_{Tuesday}(R)$. $\sigma_{Tuesday}(R)$. NC, NNC = nearby and next to nearby contract, respectively. Confidence intervals correspond to a probability level of 90%.

III. RESULTS

Consistent with other studies documenting the Monday effect in the stock market, we found *spot index returns to be lower on Mondays on the average*. The Mondays annualized average return is -4.93% which is minimal for all days of the week. (See line 1 in Table 1.) The statistical hypothesis of equal expected returns on Monday/Friday and Monday/ Tuesday must be rejected at the statistical level of .10. In addition, the confidence intervals for the mean difference returns indicate lower Monday returns. The confidence interval for $E_{Monday}(R_I)-E_{Tuesday}(R_I)$ is $(-.90, -.41)$ and the confidence interval for $E_{Friday}(R_I)-E_{Monday}(R_I)$ is $(-.04, .90)$. Both intervals are strongly asymmetric with respect to 0 indicating a relative low Monday expected return. The confidence intervals for differences of other expected returns are balanced around zero (Table 3), supporting the equal mean return hypothesis for other days.

There is no evidence of a Monday effect in the index futures market both for the nearby and the next to nearby contracts. In fact, the data suggest that in the futures market the Monday effect is slightly reversed with returns potentially higher than on other days of the week. The average return for the Monday nearby contract is 19.35%, which is second only after Thursday, and for the next to nearby contract the Monday return is 17.61%, highest for all the days of the week (Table 1, lines 2 and 3). The comparative inferences support these findings as well. As shown in Table 2, the levels of statistical significance of equal mean for adjacent days are in the same range for Monday as for other days of the week. The confidence intervals for the mean return differences have the boundaries balanced around the origin, (see Table 4), which is consistent with the fact that the equal mean return hypothesis cannot be rejected. The small asymmetry of the Monday/Tuesday and Friday/Monday confidence intervals correspond to somewhat higher Monday returns for the futures contracts.

As we mover from the nearby contract to the next to nearby contract, market efficiency improves. As shown in Table 2, the statistical significance of the equal means hypothesis increases for Monday/Tuesday from .69 to .96 and for Friday/Monday from .59 to .87. Also, the symmetry around the origin of the confidence intervals for the mean return differences improves, indicating an increased efficiency for distant contracts. While we do not have an explanation for it, we find this result particulary interesting.

The standard deviation of daily annualized returns is statistically low on Mondays both for the cash index and the futures contract. A simple inspection of lines 4, 5, and 6 of Table 1 shows the standard deviation of returns lower on Mondays and Thursdays. While mean returns are equal, the relatively low standard deviation of returns on Mondays and Thursdays persist in the futures market. The equal standard deviation of returns on

Monday versus Tuesday must be rejected at the .10 level for the cash index and all of the contracts. The same applies to the hypothesis of equal standard deviations for Thursday versus Wedneday. However, statistical significance for test of equal standard deviations in the futures contract impoved for other adjacent days both for Monday and Thursday (Table 3).

The relatively lower Monday return standard deviation reinforces the Monday mean-return effect for the cash index. Not only are mean returns lower on Mondays but they are consistently so, and the mean is more meaningful than on other days. The statistical significance of equal variances is restored for futures for some of the adjacent days. The maximum level of significance for equal standard deviation for futures return increases from .20 to .90 for Friday/Monday (Table 3). Again, we find the futures market to be more efficient than the spot index. While we find it interesting that the return standard deviation is statistically signif-icantly low on Mondays, we are short of an explanation.

Return correlation coefficients between spot and futures contracts are not significantly different for the different days of the week. The correlation coefficients range from .78 to .85 (Table 1, lines 7 and 8). No consistent pattern can be observed as one moves across days of the week or from nearby to next to nearby contracts. Albeit the futures market is more efficient than the cash index, the increase in market efficiency does not happen at an expense of their comovement as measured by correlation.

The fact that the equal mean return hypothesis cannot be rejected for the stock-index futures is theoretically important as it provides an explanation of the spot-index Monday effect. Several explanations of the Monday effect have been attempted, none of which proved satisfactory. Explanations for the observed weekend effect that have been rejected include the calendar time hypothesis, which asserts that expected return for Monday is three times the expected return for other days of the week (French [6]), the delay between trading and settlement due to check clearing (Lakonishok and Levi [10]), and measurement errors in returns (Gibbons and Hess [7]). We conjecture that *the Monday effect is due to a psychological phenomenon related to the reluctance of the human mind to admit its own mistakes.* It has to do with the aversion to cutting losses short. It is only human to postpone digestion of negative news of individual issues to the weekend when careful examination can be given to the portfolio. Such an interpreta-tion is consistent with previous empirical findings. Rogalski [12] found returns following other than weekend holidays to be consistent with other weekdays rather than with Monday returns. On the other hand, French [6] found over a period of 6 months when the New York Stock Exchange was closed on each Wednesday that Thursday returns were consistent with the Monday effect. This suggests that the Monday effect is not a holiday effect but rather a periodical holiday effect. It is more likely from a psychological standpoint that investors defer and schedule analysis of negative news for a periodical holiday than for some holiday such as the 4th of July.

As negative information is digested over the weekend selling pressure is prolonged and one would expect the Monday effect to materialize at the beginning of the trading day, when orders placed as a result of delayed analysis are executed. Indeed, using DJIA data from 1974 to 1984, Rogalski [12] found that Monday effect is actually a close to open effect. Using transaction data for 14 months ending January 1983 for all NYSE stocks, Harris [8] found that for large firms the negative Monday returns accrued before opening. He also finds a significant difference between Monday and other days of the week in the first 45 minutes of trading, when Monday returns are negative. On other weekdays during the same period returns are 5 to 10 times as large as returns accruing later in the day. While the cash-index responds to prolonged selling pressure on individual equity issues with negative news, the futures market is efficient, in the sense that it adjusts instantaneously to the negative or positive news the same.

While the Monday effect is present in the cash market, its magnitude is lower than that for earlier periods (e.g., Gibbons and Hess found an average Monday return of -32%). Smirlock and Starks [13] found that the Monday effect has "moved up" in the day. We believe that the presence of index futures has contributed greatly to the decrease of this seasonality. As program trading increases in importance as a means of arbitrage between index futures and cash, the Monday effect will decrease and eventually disappear.

IV. CONCLUDING REMARKS

This paper has investigated the intraweek effects in stock return and index futures for the S&P 500 over the period March 18, 1983 to June 27, 1986. Several observations emerge from the analysis. First, we found statistical evidence of a Monday effect for the spot index consistent with but of less magnitude than studies covering earlier periods. A seasonal effect related to small standard deviation of returns on Monday has been identified for the spot index. This seasonality persists somewhat in the index futures market. No evidence of lower Monday returns have been found for either the nearby or the next to nearby stock-index contracts and hence we assert that stock-index futures are consistent with the efficient market hypothesis.

Stock-index futures efficiency has a multiple importance. For practitioners it means that no excess profits can be derived using a strategy based on intraweek seasonality effects. In a theoretical plane it offers an explanation of the spot index Monday effect based on investor's psychology. Due to human reluctance to admit mistakes, more of the negative news is digested over the weekend, prolonging the selling pressure of the losing issues to the first trading hours on Monday. Given the price discovery function of futures, stock-index contracts reflect both negative and positive information instantaneously as it becomes available. Finally, we anticipate futures market efficiency and arbitrage between futures and cash to erode the Monday effect away, rendering the spot market free of intraweek seasonalities.

NOTES

1. Gibbons and Hess found that this effect applies to the T-bill market also.
2. French [6] simulated a strategy based on the weekend effect from 1953 to 1977 to derive an excess annual return of 7.9% over the buy and hold strategy. However, when transaction costs were considered, the buy and hold strategy consistently yielded a higher return.
3. At current fee schedules it is possible to take on and dispose of $130,000 worth of market risk at a transaction cost of $27 from off the trading floor, by buying and selling one S&P 500 contract through a futures discount broker.
4. Before June of 1984 the contracts were expiring on the third Thursday of the delivery month.

REFERENCES

1. Black, F., "The Pricing of Commodity Contracts," *Journal of Financial Economics,* 3 (June 1976), 167–179.
2. Cornell, B., "The Weekly Pattern in Stock Returns: Cash versus Futures: A Note," *The Journal of Finance,* XL, 2 (June 1985), 583–588.
3. Cross, F., "The Behavior of Stock Prices on Fridays and Mondays," *Financial Analyst Journal* (Nov.–Dec. 1973), 67–69.
4. Dyl, E. A., and E. D. Maberly, "The Weekly Pattern in Stock Index Futures: A Further Note," *The Journal of Finance* XLI, 5 (December 1986), 1149–1152.
5. Dyl, E. A., and S. A. Martin, Jr., "Weekend Effects of Stock Returns: A Comment," *The Journal of Finance,* XL, 1 (March 1985), 347–349.
6. French, K. R., "Stock Returns and the Weekend Effect," *Journal of Financial Economics* 8 (1980), 55–69.
   Gibbons, M. R., and P. Hess, "Day of the Week Effects and Asset Returns," *Journal of Business* 54, 4, (1981), 579–596.
8. Harris, L., "A Study on Transaction Data of Weekly and Intradaily Patterns in Stock Returns," *The Journal of Financial Economics* 16 (1986), 99–117.
9. Jaffe, J., and R. Westerfield, "The Week-End Effect in Common Stock Returns: The International Evidence," *The Journal of Finance,* XL, 2 (June 1985), 433–454.
10. Lakonishok, J., and M. Levi, "Weekend Effects on Stock Returns: A Note," *The Journal of Finance* XXXVII, 3 (June 1982), 883–889.
11. Lakonishok, J., and M., Levi, "Weekend Effects on Stock Returns: A Reply," *The Journal of Finance* XL, 1 (March 1985), 351–352.

12. Rogalski, R. J., "New Findings Rearding Day-of-the-Week Returns over Trading and Nontrading Periods: A Note," *The Journal of Finance* XXXIX, 5 (December 1984), 1603–1614.
13. Smirlock, M., and L. Starks, "Day of the Week and Intraday Effects in Stock Returns," *Journal of Financial Economics* 17 (1986), 197–210.

CASH VERSUS FUTURES PRICES AND THE WEEKEND EFFECT: THE CANADIAN EVIDENCE

Trevor W. Chamberlain,* C. Sherman Cheung,* and Clarence C. Y. Kwan*

I. INTRODUCTION

One of the most widely documented, but least understood, patterns of stock price behavior in the United States is the so-called weekend effect, according to which measured returns for the trading day following a weekend are, unlike any other day of the week, significantly negative.[1,2]

*Faculty of Business, McMaster University.

Financial support for this research was provided by the Social Sciences and Humanities Research Council of Canada. Research assistance by Lyle Lisitza is gratefully acknowledged.

Advances in Futures and Options Research, Vol. 3, pages 329–339.

Recent studies by Cornell [3], Dyl and Maberly [5, 6], and Junkus [12] have extended the investigation of this phenomenon by attempting to establish whether it persists in the futures markets for stock indices as well. Unfortunately, these studies have produced conflicting and what, collectively, can be described only as inconclusive results. In an effort to reconcile these results and, at the same time, establish whether the weekend effect characterizes futures markets outside of the United States, the present study was undertaken.

With regard to the Friday close to Monday close and Monday trading day periods, both Cornell and Dyl and Maberly conclude that there has been no evidence of a weekend effect in either the cash or the futures market for the S&P 500 since the introduction of futures trading. As for the period between the Friday close and the Monday open, however, Cornell reports returns that are negative and statistically significant in the cash market, but positive, albeit insignificant, in the futures market. In contrast, Dyl and Maberly, utilizing additional observations, find that the futures market, like the cash market, experiences significantly negative changes in price during the weekend nontrading period. [3,4]

Whereas Cornell and Dyl and Maberly confine their attention to the S&P 500 and its futures market, Junkus also examines the behavior of the NYSE Composite and the Value Line indexes, as well as that of their respective futures contracts. Her study focuses on close to close returns and, like Cornell and Dyl and Maberly, in their close to close period work, she finds no indication of a weekend effect in either the cash or the futures market.

On the basis of the United States evidence, the only inference that might reasonably be made is that the tendency for weekend returns in the cash market to be negative, at least for the Friday close to Monday open period, has not disappeared following the introduction of futures trading. As for the price change behavior of futures contracts for stock indexes, the inconclusive results obtained by Cornell, Dyl and Maberly, and Junkus suggest that further analysis is required.

Outside of the United States the weekend effect in the cash market for common stocks has been examined previously by Jaffe and Westerfield [11]. Their study, which involved widely followed indexes in the United Kingdom, Japan, Australia, and Canada, included, in the case of the latter, close to close returns for the TSE 300 Composite between January 1976 and November 1983. The results for the TSE 300 were similar to those produced by the early United States studies utilizing close to close returns data; that is, the mean return for Monday was negative and the hypothesis that the daily returns were equal was rejected at the 1% level.

Following Jaffe and Westerfield, the present paper begins, in the next section, by examining the daily price change behavior of the TSE 300 Composite Index, together with that of its futures, which are traded on the

Toronto Futures Exchange. It then goes on to abstract from the potentially confounding turn of the year effects identified by Rogalski [18] and Smirlock and Starks [19] in the United States cash market for common stocks by analyzing the results obtained when price changes for 6 weeks of trading around the end of each year are removed from the data set. This is followed by an examination of the daily changes in the futures-cash basis, in an effort to clarify the extent to which the price change behavior of the futures market parallels that of the cash market. Next, as a means of determining whether the weekend effect in the futures market, to the extent it exists, can be attributed to the behavior of the cash market, the results of tracking the relationships between day to day price changes in the two markets are considered. The paper concludes with a brief summary of the study's results and their implications.

II. DATA AND ANALYSIS OF DAILY PRICE CHANGES

The data, which, in the case of the cash index, were obtained directly from the Toronto Stock Exchange and, in the case of the futures, from the Toronto Futures Exchange, consist of time-ordered records of the closing levels of the TSE 300 Index between March 1978 and December 1986 and of the closing levels of futures contracts written on that index between January 1984 and December 1986. Like earlier studies the present one attempts to abstract from the effects of holidays in so far as it excludes all long weekends from the sample. Thus, the observations utilized are for "normal" 1 day and weekend periods.

Following previous studies the present one also chooses the futures contract nearest to maturity at the time of the initial observation because near contracts typically have the largest open interest and are the most actively traded. However, at the beginning of the month of expiration, it switches to the next to near contract in order to capture the shift in trading activity that appears to occur at that time. In this respect the present approach follows the switching convention adopted by Cornell.

The closing prices for each market were used to generate close to close price changes, ΔP_t, calculated as $\Delta P_t = P_t - P_{t-1}$, where P_t is the level of the TSE 300 or its futures at the close of trading on day t.[5] In order to highlight the impact, if any, of futures trading on daily price change behavior in the cash market, the observations for the latter were resolved into two subsets, representing the periods before and after the introduction of TSE 300 futures contracts on January 16, 1984.

The daily means, associated t-statistics, and standard deviations of the daily price changes for the two cash market time series are reported in A and B of Table 1. The patterns of daily means for the two series are similar; that

Table 1. Summary Statistics for the Daily Close to Close Price Changes (ΔP_t) of the TSE 300 Index and TSE 300 Index Futures

Statistic	Monday	Tuesday	Wednesday	Thursday	Friday	F_{4,n_2}
	A: Cash; March 07, 1978 to January 15, 1984					
Mean	−3.4408	1.3317	3.2051	2.0276	2.3440	6.328[a]
Standard						($n_2 = 1410$)
deviation	18.3955	15.5447	16.5151	19.0571	15.6785	
t-statistic	−3.022[a]	1.400	3.345[a]	1.840	2.550[b]	
Observations	261	267	297	299	291	
	B: Cash; January 16, 1984 to December 31, 1986					
Mean	−3.1842	0.3990	1.6267	1.5165	3.1684	3.471[a]
Standard						($n_2 = 718$)
deviation	14.5691	16.0154	15.1797	16.6314	13.2342	
t-statistic	−2.549[b]	0.293	1.313	1.117	2.922[a]	
Observations	136	138	150	150	149	
	C: Futures; January 16, 1984 to December 31, 1986					
Mean	−2.8976	0.2090	0.5685	1.2414	2.0915	1.828
Standard						($n_2 = 689$)
deviation	16.6928	17.5816	15.5980	17.7460	12.3856	
t-statistic	−1.956	0.138	0.440	0.842	2.012[b]	
Observations	127	134	146	145	142	

[a]Significant at 1%.
[b]Significant at 5%.

is, Monday's price change is negative and larger in absolute value than that of any other weekday, Tuesday's change is slightly low, and Wednesday's and Friday's changes appear to be somewhat higher than those of Tuesday and Thursday. In addition, in both periods the price changes on Monday and Friday are different from zero at reasonable levels of significance.[6]

As for the futures market, the daily means, standard deviations, and t-statistics are set out in C of Table 1. The overall patterns of these statistics are remarkably similar to those obtained for the cash market. With regard to Monday, in particular, the futures price change is negative and greater in absolute value than the price change on any other day. In addition, it is very close to being significantly different from zero at the 5% level.

The apparent existence of a weekend effect in the close to close price change behavior of the TSE 300 and its futures distinguishes the present results from those obtained by Cornell, Dyl and Maberly, and Junkus using United States data. In order to conduct a formal test for this effect, the following model was estimated for each of the cash market time series and for the futures market time series:

$$\Delta P_t = \delta_1 d_{1t} + \delta_2 d_{2t} + \delta_3 d_{3t} + \delta_4 d_{4t} + \delta_5 d_{5t} + \varepsilon_t. \tag{1}$$

ΔP_t is the daily change in price measure in week t and d_{1t} through d_{5t} represent dummy variables indicating the day of the week on which the price change is observed. Thus, for example, d_{1t} takes on a value of one if the price change occurs on a Monday and zero otherwise. The error term, ε_t, is assumed to be independently and identically distributed as $N(0, \sigma^2)$.

The coefficient δ_j in Equation (1) measures the mean price change on day of the week j (j = 1 to 5). If the price change distributions are identical for all days, the distribution means will be equal. In addition, the F-statistic for the joint hypothesis $\delta_1 = \delta_2 = \delta_3 = \delta_4 = \delta_5$ will not be significant.[7]

The F-statistics for the three sets of price changes considered are reported in the final column of Table 1. The statistics for the spot market allow rejection of the hypothesis that the daily means are equal at 1% for the periods both before and after the introduction of futures trading. However, the F-statistic for the futures market, in C, indicates that, at the 1% level, at least, the hypothesis of equal daily means cannot be rejected.

III. DAILY PRICE CHANGES AND THE TURN OF THE YEAR EFFECT

Using data for both the DJIA and 10 size based NYSE and AMEX firm portolios, Rogalski investigated whether daily returns for the month of January differed from daily returns for the other months of the year. He found that whereas the return patterns for the 11 months except January were similar to, albeit generally more pronounced than, those obtained using data for all months, the mean close to close returns for Mondays in January were consistently positive. Moreover, in the case of the DJIA, for which both opening and closing values were available, the close to open and open to close January Monday mean returns were also positive.[8]

Following Rogalski each of the price change series included in the present study was resolved into its January and non-January components.[9] Unfortunately, the number of observations available for January was insufficient to allow testing for the presence of a weekend effect. Hence, the analysis was limited to an examination of non-January price changes, the results of which are summarized in Table 2.

Comparing Tables 1 and 2, one notes that the non-January price changes are similar to those observed for all months. With one exception — Tuesday in the futures market — the signs of the price changes are identical and the overall pattern of the t-statistics is the same. As for evidence of a weekend effect, the Monday price changes not only continue to be negative, but also increase in absolute value. In addition, the t-statistic for the futures market is now significant at the 5% level.

Finally, the F-statistics obtained through the application of Equation (1)

Table 2. Summary Statistics for the Daily Close to Close Price Changes (ΔP_t) of the TSE 300 Index and TSE 300 Index Futures When Turn of the Year Data Are Excluded

Statistic	Monday	Tuesday	Wednesday	Thursday	Friday	F_{4,n_2}
	A: Cash; March 07, 1978 to January 15, 1984					
Mean	− 3.7121	1.5224	3.4109	1.3661	2.1154	6.270^a
Standard						($n_2 = 1278$)
deviation	18.0884	15.4012	16.3558	18.8803	16.0355	
t-statistic	− 3.159^a	1.547	3.427^a	1.189	2.131^b	
Observations	237	245	270	270	261	
	B: Cash; January 16, 1984 to December 31, 1986					
Mean	− 3.9309	0.1158	1.3758	1.5544	3.5214	4.478^a
Standard						($n_2 = 654$)
deviation	13.7953	16.1863	13.9360	16.5871	12.9593	
t-statistic	− 3.147^a	0.080	1.160	1.105	3.169^a	
Observations	122	124	138	139	136	
	C: Futures; January 16, 1984 to December 31, 1986					
Mean	− 3.5929	− 0.0583	0.5075	1.3284	2.4729	2.456^b
Standard						($n_2 = 625$)
deviation	16.3918	17.8525	14.5637	17.9514	12.1193	
t-statistic	− 2.330^b	− 0.036	0.403	0.857	2.318^b	
Observations	113	120	134	134	129	

^{a}Significant at 1%.
^{b}Significant at 5%.

are reported in the final column of Table 2. These statistics, like those based upon data for the entire year, indicate that the hypothesis of equal daily price changes in the spot market can be rejected, at 1%, for the periods both before and after the introduction of futures trading. In addition, and unlike the results reported in Table 1, the F-statistic for the futures market allows us to reject, at 5%, the hypothesis that the daily price changes are equal.

IV.   THE DISTRIBUTION OF DAILY CHANGES IN THE BASIS

Cornell, as part of his investigation of the S&P 500 and its futures, examined the daily change behavior of the futures-spot basis. What he discovered was that, between May 1982 and July 1984, the close to close changes in the basis on Monday were significantly positive. Moreover, the positive close to close Monday basis change was almost precisely offset by a significantly negative change on Tuesday. In addition, the data allowed him to reject, at 1%, the hypothesis that the mean daily changes, including that observed for Monday, were equal.

The daily change in the basis — that is, $(P^F - P^S)_t - (P^F - P^S)_{t-1}$ — may be viewed as the difference between the daily price changes in each of the futures and spot markets — that is, $(P^F_t - P^F_{t-1}) - (P^S_t - P^S_{t-1})$. Cornell's evidence can thus be interpreted as indicating that, among other things, the Monday close to close price change in the futures market is greater than the corresponding change in the spot market. As such, one might infer, as he does, that they "provide further evidence that the [weekend] effect is due to the peculiar behavior of cash prices" [3, p. 587].

In order to determine whether the daily change behavior of the S&P 500 basis observed by Cornell characterizes other markets as well, the daily changes in the TSE 300 basis were examined. The results of this examination, reported in Table 3, are, in some respects, similar to and, in others, different from those described by Cornell.

On Monday the basis change is positive, but, in contrast to Cornell's finding, insignificant, apparently reflecting a tendency for TSE 300 cash and futures prices to move together. As for Tuesday, whereas Cornell found a negative and significant basis change that almost perfectly offset the positive basis change on Monday, the Tuesday basis change for the TSE 300, though negative, is not significantly different from zero. On all other days the basis change is, similarly, both negative and statistically insignificant. Further, on the basis of the F-statistics in the final column of Table 3 — obtained from the application of Equation (1), with basis change substituted for price

Table 3. Summary Statistics for the Daily Close to Close Changes in the Basis $[\Delta(P^F - P^S)_t]$ for the TSE 300 over the Period January 16, 1984 to December 31, 1986

Statistic	Monday	Tuesday	Wednesday	Thursday	Friday	F_{4, n_2}
		A: All Months				
Mean	0.3835	−0.3381	−0.7942	−0.3872	−0.3097	0.717
Standard						$(n_2 = 689)$
deviation	5.7663	5.8289	6.5094	5.4141	5.3669	
t-statistic	0.749	−0.671	−1.474	−0.861	−0.688	
Observations	127	134	146	145	142	
		B: Turn of the Year Data Excluded				
Mean	0.5064	−0.3300	−0.5731	−0.3487	−0.2233	0.599
Standard						$(n_2 = 625)$
deviation	5.7256	5.9277	6.3418	5.5160	5.3106	
t-statistic	0.940	−0.610	−1.046	−0.732	−0.477	
Observations	113	120	134	134	129	

change — it is not possible to reject, at any reasonable level of significance, the hypothesis that the daily basis changes are equal. Hence, it seems quite apparent that the weekend effect persists in both the cash and futures markets for the TSE 300.

V. THE DAY-TO-DAY RELATIONSHIPS BETWEEN CASH AND FUTURES PRICE CHANGES

The various patterns identified in previous sections were based upon the summary statistics appearing in Tables 1, 2, and 3, with no direct consideration being given to whether the behavior of the futures market actually reflects that of the cash market. In order to investigate these relationships — and, in particular, the association between price changes in the cash and futures between the Friday close and the Monday close — the following equation was estimated:

$$\Delta P^F_{j,t} = \alpha_{0,j} + \alpha_{1,j} \, \Delta P^S_{j,t} + \varepsilon_{j,t}. \tag{2}$$

$\Delta P^F_{j,t}$ is the daily futures price change in week t and $\Delta P^S_{j,t}$ is the corresponding price change for the cash index. If the price change in the futures market is identical to the price change in the cash market, $\alpha_{0,j}$ will be equal to zero and $\alpha_{1,j}$ will be equal to one.

The estimates of $\alpha_{1,j}$, together with corresponding t-statistics and R^2 statistics for Equation (2), are reported in Table 4. Referring to either A or B, one observes that the daily coefficient estimates are consistently very

Table 4. The Relationship between the Daily Price Changes of the TSE 300 Index and TSE 300 Index Futures over the Period January 1984 to December 1986

Statistic	Monday	Tuesday	Wednesday	Thursday	Friday
		A: All Months			
$\hat{\alpha}^i_{1,j}$	1.0674	1.0371	0.9540	1.0053	0.9131
t-statistic[a]	30.894	32.887	26.310	37.333	25.225
R^2	0.884	0.891	0.828	0.907	0.820
Observations	127	134	146	145	142
		B: Turn of the Year Data Excluded			
$\hat{\alpha}^i_{1,j}$	1.1118	1.0415	0.9692	1.0182	0.9199
t-statistic[a]	29.512	31.084	23.815	35.642	23.588
R^2	0.887	0.891	0.811	0.906	0.814
Observations	113	120	134	134	129

[a] All t-statistics are significant at 1%.

close to one. In other words, the price changes in the cash and futures markets are, on average, almost identical. Moreover, in all cases these estimates are significantly different from zero at the 1% level. In addition, the R^2 statistics indicate that the price changes in the two markets are highly correlated. This similarity of behavior in the two markets suggests that the factor(s) contributing to the weekend effect in the cash market for common stocks most probably also persist in the futures market for stock indices.

VI. SUMMARY

This paper examined the daily price change patterns of the TSE 300 Index and of the near futures contracts written on the index. Several observations emerged from the analysis. First, measuring price changes on a close to close basis, evidence of a weekend effect was found in both the cash and futures markets. As such, the results are in sharp contrast to those obtained in recent studies involving United States data, which have suggested that for the close to close period, the effect has disappeared since the inception of futures trading.

While Cornell and Dyl and Maberly have reported negative and statistically significant returns in the cash market for the nontrading period between the Friday close and Monday open, their results are inconclusive as to whether the effect spills over into the futures market during this period. An analysis of the daily changes in the TSE 300's futures-cash basis suggests that the two markets do move together since the daily changes in the basis, including the change in Monday, are not significantly different from zero. There is thus no reason to believe, as Cornell has suggested, that the weekend effect is confined to the cash market.

Ordinary least-squares regressions of the daily futures price changes on the corresponding cash price changes also indicated that the behavior of each market was reflected in that of the other. The slope coefficients for all days are very close to one, suggesting that the price changes in the two markets were, on average, almost identical. In addition, the R^2 statistics indicate that the price changes were highly correlated.

Finally, the study considered the implications of removing late December and January price changes from the sample in order to abstract from possible turn of the year effects. However, doing so produced results for both the cash and the futures markets that are substantially the same as those based upon data for the entire year.

NOTES

1. The weekend effect was first identified by Cross [4], French [8], and Gibbons and Hess [9]. Other studies investigating this effect in the cash market for common stock include those of Lakonishok and Levi [14], Keim and Stambaugh [13], Rogalski [18], Harris [10], and Smirlock and Starks [19].

2. Negative Monday returns and other empirical regularities have also been identified in the markets for gold (Ball, Torous, and Tschoegl [1], and Ma [16]), Treasury bills (Gibbons and Hess [9]), and foreign exchange (Levi [15], Coats [2], McFarland, Pettit, and Sung [17]).

3. A significantly negative close to open return in the cash market has also been identified by Rogalski [18] and Smirlock and Starks [19].

4. Dyl and Maberly [5] ascribe Cornell's [3] results to errors in his data. When they replicated his study with the errors corrected, they found that the weekend price change in the futures market was negative, but not significantly different from zero.

5. A corresponding set of rate of return series was also calculated, and then used to conduct tests paralleling those set out in this paper. The results obtained are substantially the same as those to be described, however, and, as such, are not reported.

6. The standard deviations of the daily price changes, in contrast, do not exhibit the strong weekend identified by Fama [7] using DJIA data.

7. See Theil [20], Chapter 7.

8. Similar results, also for the DJIA, are reported by Smirlock and Starks [19].

9. More precisely, the January component of each year comprises the period of 6 weeks in which the third week encompasses the first day of trading in the new year if that day is a Wednesday, Thursday, or Friday or, if it is a Monday or Tuesday, the preceding week.

REFERENCES

1. Ball, C. A., W. N. Torous, and A. E. Tschoegl, "Gold and the 'Weekend Effect'," *Journal of Futures Markets* II (Summer 1982), 175–182.

2. Coats, W. L., Jr., "The Weekend Eurodollar Game," *Journal of Finance,* XXXVI (June 1981), 649–659.

3. Cornell, B., "The Weekly Pattern in Stock Returns: Cash versus Futures: A Note," *Journal of Finance* XL (June 1985), 583–588.

4. Cross, F., "The Behavior of Stock Prices on Fridays and Mondays," *Financial Analysts Journal* XXIX (November–December 1973), 67–69.

5. Dyl, E. A., and E. D. Maberly, "The Daily Distributions of Changes in the Price of Stock Index Futures," *Journal of Futures Markets* VI (Winter 1986), 513–521.

6. Dyl, E. A., and E. D. Maberly, "The Weekly Pattern in Stock Index Futures: A Further Note," *Journal of Finance* XLI (December 1986), 1149–1152.

7. Fama, E. F., "The Behavior of Stock Market Prices," *Journal of Business* XXXVIII (January 1965), 34–105.

8. French, K. R., "Stock Returns and the Weekend Effect," *Journal of Financial Economics* VIII (March 1980), 55–69.

9. Gibbons, M. R., and P. Hess, "Day of the Week Effects and Asset Returns," *Journal of Business* LIV (October 1981), 579–596.

10. Harris, L., "A Transactions Data Study of Weekly and Intradaily Patterns in Stock Returns," *Journal of Financial Economics* XVI (May 1986), 99–117.

11. Jaffe, J., and R. Westerfield, "The Week-End Effect in Common Stock Returns: The International Evidence," *Journal of Finance* XL (June 1985), 433–454.

12. Junkus, J. C., "Weekend and Day of the Week Effects in Returns on Stock Index Futures," *Journal of Futures Markets* VI (Autumn 1986), 397–407.
13. Keim, D. B., and R. F. Stambaugh, "A Further Investigation of the Weekend Effect in Stock Returns," *Journal of Finance* XXXIX (July 1984), 819–835.
14. Lakonishok, J., and M. D. Levi, "Weekend Effects on Stock Returns: A Note," *Journal of Finance* XXXVII (June 1982), 883–889.
15. Levi, M. D., "The Weekend Game: Clearing House vs. Federal Funds,' *Canadian Journal of Economics* XI (November 1978), 750–757.
16. Ma, C. K., "A Further Investigation of the Day-of-the-Week Effect in the Gold Market," *Journal of Futures Markets* VI (Autumn 1986), 409–419.
17. McFarland, J. W., R. R. Pettit, and S. K. Sung, "The Distribution of Foreign Exchange Price Changes: Trading Day Effects and Risk Measurement," *Journal of Finance* XXXVII (June 1982), 693–715.
18. Rogalski, R. J., "New Findings Regarding Day-of-the-Week Returns over Trading and Non-Trading Periods: A Note," *Journal of Finance* XXXIX (December 1984), 1603–1614.
19. Smirlock, M., and L. Starks, "Day-of-the-Week and Intraday Effects in Stock Returns," *Journal of Financial Economics* XVII (September 1986), 1603–1614.
20. Theil, H., *Principles of Econometrics*. New York: John Wiley, 1971.

THE EFFECT OF INDIVIDUAL STOCK OPTION EXPIRATIONS ON STOCK RETURNS BEFORE AND AFTER THE INTRODUCTION OF SP 100 INDEX OPTIONS

Joseph Vu[*] and E. Mine Cinar[**]

I. INTRODUCTION

Several studies have found that individual stock option expirations influence the return and the volatility of the underlying stock. Klemkosky [4] found significant negative stock returns in the week preceding the option

[*]DePaul University
[**]Loyola University of Chicago.

We would like to thank Ileen Malitz and Michael Long for the computer support provided and Boyd Konowalski for his research assistantship. We also appreciate comments by Beni Lauterbach, Diana Harrington, and Paul Schultz on an earlier version of this paper.

Advances in Futures and Options Research, Vol. 3, pages 341–356.

expiration and insignificant positive returns in the subsequent week. Officer and Trennepohl [6] examined the daily price changes of 152 underlying securities during 4 days surrounding option expiration and found that optionable stocks experienced some downward price pressure 2 days before option expiration. The stock price volatility was only slightly greater than the predicted volatility, however, implying that the difference was very small for distorting trading activity. Cinar and Vu [2] examined the impact of both index and individual stock option expirations on the rate of return of the underlying stocks. While the effect of index option expirations was negligible, the effect of individual stock option expirations was significant for some stocks in the sample. The biggest effects were on the volatility of the volume of stocks. Using hourly and minute-by-minute stock price data, Stoll and Whaley [8] reached the same conclusion, finding significant volume effects and only negligible price effects on expiration days of stock index options and futures contracts. Rendleman [7] suggested that cash settlement provisions of stock index futures contracts provide hedgers with an incentive to unwind stock positions through sloppy trades that could cause excess price volatility during the final hours of trading.

Observed abnormal negative stock returns prior to the option expiration date can be explained by different reasons. Traders usually sell more than one call for each round lot of stock. Near the option expiration date, if the stock price is below the exercise price, the trader may sell the stock, expecting the calls not to be exercised. If the stock price is above the exercise price, the call writer may want to buy back the calls at maturity to minimize the time value of the option, then sell the stock. Both of these actions will cause downward pressure on the stock price.

Although there is no formal theory suggesting that market index option expirations affect the prices of the underlying stocks, we might expect to see some downward price pressure on the stock price with the expiration of SP 100 index options, too. The growth of market stock indexes has been phenomenal in recent years. The volume of options on SP 100 index presently accounts for a large share of the volume in the total options traded. Recently, the market index expirations of SP 100 have been noted in financial papers and in the news media as being "manipulated" by massive sales or purchases of leading stocks. The Commodity Futures trading Commission has established a new rule, requiring exchanges to lower the ceiling on many traders' holdings in days leading up to the index expiration in an attempt to curb the potential tendency of stock-index trading effects on the stock market itself. The October 19, 1987 "crash" of the stock market has renewed interest and examination of the effects of large volume trading associated with index expirations in the market. New regulations are proposed to control the financial markets and voluntary trading limits have been adapted by some exchanges and large trading firms have increased margin requirements, dampening the volume of trades.

In our previous paper [2], in which we examined six blue-chip stocks, we found that the rate of return on the six underlying stocks was not affected. However, the volume of stock traded on the day of the expirations was statistically larger for some stocks, especially on the days their own options expired. In this study, the effect of individual stock option expirations on a large number of stocks is tested. In order to account for the potential influence of SP 100 index options, a pooled sample period and then pre- and post-SP 100 index option periods are used. The stocks in the SP 100 basket are also examined separately.

Table 1.[a]

A. The Monthly Trading Volume of SP 100 and SP 500 Index Options, 1983–1984

	SP 100	SP 500
1983 March	114,299	—
April	452,755	—
May	734,221	—
June	986,857	—
July	723,841	2,873
August	1,323,241	4,411
September	1,415,947	3,163
October	1,359,715	1,415
November	1,591,809	1,287
December	1,892,979	934
Total for 1983	10,595,664	14,093
1984 January	2,539,038	1,874
February	4,201,438	4,490
March	4,396,606	741
April	4,450,065	354
May	6,084,172	442
June	5,420,208	329
July	4,894,493	149
August	7,359,550	370
September	5,590,714	53
October	6,722,962	45
November	6,304,598	2,629
December	5,924,601	44
Total for 1984	64,288,445	11,970

B. Comparison of Trading Volumes between SP 100 and Individual Stock Options

	Stock Options, CBOE	Stock Options, All Exchanges	SP 100
1982	75,721,605	137,264,816	None
1983	71,695,563	135,658,976	10,595,664
1984	58,674,901	118,925,239	64,288,445

[a]*Source:* The Options Institute, Chicago Board of Options Exchange.

The stock indexes that are recently introduced into the market, such as the OTC index products, are disregarded in this study. One reason is these indexes have been in operation for only a short time, and another reason is that the trade volume has fallen consistently and drastically (from a combined weekly volume of 70,000 + contracts in late October 1985 to about 3,000 in late February 1986 for NASDAQ 100 and OTC 250 futures). The SP 500 is also ignored here because of the low volume of trading in recent years. Table 1 shows the relative growth of SP 100 index with respect to SP 500 as well as individual stock options during the period under observation in this study. The SP 100 was introduced on March 11, 1983 and in 1984, its volume was approximately six times that of the SP 500 (Table 1a). The trade-off between the SP 100 and individual stock options for the period covered in this study is also evident from part (b) of the table. While the SP 100 volume went from zero to 64 million in 2 years, the volume of individual stock options traded at Chicago Board of Exchange declined by about 17 million, and at all exchanges, by about 20 million. This is due to the fact that in the pre-SP 100 period, portfolio managers hedged by writing call options against stocks in the portfolio. However, after the introduction of SP 100 indexes, they have been hedging by writing on SP 100s, thereby saving on transaction costs. We would therefore expect to see less use of individual stock options.

We chose to study the impact of the SP 100 index on all stocks with options, as well as only those included in the SP 100 index. The effect of the SP 100 index on the market in general may be so strong that all stocks may be affected.

II.   THE SAMPLE

The stocks included in this study consist of all the stocks that have listed options traded at the Chicago Board of Options, American, Philadelphia, and Pacific Exchanges during the period from January 1982 to December 1984. The stocks for which the options were delisted during this time period or were introduced during this period were excluded from our study. Data were collected from the *Wall Street Journal* and stock returns were obtained from the Center for Research in Security Prices (CRSP) daily tapes. The stock returns not on CRSP tapes were excluded from this study. We also excluded stocks with missing daily returns and those whose options had changed expiration cycles. Our sample included more than 200 stocks, the data on which were partitioned into pre- and post-SP 100 index option periods. Eighty-nine of these stocks were also included in the SP 100 index basket throughout the time period under study. The first all inclusive sample is between January 2, 1982 and March 11, 1983, and the second sample covers the period between March 12, 1983 and December 31, 1984. Using the criteria described above, the overall sample consists of 2617 option expirations: the pre-SP 100 period has 1031 and the post-SP 100 period has 1586 option expirations. The "SP 100 stocks only" sample includes 1068 individual stock expirations, 445 of which belong to the pre-SP 100 period. All the individual stock options expired on the third Friday of their expiration month at 3:00 P.M. Central time and the SP 100 index options expired on the third Friday of each month at 2:00 P.M. Central time. Hence, there is a slight mismatching of 1 hour. Since we are only examining stock option data in this study at market closing time, we are actually observing the closing prices of stock options after the market index has expired and the prices have settled.

III. METHOD OF ANALYSIS

The methodology we use to examine stock returns is described in Dodd and Warner [3]. For each stock, the market model is used to calculate an excess return (AR) as follows:

$$AR_{it} = R_{it} - \hat{a}_i - \hat{b}_i R_{mt} \tag{1}$$

where R_{it} is the rate of return on stock i on day t, and R_{mt} is the rate of return on the NYSE valued-weighted index on day t. The intercept and the slope coefficients ($\hat{a}_i$ and $\hat{b}_i$) are estimated by ordinary least squares from day -240 to day -11 before the event day. Excess returns are calculated for each stock from $t = -10$ to $t = +10$, a period of 2 weeks before and 2 weeks after an option expiration date. The mean portfolio excess return is defined as

$$\overline{AR}_t = (1/n) \sum_{i=1}^{n} AR_{it} \tag{2}$$

where n is the number of stocks in the portfolio. The cumulative portfolio excess return (CAR) from 10 days before the event date to date T is computed as

$$CAR^T_{-10} = \sum_{t=-10}^{T} \overline{AR}_t. \tag{3}$$

As in any empirical work, there are problems associated with using a data base that may not satisfy the assumptions required to get best linear unbiased (BLUE) estimators with ordinary least squares. In the post-SP 100 sample period, the volatility of the data may be different than the pre-SP 100 period. Also, we might expect the volatility of the rate of return of stocks included in the SP 100 index to be larger than the volatility of the rest of the stocks. If there is a statistically significant change in volatility between the pre- and the post-SP 100 periods, this would result in the estimates of a_i and b_i being both small sample and asymptotically inefficient for the pooled sample period. Loss of efficiency would result in the loss of precision of the confidence intervals used for testing hypotheses.

To check for this, a heteroscedasticity test was conducted on the data set. Based on the test, the data were found to be heteroscedastic. The direction of the bias of the calculated variances was examined. The bias is defined as

$$E(s^2\hat{b}) - Var(\hat{b}), \tag{4}$$

where E stands for expected value of

$$s^2\hat{b} = s^2/\sum(X_i - \bar{X})^2 \tag{5}$$

and

$$s^2 = [\sum(Y_i - \hat{a} - \hat{b}X_i)^2]/(n - 2). \tag{6}$$

The bias was found to be negative. Therefore, the confidence intervals are actually narrower than expected and the significance levels are sharper. Hence, it is unnecessary to correct for heteroscedasticity in the sample since the tests for the pooled and the post-sample are more significant than stated.

IV. EMPIRICAL RESULTS

A. All Stocks

Both raw and excess returns were examined for the pooled sample, the pre-SP 100 sample, and the post-SP 100 sample. The results are given in Tables 2 to 4.

The Pooled Sample. Table 2 shows the raw and the excess returns on the stocks near the individual stock option expiration dates, respectively, for the total sample period, which covers the time periods before and after the introduction of SP 100 stocks. The table gives the average rate of return from 10 days before the individual stock option expiration (event day) to 10 days after, as well as the cumulative portfolio excess return and the percentage positive excess return. The significance levels associated with the average rate of returns are noted by asterisks. The *raw returns* in general show a significant average negative rate of return on the event day. They become positive the day after the event day (the following Monday) and become slightly cyclical.

The *excess returns* also show a significant average negative rate of return

Table 2. Daily Raw and Excess Returns Around Option Expiration in the *Pooled Sample* Period from January 1982 to December 1984 (2617 Observations)

Day Relative to Expiration	Percentage Mean Portfolio Raw Return	Percentage Mean Portfolio Excess Return	Cumulative Portfolio Excess Return	Percentage Positive Excess Return
− 10	0.311	− 0.020 (− 0.737)[a]	− 0.00020	47.03
− 9	0.056	− 0.014 (− 0.378)	− 0.00034	47.64
− 8	− 0.193	− 0.019 (− 0.614)	− 0.00053	49.42
− 7	− 0.112	0.004 (− 0.408)	− 0.00049	48.26
− 6	0.237	− 0.017 (− 0.733)	− 0.00066	48.45
− 5	0.193	− 0.040 (− 1.394)*	− 0.00106	47.93
− 4	0.055	− 0.091 (− 1.465)*	− 0.00197	47.80
− 3	− 0.045	− 0.017 (− 0.037)	− 0.00214	47.53
− 2	− 0.171	− 0.084 (− 1.973)**	− 0.00298	47.15
− 1	− 0.075	− 0.032 (0.844)	− 0.00330	46.92
0; event day	− 0.107	− 0.125 (− 3.195)***	− 0.00455	46.19
1	0.014	− 0.031 (− 0.326)	− 0.00486	47.11
2	0.064	− 0.048 (− 1.202)	− 0.00534	46.19
3	0.472	− 0.025 (0.153)	− 0.00559	46.50
4	0.163	0.026 (0.528)	− 0.00533	46.48
5	− 0.001	0.000 (− 0.341)	− 0.00525	46.15
6	− 0.171	0.013 (0.665)	− 0.00512	46.86
7	0.182	0.088 (2.370)**	− 0.00424	47.66
8	− 0.132	− 0.045 (− 1.767)*	− 0.00469	47.97
9	0.184	0.027 (0.223)	− 0.00442	48.41
10	0.207	− 0.000 (0.031)	− 0.00442	47.97

[a] t-statistics are in parentheses.
*Significant at the 10% level.
**Significant at the 5% level.
***Significant at the 1% level.

on the event day. The results are similar to the findings of Officer and Trennepohl [6]. We find a significant negative excess return on the option expiration date using the whole sample period data. There is also a statistically significant negative excess return on the Wednesday (day -2) of the expiration week. On the seventh day of trading (corresponding to Tuesday which is 10 calendar days after the expiration Friday), we get the first significant positive excess return. Hence, based on this large sample, there is evidence that option expirations cause negative excess returns on the expiration Fridays. The *cumulative* excess returns show that the negative excess returns go into steady state only after 2 weeks following the event date. In other words, after the event date, we do not see a reversal of negative excess returns. The cumulative excess returns from day -10 to the event day average about 0.5%.

To check for the effect of the outliers, the percentage positive excess returns is reported in the same table. From day -10 on, the percentage positive excess return is lowest (46%) on the event day. The values in the column generally show a percentage positive of less than 50%. Hence, the negative excess return shown is not due to an extreme outlier but is part of a trend. The result suggests that price pressure occurs around the time of option expiration.

Pre-SP 100 Options Period. Table 3 gives the raw and the excess rates of return for this period. The important difference in this table is in the event day average returns. In the case of raw returns, the average on the event day is *positive*. In the excess returns case, the average rate of return is not statistically different from zero. In other words, in the period before the introduction of SP 100 index options, we do not see any significant negative rates of return on the third Friday of the month when individual stock options expire.

Post-SP 100 Options Period. The pattern in this period, given on Table 4, is the same as the pooled sample period but different from the pre-SP 100 period. For the post-SP 100 sample, the average rate of return on the event day is negative for both raw and excess returns and statistically significant for the latter. The average excess rate of returns become positive and significant 7 trading days after the event day. However, the cumulative excess returns is still negative (-0.39%) at the end of 10 days after the event.

The effect of the post-SP 100 period is so strong that the whole sample (pre- and post-SP 100) shows the same characteristics with respect to the negative rate of return on the event day. For example, in the case of the raw returns, the average rate of return on event day is -0.375% (Table 4) in the post-SP 100 period but it is diluted to -0.107% (Table 2) when we examine

Table 3.   Daily Raw and Excess Returns Around Option Expiration in the *Pre-SP 100* Sample Period from January 2, 1982 to March 11, 1983 (1031 Observations)

Day Relative to Expiration	Percentage Mean Portfolio Raw Return	Percentage Mean Portfolio Excess Return	Cumulative Portfolio Excess Return	Percentage Positive Excess Return
−10	0.507	−0.004 (−0.067)[a]	−0.00004	46.36
−9	0.039	−0.087 (−1.557)	−0.00127	46.26
−8	−0.150	−0.053 (−0.444)	−0.00180	47.57
−7	0.011	0.016 (0.123)	−0.00164	46.84
−6	0.385	0.025 (0.681)	−0.00139	47.91
−5	0.325	0.008 (0.070)	−0.00131	48.44
−4	−0.002	−0.069 (−0.104)	−0.00200	48.01
−3	−0.005	−0.031 (−0.065)	−0.00231	47.42
−2	−0.062	−0.089 (−1.417)	−0.00320	47.23
−1	−0.064	−0.151 (−2.711)***	−0.00471	48.69
0; event day	0.305	−0.093 (−1.086)	−0.00565	47.62
1	0.069	0.041 (0.854)	−0.00523	50.04
2	−0.132	−0.066 (−0.240)	−0.00589	48.01
3	0.671	−0.018 (0.247)	−0.00607	48.78
4	0.288	0.008 (0.138)	−0.00599	47.47
5	−0.064	−0.042 (−0.927)	−0.00641	47.18
6	−0.021	−0.061 (−0.409)	−0.00702	47.13
7	0.179	0.024 (1.062)	−0.00678	47.42
8	−0.601	−0.115 (−2.283)**	−0.00793	47.52
9	0.073	0.044 (0.474)	−0.00749	49.27
10	0.335	−0.112 (−1.908)*	−0.00861	48.20

[a]t-statistics are in parentheses.
*Significant at the 10% level.
**Significant at the 5% level.
***Significant at the 1% level.

Table 4.   Daily Raw and Excess Returns Around Option Expiration in the *Post-SP 100* Sample Period from March 12, 1983 to December 31, 1984 (1586 Observations)

Day Relative to Expiration	Percentage Mean Portfolio Raw Return	Percentage Mean Portfolio Excess Return	Cumulative Portfolio Excess Return	Percentage Positive Excess Return
−10	0.183	−0.031 (−0.893)[a]	−0.00031	47.47
−9	0.067	0.034 (0.769)	0.00003	48.54
−8	−0.221	0.003 (−0.431)	0.00006	50.63
−7	−0.192	−0.004 (−0.624)	0.00002	49.18
−6	0.140	−0.044 (−1.490)	−0.00042	48.80
−5	0.107	−0.071 (−1.847)*	−0.00113	47.66
−4	0.092	−0.105 (−1.799)*	−0.00218	47.66
−3	−0.071	−0.008 (0.004)	−0.00226	47.60
−2	−0.242	−0.081 (−1.391)	−0.00307	47.09
−1	−0.165	−0.150 (−3.270)***	−0.00457	45.77
0; event day	−0.375	−0.146 (−3.228)***	−0.00603	45.27
1	−0.022	−0.077 (−1.108)	−0.00680	45.20
2	0.191	−0.037 (−1.350)	−0.00717	45.01
3	0.342	−0.030 (−0.396)	−0.00747	45.01
4	0.082	0.038 (0.567)	−0.00709	45.83
5	0.040	0.040 (0.309)	−0.00669	45.48
6	−0.269	0.060 (1.184)	−0.00609	46.68
7	0.184	0.130 (2.188)**	−0.00479	47.82
8	0.174	0.000 (−0.428)	−0.00479	48.26
9	0.256	0.016 (0.094)	−0.00463	47.85
10	0.124	0.073 (1.579)	−0.00390	47.82

[a] t-statistics are in parentheses.
*Significant at the 10% level.
**Significant at the 5% level.
***Significant at the 1% level.

the overall sample. Again in the average excess rate of returns, the rate on event day is -0.146% (Table 4) in the post-SP 100 sample but is reduced to -0.125% (Table 2) in the overall sample. Since the numbers of observations were asymptotically similar in the two samples, the effects appearing in the post-SP 100 sample must have dominated over the effect of the pre-SP 100 sample.

B.   Stocks Included in the SP 100 index

Since the introduction of SP 100 index option in March 1983, traders have switched from writing call options on individual stocks to writing on SP 100 call options on proxy portfolios. These portfolios are designed to follow the index closely, and typically contain the most liquid stocks that comprise the index. There are several scenarios illustrating that the introduction of SP 100 options can create price pressure for common stocks at option expiration. For those who write index calls against their portfolio, as expiration approaches, if the exercise price of the SP 100 index call is greater than the index, the call will expire worthless. Some traders may write another index call to pick up additional income while other traders sell stocks of their portfolios because these stocks are not needed for hedging anymore. Furthermore, selling stocks is an attractive alternative if the traders can recognize capital losses immediately. In another scenario, traders buy SP 100 puts to protect themselves. If the market declines, the traders exercise the puts to receive cash resettlement, and sell the stocks to get the capital loss.

Because the SP 100 index options improve the liquidity of the market, they bring in more market participants. Therefore, we expect the price pressure on common stock at individual option expirations to be greater after the introduction of the SP 100 index option. In this section, we examine a subsample of stocks included in the SP 100 index to see if these actively traded stocks behave differently from other stocks at their option expiration date.

The excess returns for the pooled sample, pre-SP 100, and post-SP 100 samples are given in Tables 5, 6, and 7, respectively. In the *pooled sample*, the excess returns show a significant negative effect on the event day. Similar to the results on the complete sample reported in Table 2, we also find a significant negative excess return on the Wednesday (day -2) of the expiration week. However, the significant positive excess returns appear on days 3 and 4. The cumulative mean excess returns are mostly positive, indicating that there is no evidence of price pressure for 89 stocks in the SP 100 index.

Table 6 shows the returns for 89 stocks in the SP 100 index in the pre-SP 100 option introduction period. Unlike the results of the complete sample,

Table 5.   Percentage Mean Excess Returns and Percentage Cumulative Mean Excess Returns for 89 Stocks Covered in SP 100 Index, *Pooled Sample*, from January 1982 to December 1984 (1068 Observations)

Day Relative to Expiration	Percentage Mean Portfolio Excess Return	Cumulative Portfolio Excess Return
− 10	0.0034 $(4.857)^{***,a}$	0.0034
− 9	0.0000 (0.000)	0.0034
− 8	− 0.0025 $(-4.166)^{***}$	0.0009
− 7	− 0.0013 (− 1.625	− 0.0004
− 6	0.0034 $(5.667)^{***}$	0.0030
− 5	0.0013 $(2.166)^{**}$	0.0043
− 4	0.0017 $(2.428)^{**}$	0.0060
− 3	0.0000 (0.000)	0.0060
− 2	− 0.0014 $(-2.333)^{**}$	0.0046
− 1	− 0.0005 (− 0.714)	0.0041
0; event day	− 0.0018 $(-2.571)^{**}$	0.0023
1	0.0003 (0.428)	0.0026
2	0.0006 (0.857)	0.0032
3	0.0067 $(9.571)^{***}$	0.0099
4	0.0021 $(3.500)^{***}$	0.0120
5	0.0004 (0.666)	0.0124
6	− 0.0019 $(-2.714)^{***}$	0.0105
7	0.0032 $(4.571)^{***}$	0.0137
8	− 0.0024 $(-3.000)^{***}$	0.0113
9	0.0022 $(3.143)^{***}$	0.0135
10	0.0026 $(3.250)^{***}$	0.0161

[a]t-statistics are in parentheses.
*Significant at the 10% level.
**Significant at the 5% level.
***Significant at the 1% level.

Table 6. Percentage Mean Excess Returns and Percentage Cumulative Mean Excess Returns for 89 Stocks Covered in SP 100 Index in the *Pre-SP 100 Option Introduction Period* from January 2, 1982 to March 11, 1983 (445 Observations)

Day Relative to Expiration	Percentage Mean Portfolio Excess Return	Cumulative Portfolio Excess Return
− 10	.0068 $(5.231)^{***,a}$	0.0068
− 9	− 0.0010 $(− 0.909)$	0.0058
− 8	− 0.0025 $(− 2.083)^{**}$	0.0033
− 7	0.0023 $(1.769)^{*}$	0.0056
− 6	0.0052 $(4.727)^{***}$	0.0108
− 5	0.0032 $(2.667)^{***}$	0.0140
− 4	0.0002 (0.143)	0.0142
− 3	0.0020 (1.538)	0.0162
− 2	− 0.0011 (0.917)	0.0151
− 1	− 0.0004 $(− 0.364)$	0.0147
0; event day	0.0037 $(3.364)^{***}$	0.0184
1	0.0011 (0.786)	0.0195
2	− 0.0012 $(− 1.000)$	0.0183
3	0.0102 $(7.846)^{***}$	0.0285
4	0.0025 $(2.500)^{**}$	0.0310
5	0.0004 (0.364)	0.0314
6	− 0.0009 $(− 0.643)$	0.0305
7	0.0037 $(3.083)^{***}$	0.0342
8	− 0.0067 $(− 6.700)^{***}$	0.0275
9	0.0014 (1.166)	0.0289
10	0.0025 $(2.083)^{**}$	0.0314

[a] t-statistics are in parentheses.
[*] Significant at the 10% level.
[**] Significant at the 5% level.
[***] Significant at the 1% level.

Table 7. Percentage Mean Excess Returns and Percentage Cumulative Mean Excess Returns for 89 Stocks Covered in SP 100 Index in the *Post-SP 100 Option Introduction Period* from March 12, 1983 to December 31, 1984 (623 Observations)

Day Relative to Expiration	Percentage Mean Portfolio Excess Return	Cumulative Portfolio Excess Return
− 10	0.0009 (1.000)[a]	0.0009
− 9	0.0009 (0.900)	0.0018
− 8	− 0.0026 (− 3.250)***	− 0.0009
− 7	− 0.0038 (− 4.222)***	− 0.0047
− 6	0.0021 (2.625)***	− 0.0026
− 5	− 0.0001 (− 0.142)	− 0.0027
− 4	0.0029 (3.625)***	0.0002
− 3	− 0.0015 (− 1.666)*	− 0.0013
− 2	− 0.0017 (− 2.125)***	− 0.0030
− 1	− 0.0006 (− 0.666)	− 0.0036
0; event day	− 0.0057 (− 7.125)***	− 0.0093
1	− 0.0002 (− 0.250)	− 0.0095
2	0.0018 (2.250)**	− 0.0077
3	0.0040 (4.444)***	− 0.0037
4	0.0018 (2.000)**	− 0.0019
5	0.0004 (0.500)	− 0.0015
6	− 0.0026 (− 2.888)***	− 0.0041
7	0.0028 (3.111)***	− 0.0013
8	0.0007 (0.509)	− 0.0006
9	0.0027 (3.000)***	0.0021
10	0.0027 (2.700)***	0.0048

[a]t-statistics are in parentheses.
*Significant at the 10% level.
**Significant at the 5% level.
***Significant at the 1% level.

we find a significant positive excess return on the individual option expiration date. The cumulative excess return rises steadily in both the pre- and post-2-week periods surrounding the event day. Again, there is no evidence of price pressure for the 89 stocks in the pre-SP 100 option introduction period.

Table 7 shows the returns for 89 stocks in the post-SP 100 option introduction period. The excess returns on the event day as well as days − 2 and − 3 are significantly negative. However, the excess returns on days 2, 3, and 4 are significantly positive. The cumulative excess return suggests that the price pressure exists in the 2 weeks before the individual option expiration date, but the price pressure disappears in the following 2 weeks. This result is similar to those found by Klemkosky [4] and Officer and Trennepohl [6].

One of the distinctions between the SP 100 basket stocks and the total sample is in the magnitude of the rates of return. The former are much smaller, showing that large volume stocks have lower excess returns.

V. CONCLUSIONS

Based on 2617 individual option expirations, this study shows that after the introduction of SP 100 index options, the raw and excess common stock returns become significantly negative on the individual stock option expiration days. It is interesting to note that we could not find any evidence of this effect when we studied six individual blue chip stocks previously (see Cinar and Vu [2]). On an individual stock basis, the only visible effect was on the volatility of volumes, not on rates of return. However, using a larger sample, this study finds that the average rates of return become strongly negative on the individual stock option expiration day, especially after the introduction of SP 100 index options. The result suggests that price pressure occurs around the time of individual option expirations. For 89 stocks in the SP 100, the magnitude of the rates of return is smaller, indicating that large volume stocks have smaller rates of return. Moreover, the price pressure only exists in the 2 weeks before individual option expiration date after the SP 100 index options are introduced.

Although our overall results are similar to the findings of Klemkosky [4] and Officer and Trennephol [6], the pre-SP 100 subsample results are not. We use a larger sample and a different time period. Stoll and Whaley [8] also reported a negligible stock price reaction on the option expiration days. Based on these mixed results, the reported negative stock price reaction on option expiration days are probably nonstationary over time.

REFERENCES

1. Brown, S. J., and J. B. Warner, "Using Daily Stock Returns, the Case of Event Studies," *Journal of Financial Economics* 14 (1985), 3–31.
2. Cinar, M., and J. Vu, "The Effect of Option Expirations on Stock Prices," *Financial Analysts Journal* (January/February 1987), 55–57.
3. Dodd, P., and J. Warner, "On Corporate Governance: A Study of Proxy Contests," *Journal of Financial Economics* 11 (1983), 401–438.
4. Klemkosky, R., "The Impact of Option Expiration on Stock Prices," *Journal of Financial and Quantitative Analysis* (September 1978), 507–518.
5. Kmenta, J., *Elements of Econometrics*. New York: Macmillan Company, 1978.
6. Officer, D., and K. Trennepohl, "Price Behavior of Corporate Equities Near Option Expiration Dates," *Financial Management* (Summer 1981), 75–80.
7. Rendleman, R. J., "Commentary on the Effects of Stock-Index Futures Trading on the Market for Underlying Stocks," working paper, University of North Carolina, Chapel Hill, N.C., 1986.
8. Stoll, H. R., and R. E. Whaley, "Expiration Day Effects of Index Options and Futures," working paper, Vanderbilt University, Nashville, Tennessee, 1986.

A FURTHER INVESTIGATION OF THE RISK–RETURN RELATION FOR COMMODITY FUTURES

Hun Y. Park,[*] K. C. John Wei,[**] and Thomas J. Frecka[*]

I. INTRODUCTION

The underlying process of futures price generation has been controversial since the inception of the futures market. Keynes [19] and Hicks [17] viewed the futures market as a semiefficient mechanism in which speculators ensure risk-averse investors holding stocks of commodities against changes in future spot prices. To induce speculators to enter the contract, they argued that futures prices should be downward biased estimates of expected

[*]University of Illinois at Urbana-Champaign.
[**]University of Miami, Coral Gables.

Advances in Futures and Options Research, Vol. 3, pages 357–377.

spot prices and increase over the life of the contract since futures prices must equal spot prices on the maturity date. This hypothesis, called "normal backwardation," contends that the risk premium of a futures contract is positive, where risk is measured as the variability of futures prices. On the other hand, Hardy [15] and Telser [31] viewed the futures market as a mechanism where speculators are gambling with hedgers, and thus argued that speculators are willing to enter the contract even if futures prices stay above expected spot prices. In an attempt to test the normal backwardation hypothesis, a number of studies have examined the price changes of various futures contracts, but empirical results are mixed.[1]

Recently a number of studies (e.g., Dusak [13], Bodie and Rosansky [4], Carter, Rausser, and Schmitz [6], and Baxter, Conine, and Tamarkin [2]) have analyzed futures prices in the capital asset pricing model (CAPM hereafter) framework of Sharpe [30], Lintner [20], and Mossin [22]. Inherent in the CAPM is that capital assets, under some simple assumptions, are held as a function of the expected means and variances of security returns, and that investors pay only for the systematic risk of a capital asset as measured by the covariance between the return on the asset and the return on the market portfolio. As reviewed below, previous studies ran the regression of changes in futures prices against the return on the market portfolio to estimate the systematic risk of futures contracts without testing whether the covariance relation is consistent with the CAPM.[2] Furthermore, the previous studies reached different conclusions depending upon the proxy chosen for the market portfolio, bringing into question the validity of the CAPM in estimating risk premiums for futures contracts.

The main purpose of this study is to further investigate the behavior of risk premiums for commodity futures contracts employing an alternative pricing model, the arbitrage pricing theory (APT hereafter) developed by Ross [26], in which the market portfolio does not play a crucial role. We also make use of a larger variety of futures contracts than employed in previous studies. In light of the fact that the measure of the systematic risk of a futures contract depends on the proxy used for the market portfolio, the APT seems to be a natural choice to be examined. In addition, for comparison purposes, we test whether the covariance relation of futures is consistent with the CAPM. Roll [24] pointed out some serious problems testing the CAPM for common stocks. Nevertheless, whether or not futures prices can be analyzed in the CAPM framework is a fundamental question that needs to be investigated before the theory can be used to infer anything about the risk of futures contracts.

The paper is organized as follows. Section II briefly reviews the literature concerning risk premiums for commodity futures within the CAPM framework. In Section III, we examine the risk premiums using the APT and thus eliminate the market portfolio proxy problem. In Section IV, we reexamine the risk–return relation of commodity futures in the CAPM framework for the purpose of comparing it with the APT. Section V contains a brief summary and conclusion.

II. PREVIOUS RESEARCH CONCERNING RISK PREMIUMS FOR COMMODITY FUTURES CONTRACTS

A number of empirical studies have examined the return on commodity futures in the context of the CAPM. Dusak [13], arguing that futures contracts are not different in principle from any other risky assets, ran the following market model to estimate the systematic risk of a futures contract:

$$R_{jt} = \alpha_j + \beta_j R_{mt} + e_t, \tag{1}$$

where

R_{jt} = the random percentage change in the futures price of commodity j in time period t.

R_{mt} = the random percentage change in the market portfolio m in time period t.

β_j = the measure of the systematic risk of the commodity futures j.

e_j = the random disturbance that is assumed to have mean zero and constant variance.

For the proxy for the market portfolio m in Equation (1), Dusak used the Standard and Poor (S&P) 500 common stock index. Examining 2-week holding period returns for wheat, corn, and soybean futures over the period 1952–1967, she found that systematic risk was not significantly different from zero. Based on this result, she concluded that futures contracts are not risky and that Keynes's normal backwardation hypothesis is not supported. Bodie and Rosansky [4] extended Dusak's work using quarterly returns on a buy-and-hold strategy of 23 commodity futures from 1950 to 1976. For the market portfolio, they employed a "benchmark" portfolio consisting of equal dollar amounts invested in all the available commodity futures. For the benchmark portfolio, the mean rate of return was positive, which supported the normal backwardation hypothesis.[3] However, most individual commodities had negative betas even though the returns were, in general, positive. In addition, they ran a cross-sectional regression of returns against betas. The negative slope coefficient led them to conclude that their findings were not consistent with the CAPM.

More recently, Carter, Rausser, and Schmitz [6] (CRS hereafter) criticized Dusak's work on the grounds that the proxy for the market portfolio Dusak used was not appropriate for commodity futures and that

Dusak ignored the net positions of speculators. Using an alternative index that was composed of the S&P 500 common stocks and the Dow Jones Commodity Futures Index and considering the net positions of speculators, CRS found that the betas of the same commodity futures (i.e., wheat, corn, and soybeans) were positive. Based on this result, they concluded that holding futures contracts is risky and that the theory of normal backwardation has some merit. However, subsequent studies in turn criticized the CRS study arguing that their modified CAPM was misspecified. Specifically, Marcus [21] argued that CRS overstated the value of commodity weighting in the market portfolio and that the beta estimates were biased. Baxter, Conine, and Tamarkin [2] (BCT hereafter) also pointed out that CRS substantially overstated the value of cash commodities in their weighting scheme, and argued in addition that the criticism of Dusak for the exclusion of short positions of speculators is faulty since the CAPM as formulated by Dusak does not allow short selling in the first place. With persuasive arguments, BCT used the proxy for the market portfolio, which was constructed of 93.7% of the S&P 500 common stock index and 6.3% of the Dow Jones Commodity Cash Index instead of the Futures Index. Using the same commodities, wheat, corn, and soybeans, from January 1, 1975 to December 31, 1981, BCT replicated Dusak's results, confirmed Marcus's arguments, and rejected CRS's conclusion.

III. COMMODITY FUTURES IN THE APT

As reviewed in the previous section, the measurement of the systematic risk of commodity futures contracts varies depending upon the market portfolio proxy employed. In this section, we examine the risk–return relation of commodity futures contracts in an alternative pricing model in which the market portfolio does not play a crucial role, i.e., the APT. The data and test procedures are summarized below.

A. Data

Commodity futures price data for 14 agricultural commodities and three metals (platinum, silver, and copper) were collected from a variety of sources for the 1967–1982 period. The commodities and their sources are listed in the Appendix. For the market portfolio, three measures are used. The first is the New York Stock Exchange value-weighted index obtained from the CRSP tape, the second is an equal-weighted commodity futures index that we construct using the 17 commodities, and the third is a combination of 90% NYSE index and 10% commodity futures index.[4]

A difficulty in testing the risk–return relation for commodity futures relates to developing a return series for futures contracts since they require no initial investment. We use two methods to compute the rate of return for a futures contract. The first method uses the percentage change in the futures price. The second method involves forming a portfolio that consists of buying a futures contract and investing money equal to the futures price in the riskless asset and calculating the rate of return on the portfolio (roughly the percentage change in the futures price plus the risk-free return).[5] This procedure is justified by considering a futures contract as the purchase of a capital asset (the underlying commodity) on credit (see Dusak [13]).

Quarterly returns on futures contracts were calculated for both methods by first examining changes in the price of the contract for a given commodity that was to mature soonest after the quarter's end. In some cases, the contract to mature soonest after a quarter's end was not traded at the end of both that and the preceding quarter. In that case, the next nearest contract for which the required price data were available was used. For the second series of returns (i.e., the interest-adjusted return series), the 3-month Treasury bill rate was used as the risk-free interest rate. Since the results from both series of returns are quite similar, only the results from the interest-adjusted return series are reported.[6] One may argue that monthly returns can provide more powerful tests. However, it is important to note that maturities of futures contracts are standardized in general with 3-month intervals. Thus, empirical tests using monthly returns on futures contracts may be subject to a conditional heteroscedasticity problem. Quarterly returns were chosen to overcome this problem.[7]

B. The APT and Test Procedure

The Arbitrage Pricing Theory (APT) of Ross [26, 27] begins by assuming that the return on asset i is generated by the following k linear factor model:

$$\tilde{R}_{it} = E_i + b_{i1}\tilde{f}_{1t} + \cdots + b_{ik}\tilde{f}_{kt} + \tilde{\eta}_{it}, \qquad i = 1, ..., n \text{ and } t = 1, ..., T, \quad (2)$$

where E_i is the mean return on asset i, f_{jt} is percentage change in factor j during period t, and η_{it} is a random error term. It is assumed that the f's are uncorrelated with each other and with the residuals η's. Ross [26, 27] and others have shown that if n is infinite, there exist numbers $\lambda_0, \lambda_1, ...,$ and λ_k such that

$$E_i \approx \lambda_0 + \lambda_1 b_{i1} + \cdots + \lambda_k b_{ik}. \qquad (3)$$

Roll and Ross [25] have developed a classical procedure for testing the APT. Following them, we use a GLS procedure to estimate the factor risk premiums of (3). Chen [8] has provided a chi-square statistic to test the hypothesis that any one of the risk premiums is priced as

$$T\Lambda W^{-1}\Lambda' \sim \chi^2,$$

where $\Lambda = \sum \lambda_t/T$ and $W = \sum (\lambda_t - \Lambda)'(\lambda_t - \Lambda)/T$.

One difficulty in using the APT is to determine the number of factors, which has been subject to debate. Roll and Ross used the maximum likelihood (ML) factoring method to estimate the number of factors in the common stock returns. They found that in about 88% of their groups the probability that no more than five factors are needed to explain the stock returns is higher than 0.5, and that when $\bar{\lambda}_0$ is not taken as known, in 95% of the groups three or fewer factors are associated with the risk premium. However, Dhrymes, Friend, and Gultekin (DFG) [11] and Dhrymes, Friend, Gultekin, and Gultekin (DFGG) [12] have argued that the number of factors generating returns is sensitive to the number of assets in the group and the number of time periods. Brown and Weinstein [5] used bilinear factoring procedures to test the appropriate number of factors for common stock returns. Their findings supported the three-factor version of the APT. We also apply the ML method to determine the number of factors generating commodity futures returns.

Unfortunately, when our 17 commodity futures data were factorized, the Heywood cases happened for the factors less than the sufficient number.[8] We found that five factors are sufficient for the whole period and four factors are sufficient for each subperiod if the Heywood case is allowed. When we drop assets that have communalities greater than one, the sufficient number of factors is less than three. Therefore, we report the results for only the three-factor model.[9] Since the ML method faced the Heywood problem, we used principal component analysis to estimate factor loadings and factor scores as suggested by Chamberlain and Rothschild [7] and Connor and Karajczyk [9] in testing the approximate factor structure (i.e., the unique factors are allowed to be correlated with each other).

We also test whether the residual standard error from the factor model enters the pricing relation as suggested by Roll and Ross [25], Chen [8], and Dhrymes, Friend, and Gultekin (DFG) [11].[10] In addition, we test whether the market portfolio provides any useful information concerning the pricing relation in addition to the factors. We regress the market portfolio returns against the three factors and the residual is obtained as

$$\widetilde{R}_{mt} = a_0 + a_1\tilde{f}_{1t} + a_2\tilde{f}_{2t} + a_3\tilde{f}_{3t} + \tilde{\varepsilon}_{mt}. \tag{4}$$

The residual from the market portfolio is regarded as the $k + 1$ factor. Since this additional factor is orthogonal to other factors by construction, the responsive coefficients to this additional factor for each asset can be easily computed as

$$b_{im} = \text{Cov}(\widetilde{R}_{it}, \tilde{\varepsilon}_{mt})/\text{Var}(\tilde{\varepsilon}_{mt}), \tag{5}$$

where $\tilde{\varepsilon}_{mt}$ is from (4) and m is the NYSE index, s, or the commodity futures index, f.

In sum, the following versions of the APT are used to test the risk−return relation for the commodity futures:

Model A: $\quad \tilde{R}_{it} = \lambda_{0t} + \lambda_{1t}b_{i1} + \lambda_{2t}b_{i2} + \lambda_{3t}b_{i3} + \tilde{\mu}_{it}$

Model B: $\quad \tilde{R}_{it} = \lambda_{0t} + \lambda_{1t}b_{i1} + \lambda_{2t}b_{i2} + \lambda_{3t}b_{i3} + \lambda_{5t}\sigma(\eta_{it}) + \tilde{\mu}_{it}$

Model C_1: $\quad \tilde{R}_{it} = \lambda_{0t} + \lambda_{1t}b_{i1} + \lambda_{2t}b_{i2} + \lambda_{3t}b_{i3} + \lambda_{4t}b_{is} + \lambda_{5t}\sigma(\eta_{it}) + \tilde{\mu}_{it}$ $\qquad$ (6)

$\quad C_2$: $\quad \tilde{R}_{it} = \lambda_{0t} + \lambda_{1t}b_{i1} + \lambda_{2t}b_{i2} + \lambda_{3t}b_{i3} + \lambda_{4t}b_{if} + \lambda_{5t}\sigma(\eta_{it}) + \tilde{\mu}_{it},$

where $\sigma(\eta_{it})$ represents the residual standard error from the three-factor model, and b_{is} and b_{if} represent values from Equation (5) corresponding to the NYSE common stock index and the commodity futures index, respectively.

Model A can be interpreted as the Ross version of the APT. Models B and C are alternative tests of the APT: Model B tests whether the unique factor of the standard error of the three-factor model plays a role. Model C tests whether the market portfolio provides any information in pricing commodity futures. Models C_1 and C_2 use for the market portfolio the NYSE index s and the commodity futures index f, respectively. We also used the combination of 90% NYSE index and 10% futures index for the market portfolio in a version of Model C. Since the results are not significantly different from Model C_1, they are not reported.[11]

C. Empirical Results

The first two moments of the returns on the commodity futures contracts and a correlation matrix are shown in Table 1. As expected, the correlations among related commodities such as soybeans and soybean oil are usually high. The mean rate of return for each commodity is positive, a result that is consistent with Bodie and Rosansky [4]. If judged only in terms of mean returns (as in Bodie and Rosansky), the result lends support to the Keynesian normal backwardation hypothesis.

The results on the APT models of (6) are summarized in Table 2. To examine the stability of the coefficients, we test the APT models in equally divided subperiods as well as the whole period.

From Table 2, $\bar{\lambda}_0$ is positive and significant in all four models in both the whole period and the second subperiod. But it is negative and insignificant in the first subperiod in all models except for Model A. All three factor risk premiums, $\bar{\lambda}_1$, $\bar{\lambda}_2$, and $\bar{\lambda}_3$, are insignificent in all models in all three periods except that the second factor premium is significant in the second period for Models B and C. The χ^2_{1-3} statistic, which is used to simultaneously test the

Table 1. Commodity Futures Contracts: Correlation Matrix and Quarterly Mean Return (1967–1982)

	Wheat	Corn	Oats	Soybeans	Soybean Meal	Soybean Oil	Silver	Copper	Potatoes	Platinum	Cotton	Orange Juice	Sugar	Cocoa	Bellies	Pork Hogs	Cattle
Wheat	1.0000																
Corn	0.7083	1.0000															
Oats	0.6802	0.6963	1.0000														
Soybeans	0.3817	0.6784	0.4662	1.0000													
Soybean meal	0.4157	0.6186	0.4204	0.6002	1.0000												
Soybean oil	0.2864	0.5202	0.4043	0.8847	0.2740	1.0000											
Silver	0.0631	0.0432	−0.0761	0.1197	0.0734	0.1395	1.0000										
Copper	0.0440	0.0312	−0.0846	0.2703	0.2587	0.2035	0.4707	1.0000									
Potatoes	0.4050	0.3260	0.2985	0.3180	0.2462	0.3620	0.1212	0.2804	1.0000								
Platinum	0.0488	0.0059	0.0303	0.1832	0.0811	0.1967	0.6526	0.4729	0.1170	1.0000							
Cotton	0.4666	0.3682	0.3884	0.4152	0.2336	0.4229	0.1142	0.1139	0.2655	0.1210	1.0000						
Orange juice	0.0194	−0.0257	0.0108	0.0316	0.1103	−0.0481	−0.0274	0.0994	0.0622	0.0994	−0.0167	1.0000					
Sugar	0.2807	0.3200	0.2819	0.2727	0.4158	0.1556	0.2688	0.1405	0.0096	0.1718	−0.0010	−0.1269	1.0000				
Cocoa	0.1067	0.2811	0.0800	0.4081	0.3457	0.2689	0.1614	0.2825	0.1943	0.1594	0.1265	0.0790	0.0801	1.0000			
Pork bellies	0.2196	0.2578	0.3138	0.3583	0.2883	0.2872	0.1311	0.0846	0.1642	−0.0659	0.1452	0.0131	0.1214	0.0420	1.0000		
Hogs	0.2503	0.2451	0.2759	0.3870	0.2109	0.3588	0.0749	0.0928	0.3226	0.0024	0.1722	0.0579	0.0062	−0.0401	0.7635	1.0000	
Cattle	0.0620	0.0338	0.0422	0.1677	−0.0808	0.2353	0.0045	0.1533	0.2691	0.0449	−0.0206	0.0017	−0.2039	−0.2710	0.4215	0.6326	1.0000
Mean (%)	2.063	1.788	2.114	3.867	5.504	4.390	4.907	3.547	0.337	2.824	3.330	6.135	5.832	6.851	2.626	5.337	3.500
σ	16.60	11.94	11.37	17.12	18.05	20.18	23.28	15.81	19.16	15.66	14.88	22.64	27.97	19.80	16.90	12.45	9.16

Table 2. Average Values of the Estimated Coefficients of the APT Models[a]

$$\tilde{R}_{it} = \lambda_{0t} + \lambda_{1t}b_{i1} + \lambda_{2t}b_{i2} + \lambda_{3t}b_{i3} + \lambda_{4t}b_{im} + \lambda_{5t}\sigma(\eta_{it}) + \tilde{\mu}_{it}$$

Model	$\bar{\lambda}_0$	$\bar{\lambda}_1$	$\bar{\lambda}_2$	$\bar{\lambda}_3$	$\bar{\lambda}_4$	$\bar{\lambda}_5$	χ^2_{1-3} [b]	χ^2_{4-5} [c]
			A. Whole Period (1967–1982)					
A	0.0404**	−0.0215	−0.0666	0.0281	—	—	0.361	—
	(5.771)	(−0.151)	(−0.529)	(0.220)				
B	0.0208**	−0.0501	−0.1119	−0.0264	—	0.2007**	0.892	—
	(1.962)	(−0.352)	(−0.881)	(−0.205)		(2.479)		
C_1	0.0211**	−0.0569	−0.1136	−0.0301	−0.0494	0.2049**	0.953	10.912**
	(1.981)	(−0.399)	(−0.893)	(−0.232)	(−0.230)	(2.487)		
C_2	0.0253**	−0.0659	−0.1029	−0.0267	−0.0011	0.1872**	0.815	4.429
	(2.117)	(−0.436)	(−0.809)	(−0.204)	(−0.554)	(2.053)		
			B. First Subperiod (1967–1974)					
A	0.0331**	0.2748	−0.2673	0.034	—	—	4.652	—
	(4.911)	(1.474)	(−1.511)	(0.019)				
B	−0.0099	0.1156	−0.3490*	−0.0374	—	0.5096**	4.487	—
	(−0.965)	(0.613)	(−1.966)	(−0.211)		(5.552)		
C_1	−0.0129	0.0955	−0.3603**	−0.0526	−0.0309	0.5582**	4.657	30.283**
	(−1.183)	(0.503)	(−2.026)	(−0.297)	(−1.332)	(5.261)		
C_2	−0.0109	0.1784	−0.3084*	−0.0361	0.0025	0.4752**	4.147	24.885**
	(−0.941)	(0.930)	(−1.741)	(−0.204)	(0.601)	(4.849)		
			C. Second Subperiod (1975–1982)					
A	0.0486**	−0.2990	−0.2349	0.1913	—	—	5.231	—
	(5.618)	(−1.541)	(−1.286)	(1.075)				
B	0.0789**	−0.3034	−0.2444	0.1658	—	−0.2780**	5.100	—
	(5.844)	(−1.565)	(−1.339)	(0.929)		(−2.911)		
C_1	0.0813**	−0.3245	−0.2553	0.1601	−0.0238	−0.2776**	5.484	9.759**
	(5.857)	(−1.665)	(−1.396)	(0.897)	(−1.118)	(−2.825)		
C_2	0.0814**	−0.3059	−0.2530	0.1525	−0.0008	−0.3030**	4.766	10.449**
	(5.777)	(−1.509)	(−1.364)	(0.852)	(−0.454)	(−3.098)		

Notes: [a]The numbers in parentheses represent t-statistics.
[b]χ^2_{1-3} is to test the hypothesis that $\bar{\lambda}_1 = \bar{\lambda}_2 = \bar{\lambda}_3 = 0$.
[c]χ^2_{4-5} is to test the hypothesis that $\bar{\lambda}_4 = \bar{\lambda}_5 = 0$.
**Significant at the 5% level based upon two-sided test except $\bar{\lambda}_0$.
*Significant at the 10% level based upon two-sided test except $\bar{\lambda}_0$.

joint hypothesis that $\bar{\lambda}_1 = \bar{\lambda}_2 = \bar{\lambda}_3 = 0$, is insignificant in all models in all periods. Furthermore, $\bar{\lambda}_4$ is insignificant in all periods. This result suggests that the market portfolio does not provide any extra explanation in pricing the commodity futures, regardless of which proxy, the NYSE common stock index or the commodity futures index, is used.

What is even more interesting in Table 2 is the estimate of $\bar{\lambda}_5$, the coefficient of the unique factor, $\sigma(\eta_{it})$, i.e., the standard error of the factor pricing model. $\bar{\lambda}_5$ is significant at the 5% level in all periods for all relevant models. This result indicates that something other than the factors (i.e., the unsystematic risk) is important in pricing commodity futures. Note also that the sign of $\overline{\lambda}_5$ changes from the first period to the second period. In light of the fact that no initial investment is required for futures contracts, the positive (negative) $\overline{\lambda}_5$ can be interpreted to mean that a long (short) position in the futures contract is paid for the unexpected price volatility. The last column in Table 2 shows χ^2_{4-5} statistics, which are used to test simultaneously the joint hypothesis that $\overline{\lambda}_4 = \overline{\lambda}_5 = 0$. As expected from the coefficients of $\overline{\lambda}_4$ and $\overline{\lambda}_5$, χ^2_{4-5} are significant at the 5% level in all tests except for Model C_2 when the 1967–1982 data are used. In sum, the results in Table 2 suggest that the risk–return relation for commodity futures does not conform to the APT. The residual variance appears to be the only variable that explains commodity futures pricing.

However, one should be cautious in interpreting the results. Since the returns on individual futures contracts are used in cross-sectional regressions (6), the estimates of coefficients may be subject to a nontrivial errors-in-variables problem. To overcome this problem, we used the cross-sectional-regression-test (CSRT), suggested by Shanken [29]. Using his notations, Shanken's CSRT can be summarized as:[12]

(i) Unadjusted test statistic Q:

$$Q = T e' \hat{V}^{-1} e,$$

where

T = the length of the time-series
$\hat{V}$ = an (n × n) estimated sample variance–covariance matrix for n assets
e = an (n × 1) vector of residuals estimated from the generalized least-squares (GLS) cross-sectional regression on factor loadings for n assets
  $\equiv \overline{R} - X\hat{\Gamma}$
$\overline{R}$ = time series means of security returns R_t
X = the matrix for explanatory variables, factor loadings
$\hat{\Gamma}$ = the coefficients of X
  $\equiv (X'\hat{V}^{-1}X'\hat{V}^{-1}\overline{R}.$

Basically, the unadjusted test statistic Q is defined as a sum of residual squares obtained from a GLS cross-sectional regression.

(ii) Test statistic Q^A that is adjusted for the estimation errors of factor loadings:

$$Q^A \equiv Q/(1 + \hat{\lambda}' \Delta^{-1}\hat{\lambda}) \sim T^2(n - k - a - 1, T - k - 1)$$
$$F = Q^A(T - n + 1 + a)/(n - k - a - 1)(T - k - 1)$$
$$\sim F(n - k - a - 1, T - n + a + 1),$$

Table 3. Shanken's CSRT Results on the APT for the Whole Period
(1967–1982)

A. Test for three-factor APT
   1. $F(13,48) = 2.023$ when σ is not included
   2. $F(12,49) = 1.710$ when σ is included
B. Test for three-factor plus market portfolio APT[a]
   1. $F(12,48) = 1.568$ when σ is not included
   2. $F(11,49) = 1.278$ when σ is included

Note: [a] The market portfolio was constructed in the proportion of 10% futures and 90% NYSE index.

where

$$\hat{\lambda} = [\hat{\lambda}_1, ..., \hat{\lambda}_k]$$
Δ = the sample covariance of factor scores
a = the number of extraneous variables in X.

We tested several versions of the APT based on Q^A for the whole period, 1967–1982. The results are reported in Table 3. Part A presents F-statistics for the three-factor APT. When the standard error (σ) is not included as an explanatory variable, F-value equals 2.023, which is significant at the 5% level. Therefore, we may reject the three-factor version of APT without the standard error at the 95% confidence level. However, when the standard error is included, F-value declines significantly, enhancing the probability to accept the model. The results for the three-factor plus market portfolio version of APT are reported in Part B. For comparison purpose, we report only the results on this version of APT, using 10% futures index and 90% NYSE index for the market portfolio. The F-values are, in general, lower than the previous case without the market portfolio. However, like the previous case, the probability to accept the model increases when the standard error is included. This result on Shanken's CSRT confirms the importance of the residual variance in pricing commodity futures.

The results in this section also suggest that the conflicting results in previous studies in a CAPM context may not be necessarily due to different proxies for the market portfolio. In light of the importance of the standard error (σ) in this section, the conflicting results may be because the risk–return relation for commodity futures is not consistent with the CAPM. We reexamine the return structure of commodity futures in the CAPM framework for comparison purpose.

IV. COMMODITY FUTURES IN THE CAPM

The systematic risk (i.e., the beta) of a futures contract is obtained from the following versions of the market model as

$$\widetilde{R}_{it} = \alpha_{is} + \beta_{is}\widetilde{R}_{st} + \tilde{\varepsilon}_{it} \tag{7}$$

$$\widetilde{R}_{it} = \alpha_{if} + \beta_{if}\widetilde{R}_{ft} + \tilde{\varepsilon}_{it}, \tag{8}$$

where

$\widetilde{R}_{it}$ = the return on commodity futures contract i for the period t,
$\widetilde{R}_{st}$ = the return on the NYSE common stock index for the period t,
$\widetilde{R}_{ft}$ = the return on the self-constructed futures index for the period t,
$\beta_{ij} = Cov(\widetilde{R}_{it}, \widetilde{R}_{jt})/Var(\widetilde{R}_{jt})$, where j = s or f.

The beta coefficients for the commodity futures contracts using the NYSE index as the market portfolio are presented in Table 4. Also, to test the stability of the beta, we divided the test period into four equal subperiods. From Table 4, it is clear that most of the beta coefficients are insignificant for both the whole period and the subperiods. However, all of the beta coefficients change over time and appear highly unstable.[13] The fact that some of the previous studies could not observe a risk premium may be due to this instability. However, the instability may also be due to the choice of market index.

Table 5 presents the result of the beta coefficients based on Equation (8). Using data for the entire 1967–1982 period, 15 commodities out of 17 are shown to have positive and significant beta coefficients. This result is in sharp contrast to the Table 4 results. It appears that our commodity futures index approximates the common element of variability in commodity futures returns. However, note that the beta coefficients again change significantly over the subsample periods. For example, in the first subperiod (1967–1970), only four commodities show significant beta coefficients. The number of commodities showing significantly positive betas increases to 8, 12, and 13 in subperiods II, III, and IV, respectively.

As pointed out earlier, whether or not the risk–return relation is consistent with the CAPM is a fundamental question yet to be tested, no matter what proxy for the market portfolio is used. For this purpose, we use a cross-sectional time-series regression similar to Fama and Macbeth [14] as follows:

$$R_{it} = \lambda_{0t} + \lambda_{1t}\beta_i + \lambda_{2t}\beta_i^2 + \lambda_{3t}\sigma_{\varepsilon_{it}} + \mu_{it}, \tag{9}$$

where $\sigma_{\varepsilon_{it}}$ is the standard deviation of the residual term estimated from the market models (7) and (8).

Note, however, that beta instability may cause difficulty in testing the risk–return relation since β_i in Equation (9) is assumed constant over the test period. Therefore, the results for Equation (9) should be interpreted with caution. One way to overcome this difficulty is to shorten the time

Table 4. The Estimated Beta Coefficients from the Market Model Market Index: The Value Weighted CRSP NYSE Index[a]

Commodity Futures Contracts	Whole Period (1967–1982)	Subperiod I (1967–1970)	Subperiod II (1971–1974)	Subperiod III (1975–1978)	Subperiod IV (1979–1982)
1. Wheat	−0.236(−1.028)	0.038(0.151)	0.255(0.373)	−0.928(−2.537)*	0.259(0.692)
2. Corn	−0.395(−2.482)*	−0.107(−0.420)	−0.908(−2.405)*	−0.718(−2.802)*	0.556(1.884)
3. Oats	−0.160(−1.018)	0.098(0.454)	−0.436(−1.93)	−0.459(−1.307)	0.438(1.380)
4. Soybeans	−0.614(−2.716)*	−0.252(−3.661)*	−1.038(−1.974)	−0.902(−1.933)	0.582(2.320)*
5. Soybean meal	−0.819(−3.572)*	−0.043(−0.116)	−1.958(−4.089)*	−0.954(−2.193)*	0.425(1.708)
6. Soybean oil	−0.349(−1.254)	−0.180(−1.097)	−0.718(−0.758)	−0.684(−1.360)	0.738(2.724)*
7. Silver	0.299(0.926)	0.373(0.967)	0.049(0.092)	−0.242(−1.051)	1.262(1.027)
8. Copper	0.092(0.418)	−0.499(−1.287)	0.221(0.342)	0.121(0.413)	0.848(2.097)*
9. Potatoes	−0.165(−0.620)	−0.307(−0.567)	0.070(0.108)	−0.411(−0.796)	0.488(1.097)
10. Platinum	0.306(1.420)	0.605(1.359)	−0.011(−0.023)	−0.375(−1.285)	1.226(2.425)*
11. Cottom	0.108(0.519)	0.183(1.075)	0.302(0.467)	0.083(0.197)	0.082(0.252)
12. Orange juice	−0.253(−0.804)	0.306(0.410)	0.109(0.269)	−1.310(−1.926)	−0.136(−0.187)
13. Sugar	−0.604(−1.613)	0.096(0.202)	−1.217(−1.359)	−0.764(−1.430)	0.777(0.931)
14. Cocoa	−0.00(−1.858)	0.464(1.286)	−1.028(−1.567)	−0.691(−1.444)	−0.487(−1.101)
15. Pork bellies	−0.248(−1.062)	−0.346(−1.036)	−0.486(−1.165)	−0.289(−0.437)	0.240(0.473)
16. Hogs	−0.189(−1.101)	−0.456(−1.667)	−0.141(−0.466)	−0.334(−0.715)	0.235(0.573)
17. Cattle	−0.033(−0.260)	−0.276(−1.838)	−0.192(0.698)	−0.002(−0.007)	−0.130(−0.385)

Note: [a]The numbers in parentheses represent t-statistics.
*Significant at the 5% level.

Table 5. The Estimated Beta Coefficients from the Market Model Market Index: The Equal Weighted Commodity Futures Index[a]

Commodity Futures Contracts	Whole Period (1967–1982)	Subperiod I (1967–1970)	Subperiod II (1971–1974)	Subperiod III (1975–1978)	Subperiod IV (1979–1982)
1. Wheat	1.153(5.91)*	0.741(1.45)	1.082(1.96)	1.352(5.25)*	0.767(2.16)*
2. Corn	0.944(7.36)*	0.570(1.06)	1.230(5.09)*	0.890(4.11)*	0.659(2.13)*
3. Oats	0.744(5.40)*	0.866(2.10)*	0.572(1.83)	1.204(6.34)*	0.454(1.32)
4. Soybeans	1.571(10.25)*	0.160(0.78)	2.032(4.96)*	1.790(8.06)*	0.828(3.62)*
5. Soybean meal	1.370(6.84)*	1.555(2.22)*	1.240(2.25)*	1.517(5.01)*	0.792(3.87)*
6. Soybean oil	1.564(7.10)*	−0.164(−0.45)	2.226(3.45)*	1.664(5.53)*	0.914(3.447*
7. Silver	1.185(3.86)*	0.563(0.66)	0.885(2.12)*	0.626(3.64)*	3.421(3.34)*
8. Copper	0.883(4.34)*	1.903(2.59)*	1.007(1.92)	0.484(1.81)	1.228(3.26)*
9. Potatoes	1.171(4.91)*	0.934(0.80)	1.523(3.54)*	0.690(1.39)	1.068(2.61)*
10. Platinum	0.769(3.69)*	1.291(1.33)	0.525(1.25)	0.596(2.24)*	1.851(4.41)*
11. Cotton	0.809(4.19)*	0.129(0.34)	1.216(2.46)*	0.816(2.25)*	0.194(0.56)
12. Orange juice	0.507(1.55)	4.436(3.94)*	0.025(0.07)	0.603(0.80)	0.456(0.59)
13. Sugar	1.480(4.05)*	1.233(1.01)	0.798(0.96)	1.255(2.69)*	1.810(2.29)*
14. Cocoa	0.984(3.74)*	1.184(1.54)	1.622(3.39)*	0.500(1.01)	−0.048(−0.10)*
15. Pork bellies	0.940(4.31)*	0.616(0.84)	0.648(1.81)	1.544(2.93)*	1.021(2.13)*
16. Hogs	0.710(4.45)*	0.945(1.57)	0.375(1.45)	1.102(3.34)*	0.928(2.49)*
17. Cattle	0.216(1.64)	0.038(0.11)	−0.005(−0.02)	0.367(1.33)	0.654(2.03)*

Note: [a] The numbers in parentheses represent t-statistics.
  * Significant at the 5% level.

period at the expense of increased standard error. Therefore we examine Equation (9) for two equal subperiods in addition to the whole period. We test λ coefficients of Equation (9) based on the betas estimated through Equations (7) and (8). In estimating the regression coefficients, the generalized least-squares (GLS) procedure suggested by Roll and Ross [25] is used. Let $\sum$ be the variance–covariance matrix for the commodity futures portfolios. Then

$$\lambda_t = (\lambda_{0t}, \lambda_{1t}, \lambda_{2t}, \lambda_{3t})' = [\beta^* {\textstyle\sum}^{-1} \beta^*]^{-1} {\textstyle\sum}^{-1} R_t$$

where

$$\beta^* = \begin{bmatrix} 1, & \cdots, & 1 \\ \beta_1, & \cdots, & \beta_n \\ \beta_1^2, & \cdots, & \beta_n^2 \\ \sigma(\varepsilon_{1t}), & \cdots, & \sigma(\varepsilon_{nt}) \end{bmatrix}$$

and

$$R_t = (R_{1t}, R_{2t}, \ldots, R_{nt})'.$$

If the risk–return relation conforms to the CAPM, λ_0 should be the riskless rate of return or zero-beta rate, λ_1 should be greater than zero, and $\lambda_2 = \lambda_3 = 0$ since only the systematic risk is priced linearly. [14]

Table 6 presents the average values of the estimated coefficients of the four-parameter model of (9). $\bar\lambda_0$ through $\bar\lambda_3$ are the arithmetic means of the quarterly cross-sectional regression estimates. The values in parentheses represent t-statistics. [15] Parts A, B, and C in Table 6 are for the whole period (1967–1982), and for first (1967–1974) and second (1975–1982) subperiods, respectively. When the NYSE common stock index is used to estimate the beta of commodity futures, $\bar\lambda_1$ is negative but statistically insignificant for the whole period and the second subperiod and positive but insignificant for the first subperiod. When the betas based on the self-constructed futures index are used, $\bar\lambda_1$ is negative but insignificant regardless of the time period.

$\bar\lambda_2$, which is used to measure the nonlinear relation between the return and beta, is insignificantly positive in the whole and the second subperiod but significantly positive for the first subperiod, regardless of which market index is used. Tinic and West [33] retest the Fama–Macbeth four-parameter CAPM of Equation (9) using common stock returns and find that there exists nonlinearity between the return and beta with a negative sign. Interestingly, we also find slight evidence of nonlinearity but with a positive sign for commodity futures.

More importantly, $\bar\lambda_3$ is positive and significant in both the whole period and the first subperiod. But, it is significantly negative in the second

Table 6. Regressions of the Four-Parameter Model[a]

$$\tilde{R}_{it} = \lambda_{0t} + \lambda_{1t}\beta_i + \lambda_{2t}\beta_i^2 + \lambda_3\sigma(\varepsilon_{it}) + \mu_{it}$$

Market	$\bar{\lambda}_0$	$\bar{\lambda}_1$	$\bar{\lambda}_2$	$\bar{\lambda}_3$
	A. Whole Period (1967–1982)			
NYSE stock	0.0207**	−0.0134	0.0187	0.1538*
	(1.716)	(−0.450)	(0.484)	(1.728)
Commodity futures	0.0249	−0.0324	0.0119	0.2202**
	(1.660)	(−1.141)	(0.839)	(2.538)
	B. First Subperiod (1967–1974)			
NYSE stock	−0.0172	0.0025	0.0462*	0.6585**
	(−1.421)	(0.086)	(1.848)	(4.737)
Commodity futures	−0.0053	−0.0299	0.0256**	(0.5746**
	−0.445)	(−1.269)	(2.232)	(4.702)
	C. Second Subperiod (1975–1982)			
NYSE stock	0.0670**	−0.0231	0.0589	−0.4038**
	(4.188)	(1.014)	(1.066)	(−2.221)
Commodity futures	0.0828**	−0.0661	0.985	−0.1895
	(2.989)	(−1.261)	0.778)	(−1.211)

Notes: [a]The numbers in parentheses represent t-statistics.

**Significant at the 5% level based upon

$$H_0: \bar{\lambda}_0 = 0, \ \bar{\lambda}_1 = 0, \ \bar{\lambda}_2 = 0, \ \bar{\lambda}_3 = 0.$$

*Significant at the 10% level based upon

$$H_0: \bar{\lambda}_0 = 0, \ \bar{\lambda}_1 = 0, \ \bar{\lambda}_2 = 0, \ \bar{\lambda}_3 = 0.$$

subperiod when using the NYSE stock index and insignificantly negative when using the commodity futures index. Tinic and West find similar results in the common stock market. The significant $\bar{\lambda}_3$ in Table 6 indicates the importance of the residual variance for the rate of return on commodity futures. Note that σ_ε is the residual variance from the market models, Equations (7) and (8). In light of the insignificant $\bar{\lambda}_1$ coefficients in general, the significant values of $\bar{\lambda}_3$ provide evidence that traders in commodity futures do not necessarily price the systematic risk but, instead, price the Keynesian version of the risk, i.e., the volatility of the futures price per se. This result is consistent with the APT case although the σ estimate comes from totally different models.

Overall, the results in Tables 2 and 6 indicate that the risk–return relation for commodity futures contracts conforms to neither the APT nor the CAPM. In both models, residual variance appears to be the only important variable for pricing commodity futures contracts. In addition, combining the results on the APT and CAPM tests suggest that the conflicting results of previous studies in a CAPM framework may not be necessarily due to different proxies for the market portfolio, but to the inconsistency of the risk–risk relations with the CAPM and instability.

V. CONCLUSION

Previous studies have examined risk premiums of futures contracts by estimating beta using the market model (i.e., the CAPM). However, empirical results of the studies depend on the proxy adopted for the market portfolio. The main purpose of this study was to further investigate the risk premiums of commodity futures, using an alternative pricing model (i.e., the APT) in which the market portfolio does not play a crucial role. The model is considered especially appropriate for examining the risk premiums for commodity futures contracts in light of the fact that the estimated risk premiums of the futures of previous studies in a CAPM context depend on the market portfolio proxy employed. In addition, we reexamined the risk−return relation of commodity futures in the CAPM framework for the purpose of comparing it with the APT.

Empirical results, using quarterly returns on futures contracts of 14 agricultural commodities and three metals, provided evidence that neither the APT nor the CAPM is satisfactory in explaining the risk−return relation for commodity futures contracts. In both models, the residual variance appeared to be the only important variable in pricing these assets. Our results also suggest that positive or zero risk premiums noted in previous studies in a CAPM context are not necessarily due to different proxies for the market portfolio, but instead are due to the inconsistency of the risk−return relation with the CAPM and instability. The results from our APT model tests confirm this conclusion.

In view of the evidence on the inability of the APT and the CAPM to approximate common elements in the fluctuations of commodity futures returns, identifying underlying economic variables that impact commodity futures returns is a topic that deserves future research.

NOTES

1. See Houthakker [18], Telser [32], Cootner [10], Alchian [1], Hirshleifer [16], Samuelson [28], Dusak [3], Bodie and Rosansky [4], Park [23], Carter, Rausser, and Schmitz [6], and Baxter, Conine, and Tamarkin [2].

2. The only exception, to the authors' best knowledge, is Bodie and Rosansky [4], who ran a simple cross-sectional regression of mean excess returns on commodity futures against their betas.

3. Also, to compare their results with Dusak [13], they restricted their sample to the same three commodities, wheat, corn, and soybeans, and the same time period as Dusak used, and found that their results were somewhat similar to Dusak.

4. We chose the random percentages of futures and NYSE index. However, the composition is roughly consistent with Baxter, Conine, and Tamarkin [2].

5. Consider purchasing a good at the beginning of a period (time t), where delivery of the good and payment will occur at the end of the period (time t + 1). What must be paid at time t

to ensure payment of a fixed price at time t + 1? Assume the futures price at time t for delivery at time t + 1 is F_t. Then an investor could acquire Treasury bills at time t to mature at time t + 1 in the amount F_t, and could simultaneously acquire a futures contract so as to ensure delivery at time t + 1 at price F_t. The investment in Treasury bills would cost $F_t/(1 + R_{ft})$, where R_{ft} is the risk-free interest rate from to to t + 1. The goods received at time t + 1 would have a value equal to the then-existing spot price, which would, at that time, be equal to the futures price, F_{t+1}. The investor's return would be

$$R_t = \frac{1}{F_t/(1 + R_{ft})} \{F_{t+1} - [F_t/(1 + R_{ft})]\} \approx \frac{1}{(1 + R_{ft})} \left(\frac{F_{t+1} - F_t}{F_t} + R_{ft}\right).$$

The above measure of returns on futures contracts is consistent with Dusak [13, see pages 144–147]. However, Dusak excludes the factor R_{ft} in the right-most term to convert a total return measure to a risk premium. Since the scale factor $1/(1 + R_{ft})$ is small, that factor was excluded in computing returns, both by Dusak and in this paper. (However, the primary tests were repeated here while including the factor to verify that the effect was trivial.) The return measure used is also consistent with one used by Bodie and Rosansky [4], although their justification for the measure was very different.

6. The results from the first series of returns are available upon request from the authors.

7. See also Bodie and Rosansky [4] for the use of quarterly returns.

8. Since communalities are squared correlations (when the correlation matrix is to be factorized), one would expect them to lie between 0 and 1. It is a mathematical peculiarity of the common factor model, however, that the final communality may be greater than 1. When the communality is equal to one, the case is called a Heywood; and if the communality exceeds one, it is an ultra-Heywood [see SAS Users Guide (pp. 326–327), Statistical, Ed. (1982)]. Possible causes of Heywood cases include (a) bad prior commonality estimate, (b) too many common factors, (c) too few common factors, (d) not enough data to provide stable estimates, and/or (e) the common factor model is not appropriate specification for the data.

9. The results from the one-, two-, and five-factor models are similar to those from the three-factor model and are available upon request from the authors. Also, the use of only the futures to calculate the factor loadings needed to test the APT can be justified since the APT is testable on subsets in principle.

10. Most of the previous studies in testing the APT use the total variance instead of residual variance as an additional explanatory variable. Unfortunately, the total variance contains the systematic component risk. As a result, there is a double counting problem in estimating the cross-sectional regression coefficients if the total variance is used.

11. The results are available upon requests from the authors.

12. See Shanken [29] for details. Originally, Shanken focused on empirical testing of the CAPM. However, since his CSRT test is general for any cross-sectional regression test, it is equally applicable to the APT.

13. A similar result was noted by Bernard and Frecka [3]. In that study the authors examined the ability of commodity futures contracts to hedge against unexpected specific price inflation. They found a lack of hedging ability for commodity futures contracts and attributed the results to the lack of a stable relation between commodity futures returns and unexpected inflation.

14. See Fama and MacBeth [14] for details.

15. The t-statistic is given by $\sqrt{T}(\lambda_i/S_i)$, where

$$\lambda_i = \Sigma\lambda_{it}/T$$

and

$$S_i^2 = [\Sigma(\lambda_{it} - \lambda_i)^2/T],$$

where T stands for the number of periods.

REFERENCES

1. Alchian, A., "Information, Martingales and Prices," *Swedish Journal of Economics* 76 (March 1974), 3–11.
2. Baxter, J., Conine, T., and Tamarkin, M., "On the Commodity Market Risk Premiums: Additional Evidence," *Journal of Futures Markets* 5 (Spring 1985), 121–125.
3. Bernard, V., and Frecka, T., "Commodity Contracts and Common Stocks as Hedges Against Relative Price Risk," *Journal of Financial and Quantitative Analysis* (1987). 22 (June 1989), 169–188.
4. Bodie, Z., and Rosansky, V., "Risk and Return in Commodity Futures," *Financial Analyst Journal* 36 (May/June 1980), 27–39.
5. Brown, S., and Weinstein, M., "A New Approach to Testing Asset Pricing Theories: The Bilinear Paradigm," *Journal of Finance* 38 (June 1983), 711–743.
6. Carter, G., Rausser, G., and Schmitz, A., "Efficient Asset Portfolios and the Theory of Normal Backwardation," *Journal of Political Economy* 91 (April 1983), 319–331.
7. Chamberlain, G., and Rothschild, M., "Arbitrage, Factor Structure and the Mean-Variance Analysis on Large Asset Markets," *Econometrica* 51 (September 1983), 1281–1304.
8. Chen, N. F., "Some Empirical Tests of the Theory of Arbitrage Pricing," *Journal of Finance* 40 (December 1983), 1393–1414.
9. Connor, G., and Karajczyk, R., "Performance Measure with the Arbitrage Pricing Theory: A New Framework for Analysis," *Journal of Financial Economics* 15 (March 1986), 373–394.
10. Cootner, P., "Returns to Speculators: Telser vs. Keynes," *Journal of Political Economy* 68 (August 1960), 396–404.
11. Dhrymes, P., Friend, I., and Gultekin, B., "A Critical Re-examination on the Empirical Evidence on the Arbitrage Pricing Theory," *Journal of Finance* 39 (June 1984), 323–346.
12. Dhrymes, P., Friend, I., Gultekin, M., and Gultekin, B., "New Tests of the APT and Their Implications," *Journal of Finance* 40 (July 1985), 659–674.
13. Dusak, K., "Future Trading and Investor Return: An Investigation of Commodity Market Risk Premiums," *Journal of Political Economy* 81 (December 1973), 1387–1406.
14. Fama, E., and MacBeth, J., "Risk, Return and Equilibrium: Empirical Tests," *Journal of Political Economy* 71 (May/June 1973), 607–636.
15. Hardy, C., *Risk and Risk Bearing*. Chicago, Illinois: The University of Chicago Press, 1940.
16. Hirshleifer, J., "Speculation and Equilibrium: Information, Risk and Markets," *Quarterly Journal of Economics* 89 (November 1975), 519–542.
17. Hicks, J., *Value and Capital: An Inquiry into Some Fundamental Principles of Economic Theory*, 2nd ed. Oxford: Oxford University Press, 1939.
18. Houthakker, H., "Can Speculators Forecast Prices?," *Review of Economics and Statistics* (May 1957).
19. Keynes, J., *A Treatise on Money*. New York: Harcourt Brace Co., 1930.
20. Lintner, J., "Security Prices, Risk and Maximum Gains from Diversification," *Journal of Finance* 20 (December 1965), 587–615.
21. Marcus, A., "Efficient Asset Portfolios and the Theory of Normal Backwardation: A Comment," *Journal of Political Economy* 92 (February 1984), 162–164.
22. Mossin, J., "Equilibrium in a Capital Asset Market," *Econometrica* 37 (October 1966), 763–768.
23. Park, H., "Reexamination of Normal Backwardation Hypothesis on Futures Markets," *Journal of Futures Markets* 5 (Winter 1985), 505–515.

24. Roll, R., "A Critique of the Asset Pricing Theory's Tests," *Journal of Financial Economics* (May 1977), 129–176.

25. Roll, R., and Ross, S., "An Empirical Investigation of the Arbitrage Pricing Theory," *Journal of Finance* (December 1980), 1073–1103.

26. Ross, S., "The Arbitrage Theory of Capital Asset Pricing," *Journal of Economic Theory* (December 1976), 341–360.

27. Ross, S., "Return, Risk and Arbitrage," in *Risk and Return in Finance* (I. Friend and J. Bicksler, eds.), 1977. Cambridge, MA: Ballinger.

28. Samuelson, P., "Proof that Properly Anticipated Prices Fluctuate Randomly," *Industrial Management Review* (Spring 1965), 41–49.

29. Shanken, J., "Multivariate Test of the Zero-Beta CAPM," *Journal of Financial Economics* 14 (September 1985), 327–348.

30. Sharpe, W., "Capital Asset Prices: A Theory of Market Equilibrium under Conditions of Risk," *Journal of Finance* 19 (September 1964), 425–442.

31. Telser, L., "Futures Trading and the Storage of Cotton and Wheat," *Journal of Political Economy* 66 (June 1958), 233–255.

32. Telser, L., "Returns to Speculators: Telser vs. Keynes: Reply," *Journal of Political Economy* 68 (August 1960), 404–415.

33. Tinic, S., and West, R., 'Risk, Return, and Equilibrium: A Revisit," *Journal of Political Economy* 94 (February 1986), 126–147.

APPENDIX: COMMODITY FUTURES CONTRACTS INCLUDED IN SAMPLE

		Maturity Date of Contract Used to Calculate Return for Calendar Quarter			
Commodity	Exchange	I	II	III	IV
Wheat	Chicago Board of Trade[a]	May	July	December	March
Corn	Chicago Board of Trade[a]	May	July	December	March
Oats	Chicago Board of Trade[a]	May	July	December	March
Soybeans	Chicago Board of Trade[a]	May	July	November	January
Soybean oil	Chicago Board of Trade[a]	May	July	October	January
Soybean meal	Chicago Board of Trade[a]	May	July	October	February
Pork bellies	Chicago Mercantile Exchange[b]	May	July	February	February[c]
Live hogs	Chicago Mercantile Exchange[b]	April	July	October[c]	February[c]
Live cattle	Chicago Mercantile Exchange[b]	April	August	October	February
Potatoes (Maine)	N.Y. Mercantile Exchange[d]	April[c]	November	November	March
Cotton	N.Y. Cotton Exchange[d]	May	July	October	March
Sugar	N.Y. Coffee Sugar Exchange[d]	May	September	November ('67–'70)	March
				October ('71–'82)	March
Cocoa	N.Y. Cocoa Exchange[d]	May	July	December	March
Orange juice	N.Y. Cotton Exchange[d]	May	July	November	January
Platinum	N.Y. Mercantile Exchange[d]	April	July	October	January
Copper	Commodity Exchange, Inc.[d]	May	July	October[c]	January
Silver	Commodity Exchange, Inc.[d]	May	July	October	January

[a]Price data were collected from a series of the *Statistical Annual*, published by the Chicago Board of Trade.

[b]Price data for 1972 through 1982 were collected from a series of the *Yearbook* published by the Chicago Mercantile Exchange. Data for periods prior to 1972 were collected from a series of the *Annual Summary of Commodity Futures Statistics*, published by the Commodity Exchange Authority.

[c]Represents most often used contract: in some cases where data for near contract were available, the nearer contract was used. In addition, in some cases where the contract listed above was inactive, data for the next-nearest contract were used.

[d]Price data were collected from the *Wall Street Journal* and the *Journal of Commerce*.

THE DAY-OF-THE-WEEK EFFECT FOR DERIVATIVE ASSETS:
THE CASE OF GOLD FUTURES OPTIONS

Frank J. Fabozzi[*] and Christopher K. Ma[**]

I. INTRODUCTION

In recent years, several studies have examined the so-called "day-of-the-week" effect. The studies by French [4], Gibbons and Hess [5], and others [9, 10] show that in equity markets, the mean return of Monday is lower than that of the other weekdays. Jaffe and Westerfield [7] identify the same daily effect in foreign equity markets. While strong evidence of daily seasonality has been found in various equity markets, recent studies show that this phenomenon, in general, does not carry over to the derivative asset

[*]Sloan School of Management, MIT.
[**]College of Business Administration, Texas Tech University, and University of Toledo.

Advances in Futures and Options Research, Vol. 3, pages 379–388.

market. Both Cornell [2] and Junkus [8] fail to find significant weekend effects in returns of stock index futures. Using a slightly different return measure and time period, Dyl and Maberly [3] find a weak, negative Monday effect on close-to-open S&P 500 index futures prices. However, their test statistics indicate that the Monday returns are not statistically different from other days of the week at a meaningful level of significance. Similarly, Sweeney, McBain, and Crane [14] conclude that the weekend effect concerning equity markets does not apply to the index options market.

While some empirical explanations may be provided for insignificant findings in the derivative market,[1] more importantly, there is a lack of general understanding on the relationship between the pricing (in)efficiency in cash markets and in futures markets. In particular, it is still unclear as to what extent the anomaly in the cash market, if it exists, may transmit to its derivative asset market. The purpose of this paper is to investigate the relationship of the daily effect between the derivative asset market and the underlying asset market. To examine daily seasonality properly, we seek an asset that has an extensive trading record on both the cash market and the derivative asset market. Gold futures and gold futures options are selected since gold futures contracts have been traded on both the New York Commodity Exchange (COMEX) and the Chicago Mercantile Exchange since 1975, and gold futures options have been traded on both the COMEX and Chicago Board of Trade since 1982. In addition, both Ball, Torous, and Tschoegl [1] and Ma [11] present evidence that the daily return seasonality is evident in the gold spot market. This provides a unique opportunity to examine the relationship of seasonality in the spot asset market and its derivative asset market.

The remainder of this paper is organized as follows: Section II describes the source of the data. The hypotheses, testing methodology, and empirical results are discussed in Section III. The implications and conclusions are presented in Section IV.

II. DATA

Our sample includes 9380 daily gold futures option premium observations between October 1982 and October 1986. Table 1 summarizes the sample characteristics. On average, the sample covers a diverse array of option contracts in terms of the month of expiration, the time to maturity, and the degree of in-the-money. Since long-term options may introduce some biases of illiquidity to the daily effect, there are proportionally more observations for the shorter term contracts. Corresponding to each futures option contract, daily futures prices of the same maturity are also collected for the

Table 1. Sample Description[a]

SK (Futures/Strike)	No. of Obs.	Days to Maturity	No. of Obs.	Month of Expiration	No. of Obs.	No. of Contracts
SK > 1.4	296	t > 360	506	February	781	9
1.4 > SK > 1.2	1716	360 > t > 300	593	April	931	9
1.2 > SK > 1.0	3884	300 > t > 240	1249	June	1431	9
1.0 > SK > 0.8	3264	240 > t > 180	1861	August	2029	16
0.8 > SK	220	180 > t > 120	2252	October	1645	14
		120 > t	2919	December	2563	13

"Time period: 10/04/82–9/30/86.
Number of trading days: 1002.
Number of call options contracts: 70.
Number of daily observations: 9380.

sample period. Both futures option premiums and futures prices are daily closing prices gathered from *Statistical Yearbook* published by the Commodity Exchange, Inc..

The preliminary sample is further screened to delete some well-known "abnormal" price movements over the life of typical option contracts. For the purpose of this study, daily returns immediately following holidays are deleted.[2] As Stoll and Whaley [13] document volatile options/futures price movements near expiration dates, the observations during the expiration month are also dropped from the sample.

III. HYPOTHESES, METHODOLOGY, AND EMPIRICAL RESULTS

A. Simple Tests of the Weekend Effect

In our initial tests we compared the average weekday returns for the sample of gold futures options. The daily return was computed as follows:

$$R_t = \ln(P_t/P_{t-1})$$

where ln is the natural logarithm and P_t and P_{t-1} are closing prices on day t and t − 1, respectively. Part A of Table 2 shows the mean return for each weekday. The computed t-statistics indicate that the mean return for Monday, Tuesday, and Thurday is significantly different from zero at the 1% level.

To test the hypothesis that the Monday return is significantly different from other weekday returns, the following model is estimated:

$$R_t = d_1 + \sum_{t=2}^{5} d_t D_t + e_t \qquad (1)$$

Table 2.   A: Average Returns for Weekdays

	Monday	Tuesday	Wednesday	Thursday	Friday
Mean return	-1.292^*	-2.737^*	-0.524	-2.471^*	-0.551
Standard deviation	17.706	13.710	15.100	14.506	15.220
T-value	-3.032	-8.720	-1.524	-7.501	-1.566
Number of observations	1731	1908	1932	1939	1870

*Significant at the 1% level.

Table 2.   B: Regression Statistics for Equation (1):
$$R_t = d_1 + d_2D_2 + d_3D_3 + d_4D_4 + d_5D_5 + e_t$$

	d_1	d_2	d_3	d_4	d_5
Estimate	-1.292^*	-1.445^*	0.768	-1.179^*	0.741
Standard error	(0.376)	(0.507)	(0.505)	(0.505)	(0.510)

$N = 9380$, $R^2 = 0.004$, F-value = 8.96, Prob > F = 0.0001

*Significant at the 1% level.
**Significant at the 5% level.

where e_t is the error term and D_2 through D_5 represent dummy variables indicating the day of the week return (e.g., D_2 is equal to 1 if the return occurs on a Tuesday, with D_3 through D_5 equal to 0). The intercept, d_1, represents the average Monday return. The coefficients of dummy variables measure the average difference in returns between Monday and each of the other weekdays.

Part B of Table 2 summarizes the regression estimates for Equation (1). The Monday return is significantly higher than the Tuesday return and Thursday return at the 1% level. While this evidence reveals some daily effect in option returns, it is different from the general finding of the negative weekend effect in equity markets.

B.   Bull and Bear Market Periods

The seemingly different daily seasonality in futures option returns compared to equity returns requires a further investigation. Jaffe, Ma, and Westerfield [6] and Ma [11] demonstrate that the standard weekend effect may reverse itself in a bull market. Rogalski [12] also finds that the weekend effect in January, generally a bullish month, turns positive. Since the metal market was bullish during late 1982, 1985, and 1986, it is not surprising that a significantly lower Monday return is not prevalent over the entire sample period due to the averaging procedure. However, if there is a bull market and bear market weekend effect, the Monday return should be significantly higher (lower) than other weekday returns in a rising (declining) market period.

To test this hypothesis, we divided the entire sample into bull market and bear market subsamples. Since any classification scheme suffers from its arbitrary nature, three alternative criteria are used to classify the subsamples. The five observations in each week are included in the bull or bear

Table 3. Regression Statistics over Bull/Bear Markets

Coefficient	Criterion A		Criterion B		Criterion C	
	Bull	Bear	Bull	Bear	Bull	Bear
A: Regression Statistics of Equation (1) over Bull/Bear Markets $R_t = d_1 + d_2 D_2 + d_3 D_3 + d_4 D_4 + d_5 D_5 + e_t$						
d_1 (Mon)	0.775	-2.853^*	8.002^*	-11.080^*	8.855^*	-13.789^*
	$(1.29)^a$	(-6.24)	(16.92)	(-26.01)	(22.53)	(-32.52)
d_2 (Tue)	-4.066^*	0.507)	-3.569^*	2.760^*	-3.504^*	2.285^*
	(-4.93)	(0.80)	(-5.23)	(4.84)	(-6.35)	(3.95)
d_3 (Wed)	-2.312^*	3.105^*	-1.183	3.675^*	-1.694^*	2.975^*
	(-2.81)	(4.90)	(-1.78)	(6.34)	(-3.15)	(5.02)
d_4 (Thr)	-3.429^*	0.514	-2.367^*	2.204^*	-2.541^*	2.156^*
	(-4.16)	(0.81)	(-3.49)	(3.87)	(-4.60)	(3.76)
d_5 (Fri)	-1.526	2.427^*	-1.528^{**}	3.365^*	-1.821^*	2.444^*
	(-1.83)	(3.82)	(-2.31)	(5.70)	(-3.38)	(4.06)
N	4052	5267	4455	4923	5139	4239
R^2	0.007	0.0007	0.007	0.010	0.008	0.007
F-value	7.56^*	9.48^*	7.67^*	12.23^*	10.89^*	7.39^*
B: Regression Statistics of Equation (2) over Bull/Bear Markets $RF_t = b_1 + b_2 D_2 + b_3 D_3 + b_4 D_4 + b_5 D_5 + \eta_t$						
b_1 (Mon)	0.313^*	-0.213^*	1.098^*	-1.126^*	0.794^*	-0.937^*
	(3.86)	(-3.38)	(27.45)	(-14.08)	(15.27)	(-11.29)
b_2 (Tue)	-0.747^*	0.032	-0.382^*	0.056	-0.407^*	-0.082
	(-6.67)	(0.36)	(6.70)	(0.52)	(-5.58)	(-0.73)
b_3 (Wed)	-0.381^*	0.457^*	-0.102	0.408^*	-0.139	0.311^*
	(-3.40)	(5.25)	(-1.82)	(3.78)	(-1.96)	(2.68)
b_4 (Thr)	-0.489^*	0.090	-0.257^*	0.195	-0.340^*	0.161
	(-4.37)	(1.03)	(-4.51)	(1.85)	(-4.66)	(1.44)
b_5 (Fri)	-0.462^*	0.108	-0.345^*	0.108	-0.319^*	-0.038
	(-4.09)	(1.24)	(-6.16)	(0.98)	(-4.49)	(-0.32)
R^2	0.011	0.007	0.015	0.004	0.008	0.004
F-value	11.57^*	9.14^*	16.56^*	4.57^*	10.64^*	4.17^*

*Significant at the 1% level.
**Significant at the 5% level.
^{a}T-values in parentheses.

market sample based on the following classification schemes:

A. The daily observations of the current week are classified into the bull (bear) market sample, if the performance of the *gold futures option* over the previous week (Friday to Friday) was positive (negative). This criterion classifies the sample on an *ex ante* basis and results in 4052 observations in the bull market sample and 5267 observations in the bear market sample.

B. On an *ex post* basis, each option premium is classified into the bull (bear) sample if the underlying *futures* return is positive (negative). Accordingly, there are 4455 observations in the bull market sample and 4923 observations in the bear market sample.

C. Each option premium is classified into the bull (bear) sample if the *actual option return* is positive (negative). This criterion results in 5139 observations in the bull market sample and 4239 observations in the bear market sample.

Equation (1) is estimated for both the bull and bear subsamples for each of the three classification schemes. Part A of Table 3 summarizes the regression estimates. While most of the estimates are significant at the 1% level, it is clear that the sign reverses itself between bull and bear market periods. The result holds for all three classification systems. These results suggest that strong daily seasonality exists in the returns of gold futures options. Specifically, the Monday return is higher than the other weekday returns in a rising market and lower in a declining market.

C. Seasonality in Returns of Underlying Futures Contracts

Given the close association between futures option returns and returns of the underlying futures, the seasonality we have just demonstrated in futures option returns may be merely a reflection of the seasonal pattern in their underlying futures returns. To explore this possibility, the seasonality of the underlying futures return is first examined by estimating Equation (2) with futures returns.

$$RF_t = b_1 + \sum_{t=2}^{5} b_t D_t + \eta_t \qquad (2)$$

where η_t is the error term and RF_t is the daily futures return for weekday t. The results are presented in Part B of Table 3.

The results indicate that the associated futures returns also exhibit significant bull and bear market weekend effects. That is, for the three bull/bear classification schemes, most of the dummy variables (non-Monday) are significantly negative in bull market samples at the 1% level. In bear market samples, most signs are positive but not significant.[3]

However, Wednesday returns are significantly higher than Monday returns in all three cases. Consequently, it is possible that the seasonality associated with option returns is only a manifestation of seasonality in the underlying futures returns. At this point, it is not yet clear as to what extent the observed seasonality in futures options is endemic to the gold futures option market itself.

To investigate this, we isolated the unique seasonality in gold futures options by factoring out the seasonality from the underlying futures returns by modifying Equation (1) as follows:

$$R_t = a_0 + a_1ST + a_2T + b_0RF_tDM + b_1RF_tDNM + \sum_{t=2}^{5} d_tD_t + \varsigma_t \qquad (3)$$

where

ς_t = the error term,
T = time to maturity in terms of a year,
ST = ratio of the current futures price divided by the striking price,
DM = dummy variable for Monday,
DNM = dummy variable for non-Monday,

and d_t and D_t are defined as before. Since the sample includes both time series and cross-sectional data, it is heterogeneous in terms of times to maturity as well as striking price. Since these differences might systematically affect option returns, their impact should be properly assessed while the daily seasonality is being identified. Consequently, in Equation (3), the inclusions of ST and T are to control the heterogeneous nature of the sample. The impact of underlying futures seasonality is captured by the interaction terms, RF_tDM and RF_tDNM. If the futures option return is affected by the underlying futures return, the coefficients of the two interaction terms, b_0 and b_1, should be significantly positive. Futhermore, if the futures return has varying impacts on futures option returns across different weekdays, b_0 and b_1 should be significantly different. The significant difference between b_0 and b_1 would imply that the seasonality in futures returns does not carry over completely to the futures option market. On the other hand, the coefficients of the original dummy variables, D_ts, measure the futures option seasonality, which is independent of the seasonality in futures returns.

Table 4 presents the results of testing Equation (3) over various subsamples. The estimates of b_0 and b_1 are significantly positive at the 1% level. Furthermore, the difference tests at the bottom of Table 4 also suggest that b_0 and b_1 are significantly different for each of the bull/bear market classification systems. This supports the hypothesis that there is a strong impact from underlying asset returns, and that the underlying seasonality is

Table 4. Regression Statistics of Equation (3) over Bull/Bear Markets:
$R_t = a_0 + a_1ST + a_2T + b_0RF_tDM + b_1RF_tDNM + \sum_{t=2}^{5} d_tD_t + \zeta_t$

Coefficient	Criterion A		Criterion B		Criterion C	
	Bull	Bear	Bull	Bear	Bull	Bear
a_0 (Mon)	4.246	−0.167	12.950[*]	−12.254[*]	13.650[*]	9.690[*]
	(2.41)[a]	(−0.12)	(8.47)	(−9.57)	(11.56)	(7.69)
a_1	−5.530[*]	−3.057[*]	−4.324[*]	−0.715	−3.590[*]	−28.724[*]
	(−3.79)	(−2.84)	(−3.49)	(−0.71)	(−3.95)	(−26.26)
a_2	3.971[*]	1.672[**]	−1.575	5.314[*]	−2.500[*]	14.914[*]
	(4.30)	(2.22)	(−1.94)	(7.61)	(−3.86)	(23.19)
b_0	2.657[*]	3.138[*]	3.435[*]	1.371[*]	3.160[*]	1.154[*]
	(23.51)	(28.27)	(18.37)	(16.52)	(22.73)	(16.72)
b_1	10.216[*]	9.504[*]	4.790[*]	5.676[*]	5.362[*]	5.313[*]
	(10.14)	(9.57)	(4.93)	(6.36)	(6.67)	(6.98)
d_2 (Tue)	−2.574[*]	0.914	−5.566[*]	3.586[*]	−4.363[*]	2.308[*]
	(−3.37)	(1.56)	(−8.20)	(6.32)	(−8.22)	(4.55)
d_3 (Wed)	−1.790	2.170[*]	−4.160[*]	3.987[*]	−3.454[*]	2.530[*]
	(−2.35)	(3.70)	(−6.16)	(6.98)	(−6.60)	(4.90)
d_4 (Thr)	−2.567[*]	0.735	−4.863[*]	2.837[*]	−3.673[*]	1.997[*]
	(−3.37)	(1.26)	(−7.15)	(5.03)	(−6.89)	(3.99)
d_5 (Fri)	−0.762	2.574[*]	−3.677[*]	3.998[*]	−3.003[*]	2.380[*]
	(−0.99)	(4.38)	(−5.55)	(6.85)	(−5.78)	(4.52)
N	4052	5267	4455	4923	5139	4239
R^2	0.153	0.155	0.087	0.081	0.118	0.271
F-value	91.48[*]	120.46[*]	53.02[*]	54.09[*]	85.96[*]	196.21[*]
$H_0: b_0 = b_1$	10.55[*]	9.01[*]	1.94[**]	6.79[*]	3.82[*]	7.70[*]

[*]Significant at the 1% level.
[**]Significant at the 5% level.
[a]T-values in parentheses.

not fully transmitted to futures option returns. Again, most estimates of the d_ts are significantly positive for bull market samples and negative for bear market samples at the 1% level. The same pattern is evident in each of the three classification systems. Consequently, there is a daily effect that is unique to gold futures option markets.

IV. IMPLICATIONS AND CONCLUSIONS

In this paper, strong daily effects are identified in both gold futures option returns and in underlying futures returns. While part of the seasonality in futures options is carried over from the underlying futures markets, there is an independent daily seasonality in the gold futures option market. The results add to the recent evidence of bull and bear market weekend effects in equity markets. Similar to findings in the gold spot market, the weekend effect, in its derivative asset market, also reverses itself between bear and bull market periods. Since the evidence clearly indicates that the daily effect varies for different market periods, future research for both cash and derivative assets should recognize the bias of using a pooled bull/bear sample period to test the daily effect.

NOTES

1. Several explanations may be offered for their findings. First, the same studies by Cornell [2] and Junkus [8] demonstrate that for stock returns, the typical weekend effect, i.e., low Monday and high Friday returns, is not prevalent in the post-1980 period. Since index futures and index option contracts started trading after 1982, the findings of insignificant differences in daily returns may be attributed to the lack of weekend effects in underlying cash markets during the same time period. Furthermore, as shown by Jaffe, Ma, and Westerfield [6], and Ma [11], the traditional weekend effect is not evident in a rising market. In this case, Monday returns are significantly higher than other weekday returns. The weekend effect, therefore, reverses itself from bear to bull markets. This may explain the reason that a low Monday return is not observed in the post-1982 period in both cash and futures markets, since the bulk of that period has been a rising market.

2. Both Cornell [2], Junkus [8], and Dyl and Maberly [3] use this procedure.

3. One reason for the insignificance is that the sample has been divided into subsamples using the ex post performance of futures option returns (Criterion C).

REFERENCES

1. Ball, C. A., W. N. Torous, and A. E. Tschoegl, "Gold and the 'Weekend Effect'," *Journal of Futures Markets* 2 (1982), 175–182.
2. Cornell, B., "The Weekly Pattern in Stock Returns: Cash versus Futures: A Note," *Journal of Finance* 40 (1985), 583–588.
3. Dyl, E. A., and E. D. Maberly, "The Weekly Pattern in Stock Index Futures: A Further Note," *Journal of Finance* 41 (December 1986), 1149–1152.
4. French, K. R., "Stock Returns and the Weekend Effect," *Journal of Financial Economics* 8 (March 1980), 55–69.
5. Gibbons, M., and P. Hess, "Day of the Week Effects and Asset Returns," *Journal of Business* 54 (1981), 579–596.
6. Jaffe, J. F., C. K. Ma, and R. Westerfield, "A Twist on the Monday Effect in Stock Prices," *Journal of Banking and Finance*, forthcoming.
7. Jaffe, J. F., and R. Westerfield, "Patterns in Japanese Common Stock Returns: Day of the Week and Turn of the Year Effects," *Journal of Financial and Quantitative Analysis* 20 (1986), 261–272.
8. Junkus, J. C., "Weekend and Day of the Week Effects in Returns on Stock Index Futures," *The Journal of Futures Markets* 6 (1986), 397–408.
9. Keim, D., and R. Stambaugh, "A Further Investigation of the Weekend Effect in Stock Returns," *Journal of Finance* 39 (1984), 819–834.
10. Lakonishok, J., and M. Levi, "Weekend Effects on Stock Returns: A Note," *Journal of Finance* 37 (June 1982), 883–889.

11. Ma, C. K., "A Further Investigation of the 'Day-of-the-Week' in the Gold Market," *The Journal of Futures Markets* 6 (1986), 409–420.
12. Rogalski, R., "Discussion," *Journal of Finance* 39 (March 1984), 835–837.
13. Stoll, H., and R. Whaley, "Expiration Day Effects of Index Options and Futures," Research Report for the SEC, Vanderbilt University, 1986.
14. Sweeney, R. J., M. L. McBain, and S. E. Crane, "On Option Pricing: An Examination of Day of the Week Effect and Delays in the Opening," Working paper 86-122, Marquette University, 1986.